THE CAMPBE

Stephen Boardman

THE CAMPBELLS
1250–1513

ORIGIN

This edition published in 2019 by
Origin, an imprint of Birlinn Ltd
West Newington House
10 Newington Road
Edinburgh EH9 1QS

www.birlinn.co.uk

Originally published by John Donald in 2006

Copyright © Stephen Boardman 2006

ISBN 978 1 912476 6 33

British Library Cataloguing-in-Publication Data
A Catalogue record is available on request from the British Library

Typeset by Hewer Text UK Ltd, Edinburgh
Printed and bound by Gutenberg Press Ltd.

Contents

Acknowledgements	vii
Abbreviations	ix
List of Illustrations	xiii
List of Maps	xv
List of Genealogical Tables	xv
Maps	xvii
Genealogical Tables	xxi
Introduction: The Way of the Wild Ash	1
1. The Sons of Arthur? Clan Campbell in the Thirteenth Century	9
2. The Storm Petrels: Clan Campbell, Robert I and the Wars of Independence	36
3. The Steward's Shirt of Mail: Gillespic of Arran	56
4. The Lords of Argyll	94
5. The Albany Stewarts	118
6. The Foes of Friendly Duncan	141
7. On the Edge and in the Middle: The Early Career of Colin, 1st Earl of Argyll	166
8. Courting the Savage?	202
9. 1488–1492: Argyll Ascendant	238
10. The Fall of the House of Sorley	259
11. Loch, Stock and Barrel: the Economy of Campbell Lordship	291
12. The Red Road	311
Bibliography	343
Index	355

Acknowledgements

The views, thoughts and expertise of a great many friends and colleagues have helped to shape this book. The debts I have incurred range
over a number of institutions and subject areas, testimony to the spirit of co-
operation and generosity that binds together those cheerful souls engaged in
the study of medieval Scottish history. I am particularly grateful to the
following individuals for specific help, general advice and friendship. At
Aberdeen University, Dr David Ditchburn, who provided helpful comments on an early draft of Chapter 11; at St Andrews, Professor Keith
Brown, Professor Roger Mason, Dr Michael Brown and Alex Woolf; at
Glasgow, Dr Dauvit Broun, Dr Martin MacGregor, Professor Thomas
Clancy and the rest of the 'video-link' crew. At Edinburgh, all my current
colleagues in the Scottish History, History and Celtic subject areas,
especially Dr James Fraser, Dr Ewen Cameron, Professor Willie Gillies
and Dr Wilson MacLeod. David Sellar, from the Faculty of Law, has been
extremely generous with insights and information from his own studies of
the Clan Campbell and other Highland and Hebridean families and also
read Chapter 1 in advance of publication. Professor Geoffrey Barrow has
responded to a number of enquiries with swift, courteous and invariably
useful replies. As ever, the misfortune of reading and commenting on the
entire text fell on my former supervisor, Dr Norman Macdougall, who
performed this unhappy task with characteristic good grace and humour. I
should also like to thank my publisher, Dr John Tuckwell, not only for his
input to this particular volume but also for his long commitment to the
production of serious studies of Scottish history. Needless to say, the author
alone remains responsible for all intellectual, factual or grammatical out-
rages that still lurk within these covers.

Outwith the academic community I should like to thank a man I have
never met, Mr A.B.W.McEwen, for his challenging and interesting
observations on genealogical matters delivered regularly in commendably
forthright letters from Maine. The excellent hospitality of Alastair Campbell of Airds and his family in and around Taynuilt was very much

appreciated, as was his help in accessing the Argyll Muniments at Inveraray for a limited period of time. Thanks are also, of course, due to the Duke and Duchess of Argyll for allowing me to consult the papers at Inveraray.

Turning to home, I would like to express my deep gratitude to Sheila for putting up with her less than exemplary spouse. Kirsty and Catriona remain a constant source of joy, entertainment and expenditure. The unlikely adventures of Beano, Whisky, Oda, Sugar, Polo and Raray continue to put the cares of teaching, research and publication into proper perspective.

Work on the final stages of the book was greatly assisted by an award from the AHRB Research Leave scheme.

Abbreviations

Aberdeen-Banff Illustrations   *Illustrations of the Topography and Antiquities of the Shires of Aberdeen and Banff* (Spalding Club, 1847–69).

Abdn. Counc.   *Extracts from the Council Register of the Burgh of Aberdeen* (Spalding Club, 1844–48).

AC   *Annála Connacht: the Annals of Connacht, AD 1224–1544*, ed. A.M. Freeman (Dublin, 1944).

ADA   *The Acts of the Lords Auditors of Causes and Complaints*, ed.T.-Thomson (Edinburgh, 1839).

ADC   *The Acts of the Lords of Council in Civil Causes*, edd. T.Thomson and others (Edinburgh, 1839 and 1918–).

ALC   *The Annals of Loch Cé*, ed.W.M.Hennessy (Rolls Series, 1871).

ALI   *The Acts of the Lords of the Isles, 1336–1493*, ed. J. and R.W.Munro (SHS, 1986).

APS   *The Acts of the Parliaments of Scotland*, edd. T.Thomson and C.Innes (Edinburgh, 1814–75).

AT   Argyll Transcripts, made by 10th Duke of Argyll (photostat copies of extracts in the Department of Scottish History, University of Glasgow).

AU   *Annals of Ulster*, ed. W.M.Hennessy and B.McCarthy (Dublin, 1887–1901).

Bannatyne Misc.   *The Bannatyne Miscellany* (Bannatyne Club, 1827–55).

Bellenden, *Chronicles*   *The Chronicles of Scotland compiled by Hector Boece*, translated into Scots by John Bellenden 1531 (STS, 1938–41).

Brechin Registrum   *Registrum Episcopatus Brechinensis* (Bannatyne Club, 1856).

Cambuskenneth Registrum   *Registrum Monasterii S. Marie de Cambuskenneth* (Grampian Club, 1872).

Cawdor Bk   *The Book of the Thanes of Cawdor* (Spalding Club, 1859).

CDS   *Calendar of Documents Relating to Scotland*, ed. J.Bain (Edinburgh, 1881–8).

Chron. Auchinleck (McGladdery)   The 'Auchinleck Chronicle', Appendix 2 in C.McGladdery, *James II* (Edinburgh, 1990).

Chron.Bower (Watt)   Walter Bower, *Scotichronicon*, ed.D.E.R.Watt, 9 vols. (1987–1998).

Chron. Extracta   Extracta e Variis Cronicis Scocie (Abbotsford Club, 1842).

Chron. Fordun   Johannis de Fordun, Chronica Gentis Scotorum, ed.W.F.Skene (Edinburgh, 1871–2).

Chron. Pluscarden   Liber Pluscardensis, ed. F.J.H.Skene (Edinburgh, 1867).

Chron.Wyntoun (Laing)   Androw of Wyntoun, *The Orygynale Cronykil of Scotland*, ed. D.Laing (Edinburgh, 1872–79).

CPL   Calendar of Entries in the Papal Registers relating to Great Britain and Ireland: Papal Letters, edd. W.H.Bliss and others (London, 1893–)

CPL Benedict XIII   Calendar of Papal Letters to Scotland of Benedict XIII of Avignon, 1394–1419 (SHS, 1976).

CPL Clement VII   Calendar of Papal Letters to Scotland of Clement VII of Avignon, 1378–1394 (SHS, 1976).

CPNS   W.J.Watson, *The History of the Celtic place-names of Scotland* (Edinburgh, 1926).

CPP   Calendar of Entries in the Papal Registers relating to Great Britain and Ireland: Petitions to the Pope, ed. W.H.Bliss (London, 1896).

CSP Scot.   Calendar of the State Papers relating to Scotland and Mary, Queen of Scots, 1547–1603, edd. J.Bain and others (Edinburgh, 1898–).

CSSR   Calendar of Scottish Supplications to Rome (SHS and others, 1934–).

ER   The Exchequer Rolls of Scotland, edd. J. Stuart and others (Edinburgh, 1878–1908).

Foedera   Foedera, Conventiones, Litterae et Cuiuscumque Generis Acta Publica, ed. T.Rymer, Record Commission edition (London, 1816–69).

Fraser, *Colquhoun*   W.Fraser, *The Chiefs of Colquhoun and their Country* (Edinburgh, 1869).

Fraser, *Douglas*   W.Fraser, *The Douglas Book* (Edinburgh, 1885).

Fraser, *Eglinton*   W.Fraser, *Memorials of the Montgomeries Earls of Eglinton* (Edinburgh, 1859).

Fraser, *Keir*   W.Fraser, *The Stirlings of Keir* (Edinburgh, 1858).

Fraser, *Lennox*   W.Fraser, *The Lennox* (Edinburgh, 1874).

Fraser, *Menteith*   W.Fraser, *The Red Book of Menteith* (Edinburgh, 1880).

Frasers of Philorth   The Frasers of Philorth, ed. A.Fraser, Lord Saltoun (Edinburgh, 1888).

Glas. Reg.   Registrum Episcopatus Glasguensis (Bannatyne and Maitland Clubs, 1843).

HMC Reports of the Royal Commission on Historical Manuscripts (London 1870–).

Holyrood Liber Liber Cartarum Sancte Crucis (Bannatyne Club, 1840).

HP Highland Papers, ed. J.R.N.Macphail (SHS, 1914–34).

Inchaffray Chrs. Charters, Bulls and other Documents relating to the Abbey of Inchaffray (SHS, 1908).

IR Innes Review

James IV Letters The Letters of James the Fourth, 1505–13, edd. R.K.Hannay and R.L.Mackie (SHS, 1953).

Laing Chrs. Calendar of the Laing Charters, 854–1837, ed. J.Anderson (Edinburgh, 1899).

Lamont Papers An Inventory of Lamont Papers (SRS, 1914).

Lennox Cartularium Cartularium Comitatus de Levenax (Maitland Club, 1833).

Lesley, *History* J.Lesley, The History of Scotland from the Death of King James I in the Year 1436 to the Year 1561 (Bannatyne Club, 1830).

Lindores Liber Liber Sancte Marie de Lundoris (Abbotsford Club, 1841).

Maidment, *Analecta* Analecta Scotica [ed.J.Maidment] (Edinburgh, 1834–7).

Maitland Misc. Miscellany of the Maitland Club (Maitland Club, 1833–47).

Moray Reg. Registrum Episcopatus Moraviensis (Bannatyne Club, 1837).

Mort.Reg. Registrum Honoris de Morton (Bannatyne Club, 1853).

Munro Writs Calendar of Writs of Munro of Foulis, 1299–1823, ed. C.T.McInnes (SRS, 1940).

Myln, *Vitae* A.Myln, Vitae Dunkeldensis Ecclesiae Episcoporum (Bannatyne Club, 1831).

NAS National Archives of Scotland.

Nat. MSS. Scot. Facsimiles of the National Manuscripts of Scotland (London, 1867–71).

Newbattle Registrum Registrum S. Marie de Neubotle (Bannatyne Club, 1849).

NLS National Library of Scotland.

OPS Origines Parochiales Scotiae (Bannatyne Club, 1851–5).

Palgrave, *Docs. Hist. Scot.* Documents and Records illustrating the History of Scotland, ed. F.Palgrave (London, 1837).

Pais. Reg. Registrum Monasterii de Passelet (Maitland Club, 1832).

PSAS Proceedings of the Society of Antiquaries of Scotland (1851–).

RCAHMS *Argyll* *Royal Commission on the Ancient and Historic Monuments of Scotland, Inventory of the Ancient Monuments of Argyll* (Edinburgh, 1971–92).

RMS *Registrum Magni Sigilii Regum Scotorum*, edd. J.M.Thomson and others (Edinburgh, 1882–1914).

Rot.Scot. *Rotuli Scotiae in Turri Londinensi et in Domo Capitulari Westmonasteriensi Asservati*, edd. D.Macpherson and others (1814–19).

RRS *Regesta Regum Scottorum*, edd. G.W.S.Barrow and others (Edinburgh, 1960–).

RSS *Registrum Secreti Sigilii Regum Scottorum*, edd. M.Livingstone and others (Edinburgh, 1908–).

Scalacronica *Scalacronica, by Sir Thomas Gray of Heton Knight* (Maitland Club, 1836).

SGS *Scottish Gaelic Studies*

SGTS Scottish Gaelic Texts Society

SHR *Scottish Historical Review.*

SHS Misc. *The Miscellany of the Scottish History Society* (SHS, 1893–).

SP *The Scots Peerage*, ed. Sir J.Balfour Paul (Edinburgh, 1904–14)

Spalding Misc. *Miscellany of the Spalding Club* (Spalding Club, 1841–52).

SRS Scottish Records Society.

SS Scottish Studies.

Stevenson, *Documents* *Documents Illustrative of the History of Scotland, 1286–1306*, ed. J.Stevenson (Edinburgh, 1870).

Stevenson and Wood, *Seals* *J.H.Stevenson and M.Wood (eds.), Scottish Heraldic Seals* (Glasgow, 1940).

SWHIHR The Society of West Highland and Island Historical Research.

TA *Accounts of the Lord High Treasurer of Scotland*, edd. T.Dickson and Sir J.Balfour Paul (Edinburgh, 1877–1916).

Taymouth Bk. *The Black Book of Taymouth* (Bannatyne Club, 1855).

TGSI Transactions of the Gaelic Society of Inverness.

Vet.Mon. *Vetera Monumenta Hibernorum et Scotorum Historiam Illustrantia*, ed. A.Theiner (Rome, 1864).

Watt, *Dictionary* *D.E.R.Watt, A Biographical Dictionary of Scottish Graduates to A.D. 1410* (Oxford, 1977).

Watt, *Fasti* *D.E.R.Watt, Fasti ecclesiae Scoticanae medii aevi ad annum 1638*, 2nd draft (SRS, 1969).

List of Illustrations

1. The bell tower of the collegiate kirk of Kilmun
2. Timothy Pont's map of Argyll
3. The tomb of Duncan 1st Lord Campbell and Lord of Loch Awe
4. The tomb of Duncan's wife at Kilmun
5. Illustration of a clarsach from *Liber Pluscardensis*
6. Detail from the 'Scots Roll'
7. Innis Chonnel Castle
8. Detail from the 'Scots Roll'
9. Gatehouse of Dunstaffnage Castle
10. The castle of Menstrie near Stirling
11. Sir Colin Campbell of Glenorchy
12. Duncan Campbell of Glenorchy
13. 'A Campbell Trinity': Duncan Campbell of Loch Awe, Colin first of Glenorchy and Archibald, first earl of Argyll

List of Maps

1. Major territorial divisions of Argyll
2. Lands to be incorporated in the proposed sherriffdom of Lorn, 1293
3. Principal castles, churches and burghs

List of Genealogical Tables

1. The ten generations above Colin Mór
2. The Loch Awe and Ardscotnish Campbells: A conjectural genealogy
2a. The Loch Awe and Ardscotnish Campbells: as per A.B.W.McEwen
3. Principal Cadets of the Loch Awe Campbells
4. East and West, significant Campbell marriages in the fifteenth century

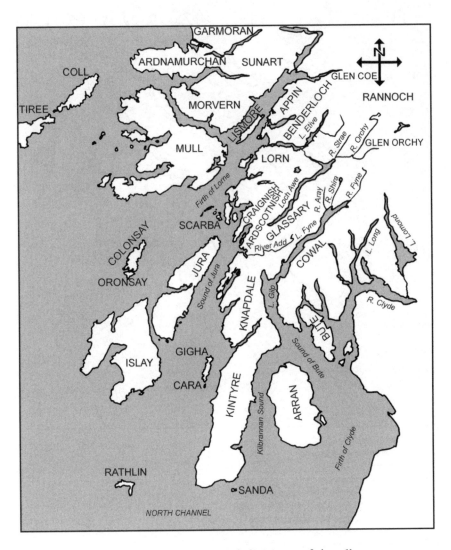

MAP I: Major territorial divisions of Argyll

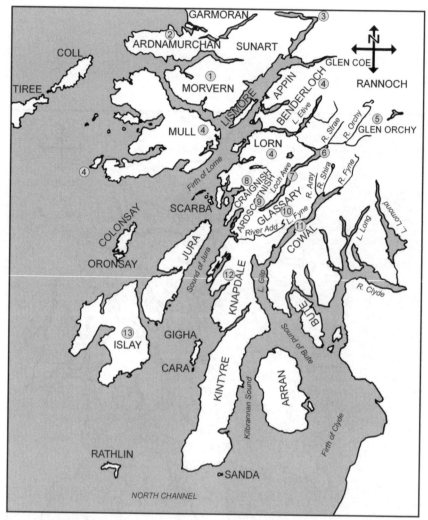

Key to Map 2

1 'Cineal Bhaodain' (Morvern)
2 Ardnamurchan
3 'Lochelve' (Locheil)
4 The lands of Alexander MacDougall (Lorn, Mull, Lismore and the small islands)
5 The lands of John of Glenorchy (Glenorchy)
6 The lands of Gilbert [McNaughton] (Upper Loch Awe)
7 The lands of Malcolm MacIver (Middle Loch Awe)
8 The lands of Dugald of Craignish (Craignish)
9 The lands of John MacGilchrist (Ardscotnish)
10 The lands of Master Ralph of Dundee (Glassary)
11 The lands of Gillespie MacLachlan (Strathlachlan)
12 The Earl of Menteith's lands in Knapdale
13 The lands of Angus son of Donald of the Isles (Islay)

MAP 2: Lands to be incorporated in the proposed sherriffdom of Lorn, 1293

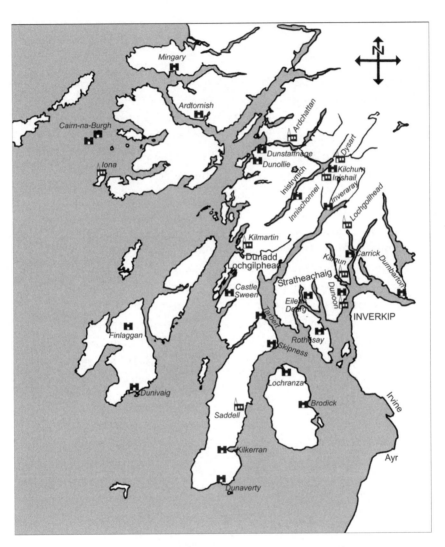

MAP 3: Principal castles, churches and burghs

TABLE I: *After Sellar, 'Earliest Campbells', p.117*

MS1467	Kilbride MS	MacFirbis
?IUBUR	AMBROSIUS	IOBHAR
ARTHUR	ARTHUR	ARTHUR
MEIRBI	SMERBI	SMEIRBE
?EIRENAIA	FERADOIG	FERADOIGH
DUIBNE	DUIBNE	DUIBNE
MALCOLM	MALCOLM	MALCOLM
GILLESPIC	DUNCAN	DUNCAN
DUNCAN	GILLESPIC	EOGHAN
DUGALD	DUGALD	DUGALD
GILLESPIC	GILLESPIC	GILLESPIC
COLIN	COLIN	COLIN

The Ten Generations above Colin Mór

TABLE 2: *The Loch Awe and Ardscotnish Campbells: A conjectural genealogy*

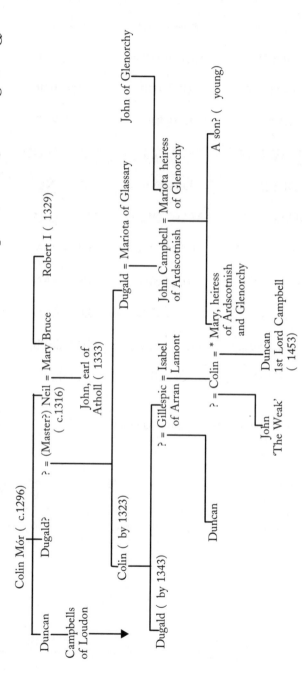

* The papal dispensations obtained in 1366 for Colin and Mary's marriage give an account of the connection between the couple (expressed in terms of degrees of consanguinity) that is incompatible with the relationship suggested in the above genealogy or, indeed, the alternative genealogy of the Loch Awe and Ardscotnish families provided in Table 2a.

TABLE 2A: *The Loch Awe and Ardscotnish Campbells: as per A.B.W. McEwen*

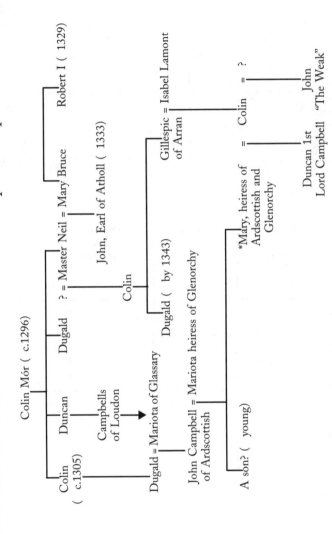

* See note in Table 2

TABLE 3: *Principal Cadets of the Loch Awe Campbells*

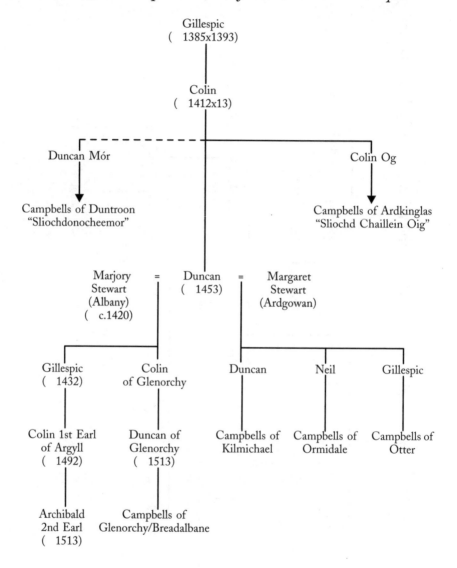

Gillespic
(1385x1393)

Colin
(1412x13)

Duncan Mór

Campbells of Duntroon
"Sliochdonocheemor"

Colin Og

Campbells of Ardkinglas
"Sliochd Chaillein Óig"

Marjory = Duncan = Margaret
Stewart (1453) Stewart
(Albany) (Ardgowan)
(c.1420)

Gillespic   Colin
(1432)   of Glenorchy

Duncan   Neil   Gillespic

Colin 1st Earl   Duncan of
of Argyll   Glenorchy
(1492)   (1513)

Campbells of   Campbells of   Campbells of
Kilmichael   Ormidale   Otter

Archibald   Campbells of
2nd Earl   Glenorchy/Breadalbane
(1513)

TABLE 4: *East and West, significant Campbell marriages in the fifteenth century*

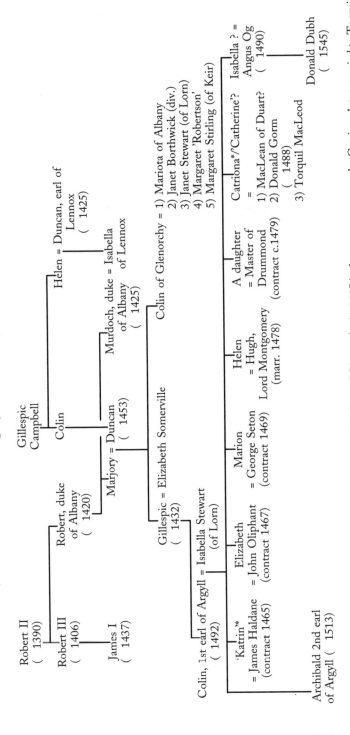

* It is uncertain whether the 'Katrin' contracted to James Haldane of Gleneagles in 1465 is the same woman as the Catriona later married to Torquil MacLeod and/or the 'Catherine' mentioned in seventeenth-century sources as the partner of MacLean 'of Mull' and Donald Gorm

The Way of the Wild Ash

In 1938 Hector McKechnie published a history of the Lamonts of Cowal. He opened his work with a brief summary of the fortunes and qualities of the great Gaelic families of medieval Scotland. 'A dignity unequalled attached to the proud McDonalds under the Lords of the Isles, although they split into factions later. Thereafter unrivalled success attended the sleekit Campbells, who combined claymore and parchment as never Celts before, and encroached on all their neighbours. They were copied in the north by the greedy MacKenzies, who could pass the fiery cross from sea to sea through lands they had grasped from others . . .'[1] Naturally, MacKechnie also included the Lamonts amongst those who had fallen victim to the overweening ambitions of the Campbell lords. The author returned to his happy theme of Campbell iniquity when he suggested that the family followed 'the way of the Wild Ash', a vigorous fast-growing tree that overshadowed and eventually destroyed all its neighbours.[2]

McKechnie's excitable prose is fairly typical of the way in which the apparently relentless growth of Campbell lordship in medieval Scotland has been explained and stigmatised in both popular and academic histories. One of the most influential academic works available for consultation by McKechnie and other nineteenth- and twentieth-century authors dealing with the history of individual Highland families was W.F. Skene's *The Highlanders of Scotland*, first published in 1837. In Skene's estimation the undoubted effectiveness of the medieval Clan Campbell was built on a 'policy characterised by cunning and perfidy, though deep and far sighted, and which obtained its usual success in the acquisition of great temporal grandeur and power'.[3] Campbell 'cunning', 'policy' and foresight, and the way in which these qualities marked the family off from its neighbours, became a standard theme of scholarly writing on the Highlands. In 1859, Cosmo Innes claimed that although the Campbells had replaced 'the great ancient lords of Argyll, the Isles, and Lorn . . . theirs was a different rule from that of the pirates and rude princes, their predecessors'. Despite the power they wielded, 'which they might easily have made independent, over the Celts of the remote and inaccessible mountains and isles, the Campbells from the beginning, attached themselves to the Scotch court'. Their success depended on 'the personal character of the race, predominating alike in policy and force over all their neighbours'.[4]

The full significance of the judgements delivered by Skene and Innes is only apparent when set against the background of contemporary views of the historical development of the Scottish kingdom and the supposed attributes of the Gael. For many in the nineteenth century, the story of late medieval Scotland had been distinguished by a long struggle for supremacy between the Gael and the Saxon or Teuton and their respective languages and cultures. In this great confrontation the Scottish monarchy, at least from the reign of David I (1124–1153) onward, was explicitly identified with the interests of Lowland 'teutonic', English-speaking Scotland. The champions of the late medieval Gael, by contrast, were the MacDonald Lords of the Isles. Military and political clashes between the Lordship and the crown or its agents, such as the famous Battle of Harlaw (1411), tended to be seen and explained in terms of this fundamental cultural and 'racial' division. A rather extreme expression of this view was to be found in the, perhaps inappropriately titled, *Book of Bon-Accord*, published two years after Skene's *Highlanders*. Talking of Harlaw, the author helpfully placed the confrontation into its historical context by describing the battle as 'one of the conflicts in that great war between the Celtic and the Saxon races – between barbarism and civilisation – which beginning with the Pretender Donalbane, in the eleventh century, was only finally ended on the Moor of Culloden . . .'.[5] In this historical scheme, the Campbells' association with the 'Scotch' court and their disinterest in achieving 'independent' rule over the 'Celts' of the western Highlands and Islands made their position seem unnatural and 'ungaelic'. If there was a war between Celt and Teuton, then Campbell success seemed to depend on collaboration with the enemies of the Gael. Even Skene's emphasis on Campbell prescience and lust for 'temporal grandeur' may have had an unsettling resonance for a nineteenth-century readership. The 'Celtic' peoples of Britain and Ireland were thought to exhibit certain distinctive racial characteristics, such as emotional impulsiveness, a lack of interest in material acquisition, and a heightened artistic and spiritual sensibility, that could be contrasted with the more stolid virtues of the Saxon.[6] Skene's short description of the Campbells implied, intentionally or otherwise, that the family had a mindset that was in many ways 'non-Celtic'.

The rather hostile view of Clan Campbell found in Skene as a predatory, scheming and almost quisling presence within Gaelic Scotland was thus partly shaped by the concerns of Skene's own age, but also by his study of the literary and historical works of earlier periods. Particularly influential in this latter category were the Gaelic poets in the service of various branches of Clan Donald in the seventeenth century, such as Iain Lom, who lamented the passing of Clan Donald power and unity while savaging contemporary Campbell duplicity and cravenness. Iain Lom's assertion that 'The sharp stroke of short pens protects Argyll' is a memorably pithy comment on the perceived Campbell manipulation of the legal forms and machinery of Lowland Scotland to destroy fellow Gaelic families and lords in the west during the seventeenth century.[7] However, the idea that the Campbells' historic mission was to achieve the ruin of the Clan Donald in the interests of the crown was not simply a creation of the family's opponents. By the end of the sixteenth century, if not before, Campbell earls seem to have consciously promoted the notion that their ancestors had indeed played a critical role in the 'daunting' of the Isles and had acted as representatives of law, order and civilisation in the wild frontier lands of the Scottish and English realms. The historical interpretation not only justified the family's prominence in the Scottish polity and the special privileges it enjoyed, but it also acted, in a sense, as the Campbells' business card, outlining their reliability and their usefulness in pest control and eradication in the Highlands, Islands and, potentially, Ireland.[8]

The notion that the spread of Campbell power involved the steady and deliberate destruction of older and more prestigious Gaelic lordships has become a potent element in the popular and scholastic imagination. Nineteenth- and twentieth-century histories of the Highlands (such as MacKechnie's) are littered with the supposed victims of Campbell aggression and duplicity, although the most notable and significant casualties are taken to be the MacDougalls and the MacDonalds. In the latter case, Campbell territorial and political advances have been used to track and explain the decline and then disintegration of the great Clan Donald hegemony over the Isles. In some popular histories the entire sweep of Highland history has been reduced to a long-running feud between the Campbells and Clan Donald.[9] Moreover, the two families have also been taken to symbolise and represent opposed forces and long-term processes affecting the culture, language and economy of the Highlands and the Hebrides. Campbell expansion at the expense of other kindreds has not been seen as part of the natural rise and fall of west-coast lordships according to changing political and dynastic fortunes, but as an indicator of a much more sinister and inexorable assault upon the very fabric of Gaelic society. In more scholarly works a large part of the Campbells' political and territorial success is attributed to their adoption of 'alien' traditions of lordship, integration into the Lowland political community, to their close relationship with the Scottish crown, and to the sheer guile exhibited by a succession of Campbell lords. Where the Campbells are said to have become in the late medieval period 'the most feudal of Celtic kindreds, basing their expansion on feudal charters, the newly created sheriffship of Argyll, and an aggressive adoption of Lowland ways', the MacDonalds, 'in contrast, fostered a renewed, self-conscious pan-Celtic Gaeldom'.[10] In many ways this judgement reflects the generally hostile nineteenth-century Gaelic historiographical tradition that portrayed Clan Campbell as somehow 'ungaelic', a conduit by which corrosive alien practices were introduced into the Gaelic west at the behest of the Lowland monarchy. In the Gaelic tradition the Campbell-MacDonald rivalry remains 'a dialectical opposition of resistance to and collaboration with the central authorities'.[11] The Campbells' willingness to act as royal representatives in the west and their rivalry with the Clan Donald are seen as inseparable features of their history and policy. The dominance achieved by Clan Campbell in Argyll by the end of the medieval period is explained largely through the assertion that the family acted 'as agents of the Scottish crown in destroying the overmighty Macdonalds'.[12] More-over, the results of the fall of the MacDonald lordship of the Isles and the Campbell ascendancy are often portrayed as utterly disastrous for Gaelic culture and society in a wider sense. At the political level the loss of the guiding hand of the Lord of the Isles allowed local rivalries and feuds in the Hebrides to run unchecked. 'These were skilfully fomented by the central government and by its agent Argyll. It was indeed this use of diplomacy and stratagems rather than open violence that won the Camp-bells such hatred. The utter barbarity of the history of the Highlands from roughly 1475 to 1625 was largely the result of the "daunting of the Isles" and the destruction of the Macdonald lordship.'[13] Aside from being more or less directly responsible for most of the violence that afflicted Highland Scotland in the century and a half after 1475, the Campbells had other charges to answer in relation to their long campaign against the Clan Donald. The disappearance of the great MacDonald lords as patrons and defenders of Gaelic culture has been a suitable subject for lamentation from the sixteenth century to the present day. In some accounts Gaelic cultural and linguistic vitality in the medieval period has become virtually synonymous with the political and territorial fortunes of the Lordship of the Isles. Indeed, the cultural role of the medieval Lords of the Isles has been emphasised to such an extent that they can appear almost as the curators of a beleaguered institute for Gaelic studies fighting compulsory closure, rather than potent, aggressive and expansionist aristocrats whose principal and immediate concern lay in securing or augmenting their lands, status and wealth. The idea of the Lordship of the Isles as an unalloyed political expression of Gaelic identity in the Middle Ages is a powerful and evocative one, especially for literary scholars and historians chiefly concerned with issues of Gaelic culture and language. The identification of the Lordship with the wider story of the Gaelic language has probably been strengthened with the much more recent withering of Gaelic as a spoken language in areas of mainland Scotland and its tenacious survival in the Hebrides, the heartland of former lordship territories. John Bannerman's seminal and perceptive survey of the medieval Lordship of the Isles, for example, concluded: 'It is perhaps not too fanciful to see the Lordship, a comparatively recent manifestation of a highly successful native political and social unit and only marginally indebted to foreign influences, as a contributory factor in the continuing existence of the Gaelic language and culture in Scotland today.'[14]

If Campbell lords have long been portrayed as calculating villains to be set against the noble but doomed leaders of Clan Donald, recent work has begun to question some of the historical assumptions underlying this picture. In penetrating studies of the Lordship of the Isles, John Bannerman made two important points in relation to Clan Campbell. First, there was, in fact, little or no real evidence for any sustained political and territorial conflict between the Clan Donald and Clan Campbell in the medieval period. Second, the ruling elite within Clan Campbell, far from abandoning or rejecting Gaelic cultural forms, remained significant patrons of the activities of the Gaelic learned orders well into the sixteenth century. In these two areas, the political and cultural, Bannerman implied a certain measure of Campbell subservience towards the Lords of the Isles, whose position at the apex of Gaelic society was unquestioned.[15] The importance of the Campbells as cultural patrons within the Gaelic world has become even more obvious through the careful and illuminating scholarship of Willie Gillies and Martin MacGregor.[16] What emerges is a picture of Campbell lordship in the medieval period as one of the great bastions of Gaelic learning and culture. Historical studies proceeding from a rather different angle have also served to blur the previously sharp distinction between Clan Donald and Clan Campbell in terms of the way the families functioned as lords of men and land. Billie and Jean Munro's collection of the *Acts of the Lords of the Isles* and Alexander Grant's acute analysis of the Clan Donald adoption of charter lordship have tended to suggest that the Lords of the Isles were rather more adaptable, innovative and pragmatic than their reputation as conservative guardians of tradition might suggest.[17] This pragmatism extended into the area of the Lords' relationship with the Scottish crown, which was not a tale of unremitting hostility fired by deep-rooted cultural animosity – on either side. In the course of the fifteenth century, as Clan Donald chiefs sought to secure their hold on the earldom of Ross, they became more rather than less involved with Scottish court politics, entered more marriage and political alliances with Scottish magnates, and held and discharged important crown offices. The great and fatal clashes of the fifteenth century arose from a background of growing engagement rather than disengagement. Increasingly, then, the Clan Campbell and Clan Donald do not appear as implacable adversaries, but as travellers along parallel paths, faced by similar difficulties, choices and opportunities, buffeted by the same historical and political pressures.

Some of the themes and debates outlined above are briefly addressed in the course of the present study. However, the bulk of what follows is a political narrative dealing with the fortunes of the main line of the Campbell family from its emergence in historical record in the mid-thirteenth century to the spectacular demise of the second Campbell earl of Argyll at the battle of Flodden in 1513. There is no conscious attempt to defend Campbell lords against charges of opportunism, ruthlessness and aggression, not least because these qualities were amongst the essential prerequisites for the successful exercise and extension of aristocratic power in late medieval Scotland. Those hardy souls who follow the story through and achieve a merciful release alongside Earl Archibald on Branxton Hill may well feel that history has been rather unkind to the medieval lords of Loch Awe. On the whole, the damaging depiction of Campbell regional power as resting entirely on a policy of co-operation with the Scottish crown appears rather simplistic and misleading. At a more fundamental level, the tale of Clan Campbell should also perhaps raise questions about the historical framework in which late medieval Gaelic Scotland is studied. For those who continue to regard the period as one dominated by a struggle between an undifferentiated Gaelic community and an 'anglicising' Scottish monarchy, the Campbells will still appear as an anomaly – a family out of step with the traditions and attitudes of the region they governed. From the viewpoint of a political historian largely concerned with the development of the Scottish kingdom, however, the achievement of Clan Campbell is indicative of a wider success story, namely the integration of lords from Gaelic areas and backgrounds into a political community focused on the Scottish crown. At some level this process may have relied on, or encouraged, a measure of cultural accommodation, but as the Campbell lords themselves proved, political loyalty to the Scottish crown was not, in itself, incompatible with the maintenance of claims to a leading role in Gaelic society.

Notes

1. H. MacKechnie, *The Lamont Clan, 1235–1935* (Edinburgh, 1938), 1.
2. *Ibid.*, 70.
3. W.F. Skene, *The Highlanders of Scotland* (Stirling, 1902), 359.
4. *Cawdor Bk* (ed. C. Innes), xxii.
5. *The Book of Bon-Accord* (Aberdeen, 1839), i, 37; see also Skene's depiction of Harlaw and the struggle over Ross in his *Highlanders*, 89–90. 'It was at once perceived by Government, that however undeniable this claim (to Ross) might be, to admit it would be to concentrate the whole power which the Gael still possessed collectively in the person of one chief, and that by means of that union he would become so formidable an opponent, as to render the result of any struggle . . . between the two races, a matter of considerable doubt. The government therefore resolved to oppose the claim . . . by every means in its power, and . . . a fictitious claim to the title was raised in the person of the son of the governor. The lord of the Isles flew to arms in order to vindicate his right, and that struggle was commenced between the government and these powerful lords, which in all probability would have been successful on the part of the Gael, had it not been for the energy and military talent of King James I, and which was not brought to a conclusion till the forfeiture of the last lord of the Isles in 1493.'
6. P. Sims-Williams, 'The visionary Celt: the construction of an ethnic preconception', *Cambridge Medieval Celtic Studies*, 11 (1986).
7. *Orain Iain Luim: Songs of John MacDonald, Bard of Keppoch* (SGTS, 1964). For a good discussion of the impact of the work of these seventeenth-century Clan Donald poets on the reputation of Clan Campbell within Gaelic historiography, see W. Gillies, 'Some aspects of Campbell History', *TGSI*, 50 (1978), 265–295.

8. Hints of the presentation of the Campbell past in this way to a Lowland audience can be found in the early sixteenth-century chronicles of Hector Boece and his vernacular translators. In 1516, Colin, 3rd earl of Argyll, claimed that in the years since the battle of Flodden (1513) he had been heavily engaged in the 'defens of my Kingis landis fra the men of the Ylis, quhilkis of ald hes beyn trowblus'. NAS CS5/xxix, f.210. In 1596, Denis Campbell, dean of Limerick, in communication with the English government, outlined his family's historic role in dealing with the inhabitants of the west of Scotland, the Hebrides and Ireland. According to the dean, the Campbells as a kindred were 'Trusti, valiant and civillie-inclined'. *CSP Scot.*, xii, 201–211; *Maitland Misc.*, iv, 37–57. Seventeenth-century Campbell histories/genealogies were unequivocal in emphasising the loyalty of the family to the crown and its prominent role in the suppression of Hebridean rebellion in the past. See *HP*, ii, 69–111; Lord Archibald Campbell, *Records of Argyll* (Edinburgh, 1885).

9. E.g., O. Thomson, *The Great Feud: The Campbells and the MacDonalds* (Stroud, 2000).

10. M. Lynch, *Scotland: A New History* (Edinburgh, 1990), 67.

11. John MacInnes, 'Gaelic poetry and historical tradition', in *The Middle Ages in the Highlands* (Inverness, 1981), 142–163. See also in this article the suggestion that 'The house of Argyll rose to power and pre-eminence by service to the Scottish crown', p.156.

12. E.R. Cregeen, 'The Changing Role of the House of Argyll in the Scottish Highlands', in *History and Social Anthropology*, ed. I.M. Lewis (London, 1968), 153–192, at 153.

13. Cregeen, 'House of Argyll', 156. The footnote for this argument expands on the theme by claiming that 'the deliberate destruction of the ordered system of government and the political and social equilibrium represented by the Lordship of the Isles' gave rise to feuds that were 'systematically encouraged by government and the Argylls'.

14. J.W.M. Bannerman, 'The Lordship of the Isles', in J. Brown (ed.), *Scottish Society in the Fifteenth Century* (London, 1977), 209–240, at 240.

15. Bannerman, *op.cit.* and 'The Lordship of the Isles: Historical Background', Appendix II, in K.A. Steer and J.W.M. Bannerman, *Late Medieval Monumental Sculpture in the West Highlands* (Edinburgh, 1977), 201–213.

16. W. Gillies, 'Campbell History', *TGSI*, 50 (1978), 265–295. This important article surveys the Campbells' reputation as an 'ungaelic' family and, through a close study of Campbell patronage of Gaelic poets, hints at its inappropriateness; M. MacGregor, 'Church and culture in the late medieval Highlands', in *The Church in the Highlands*, ed. James Kirk (Edinburgh 1998), 1–36; Ibid., 'Surely one of the greatest poems ever made in Britain': The Lament for Griogair Ruadh MacGregor of Glen Strae and its Historical Background', in *The Polar Twins: Studies in Scottish Literature and Scottish History*, eds. D. Gifford and E.J. Cowan (Edinburgh, 2000), 114–153.

17. *Acts of the Lords of the Isles, 1336–1493*, eds. J. Munro and R.W. Munro (Scottish History Society, 1986).(Hereafter *ALI*); A. Grant, 'Scotland's "Celtic Fringe" in the late middle ages: the MacDonald Lords of the Isles and the kingdom of Scotland', in R.R. Davies (ed.), *The British Isles, 1100–1500* (Edinburgh, 1988).

ONE

The Sons of Arthur?
Clan Campbell in the Thirteenth Century

L ate in the summer of 1306 Robert Bruce, King of Scotland, and a
weary band of his supporters made their way through the earldom of
Lennox to the shore of Loch Long.[1] King Robert and his men had
travelled a long, bitter and bloody road to reach the salt sea; behind them
lay crushing military defeats at Methven and Dail Righ, and a doleful
litany of kinsfolk and allies killed, captured or executed.[2] Indeed, the
clamour of remorseless pursuit was still with Robert and his remaining
partisans as they waited on the shore of the 'Loch of Ships'. According to
John Barbour, writing his account of Robert's kingship in the 1370s, the
beleaguered monarch hoped for news of a fleet under the command of Sir
Neil Campbell. Neil had left Bruce's company a few days earlier in order to
muster a galley force that could carry the king and his men to the relative
safety of Kintyre.[3] As King Robert's followers gazed out to catch a glimpse
of sail in the Firth of Clyde, they may well have pondered the nature of the
man upon whom they waited. The king himself would have had few
concerns about the fidelity of Neil Campbell, or his capacity to bring the
promised fleet to the rendezvous, for by 1306 Sir Neil already had a long
history of personal service to Robert and his family; Campbell would come
if he was able. Neil's unyielding loyalty to the Bruce king and his ability to
raise a galley force in 1306 reflected the political and personal alliances and
territorial interests which the Campbell kindred had built in Argyll,
Cowal and other territories fringing the Firth of Clyde over the closing
decades of the thirteenth century.

It is customary, but slightly misleading, to point to the relationship
between Sir Neil and Robert I as the decisive factor in the development of
Campbell power in late medieval Scotland. Bruce's eventual triumph, it is
argued, handed regional supremacy in Argyll to the king's ally, Sir Neil,
and his descendants. From that point Campbell lordship was characterised
by its close co-operation with the Scottish crown and entered an apparently irresistible and relentless phase of expansion.[4] The reality was less

neat. The family would certainly prosper as a result of its association with the hero-king, but the advance was fitful and interrupted by dramatic setbacks and shifts of political and territorial focus. Moreover, the story is not to be told in the simple passing of a burgeoning Campbell lordship from father to son. Early in the fourteenth century the predominance of the Campbell line represented by Sir Neil and his descendants was by no means natural or assured. The effective leadership of the wider kindred would pass at various points to a number of men from other branches of the family in the tumult of civil and national war in the years after 1306.

Although Neil Campbell is the first member of the family for whom the outlines of a career can be discerned, recent historians have properly laid stress on the fact that Clan Campbell was a well-established kindred with wide-ranging territorial interests long before the end of the thirteenth century.[5] The earliest surviving genealogy relating to the family is contained in a collection dating from c.1400 (MS. 1467) that records the descent of a number of the leading Gaelic aristocratic kindreds in the Hebrides, Argyll and the Scottish west coast.[6] In his ground-breaking study of the origins of the family, David Sellar collated the Campbell genealogy found in MS.1467 with genealogies preserved in the sixteenth-century Kilbride MS (now lost) and the seventeenth-century collection of the Irish genealogist Duald MacFirbis.[7] Despite some minor inconsistencies, the various genealogical tracts presented a broadly consistent picture of the descent of late medieval Campbell lords. Taking the genealogies studied by Sellar in conjunction with contemporary references to individual Campbell lords in other sources, Neil emerges as the representative of an aristocratic lineage that could trace its descent with reasonable certainty back into the twelfth century. (see Table 1). Neil himself was the son of the well-attested Colin (d.c.1296), probably the Cailean Mór from whom subsequent Campbell chiefs were said to derive their distinctive Gaelic style MacCailein Mór.[8] Colin's own father, Gillespic, appeared in royal record in 1262–3 and 1266. For the generations beyond Gillespic we rely largely on the sometimes conflicting genealogies examined by Sellar. These agree that Gillespic's father was named Dugald, while MacFirbis' genealogy alone asserts that this man was the first of the line to bear the name Campbell, probably derived from the Gaelic byname Caimbeul, indicating a wry or twisted mouth.[9] Above Dugald the genealogies show some divergence but, importantly, all claim that Dugald's father or grandfather was named Duncan. In a charter issued by

David II in 1369 the then Campbell chief had confirmed to him the lands and rights held by his progenitor, one Duncan 'Macdowne' (MacDuibne), in the lordship of Loch Awe and elsewhere in Argyll.[10] The 1369 charter makes it clear that in the fourteenth century Duncan MacDuibne was regarded as a prominent ancestor from whom the Campbell lineage claimed to derive rights to land and lordship in Loch Awe. The terms of the royal grant suggest that elements of the Campbell genealogy recorded c.1400 were in place by 1369 and, as Sellar has argued, also support the assertion made in later family histories that the Campbells emerged from an earlier kindred that originally bore the name MacDuibne or O'Duibne.[11] Beyond the Duibne, from whom the family name MacDuibne or O'Duibne was said to derive, the Campbell genealogies record a series of rather bizarre names that seem to have a strong 'British' resonance. Sellar goes on to argue that this belief in 'British' descent represented the earliest strand of Campbell thinking as to the origins of their own family. Thus the Campbell genealogy in MS.1467 extended back from the chief alive in 1400, Colin, to the legendary British king Arthur, son of Uther Pendragon 'the undisputed king of the world'.[12] The Arthurian/British descent claimed for Clan Campbell remained a constant feature of Gaelic poems and genealogies produced for the family in the medieval and early modern periods.[13] This fact, combined with the early concentration of family members in and around the Firth of Clyde, might suggest that the kindred's origins genuinely lay in a district where the influence and prestige of the old British kingdom of Strathclyde still lingered, and Sellar has argued plausibly that the earldom of Lennox was a likely area for the genesis of the family.[14]

   The picture of Clan Campbell at the end of the thirteenth century as a family with rights in Loch Awe that could be traced back to a Duncan MacDuibne and whose general pre-eminence on the borders of Argyll/Lennox reflected its descent from Old British stock is a compelling and persuasive one. However, some interesting problems remain. One is the fact that it is very difficult to identify the 'core' Campbell estates in this period with any precision. Despite the family's reputedly ancient association with Loch Awe the bulk of the surviving evidence, as Sellar notes, seems to point to the Lennox and the Firth of Clyde as the area in which thirteenth-century Campbell lords exerted most influence. By the 1290s there were a number of prominent Campbells holding land or office in this region.[15] A potentially useful snapshot of landholding in Argyll and other

west-coast lordships was provided in February 1293, when King John
Balliol's first parliament ratified plans for the creation of three new west-
coast sheriffdoms based on Ross, Lorn and Kintyre and listed the estates
of individual landowners that were to be incorporated within the prospective new jurisdictions.[16] A Colin Campbell, almost certainly the
father of Bruce's companion Sir Neil, was noted as holding lands that
were to be included in the new sheriffdom of Lorn. At first sight this
would seem to refer to the Campbells' 'ancestral' holdings in Loch Awe,
but the sequence in which the landowners were named is curious and
seems to suggest that wherever Colin's estates lay, they were not in Loch
Awe.[17] Certainly, Colin's name did not appear where it might be expected
alongside others who demonstrably held land in mid-Argyll and Loch
Awe. The classification of Loch Awe landowners seems to have retained
the north-to-south organisation of the wider listing and to have named
the lords of the principal secular lordships running down the loch. In
many cases these secular lordships corresponded to the local parish
boundaries. Thus the lands of John of Glenorchy (Glenorchy), were
followed by those of Gilbert (MacNaughton) (Upper Loch Awe; the
parishes of Inishail and Kilmorich),[18] the lands of Malcolm MacIver
(Middle Loch Awe: Kilchrenan parish?), the lands of Dugald of Craignish
(Craignish), the lands of John MacGilchrist (Ardscotnish; Kilmartin
parish?),[19] the lands of Master Ralph of Dundee (Glassary) and the lands
of Gillespic MacLachlan (Strathlachlan). The list continued with the
estates of the earl of Menteith in Knapdale and the holdings of Angus son
of Donald of the Isles (presumably in Islay?) and rather strangely ended
with those of Colin Campbell. It is impossible to identify any lordship
held by Colin that could have lain to the south of the lands of Angus Mór
MacDonald.[20] If the location of Colin's estates remains rather mysterious,
we can at least suggest that the Campbells were not regarded by the crown,
or anybody else, as enjoying any special or superior status in Loch Awe in
1293. The problematic position of the lordship of Loch Awe will be
returned to later. Other Campbell lords were named in the list of men
whose lands were to be incorporated in the new sheriffdom of Kintyre to
be administered by James the Steward. Thomas Campbell was clearly a
close kinsman of Colin, while the individual identified as Duncan Dubh
has been claimed as an ancestor of the MacArthur Campbells of Strachur.[21] The descendants of these men seem to have held estates in
northern Cowal; if this reflected earlier patterns of possession, then

the 1293 legislation might suggest the existence of a number of Campbell lineages clustered in the area between the heads of Loch Fyne and Loch Long.[22] Accounts of the family's military exploits in 1306 and 1334 also indicate the early influence of the Campbells in the sea lochs that opened into the Firth of Clyde. In 1306, as we have seen, Robert I expected a Campbell galley force to come to his rescue on the shores of Loch Long, while in 1334 Robert's grandson, Robert the Steward, also relied on Campbell galleys to undertake assaults on English forces in Dunoon and Bute.[23]

However, thirteenth-century references to individual Campbell lords were not confined to the Clyde, and at least some suggest a link to another area rich in Arthurian/British associations to the east of Stirling. On the two occasions when he appeared in record, Sir Neil's putative grandfather, Gillespic, was associated with this region. At some point in 1262–3 Gillespic received a royal gift of the lands of 'mestreth and sawlchop', taken to be Menstrie and Sauchie in Stirlingshire, while three years later, on 4 March 1266, he witnessed a charter issued at Stirling by Alexander III in favour of the abbey of Lindores.[24] Menstrie remained in the hands of Gillespic's descendants into the sixteenth century and it is tempting to suggest that the occupation of the estate in 1263 was, or swiftly became, heritable.[25] The appearance of Gillespic's grandson, Neil, as a witness to a grant of 1282 in favour of Cambuskenneth abbey reinforces the impression that in the second half of the thirteenth century the family had a number of ties to the aristocratic society of Stirling and Clackmannan.[26] The Campbells' claim to Arthurian/British ancestry would not have been out of place in this geographical context, for Stirling was commonly regarded in late medieval Scotland as marking the boundary between the ancient British and Scottish kingdoms, and as a stronghold with explicit connections to King Arthur. In 1365 David II boasted to the visiting chronicler Jean Froissart that the royal castle at Stirling was the site of King Arthur's Snowdon. In the 1420s a Burgundian knight received a similar 'Scottish heritage tour', in which Arthur's role as the builder of Stirling Castle was highlighted. In the fifteenth century the royal herald associated with Stirling castle was named 'Snawdoun', while the castle's Arthurian past and alternative name of 'Snawdonwest' was advertised by an unknown Scot travelling in England during the 1470s.[27] On the whole, Stirling's Arthurian/British associations seem to reflect a rather antiquarian late medieval literary and cultural enthusiasm for the British past that affected much of the aristocracy of western Europe. It would be worthwhile to look at Campbell claims to British descent in the same context. While it is certainly possible that the Campbells and other Scottish families that asserted Arthurian ancestry were genuinely of Old British stock, the cult of Arthur and 'British' kingship had also enjoyed a much more recent revival in the wake of the appearance of Geoffrey of Monmouth's *Historia Regnum Britanniae* (History of the Kings of Britain) in or around 1136. Monmouth's work spawned a wide interest in Arthur as well as other British kings of dubious authenticity.[28] As a result, it is well nigh impossible to disentangle any genuine and early 'British' legacy from a relatively late accommodation with the Arthurian pseudo-history invented by Geoffrey.

One interesting aspect of the Campbell avowal of Arthurian descent, however it arose, is that in a thirteenth-century context it would seem to be another factor which aligned Clan Campbell with the interests of the Stewart family, the rising regional power in the Firth of Clyde. The Campbells' supposed 'British' origins certainly marked the family off from most of their neighbours in Cowal, Knapdale and mid-Argyll. The Lamonts, MacSweens, MacGilchrists and MacLachlans, for example, regarded themselves as related branches of a wider kindred descended from a common ancestor, and ultimately traced their origins back to an eleventh-century Irish prince.[29] However, as twelfth-century Breton incomers to the British Isles, the Stewarts could genuinely claim 'British' ancestry.[30] The assertion of a descent from illustrious figures in the British past was used by a number of noble families across the British Isles in the twelfth and thirteenth centuries to provide a historical precedent for the aggressive creation of new aristocratic supremacies in areas once reputedly held by the British kings and for the expulsion or subjugation of established landowners. It may not be coincidence that, to judge by the use of Arthur as a Christian name, the cult of Geoffrey of Monmouth's all-conquering king seems to have flourished in and around areas of Stewart lordship in the Firth of Clyde in the thirteenth century.[31] The period was also notable for the rapid expansion of Stewart interests from their core lordship of Renfrew. The advance of Stewart lordship across the Firth of Clyde can be tentatively traced through resignations and grants made by local landowners in favour of the abbey of Paisley, a Stewart foundation and the long-established ecclesiastical focus for the family. By c.1200 the Stewarts had become the dominant lords in Bute, and during the 1230s the rocky Cowal peninsula, lying to the north of the island, also fell under their sway.[32] Around the middle of the century Arran and Knapdale were added to the growing Stewart empire and eventually seem to have been absorbed into the personal lordship of Walter Stewart, the younger brother of Alexander, the fourth High Steward.[33] Prominent families in the areas affected were displaced or found their independent status challenged as the Stewarts steadily acquired lands and jurisdiction. The most notable casualties were the MacSweens, the possessors of extensive estates in Knapdale and Kintyre, including the great fortresses at Skipness and Castle Sween. From 1261 onwards, there were distinct indications of a concerted Stewart campaign to force MacSween recognition of their lordship in the region.[34] At least some members of the MacSween kindred were unwilling to subject themselves to Stewart control, and played a prominent part in supporting the expedition of the Norwegian king Haakon IV in 1263.[35] The ultimate failure of the expedition left the family vulnerable to retaliation and expulsion from their estates. By the close of the thirteenth century the MacSweens had been forced into exile in Ireland, where they carved out a lordship around Fanad, while the banners of Walter Stewart flew above Skipness and Castle Sween.[36]

Early in the 1260s Walter also laid claim to the earldom of Menteith by right of his wife, Mary of Menteith. The successful prosecution of this claim meant that Walter Stewart's descendants adopted Menteith as a surname. The earldom had had a convoluted recent history. In 1213 the then earl, Maurice, had resigned Menteith in favour of his younger brother, also Maurice. The elder Maurice, however, was to retain possession of certain lands for his own lifetime, while others were to be used to provide a tocher, or marriage portion, for his daughters. The lands given to Maurice the elder's daughters 'and their heirs to come', to be held from Maurice the younger and his heirs, were Savelin (Saline?), 'Mestryn', 'Keneltone' and 'Stradlochlin'.[37] The 'Mestryn' mentioned here as an estate to be held by one of Maurice's daughters and her heirs is usually equated with Menstrie, i.e. the lordship that, as 'Mestreth', was later assigned to Gillespic Campbell in 1262–3.[38] The possibility that the Campbells were in some way involved in the division of the Menteith inheritance is intriguing, especially given the wider struggle over the earldom in the mid-thirteenth century. On the death of the younger Maurice, shortly before January 1234, Walter Comyn, the husband of

Maurice's daughter Isabella, had assumed the title of earl.[39] Following Walter Comyn's own death in 1258 Countess Isabella swiftly remarried, this time to an English knight named John Russell. The liaison provoked opposition, and accusations that the countess had poisoned her first husband. At this point Countess Isabella and Russell were forced to flee the kingdom and Walter Stewart advanced his claim to the vacant earldom as the husband of Mary of Menteith. It was long assumed that this Mary was a younger sister of Isabella, but in 1975 Archie Duncan put forward the suggestion that Mary was, in fact, a daughter of the elder Maurice and thus Isabella's cousin rather than her sister.[40] Walter Stewart was styling himself earl of Menteith by 17 April 1261, when he witnessed a grant to the abbey of Paisley.[41] The displaced Countess Isabella and her husband John Russell continued the struggle, having the agreement of 1213 inspected by Henry III of England in September 1261 and appealing for papal intervention. The dispute would be carried on by Countess Isabella's daughter, also Isabella, and her husbands; it eventually rumbled on into the fourteenth century. If Walter Stewart's claim to Menteith depended, as Duncan suggests, on the revival of the rights of the descendants of the elder Maurice of 1213, it is tempting to speculate on the position of Gillespic Campbell in Menstrie in 1262–3. It is, of course, perfectly possible that Menstrie had fallen to the crown through forfeiture or sale after 1213 so that the gift of 1262–3 need not imply that the Campbell lord had any hereditary claim to the estate. Certainly, later Campbell genealogies give not the slightest hint that the Campbell lords most likely to be active around 1213 concluded a marriage to an heiress from a comital family.[42] Nevertheless, it is worth noting that an interest in the Menteith inheritance would square remarkably well with the geographical spread of Campbell estates, from Stirlingshire to Cowal, by the end of the thirteenth century.[43] Moreover, if the MacFirbis genealogy is correct in identifying Gillespic's father, Dugald, as the first individual to actually bear the name Campbell, this would imply that the various 'Campbell' lords noted at the end of the thirteenth century were all grandsons or great-grandsons of this man and that he had held sufficient land or influence to provide for several cadet families.[44] The emergence of a widely ramified family sharing a name that only came to be used in the first half of the thirteenth century suggests either that Dugald managed to lay exclusive claim to a substantial part of the resources held by his father as a member of the MacDuibne kindred, or that he himself was responsible for a rapid accumulation of territory. The Campbells' 'historical horizon' as 'Campbells' and, perhaps, as holders of estates stretching from Argyll to Stirlingshire does, therefore, seem to lie in the first half of the thirteenth century.

There were clearly a number of circumstances, besides an interest in the Menteith inheritance, that might explain the expansion of Campbell or proto-Campbell MacDuibne interests in the Firth of Clyde and elsewhere in Argyll in the thirteenth century. For much of the period the issue of ultimate sovereignty in Argyll and the Isles was a matter of open, and occasionally violent, dispute between the Scottish and Norwegian crowns. The flashpoints in this conflict, the military expeditions led by Alexander II against Argyll in the 1220s and 1249, and the Norwegian crown's bellicose responses in 1230 and 1263, are well-known and much analysed.[45] In such a situation a rapid turnover in land ownership and occupation might be anticipated. The punitive expeditions led or promoted by Alexander II and Alexander III into the west in the 1220s, 1240s and 1260s were later said to have caused major re-settlements of land and office.[46] Although the long-term effect of these royal raids may be exaggerated, there is little doubt that aristocratic lordships and ecclesiastical institutions firmly tied to the interests of the Scottish crown increased their influence and authority inside Argyll as the century progressed. Although we can say nothing in detail about the conduct and political alliances of Campbell lords during this period, by the end of the thirteenth century the family were clearly reconciled to a role in the service of Stewart overlords and this probably reflected a reasonably long-standing association.

By the 1290s Gillespic Campbell's son, Colin, was unequivocally part of the affinity of James the Steward, the son of Alexander and the nephew of Walter, earl of Menteith, and was active in a number of lordships bordering the Firth of Clyde. In 1293, for example, the Steward and his brother John stood as pledges for Colin Campbell in a transaction involving lands in the Steward's lordship of Kyle.[47] In January 1295, Sir Colin witnessed a charter by James in favour of Paisley Abbey at a major centre of Stewart lordship, the Blackhall of Paisley. In the following year Colin attested the arrangements for James' marriage to Giles or Egidia de Burgh, sister of Richard de Burgh, earl of Ulster.[48] Colin also witnessed an undated charter by Malcolm, earl of Lennox, in favour of Sir John of Luss in the company of the Steward and a number of his retainers.[49] At around the same time he received a grant of lands in the lordship of Cowal from John Lamont.[50]

However, the Steward was not the only great figure in the south-west of Scotland with whom Colin Campbell was associated. David Sellar has suggested that Colin's mother was Effrica of Carrick, the niece of Neil, earl of Carrick.[51] Such a match would have given the Campbells an early link with the Bruce family, for Earl Neil's daughter and heiress, Marjorie, married Robert Bruce and carried to him the title earl of Carrick. The eldest son of this marriage, also Robert, was the future king.[52] Colin Campbell's position as a kinsman of the Bruce earls of Carrick might explain his nomination by the Bruce family to take part in the arbitration of the contesting claims of Robert Bruce and John Balliol to the Scottish throne in June 1291.[53] In November 1292, at Berwick, a Master Neil Campbell, usually identified as Colin's brother, was one of the Bruce auditors required to acknowledge the decision of the court in favour of John Balliol.[54] In the following year, Master Neil was openly in the service of Robert, earl of Carrick, voyaging to Bergen in Norway to deliver clothes and furniture to the earl's sister, Isabella, queen of Norway.[55]

The failure of the Bruce claim to the throne in 1292 was undoubtedly a blow to the family and its supporters in the west. The newly established Balliol regime might well have anticipated some measure of resistance to its authority from those families and areas most closely associated with championing the Bruce claim to the kingship. Bruce attempts to ensure that the representative of their right should not render homage to the new king hardly suggested that they were reconciled to the decision. The Bruce interest lay like a shadow behind Balliol's kingship, a potential focus for internal political dissent and external manipulation. King John, however, had his own powerful domestic allies, whose influence extended into the west and more than matched that of the earl of Carrick and his affinity. King John's brother-in-law was John Comyn, lord of Badenoch and Lochaber. Comyn's own brother-in-law was Alexander MacDougall, lord of Argyll, one of the most prestigious and powerful west-coast lords. The Balliol-Comyn-MacDougall axis was the cornerstone of Balliol rule.

As we have seen, one of the first acts of the Balliol government, in February 1293, was to put forward plans for the creation of new sheriff-doms in the west. The arrangement seems like a sensible extension of the authority of the Scottish crown into the west, an attempt to regulate landholding and justice in an area that had been formally subject to the

Scottish crown since the treaty of Perth of 1266. One of the proposed sheriffdoms was that of Lorn, to be administered by Alexander of Argyll.[56] At some point shortly after the creation of the Lorn jurisdiction, Alexander was given powers to receive into the king's peace men within the new sheriffdom who were willing to take their lands at farm and who offered sufficient 'securities' that they would render the appropriate services. It seems likely that similar powers were granted to the other new sheriffs, the earl of Ross for Skye and James the Steward for Kintyre.[57] Although the arrangements have been seen as desirable in terms of the extension and consolidation of royal authority, the effect on the ground was to hand extensive rights to three powerful magnates who could not always be guaranteed to distinguish between royal needs and those of their own affinities. What is certain is that in the early 1290s the earls of Ross, bolstered by their wide-ranging new rights, were waging what they later described as an open war against the recalcitrant MacRuairies of Garmoran.[58] Alexander MacDougall's exercise of the Lorn sheriffship may also have produced a cluster of dissatisfied local opponents who found the regional agent of the Balliol regime a dangerous and discomfiting foe. One man who may have been rather unhappy with the incorporation of his family's recently acquired Knapdale lands into the sheriffship of Lorn was the earl of Menteith.

Although the Great Cause had the potential to identify and consolidate two opposed political 'blocs' inside the Scottish polity, given time and the sensible use of patronage, Balliol would surely have consolidated his position and engineered support even from those who had been identified with the Bruce claim. The demands of Edward I ensured that Balliol was denied the opportunity to secure his kingship. When war began in March 1296 disaster was heaped on disaster for King John. Edward I's brutal sack of Berwick at the end of March 1296 was followed by the wholesale defeat of the Scottish host at Dunbar on 27 April. In the aftermath of Dunbar many of the Scots nobility submitted to the English king. By 2 July King John himself had been forced to surrender his kingdom to Edward I. The hapless John was ceremonially humiliated and taken as a prisoner from his own realm.[59]

In order to consolidate his hold on Scotland, Edward I toured the kingdom in July and August, collecting oaths of loyalty from those who held significant estates within the realm.[60] Amongst the Scottish noblemen who submitted to Edward I was Alexander of Argyll, who appeared at Elgin to render his fealty to the English crown. Edward was evidently unimpressed with MacDougall's submission, particularly as Argyll's eldest son and heir, John, failed to render an oath of allegiance. On 10 September Edward made arrangements for a concerted offensive to neutralise the threat posed by John of Lorn. The English king did not have to look far to find men willing to take on the MacDougalls in Argyll, and essentially recruited the entire Stewart/Menteith affinity into his service. One of the chief agents of the English crown was to be Alexander, earl of Menteith, who received a commission to occupy Alexander and John MacDougall's castles and lands.[61] The men of James the Steward in Cowal, Bute and Rothesay, and the burghs of Ayr, Renfrew, Dumbarton and Glasgow, as well as the men of Ross and John Comyn's lordships of Badenoch and Lochaber, were instructed to support Menteith's move against the lordship of Argyll. Edward also demanded the support of the barons of Argyll and Colin Campbell, described as bailie of Loch Awe and Ardscotnish.[62] This was in fact the first occasion on which the Campbells were explicitly identified as exercising any form of authority in Loch Awe. Despite the later association of the Campbells with the area there is no direct evidence to connect the family to the lordship in the thirteenth century and certainly nothing to indicate that they enjoyed extensive rights over other landowners as descendants of the Duncan MacDuibne mentioned in the charter of 1369.[63] In fact, the bailiary arrangement suggests that in 1296 the rights of lordship over Loch Awe and Ardscotnish lay with Edward I. Moreover, the existence of a royal bailiary of Loch Awe and Ardscotnish was almost certainly not the invention of Edward I in his quest to undermine MacDougall power in 1296, for King John had also addressed commands to his bailie of Loch Awe and Ardscotnish in 1293.[64] It is not inconceivable that these two lordships had come under the direct jurisdiction of the Scottish crown much earlier in the thirteenth century. Alexander II and Alexander III had both issued charters dealing with lands (and particularly the possession of castles) in Loch Awe that implied that the estates and strongholds involved were held directly of the king rather than from an intermediate lord.[65] An interesting indication of the way in which Loch Awe and mid-Argyll were opened up to secular and ecclesiastical lordship based further to the east came in the resignations of the parochial churches of Inishail and Kilmorich by MacNaughton lords in favour of Inchaffray Abbey. Both resignations were witnessed by Malise, earl of Strathearn, and Clement, bishop of Dunblane, two of the driving forces behind the mid-thirteenth-century royal campaigns in Argyll.[66] The retention of royal rights in Loch Awe and Ardscotnish may have been regarded as essential for the maintenance of the crown's control over the recently annexed province, with Loch Awe, in particular, providing a land route from eastern Scotland into the heart of Argyll.

In 1296, then, the stage was set for a co-ordinated assault on the position of the MacDougall lords, in which Colin Campbell, the newly created bailie of Loch Awe and Ardscotnish, could be expected to play a leading role in support of the earl of Menteith. This, surely, provides the political context for the traditional tale of the death of Sir Colin in a clash with John of Lorn on the borders of Loch Awe and Lorn, an event that could have occurred at any stage after the commission of 10 September 1296.[67] Sir Colin's death was not the only fatality inflicted by the MacDougall lords of Argyll as they sought to defend themselves against the men assigned to bring them to heel in 1296. Letters usually dated to the summer of 1297 from Alexander of Islay to Edward I indicate that Alexander of Argyll had mounted a spectacular counter-offensive, raiding Clan Donald lands and striking against targets across the Firth of Clyde. In 1299 Alexander of Argyll caught up with Alexander of Islay and killed him 'together with a countless number of his own people that were slaughtered around him'.[68]

While others struggled to contain the lords of Argyll, the Clan Campbell seem to have dropped out of the fierce military competition within the province. The transmission of Campbell estates and leadership of the kindred after Sir Colin's death may have been disputed, and was by no means as straightforward as the traditional genealogies might suggest. In 1301–2, two of Colin's sons, Donald and Neil, suddenly appear as active and influential personalities in the service of Robert Bruce, earl of Carrick (the future Robert I), outwith Argyll. By that stage the brief Campbell hold on the bailiary of Loch Awe and Ardscotnish had probably already been lost. Alexander of Argyll and his sons had submitted to Edward I in the summer of 1301 and, by 1304 at the latest, the lord of Argyll had been made responsible for the inbringing of royal revenues from Loch Awe and Ardscotnish.[69]

Although Campbell tradition unequivocally regards Neil as the elder son of Sir Colin, the contemporary evidence, such as it is, might suggest that Donald enjoyed this distinction.[70] Moreover, although by the time of his death (c.1316) Sir Neil was the dominant figure in Clan Campbell, there is no indication that he was initially regarded in this light. Indeed, after his first appearance as a witness to the 1282 grant in favour of Cambuskenneth Abbey, Neil Campbell simply disappears from sight for two decades.[71] Given these circumstances, speculation that the clerical Master Neil, who was notably active in the service of the Bruce family throughout the 1290s, might be one and the same as Neil, Colin's son (and thus a cleric who abandoned the religious life in order to pursue a career as a secular lord), is attractive, but unprovable.[72]

What is clear is that from 1300 Neil Campbell and, to a much lesser extent, his brother Donald built their careers and reputations on their unswerving loyalty and service to Robert the Bruce. Throughout these uncertain years the Campbell brothers were invariably in step with the political dance of the earl of Carrick, and Neil, at least, seems to have been part of Carrick's personal affinity. Bruce became a joint guardian of the kingdom after the defeat of the Wallace-led host at the battle of Falkirk in 1298, but resigned before May 1300.[73] Bruce seems to have become increasingly disenchanted with the determination of his fellow guardians to negotiate the restoration of John Balliol to the Scottish throne. Alarmed by the apparent success of the diplomatic initiatives of the pro-Balliol guardians, Bruce was driven to seek an accommodation with another man bitterly opposed to the restoration of Balliol, namely Edward I. Early in 1302, Robert came into the peace of the English king.[74] Amongst the men who followed Bruce into the service of the English crown was Sir Neil Campbell. On 13 February 1302, Neil received a grant from the English king of lands in Cumberland that belonged to the heir of the deceased Hubert de Multon, along with the right to marry Hubert's widow, Margaret. The grant was one of a cluster of remissions and concessions issued to Carrick's followers by Edward I in the wake of Earl Robert's shift of allegiance.[75] It also seems likely that it was around this time that Neil and his brother Donald received from Edward the lucrative ward of the two daughters and heiresses of Andrew of Crawford, lord of Loudoun, Draffan and Lochmartnaham.[76]

For the next four years, the Campbell brothers followed the lead of the earl of Carrick and served the English war effort in Scotland with a fair degree of enthusiasm. Donald was one of the knights retained in the service of Sir John Botetourte, the English justiciar of Galloway, in campaigns in the south-west of Scotland, and eventually acted as sheriff of Wigtown for the English administration in 1304–5.[77] In 1304, Neil himself served in the retinue of Richard de Burgh, earl of Ulster, and appeared as part of the great host besieging one of the last bastions of Scottish resistance, Stirling Castle.[78] Neil's connection to the earl of Ulster was not as surprising as it first appears, since in 1302 the earl of Carrick had married de Burgh's daughter Isabella. Neil's service to Earl Richard undoubtedly reflected de Burgh's position as Bruce's new father-in-law.

When the garrison of Stirling eventually surrendered to Edward I's forces on 20 July 1305, it seemed that the English king's triumph in the struggle for control of the Scottish kingdom was complete. Already, in February 1304, the Scottish guardian, John Comyn of Badenoch, had negotiated the surrender of most of the principal leaders of Scottish resistance to Edward's regime.[79] After the fall of Stirling, Edward now had to find a way to govern the annexed northern kingdom as its accepted lord. The process was likely to be complicated not only by the resentment of many Scots at the dissolution of the institutions of Scottish kingship and the infringement of the rights and liberties secured by, and vested in, those institutions, but also by the tensions created as former opponents of the English crown sought the restoration of estates and offices which, in many cases, had been assigned to other men. During 1305, Bruce and his supporters, including Neil and Donald Campbell, became acutely aware of the disadvantages of serving an English monarch intent on securing his hold over the entire Scottish aristocratic community, and not simply concerned with rewarding the earl of Carrick and his adherents.

In March 1305, Carrick attended a Parliament at Westminster as one of the three Scottish commissioners (the others being Robert Wishart, bishop of Glasgow, and Sir John Mowbray) consulted by Edward I on the arrangements to be made for the future governance of Scotland.[80] It was agreed that a full panel of Scottish representatives should attend a parliament at Westminster later in the year in order to finalise arrangements for the administration of Scotland.[81] Earl Robert's prominent role in the March negotiations at Westminster and the personal concessions he obtained from Edward I at the same time represented the high point of Bruce's influence with the English crown.[82] By the time the parliament actually met to discuss the future governance of Scotland, in September 1305, the relationship between the earl and Edward I's government was decidedly less cordial.

The troubles experienced by Sir Neil Campbell during 1305 undoubtedly reflected and aggravated those of his Bruce master. Neil seems to have accompanied Earl Robert to the discussions of March 1305; Campbell was certainly physically present and transacting business in Westminster during Lent of that year.[83] The Campbell lord's problems centred on a long-running dispute over the wardship of the two Crawford heiresses that had been granted to Neil and his brother in 1302. Sir Robert Keith, who claimed to have purchased the wardship of the heiresses from king John Balliol, contested the right to the ward and marriage of the young sisters. Keith had been a leading figure in Scottish resistance to Edward I during the 1290s, before being captured and imprisoned in 1299. Sometime in 1303, Keith obtained his release under terms that expressly allowed him to recover his lands and rights with the support of the English crown.[84] By November 1303 Keith had begun legal proceedings to recover possession of the heiresses from Neil Campbell and his brother.[85] The Campbells were prohibited from arranging the marriages of the Crawford sisters before the king's council in Scotland discussed the legal rights of the contesting parties. Regardless of this ban, Neil seems to have married (or arranged a marriage for) the younger sister, Alice, and was thereafter summoned before the king's council for contempt.[86] Eventually, the case was decided in Keith's favour at a parliament in London, perhaps that of March/April 1305, but more probably the assembly in September of the same year.[87] After the judgement, Edward I ordered his Scottish chancellor and chamberlain 'to allow [Keith] to have these children, and to distrain Sir Dovenald Chambel and Sir Nel Chambel by their lands and bodies'.[88]

The deterioration of the relationship between the Campbell brothers and Edward I's administration during 1305 may well have been exacerbated by the grants made by Edward in favour of one of his household knights, Sir John Dovedale, who had been active in the king's Scottish campaigns.[89] At some point in 1305 the king assigned the lands of one Sir Colin Campbell to Dovedale, because Colin had died leaving an underage son and heir.[90] Later in the year, and again probably at the Westminster parliament of September 1305, Dovedale successfully petitioned the king for the ward and marriage of Sir Colin's infant heir.[91] The identity of this Sir Colin Campbell is problematic. It would seem unlikely that the Colin who was Donald and Neil's father could leave an under-age heir in 1305. One possibility is that the Colin who died c.1304–5 was an otherwise unrecorded younger brother of Neil and Donald who had claims on his father's inheritance because Neil and Donald were considered to be illegitimate.[92] If this were the case, then the Dovedale grant would have seen the core Campbell estates and custody of Neil's infant nephew pass to one of Edward I's knights. Alternatively, Sir Colin may have been the man captured by the English in 1296 and described then as 'Nicholas (Colin) Doncandouesone'.[93] In any event, Edward I's grant gave over rights to Campbell property and the wardship of an important Campbell heir to one of the king's own favoured retainers.

The Dovedale grant and the judgement in favour of Keith against Carrick's adherents were symptomatic of the changing pattern of the English king's patronage during 1305. While Carrick's influence declined, Sir Robert Keith's star was very much in the ascendant. Keith had been chosen in May as one of the ten Scottish representatives to attend the meeting in September that would settle the arrangements for Edward's administration of Scotland.[94] In the ordinance issued in September, Keith was appointed justiciar between the Forth and the Mounth alongside the Englishman Sir William Inge.[95] The high favour in which Keith was held was confirmed on 26 October when he was one of four men (the others being the bishop of St Andrews, the Chamberlain John de Sandale and John de Kingston) to whom custody of the kingdom was assigned until the arrival of the lieutenant nominated in the September Ordinance, the king's nephew John of Brittany.[96] In contrast, the Ordinance of September 1305 was notable for the eclipse of Bruce interests in all of the areas where the earl and his adherents had been active after 1302. Although Earl Robert was given a place on the council assigned to John of Brittany, he secured no judicial or administrative offices, even in the sheriffdoms of Ayr, Lanark or Wigtown, where he or his supporters had acted as sheriffs for the English administration in the recent past. In the month following the drawing up of the ordinance, Bruce lost a long-running dispute with Ingram de Umfraville over lands in his own earldom of Carrick.[97]

As 1305 drew to a close, the earl of Carrick and Sir Neil Campbell could hardly have viewed the Edwardian settlement of Scotland with any relish. There was also, of course, the issue of the long-cherished Bruce claim to the Scottish throne. Carrick's determination to prepare the ground for a future vindication of his claim to be king, perhaps alongside a desire to deal with the more short-term damage inflicted on his interests during 1305, prompted Bruce to arrange a meeting with John Comyn, lord of Badenoch, in February 1306.[98] The fateful meeting ended in a clash between Bruce and Comyn that left the lord of Badenoch and his uncle dead. The overwhelming testimony of near-contemporary and later chronicle tradition suggests that the two men, who had a long history of violent personal enmity, quarrelled as Robert sought Comyn's support for any future attempt to make good the Bruce claim to the kingship.[99] Given Bruce's actions in the immediate aftermath of Comyn's death, this interpretation of the substance of the February meeting is both logical and understandable. Some of the chronicle accounts dealing with the episode add another element to the dispute in the Greyfriars kirk by suggesting that Bruce also aired a number of retrospective grievances. In particular, it was alleged that Comyn had broken a mutual indenture and agreement between the two men by undermining Robert's reputation with Edward I.[100] As Barrow argues, much of this was undoubtedly invented (in the Scottish sources at least) to blacken the reputation of the lord of Badenoch. Yet the notion that Bruce and his men had fallen from Edward's favour in the months before February 1306 seems to have some substance. Given the relative success of men attached to John Comyn in obtaining offices under the terms of the Ordinance of September 1305, Carrick may also have had some grounds for suspecting that his rival had influenced the English king.[101]

Sir Neil Campbell and his brother were amongst the first men to actively support Bruce's cause in the wake of Comyn's death, being noted in English sources as leaving Edward I's allegiance in February 1306.[102] Sir Neil may have joined Bruce's entourage during the Earl's whirlwind campaign against English forces and Comyn allies in the south-west of Scotland in the immediate aftermath of Badenoch's demise. Campbell almost certainly attended Bruce's inauguration as king on 25 March 1306, six weeks after John Comyn's death, in the abbey kirk of Scone.[103] Neil was one of the new king's men involved in the intimidation and seizure of Malise, earl of Strathearn, the earl of Buchan's brother-in-law, in the immediate aftermath of the ceremony at Scone.[104]

Sir Neil and Donald Campbell's instantaneous adherence to the Bruce cause in February 1306 was hardly a surprise. The record evidence from 1301–2 onwards indicates that both men were already part of the earl of Carrick's political affinity, advantageously entering Edward I's peace in 1302 in a deal brokered by Earl Robert and falling from grace in 1305 alongside their patron. Moreover, the setbacks experienced by the brothers during 1305 ensured that they had no incentive to support the system and personnel of government established by the Ordinances of the previous

September indeed, quite the reverse. When Bruce asked for the support of his allies in his audacious resurrection of Scottish kingship in the early spring of 1306, Neil and Donald clearly had little hesitation in joining their lord. Like most of those who followed Bruce in the early months of 1306, the Campbell brothers were soon to suffer for their decision.

Notes

1. *John Barbour; The Bruce*, ed. A.A.M. Duncan (Edinburgh, 1997), 130–133, 138–41. (Hereafter *The Bruce* (Duncan))
2. G.W.S. Barrow, *Robert Bruce and the Community of the Realm of Scotland*, 3rd edition (Edinburgh, 1988), 153–64. (Hereafter, Barrow, *Bruce*)
3. *The Bruce* (Duncan), 138–41. Barbour's depiction of these events has to be treated with caution, since there are indications that his account of the career of Robert I was heavily influenced by the concerns and personalities of the Scottish court in the 1370s.
4. M. Lynch, *Scotland: A New History* (London, 1991), 67.
5. W.D.H. Sellar, 'The Earliest Campbells – Norman, Briton or Gael?', *SS* 17 (1973), 109–126, at 110, 122; Barrow, *Bruce*, 289.
6. NLS, MS.72.1.1. I should like to thank Ronnie and Marie Black, currently working on an edition of MS.1467, for their helpful comments on the Campbell genealogy in the manuscript. For Sellar's discussion, see 'The Earliest Campbells', 109–125.
7. Sellar, 'Earliest Campbells', 117–8.
8. Sellar, 'Earliest Campbells', 111.
9. Sellar, 'Earliest Campbells', 115.
10. *RRS*, vi, 454–5, no.429.
11. Sellar, 'Earliest Campbells', 111–2. As we shall see, there were particular circumstances underlying the 1369 grant that may have encouraged a certain exaggeration of Duncan's influence and territorial holdings in Loch Awe.
12. Willie Gillies has pointed out that this phrase may have been intended as an ironic comment rather than a statement of fact.
13. W. Gillies, 'Some Aspects of Campbell History', in *TGSI*, 50 (1978), 256–96.
14. Sellar, 'Earliest Campbells', 109–110, 119–122. for a review of the evidence indicating a Campbell connection to the Lennox.
15. Sellar, 'Earliest Campbells', 119–122. In 1289 one Dugald Campbell had appeared as a deputy of the sheriff of Dumbarton. *ER*, i, 38. In contrast, 'Ane Accompt of the the Genealogie of the Campbells', a seventeenth-century Campbell genealogy that included much earlier material, implied that the Campbell line had acquired control of all three territorial divisions of Loch Awe by the end of the eleventh century! *HP*, ii, 80–2.
16. NAS Parliamentary Acts, PA 1/2; *APS*, i, 447.
17. Generally the catalogue seems to run geographically from the north of the sheriffdom to the south. Thus, 'Cineal Bhaodain' (Morvern) was followed by Ardnamurchan, Locheil?, Alexander MacDougall's lands (Lorn, Mull, Lismore and the small islands?), the lordships of Mid-Argyll examined below, the earl of

Menteith's lands in Knapdale and the lands of Angus son of Donald of the Isles [Islay?]. In the nineteenth-century printed edition of the acts of parliament the third territory annexed to the sheriffship of Lorn was described as 'Bothelve', a name that cannot be matched to any known territorial divisions in or bordering Lorn. However, in the original manuscript (NAS PA 1/2) the first letter of the name, although partially erased, appears more likely to be 'L' rather than 'B', giving perhaps the name 'Lochelve'. I am grateful to Professor Barrow for the suggestion that this might represent Locheil.

18. The dominant position of the MacNaughtons at the northern end of Loch Awe earlier in the century is suggested by a grant of 1257 in favour of Inchaffray Priory by Aedh son of Malcolm MacNaughton, with the consent of his brother Sir Gilbert, of the kirk of St. 'Findoce de Ichealt (Inishail). *Inchaffray Chrs.*, no.lxxxv, pp.75–6. Some ten years before this grant another of Malcolm's sons, Gilchrist, had given over to Inchaffray the kirk of Kilmorich, the parish at the head of Loch Fyne. *Ibid.*, nos. lxxiii, lxxiv, pp.64–5. In 1267 the same Gilchrist had received a grant from Alexander III of the castle of Fraoch Eilean in the northern reaches of Loch Awe. NAS RH6/55; *HP*, i, 107.

19. In 1240 a Gillespic MacGilchrist had been granted the lands of Fincharn at the southern end of Loch Awe. *HP*, ii, 114–15, 121–4, 227–45; G.W.S. Barrow, *The Anglo-Norman Era in Scottish History* (Oxford, 1980), 138. (Hereafter, Barrow, *Anglo-Norman Era*)

20. One possibility is that Colin's lands were scattered throughout the proposed sheriffdom. Alternatively, the listing may have moved north again to indicate lands around the head of Loch Fyne that were not to be part of the neighbouring sheriffdom of Kintyre. Colin Campbell's principal estates in 1293 could thus, conceivably, have lain in the parish of Kilmalew on the western shore of Loch Fyne. The parish kirk of Kilmalew was adjacent to Inveraray, a site that would later emerge, before 1432, as one of the principal centres of Campbell lordship in the region. Moreover, in terms of secular lordship, parts at least of the parish, such as Glen Shira, were later identified as lying in the barony or lordship of Loch Awe. Campbell claims to have an early interest in Loch Awe could also, then, have been based on landholding in Kilmalew. In addition, if Colin's estates lay on the shores of Loch Fyne they may well have marched with the territories of other Campbell lords who appeared in the 1293 act.

21. *HP*, ii, 83–4; Sellar, 'Earliest Campbells', 116. The Kintyre sheriffdom was to cover all the lands of Kintyre, the lands of two Lamont chiefs, the island of Bute, and finally the lands of Thomas Cambel and Duncan 'Duf'. *APS*, i, 447.

22. Strachur itself lay in Kilmaglas parish on the eastern shore of Loch Fyne opposite Kilmalew parish although it is not clear exactly when the MacArthur Campbells obtained possession of these lands. Again at a later date, MacArthur Campbell landholding interests extended into Lochgoil parish and lands around the head of Loch Long. The seventeenth-century Campbell history mentions one Taius Coir (i.e Tavish – Thomas) 'who conquiest Cowall from the Lamonds being a man of great valor and couradge: from him descended the Clanntavish Campbells such as the house of Leanach Netherrudill and others'. *HP*, ii, 82. The chronology of the history makes this man an impossibly early figure. The Thomas active in 1293 may be meant, especially given the connection with Cowal. By the middle of the fourteenth century there were a number of

Campbell families who held estates in Loch Goil parish and around the head of Loch Long. Whether these groups were descended from the Thomas and Duncan mentioned in 1293 is impossible to say.

23. *The Bruce* (Duncan), 130–33 (where the fact that Sir Neil Campbell had kinsmen living nearby is emphasised), 138–41; *Chron.Wyntoun* (Laing), ii, 414; *Chron. Bower* (Watt), vii, 102–5.

24. NAS E38/1 f. 8v., *ER*, i, xlv, 24. The lands were included in the account rendered by the sheriff of Stirling so certainly lay in that shire. The grant may have been related to wider events in 1263, most particularly the arrival in the Hebrides of a great Norse war-fleet under the command of Hakon IV which aimed to re-assert the rights of the Norwegian crown in the Hebrides and Argyll. See E.J. Cowan, 'Norwegian sunset-Scottish dawn: Hakon IV and Alexander III', in N.Reid, ed., *Scotland in the Reign of Alexander III* (Edinburgh, 1990), p.121 for Norwegian attacks on Lennox and the earldom of Menteith and the Scots' garrisoning of Stirling Castle; *Lindores Liber*, 8. The witnesses included William, earl of Mar, John Lamberton (the man who had acted as sheriff of Stirling in 1263), John de Lindsay, John Hay and 'Gilascoppe Cambell'.

25. The next reference to Menstrie in Campbell possession dates to *c*.1320. See below p. 43

26. *Cambuskenneth Registrum*, 67–70. As *Nigello filio Colini Cambell*. The grant by William of Kinnimond was also witnessed by, amongst others, Richard of Callendar, the constable of Stirling, Richard 'called Prethir', a burgess of Stirling, and a Gilchrist Magilmore and his brother Gillespic. The grant was sealed with the seals of the bishop of Dunblane, the sheriff of Stirling, and the communities of Stirling and Linlithgow. Moreover, at the start of the fourteenth century, a Colin son of Neil Campbell appeared briefly as lord of Tillicoultry. *Cambuskenneth Registrum*, 222. If the Neil referred to here as 'deceased' was Bruce's companion, then the charter must date to a period after *c*.1315. The witnesses included Nicholas of Lochmaben, Thomas of Tillicoultry, vicar of Auchterarder, John Lardner, burgess of Stirling, and Forsyth de Alweth (Alloa). Of these men Nicholas of Lochmaben may be the man holding the kirk of Skirling in Peeblesshire in 1296, having been presented in July 1275. Watt, *Dictionary*, 358; *Rot.Scot*, i, 25; *Glas. Reg.*, i, 191; G.W.S. Barrow, *The Kingdom of the Scots: Government, Church and society from the eleventh to the fourteenth century* (London, 1973), 248. (Hereafter Barrow, *Kingdom*) The Campbells could not have held this lordship for long for it was a heritable possession of the earls of Mar. NAS GD 124/1/513 Grant of 21 December 1262 by Alexander III to William, earl of Mar, of the lands of Tillicoultry; *RMS*, i, 502. Donald, earl of Mar, was in exile in England between 1306–1327 and the Campbell grant thus probably dates to the period *c*1316X1327. *RMS*, i, no.145; Barrow, *Bruce*, 274 (although see also *RMS*, i, no.145).

27. Baron H. Kervyn de Lettenhove, *Oeuvres de Froissart publiées avec les variants des divers manuscrits*, 25 vols. (Brussels, 1867–77), ii, 313; Philippe Contamine, 'Froissart and Scotland' , in *Scotland and the Low Countries, 1124–1994*, ed. G. Simpson (East Linton, 1989), 43–58 at 55; *Oeuvre de Ghillebert de Lannoy, voyageur, diplomate et moraliste* (Louvain 1878), 168; *CDS*, iv, no.1067; William Worcestre, *Itineraries*, ed. John H. Harvey (Oxford 1969), 6–7. See also Sir David Lindsay's *Complaynt of the Papingo* (1530). *The Works of Sir David Lindsay*

of the Mount, 1490–1555, ed. Douglas Hamer, (STS, 1931), i, 75; *Chron. Bower* (ed.Watt), iv, 473–5; v, 355–7.

28. See Julia C. Crick, *The Historia Regum Brittannie of Geoffrey of Monmouth*, vol. iv: *Dissemination and Reception in the Later Middle Ages* (Cambridge, 1991) for an estimation of popularity and influence of Monmouth's 'history'; Sellar, 'Earliest Campbells', 119–120 for an argument that stresses the possibility of a genuine British descent for a number of Lennox/Strathclyde families.

29. See W.D.H. Sellar, 'Family origins in Cowal and Knapdale', *SS*, xv (1971), 21–37 for a discussion of these families and a strong argument in favour of the historical authenticity of these genealogies.

30. For a discussion of the Stewarts' apparent promotion of their British origins in the fourteenth century, see S. Boardman, 'Late Medieval Scotland and the Matter of Britain', in E.J. Cowan and R.J. Finlay, eds., *Scottish History: The Power of the Past* (Edinburgh, 2002), 47–72, at 51–54.

31. See Fraser, *Eglinton*, 18–19 (Arthur of Ardrossan *c.*1200). In the closing decades of the thirteenth century James the Steward's retainers included one Arthur of Dunoon, who may well have acted as the constable of Dunoon Castle. *Lennox Cartularium*, 21, *Pais. Reg.*, 92–6. Arthur Galbraith (1294), *Pais. Reg* ., 203*. The appearance in the 1290s of Arthur as a Christian name in the Campbell lineage later associated with Strachur may thus be part of a regional pattern.

32. At least there are indications of Stewart lords attempting to exercise the rights of overlords in these areas, particularly through the transfer of ecclesiastical rights over local kirks to their own foundation at Paisley. *Paisley Reg.*, 15, 132, 133, 137, 138, 308; G.W.S. Barrow and A. Royan, 'James Fifth Stewart of Scotland, 1260(?)- 1309', in K. Stringer (ed.), *Essays on the Nobility of Medieval Scotland* (Edinburgh, 1985), 166–194, at 167–9; Barrow, *Anglo-Norman Era*, 67–8.

33. *Pais. Reg* ., 132.

34. In 1261 Dugald MacSween gave over the rights of patronage of the kirk of St. Colmanell in his lands of Kintyre, with the chapel of St. Columba next to his Castle of Skipness, to the Abbey of Paisley. Walter Stewart, earl of Menteith, witnessed this transaction and in the following year confirmed the arrangement, implying that he claimed rights of lordship in both areas.

35. W.D.H. Sellar, 'Cowal and Knapdale', 21. See Cowan, 'Norwegian Sunset, Scottish Dawn', 121–2, for an account that emphasises the anti-Stewart nature of much of the military activity during 1263, and in particular the assault on Walter's recently acquired earldom of Menteith.

36. G.A. Hayes-McCoy, *Scots Mercenary Forces in Ireland (*1565–1603) (Dublin, 1937), 22, 30–35; R.A.McDonald, *The Kingdom of the Isles, Scotland's Western Seaboard, c.*1100–*c.*1336 (East Linton, 1997), 155 (hereafter McDonald, *Kingdom of the Isles*); K.Simms, *From Kings to Warlords* (Woodbridge, 1987), 122–24.

37. *CDS*, i, no.2276; *Calendar of Patent Rolls, Henry III*, 1258–1266 (London, 1901–13), 175–6.

38. The place-name identifications are not certain but were accepted by W.J. Watson in his seminal study of 'Celtic' place-names in Scotland. *CPNS*, 264, 377.

39. *Holyrood Liber*, 52; *SP*, vi, 127.

40. The case remains unproven either way. A.A.M. Duncan, *Scotland: The Making of the Kingdom* (Edinburgh, 1975), 584, note 34.

41. *Pais. Reg.*, 120–1.

42. *HP*, ii, 83–5.
43. Aside from the earldom itself twelfth-century earls of Menteith seem to have enjoyed some judicial responsibility for the inhabitants of Cowal and Kintyre. Whether this reflected territorial rights in these areas is not certain. *APS*, i, 372.
44. Sellar, 'Earliest Campbells', 115, 117. MacFirbis thus places the emergence of the Campbells from the earlier MacDuibne kindred far later than the seventeenth-century genealogies.
45. Brown and Duncan, 'Argyll and the Isles in the earlier Middle Ages', *PSAS*, 90 (1956–57), pp.192–220; G.W.S. Barrow, *Kingship and unity : Scotland, 1000–1306* (London, 1981), Ch. 6; E.J. Cowan, 'Norwegian Sunset, Scottish Dawn'; R.A. McDonald, *The Kingdom of the Isles*.
46. A later chronicle described Alexander II's punitive raids on Argyll in 1221–2 and recorded that some of the beleaguered Argyllsmen 'gave hostages and a great deal of money, and were taken back in peace: while others, who had more deeply offended against the king's will, forsook their estates and possessions and fled. But our lord the king bestowed both the land and goods of these men upon his own followers at will; and thus returned in peace with his men'. *Chron.Fordun*, ii, 284. See Brown and Duncan, 'Argyll and the Isles', *PSAS*, 90 (1956–57), pp.192–220, for an estimation of the likely source of the Fordun/Bower accounts. D. Broun's analysis of 'Fordun's' chronicle would suggest that the account of the expedition dates from the 1280s rather than the 1380s. See Dauvit Broun, 'A New Look at *Gesta Annalia* attributed to John of Fordun', in *Church, Chronicle and Learning*, ed. Barbara E. Crawford (Edinburgh 1999), 9–30.
47. *Newbattle Registrum*, 137–40. Colin, described as the son of the deceased 'Gylascop Kambel', bought the estate of Symington from Sir William Lindsay. The agreement was finalised at the Steward's burgh of Renfrew. The pledges for Campbell's obligation to continue the payment of an annual rent to Lindsay (in reality the abbey of Newbattle) were the Steward and his brother, William Fleming of Barochan and Duncan Fleming. William Fleming may have been the constable of Dumbarton Castle who acted alongside Dugald Campbell in rendering the Dunbartonshire shrieval accounts of 1288/9. Cf. *RMS*, i, 82; *RMS*, i, app 2, 1040.
48. *Pais. Reg.*, 92–6. The witnesses included Robert, bishop of Glasgow, John Stewart, the Steward's brother, Andrew Fraser, John de Soules, Colin (Nicholas) Cambell, Reginald de Crawford, Arthur de Dunoon, knights, Galfrido de Caldcot, William de Shaw, Alexander de Normavilla, Patrick de Louwell, clerks, Gilbert de Conisgburg, John Pride, Gilifio de Estwode, Walter son of Gilbert; Stevenson, *Documents.*, ii, no.401.
49. Fraser, *Colquhoun*, ii, 274–5; *Lennox Cartularium*, 20–1. Colin appeared as a witness behind Reginald de Crawford and Arthur of Dunoon whom he had preceded in the January 1295 charter. The other witnesses were Hugh Danielston, Finlay of Houston, Duncan filio Auleth (son of Aulay) (all knights) and Gilbert de Coningsbergh, lord of Abirdalgy.
50. Argyll Transcripts (AT), *c.*1295; *Lamont Papers*, 7–8, no.10. The witnesses were Lennox men and Dumbarton-based lords and included Duncan MacAulay, Dugald Cambel, Giles the chaplain, William Fleming (of Barrochan?), Donald 'McAuchol' and James Marshall. Duncan son of Aulay and Donald 'McAuchol' were associated with the earl of Lennox in a dispute with the bishop of Glasgow in 1294. *Pais. Reg.*, 203*.

51. Sellar, 'The Earliest Campbells' at 116–7. A marriage between a daughter of Colin of Carrick and Gillespic would explain, as Sellars suggests, the naming of two of Gillespic's son, Colin and Neil.

52. Sellar, 'The Earliest Campbells' at 116. Sellar's argument is based on a Campbell genealogy of the seventeenth century which claims Gillespic married the daughter of Colin, Lord of Carrick. Sellar has demonstrated that there was a 'Nicholas' or Colin, son of Donnchad, earl of Carrick, and brother of Neil, earl of Carrick, alive in the middle of the thirteenth century. In correspondence A.B.W. McEwen has argued that Gillespic could have married one of Neil's four daughters. In the latter case Colin Campbell would have been a first cousin of the future king.

53. Palgrave, *Docs. Hist. Scot.*, Illustrations, no.11; Barrow, *Bruce*, 39

54. Watt, *Dictionary*, 74; Palgrave, *Docs.Hist.Scot.*, Illustrations, no.5; *Foedera*, i, 767. In correspondence A.W.B.McEwen has made the ingenious suggestion that Master Neil was not the brother but a son of Sir Colin who later abandoned his clerical career. McEwen points out that despite the appearance of Neil son of Colin as early as 1282 there are no subsequent references to him until 1302. In the interim the only Neil Campbell on record is Master Neil. Most tellingly, Master Neil is the only Campbell of that name noted in the various submissions to the English crown made *c.*1296. If Neil was a Master by 1292 this would suggest that he was born *c.*1268 or earlier given that cure of souls has to be by someone of 25.

55. *CDS*, ii, 158–9.

56. For a discussion of the scheme, see Duncan and Brown, 'Argyll and the Isles' at 216–8.

57. Duncan and Brown, 'Argyll and the Isles', 217 and appendix VI.

58. *CDS*, ii, nos. 1631, 1632.

59. Barrow, *Bruce*, 71–4.

60. *Ibid.*, 76–8.

61. *Rot.Scot.*, i, 31.

62. *Ibid.*, 31–2.

63. *RRS*, vi, 454–5, no.429.

64. *APS*, i, 448; *Foedera*, ii, 786. Loch Awe and Ardscotnish were still being treated as royal lands in 1304–5, and their status probably did not change until 1315. *CDS*, ii, no.1646, p.439.

65. See *HP*, i, 107, ii, 121, Barrow, *Anglo-Norman Era*, 137–41. It has been claimed that the minority government of Alexander III temporarily treated all of Argyll as a royal bailliary during Ewen of Argyll's exile from the realm between 1249 and 1255. See Duncan and Brown, 'Argyll and the Isles', 211. The evidence for the existence of a bailliary of Argyll is not overwhelming, resting on the appearance of one Richard 'Sticlaw' described as 'ballivo domini Regis' (with no indication of the geographical extent of his office) in September 1250 as a witness to a piece of ecclesiastical business in Cowal. *Pais.Reg.*, 134; *Foedera*, i, 761.

66. *HP*, i, 107, ii, 121; Duncan and Brown, 'Argyll and the Isles', 208–9, 210–11, for the role of Bishop Clement. The process seems analogous to the much better understood expansion of the influence of Paisley abbey alongside Stewart secular lordship in the Firth of Clyde.

67. *HP*, ii, 84–5. The exact date of Sir Colin's death is uncertain. Because of confusion over the Latin rendering of Colin's name as Nicholas, later writers thought that the beneficiary of the grant of 10 September 1296 was his son Neil and thus attempted to locate Sir Colin's death before that date.

68. *AU*, ii, 392–3, although Sean Duffy has suggested that the man killed in 1299 was not Alexander Óg but his uncle. For contrasting views, see S. Duffy, 'The "Continuation" of Nicholas Trevet: a new source for the Bruce invasion', *Proceedings of the Royal Irish Academy*, xci (1991), 311–12 and W.D.H. Sellar, 'MacDonald and MacRuairi pedigrees in MS 1467', *West Highland Notes and Queries*, xxviiii (1986), 7.

69. Stevenson, *Documents*, ii, pp.429–30, no.610; *CDS*, ii, no.1646.

70. In any documents in which they appeared together, Donald was invariably listed first. *RRS*, v, no.385, pp.629–30; *CDS* v. no. 523.

71. It seems odd, for example, that Neil does not feature in the lists of submissions gathered by the English crown c.1296.

72. See note 54. Master Neil swore fealty to Edward I at Berwick on 28 August 1296 or shortly beforehand, when he was noted as hailing from the county of Ayr. *CDS*, ii, nos. 675, 823, p.199, p.205 (where 'Mestre Neel Cambel' appears amongst a number of men from Carrick and Ayrshire), no.961; *APS*, i, 447, 289. On 11 June 1297 Master Neil obtained a safe-conduct alongside a number of other Scottish lords to visit Scotland and return before 1 August. Stevenson, *Documents*, ii, no.434, p.175; *CDS*, ii, no.961. The near-contemporary example of Master Ralph of Dundee does not provide an exact parallel, for Ralph retained his clerical title.

73. Barrow, *Bruce*, 110–12.

74. Barrow, *Bruce*, 121–22; E.L.G. Stones, *Anglo-Scottish Relations, 1174–1328, Some Selected Documents* (London, 1965), no.32 (Hereafter Stones, *Documents*); E.L.G. Stones, 'The Submission of Robert Bruce to Edward I, c.1301–2', *SHR*, xxxiv (1955), 122–34; A.A.M. Duncan, review of Barrow's *Robert Bruce*, *SHR*, xlv (1965), 184–201, at 194–8. Bruce had entered the English king's service before February 16 1302; N. Trivet, *Annales*, ed.T.Hog, 397.

75. *CDS*, ii, no.1289. Three days after the grant to Campbell, Edward issued a pardon 'at the instance of Robert Bruce, earl of Carrick' to one Hector Askeloc for offences committed in Cumberland and elsewhere. In April 1302 another Carrick adherent, Patrick de Trump, was restored to lands in Cumberland after coming to the king's peace with the earl. All this suggests that the earl had also petitioned on behalf of Campbell, who otherwise had no connection to Cumberland. *Ibid.*, nos. 1291, 1302, 1303.

76. *Ibid*, ii, no.1406. Although the suggestion that the king had given the ward to Neil and Donald before Sir Robert Keith came to peace in 'the first war' might indicate a date in the 1290s? Robert Keith, the Marischal, was captured by the English in 1299 and subsequently imprisoned in Bristol. Barrow, *Bruce*, 113; *Chron. Rishanger*, 442; *CDS*, ii, nos 1147–8, 1159.

77. *Ibid.*, ii, no. 1437, 1439; *Ibid.*, v, no. 408. Donald seems to have been particularly active in the south-west. In August 1304 he was one of the assise of 'men of the counties of Roxburgh and Dumfries' who found in favour of the earl of Carrick's rights to be free from the interference of royal officers in the lordship of Annandale. *Ibid.*, ii, No. 1588. As late as 1305–6, Donald was still apparently

active in the English military effort in the south-west as a member of the affinity of John Saint John. *CDS*, v, no. 514.

78. Palgrave, *Docs. Hist. Scot.*, 274, no. cxxvi. On 27 June 1304, at Stirling, Sir Neil Campbell received letters of protection from Edward I because he was in the king's service. This may have been intended to halt proceedings over the Crawford inheritance. *Calendar of Chancery warrants preserved in the Public record office* (London, 1927–), i, 225. Quite when Sir Neil joined the Irish force is unclear. The Irish besieged the Stewart castles of Inverkip and Rothesay, taking the latter and giving it to the command of John Bisset. Barrow, *Bruce*, 126–7. J.F. Lydon, 'Edward I, Ireland and Scotland, 1303–4', in *England and Ireland in the later Middle Ages* ed. J.F. Lydon (Dublin, 1981), 43–61, at 50.

79. Barrow, *Bruce*, 129–30.

80. *Memoranda de Parliamento*, 1305 (Rolls Series, 1893), xl, xlix, 14–16, 293.

81. The parliament, originally scheduled for July 1305, was twice postponed and eventually met in September 1305. *CDS*, ii, nos.1669, 1678.

82. *CDS*, ii, nos. 1657, 1658.

83. Neil sold the Multon wardship to one Richard le Brun at Westminster in Lent in the 33rd year of Edward I's reign (i.e. between 3/3/1305 and 18/4/1305) for the sum of £120. *Calendar of Close Rolls, Edward I, 1302–1307* (London, 1908), 496–7.

84. *CDS*,ii, nos.1978, 1147,1148, 1159.

85. *CDS*, ii, no. 1406. Neil denied that he had acted in contempt of the king's council, because Alice was not in sasine at the time of the prohibition.

86. *Ibid.*, Unfortunately the dating of these events remains very unclear as they are alluded to as part of an undated commentary which starts with the initial prosecution of Keith's case at Dunfermline around Martinmass 1303.

87. *CDS*, v, no. 523. The exact date of the parliamentary judgement is not given, but the two parliaments of 1305 were the only recorded Westminster assemblies after October 1302. *Handbook of British Chronology*, 3rd edition (1986), 550–1. Since there is no indication that Keith was in London for the Lent parliament, this might suggest that the September meeting saw the prosecution of his case against the Campbells.

88. *CDS*, v, no. 523.

89. *CDS*, ii, no.1470.

90. *CDS*, ii, no.1628; Palgrave, *Docs. Hist. Scot.*, 310–11 which seems to be a confirmation of the gift of 'Nichol' Cambel's lands to Dovedale on 15 August 1306 after Bruce's seizure of the crown. Barrow, *Bruce*, 327 takes this as a reference to Sir Neil Campbell's lands, but Colin is probably meant.

91. *CDS*, ii, nos.1628, 1717.

92. Again, this suggestion stems from the correspondence of A.B.W. McEwen. The notion of Neil and Donald's illegitimacy would, of course, chime well with McEwen's idea that Neil was initially meant for a career in the kirk.

93. *CDS*, ii, p.177; Sellar, 'Earliest Campbells', 114. This Colin's father, 'Duncan Dubh', may well be the man recorded as a landowner in the sheriffdom of Kintyre in 1293. Despite the use of the patronymic in 1296, Colin's putative brother, Arthur, habitually used the surname Campbell.

94. *CDS*, ii, no.1691.

95. *Ibid.*, no.1691. An annual salary of 40 merks was assigned to Keith's office in October 1305. *CDS*, ii, no.1706.

96. Barrow, *Bruce*, 139.
97. *CDS*, ii, no.1691; Stones, *Documents*, no.33. Carrick himself had briefly held the sheriffships of Ayr and Lanark. In 1305 Ayr was assigned to Sir Godfrey Ross, who had submitted to the English with Sir John Comyn in February 1304, and Lanark to Sir Henry Sinclair. The office of sheriff of Wigtown went to Thomas MacCulloch. *CDS*, ii, nos.1420, 1437, 1657, 1658 1696, 1741.One of the principal targets of Bruce on the day of Comyn's death was Sir Richard Siward, the new sheriff of Dumfries, who was captured by Bruce and Seton on the same day in Dumfries Castle. A.A.M. Duncan explains the cooling of Edward and Robert's relationship as arising from Robert's consistently held and expressed desire to re-establish Scottish kingship. Duncan, review of Barrow's *Bruce* , at 198–9. E.V. Barron, *The Scottish War of Independence*, 2nd edition (Inverness, 1934), 168–174.
98. Barrow, *Bruce*, 139–44.
99. For a judicious discussion of these accounts and the events surrounding Comyn's death, see Barrow, *Bruce*, 139–41; A. Young, *Robert the Bruce's Rivals: The Comyns, 1212–1314* (East Linton, 1997), 197–200.
100. *The Chronicle of Walter of Guisborough* (Camden Society, 1957), 366–7; *Scalacronica*, 129–30; *Chron.Fordun*, i, 337–40; ii, 330–33.
101. Young, *op.cit.*, 192–5. There may even have been an 'indenture' – exchanges of such generally worded bonds were common in late medieval Scotland, and were often designed to re-establish amicable relations between parties known to be on bad terms. As Duncan argues, an exchange of indentures between Bruce and Comyn might well have been expected after Comyn's submission to Edward I in February 1304 to deal with any animosities built up over the previous two years when the two lords and their followers had been actively campaigning against each other. In 1304 what might these agreements be about? The need for a general cessation of hostilities and abandonment of grudges is obvious, but the deal may also have looked forward to the wider settlement of Scottish affairs. Duncan, review of Barrow's *Bruce*, 70, 78–80.
102. *Calendar of Close Rolls, Edward I, 1302–1307*, pp.496–7. Here Campbell's fall from allegiance to Edward I was curiously dated to the Thursday after the purification of the Virgin Mary (2 February), 1306, a week before the lord of Badenoch's death.
103. Barrow, *Bruce*, 148–151.
104. Fraser, *Menteith*, i, 513–4; Palgrave, *Docs.Hist.Scot.*, 319–21.

TWO

The Storm Petrels: Clan Campbell,
Robert I and the Wars of Independence

I n the weeks after the Lord of Badenoch's death Bruce's opponents both
in Scotland and England seem, at first, to have been stunned by the
speed and dynamism of King Robert's coup, but by 5 April an enraged
Edward I had appointed his capable half-cousin Sir Aymer de Valence
(who was also the murdered John Comyn's brother-in-law) as his
lieutenant in Scotland.[1] De Valence advanced to Perth, while Robert
seems to have stationed his forces in the lordships to the west and north of
the burgh.[2] On 19 June 1306 Bruce's army was surprised and routed at
Methven near Perth by Edward's lieutenant; King Robert's much depleted
force was forced to retreat west along Loch Tay and into Glen Dochart.
At a location known as Dail Righ, near Tyndrum, Bruce's followers met
with a second defeat at the hands of a host that John Barbour later claimed
was under the command of John of Lorn, the son of Alexander of Argyll.[3]
After the defeat at Dail Righ Bruce was reduced to the status of a fugitive,
surrounded by enemies and supported by a small and increasingly desperate band of noblemen that included, again according to John Barbour, Sir
Neil Campbell.[4] Neil's presence in this select band need not be doubted,
but other aspects of Barbour's presentation of the Campbell lord should be
treated with caution. Barbour was writing in the 1370s for the court of
Robert II (1371–1390) where Neil's grandson, Gillespic, was very much in
favour.[5] The tale of Neil's decisive role in the gathering of a galley force to
spirit the refugee king away from the Scottish mainland in the autumn of
1306 may well reflect Gillespic's desire to emphasise the heroic part his
grandfather had played in Bruce's struggle for the throne.[6] However, even
if his descendants magnified Neil's deeds and importance, there can be
little doubt that he was a trusted member of Robert's entourage. He may
well have accompanied the king during the mysterious months over the
winter of 1306–7 when Bruce and his supporters simply disappeared into
the west.[7]

Campbell's role in Bruce's stuttering but eventually triumphal return to

Scotland in February 1307 centred on dealing with Bruce's rivals and enemies in the west and central Highlands. Sir Neil's relatively rare appearances in record and chronicle accounts confirm both his closeness to the king and his part in the eradication of opposition to the Bruce regime along the Firth of Clyde and in Argyll.

When Bruce returned to the earldom of Carrick in February 1307, he was faced by a formidable coalition of foes both Scots and English, co-ordinated by the energetic Aymer de Valence. In the west Bruce and his men had to contend with a number of obstacles and threats. Alexander of Argyll and his son John were great figures in Gaelic Scotland – major territorial lords and military leaders and the figureheads of the provincial aristocracy of Argyll. They were also kinsmen of the slain Comyn lord of Badenoch, intent on revenging Comyn's death and preserving their lordship against the allies of the 'usurper' Bruce. In the 1290s Edward I had encouraged the MacDonalds and the Campbells to take on MacDougall lordship under the leadership of Alexander, earl of Menteith. That earlier attempt to shake MacDougall power had ended with the deaths of Alexander MacDonald and Sir Colin Campbell; there could be no certainty that the MacDougalls would be any easier to displace after 1307.[8] Another formidable opponent was Sir John of Menteith, who in 1307 represented a threat to Robert I's interests in the west that was almost as serious as that posed by the MacDougall lords of Argyll. Menteith was one of the most remarkable figures of the early fourteenth century. The second son of Walter Stewart, earl of Menteith, Sir John was a figure of some influence but with little prospect of a substantial inheritance. After the death of Earl Walter the earldom passed to Sir John's brother Alexander. The outbreak of war in 1296, however, transformed the prospects of the bellicose Sir John. Captured by the English at Dunbar in 1296, Menteith seems to have won his freedom by serving with Edward I in Flanders during 1297.[9] The relationship established between Menteith and King Edward as a result of their shared military adventure in 1297 seems to have been reasonably cordial, perhaps even warm. Sir John's links to the English king may explain why, even when he was identified with the Scots lords defying Edward I during the long political stalemate after 1298, he appeared as an envoy in the negotiations between the English crown and its Scottish enemies.[10] In contrast to Bruce and his adherents, Sir John did extremely well out of Edward I's attempted settlement of the government of Scotland in the years 1304–5. In March 1304, a month after

John Comyn negotiated terms with Edward I, the English king appointed Menteith as sheriff and constable of Dumbarton.[11] Thereafter, Sir John's personal loyalty to the English king, and his relish for aggressive military lordship, made him an invaluable ally in Edward's attempts to control the northern kingdom. Menteith's most notable and infamous service was, of course, the part he played in the capture of William Wallace in August 1305.[12] With the launch of the Bruce rebellion in 1306, Sir John faced something of a dilemma. John's nephew, Allan, earl of Menteith, supported Robert's claim to the throne and Bruce obviously thought it was worth the effort to make a personal appeal to John to follow his kinsman's example and to hand over control of the vital castle of Dumbarton to the Bruce cause.[13] John refused, and events soon justified his decision, for after the defeat at Methven his nephew Allan was captured by the English. Edward I's subsequent decision to forfeit Earl Allan and to assign the earldom of Menteith with its associated territories to Sir John Hastings (who had a hereditary claim as a descendant of the thirteenth-century Comyn earl of Menteith) may have tested Sir John's loyalty. However, the English king was not about to alienate one of his most useful Scottish adherents; within a month of the grant of Menteith to Hastings, Sir John had been given the earldom of Lennox, forfeited by Earl Malcolm because of his support for Bruce.[14] From his near impregnable base at Dumbarton, Menteith deployed a naval force that operated against Bruce and his supporters in the Firth of Clyde throughout 1306–7. It was Menteith who had mounted the relentless pursuit of Bruce and his fugitive band in Kintyre in the autumn of 1306 and who maintained the search for Robert in the Western Isles after his disappearance. Menteith's continued hold on Dumbarton was clearly a major obstacle to the Bruce cause, providing a secure base for hostile naval forces and restricting the ability of King Robert's allies to launch operations against the MacDougall lords of Argyll and other west-coast enemies. Unlike the MacDougalls, however, Menteith was a man who had previously enjoyed good relations with the Bruce family and a number of individuals who supported King Robert's cause in 1306–7.[15] These personal connections and the death of Edward I paved the way for the transfer of Menteith's allegiance to Robert I. During 1308 the great fortress at Dumbarton was surrendered to King Robert in mysterious circumstances. Sir John was able to attend the parliament held by Robert I at St Andrews in March 1309 alongside Neil, Donald and Thomas Campbell.[16] Thereafter, Sir John was clearly militarily active on behalf of the Bruce cause in the west, and in the vanguard of the political/ military establishment built up by Robert to defend the western borders of his kingdom and to carry the war against English interests in Ireland and elsewhere.[17] Sir John Menteith and his successors carved out a maritime lordship in the Firth of Clyde that embraced Arran and much of Knapdale. By 1320 John was also styled guardian of the earldom of Menteith, despite the fact that his nephew, Murdoch, was of age and apparently in possession.[18] The Menteith lordship was to provide an important military and political focus for various branches of the Clan Campbell in the early decades of the fourteenth century. Indeed, one aspect of the return of Sir John Menteith to the Bruce fold in 1308 may have been the marriage of his daughter or granddaughter to Sir Neil Campbell's son, Colin.[19]

The defection of Sir John Menteith allowed King Robert and his allies to intensify their assault on John MacDougall, who had been notably active in support of English attempts to dispose of Bruce in 1307.[20] The course and timing of the campaigns against the MacDougalls are rather uncertain, but it seems that the lords of Argyll had to face at least two major expeditions personally led by the king into their own province in 1308/9.[21] Sir Neil Campbell may well have played a prominent part in both campaigns. Neil was certainly with the king on 7 August 1309 when Robert issued a charter at a location known as 'Lochbren' alongside Malcolm, earl of Lennox, and Sir John Menteith at a point when the king may have been about to unleash his final assault on the MacDougall lords.[22] The siege of Dunstaffnage related by John Barbour would, then, have occurred in the autumn of 1309, a supposition reinforced by the appearance of Robert I in Dunstaffnage on 20 October 1309 and the arrival of the MacDougalls as political exiles in Ireland before the end of the year. From his new base in the English crown's Irish lordship John MacDougall became a consistent irritant to the Bruce regime in the west, co-ordinating naval operations across the North Channel on behalf of the English crown.[23]

The expulsion of the MacDougalls and their supporters from Argyll encouraged the dismemberment of their political and territorial lordship by Bruce's allies in the west, although any gains would have to be defended against MacDougall incursions and perhaps local hostility. The dispersal of MacDougall lands and strongholds in the immediate aftermath of their defeat in 1309 is difficult to trace, although various branches of Clan Campbell, the Clan Donald and the MacLeans of Mull would seem to have been the main beneficiaries.

The favour shown by Robert I to the Campbells in the west was undoubtedly secured by Sir Neil Campbell's close personal relationship to the king, with the Campbell lord playing a prominent role in the king's affairs in all areas of the kingdom. In September 1308 Neil seems to have been involved in negotiations at Cambuskenneth to allow the return of southern lairds to King Robert's allegiance, while he and his brother Donald attended the king's first parliament held in St Andrews in March 1309.[24] Neil also acted as an envoy for the king in negotiations with representatives of the English crown in 1309 and 1314.[25] Sir Neil received a substantial reward for his loyal service to Robert with a prestigious marriage to the king's sister, Mary Bruce. Mary, like many of the female relations of the king, had been captured in 1306 and had spent the intervening years in prison in England. She was probably released around October 1314 as part of a group exchanged for the earl of Hereford, who had been captured in the aftermath of Bannockburn.[26] The exact date of the marriage is unknown, but it was a fruitful union, culminating in the birth of a son, John. Robert I bestowed on his sister and brother-in-law and their young son a grant of all the lands that had belonged to David of Strathbogie, earl of Atholl, forfeited for his defection to the English on the eve of Bannockburn.[27] It seems likely that the promotion of Neil's infant son by Mary Bruce as a future earl of Atholl briefly gave control of the great earldom to the king's brother-in-law. The Campbell advance into Atholl was part of a great redistribution of lordships running from Perthshire to Argyll to Robert I's own kinsmen and trusted associates.[28]

The distribution of royal favours to Neil's offspring did not stop with the earldom of Atholl. On 10 February 1315, Sir Neil's son by an earlier relationship, Colin, received a grant from Robert I of all the lands of Loch Awe and Ardscotnish in free barony, holding them 'as the rest of our barons in Argyll hold their baronies of us' for the service of a galley of forty oars for forty days.[29] The grant, with its prominent exaction of galley service, may well have been part of the king's preparations for his brother Edward's great expedition to Ireland, which would be launched in May of that year.[30] The 1315 grant has usually been regarded simply as confirming the Campbells' longstanding possession of Loch Awe and Ardscotnish. However, as we have seen, for at least two decades before 1315 Loch Awe and Ardscotnish seem to have been royal lordships, administered on the crown's behalf by local bailies.[31] It seems likely that the bailie was usually the MacDougall lord of Argyll; the only point at which a Campbell lord was said to be responsible for these lordships coincided with Edward I's assault on the MacDougalls in 1296. After 1296 the English crown continued to administer the lordships through royal bailies and to extract revenues from the king's lands there; by 1304, Edward's bailie was once again Alexander of Argyll.[32] Prior to 1315 there was little indication that Campbell landholding and social influence inside Loch Awe and Ardscotnish was any more significant than that of a number of other lords such as the MacNaughtons, MacGilchrists and MacIvers. The grant to Colin Campbell, then, rewarded the family for their loyalty and, perhaps, their role in the suppression of MacDougall loyalists in Loch Awe and Ardscotnish. Certainly a number of local families, such as the Mac-Naughtons, had remained faithful to the MacDougall lords who had long directed the affairs of their province.[33] The 1315 grant was no doubt intended to make the Campbell ascendancy in the area more permanent by transferring to them baronial powers, presumably with possession of any lands previously directly held by the crown and rights of jurisdiction and feudal superiority over other landowners in the area. In fact, the superior status of Campbell lords in relation to other influential families in Loch Awe and Ardscotnish seems to have been long contested and, in some cases, only secured much later in the fourteenth century. Certainly, the accumulation of rights of church patronage and overlordship was a gradual and piecemeal process, often dependent on the failure of male descent in other lineages rather than the terms of the 1315 grant. Robert I's gift of Loch Awe and Ardscotnish may, then, have been akin to other 'speculative' grants of west-coast lands and lordships made by the king in favour of his allies where the long-term prospects for the grantees were by no means assured.

The transfer of Loch Awe and Ardscotnish to Colin may also have reflected a realisation that Sir Neil Campbell was nearing the end of his long career in Robert I's service. Neil appeared as a witness to a royal charter issued at Arbroath on 15 February 1315, five days after the grant to his son. This was his last recorded activity, although his seal may have been attached to an entailing of the crown at Ayr on 26 April 1315; Neil probably died shortly after this event.[34] Since 1300 Sir Neil had spent his life in the service of Robert Bruce. The trials had been many, but the rewards had been great; Neil had flown his course through the storms of war and, at the end, left a considerable legacy to his sons. Colin was established as lord of Loch Awe and Ardscotnish; John, the infant son of

Neil and Mary Bruce, could expect the protection and patronage of his royal uncle and seemed destined for a prominent place in the new political community being fashioned by the king. With Neil's death, however, Fortune's favour settled on other men.

The career of Colin Campbell, who can legitimately be described as the first Campbell lord of Loch Awe, was both brief and obscure. Colin seems to have accompanied Robert I and Edward Bruce to Ireland where, according to Barbour, he managed to rouse the king's wrath by a display of reckless bravery that countermanded the king's orders and resulted in the Campbell lord having his horse killed under him.[35] Aside from John Barbour's reference to his impetuosity during the Bruce campaigns in Ireland there is next to nothing known of his life. Despite this, he is clearly the historical basis for a curious vernacular verse poem first attested in the sixteenth century, *Ane Taill of Sir Colling ye Knyt*.[36] The story, in summary, tells of a knight who fights for Robert Bruce in Ireland, who weds the daughter of a king of Argyll and kills a three-headed monster threatening the region, thereby winning control of the province. Tales involving the defeat of fearsome monsters in specific localities were quite common features of family origin legends in the late-medieval and early-modern period, although few seem to have formed the basis of an extended 'romance'. Curiously, a Gaelic poem of the early sixteenth century traced the line of the then earl of Argyll, Archibald, back through his ancestors to this Colin and did not extend beyond him to laud Neil or his father Colin.[37] Since the Colin who died c.1296 is normally regarded as the Cailean Mór from whom the chiefly style MacCailein Mór derived, his omission from a poem extolling the virtues of Earl Archibald's illustrious predecessors might seem odd.[38] The posthumous prominence of Neil's son Colin may not be unrelated to the dynastic struggles that broke out within Clan Campbell following Colin's death. The young lord does not seem to have long survived his father, and was almost certainly dead by 1323, if not before; it is not entirely clear that he survived the Bruce campaigns in Ireland and, in particular, the carnage of Edward Bruce's last battle as king of Ireland at Fochart on 14 October 1318.[39]

Colin's early death left his two young sons, Dugald and Gillespic, in a vulnerable position. Although Dugald was the heir to the lordships created by the 1315 grant, the early decades of the fourteenth century were not conducive to the upholding of the rights of minors in lordships which were vital for both the kindred and the kingdom. Robert I's own entailing of the crown in 1315 had shown that immediate military necessity and political expediency were powerful arguments in determining succession arrangements.[40] After Fochart the kingdom's western approaches were once again vulnerable to incursions from Scottish exiles and agents of the English crown in the north of Ireland. Other members of Clan Campbell and the royal government had a vested interest in seeing Campbell lands and military resources under the control of an active adult male. Thus the deaths in rapid succession of Sir Neil and Sir Colin saw the leadership of the family assumed by the heads of other branches of the kin, who dominated Robert I's patronage as he attempted to consolidate his political hold on Argyll and the Hebrides during the 1320s. The most significant and threatening figure as far as the sons of Colin were concerned was one Dugald Campbell. Dugald's exact relationship to the young men remains a matter of conjecture, but he emerged in the 1320s as the effective leader of the family and a major player in Robert I's governance of the west. It seems most likely, although by no means certain, that Dugald was a son of Neil Campbell and thus the uncle of the younger Dugald and Gillespic.[41] (See Tables 2 and 2a)

The elder Dugald was the beneficiary of a series of grants from the king in the 1320s that confirmed the Campbell lord's active role in the military settlement of Argyll and the Isles by the king's partisans. However, the number of Campbells of various generations bearing the name Dugald makes precise attribution difficult.[42] At some point, probably c.1321, Robert I granted a Dugald Campbell the island of Torsay along with a block of territory running north from the northern shore of Loch Melfort.[43] The lands, which were probably former MacDougall holdings, were to be held for the service of a galley of twenty-six oars. The Torsay grant appears to have been associated with a further gift in favour of Dugald, namely the lands of Menstrie.[44] A Dugald Campbell son of Neil, perhaps but not certainly the same man, also obtained about this time a grant of 'sundry' lands in Argyll for the service of a galley of eighteen oars.[45]

More worryingly for Colin's sons, the ambitions of Dugald Campbell seem to have stretched to lands that had been held by their father. Control of the lordship of Ardscotnish was certainly in dispute in the early 1320s, with the issue being raised in a meeting of the three estates at Scone on 3 August 1323. On that date an agreement (concordia) was reached between 'Dugallum' Campbell son of Sir Colin Campbell and 'Dugallum' Campbell son of Neil over 20 merks' worth of land in Ardscotnish along with the right to present clerics to the kirk of Kilmartin. The latter right had been explicitly given to Colin Campbell and his heirs as barons of Ardscotnish in the charter of 1315, and it is difficult to see how one of the parties whose claims were involved in the agreement could not be Colin's young son Dugald.[46] The agreement of 1323 seems to have left Ardscotnish in the hands of Dugald son of Neil, and the arrangement may soon have attained a semi-permanent aspect; Dugald's descendants were to hold Ardscotnish quite independently of the Loch Awe family until the 1360s. The line descended from Dugald also seem to have obtained possession of Menstrie, which makes it likely that he was the beneficiary of the linked grants of Menstrie and Torsay outlined above. The territorial and political legacy handed down by Dugald was sufficient for his descendants to establish their independent right to significant Campbell estates, an autonomy reflected in the emergence of a kindred name, the MacDougall Campbells, that commemorated their founder and defined the lands to which they were entitled.

Dugald Campbell clearly had an active part in the consolidation of the king's plans for the Firth of Clyde. In or around 1321 the king instituted a new sheriffdom of Argyll, centred on a proposed burgh, port and castle at Tarbert in Kintyre.[47] Tarbert was the most important part of an interlinked military and judicial system that covered much of Argyll through dependent constabularies at Dunoon and Dunstaffnage.[48] By 1326 Dugald Campbell was sheriff of the newly constituted Argyll sheriffdom, and responsible for the collection of royal revenues from the area.[49] At the same time Dugald acted as bailie of Atholl, presumably on behalf of the young John Campbell, perhaps Dugald's own half-brother.[50] Dugald further consolidated his position in the west through a marriage to Margaret, the sister of John of Glassary, who granted to his new brother-in-law extensive estates inside Argyll.[51] Dugald son of Neil thus exercised authority across an area stretching from Atholl to Argyll, and his usefulness to the crown clearly made concessions desirable.

Dugald was not the only member of Clan Campbell to profit in royal service after 1318. The disaster at Fochart had transformed the situation in the west in terms of Robert I's ability and willingness to grant lands to his agents in the region and the strategies he followed to attain control. After the exile of the MacDougalls in 1309, Robert I seems initially to have relied on co-operation with the remaining branches of the Clan Sorley, the MacRuairies and the Clan Donald to control the region. Various grants to Angus Óg of Islay and his son Alexander suggest the advance of Clan Donald at the expense of both the MacDougalls and the Comyns.[52] The deaths of the heads of the Clan Donald and the Clan Ruairi at Fochart, both apparently leaving under-age heirs, allowed or forced Robert I to adopt a radical new strategy in the west. In or around 1321, as we have seen, the king founded a new sheriffdom of Argyll, centred on Tarbert in Kintyre.[53] At the same time Robert began to dismember the mainland lordship of the MacDougalls, creating a series of free baronies in Lorn, Benderloch and Appin to be held directly of the crown for galley service. Territorial rights, concessions or privileges granted to the Mac-Donalds and the MacRuairies prior to 1318 were simply ignored as the king's partisans, their actions justified by military expediency and spurred by private ambition, attempted to build and consolidate extensive lordships in Argyll. The pivotal figures in the process appear to have been the warlike Sir John Menteith and his son and namesake.[54] Among the men who were linked to Menteith's lordship were three Campbell lords, Sir Donald (Neil's brother), Sir Thomas and Sir Arthur.[55] Of these, the most aggressive and ambitious was Sir Arthur who, with his son, also Arthur, assumed the leading role in the dismemberment of the MacDougall lordship in Lorn. At some point in the early 1320s Robert I made Sir Arthur constable of the former MacDougall stronghold of Dunstaff-nage.[56] It is unclear who had acted as custodian of Dunstaffnage since the siege of 1309, although Barbour asserted that Bruce handed care of the fortress to an unidentified 'good warden' to whom he gave 'bath men and met/ Sua that he lang tyme thar mycht be/ Magre thaim all off that countre'.[57] In a grant that may have been issued at the same time as that for the constableship of Dunstaffnage, Sir Arthur received a variety of MacDougall estates in Lorn and Benderloch, including Dunollie (the site of another major MacDougall castle), Ardstaffnage and Inverawe in free barony.[58] In the last year of his life, Robert I extended the grip of Sir Arthur (or his son) on mainland Argyll with a grant of various lands in Appin for the service of a ship of twenty oars.[59]

However, the ambitions of Sir Arthur and his family were not confined to former MacDougall lands. From their new strongholds in Lorn, Sir Arthur and his son could contemplate acquisitions still further north, in the lordship of another branch of the great Clan Sorley, the MacRuairis of Garmoran. The death of Ruairi MacRuairi at the battle of Fochart had left the lordship vulnerable, and not simply because Ruairi's heir, Ranald, was under-age. Ruairi and his brother Lachlan, who may well have been the effective leader of the clan until *c.*1308–9, were both illegitimate sons of Allan mac Ruairi.[60] The brothers' legitimate sister, Christina, was married to Duncan, the son of Donald, earl of Mar. There is nothing to suggest that Duncan ever sought to take advantage of his wife's claims to be Allan's 'heir'. There was, however, an ever-present threat that Christina's 'rights' could be exploited in an attempt to disrupt her brothers' control of Garmoran. Robert I had a personal interest in the issue since his first wife, Isabella, was Duncan of Mar's sister, while Bruce's own sister had married Duncan's brother Gartney, earl of Mar; Christina was thus the king's sister-in-law twice over. Christina and Duncan appear to have had a son, Ruairi, who might have expected the support of his royal uncle in pursuit of his rights in Garmoran. Instead, Robert I consented to, and may well have arranged, Christina's resignation of her claims to Garmoran in favour of her brother Ruairi, a deal that secured for the king the military and political support of one of the most powerful west-coast kindreds.[61]

Through his deal with the king over the Garmoran lordship and his subsequent service to the Bruces in Scotland and Ireland, Ruairi MacRuairi seemed to have guaranteed the place of his heirs in the Bruce settlement of the Hebrides. However, in the aftermath the death of the MacRuairi Rí Innse Gall alongside Edward Bruce at Fochart, King Robert's agents in the west re-opened the issue of the MacRuairi inheritance. In an undated charter Christina, described as the daughter and heiress of Alan son of Ruairi, gave to Arthur Campbell, son of Sir Arthur Campbell, the lands of Moidart, Arisaig and Morar, with the isles of Eigg and Rum and the small islands belonging to them along with 'the island which is called dry island' (i.e. Eilean Tioram – the site of the chief MacRuairi stronghold). Arthur and his heirs were to supply one ship of twenty oars in the common army of the king of Scotland.[62]

The extent of the lands to which Arthur Campbell and his son laid claim across Lorn, Benderloch, Appin and Garmoran in the 1320s was thus truly staggering. Turning these claims into meaningful lordship, of course, was rather a different matter. Ruairi MacRuairi's son, Ranald, was undoubtedly regarded as the proper heir to the Garmoran lordship by most of his kin. Sir Arthur Campbell and his heirs would have to pursue a long and bitter struggle against one of the most militarily powerful kindreds in the west if they were to make good their claims. Sir Arthur was not, however, without intimidating allies of his own. The witnesses to Christina's grant included Sir John Menteith, Sir Donald Campbell, Sir Alexander McNaughton, Sir Ewen MacIver, Sir Duncan son of Thomas Campbell, and Neil and Donald MacLean. This was effectively a roll call of the Bruce partisans who were most active in carrying war against the MacDougalls and their allies in the west in the early 1320s. The involvement of Sir John Menteith, Sir Donald Campbell and the MacLeans in Christina's resignation gave any scheme for the annexation of MacRuairi estates north of Loch Linnhe by the MacArthur Campbells far greater credibility, for it potentially united the maritime power of a set of mutually supporting allies, prominent in defence of the Bruce interest in the Firth of Clyde, the Sound of Mull and the Firth of Lorn. Sir John Menteith (depending on the date of the arrangement either the man who turned to the Bruce cause in 1308–9 or his son) had command of the strongholds at Castle Sween, Skipness, Lochranza and perhaps Brodick, while his kinsman, Walter the Steward, held Dunoon, Rothesay and possibly Dunaverty. Robert I consolidated the Menteiths' role in the Firth of Clyde with a grant, in 1323, of the lands of Glen Breackerie in Kintyre, and Ailsa Craig.[63] Of the other witnesses, Sir Donald Campbell had acquired extensive interests inside the lordship of Argyll, receiving a grant of lands in Benderloch from Robert I.[64] The other Campbell witness, Duncan son of Thomas, represented a lineage that had been identified as landowners in the sheriffdom of Kintyre proposed by King John Balliol in 1293.[65] The family seems to have been closely tied to the Menteiths of Knapdale and Arran.[66]

Alexander MacNaughton and Ewen MacIver were probably the senior representatives of families with extensive estates inside Loch Awe and mid-Argyll. MacNaughton had originally maintained his allegiance to the MacDougall lords of Argyll, but by this stage he had clearly switched his support to Bruce (apparently bringing with him tales of Robert I's valour against his MacDougall opponents, which also happily explained Mac-Naughton's change of heart).[67]

The appearance of the two MacLean brothers is also significant. The MacLeans, like the Campbells, prospered in the service of Robert I after 1306. The link to the crown, again as in the case of the Campbells, may have built on ties of kinship with the Bruce king through a common descent from the earls of Carrick.[68] At any rate, Neil and Donald, alongside a third brother John, were in royal service by 1326 at the latest, when they received payment for various tasks undertaken in and around the king's castle, burgh, and military and administrative centre at Loch Tarbert.[69] In 1329, the year of Robert I's death, Neil MacLean was acting as Constable of the castle of 'Scraburgh', perhaps either Cairn na Burgh Mór or Beg in the Treshnish Isles, near Mull.[70]

By the end of Robert I's reign Clan Campbell had attained a commanding position around the Firth of Clyde and in Argyll. Further east, title to the earldom of Atholl lay in the hands of the young John Campbell. At first sight, then, the idea that the family's fortunes were founded on and guaranteed by their support for Robert I seems to be valid. But the impression of the continuous growth of Campbell power after 1306 is misleading. The family had embarked on many roads under the first Bruce king, but in the end most turned out to be cul-de-sacs. In the aftermath of the king's death the Campbell interests in Atholl and Argyll were swept away as displaced and dispossessed lords returned to claim their own. The future greatness of Clan Campbell did not lie with Sir Arthur and his son and their temporary military ascendancy in Lorn, Benderloch, Appin and Garmoran, nor with John Campbell and the earldom of Atholl, or the descendants of Dugald son of Sir Neil Campbell, sheriff of Argyll and bailie of Atholl for Robert I. Instead, the foundations of the powerful and enduring lordship of the later Middle Ages would be laid by a figure who was of little weight or consequence during the reign of Robert I.

The young Gillespic of Arran, second son of the ill-starred Colin, was hemmed in by kinsmen and rivals who had played a much greater and more dynamic part in the first phase of the Wars of Independence.[71] However, Gillespic's hour upon the stage was drawing near. An unforeseen consequence of the disasters that overwhelmed other branches of the family in the 1330s and 1340s was the clearing of Gillespic's path to the undisputed leadership of his kin. Over a long life Gillespic would transform the status of the Loch Awe Campbells, recovering his father's estates, unifying the Loch Awe and Ardscotnish lines through marriage, and presiding over a huge expansion of Campbell interests in Cowal and elsewhere before eventually becoming the king's lieutenant in Argyll. Gillespic's lordship was very much his own creation, but for much of his career his fortunes were intertwined with those of Robert the Steward (who became king as Robert II in 1371). The rise of the Stewart family to dominate fourteenth-century Scottish aristocratic society also brought a large number of Stewart adherents from south-western Scotland to national prominence. According to tradition the MacRaes of Kintail and Wester Ross were known as MacKenzie's 'shirt of mail', on account of the military services and security they provided on the western borders of MacKenzie lordship in Ross. The Steward was similarly blessed, for his lands and lordships on the Firth of Clyde were under the protection and care of Gillespic of Arran. It was as the Steward's 'shirt of mail' that Gillespic Campbell established the lordship on which later generations of his family would build.

Notes

1. Barrow, *Bruce*, 153; *CDS*, ii, no.1754.
2. Barrow, *Bruce*, 153–4.
3. Barrow, *Bruce*, 160; also *The Bruce* (Duncan), 112–121, especially note 1, p.112 for an interpretation which places some doubt on the identification of John of Lorn and the suggestion that the real leader of the force encountered by Bruce was the local lord in Glen Dochart. This seems plausible given Bruce's actions against the established lords of these areas after his return in 1307.
4. *The Bruce* (Duncan), 104.
5. See below, p. 95.
6. *The Bruce* (Duncan), 130–1, 138–141. Interestingly, the Annals attached to John of Fordun's chronicle have nothing to say about Sir Neil, and identify Bruce's constant companions in this period as Malcolm, earl of Lennox, and Gilbert Hay. Similarly, where Barbour stresses the contribution of Angus Óg Mac-Donald to Bruce's survival, the Annals concentrate on an entirely different figure, Christina MacRuairie of Garmoran. Since Robert II was the father-in-law of John MacDonald of Islay in the 1370s, it would seem that Barbour was very much interpreting this critical stage of Bruce's career from a later Stewart perspective. The Annals, on the other hand, seem to have been thoroughly anti-Stewart in tone and sentiment. See S. Boardman, 'Chronicle Propaganda in Fourteenth-Century Scotland: Robert the Steward, John of Fordun and the "Anonymous Chronicle" ', *SHR*, lxxvi (1997), 23–43, and Dauvit Broun, 'A New Look at *Gesta Annalia* attributed to John of Fordun', in *Church, Chronicle and Learning*, ed. Barbara E. Crawford (Edinburgh 1999), 9–30.
7. The best discussion of this episode is provided in Barrow, *Bruce*, 166–71.
8. For a thoughtful examination of the MacDougall lordship (and much else), see W.D.H. Sellar, 'Hebridean Sea Kings: The Successors of Somerled, 1164–1316' (hereafter, Sellar, 'Hebridean Sea Kings'), in *Alba: Celtic Scotland in the Middle Ages* (East Linton, 2000), eds. E.J. Cowan and R.A. McDonald, 187–218.
9. *CDS*, ii, nos.742, p.177 (Menteith as a prisoner in 1296); Stevenson, *Documents*, ii, p.136 (his move from Nottingham Castle to the king at Winchelsea before his release in August). See M.Prestwich, *Edward I* (London, 1988), 392–4 for the sailing of Edward's expeditionary force on 24 August.
10. Stevenson, *Documents*, ii, no.626, p.453.

11. On 20 March 1304, Stevenson, *Historical Documents*, ii, no. 635, p.474.

12. For Menteith's role in the capture of Wallace, see Barrow, *Bruce*, 136; Palgrave, *Docs.Hist.Scot.*, 295 (but see Barrow, *Bruce*, 353, note 32). The relationship between John and Edward seems to have become even closer after the capture of Wallace. In issuing a safe-conduct to merchants of St Omer at the request of Sir John Menteith Edward claimed that he would have given the concession 'to no other than himself'. *CDS*, ii, no.1719.

13. In the immediate aftermath of Comyn's death, Robert attempted to secure a number of castles in the south-west, particularly those of strategic significance on or near the Firth of Clyde such as Ayr, Rothesay, Inverkip and Dunaverty. See Barrow, *Bruce*, 149; Stones, *Relations*, no.34, pp.266–9.

14. Palgrave, *Docs.Hist.Scot.*, pp.353–4. *CDS*, ii, no.1771. Edward's grant of May 22 1306 to John de Hastings and his heirs of the earldom of Menteith in Scotland included the Isles and all other forfeited lands of Allan, lately earl of Menteith, a rebel with Robert the Bruce; excepting the lands in the earldom granted by charter to Edmund de Hastings; *The Bruce* (Duncan), 168–9. Sir John Hastings of Abergavenny was noted as the keeper of Brodick Castle on Arran when it was subjected to an attack by Bruce's supporters James Douglas and Robert Boyd; *CDS*, ii, no.1786 June 16 1306, mentioning the grant of Lennox to Sir John.

15. Sir John Menteith was one of the men involved in the so-called 'Turnberry Band' of 20 September 1286, a much-discussed agreement that, at the least, showed an early interaction between his family and the Bruce earls of Carrick. The other men involved in the bond included John's brother Alexander, and his father, Walter, earl of Menteith, as well as their close kinsmen, James the Steward and his brother. Stevenson, *Historical Documents*, i, no.12.

16. *APS*, i, 459. Indeed, the seals of Donald and Neil (described as brothers) and Sir John were all placed on the same tag. One version of Bower's *Scotichronicon* included two stories that purported to explain how Menteith was eventually reconciled to the Bruce cause. Both tales were hostile to Menteith and portrayed him as a habitual traitor. *Chron. Bower* (Watt), vi, 447–9. A royal charter in favour of Melrose Abbey may have been issued at this parliament or during one of Robert's Highland campaigns. The witnesses included Malcolm earl of Lennox, Edward Bruce, James Stewart, John Menteith, Alexander Lindsay, Donald 'Cambel' and Neil 'Cambel'. *RRS*, v, no.385, pp.629–31, where Duncan argues for a charter date August 1308 X July 1309.

17. For Menteith as a target for the English crown after 1308, see *Rot. Scot.*, i, 90. For service in Ireland, *Chartularies of St Mary's Abbey, Dublin*, ed. J.J. Gilbert (London, 1884), 299, 344.

18. Sir John was thus styled as one of the noblemen named in the 1320 baronial letter to Pope John XXII now known as the 'declaration' of Arbroath. For the translated text, see A.A.M. Duncan, *The Nation of the Scots and the Declaration of Arbroath* (Historical Association, 1970), pp.34–37.

19. *HP*, ii, 91. The seventeenth-century Campbell genealogy asserted that Neil's son Colin married one 'Helena daughter to Sir John More whom Colvin supposes to have been the son of the Earle of Lennox'. The identity of this John Mór is problematic, for it is difficult to find a son of the contemporary earls of Lennox named John. However, John Menteith had briefly been provided to this title by Edward I and, if the tales preserved by Walter Bower are correct, he had

attempted to retain the earldom in his negotiations with Robert I in *c*.1308. Curiously, these tales also suggested that Menteith's reconciliation with Bruce and his followers and his restoration as a respectable public figure were partly due to the connections established by his daughters. *Chron. Bower* (Watt), vi, 447–9.

20. *CDS*, ii, no.1957.

21. McDonald, *Kingdom of the Isles*, 175–180, provides a summary of the conflicting interpretations of the timing and objectives of these expeditions. See also Barrow, *Bruce*, 179–80; *The Bruce* (Duncan), 366.

22. *Cawdor Bk.*, 4; *RRS*, v, no.9. If 'Lochbren' can be taken to mean Lochbroom, then the charter would support Duncan's argument that the king's appearance in the far north, in company with three lords noted for their ability to mobilise naval forces, marked the point at which Robert launched his decisive strike against the MacDougalls. An alternative suggestion, made by G.W.S. Barrow, is that the place-name Loch Bren does not indicate Loch Broom, but rather a location in the parish of Bren in Easter Ross.

23. *RRS*, v, no.10; Sellar, 'Hebridean Sea Kings', at 214–8.

24. The dating of the 1308 bond has been variously given as 8, 9 or 24 September at Cambuskenneth, and the men involved as Neil, Gilbert Hay and Alexander Seton. The Cambuskenneth connection is interesting given earlier Campbell appearances at this location. The bond may have resulted from negotiations designed to allow a number of southern landowners to withdraw from English allegiance. At least two prominent Scots, Robert Keith and Thomas Hay, came over to Bruce around Christmas 1308. *CDS*, iii, no.245; *Calendar of Close Rolls Edward II*, no.245. Negotiations are likely to have been underway some time before this, and the change of allegiance only attested in December 1308 when there was a major Bruce raid on English interests in Lothian; Barrow, *Bruce*, 187. *Rot. Scot.*, i, 61. That the allegiance of Hay and Seton was new or uncertain is suggested not only by the terms of the bond, but also by Seton's evident return to the service of the English crown by 20/2/1312 when he took part in an English shrieval inquest in Edinburgh. Neil's involvement in the 1308 bond could have reflected his position as Bruce's representative, but it might also have been required because of some particular tension between him and these men. Were they associates of Robert Keith? George MacKenzie, *The lives and characters of the most eminent writers of the Scots nation; with an abstract and a catalogue of their works; their various editions; and the judgment of the learn'd concerning them*, 3 vols. (Edinburgh 1708–22), iii, 210; NLS, Adv.Ms.35.3.7, p.318. The seal tags on the document issued by the 1309 parliament included the names of Donald and Neil. *APS*, i, facsimile facing p.459.

25. On 21 August 1309 Sir John Menteith and Sir Neil had a safe-conduct from Edward II, as ambassadors of Robert I, to treat for peace with Richard de Burgh, earl of Ulster, commissioner of the English king. Campbell had, of course, earlier served in de Burgh's retinue at the 1304 siege of Stirling. *CDS*, iii, no.101, *Foedera*, ii, 85. In September 1314 Neil was one of the men included in a request for an English safe-conduct (the others were Roger Kirkpatrick, Robert Keith and Gilbert Hay). *RRS*, v, 328–9 no.40.

26. Certainly Mary may have been the unnamed sister of Robert I mentioned in October 1314, *CDS*, iii, no.393, *Foedera*, ii, 256; Barrow, *Bruce*, 162, 231; Mary's

captivity can be traced through to Michaelmas 1312, *CDS*, iii, nos.131 (30 March 1310), 227 (to 24 June 1311), 244 (8 February 1312), 248 (5 March 1312), 340.

27. *RMS*, i, App. 2., no. 639; *RSS*, v, nos. 394, 497; *APS*, i, 481.

28. The barony of Glendochart and the lordship of Fortingall, for example, were given over to members of the Menzies family. *RMS*, i, App. 2., nos. 465, 476–7. See also *RMS*, i, App. 2., no. 568. Between 1320 and 1329 Strathgartney was given to Sir John Menteith and his wife Elena of Mar, the King's niece. *RSS*, vi, no.212; *APS*, i, 524.

29. *RRS*, v, no.46, pp.333–4; *RMS*, i, App 1, 106; Argyll Muniments, Inverary, Argyll Charters.

30. See C. McNamee, *The Wars of the Bruces* (East Linton, 1997), Ch. 5, for a good summary of the latest research on this episode.

31. *APS*, i, 448; *Foedera*, ii, 786.

32. *CDS*, ii, no.1646, p.439.

33. *The Bruce* (Duncan), 118–9.

34. RRS, v, nos. 48,58 (although this depends on the accuracy of the seventeenth-century antiquarian Balfour of Denmylne's description of seals attached to the tags of this document). Mary Bruce married, after Sir Neil's death, Sir Alexander Fraser. The marriage produced a son John who was referred to in a charter of 6 April 1327 when he must have been very young. *RRS*, v, no.320; *Frasers of Philorth*, i, 67; *RMS*, i, App. 2., no. 483. Neil must have died before his son Colin if the appearance of Colin Campbell lord of Tillicoultry, son and heir of the deceased Neil Campbell refers to these two men. *Cambuskenneth Registrum*, no.222. Colin himself died young, probably before *c.*July 1323. *RRS*, v, no.394. All the indications, therefore, are that Neil died shortly after the grant of Loch Awe and Ardscotnish to his son.

35. *The Bruce* (Duncan), 586.

36. M. Stewart, 'A Recently-Discovered Manuscript: "ane taill of Sir colling ye knyt"', *SS*, 16 (1972), 23–39.

37. *Scottish Verse from The Book of the Dean of Lismore*, ed.W.J. Watson (SGTS, 1937) (hereafter, *The Book of the Dean*), xx (pp.158–165), notes pp.290–1.

38. The genealogies preserved in MS 1467 and the collection of MacFirbis both name Neil's father as 'Ailin Mór' for 'Cailin Mór'. I should like to thank Ronnie and Mairi Black for their helpful comments on these manuscripts.

39. Although it seems most likely that he died around 1322–3. For the Irish campaigns, see McNamee, *The Wars of the Bruces*, 184–6. Irish chronicles made no mention of Colin Campbell but did record the presence of a 'Dominus Johannes Cambell' on the campaigns of the Bruce brothers in Ireland, alongside the earl of Moray, John Menteith, John Stewart and Philip Mowbray. *Chartularies of St Mary's Abbey, Dublin*, ed. J.J. Gilbert (London, 1884), 299, 344.

40. *RRS*, v, no.58.

41. The earliest direct comment on Dugald is to be found in the seventeenth-century genealogy of the Campbells where it was suggested that he was a son of Sir Neil Campbell from an association with Margaret, daughter to Sir John Cameron. 'This Dugald Campbell son to Sir Neill had a son called John and that John had a daughter called Mary who was afterward married to her own cousin Coline Iongantich.' *HP*, ii, 89. As we shall see, the genealogy is certainly accurate in depicting the later marriage between the two Campbell families, and

it is tempting to accept the stated relationship between Dugald and Neil Campbell. However, A.B.W. MacEwen has advanced an ingenious argument that the Dugald active in the 1320s was the son of the hitherto unidentified Colin Campbell, the son (and the legitimate heir) of the Colin who died c.1296. In MacEwen's scheme it was this younger Colin who left an under-age heir (Dugald) whose ward was assigned to Sir John Dovedale by Edward I. See Table 2a. Dugald would thus have represented the senior line descended from Colin (d.1296), a fact that would justify Dugald's 'reclamation' of estates from his cousins. Much depends on the interpretation of a note of an agreement between a Dugald son of Neil and a Dugald son of Colin from 1323 to be discussed in greater detail below.

42. There was clearly a Dugald Campbell alive and active as an adult in the last decade of the thirteenth century. This Dugald rendered the accounts of the sheriff of Dumbarton in 1289 and, presumably the same man, witnessed a charter in favour of Sir Colin, c. 1295, and rendered homage to Edward I on 28 August 1296 for lands in the county of Perth. Sir Colin is reputed to have had a son named Dugald and it is possible that these three appearances relate to him, although the evidence here is not conclusive. *ER*, i, 38; Sellar, 'Earliest Campbells', 114.

43. *RRS*, v, no.27, p.315, gives the terms of the charter and dates it 24 January in the seventh year of the King's reign (giving 1313). Kilchoan, Degnish, Auchinaclosh, Auchnasaul, Caddleton, 'Garpyng', Ardincaple, Ragray, Kilninver, Esgeallan, Clachanseilach, Leternacrosh, Scamadill, the 1d of Kilveran, 1d of Leternamuck and Toresay. The detailed list is derived from an Argyll inventory of the seventeenth century, and the designation of Dugald as 'of Lochaw' was probably a mistaken interpolation by the compiler of that source. *RMS*, i., App 2, no.363 dated what seems to have been the same grant to c.1321.

44. *RMS*, i, App.2., nos. 363, 364. The first is described as a charter to Dowgalli Campbell (Dugaldi Cample) of the lands of Gillitenval (insula de Dorsa et terris de Deginiche – i.e. Torsay and Degnish). Index A. In Index B as a charter to Dugald Campbell of the isle of Torsa with many other lands. No.364 is a charter (Index A) to 'dicti Dugaldi [Carta Dugaldi Campbell] de terris de Mestour [Nestre]', and in Index B as one to Dugald Campbell, of the lands of Menstrie in Clackmannanshire.

45. *RMS*, i, App.2., no.352. Index A describes a charter to 'Dungalli? Campbell de terris de Ardsoir etc.' This charter is given alternatively as one to 'Duncani? Campbell filii Nigelli de terris de Ordefore Neog' Index A. In Index B this charter is described as one to Dugald Campbell, of sundry lands in Argyll, or 'Carta Dugalli Cambell filii Nigelli of mani lands: Inveniendo annuatim unam navem octodecim remorem sufficientem ad opus nostrum proprium cum ipsa indiguerimus'.

46. *RMS*, i, App. 2, 695. MacEwen's alternative argument would be that the Dugald son of Colin involved in the 1323 agreement was not the son of Colin son of Neil but the son of Colin son of Colin Mór. Against this interpretation we might note that explicit rights of Campbell lordship over Ardscotnish seem to have been established only in Neil's lifetime so that there would have been no legal basis for a transfer of title to a man descended from Neil's father.

47. *RRS*, v, p.242.

48. J.G. Dunbar and A.A.M. Duncan, 'Tarbert Castle; a contribution to the history of Argyll', *SHR*, l (1971), 1–17, at 14–16.
49. *ER*, i, 52.
50. *ER*, i, 52. John was probably born sometime after 1314 and so would have been a minor in 1326. Atholl thus seems to have been made a royal bailliary during John's minority under the charge of one of John's nearest kinsmen.
51. Argyll Muniments, Inveraray, Argyll Charters; *HP*, ii, 132–4. The appearance of John Cameron of Baledgarno as a witness may inspire further confidence in the family relationships laid out in the seventeenth-century Campbell genealogy since it was claimed there that Neil's son Dugald was the product of a liaison with a daughter of John Cameron. Cameron may thus have witnessed as Dugald's father or brother-in-law. Another witness to the charter was Gilbert Hay, lord of Erroll, who, depending on the date of the charter, was, or was about to become, Robert I's constable.
52. *RMS*, i, App.2, nos. 56 (Cenel Baden and Ardnamurchan), 57 (Lochaber), 58 (Duror and Glencoe) to Angus Óg of Islay, 59 (Moidart and Knoidart) to Ruairi mac Allan. *RMS*, i, App. 1, no.9.
53. See N. Murray 'A House Divided Against Itself: A Brief Synopsus of the History of Clann Alexandair and the early career of 'Good John of Islay' c. 1290–1370' in *Rannsachadh na Gàidhlig 2000*, edd. c. ÓBaoill and N. R. McGuire (Aberdeen, 2002), 221–230 for discussion of Clan Donald leadership in the early fourteenth century, *RRS*, v, p.242.
54. The elder John Menteith seems to have died either *c.*1318 or (as argued by Duncan in *RRS*, v, p.iii) as late as *c.*1323.
55. All three Campbell lords witnessed a charter issued 1309 X 1323 by Sir John (described as the son of Walter, earl of Menteith) in favour of Ewen Finlayson (a Lamont) of the lands of Ardmernock and others in Cowal. The other witnesses were Sir Alexander Menzies, Sir Finlay, rector of Dunoon, John son of Gilbert, John son of Roman (Lauman). *Lamont Papers*, no.13, p.9.
56. *RMS*, i, App. 2, nos. 353, 368. To Arthur Campbell of constabulary of Dunstaffnage and mains thereof, which Alexander Argyll had in his hands. Duncan argues that this grant should be dated to *c.*1321 on the basis that it appears in a roll associated with other grants from the 16th year of Robert I's reign. *RRS*, v, p.242. This individual could be either Sir Arthur Campbell senior or junior. Duncan suggests that the grant of the constabulary was part of the creation of the new sheriffdom of Argyll and that Dunstaffnage represented a dependent constabulary of Tarbert.
57. *The Bruce* (Duncan), 366–7.
58. Unusually in the context of Robert I's west-coast grants, the service specified was for a quarter of a knight rather than providing a galley. *RRS*, v, no.393, p.639. Duncan speculates that the charter was either issued in 1306X20 or, more probably, 25 March 1321X24March 1322. *HP*, iv, 195–6. *RMS*, i, App.2, no. 372. See also *RRS*, v, no. 366 p. 617. 6 February 1329; *HP*, iv, 196–7.
59. *RRS*, v, no. 374, p. 622. 3 April 1329. Probably issued at Whithorn. The same grant as *RMS*, i, App. 2, 620.
60. *RMS*, i, App. 1, 9; Lachlan was married to the daughter of Alexander of Argyll. Stevenson, *Documents*, ii, no.610, pp.429–30; *Ibid.*, no.445, p.189; *CDS*, ii, no.1633; *CDS*, iv, p.400; *APS*, i, 477.

61. *RMS*, i, App. 1, no.9. The undated charter by Robert I confirmed to Ruairi son of Allan the lands resigned by Christian daughter of the deceased Allan son of Ruairi to the king. The lands were to be held by Ruairi and his heirs male from the King and his heirs for the service of a boat of twenty-six oars with men and victuals in the King's army when required. If Ruairi did not produce male heirs, the lands were to return to Ruairi son of the said Christian (presumably by Duncan of Mar). The name of Christian's son may simply reflect the adoption of the name of his maternal grandfather, but it also seems to mark the boy as a potential successor to the MacRuairi lordship. The deal would seem to have been made very early in Robert I's reign; it is not inconceivable that it was concluded over the winter of 1306–7. The Annals attached to Fordun's chronicle noted that Christian (styled of the Isles) aided the King during his sojourn in the Hebrides in 1306–7. *Chron.Bower* (Watt), vi, 327.

62. Library of the Faculty of Procurators, Glasgow, Bound vol. 'Charters etc. 1423 to 1708'. Since Christian is described as a widow, and no longer uses the name 'of Mar', we can assume that this charter was issued after the death of Duncan of Mar.

63. NAS GD 124/1/1113; see *RRS*, v, no.239. Glen Breackerie runs to the sea near Dunaverty Castle. See also *RMS*, i, App. 2, no. 661 for a grant of Kintyre in favour of Walter's son Robert (the King's grandson).

64. *RMS*, i, App. 2, no.660. The exact date of the grant is not given, but it was certainly before February 1329, when Donald resigned the lands in favour of his son Duncan. *RRS*, v, no. 366, p.617. 6 February 1329; *HP*, iv, 196–7. The lands were to be held in free barony and for the service of a galley of twenty-six oars. Effectively, then, the lordship of Argyll was being carved up into a series of Campbell baronies to be held directly of the Crown for galley service.

65. *APS*, i, 447. 'Terra domini Thomae Cambel.'

66. After Sir John Menteith negotiated his release from English captivity in 1297 he stood as surety for the release of a number of other men, including Thomas Campbell, who were to fight with him on Edward I's Flanders campaign of 1297. *Foedera*, i, 867, 872, 889; *Rot.Scot.*, i, 44, 45.

67. *The Bruce* (Duncan), 118. Barbour was very likely to have had a good source for this tale, as Robert II's mistress, Mariota Cardeny, had been first married to Alexander MacNaughton of that Ilk.

68. N. MacLean-Bristol, *Warriors and Priests: The History of the Clan Maclean, 1300–1570* (East Linton, 1995), 9–11.

69. *ER*, i, xxiii, 57.

70. *ER*, i, 238; *Chron.Bower* (Watt), i, 189, 347; RCAHMS *Argyll*, iii, 184–90, no.335.

71. The by-name 'of Arran' was given to Gillespic in an early sixteenth-century poem addressed to his descendant Archibald, 2nd earl of Argyll. *The Book of the Dean*, xx (pp.158–165).

THREE

The Steward's Shirt of Mail: Gillespic of Arran

The death of Robert I brought a new age of war and ruin to the king's supporters in the west. The network of stone and ships that had underpinned the Bruce ascendancy in Argyll and the Hebrides did not long survive the king. However, from the wreck of Campbell power a new leader rose to achieve an unprecedented level of control over other branches of the kin and, by the end of his life, to dominate much of Argyll. The tale of Gillespic of Arran was wound about the lives of two other long-lived aristocrats whose careers ran parallel to, and synchronised with, his own. Between them, Gillespic Campbell, John MacDonald of Islay, and Robert the Steward of Scotland built the great lordships that would govern the politics of Gaelic Scotland until the end of the fifteenth century.

In the immediate aftermath of Robert's death the militarised lordships held by his committed lieutenants looked capable of survival and of sustaining the hold of the king's infant son, David, on the kingdom. Above all, the most impressive of Robert's warlords, Thomas Randolph, earl of Moray, exercised the office of guardian of the kingdom for the young monarch with a steely conviction and ruthlessness.[1] Outwith the kingdom's marches, however, the forces and interests that had been held at bay during Robert's reign were recovering their strength and ambition. The young English king, Edward III, seems to have regarded the treaty of Edinburgh/Northampton as a shameful surrender of English royal rights and a personal humiliation. He was intent on restitution and revenge. The English king had many men prepared to carry forward his agenda in Scotland. Edward Balliol, the son of King John, looked to recover the lordship wrested from his family by the usurper Bruce. Already the focus of a great conspiracy against Robert I in 1320, Balliol's hour seemed to have arrived with the death of the first Bruce king and the accession of the infant David.[2] Balliol could count on the support of all those lords, English or Scots, whose heritage had been denied them by the Bruce regime. Like the Bruce rebellion of 1306, the Balliol intervention of the

1330s involved an aggregation of individual aristocratic interests and grievances grouped around a central claim to the Scottish throne. Unlike that of 1306, however, the movement was first sponsored and then openly sustained by the English crown.

In July 1332 Edward Balliol and his supporters, collectively known as the Disinherited, were ready to trust the judgement of their cause to battle and set sail from England to land on the Fife shore at Kinghorn on 6 August.[3] The path had been smoothed for Balliol and his supporters by the sudden death of the Scottish guardian, Randolph, on 20 July. On 11 August Balliol's small force was engaged at Dupplin Moor by a far larger army under the command of the new Scottish guardian, Donald, earl of Mar. Mar's force was badly led and deployed and in the ensuing shambles the guardian and a number of leading noblemen were killed.[4] Military victory allowed Balliol to be crowned at Scone on 24 September 1332, but the new 'king' was constantly harassed by Bruce partisans and had been forced to flee to Carlisle by the end of the year.[5] At this point Edward III decided to take a direct hand in the war in the northern kingdom, offering Balliol military aid in mounting a siege of Berwick. In May 1333 the English king arrived in person to conduct the siege.[6] The defenders were forced to agree the surrender of the burgh and castle if they were not relieved by 20 July. On 19 July a Scottish host under the command of yet another new guardian, Archibald Douglas, made a determined attempt to break the siege. At Halidon Hill near Berwick the Scottish army suffered a catastrophic reverse, during which Douglas and many other Scottish noblemen were killed.[7] The follow-up to the crushing English victory at Halidon was sustained in a way that Balliol's at Dupplin the previous year had not been. The renewed war now directly threatened the interests of the Campbells and their political patrons in the west.

In the deep winter of 1333/4 the future for the various branches of the Clan Campbell seemed bleak. Supporters of the Bruce cause in the west had been greatly weakened by the events of the previous two years. The death of Thomas Randolph had removed a man who had been active both in Wester Ross and Argyll after Robert I's death.[8] The shattering victories of Edward Balliol, the Disinherited and the English crown at Dupplin Moor and Halidon Hill had seen a further loss of key personnel. On the slopes of Halidon John Campbell, the young earl of Atholl, had been killed; with the passing of the childless earl, Campbell ambitions in Atholl were extinguished. Moreover, the political and military effectiveness of the Stewarts had been dealt a critical blow with the death of James Stewart of Durisdeer at Halidon. James was the uncle and guardian of the young heir to the Stewartry, Robert, and had led the Steward's men in war since the death of his brother Walter in 1327.[9] After Halidon the young lord Robert was in a perilous position. The triumphant Edward III and Balliol followed up their military success by forfeiting the Steward's ancestral lands in the Stewartry and the lordships of the Firth of Clyde. These were assigned over to David of Strathbogie, the restored earl of Atholl, as the representative of the new regime in the summer of 1333.[10] With Balliol's agents closing in, Robert made a frantic overnight dash from his hiding place in Rothesay to join his fugitive king David II in the relative safety of Dumbarton Castle on the Clyde, held by Sir Malcolm Fleming.[11]

At the nadir of his fortunes Robert turned again to his family's Campbell supporters in the Firth of Clyde. During the long winter months in Dumbarton the Bruce partisans seem to have decided on a twofold military/diplomatic strategy with which to greet the coming spring.[12] At the end of April, or in early May, 1334 the ten-year-old David II set sail from Dumbarton on a French vessel to seek the protection of the French king and to begin a seven-year political exile.[13] Robert the Steward also took to the waters of the Firth of Clyde in April/May, although on a more warlike mission, for Robert was embarking on a campaign to drive out the Balliol loyalists who were occupying his patrimony. According to later chronicles, the Steward's principal supporter in this enterprise was one 'Dowgal Cammell' who resided at nearby Loch Awe and who had 'a gret affectyown' for the young Robert.[14] It seems likely that this Dugald was the eldest son of Sir Colin Campbell, who had now assumed an active role in the military affairs of the family.[15] The Steward's small force eventually sailed out into the Firth of Clyde, presumably on Campbell galleys.[16] Robert's first target was Dunoon Castle in Cowal, a fortress that dominated the routes from the Holy Loch, Loch Long and the mouth of the Clyde south to the open sea.[17] The arrival of the Steward's army is said to have swiftly forced the surrender of the castle by negotiation.[18] The Steward's expedition and David II's flight from Dumbarton seem to have been co-ordinated. It may well be that the Steward/Campbell assault on Dunoon and the nullification of the pro-Balliol garrison were partly designed to give the French ships carrying David II into political exile a fighting chance of reaching the North Channel undetected by the king's enemies.

The successful attack on Dunoon is said to have sparked a spontaneous rising by the inhabitants of Bute, who killed the Balliol-appointed sheriff and captured Rothesay Castle.[19] By 25 May 1334 the Steward had returned in triumph to the island from where he issued a charter in favour of Iver Campbell, son of Sir Arthur Campbell, of the castle and bailiary of Rosneath on the north shore of the Clyde.[20] Rosneath may have been another fortress to fall to the Steward's forces in the spring of 1334. By May 1334, then, the Bruce/Stewart partisans were in possession of a network of mutually reinforcing strongholds, Dumbarton, Rosneath, Dunoon and Rothesay, which gave them effective control over much of the Firth of Clyde.

The response of Edward III and Edward Balliol to their losses in the region was a diplomatic and military offensive that culminated in a co-ordinated assault on Bruce supporters during the summer of 1335.[21] As early as April 1335 Edward III was making arrangements for the assembly of a fleet and army in Carlingford Lough that would supplement the advance of the king's army into Lowland Scotland.[22] In July 1335 Edward III led his army across the Solway while another force under Edward Balliol moved through the eastern March.[23] Resistance on the part of those upholding the Bruce claim to the throne seems to have been nominal as the army of the English king swept through the south-west, including the Steward's recently reclaimed lordships of Cunningham and Kyle.[24] Edward III and Balliol were able to link their forces and hold a council of war at Glasgow before moving north to Perth.

If the storm of war had appeared to bypass the Steward's Campbell adherents in the Firth of Clyde, then the respite was only temporary. On a date between 23 and 28 August 1335 Edward's Irish fleet set sail, carrying the troops and siege engines of the justiciar of Ireland, John Darcy, and the earls of Desmond and Ormond.[25] One of the principal targets for the fleet was Rothesay Castle on Bute, which had been won back for the Steward the previous summer.[26]

The resolve of Bruce adherents in the Hebrides and Argyll to fight on in the interests of an exiled king against apparently irresistible odds may well have wavered.[27] Even before the arrival of Edward III's fleet in the Firth of Clyde, the Steward had sounded out the possibility of reaching an accommodation with the English king.[28] In September 1335, while Rothesay Castle was being pounded by the great war-engines brought by John Darcy from Dublin, the Steward apparently made his submission

to Edward III at Edinburgh.[29] Certainly, by the end of the month Andrew
Murray had replaced the Steward as guardian of the Scottish kingdom for
the exiled David II.[30] Dugald Campbell may well have come to terms with
the Balliol/English regime at the same time as his Stewart patron; it seems
that at some point between 1335 and 1342 Dugald, like a number of other
Argyll lords, left David II's allegiance. Any submission made by the
Steward seems to have been short-lived, but by the following year Edward
III and Edward Balliol had found a more useful and reliable western ally in
the shape of John MacDonald of Islay. At Perth on 12 September 1336
John completed an indenture with Edward Balliol by which the lord of
Islay was given title to a great sweep of lordships, including Kintyre and
Knapdale, in return for his undertaking to 'damage' Edward's enemies.[31]
The casual granting away of the Stewart and Menteith lordships of
Kintyre and Knapdale makes it unlikely that the Steward was still
associated with the Balliol regime at this point.[32]

In the aftermath of the military campaigns of 1334–5 a silence falls on the
fate and fortune of the Campbell lords in Argyll. The next reference to the
family does not occur until 4 July 1342, by which time there had been
considerable change in the political landscape. In 1338, on the death of
Andrew Murray, Robert the Steward had assumed the guardianship of the
kingdom on behalf of the exiled David II. Despite his occupation of the
guardianship the personal and political relationship between David and
his nephew and heir-apparent was less than cordial. The exiled king seems
to have mistrusted Robert from an early point in his career, and instead
favoured John Randolph, son of the guardian who had died in 1332, as his
chief and most reliable agent in the Scottish kingdom. David II returned
from his French exile in 1341 but the king's presence in Scotland did little
to warm the relationship with his nephew.

The situation in Argyll on David's return to Scotland in 1341 remains
obscure, and it was not until 1342–3 that the King made a determined
personal intervention in the affairs of the west. The major lord in the
southern Hebrides, John MacDonald of Islay, seems to have retained his
allegiance, nominal or otherwise, to the Balliol cause and the English
crown throughout the late 1330s and early 1340s.[33] MacDonald may have
wielded some influence over the families of mainland Argyll. Given that
the remnants of the MacDougall kindred were also in English/Balliol
service and apparently active in their old territories during the 1330s, it is
perhaps no surprise that many lords in Argyll seem to have drifted from

Bruce allegiance prior to David II's return to Scotland.[34] Over the following two years King David II forfeited a series of estates belonging to men who were said to be, or to have died as, rebels against the king's faith and peace (although there is no guarantee that this necessarily indicates support for the Balliol cause).[35] Included in the latter group was Dugald Campbell, the man who had provided the military backing for the Steward's assault on Dunoon in 1334. On 4 July 1342 David II granted to Gillespic Campbell and his male heirs all the (unspecified) lands that had belonged to his deceased brother Dugald, and which then pertained to the king by forfeiture because Dugald had died as a rebel.[36] The fact that Gillespic was restored only to lands held 'by just title' by his brother, and not to those held by his father, was probably a significant limitation that protected the position of, amongst others, the Ardscotnish Campbells.

The nature of Dugald's crimes against the crown remains unknown and it is uncertain whether they were committed before or after David's return to the kingdom. It is conceivable that Dugald had died some time before 1342 and that his forfeiture was imposed retrospectively by the first parliament held by David in September 1341, perhaps partly to inconvenience Dugald's patron, Robert the Steward.[37]

At any rate, the 1342 grant confirmed Gillespic in control of his brother's lordships and lands. It seems likely that Gillespic shared his deceased brother's 'gret affectyown' for the Steward; at the very least Gillespic was linked by both family and personal history to Steward lordship in the region. In a later Gaelic poem Gillespic was given the by-name 'of Arran', a description that might suggest he was raised or fostered on the island.[38] This was not wholly unlikely, since Gillespic's mother may have been a daughter or granddaughter of the buccaneering Sir John Menteith whose son and grandson came to dominate Arran, Knapdale and Strathgartney during the first half of the fourteenth century.[39] Gillespic was certainly linked at an early point to the Steward's lordship of Cowal, where he received a grant of the lands of Kinlochstrevin from Robert. At around the same time Gillespic married an Isabella Lamont, a bride undoubtedly drawn from one of the Lamont lineages that dominated much of the southern part of Cowal.[40]

Gillespic had escaped unscathed from the threat to the family's lordship raised by Dugald's forfeiture, and by the following year he was a direct beneficiary of the reassertion of royal power in the west. On 2 May 1343, Campbell apparently received a grant of the lands and barony of Melfort because of the forfeiture of the heirs.[41] The gift of Melfort came at a point when David II was stepping up the pressure on John MacDonald and Ranald MacRuairi of Garmoran. The king may not have been particularly fond of Robert the Steward, but the power and local effectiveness of the Stewart affinity (including Gillespic Campbell) made it indispensable to the crown in the attempt to coerce the lords of the west. In the month following the grant of Melfort, on 12 June at Ayr, both John MacDonald of Islay and Ranald MacRuairi of Garmoran came to terms with David II.[42] The two men were confirmed in their possessions (including lands, islands and castles obtained from the MacDougalls), but John's claim to the Stewart lordship of Kintyre was pointedly ignored. At around the same time David confirmed the territorial position of a number of other Hebridean lords.[43]

It may also have been in the summer of 1343 that the king imposed a new territorial and political settlement in mid-Argyll. A series of forfeitures saw the king redistribute lands to a number of local men. Besides the gift of Melfort to Gillespic Campbell, the king granted Alexander Mac-Naughton unspecified estates forfeited by a member of Clan Donald and an individual known as Dungall the parson.[44] In addition, Arthur Campbell and Dugald of Craignish received grants from David asserting that they should be subject to no-one for their lands save the king.[45] Finally, in 1346, the lands of another Argyllshire baron, John son of Ewen Mac-Gilchrist, were forfeited by his heir and given over to Gilbert of Glassary.[46] The overall impression created by David II's grants is that Gillespic Campbell hardly dominated local society and royal patronage in mid-Argyll. The region still abounded with lords of middling stature, such as the MacNaughtons, the Glassarys, the MacArthur Campbells and the lords of Craignish, who were acutely conscious and assertive of their independence from any local overlord.

By the mid-1340s, then, David II seems to have gone some way towards re-establishing mid-Argyll as a centre for royal influence in the west. In October 1346, however, the political status quo in Argyll, and Scotland in general, was shattered by the capture of David II at the Battle of Neville's Cross, near Durham, as the Scots king drove a punitive raid through the northern English counties.[47] One of the few Scots lords to make it off the battlefield was Robert the Steward, whose conduct attracted critical comment from both English chroniclers and Scots who were sympathetic to the captured king.[48] Nevertheless, the Steward, as David's nephew and nearest heir, now assumed the office of guardian of the kingdom for the absent monarch. The Steward's guardianship was distinguished by his relentless accumulation of vacant lands and titles across the central Highlands for himself and his immediate family. The Steward's allies also prospered under the new benevolent regime. As the Steward's gaze shifted from the Firth of Clyde to the Perthshire earldoms of Atholl and Strathearn, he seems to have regarded the exercise of personal lordship in his western holdings of Cowal and Kintyre as an increasingly onerous duty. Between 1346 and 1357 Robert, wrapped up with the affairs of guardianship and territorial acquisition further east, effectively withdrew as an active lord in the Firth of Clyde.

One plank of Robert's strategy was the conclusion of a marriage alliance with John MacDonald of Islay in 1350.[49] The marriage of Robert's daughter to John may have coincided with a deal between the two men over the contentious lordship of Kintyre.[50] Elsewhere in the Firth of Clyde the Steward encouraged or tolerated a process by which title and territorial rights held in Cowal and Knapdale by himself or his Menteith kinsmen and allies were signed over to Gillespic Campbell, who effectively replaced Stewart lordship across much of the region.

In the years of the Steward's guardianship, then, the steady retreat of Stewart/Menteith lordship allowed Gillespic Campbell to make a number of highly significant gains in Arran, Cowal and Knapdale. Aside from the Steward's general disengagement from affairs in the west, the most important grants in Gillespic's favour seem to have arisen from succession problems in the Menteith family. In the 1350s John Menteith, lord of Knapdale, Arran and Strathgartney, was nearing the end of his life with no male heir.[51] In the early 1350s the Steward made a concerted attempt to arrange affairs inside the lordships of Knapdale and Arran to his own benefit before Menteith's death. Sir John's nearest relative appears to have been his sister Christian, by 1350 the widow of Sir Edward Keith of Sinton.[52] Christian's marriage to Keith produced a child, a daughter Janet, who as the niece of Sir John was a potential heir to the lordships of Knapdale, Arran, and Strathgartney.[53] Shortly before 6 December 1352, Sir Robert Erskine, Chamberlain of Scotland for the imprisoned David II, applied for a papal dispensation to allow his marriage to the widowed Christian. Although the action of the king's chamberlain could be seen as a threat to the Steward's hopes of controlling the descent of Knapdale and Arran, the reality may have been more complex. Erskine was, despite his royal office, also on good terms with the Steward. Sometime in the period 1349–52, the guardian made two major grants of lands and rights in Renfrewshire in Erskine's favour; these may have been designed to ensure Erskine's acquiescence in the descent of Arran and Knapdale to the Steward after Menteith's death.[54] Meanwhile, at around the same time, Sir John Menteith gave over control of the core estates and castles in his lordships of Arran and Knapdale to Gillespic Campbell in a move probably designed to secure Stewart influence on the ground. In a charter dating to 1346x57, Menteith gave over the castle of Lochranza and 'Mo-Laise's island, or Holy Island, in Lamlash Bay to the Campbell lord.[55] On 29 November 1353 Menteith followed this up with a grant of a great swathe of land inside Knapdale, perhaps with the custody of Castle Sween, in Gillespic's favour.[56] The grants, at least one of which was witnessed by Robert the Steward, theoretically ensured that a man loyal to the heir to the throne was installed in key strongholds in Arran and Knapdale long before Menteith's death. Given the 'digging in' of the Steward's adherent in the west, and the apparent deal between Erskine and the Steward over the rights vested in Christian Menteith and her daughter, it was hardly a surprise that after the death of Sir John Menteith, on a date between May 1360 and July 1366, Robert assumed effective control of Knapdale and Arran.[57]

Knapdale and Arran were not the only areas where the Steward's interests were potentially under threat in the early 1350s. In 1346 John Graham, earl of Menteith, was executed after his capture by the English at the battle of Neville's Cross.[58] Graham left a widow, Mary, countess of Menteith in her own right, and a daughter and heiress, Margaret. The Menteith earls held extensive lands in Cowal as tenants of the Steward. After John Graham's death it seemed likely that his daughter would transmit possession of the earldom and the earl's lands inside Cowal, to any future husband. The issue of Margaret's marriage certainly provoked a great deal of interest in royal circles. When, in November 1348, a papal dispensation was issued allowing Margaret's marriage to John Murray, it was noted that King David's wife had supplicated on behalf of the couple.[59] John Murray seems to have died shortly after 11 April 1351, for by 15 August 1352 a papal dispensation was being sought for Margaret's marriage to Thomas, earl of Mar.[60] The Steward seems to have pre-empted any interference by Margaret's husbands in Cowal by approaching Margaret's mother, the widowed countess Mary, and persuading her to resign all the lands she held in the lordship to Gillespic Campbell. Thus, on an unknown date between 1350 and 1358, Mary gave over to Gillespic Campbell the lands of Kilmun in eastern Cowal with the patronage of the kirk, along with all the lands she held in Cowal from the Steward.[61] However, Gillespic's hold on the Menteith lands in Cowal was unlikely to remain unchallenged. Those men who married Countess Mary's daughter would surely have viewed the countess's resignations as a flagrant piece of sharp practice by the Steward that effectively disinherited Margaret Graham. The countess's daughter had a varied marital career; with each of Margaret's remarriages Gillespic faced a potential threat in the form of a new husband who might be inclined to dispute the settlement made by Countess Mary as an unjust alienation of lands. There would be plenty of scope for royal intervention in the Menteith inheritance in the years after David II's release and his return to Scotland in 1357.

By the time of King David's homecoming the political situation in the west had been transformed by the remarkable rehabilitation of the head of the MacDougall kindred, John Gallda. John was the grandson of Robert I's implacable enemy John of Lorn. If the younger John's supposed Gaelic byname, 'the foreigner', is properly applied to him, then he was probably raised in exile outwith Argyll. It is most likely that he was brought up in England, where his father, Allan, had served in the household of Edward II.[62] After the death of the elder John of Lorn in September 1316 the affairs of the MacDougalls were rather obscure. Despite the family's long exile, the ecclesiastical hierarchy inside the province seems to have remained loyal to, and dominated by, the displaced lords of Argyll.[63] Moreover, the Balliol invasions of Scotland in the 1330s may have offered an opportunity for a limited comeback. During 1334 Ewen MacDougall, perhaps John Gallda's uncle, seems to have been active in Lismore, while in 1338 John Gallda himself was part of the English garrison of Perth, from where he issued a charter of lands in Lorn in favour of his aunt, Mary, the wife of John Stirling.[64] In the following year, after a long siege, Perth fell to pro-Bruce forces commanded by the Steward as guardian of the kingdom.[65] Thereafter, John disappears from record before suddenly resurfacing in the west during 1354.

On 8 September 1354 John, Lord of the Isles, came to an agreement with John 'of Lorn', styled lord of Argyll. The agreement was designed to settle the conflicting claims of the two men to territories in Argyll and the

Hebrides. By the terms of the accord John of Lorn was to abandon claims to any lands, islands and castles for which John of Islay had received charters from David II and Robert I.[66] The list included Cairn na Burgh Mór and Cairn na Burgh Beg, the island of Mull, Dun Chonnuil, the upper part of Jura and the island of Tiree. John of Islay, however, was to give the island of Coll and a portion of land on Tiree to John of Lorn. John of Lorn's use of the title 'lord of Argyll' suggests his ambition to rebuild the lordship held by his great-grandfather and, perhaps, that he had already recovered control of some of his family's mainland territories. It was clear that John of Lorn was in possession of at least one of the castles he was supposed to cede to John of Islay, for he was required to deliver three hostages to guarantee the handing over of Cairn na Burgh Mór. At around the same time as his agreement with the Lord of the Isles, and certainly before December 1355, John of Lorn also concluded a mutual alliance (confederatio) with Gillespic Campbell, lord of Loch Awe.[67] It seems likely that this lost agreement aimed, like the Islay/Lorn concord, to settle conflicting claims to land and castles in Argyll.

In 1354–5, then, the threat of John's prosecution of claims to his family's forfeited estates became one that the lord of Islay and the lord of Loch Awe no longer felt able to ignore. The inference must be that both men were worried about the possibility of a restoration of Lorn's ancestral lordships and sought to secure their interests by concluding deals with the MacDougall lord that specifically guaranteed their possession of former MacDougall lands. The sudden concern must relate to the negotiations, ongoing in 1354, to secure the release of David II from imprisonment in England.[68] John Gallda was much favoured by the Scottish monarch, not least, perhaps, because he was untainted by any association with the Steward. It seems likely that John and King David met while the Scottish king was imprisoned in England after Neville's Cross. The two men, representatives of families that had been inveterate foes in the early fourteenth century, struck up an improbable friendship and political alliance. For the remainder of his life David would favour John of Lorn, most notably arranging a marriage between his niece, Janet, and the lord of Lorn.[69]

Gillespic Campbell could hardly have looked upon the prospect of David II's ransoming with unrestrained glee, given that the king was apparently thoroughly committed to a restoration of the power and influence of the MacDougall lord in the west. However, despite the misgivings of the Steward and his adherents, the general political and diplomatic situation began to build support for David's release.[70] In October 1357 David II obtained his freedom and returned to his kingdom.

The king soon displayed his determination to support and regulate the position of John MacDougall. On 23 January 1358 David, of his 'special grace', granted to MacDougall all possessions, lands and rents which had belonged to Sir Alexander of Lorn (John's great-grandfather) in the lordship of Lorn, along with the castles and fortalices which were then in the possession of John of the Isles.[71] David's gift invalidated all Robert I's grants made in favour of the MacArthur and Loudoun Campbells and more pointedly overturned John of Lorn's three-year-old agreement with John of Islay.[72]

If Gillespic was in any way perturbed by the extent of the MacDougall restoration, his anxieties would have been swiftly allayed by the issuing of a royal charter in his favour two days after David's grant to John of Lorn. By the terms of the grant Gillespic was confirmed in all the lands that had belonged to his father, Sir Colin (which were once again described as belonging to the king because of the forfeiture of Gillespic's brother Dugald). It seems likely that the confirmation was required largely because David had revoked grants of royal land from his first period of rule, but the gift also effectively ruled out any restoration of MacDougall interests in Loch Awe and Ardscotnish.[73] More importantly, the 1358 grant significantly strengthened Gillespic's position as lord of Loch Awe by specifying that the lands were to be held 'in the same manner as Colin' with the castles constructed in the same lands and patronage of the kirks.[74] In confirming the terms of the charter of 1315 the 1358 grant extended Gillespic's rights well beyond those he could claim through King David's earlier gift of 1343. In particular, the powers now granted to Gillespic struck at the independent status and territorial rights of families such as the MacNaughtons and MacIvers in Loch Awe and the MacDougall Campbells in Ardscotnish.

By the end of January 1358 the respective spheres of influence of the MacDougall and Campbell lords were fairly precisely defined; the march between Loch Awe and Lorn now marked the division between the territorial and political interests of the two men. This situation may well reflect the substance of the agreement made between Gillespic and John in the mid-1350s, a settlement that seems to have been reinforced by a marriage alliance between the two families.[75] Although John had used the title 'lord of Argyll' in 1354, the 1358 restoration did not come close to resurrecting the wider regional hegemony enjoyed by his family prior to Robert I's reign.[76]

The turbulent years of the Wars of Independence had not, therefore, produced a permanent and total collapse of the great MacDougall lordship and a rampant expansion of Campbell power in its place. The parchment empire of the MacArthur and Loudon Campbells in Lorn and Garmoran proved to be nothing more than a chimera that crumbled to dust and ashes in the face of local opposition and indifference. The enduring advance made by the Campbell lords in this period was both less dramatic and more significant. In 1293 John Balliol had envisaged a sheriffdom of Lorn that embraced all of mid-Argyll down to the marches of Knapdale and Cowal. By 1358 the extension of control from Lorn over this area was inconceivable; the events of that year confirmed that Loch Awe was now within the orbit of Campbell control, and thus linked to a lordship with a political and social centre further to the south in the Firth of Clyde.

The remainder of Gillespic's life would see a great entrenchment and intensification of the family's territorial power and jurisdiction inside mid-Argyll and Cowal through the shrewd manipulation of marriage alliances and the acquisition of the rights of widows and others unable to enforce their claims to land in the region. There were few spectacular advances, but instead a steady accumulation of lands and lordly rights that gradually consolidated the political and social pre-eminence of the Loch Awe line amongst the various branches of Clan Campbell and the wider community of the 'barons of Argyll'. At the forefront of this process rode Gillespic's son and eventual heir Colin Iongantach, 'Colin of the wonderful conceits' as he was later remembered in the family histories.[77]

Colin was one of the sons produced by Gillespic Campbell's marriage to Isabella Lamont.[78] By the late 1350s Colin was already a powerful and significant figure in his own right. In the autumn/winter of 1361 he was at the centre of a series of transactions that greatly expanded the Loch Awe Campbells' influence inside mid-Argyll. On 27 October 1361, the young Campbell lord was appointed bailie of the lands of Gilbert of Glassary within the sheriffdom of Argyll.[79] Significantly, the arrangement specified that Campbell was to aid Gilbert in any dispute he had with Colin's kinsmen. This was almost certainly a reference to a conflict that had been running since at least 1355 between Gilbert and John Campbell of Ardscotnish. The animosity between the two men arose from the arrangements for the marriage of John's father, Dugald, to Margaret, Gilbert's aunt, earlier in the century. The match had included a substantial grant in Dugald's favour of lands at the southern end of Loch Awe and Glen Add in Glassary by Gilbert's father, John of Glassary.[80] An inquest held at Inverleckan on Loch Fyne on 25 August 1355 had declared that John's gift of one third of Glassary to Dugald and Margaret in heritage took place after John had become insane.[81] Armed with the findings and moral authority of the inquest, Gilbert appears to have gone looking for local allies to force the Campbells of Ardscotnish to acknowledge that the alienation was illegal and to allow the lands to revert to himself as John of Glassary's heir. Certainly, the dispute with Campbell of Ardscotnish may explain John of Lorn's issuing of a bond promising to defend Gilbert against all others on 19 December 1355, four months after the Inverleckan inquest had cast doubt on the validity of John of Glassary's earlier grant.[82] John of Lorn may have had his own quarrels with the Ardscotnish Campbells, particularly if the Dugald who received extensive grants inside Lorn in the 1320s was the founder of the Ardscotnish family. The situation became more serious for John Campbell of Ardscotnish during 1358 when his kinsman Colin Campbell of Loch Awe also bound himself to support Gilbert of Glassary. On 31 March 1358 Colin and Duncan, son of John Lamont, obliged themselves to defend Gilbert lord of Glassary against all men, excepting their prior allegiance to David II, Robert the Steward and Gillespic Campbell, and especially to give no assistance to John Campbell, lord of Ardscotnish.[83] It is difficult to escape the impression that the early months of 1358 were a period that John Campbell of Ardscotnish would be keen to forget. In January he had seen a co-ordinated settlement of affairs in Argyll that restored John Gallda MacDougall to his great-grandfather's estates and Gillespic Campbell to the lands and lordships held by his father Colin. Since Colin had been given the lordship of Ardscotnish in 1315, the grant was an implicit threat to John Campbell's independent status, although the bond of March 1358 continued to acknowledge him as 'lord' of Ardscotnish. With the pressure mounting, Campbell of Ardscotnish may have attempted to resolve the controversy by making a substantial grant from his Glassary lands to Gilbert for his lifetime.[84] The 1361 bailiary was thus the culmination of a long process in which Gilbert of Glassary had become dependent on the Campbells of Loch Awe in his effort to exploit his Argyllshire estates. The bailiary represented a considerable addition to the territory under the effective control of the Loch Awe Campbells, for besides Glassary Gilbert also held title to lands forfeited by the MacGilchrist lords of Ederline at the southern end of Loch Awe.[85]

In the same period Colin Campbell's hold on the region was intensified with his acquisition of the property rights of one Christina of Craignish in the lordships of Craignish and Loch Awe. On 16 August 1361, Christina, described as the daughter and heiress of the deceased Dugald of Craignish and as the widow of Alexander MacNaughton, sold her part of the barony of the deceased Alexander for a certain sum of money and cows given to her 'in my necessity' by Colin Campbell.[86] On 11 November, Christina also sold Colin her rights in 'her whole barony' in Craignish.[87] The theoretical rights and privileges of widows and heiresses were not always upheld or recognised in the face of the hostility and indifference of male kinsmen and it was common for impoverished women to seek the assistance of powerful outside agents in order to obtain redress. It may be that Christina had first applied for the support of the church, the institution that was responsible for the upholding of the laws of marriage. Certainly John, archdeacon of Argyll, witnessed both of Christina's resignations in favour of Colin Campbell. The attractions for Colin and Gillespic Campbell were obvious: an up-front investment of cattle and coinage gave them a legal claim to the entire lordship of Craignish as well as a portion of the lands that had been held by Alexander MacNaughton. The transfer of Christina's temporary rights as MacNaughton's widow may have had a particularly significant effect on the position of the Campbells within Loch Awe. Late in the thirteenth century, as we have seen, the Mac-Naughtons seem to have been the dominant lords in Upper Loch Awe (Inishail parish). Despite their, as it transpired, unwise loyalty to the MacDougall lords of Argyll the MacNaughtons had been reconciled to the Bruce regime without a complete loss of local influence and territory.[88] However, the death of Alexander MacNaughton seems to have sparked a deep-seated succession crisis in the family around the middle of the fourteenth century that ended with their principal estates scattered amongst co-heiresses.[89] Colin Campbell's acquisition of Christina's rights as MacNaughton's widow placed him in a powerful position to interfere in the division of MacNaughton lands.

The exploitation of Christina of Craignish's rights in Craignish itself faced a more serious obstacle. Christina's father, Dugald of Craignish, had been succeeded as head of kin by his brother Malcolm, who now faced the prospect of the family's lands passing to the control of the Loch Awe Campbells. It is no surprise that the Craignish family history includes a vitriolic and wholeheartedly misogynistic account of the 'treachery' of Christina in her dealings with Colin of Loch Awe.[90] Malcolm and his heirs, however, were not to be easily displaced; eventually the Loch Awe Campbells had to settle for the Craignish line retaining possession of their estates, but holding of the lords of Loch Awe rather than directly from the crown.[91]

A third positive development for Gillespic and Colin Campbell in the autumn of 1361 came with the marriage of Margaret Graham, the heiress to Menteith, to Robert Stewart, the son of the Campbells' patron Robert the Steward.[92] Margaret Graham's latent claims to Menteith estates in Cowal had remained a threat to the Campbell lords throughout the 1350s. On a date before 24 February 1359 Margaret's second husband, Thomas, earl of Mar, had divorced her.[93] Margaret had perhaps already struck up a relationship with John Drummond of Concraig before her divorce, and shortly before April 1360 applied for a papal dispensation to sanction retrospectively her liaison with Drummond and legitimise their off-spring.[94] The legitimisation of Drummond's marriage to Margaret and his associated attempts to exploit his wife's inheritance seem to have provoked a feud between John and his allies and the Menteiths of Rusky. The feud was eventually brought to arbitration in May 1360, when it was noted that Gillespic Campbell and his son were involved in the action against Drummond.[95] An attempt by Drummond to invalidate the grants made by Mary, countess of Menteith, in the 1350s would provide an obvious explanation for Campbell animosity towards John, but there is no direct evidence that such a development underlay Campbell involvement in the dispute. John Drummond seems to have died shortly after the arbitration of May 1360, and had presumably expired before Robert Stewart applied for the papal dispensation to marry Margaret that was granted on 9 September 1361. Robert Stewart's hold on Menteith promised an end to the possibility that Campbell gains in Cowal could be reversed, for the relationship between Gillespic, Colin and Robert's father was good. It was the Steward himself who had engineered the grants in Gillespic's favour, and in the 1350s Colin openly acknowledged Robert as his lord.

By the end of 1361, then, the personal lordship of Colin Campbell in theory embraced both Glassary and Craignish, while the Campbell holdings in Cowal, briefly threatened, now seemed secure. However, the family was about to be caught up in the fallout from the worsening relationship between its political patron, the Steward, and his uncle David II. The Steward and the king had never been on particularly friendly terms, but in the early 1360s the two men were on the verge of a major conflict. In the years after his return to Scotland, David had clashed with Robert over a number of specific territorial issues, notably the destination of the earldom of Fife.[96] More generally, David's proposals to alter the succession in favour of a younger son of Edward III in order to obtain more favourable terms for the repayment of his English ransom had alienated his nephew and other noblemen who were uncomfortable with the king's dealings with the English crown. Feelings of disquiet had been heightened by suspicions over David's 'misuse' of the money raised for his ransom. There was also an expectation that a number of major noblemen, including the Steward and the earl of Douglas, were to be handed over to the English as a guarantee for continued payment of the outstanding amount in 1363. These tensions were exacerbated by David's clashes with the earls of Angus and Mar in 1361 and 1362, which had resulted in Angus's death in royal custody and Mar's exile.[97] Worries about the king's plans for the destination of the childless Mar's earldom increased the disaffection of William, earl of Douglas, Mar's brother-in-law and likely heir. Finally, the king's proposed marriage to Margaret Drummond, the widow of Sir John Logie, in 1363 opened up the prospect of royal patronage and favour being bestowed on Margaret's Drummond and Logie kinsmen. This last consideration may have been particularly important for Gillespic and Colin Campbell, for the king's bride-to-be was the sister of the John Drummond with whom they had been at feud in 1360. If John's marriage to Margaret Graham had indeed produced heirs, then it seems likely that the Drummond line could now expect royal support for its long-term claim to the Menteith inheritance.

Early in 1363 the Steward, his sons John, lord of Kyle and Robert, lord of Menteith, William, earl of Douglas and Patrick, earl of March, set their seals to a resolution calling for the reform of royal government and specifically complaining about the squandering of the ransom money. The petition was either issued to justify an armed insurrection against David's rule that had already begun, or its rejection provoked the rebellion led by the Steward, Douglas and March that was apparently underway by mid-March 1363.[98] The Steward's participation in the revolt was not long-lived, and by 24 April Robert had abandoned his allies and rejoined the king, perhaps in time to witness David's marriage to Margaret Drummond at Inchmurdo in Fife. On 14 May 1363 the Steward renewed his fealty to David II in a ceremony at Inchmurdo.[99]

The role of Gillespic and Colin in the events of 1363 remains unrecorded, but on 25–6 May, David II confirmed the grants of Cowal lands made by Mary, countess of Menteith, in the 1350s. On 11 October there was a further royal confirmation of these grants.[100] Some anxiety over the king's attitude was to be expected if, as seems likely, Gillespic and Colin had been active on behalf of the Steward in the revolt. However, the royal charters of May and October 1363 were in no way a general confirmation of Campbell lands threatened with forfeiture in the aftermath of the failed rebellion of 1363. The concentration on securing title to the former Menteith estates in Cowal may reflect the Campbells' concern that these lands were especially vulnerable after the king's marriage to Margaret Drummond. The grants may then represent David coming to terms with some of the Steward's most committed adherents in the aftermath of a major revolt that had threatened the king's hold on the realm, or a reward for Campbell inactivity during the rebellion.

Indeed, despite the strained relationship between the Steward and David II after 1363 the royal establishment seems to have shown considerable favour to Colin of Loch Awe. Most notably, in the autumn of 1364, Colin received a very significant grant from Sir Robert Erskine, the royal chamberlain, who had been restored to that office on 1 April 1363 in the midst of the political confrontation between the king and the Steward and his allies.[101] Although normally seen as an out-and-out David II loyalist, Erskine seems to have had an ambivalent relationship with the Steward and his family that was not unremittingly hostile. At any rate, on 14 August 1364, Erskine gave Colin, son of Gillespic of Loch Awe, the ward and marriage of the son and heir of John Campbell of Menstrie.[102] Who was John Campbell of Menstrie and to what estates was his offspring heir? It seems probable that John was none other than the lord of Ardscotnish who had been engaged in the long dispute with Gilbert of Glassary in the 1350s. As noted earlier, the lordship of Menstrie had been granted to a Dugald Campbell (John's father?) early in the 1320s. Moreover, at around this time (1364), the Ardscotnish line ended in an heiress, Mariota Campbell. By 16 January 1366, a dispensation had been applied for to allow the marriage of Mariota, daughter of John Campbell, to John, the son of Colin Campbell.[103] It seems possible that this Mariota was a sister of the son and heir of John Campbell whose ward was purchased by Colin in 1364 but who must have died shortly thereafter. Alternatively the nineteenth-century calendar of the document may have misrepresented 'daughter and heir' as 'son and heir'. (see Table 2 and 2a) Besides claims to Ardscotnish and Menstrie, Mariota also brought with her rights to her mother's estates of Glenorchy. On 5 April 1358 David II had confirmed to Mariota of Glenorchy, daughter of the deceased John of Glenorchy, and John Campbell (of Ardscotnish), her spouse, all the lands of Glenorchy with their appurtenances in the sheriffdom of Argyll.[104] Control of Mariota Campbell's ward and marriage, then, gave Colin Campbell an immediate claim to authority over Ardscotnish, Glenorchy and Menstrie, with the opportunity to annexe these lordships permanently to the Loch Awe line through marriage. Although Colin's plan in 1366 seems to have been to marry Mariota to his son John, by 1372 Colin had decided to marry the heiress himself.[105]

Thus, in three short years, Colin had acquired claims to lordship over four major territorial divisions in and around mid-Argyll, Glassary, Craignish, Glenorchy and Ardscotnish, to add to the lordships of Loch Awe and Kilmun held by his father. The rapid acquisition of these rights inevitably led to resentment. The male line of the Craignish kindred, as noted above, were not inclined to accept Colin's claims to exercise control within their territory. The most serious reaction, however, seems to have developed in the lordship of Ardscotnish. The seventeenth-century genealogy/history of the Campbells contained a number of elaborate and sometimes obviously fanciful stories about the earl of Argyll's medieval ancestors. However, the work also seems to have incorporated older and surprisingly accurate, or at least plausible, accounts of the affairs of individual Campbell chiefs. This may be particularly true for the section of the genealogy that deals with tensions and family disputes within the kindred in the late fourteenth and early fifteenth centuries. One such tale narrated that Colin 'narrowly escaped with his Lyfe from the Clanchallum in Ardscotnish who thought to burn him alive in a house that they might get the estate brought to Duncan Skeodnaisch [of Scotnish]'. This Duncan was said in the account to have been a brother of Colin Campbell fostered with the Clanchallum in Ardscotnish (hence his byname). The assassination attempt ended with Colin's escape from the house, his coat of mail (*luireach*) 'so hott with the fyre that he rann into a pool . . . under

Kilmartine towne . . . which . . . to this day [is] called in Irish linge na Lureach that is the Lureach's pool'.[106] All this might be dismissed as fanciful if it were not for the fact that Colin did, in fact, have a brother named Duncan whose one appearance on record was as a witness to a charter by John Campbell of Ardscotnish.[107] The conditions of the late 1360s, with Colin Campbell of Loch Awe threatening to impose his authority on Ardscotnish families, would have provided an entirely believable context for the local kindreds to press the claims of their own candidate for the chieftainship. The failure of the attempt to displace Colin with the Ardscotnish-raised and -based Duncan ensured that possession of Ardscotnish estates and control of the lordship's kirk came to be dominated by Colin's sons and their descendants.

The rise of the Loch Awe Campbells to a position of supremacy in mid-Argyll was reflected in the status accorded Gillespic Campbell by David II's government in its dealings with the Hebrides and Argyll during the 1360s. The crown administration evidently viewed Gillespic as one of the leading figures in the west, ranking alongside John MacDonald of Islay, John of Lorn and Robert the Steward, in terms of his power and influence. King David's relationship with this group of west-coast magnates, indeed Gaelic Scotland as a whole, was soured by a number of factors. Perhaps the most significant issue complicating David's transactions with these men was his need to raise money to pay for his English ransom. The financial burden imposed by the Treaty of Berwick would have to be met by new exactions on the king's loyal subjects unless David could broker an improved deal with the English crown. David's negotiations with Edward III during 1363-4 proposed changes to the Scottish succession that would have seen one of the English king's sons accepted as heir to the Scottish kingdom in return for the annulment or substantial reduction of the sum owed to the English crown. However, the Scottish king's scheme had foundered in the face of Edward III's insistence that he should be made heir-presumptive and internal political opposition headed by the Steward, who sought to defend his position as David's heir.[108] Despite the rejection of the English succession proposal, David continued his attempts to reach an accommodation with the English crown that would reduce the financial burden on the kingdom. In January 1365 David's envoys returned from London with a series of proposals, including the suggestion that the king's men might wage war in the English interest in Ireland.[109] Such an undertaking would have been attractive to Edward III and, more particularly, to his son Lionel, duke of Clarence, who had claims to the earldom of Ulster and the lordship of Connacht and who had acted as lieutenant of Ireland since May 1361.[110] Other issues raised in the Anglo-Scottish negotiations of early 1365 may also have been designed to aid Lionel's position in the Irish Sea world. Lionel, rather than his younger brother John of Gaunt, may have been the intended beneficiary of proposals that a son of Edward III should receive £1,000-worth of land in Galloway that had belonged to Edward Balliol, along with the Isle of Man.[111] Intriguingly, the English chronicler Henry Knighton asserted that in 1356 Edward Balliol had resigned his rights in Scotland in favour of Lionel. The statement is normally taken to refer only to Balliol's claim to the Scottish throne, but (if Knighton's account is accurate) Lionel may have been regarded in 1365 as a man with legitimate rights in relation to the Galloway lands formerly held by Edward Balliol and his ancestors.[112] If that was the case, then the overall settlement envisaged in 1365 could have provided the Irish lieutenant with a lordship embracing much of Galloway, Ulster and Man, along with the promise of Scottish military service in the north of Ireland. The Duke of Clarence, as Edward III's second surviving son, had already loomed large in the Anglo-Scottish negotiations surrounding the succession to the throne. Indeed, Walter Bower later claimed that it was Lionel, rather than Gaunt, who was seen as a potential successor to David II.[113] A.H. Diverres has also discerned faint indications in Jean Froissart's Arthurian romance, Meliador, that Clarence may have been the central figure around whom hopes of Anglo-Scottish settlement were based.[114] Froissart was in the household of Edward III's queen and visited Scotland during 1365 and was thus thoroughly well-versed in the issues under discussion during that year.[115] The central storyline of Meliador, the chivalric competition for the hand of the daughter (Hermondine) of the Scottish king Hermond, was indirectly concerned with the issue of succession to the Scottish kingdom. The hero Meliador is the son of the Duke of Cornwall, a title that may have suggested links to the English royal house in the 1360s. As with many romances, the action of Meliador essentially takes place within an imaginary landscape, but Diverres may have been right to see significance in the fact that in journeying from Wales to Ireland the hero of the tale has to cross a river 'Clarense'.[116]

The possibility of military aid for the English crown in Ireland required the approval of those Hebridean and west-coast lords who would supply the manpower for any expedition. Thus, John of Lorn (styled John of Argyll, lord of Lorn) and Gillespic Campbell were among the men summoned to a general council at Perth in July 1365 to instruct the king's envoys. It was decided that one of the offers that the Scottish negotiators could put forward in order to obtain a peace was that a force drawn from the Hebrides and west coast might assist the English crown in the Irish wars for a period of five years. The stipulation that this force would be available for service for only three months in each year is significant, for this presumably reflected the availability of Hebridean and west-coast manpower for extended summer campaigns in Ireland between the sowing and harvesting of crops. The recruitment of Hebridean soldiers by Irish lords for campaigns against their local enemies in Ireland, Anglo-Irish lords, and the agents of the Dublin government was a well-established feature of the relationship between the two areas. The deal being proposed in 1365 would have allowed the English crown to utilise the military capacity of Argyll and the Hebrides in pursuit of its own objectives in Ireland and to deny these resources to those defying the lieutenant's authority.[117]

However, the Anglo-Scottish negotiations made little headway, and by the summer of the following year the royal administration began to lay plans to allow the collection of the sums required to pay the English ransom if no less exacting deal could be struck.[118] The crown ordered a re-evaluation of all secular and ecclesiastical property, the real value of which had fallen because of the demographic and economic slump of the early fourteenth century. The re-evaluation prepared the ground for a contribution to be levied on lands and goods in order to pay for various crown expenses (a great slice of the crown's revenue from the customs having been assigned to meet the ransom payments). Resistance to the levying of the contribution in areas at the edge of the crown's effective authority was evidently anticipated. The parliament of July 1366 urged the crown to take action against the 'rebels' of Atholl, Argyll, Badenoch, Lochaber and Ross, who should be forced to acknowledge the authority of the common law and to pay the contribution. The task of exploiting the resources of the entire realm in order to pay the English ransom threw the varying levels of royal control over the regions of the kingdom into sharp relief. From the parliament of July 1366 onwards, meetings of the three estates held by King David reveal a growing resentment at the relatively light involvement of the inhabitants of the Scottish west coast in meeting the cost of the financial burden placed on the kingdom. The participation of representatives from the Scottish burghs in the parliaments of the 1360s added a new element to the assembly that was especially aware and resentful of the financial imbalance. David II may well have encouraged rather than suppressed these tensions, for the whole issue was politically awkward for the Steward. The Steward could hardly hope that other areas of the kingdom would willingly pay the price of his political triumph in scuttling David's negotiations over the succession, if Robert's own lordships and those of his kinsmen and allies in the north and west of the kingdom were exempt from, or resistant to, the increased financial demands resulting from the failure of those negotiations.

The drive to bring the west into line in terms of financial contributions highlighted the lack of effective sanctions available to the crown to enforce compliance with royal decrees in the region. In other areas of the kingdom royal officers could pursue those who refused or avoided their financial obligations; in much of the west the infrastructure of royal government and justice was non-existent or nominal. Inevitably, then, from the viewpoint of the crown, the lack of responsiveness to financial demands became entwined with the issue of non-adherence to the common law. By the time of the parliament of June 1368, David's government had adopted a new strategy and a new vocabulary in its dealings with west-coast lords. The parliament asked that Islesmen and Highlanders should be restrained by the king and the Steward from doing damage to others. The fact that the Steward was ranked alongside the king in this task was significant, for Robert was clearly thought to have a particular influence in these regions. At the parliament, oaths were extracted from the Steward, two of his sons, and the earl of Mar, by which they promised to govern the behaviour of the inhabitants of their lordships and to prevent malefactors from crossing their lordships or being received within them.[119] The issue at stake here was probably the launching of cattle raids by some of the inhabitants of these areas on surrounding lordships and communities.

These raids and counter-raids were part of the social fabric of upland pastoral zones, an accepted, indeed lauded, aspect of local lordship. Communities that were potentially vulnerable to small-scale forays developed their own means of protecting themselves. The most effective defence, of course, was to intercept the raiding party either before it reached its objective or at least before it made off with its plunder. A number of references attest to the practice of maintaining watchmen who would guard well-known routes and passes to give advance warning of raiding parties. A century later, in 1467, for example, the royal government was paying watchmen to guard the passes between Lorn and the royal earldom of

Menteith in order to protect 'the king's lieges'.[120] The lack of such early intelligence could have disastrous consequences. In January 1392 an unusually large foray descended on Lowland Angus from Atholl.[121] Sir David Lindsay of Glen Esk, the major magnate in Angus, received no early warning of the arrival of the Atholl men despite his posting of a 'spy' 'up in to the land'.[122] In this context, Lindsay's 'spy' was probably a 'watchman'. Taken by surprise, the lords of Angus had little time to co-ordinate their pursuit of the powerful raiding party. A hastily assembled force, apparently based on the household and retinue of Sir Walter Ogilvy, sheriff of Angus, was the first to catch and engage the raiders near Glasclune. Ogilvy's retinue was cut to pieces and the sheriff killed, while Sir David Lindsay and Sir Patrick Gray were carried from the field badly wounded.

Once a raiding group had physically escaped into areas where royal officers had little authority, the problems in identifying and tracing the culprits and recovering stolen cattle and other goods were legion. The solution put forward by David II's government in 1368 was to force major Highland lords to enter into contractual obligations with the crown to regulate the activities of men within their own lordships and to police the movement of others through them. Failure to comply with these terms would allow the crown to impose penalties and sanctions on the 'responsible' lords. Writing in the 1440s, the chronicler Walter Bower praised David's use of these obligations as an original and highly effective means of controlling the affairs of Highland Scotland.[123] It is unlikely that David's policies were as innovative as Bower suggests, but the securing of contractual guarantees from Highland lords as to the behaviour of men within their lordships was a tactic re-employed by a number of later monarchs. The practice eventually evolved into the system of 'bonds' used by James IV and developed further by the administration of James VI.

The Steward was not the only magnate picked out for the rendering of sureties in 1368. The parliament demanded that John of the Isles, John of Lorn and Gillespic Campbell should also be summoned to the king and give in sureties that the community of the realm would be unharmed by them, their men and adherents. They were also to agree that they and their men would share the burdens of their peers and neighbours, presumably a reference to the ongoing unresponsiveness of these lords to the crown's financial demands.[124] The legislation identified Gillespic as one of the three most powerful and influential west-coast magnates.

The issue of law and order and the contributions that Highland lords should make to the crown surfaced again in the parliament of 6 March 1369, which was attended by both John of Lorn and Gillespic. The parliament reiterated the action that the Steward and his sons were to take for the pacification and rule of the Highlands in terms of moving against trespassers and responding to the king's officers in rendering contributions. It was asserted that other lords having lands and lordships in the Highlands, including John of Lorn and Gillespic Campbell, should oblige themselves in similar fashion 'for all being, or about to come, within their lordships lands and bounds'.[125] Gillespic may have been able to turn the royal pressure for the rendering of oaths to his own advantage. The drive to secure an adequate financial basis for David's kingship had resulted in a sweeping revocation of alienations of crown lands and rents in September 1367.[126] One aspect of the revocation that may have affected Gillespic Campbell was the stipulation that all regalities, liberties, infeftments or renewals of infeftments made since the death of Robert I by which the crown lost wardships, reliefs, marriages and suits of court and other services should be nullified. The grants made in Gillespic's favour of the lordship of Loch Awe may well have come under the terms of this revocation. Ancient liberties, regalities and immunities, however, were to remain valid. On 15 March 1369, during or shortly after the parliament, the king issued a charter that confirmed Gillespic's claims to Craignish, Melfort, Strachur, Over Cowal and 'Kyldachanane'.[127] The last-named seems to represent the secular lordship associated with the parish of 'Kyldachanane', i.e. Kilchrenan, in other words Loch Awe.[128] The royal grant may well have coincided with Gillespic's rendering of the obligation specified in the parliamentary legislation and thus effectively mapped out areas for which Gillespic was to be held responsible. In addition, the charter confirmed Gillespic in all the liberties enjoyed by his progenitor, Duncan MacDuibne, in the barony of Loch Awe and any other lands that had belonged to Duncan in Argyll. The charter also confirmed Gillespic in Duncan's liberties in respect to the free tenants and barons of that part (Loch Awe?). This stipulation is curious for, as we have seen, there is nothing to suggest that the Campbell claim to exercise authority over the free tenants and barons of Loch Awe pre-dated the 1315 grant of Loch Awe and Ardscotnish to Gillespic's father Colin. Although the possibility that Duncan MacDuibne had been 'lord' of Loch Awe should not be discounted out of hand, it may be that the situation outlined in the 1369 grant was a convenient embroidering of the truth for both the royal government and Gillespic Campbell. At the time of the grant Gillespic was pledging himself to control the inhabitants of his lordships. Yet his claim to authority over other lords in Loch Awe rested on the charters granted to him by David II in 1343 and 1358, both of which fell within the terms of the 1367 revocation. Technically, the only liberties that could survive the revocation were those that were considered to be 'ancient' and long-established. The notion that Gillespic's power in Loch Awe derived from a distant ancestor thus allowed the crown to confirm the Campbell lord's authority in the lordship and make him liable for the behaviour of its inhabitants.

Despite the deal with the royal administration in 1369, Gillespic was noted as being contumaciously absent from the next parliament at Perth in February 1370. Gillespic's absence may not have been entirely unrelated to the fact that the assembly once more addressed the issue of the light contribution of Highland lords to the expenses of royal government. The financial discussion in the parliament began with a complaint about the level of prises, i.e. the compulsory purchase of goods to support the royal household, taken by the crown. Thereafter, suggestions were made as to how the financial burden on Lowland parts, which contributed heavily to the exchequer through the customs on wool production, might be eased. One idea was that the king's chamberlain could take an annual levy of victuals, such as oats and marts, that were produced in Highland parts. Alternatively, it was proposed that the royal court might reside in these Highland areas so that they made a direct contribution to the burden of supporting royal government equal to that of the Lowlands. The areas specified were Kintyre, Knapdale and Arran and the lordships of John of Islay, John of Lorn and Gillespic Campbell.[129]

The complaints raised in the 1370 assembly may reflect genuine long-term changes in the financial basis of royal government. The collapse of the system of royal thanages had left the Bruce dynasty dependent on the revenues generated by the royal customs levied and collected in the burghs, a fact made more obvious by the ransom payments of the 1360s.[130] Moreover, the decline of the thanages must have meant that the demand for prises had also become focused on a narrower geographical area; since David II resided almost exclusively in and around Edinburgh, the burgh, and perhaps Lothian in general, *was* bearing the cost of royal government to an unprecedented degree. This fact inevitably affected the govern-mental view of other areas of the kingdom. As the economic and fiscal input from English-speaking burghal Scotland became more crucial for the royal administration, the 'failure' of much of Gaelic-speaking Scotland to contribute in the same way became evidence for a 'Highland problem' and suggestive of a disloyalty to the crown. The open acknowledgement of the Scottish king's political superiority, the rendering of tribute and the provision of military service were no longer sufficient to guarantee that royal goodwill would be extended to Highland magnates.

In February 1371 David II died unexpectedly in Edinburgh and the tensions in the crown's relationship with west-coast magnates immediately eased. The kingship passed to David's nephew, Robert the Steward, a man with extensive interests in Gaelic Scotland and Gillespic's own regional lord. The advent of the Stewart dynasty brought the Campbell lord into direct and intimate contact with the new royal court, a fact that was clearly important for the subsequent development of the power of Clan Campbell. It would be utterly misleading, however, to portray the rise of Gillespic and his descendants as somehow dependent on this cosy relationship with the Stewart monarchy. By the time of David II's death, Gillespic and his son Colin already effectively controlled mid-Argyll and the elder Campbell was ranked alongside John MacDonald and John MacDougall as a great figure in Gaelic Scotland. Gillespic's status had been won in a period when the king was either absent or displaying a marked indifference, or open hostility, towards the ambitions of the Campbells of Loch Awe. As we have seen, the historiography of Gaelic Scotland has encouraged the idea that there is a contrast to be drawn between the Campbell and the MacDonald and MacDougall lordships in terms of method, aim and values, the latter representing in some way a more intensely Gaelic style of political leadership and social organisation.[131] However, while the growth of Campbell power may have been boosted by the personal relationship of Campbell chiefs with Robert I and Robert II, this was hardly the same as a commitment to an abstract royal interest, to the mores of Lowland society, or to the promotion of governmental rights in Argyll and the west. In structural terms, the rise of the lords of Loch Awe diminished rather than increased royal influence in Argyll. In 1290 mid-Argyll had been a region with no single dominant magnate, but one in which a number of lesser landowners held directly of the crown. The crown also had, in the shape of Loch Awe and Ardscotnish, extensive lands and direct rights of lordship in the region. By 1382, when Gillespic was granted a hereditary royal lieutenancy in mid-Argyll, the entire region was effectively under the sway of one aristocratic dynasty that stood between the crown and the other landowners in the district.[132] Moreover, the power and status enjoyed by the Campbell lords were only partly derived from their role as royal lieutenants of Argyll. The wide powers and financial rights delegated to the Campbell lieutenants suggested a high level of independence and autonomy that extended well beyond that of royal representatives elsewhere in the kingdom. The royal lieutenancy of 1382 represented the culmination of the process of Campbell expansion in mid-Argyll, not its beginning.

The other 'unique' features supposedly underlying the advance of Campbell power in the period prior to 1371 should also be viewed with suspicion. The Campbells' use of feudal charters has been examined elsewhere; it will suffice to note here that the issuing of charters was a practice also embraced by the MacDonald Lords of the Isles and a number of other Argyll lords.[133] If the ability to have legal documents drawn up in Latin or Scots bestowed a mystical advantage in political and social affairs on those lords who indulged in the practice, it was hardly an advantage confined to Clan Campbell.

Finally, it is difficult to view Gillespic as a shining example of the aggressive adoption of 'Lowland ways' that was supposed to characterise the Campbell chiefs. If anything, the cultural affiliation of fourteenth-century Campbell lords seems to have been developing in precisely the opposite direction. Gillespic, the son of Sir Colin Campbell and grandson of Sir Neil, displayed a complete indifference to the marks and ranks of aristocratic distinction that dominated and graded Lowland society. If the lord of Loch Awe deigned to become a knight it was only towards the very end of his long career. In the 1360s this resulted in the absurdity of Gillespic's name being recorded in parliamentary sederunts behind that of knights, including his own kinsman, Sir Andrew Campbell of the Loudon line, whose power, wealth and political importance were a fraction of those of the lord of Loch Awe.[134] Gillespic of Arran's social world revolved predominantly, if not exclusively, around Gaelic Scotland. He and his sons and daughters drew their marriage partners from the Gaelic aristocracy of the Firth of Clyde, Highland Perthshire and the Hebrides.[135] Gillespic's family also seems to have been absorbed in the system of fosterage that linked Gaelic aristocratic households and, as a by-product of the political and social contacts established, encouraged a corporate view of their literary and historical inheritance.[136] In the 1360s Gillespic was unambiguously regarded by the three estates as a 'Highland' magnate, while members of his immediate family identified themselves in papal supplications explicitly as Highland Gaelic-speaking Scots.[137] As Gillespic battled to the top of an aristocratic society intensely aware of its part in the Gaelic world, it is difficult to see how an identification with Lowland ways or values could have been of any benefit.

The explanation for Gillespic's steady rise to regional dominance does not, therefore, lie in an early and far-sighted reading of inexorable historical processes and the development of strategies to take advantage of these. A number of short-term factors undoubtedly fed into the Campbell successes: the Bruce and Stewart links; the misfortunes of the MacDougalls; the failure of male lines in other kindreds. The ability to attract and take advantage of these opportunities, however, rested on the usefulness and effectiveness of Clan Campbell as a military power. Although it is customary to highlight the sheer military (especially maritime) power of the MacDonald lordship as a key factor in the growth of the Lordship of the Isles, the success of Campbell lordship tends to be treated as dependent largely on careful planning and on shrewd thinking. Yet, on the two occasions on which the Campbells force themselves into literary record in the fourteenth century it is because of the ability of the leader of the family to raise a significant galley force for the use of his political patrons. In the negotiations of 1365 for the deployment of Scots troops in Ireland, Gillespic Campbell was clearly regarded as one of the men who would be responsible for the raising and transportation of the force. The image of Clan Campbell as a 'mainland' clan with its heartland around Loch Awe, as opposed to the great island-based families of the Hebrides, has undoubtedly helped to obscure the fact that from an early stage the family possessed a powerful naval presence in the Firth of Clyde.[138] A brief glance at the lands held by (or at least granted to) Gillespic, regardless of the estates held by other branches of the family, around the shores of Cowal, Arran and Knapdale reveals a lordship utterly dependent on maritime links.

In the years to 1371, then, the Campbells' rise to power was hardly an anomalous intrusion into the west. Gillespic of Arran's status as one of the leading lords of Gaelic Scotland was no more questioned by contemporaries than that of John MacDonald of Islay, another figure who enjoyed a meteoric political and territorial advance in the fourteenth century. The Campbell hegemony in mid-Argyll represented the triumph of a powerful and well-established local dynasty, able to ride out and take advantage of the disturbances of the fourteenth century, and it resulted in a lessening of royal influence in the region in institutional terms.

With the accession of Robert the Steward to the throne the Campbells entered a new phase in the development of their lordship. For the next half-century Campbell chiefs would have direct and close links to the royal court. However, Gillespic and his successors were to find that this relationship brought with it dangers as well as opportunities.

Notes

1. *Chron. Wyntoun* (Laing), ii, 377–80; Nicholson, *Later Middle Ages*, 123.
2. M. Penman, 'A fell conuiracioun agayn Robert ye douchty king: the Soules conspiracy of 1318–20', *IR*, 50 (1999), 25–57; Barrow, *Bruce*, 322–3.
3. Nicholson, *Later Middle Ages*, 125; R. Nicholson, *Edward III and the Scots: the formative years of a military career, 1327–1335* (London, 1965) (Hereafter Nicholson, *Edward III*), pp.77–9.
4. Nicholson, *Later Middle Ages*, 126; Nicholson, *Edward III*, pp.85–93.
5. Nicholson, *Later Middle Ages*, 127.
6. *Ibid.*, 128–9.
7. *Ibid.*
8. *Chron. Wyntoun* (Laing), ii, 377–80; Fraser, *Lennox*, ii, 23.
9. *The Bruce* (Duncan), 710.
10. Nicholson, *Later Middle Ages*, 129.
11. *Ibid.*
12. *Ibid.*, 130.
13. *Ibid.*
14. *Chron.Wyntoun* (Laing), ii, 414; *Chron.Bower* (Watt), vii, 102–5. Both accounts are derived from the same source, a chronicle apparently compiled late in the fourteenth century. The tale may have been influenced by Barbour's account of the role of Neil Campbell in Robert I's escape from the Lennox in 1306 for there are similarities of theme and language.
15. The specification of Loch Awe makes it unlikely that Dugald of Ardscotnish is intended, although any source composed late in the fourteenth century may have assumed that a Campbell of Loch Awe was involved. Moreover, the only family that can be firmly associated with the Steward's military expedition in the Firth of Clyde on the basis of record evidence was the MacArthur Campbells. However, that a Dugald, son of Colin Campbell, was linked to the Steward and Sir Malcolm Fleming in Dumbarton at around this time is confirmed by his appearance as a witness to an undated charter issued by Robert from Dumbarton. NAS RH1/2/112. The charter was in favour of one Robert Wallace of lands in the barony of Kyle. The witnesses included Malcolm Fleming, the custodian of Dumbarton, and 'Dugallo Cambell' son of Colin Cambell, Thomas de Charteris and Hugh de Blare. It is difficult to date this charter other than to the period before Dugald's death. Evidence for the direct involvement of Dugald's brother, Gillespic, in the 1334 campaign, despite being accepted by

the author in earlier work, is not conclusive. A charter by Robert the Steward granting Gillespic the lands of Kinlochstriven in Cowal could, in fact, date from any period prior to 1371; the date of c.1335 assigned to it in the Argyll Inventory may be correct, but was probably consciously chosen in order to suggest that Gillespic had played a leading role in the conflicts of 1334.

16. *Chron. Bower* (Watt), vii, 102–5.
17. As outlined in Chapter 1, the Stewarts had been the dominant lords in Cowal since the middle of the thirteenth century and Dunoon may well have been a long-term possession of the family. See Barrow and Royan, 'James Fifth Steward of Scotland', 167–8; Barrow, *Anglo-Norman Era*, 68–70; *Rot.Scot.*, i, 31.
18. *Chron. Bower* (Watt), vii, 102–5.
19. *Ibid.*
20. *HP*, iv, p.11. A charter dated on Bute on 25 May 1334.
21. R. Nicholson, *Edward III*, 218–222. In advance of the fleet an English emissary, Andrew Leynagh, warden of the Franciscans of Kildare, was sent to John of the Isles to try to bring him into the service of the English king.
22. Nicholson, *Edward III*, 197.
23. *Ibid.*, 202.
24. *Ibid.*, 205.
25. *Ibid.*, 219.
26. See Nicholson, *Edward III*, 221 note 5.
27. Long before his fleet set sail, John Darcy had been in contact with John of the Isles in an attempt to entice the lord of Islay into English service. *Ibid.*, 221. In June 1335, Edward III had specifically appointed John Darcy to welcome Scots into the English king's peace, including those who had played a significant part in the 'rebellions' of 1334; *Rot.Scot.*. i, p. 351.
28. Nicholson, *Edward III*, 215. David of Strathbogie, earl of Atholl, had entered negotiations with Edward III and Balliol on 7 August 1335 and reached an agreement at Perth on 18 August. Strathbogie's envoys were also empowered to act on behalf of Robert the Steward although, as Nicholson notes, the Steward's position was in no way addressed by the proposed settlement of 18 August.
29. Nicholson, *Edward III*, 227; *Scalacronica*, 166. One piece of evidence that tends to support the notion of ongoing negotiations between the Steward and the English crown is Edward III's issuing of a safe-conduct in October 1335 for Nigel Carruthers, the Steward's 'chancellor'. *Rot.Scot.*, i, 382.
30. Nicholson, *Edward III*, 227; *Chron.Fordun*, i, 359–60. Although the account preserved in the Annals attached to Fordun's chronicle seems to preserve two quite separate traditions, first having Andrew made guardian at Dumbarton in the feast of St. Mathew (21 September) and then, sometime after 30 November, attending a meeting of the great lords at Dunfermline where they approved of his creation as guardian.
31. *ALI*, 2–4. The gift also included Islay, the island of Gigha, half of Jura, the islands of Colonsay, Mull, Skye, Lewis, the lands of Morvern and Ardnamurchan. The gift thus included territory formerly held by the MacDougalls and the MacRuairis.
32. The rights of other figures associated with the Balliol regime were guaranteed by the agreement. The claims of David of Strathbogie's heir in Lochaber, for example, were specifically protected in Edward Balliol's grant. Another curious

omission was the mainland territories of the MacDougall kindred. Although MacDougall island lordships and areas such as Ardnamurchan were given over to John of Islay, Lorn, Lismore, Appin and Benderloch were not mentioned. This presumably reflected the fact that John MacDougall was active on behalf of the Balliol regime; he was certainly serving in the pro-English garrison at Perth in 1338. The division of lands between John of Islay and John MacDougall laid out in the agreement of 1354 discussed below may, then, have been first established by the Balliol regime in 1335–6.

33. Murray 'A House divided' 225–6; *ALI*, lxxv.
34. See W.D.H. Sellar, 'MacDougall pedigrees in MS 1467', *Notes and Queries*, SWHIHR, 1st series, xxix (1986), 3–16; Sellar, 'Hebridean Sea Kings' , 217 n.158.
35. *RRS*, vi, nos. 54, 69, 488.
36. *RRS*, vi, no.54, pp.97–8; Argyll Muniments, Inveraray, Unbundled Charter. The charter was issued at Dumbarton and was witnessed by Robert the Steward, Maurice Moray, Malcolm Fleming, Thomas de Charteris, chancellor, Thomas Boyd, and Andrew de Buttergask.
37. David was in Dumbarton on 11 August 1341. *RRS*, vi, no.32, pp. 79–80. This visit occurred before the Steward had appeared as a witness to any royal charters. While in Dumbarton, David must have received reports about the political situation in Lennox and Argyll. The trip was made shortly after the king had summoned a parliament that would meet at Scone by 17 September 1341. *RRS*, vi, no.33, pp.80–1. If we assume a forty-day notice of the intention to hold a parliament, then this would take us to a week or so before the king's appearance in Dumbarton – it seems likely that 17 September was just about the start of the parliamentary session as the parliament was still in session on 22 September; *RRS*, vi, no.36, p.83.
38. *Book of the Dean*, xx, stanza 17.
39. *HP*, ii, 91.
40. The name of Gillespic's wife is attested in a much later grant of 12 March 1440 by Gillespic's grandson Duncan. NAS RH6/304. The date of the Kinlochstriven grant is unknown. The abstract of the charter suggests only that it was issued before 1357.
41. *RRS*,vi, no.69, p.109, Addenda, p.527. Although the source for this is a seventeenth-century inventory.
42. *RRS*, vi, nos.72, 73.
43. *RRS*, vi, nos.485–487.
44. *RRS*, vi, no.488. Like the Campbell grant, MacNaughton's gift was made in a male entail. For a discussion of the Campbell use of male entail charters, see S. Boardman, 'The Campbells and charter lordship in medieval Argyll', in S. Boardman and A. Ross (eds.), *The Exercise of Power in Medieval Scotland*, c.1200–1500 (Dublin, 2003), 95–117.
45. *RMS*, i, App. 2., nos.867, 868. Grants recorded in the lost rolls are very difficult to date, but the surrounding entries are dominated by charters dating from the period 1341–3.
46. *RRS*, vi, no.103.
47. Nicholson, *Later Middle Ages*, 145–8; M.A. Penman, 'The Scots at the Battle of Neville's Cross, 17 October 1346', *SHR*, lxxx (2001), 157–80; Boardman, *Early Stewart Kings*, 7–8.

48. Boardman, 'Chronicle Propaganda in Fourteenth-Century Scotland: Robert the Steward, John of Fordun and the "Anonymous Chronicle" ', *SHR*, 76 (1997), 23–43, at 35, 39–40.

49. *Vet.Mon.*, 294.

50. In *c.*1346 David had confirmed the lordship of Kintyre to Robert in a charter that contained an entail in favour of Robert's sons John and Walter. *RMS*, i, App. 2, no.1066.

51. This John Menteith was identified in 1359 as the son of Sir John Menteith and Helen or Elena of Mar. NAS GD 124/1/514.

52. That is, if the John Menteith of 1359 is one and the same with the Sir John Menteith, lord of Arran, Skipness and Knapdale who issued a charter on 21 May 1343 in favour of Sir Edward Keith, the son, and Christian his spouse, Menteith's sister. NAS Mar and Kellie Collection GD124/1/1050; *HMC Supplementary Report on the MSS of the Earl of Mar and Kellie*, 4. The sequence of three Menteith lords bearing the name John obviously leaves scope for some confusion over the family relationships.

53. *HMC Supplementary Report on the MSS of the Earl of Mar and Kellie*, 6–7, 8, 9; *Aberdeen-Banff Illustrations*, iv, 197–8. An explanation produced in 1447 of the relationship between Lord Robert Erskine and Gartney earl of Mar. GD 12/13.

54. *HMC Supplementary Report on the MSS of the Earl of Mar and Kellie*, 4–5. *RRS*, vi, no.119. Erskine's marriage to Christina was not popular with Sir John's male Menteith relatives, who perhaps realised that Erskine and the Steward were effectively bypassing their own claims to be treated as Sir John's heirs. A second dispensation for Robert and Christina's marriage, obtained in 1355, suggested that the match would help to bring to an end a feud in which Robert had wounded and imprisoned Walter Menteith and his brothers, Christina's cousins. Although it was something of a commonplace to claim that a marriage was essential to bring about reconciliation between the families of the prospective partners, the unusual inclusion of details of the violence suggests that, in this case, there may have been some truth in the couple's representations. It seems likely that the confrontation took place after the initial marriage. The second dispensation for their marriage was obtained on 6 March 1355 and narrated that they had first applied in the time of Clement VI who had died on 6 December 1352. *CPP*, i, 286; *CPL*, iii, 564. The second dispensation specified that king David approved of the match.

55. AT. The witnesses were Robert Steward, guardian of the realm (dating the charter to 1346–57), Sir William Cunningham, Laurence, archdeacon of Argyll, and John son of Gille-Coluim Lamont. For the identification of Molasse's isle, see *Chron.Bower* (Watt), i, notes, p.187; *CPNS*, 305–6; *Oxford Dictionary of Saints*, ed. D.H.Farmer (Oxford, 1992), 256.

56. Argyll Muniments, Inveraray, Bundle 1107; Fraser, *Menteith*, ii, 235–8. Charter issued by Menteith at Castle Sween. The granting away of the rights of ward and relief suggests an attempt to minimise the possibility of interference in the lands by Menteith's eventual heirs. *HMC Report*, 9, p.232.

57. *APS*, i, 500.

58. *Chron. Bower* (Watt), vii, 260–1

59. *Vet. Mon.*, 290.

60. *Moray Reg.*, 296–7; Fraser, *Menteith*, i, 121–3.

61. The witnesses date the charter to 1350–1358 and would indicate that the document was issued at Dunblane or perhaps Stirling. Sir Robert Erskine, described as Chamberlain of Scotland, held that office between 1350 and 1358; it cannot date to his second spell in the office in 1363–4 since one of the witnesses, William, bishop of Dunblane, was dead by 18 June 1361. The other witnesses were Michael, deacon of Dunblane, Brother Richard Farbar, prior of the Dominican house in Stirling, Walter of Menteith, John Drummond, and Laurence, archdeacon of Argyll. Maidment, *Analecta*, 2nd series, pp. 15–16. At around the same time and with the same witnesses, the countess granted out all the lands she held of the Steward of Scotland within the barony of Cowal. In May 1363, in the midst of a major rebellion against David II, the King confirmed the charter by the deceased Maria or Mary, countess of Menteith, to Gillespic of the barony of Kilmun and other lands in Cowal. A later note, apparently referring to the same charter, described this grant as conveying to Gillespic all the lands held by the countess of the Steward in the barony of Cowal, together with the lands of Kilmun. *RRS*, vi, no.293, pp. 323–4, and addenda. pp.528–9. Although the Steward did not witness the transaction, he must have approved of the grant as the immediate superior of the lands. *Vet.Mon.*, no.644.

62. D. Sellar, 'Hebriden Sea Kings', 216–7 ; see *CDS*, iii, no. 647, 684.

63. Watt, *Fasti* (2nd draft), pp.26–7. The bishop of Argyll between 1342 and 1362 was Martin de Argyll, probably a MacDougall.

64. See D. Sellar, 'Hebridean Sea-Kings', 217; *OPS*, II, Part 2, 828; *RMS*, ii, no.3136.

65. *Chron. Bower* (Watt), vii, 141–3. John may have been one of those who were allowed to depart with Thomas Ughtred, the commander of the garrison. However, other pro-Balliol Scots in Perth, such as John Logie, seem to have been restored to their estates after negotiating their own terms of surrender with the Steward.

66. *ALI*, no.5, pp.5–8. At the same time John of the Isles obliged himself to accept no letters, gifts or feu from any king or guardian of Scotland over the lands conceded to John of Lorn.

67. *HP*, ii, 142. The alliance was referred to in a document issued by John of Lorn in December 1355 at the kirk of Saint Keraldi on the south side of Loch Etive. This was one of the earliest occasions on which Gillespic was actually styled Lord of Loch Awe.

68. M.A. Penman, *David II, 1329–71*, (East Linton, 2004) (hereafter Penman, *David II*), 250–253.

69. S. Boardman, 'The Tale of Leper John and the Campbell Acquisition of Lorn', in E.J. Cowan and R.A. McDonald, eds., *Alba: Celtic Scotland in the Middle Ages* (East Linton, 2000) (hereafter Boardman, 'Leper John'), 219–247, at 231–32; *ER*, ii, 106, 352; *RMS*, i, no.237; *RRS*, vi, no.165.

70. Penman, 'David II', 256–63.

71. *RRS*, vi, no.165, pp. 202–3. It is unclear whether this means the castles detailed in the 1354 agreement or strongholds held inside Lorn by John of Islay. The former seems more likely.

72. Assuming that the castles referred to here are those listed in the agreement between Islay and Lorn in 1354. This would also suggest that Lorn's restoration was meant to embrace Mull and the other island properties. At this stage John of Islay actually appears to have been in Edward III's allegiance, so David II may

have felt that he was not a suitable custodian for any of the fortresses detailed in the 1354 concord.

73. Argyll Muniments, Inveraray, Argyll Charters; *RRS*, vi, 203.
74. *RRS*, vi, 203. The lands and rights were to descend according to the terms of a general entail in favour of Gillespic's heirs and assignees of the surname Cambell. This is interesting since it suggests that Gillespic did not wish to name a specific heir at this point.
75. In 1362 Gillespic's son Colin applied for a dispensation to marry Katherine de Lorn, undoubtedly a kinswoman of John Gallda. K.A. Steer and J.W.M. Bannerman, *Late Medieval Moumental Sculpture in the West Highlands*, RCAHMS (Edinburgh, 1977) (hereafter Steer and Bannerman, *Monumental Sculpture*), Appendix II, 204.
76. As Sellar has noted, John used the style 'of Lorn' rather than 'of Argyll' and this may imply an acceptance that his lordship would operate in a more restricted area than that of his predecessors. Sellar also discusses the way in which the style 'of Lorn' was retrospectively applied to John's grandfather in Barbour's *Bruce*. Sellar, 'Hebridean Sea-Kings', 215–6.
77. *HP*, ii, 91–2. Although the *Records of Argyll* assign this epithet elsewhere.
78. NAS Register House Charters RH6/304.
79. *HP*, ii, 146–7. The agreement was concluded in the Campells' newly-acquired kirk of Kilmun in Cowal. Colin's father, Gillespic, also stood as a surety for the terms of the agreement.
80. Argyll Muniments, Inveraray, Argyll Charters; *HP*, ii, 132–4.
81. *HP*, ii, 138–140.
82. *HP*, ii, 142–3.
83. *HP*, ii, 143–4. Although it is unclear from the bond whether the problem, in reality, was that these men had been supporting John Campbell in his resistance to Gilbert's claims.
84. *HP*, ii, 140–2. Unfortunately the charter is undated. The witnesses included Adam and Laurence, vicars of Glassary and Ardscotnish, Donald 'McMcpersun', Duncan son of Gillespic Campbell, 'Cristino Huasmabene' and Roderico et Yuaro filiis M'Gillecoan. Two of these witnesses were members of the inquest of August 1355.
85. *RRS*,vi, no.103. On 20 May 1358 David II confirmed the grant made in 1346 by which Gilbert was to receive the lands forfeited by the heirs of John mac Ewen MacGilchrist. *HP*, ii, 144–5.
86. Argyll Muniments, Inveraray, Argyll Charters; NAS RH1/2/87; *SHS Misc.*, iv, 292.
87. AT, at date; NAS RH1/2/87; HMC Report, iv, Appendix, 477; *SHS Misc.*, iv, 292. Despite the apparent gap of almost three months between the issuing of these charters they were curiously similar. Both were issued at Kilmartin Church in front of the same witnesses. Both had exactly the same penalty clauses. Moreover, Christina's style as heiress of Craignish in the August indenture suggests that the future of the Craignish lands was already under discussion.
88. *RRS*, vi, no.488.
89. *Ibid*. The charter of 1343 was a male entail which made clear that Alexander's son and heir was Duncan and that he had at least two other sons, Gilchrist and John, who were named as heirs to the entailed estates should Duncan's line fail. The

charter did not cover Alexander's main estates. In 1375 and 1403 the Campbells of
Loch Awe picked up claims to lands in the barony of upper Loch Awe from men
and women whose rights were based in some way on their relationship to either
Duncan or Alexander MacNaughton. Thus in April 1475 John of Prestwick,
described as the son and heir of 'Mariote anechel', resigned his rights to part of
the island of Inishail and patronage of the kirk to Colin Campbell of Loch Awe.
Argyll Muniments, Inveraray, Argyll Charters. In 1403 a Margaret daughter of
Gilchrist 'Macgillegeachan' resigned her rights to a sixth part of lands lying in
Glen Shira which, it was specified, had belonged to Alexander MacNaughton.
Argyll Muniments, Inveraray, Argyll Charters.

90. *SHS Misc.*, iv, 216–220.
91. See Boardman, 'The Campbells and charter lordship', 99–100.
92. *Vet.Mon.*, 317.
93. *Rot.Scot.*, i, 836. An indenture made by Mar with Edward III on that date
    includes a stipulation that he would serve Edward III for £400 or a wife of equal
    value. He was presumably free to marry at that point.
94. *Vet.Mon.*, 315. Before their marriage Margaret granted the lands of Aberfoyle in
    the west of Menteith to Drummond and to any children born between them.
    David II confirmed the grant on 12 November 1361. *RRS*, vi, no.264 At some
    stage Drummond also seems to have been granted the lands of Rosneath in
    Lennox by Margaret's mother, Mary, countess of Menteith. *RMS*, i, no.505,
    although whether this was part of a marriage settlement is impossible to say.
95. Fraser, *Menteith*, i, 239–46.Though the substance of the dispute is not made
    clear in the arbitration.
96. Boardman, *Early Stewart Kings*, 13–14; Penman, *David II*, 102–4, 236–7,
    268–9.
97. A.A.M. Duncan, 'The 'Laws of Malcolm MacKenneth'', in A. Grant and K.
    Stringer, eds., *Medieval Scotland: Crown, Lordship and Community* (Edinburgh,
    1993), 264–5; Boardman, *Early Stewart Kings*, 17–18; Penman, *David II*, 274–82.
98. Boardman, *Early Stewart Kings*, 18–19; Penman, *David II*, 283–94.
99. *Chron.Bower* (Watt), vii, 330–333.
100. *RRS*, vi, nos 293, 304.
101. *ER*, ii, 169–70.
102. *HMC Report*, iv, p.483. The original of this document was not located during a
     brief search of the Inveraray archive and the nineteenth-century report provides
     no Christian name.
103. AT, at date; Registrum Aven. Vol 162, f514. Registrum Vaticanum vol. 255,
     f36.
104. Argyll Muniments, Inveraray, Argyll Charters; *RRS*, vi, no.180, pp.214–5; *RMS*,
     i, App.2., no.1234.
105. *CPL*, iv, 56, 183.
106. *HP*, ii, 91–2. The putative relationship between Duncan and the Campbells of
     Ardscotnish may explain the apparent conflation in the traditional genealogy of
     the Campbells of Ardcotnish and the descendants of this Duncan. *Ibid.*, 89, 91.
107. *HP*, ii, 140–1.
108. Penman, *David II*, 311–325. A.A.M Duncan (ed.). 'A question about the
     succession, 1364' in *SHS Misc*, xii, 1–57, at 5–20.
109. *APS*, i, 495–6.

110. S. Duffy, *Ireland in the Middle Ages* (London, 1997), 152–7; B. Smith, 'Lionel of Clarence and the English of Meath', *Peritia* 10 (1996), 297–302.

111. *APS*, i, 495. For an argument in favour of Gaunt as the intended recipient, see Penman, *David II*, 333.

112. G.H. Martin ed. and trans., *Knighton's Chronicle, 1337–1396* (Oxford, 1995), 136–7.

113. *Chron. Bower* (Watt), vii, 322–3. Duncan 'A question', 12, 54–57.

114. A.H. Diverres, 'The Geography of Britain in Froissart's *Meliador*', in *Medieval Miscellany Presented to Eugene Vinaver* (New York, 1965), 97–112; Ibid., 'Froissart's *Méliador* and Edward III's Policy towards Scotland', *Mélanges offerts à Rita Lejeune* (Gembloux, 1969), 1399–1409.

115. P. Contamine, 'Froissart and Scotland', in G.G. Simpson ed., *Scotland and the Low Countries, 1124–1994* (East Linton, 1996), 43–58.

116. Diverres, 'Geography', 98–9. The temptation to read all aspects of such a literary work as a literal commentary on contemporary conditions and aspirations has to be resisted.

117. See S. Duffy, 'Bruce Brothers and the Irish Sea World', *CMCS* 21 (Summer 1991), 55–86; *APS*, i, 497.

118. *APS*, i, 497.

119. *APS*, i, 503.

120. *ER*, vii, 487; For much later references to the maintenance of 'watchmen' see *The Dewar Manuscripts*, vol. 1 ed. Rev. J. Mackechnie (Glasgow, 1964), 93, 117; for a coastal variation of this early warning system in the Irish Sea that relied on the lighting of beacons see A.W.Moore, *A History of the Isle of Man* 2 vols. (London, 1977), i, 327–9, 335; W.D.H. Sellar and A. Maclean, *The Highland Clan MacNeacail (MacNicol)* (Waternish, 1999), 11 for the suggestion that the fifteenth-century arms of MacLeod of Lewis depicted a warning beacon afire.

121. *Chron.Wyntoun* (Laing), iii, 58–60.

122. *Ibid.*, 58.

123. *Chron. Bower* (Watt), vii, 358–61.

124. *APS*, i, 503.

125. *APS*, i, 506–7. The emphasis on lands about to come into the lords' possession may have been necessary because both Gillespic and John of Lorn were about to receive major grants from the Crown.

126. *APS*, i, 501–2; *RRS*, vi, nos. 382, 384. The revocation was said to cover alienations of royal lands reaching back to the time of Robert I or Alexander III.

127. *RRS*, vi, 454–5, no.429.

128. *OPS*, ii, part 1, 120–128.

129. *APS*, i, 508.

130. A. Grant, 'Thanes and Thanages, from the Eleventh to the Fourteenth Centuries', in A. Grant and K.J. Stringer, eds., *Medieval Scotland: Crown, Lordship and Community* (Edinburgh, 1993), 39–79.

131. See Introduction above, pp. 1–7.

132. Argyll Muniments, Inveraray, Bundle 1107; *RMS*, ii, no. 1431.

133. See Boardman, 'The Campbells and charter lordship', 96, 105–6. Grant, 'Scotland's 'Celtic Fringe'', 118–141.

134. *APS*, i, 497 (1465), 506 (1369), 545 (1371). Gillespic may have become a knight by 1385x1388. See *HP*, iv, 17–18.

135. Gillespic was married to Isabella Lamont. Gillespic's daughter Helen married a son of John of Islay and, after his death, Duncan, the future earl of Lennox. Theiner, *Vet.Mon.*, 348.
136. See *HP*, ii, 92 for a sequence of more or less plausible bynames for Campbell lords attributed to their place of fosterage.
137. *APS*, i, 497, 503, 506–8; *CPL*, iv, 56.
138. For an expression of this view, see G.A. Hayes-McCoy, *Scots mercenary forces in Ireland (1565–1603)* (Dublin, 1937), 103.

FOUR

The Lords of Argyll

I n February 1371 Robert the Steward, the long-standing patron of Gillespic Campbell of Loch Awe, became king of Scotland. The Steward's accession to the throne promised to transform the relationship between the crown and the Gaelic aristocracy of the west. The Steward's great network of allies and retainers suddenly found themselves 'king's men', with direct access to a royal court that seems to have been comfortable with Gaelic Scotland on a cultural and social level.[1] A variety of lordships around the Firth of Clyde were instantly absorbed into the royal patrimony. The new king's established friends and kinsmen in the region might expect to prosper in the years after 1371, while his adversaries could anticipate less charity. For the Campbell lords of Loch Awe the reign of Robert II would be distinguished by a steady tightening of the family's grip on the province of Argyll. Campbell lordship advanced in two interrelated ways. First, the rights and claims to land acquired by Gillespic and his son Colin in the 1360s were gradually transformed into real local domination and exploitation by the settlement of Colin's brothers and sons in newly won estates and offices. The promotion of Colin's immediate family generated local opposition and also tensions within the wider Campbell kindred, but on the whole these were overcome; by the early fifteenth century the exercise of local lordship across mid-Argyll was dominated by the sons and grandsons of Gillespic of Arran.

The entrenchment of local power went hand in hand with, and fed off, the advance of the Campbells of Loch Awe to the status of regional overlords of Argyll, wielding wide-ranging judicial powers and claiming the title 'lord of Argyll'. The rise to dominance on this wider stage was accelerated, if not initiated, by the rapid collapse of the position of Gillespic Campbell's chief rival for social and political influence in mainland Argyll, John MacDougall of Lorn. MacDougall was the nephew by marriage of the recently deceased David II and appears to have been well regarded by that king. This was not a relationship calculated to endear him to the new Stewart monarch after 1371.[2] Certainly, John was swiftly removed from the lands and offices in western Perthshire that he had acquired in David II's reign, to be replaced by Robert II's sons.[3] The general hostility of the Stewart court towards the MacDougalls of Lorn permeated John Barbour's *Bruce*, written for Robert II *c*.1375–6.[4] Barbour's work emphasised the role of John's grandfather (and namesake) as Robert I's most resolute and irreconcilable enemy.[5] On the other hand Barbour played up the role of the ancestors of Robert II's own west-coast allies, John of Islay and Gillespic Campbell, particularly in the desperate winter of 1306–7. Barbour's depiction of the MacDougalls would hardly have been possible or appreciated during the reign of David II, when John Gallda, the king's nephew, enjoyed the favour of the crown. However, the final blow to the status of the MacDougall lords of Argyll came not from the hostility of the new king, but from the failure of John to produce a legitimate male heir before his death some time between 1371 and 1377.[6]

John's passing gave rise to a struggle for political and social status in the west that operated on two levels. The most obvious issue was who should succeed to John's estates, castles and offices inside Lorn. In the years after 1377, a number of candidates advanced claims to all or part of the lordship of Lorn. John left two legitimate daughters by his marriage to the niece of David II. At some point the girls were married to two brothers from the Stewart of Innermeath family, and by 1388 these men were openly pressing the claims of their wives to be recognised as joint heiresses to Lorn.[7] The Stewarts of Innermeath could anticipate resistance from a number of others who thought they had legitimate rights in the lordship. Most obviously, the wider MacDougall kindred had little incentive to recognise the status of John's daughters as heiresses. The effective leader of the family after 1377 seems to have been an Allan MacDougall, perhaps an illegitimate son of John himself.[8] The entrenched local power of Allan and his kinsmen would not be easily swept aside by the incoming Stewart lords. There were other threats to the Stewarts' position in Lorn. The death of John Gallda had awakened old memories of the attempted settlement of the territory by Robert I. The MacArthur Campbells of Strachur, in particular, had an impressive array of long-redundant charters granting them lands in Appin, Benderloch and Lorn. In the 1380s, the Strachur Campbells armed themselves with parchment and went in search of allies to enforce their claims.

They found a willing partner in the neighbouring lordship of Lennox. The re-ignition of the dormant MacArthur Campbell claims in Lorn and

Benderloch coincided with the emergence of a new leader in the earldom of Lennox in the summer of 1385. By 8 May 1385 the aged Walter of Faslane, lord of Lennox, had given over control of the earldom to his son and heir Duncan, with a royal charter of that date confirming Duncan as earl following on the resignation of Walter and his wife Margaret.[9] Gillespic Campbell, who was Earl Duncan's father-in-law, witnessed the king's grant. Gillespic was also present when, perhaps also in the summer of 1385, Earl Duncan received a grant from Iver Campbell of Strachur of lands in Lorn and Benderloch. The charter dealt with lands that had been gifted to Arthur Campbell in the reign of Robert I.[10] The assigning over of the MacArthur Campbell claims in Lorn to the newly established earl of Lennox in a charter witnessed by the earl's father-in-law, Gillespic Campbell, whose lordship marched with the southern flank of Lorn, was clearly ominous for all those, both MacDougall and Stewart, who claimed to be the heirs of John Gallda. The entire arrangement suggests that a co-ordinated Campbell/Lennox campaign was to be unleashed in Lorn during or shortly after 1385.

However, the grand ambitions of Earl Duncan and Gillespic seem rapidly to have foundered. In 1388 the political tide turned decisively in favour of the Stewarts of Innermeath. The upturn in Stewart fortunes coincided with the arrest of Robert II on 7 February 1388 by one of his own men, David Fleming.[11] The king's arrest seems to have been part of a coup launched by the heir to the throne, John, earl of Carrick. The immediate result of the king's temporary removal from power was a commitment of the kingdom to an intensification of war with England, a policy supported by prominent Carrick allies such as James, 2nd earl of Douglas, and endorsed by a general council held in Edinburgh in April 1388.[12] The council of April 1388 also saw royal confirmation of a deal between John and Robert Stewart of Innermeath, by which Robert and his wife resigned their claims to Lorn, Benderloch, Appin and Lismore in favour of John and his partner. The consolidation of the Stewart claim to Lorn and its explicit ratification by the crown in April 1388 may have been linked to attempts to undermine the position of Earl Duncan within the Lennox. Although he was openly acknowledged as earl between May 1385 and August 1387, at some point before 19 August 1388 Duncan found himself under pressure to restore the liferent rights of his mother and father inside Lennox. The two parties concluded their differences in Stirling around 19 August 1388, some two weeks after Carrick's regime had been fatally weakened by the death of

James earl of Douglas at the battle of Otterburn.[13] Earl Duncan's loss of full control in Lennox, combined with the death of his father-in-law Gillespic Campbell sometime between 1385 and 1393, meant that the successful prosecution of the MacArthur Campbell rights in Lorn was far less likely. However, the claims in the northern lordship were not lightly abandoned. A second agreement between the Lennox family and the MacArthur Campbells, probably made in the early 1390s, saw Earl Duncan return to Arthur (Iver Campbell's son) one third of the lands in Lorn and Benderloch (and others) given to the earl by Iver in the grant of 1385 x 1388. The arrangement suggests that Earl Duncan and Arthur were still actively seeking powerful allies to assist in the pursuit of their rights, for it raised the possibility that Arthur's claims could be vindicated through the marriage of one of the earl's daughters to Alexander MacDonald, the lord of Lochaber.[14] The earl of Lennox and Arthur Campbell clearly envisaged employing the considerable military power of Alexander of Lochaber in Lorn.

In the end, however, nothing came of the grandiose schemes of Earl Duncan and the MacArthur Campbells. The political tensions in and around the lordship of Lorn seem to have been resolved by the emergence of a regional magnate who managed to absorb all the conflicting parties into his personal lordship during the 1390s. The growing influence of Robert, earl of Fife and Menteith, the second surviving son of Robert II, in the south-western Highlands was a notable feature of the closing decades of the fourteenth century. Initially, Fife's personal and political links all seem to have lain with the Lennox family and the MacArthur Campbells. In the 1360s Duncan, the future earl of Lennox, had acted as godfather at the baptism of Fife's eldest son and heir, Murdoch.[15] The link between Robert and Duncan became far closer early in the 1390s. In a marriage contract of February 1392 between the two men it was agreed that Robert's son Murdoch would marry Duncan's eldest daughter Isabella, to whom the inheritance of the earldom would fall (Duncan having produced no legitimate male heirs).[16] Robert III confirmed the entailing of Lennox in favour of Murdoch on 8 November 1392.[17] Duncan's willingness to allow the earldom to pass from the Lennox line may be explained by a number of factors. Duncan, who was probably under fifty when the agreement was made, may not entirely have abandoned hope that he could produce a legitimate male heir.[18] If that was the case, then the deal offered a number of clear short-term advantages. First, it gave Duncan the support of Earl Robert, at that stage guardian of the kingdom, in his apparently ongoing struggle with his father Walter for full control of the Lennox.[19] Moreover, the place of Murdoch as Duncan's heir by entail encouraged the guardian to make a series of grants in favour of Lennox in anticipation of the fact that the ultimate beneficiary would be his own son.[20]

Aside from his links with Earl Duncan, Fife was also associated with the MacArthur Campbells of Strachur, who had been his tenants in the lordship of Glen Dochart since 1374.[21] Fife's relationship with Duncan and the MacArthur Campbells raises questions about his attitude to the proposed Lennox/Campbell advance into Lorn. Although there is no direct evidence that Fife supported the plan, its successful prosecution by Earl Duncan would, after 1392, have expanded the territorial lordship destined to descend to Robert's son Murdoch. Moreover, the inclusion in the second Campbell/Lennox agreement of the clause relating to the marriage of Duncan's daughter to Alexander MacDonald of Lochaber may be significant. Fife was certainly exercised over the issue of the marriages of Duncan's daughters. The 1392 agreement, aside from des-ignating Isabella of Lennox as her father's heir, also stipulated that Earl Robert was to arrange for the marriage of one of her sisters, either Elizabeth or Margaret, 'at his awin costage'. The marriage of the remaining sister was to be arranged by Lennox and Fife's son Murdoch. Since Alexander MacDonald *was* eventually married to Elizabeth of Lennox after February 1392, it seems reasonable to assume that Earl Robert and his son negotiated this match with its clear ramifications for the pursuit of Lennox/Campbell claims in Lorn.[22]

Despite the apparently formidable political and military coalition ranged against him in the early 1390s, John Stewart successfully con-solidated his lordship in Lorn. If Fife had initially supported moves against John in 1392/3, by the mid-1390s the two men were reconciled. John was to be found as a witness to a perambulation conducted by Earl Robert in Fife in 1395, while shortly after 27 September 1397 John's son Robert married Fife's daughter Johanna.[23] Thereafter, John was a regular witness to Fife charters.[24] Inside Lorn itself, Stewart reached an accom-modation with Allan MacDougall, the male heir of John Gallda. In 1450 Allan's grandson John Ciar MacDougall still held extensive lands and offices inside Lorn under terms that suggest that the incoming Stewart lords had been forced to make significant concessions in order to be accepted as overlords.[25] The MacDougalls retained the office of bailie of the entire lordship of Lorn for the Stewart lords, along with the apparently heritable right to foster the heir to the lordship. The fosterage clause ensured the continuing influence of the MacDougalls and may help to explain the swift absorption of the newly established Stewart lords of Lorn into the Gaelic cultural world.[26]

Although the death of John Gallda did not, in the end, result in a direct expansion of Campbell lordship into Lorn, the relegation of the Mac-Dougalls to a subordinate position within their own territorial heartland had implications for the regional status of the Campbells of Loch Awe. By the early 1380s Gillespic Campbell was unquestionably the most powerful magnate in mainland Argyll. As early as 1369, David II had recognised and confirmed Gillespic's hold over most of the lordships in mid-Argyll and had armed him with vague jurisdictional rights over the inhabitants of Loch Awe. The Campbells' entrenched power and authority in mid-Argyll was explicitly recognised and augmented in 1382, when Robert II granted Gillespic and his son Colin a hereditary royal lieutenancy. The lieutenancy covered an area apparently bounded on the north by the Lordship of Lorn, on the east by Loch Long, on the south by Knapdale, and on the west by the Atlantic.[27] The creation of the royal lieutenancy only superficially supports the view that the Campbells' power rested on their close relationship with the Scottish crown and their role as royal agents in the west. In reality, Gillespic had already achieved political supremacy in the area covered by the lieutenancy. Moreover, the terms of the grant hardly suggest that the Campbell lords were to be ranked alongside other royal judicial officers to be appointed and dismissed at the behest of the crown. The powers handed over were extensive, and the lieutenancy was heritable. The Campbell lords certainly thought of their dominance in Argyll as having deeper roots and a wider social significance than the temporary exercise of delegated royal authority. By 1395 Colin was openly using the style 'Dominus de Ergadia', a title that had last been employed by John Gallda MacDougall in 1354.[28] Thereafter, the status of Colin and his descendants as 'Lords of Argyll' seems to have been widely recognised, both within and outwith the province, although never explicitly by the Scottish crown.[29]

What was the basis of Colin's claim to be lord of Argyll and what did the lordship mean in practical terms? Individuals bearing the title of king, ruler or lord of Argyll had appeared in a variety of contexts from the tenth to the twelfth centuries, although the extent of the territories and powers claimed by those who used these styles remains obscure.[30] However, around the turn of the thirteenth century a more precise (and restricted) definition of Argyll seems to have been established in terms both of secular lordship and ecclesiastical organisation. A recent suggestion is that the foundation of the diocese of Argyll, probably in the 1180s and certainly by 1193, reflected the permanent political division of the secular lordship of the Isles and Man between the descendants of Somerled and the royal Manx line founded by Godfrey mac Aulay.[31] In this interpretation the boundaries of the new diocese effectively mirrored the territory held by Somerled's sons in mainland Scotland, along with the island of Lismore, where the chief church of the diocese was located. By 1225 the descendants of Somerled's son Dugald had adopted the style 'de Ergadia' (of Argyll), and they continued to dominate the lordship of the region despite the increasing influence and activity of Scottish kings in Argyll and the Isles as the thirteenth century progressed.[32] There is little contemporary evidence as to how the MacDougall lordship functioned inside Argyll, or what rights, privileges and duties were enjoyed and discharged by the ruling aristocratic dynasty. How far the diocesan structure and the century-long supremacy of the MacDougall lords of Argyll helped to foster a sense of a self-enclosed community is also difficult to say. There are, however, fleeting indications that some social, tenurial, political and military structures or obligations were organised on an 'Argyll-wide' basis, embracing the territories running from Cowal in the south to Lorn in the north. The obligation to provide men for the hosting of Argyll, for example, was explicitly mentioned in a grant of lands in Cowal in the 1290s. The right to summon and lead the host of Argyll presumably lay with the acknowledged lord of the province.[33]

The long association of MacDougall lords with the leadership of the provincial aristocracy of Argyll was shaken by the civil wars of the early fourteenth century and then permanently broken after the death of John Gallda. Rights to John's own lands and estates passed to the new Stewart lords of Lorn, but pretensions to wider authority within Argyll fell to the rising power in the province, the Campbells of Loch Awe. How did the Campbell lords justify and secure this new status? Clearly the Campbell claim could not rest on the idea that Gillespic and his son were the 'heirs' of the MacDougall lords in terms of bloodline and inheritance. Instead, the shift may have depended on the notion that the provincial lordship was not the private possession of the MacDougalls, but a quasi-public responsibility that had to be effectively discharged and that therefore could be transferred elsewhere with the eclipse of MacDougall power. The rapid advance of the Campbells during the 1360s and 1370s meant that few could have argued they were not the obvious successors to provincial supremacy. Whether imposed on the province by the sheer power of the Campbell lords or by the creation of the royal lieutenancy in 1382 (or a combination of the two), the Campbell ascendancy may still have been legitimised by the 'consent' of the wider community. The notion that Argyll should naturally have an aristocratic leader seems to have survived the political upheavals of the early fourteenth century, despite Robert I's policy of undercutting MacDougall lordship by creating new sheriffdoms and independent baronies to be held directly of the crown.[34] There is certainly plenty of evidence for the existence of a self-conscious and distinct regional aristocratic community in Argyll in the thirteenth and fourteenth centuries, not least through the regular appearance of the phrase the 'barons of Argyll' in contemporary record.[35]

If a form of communal assent played a role in the making of the Campbell lord of Argyll, the possibility of comparison with contemporary Irish Gaelic lordships inevitably springs to mind. The importance of inauguration ceremonies at customary sites, whereby a new lord was proclaimed and acclaimed by the men of his territory or imposed by a superior lord, was a notable feature of the political landscape in late medieval Ireland.[36] Unfortunately, there is little or no contemporary evidence for the conduct of these ceremonies and the existence of associated ceremonial centres in late-medieval Argyll. This may reflect simply a lack of the kind of detailed sources available for some Irish lordships. However, it is also possible that the absence of Scottish references or examples was the product of real differences in the structures and traditions of lordship.[37]

The 1382 grant of a heritable royal lieutenancy in favour of the Campbell lords effectively resurrected and sanctioned the role of regional military and judicial overlord in Argyll, although the territorial heartland of the lordship had shifted from Lorn to mid-Argyll. Whether the royal grant simply confirmed the Campbells' assumption of social, political and military leadership of the barons of Argyll, or was designed to help the lord of Loch Awe achieve this end against local opposition, remains unclear. In any case, although the crown never officially acknowledged the title 'lord of Argyll', the lieutenancy grant effectively provided a charter formula to describe and secure the powers claimed by Gillespic and Colin as provincial overlords.

One of the effects of Colin's consolidation of his position as the overlord of Argyll was that it allowed him to cement his own immediate family's control over the lordships and territories that had been swiftly acquired during the 1360s and 1370s. The right to deal with feudal casualties that theoretically fell to the crown inside the lieutenancy was a particularly important concession, for it made even lords who held their land directly from the king vulnerable to the ambitions of the lords of Loch Awe. The closing decades of the fourteenth century, then, were notable for the entrenchment of Colin Iongantach's sons in the lordships obtained by their father. Vague claims to superiority were slowly transformed into real possession and exploitation of estates. Across mid-Argyll and Cowal a number of families, including other branches of Clan Campbell, resented the rapid accumulation of rights of lordship by the Loch Awe line and struggled to hang on to as much of their former territorial and political power as possible. Thus, in Craignish, Ardscotnish, Over Cowal and Strachur, Colin faced the problem of dealing with entrenched local kindreds either by reaching an accommodation with them or by displacing them entirely. The Clan Mac-Dougall Craignish were perhaps the most successful of the mid-Argyll kindreds in retaining local influence under their new overlords. By the mid-fifteenth century the family had secured their position as tenants of the lords of Loch Awe in Craignish and maintained a monopoly of local judicial and administrative offices.[38] The successful integration of the Craignish kindred into the Campbell lordship was reflected in the adoption of the Campbell surname and the development of a genealogical tradition that presented the Clan MacDougall Craignish as a cadet branch of the Campbells of Loch Awe.[39] The fate of the established kindreds in Ardscotnish was less happy. As we have seen, Colin married Mariota or Mary Campbell, the putative heiress of Ardscotnish (and Glenorchy) sometime between 1366 and 1372.[40] A number of families linked to the Ardscotnish Campbells responded to the intrusion of Colin by supporting the claims of his brother Duncan to the wider Campbell lordship. The failure of the attempt to assassinate Colin allowed the Loch Awe Campbells to secure their hold on Ardscotnish. By 1411 Duncan Campbell, one of the two sons of Colin bearing that name,

was styled lord of Ardscotnish. It seems most likely that this was Duncan
Mór, the progenitor of the Campbells of Duntroon, who was certainly in
possession of a large number of Ardscotnish estates early in the fifteenth
century.[41] Meanwhile, the parish kirk of Ardscotnish at Kilmartin came
into the hands of John, another of Colin's sons.[42]

Yet another of Colin's sons, Colin Óg, was established as a lord with
extensive estates in the parishes of Kilmorich and Lochgoilhead at the
heads of Loch Fyne and Loch Long. The cadet branch founded by
Colin Óg, the Campbells of Ardkinglas, became one of the most
important families within the fifteenth-century Clan Campbell. The
origins of Loch Awe Campbell lordship and landowning in the north of
Cowal are uncertain, although as we have seen there is some evidence to
suggest that branches of Clan Campbell had been established in that
area as early as the thirteenth century.[43] The dominance of the Loch
Awe Campbells in the region seems, however, to have been a fourteenth-century development that involved the assertion of superiority
over already-established Campbell lineages such as the Strachur Campbells. The Loch Awe Campbells' dominant position in the north of
Cowal was certainly established as early as 1369 when David II confirmed the secular lordship of Over Cowal, which embraced the parish
of Lochgoilhead and may have included Kilmorich, in Gillespic Campbell's possession.[44] By 1380 Colin Iongantach was attempting to exercise
rights as lord of Over Cowal by presenting his own nominees to the
parish kirk of Lochgoilhead.[45] In the 1390s it was clear that Colin's son,
Colin Óg, was being promoted as the local heir to his father's rights
and influence. The marriage alliances concluded by Colin Iongantach
were obviously designed to strengthen the younger Colin's burgeoning
lordship in the north of Cowal. In June 1396, Colin Óg supplicated the
Pope to allow his marriage to Christian, daughter of Robert Lamont of
Inveryne, head of the most influential family in the south of Cowal.[46]
At around the same time Colin Óg's sister, Christian, was married to
Duncan MacFarlane, son and heir of the deceased Malcolm MacFarlane, lord of Arrochar at the head of Loch Long.[47] The consolidation of
the Loch Awe Campbells in the lands around the heads of Loch Fyne
and Loch Long affected other branches of Clan Campbell. In the
second half of the fourteenth century an independently established
Campbell lineage, the Campbells of Gaunan, held estates within the
parish of Lochgoilhead. By 1428, perhaps because of a failure in the

male line, these lands had also been absorbed into the lordship of John Campbell of Ardkinglass, the son of Colin Óg.[48]

Colin Iongantach's settlement of land on his sons went hand in hand with his arrangements for the succession to the wider Campbell lordship. At some point before 6 February 1393 Colin had evidently decided that Duncan, his son by Mariota Campbell, the heiress of Ardscotnish and Glenorchy, should be his heir.[49] The traditional histories of Clan Campbell hint that Duncan was preferred to the lordship ahead of an elder son of Colin and Mariota, John, or 'John Annan, that is weak John'.[50] The same account suggests that by the 'advice of his friends he [John] resigned the Inheritance to his brother Duncan Anadh, reserving the Straith of Craignais to himself'. Although John could have been a full brother of Duncan, it seems more likely that he was an elder half-brother, effectively excluded from the wider inheritance because only a son of Mariota Campbell could unite the lordships of Ardscotnish and Glenorchy to the Campbell patrimony.[51]

The pre-eminence of Duncan and his successors within the Clan Campbell was further enhanced by Duncan's marriage to a daughter of the king's son, Robert, earl of Fife and Menteith, sometime in the 1390s. Duncan's prestigious match with Marjory Stewart also maintained the Campbells' direct link into the heart of Scottish politics, for Robert of Fife's influence in royal government rivalled that of his brother, Robert III. That the marriage reflected an increasingly close association between Fife and the Campbell lords is suggested by Duncan's appearance on a perambulation conducted by Earl Robert in Fife on 6 July 1395.[52] However, Colin and Duncan were not simply Fife's men. Most obviously, the Campbells could hardly afford to disregard the interests of Robert III, who remained the overlord of Cowal and a source of patronage for members of the family on the Firth of Clyde.[53] The royal court still occasionally found its way to Bute, and Robert III evidently retained a close interest in the affairs of Cowal families.[54] The continuing involvement of the king's family in the region is suggested by the fact that Robert III's eldest son and heir, David, took the title duke of Rothesay in April 1398.[55] Overall, then, the Campbells' position on the Firth of Clyde must have become increasingly uncomfortable as the struggle for supremacy between Fife and the king and his family intensified in the 1390s.

Added to this tension at the heart of royal government was the growing hostility between the various branches of the Stewart family and the Clan

Donald. The general council that saw the creation of Prince David's dukedom was also notable for the preparation of a great military campaign against various members of the Clan Donald. The leaders of the expedition were to be Rothesay and his uncle Robert, who had been created duke of Albany at the same time as David received his title. The scarcity of reliable chronicle evidence makes it difficult to pin down the precise events that precipitated the military activity of 1398. Throughout the 1390s the major figures in the royal dynasty had in fact been quite happy to involve their Clan Donald kinsmen in the affairs of the kingdom. In particular, Albany (as earl of Fife and Menteith) had, from 1389 onwards, made a series of alliances with Hebridean lords as part of the political and military campaign against his younger brother Alexander, earl of Buchan.[56] Fife's eagerness to wreck his brother's lordship in the central Highlands and Ross apparently persuaded the then guardian to arrange prestigious marriages for both Donald of the Isles and Alexander of Lochaber.[57] Fife's strategy of alliance with Donald of the Isles and his brothers seems to have collapsed completely by the winter of 1397–8.[58] There were clearly a number of areas where the advance of Clan Donald interests might arouse opposition and anxiety. The most vociferous (or at least best recorded) complaints emerged from Moray, with the evidence suggesting that Alexander of Lochaber had extended his lordship rapidly through the Great Glen so that by the late 1390s his adherents were raiding or simply occupying estates around Inverness and the Moray coastal plain.[59] The condemnation of Donald's brother John of Dunivaig by the council of 1398 might also indicate problems on the Firth of Clyde, where royal Stewart lordships in Cowal, Bute and particularly Arran were vulnerable to seaborne raids from Clan Donald-controlled Kintyre. The language of the 1398 council strongly supports the notion that one of the major problems was widespread raiding. The council demanded that decisive action should be taken against the king's rebels and, in particular, that sureties had to be obtained from Donald, Alexander and John, lord of Dunivaig and the Glens, and the 'perdones and vastatores' in their service.[60] Whether these raids had simply intensified, or in 1397–8 assumed a new pattern and purpose that required an immediate response, is difficult to tell.

Whatever the precise objectives of the summer campaign of 1398, Colin Campbell, 'Dominus de Ergadie', was clearly one of the men upon whom the military success of the expedition depended. Whether Colin was also one of the men who had encouraged a direct royal intervention is impossible to say, and there is nothing to suggest that the Campbells were especially enthusiastic over the prospect. Nevertheless, Colin and his kinsman the MacArthur lord of Strachur were in Dumbarton by 20 July 1398, probably anticipating the arrival of Robert III and other lords for the hosting against the Lord of the Isles and his brothers.[61] As a result of the expedition Donald of the Isles seems to have submitted himself to royal authority, and briefly taken his younger brother Alexander into custody. By the following year, however, Alexander had been released and Donald was once more summoned to the Scots parliament.[62]

For the Campbells, any problems created by the activities of Clan Donald were soon superseded by a wider political crisis as the rivalry between Albany and the heir to the throne, Prince David, steadily grew more intense. In January 1399 the twenty-one-year-old Rothesay was made lieutenant of the realm in place of his incapacitated father.[63] Albany's status and position were protected by the stipulation that Rothesay was to rule with the advice of a council of twenty-one men, headed by Albany himself. Late in 1401 this arrangement broke down as Rothesay rejected the constraints placed on him by the council and attempted to establish an independent right to govern in his own name. Albany's reaction was to arrange Rothesay's arrest and imprisonment in Duke Robert's castle of Falkland in Fife.[64] In March 1402, Rothesay died in Falkland, either of dysentery, as Albany claimed, or of starvation, as Albany's opponents asserted. One of Rothesay's principal supporters, his maternal uncle Malcolm Drummond, lord of Mar, was similarly impri-soned in conditions that eventually led to his death.[65] The Campbells' position in the unfolding political drama is difficult to discern. Duncan's marriage to Albany's daughter would seem to ally the family with Duke Robert. Yet the Campbells also seem to have incurred the duke's displeasure at some point late in 1401 or early in 1402 as a Duncan Campbell, perhaps Colin's son and heir, spent at least six months before July 1402 in Albany's custody in Stirling Castle.[66]

The death of the heir to the throne was clearly a traumatic event that was likely to be especially keenly felt on the Firth of Clyde, where the territorial interests of Albany and the royal line were thoroughly inter-meshed. For two years after Rothesay's demise Albany and his allies dominated royal government and policy, while Robert III retreated into what amounted to internal exile on his ancestral estates in the west.[67]

From the middle of 1404, however, Robert III began slowly to recover some of his political authority, largely by advancing the territorial and political interests of his remaining son, Prince James (the future James I).[68] On 10 December 1404, at Perth, Robert III created a huge regality for the ten-year-old James, which embraced the baronies of Renfrew, Cunningham, Kyle-Stewart, the islands of Bute, Arran and the two Cumbraes, along with Cowal, Knapdale, the lands and earldom of Carrick and other lesser estates in Lothian.[69] The Campbells, with their extensive interests in Cowal and their claims to land in Knapdale and Arran, could hardly ignore the foundation of this integrated personal lordship.[70] In the years after 1402 Colin and Duncan seem, in fact, to have been more than eager to associate themselves with Robert III's family and the rising star of the heir to the throne. On 20 June 1404 at Rothesay Castle Robert III gave over to Colin Campbell various lands in lower Cowal resigned by the king's own illegitimate son, John Stewart of Ardgowan. The extent to which relatively low status men from the Firth of Clyde had unprecedented access to the royal court in Robert III's period of exile in the Stewartry is suggested by the appearance of two Campbell clerics, Finlay, rector of Loch Awe, and Celestine MacGillemichael, rector of St Maelrubha of Melfort, as witnesses to this royal charter.[71] Later in the year, on 19 October 1404, a papal mandate in favour of Neil 'Colini Cambel', the archdeacon of Argyll, described Neil as kinsman of James, duke of Rothesay, son of Robert, king of Scots. The style presumably reflected the wording of Neil's original supplication and may have been meant to indicate James and Robert's support.[72] Neil's claim to be Rothesay's kinsman probably referred to the link established by the marriage of his brother Duncan to Albany's daughter, Marjory Stewart, James' cousin. One of the unanticipated results of King Robert's political eclipse on the national stage, then, seems to have been the return of the king as a regional lord on the Firth of Clyde.

The potential consolidation of Prince James' authority inside the Stewartry and elsewhere came to an abrupt halt in the spring of 1406 as a plague of misfortunes descended on the royal house. In February 1406, Prince James, accompanied by two of his father's principal advisors, Henry Sinclair, earl of Orkney, and Sir David Fleming of Biggar, entered East Lothian with a 'strong band'. The aim of this force remains unclear, but it provoked a devastating military response from Sir James Douglas of Balvenie and a number of Lothian lairds that ended with the death of

Fleming during a confrontation at Long Hermiston Moor. In response to the threat of involvement in an open battle, or perhaps as part of a long-laid plan to remove the heir to the throne from the kingdom before the death of his father, Prince James and Orkney were rowed to the Bass Rock. There they waited for a month before boarding a ship intended to carry them to the French court. Instead, the *Maryenknecht* was intercepted by English privateers off Flamborough Head, and the heir to the throne soon found himself in the custody of the English king, Henry IV.[73] The capture of Prince James was compounded by the death of Robert III in Bute on 4 April 1406.[74] After the king's death provision for the governance of the realm had to be made. With the heir to the throne in captivity in England, the three estates turned once more to the duke of Albany, who in June 1406 was made Governor of the kingdom. Albany's adoption of the title of Governor and his issuing of charters in his own name, dated by the years of his governorship, have been seen as an indication of Duke Robert's vaulting ambition and his ultimate aim to claim the throne from his nephew. However, the most recent study points out that Albany's new status was perfectly justified in legal and constitutional terms and was supported by a wide political consensus.[75]

With the death of Robert III and the forced exile of his son and heir James, any developing Campbell association with the 'royal' alternative to Albany Stewart lordship on the Firth of Clyde withered on the vine. In the years after 1406 Albany steadily extended his political authority into the Stewartry, the great regality created for Prince James in December 1404, where loyalty to the vulnerable royal line might be expected to be most intense. The lordships that made up the Stewartry were unequivocally the personal inheritance of the heir to the throne, but while James was a minor, his uncle would act as his tutor and be responsible for the day-to-day running of affairs within the regality. In some cases, the acknowledgement of Albany's rights inside the Stewartry by individual noblemen may have been extracted by the application of political pressure. Whether Albany's accommodation with Colin Campbell also involved an element of coercion is uncertain, but by 5 May 1407 any tensions between the two men had evidently been resolved. On that date, at Stirling, Colin resigned various lands in the hands of the Governor, who thereafter issued a charter that confirmed Colin in the baronies of Loch Awe, Glenorchy and Over Cowal, and all other lands held in chief from the king in Argyll. In addition, Albany confirmed Colin in the lands of Ardenslate, Dalilongart,

Glen Kin and Glen Lean (i.e. the lands given over to Colin by John Stewart of Ardgowan in 1404) and Lochstrivenhead and all other lands held in chief from the Steward of Scotland in the bailiary of Cowal Stewart.[76] The witness list to the charter was dominated by men with interests in the earldom of Lennox, including Earl Duncan, Walter and John Buchanan, John Stewart of Darnley, Humphrey Colquhoun and Murdoch of Leckie.

The years of the Albany ascendancy may have strengthened Campbell links to the Governor and his family. In a strategic sense, the goodwill of the Lord of Argyll probably became more pressing for Albany as a result of his long-standing struggle with Donald, Lord of the Isles, for control of the earldom of Ross. Although the main theatre for the struggle obviously lay in Ross itself, the military and political conflict spilled over into other areas. The most spectacular clash between Donald's forces and Albany's agents occurred at Harlaw, barely eleven miles from Aberdeen, in July 1411.[77] Although the battle itself seems to have been a bloody stalemate, Albany responded with punitive expeditions against the lordship in both Ross and the west.[78] In particular, in the following summer Albany was said to have 'gathered three forces to attack the Lord of the Isles who came to him [Albany] at Lochgilp and offered oaths and hostages to keep the peace'.[79] Albany's expedition to Lochgilp has left little trace in the record, and the attitude of Colin Campbell and his son to the entire affair is difficult to gauge. However, it seems inconceivable that Colin and Duncan Campbell, whose royal lieutenancy in mid-Argyll extended to Lochgilp, were not involved in some way.[80]

If Colin Campbell participated in Albany's expedition, it was one of the last acts of his long and remarkable life. By 19 January 1414 Colin of the wonderful conceits was dead.[81] In temporal affairs Colin had been a great and successful figure according to the values and ambitions of a man of his status and time. He had greatly expanded the territories and offices to be handed down to his successors, and had provided generously for his numerous offspring. At the time of his death he was the royal lieutenant of mid-Argyll (in the estimation of the crown), lord of Argyll in the minds of many others. He also bequeathed to his son and heir, Duncan, an apparently cordial relationship with the Governor of the Scottish realm, Robert, duke of Albany, Duncan's father-in-law. The amicability of the relationship was attested in the immediate aftermath of Colin's death when Duke Robert granted to Duncan, 'his dearest son', the relief owed to the Governor for all Colin's lands. As son-in-law of the Governor and hereditary royal lieutenant in Argyll, Duncan already seemed to justify his by-name of 'the fortunate'. The years after 1414 would surely see a further consolidation of Campbell power in the west with the blessing of the Albany Stewarts. Away to the south, however, a fatal storm was brewing. The fate and feelings of the imprisoned James I, almost seven years a captive by the time Duncan Campbell succeeded his father, might have seemed a remote irrelevance for the lord of Loch Awe in the winter of 1413–4. It cannot have been entirely clear that the king would ever return; indeed, it would be a further decade before he was restored to his realm. However, in 1424 James did return, with the force and malevolence of a hurricane. The full fury of the tempest would be unleashed on the Albany Stewarts and their allies, and would scour Argyll and the Lennox. Duncan the fortunate could do little more than hope that the fates would deliver him from the storm.

Notes

1. See S. Boardman, 'The Early Stewart court and the Gaelic World', in M. McGregor and D. Broun, eds., *Miorum Mór nan Gall: the Great Ill-will of the Lowlander? Lowland Perceptions of the Highlands*, (forthcoming).
2. See Boardman, 'Leper John', 231–2. Robert II may even have regarded the MacDougall lord as a potential danger to the security of the newly established dynasty.
3. *RMS*, i, no.237. A grant of the king's lands of Glenlyon in March 1369; *ER*, ii, 352 (acting as bailie of the Appin of Dull in 1370–71); *RRS*, vi, no.165. The combination of Lorn, Glenlyon and the Appin of Dull clearly made John of Lorn a major figure in the Highlands at the end of David II's reign.
4. *The Bruce* (Duncan), 112–121, 248–52, 258–62, 342–5, 360–66, 564–7.
5. See *Ibid.*, 342–5, 366. Did this act as an implicit criticism of David II's attempt to reinstate MacDougall lordship in Argyll?
6. Boardman, 'Leper John', 231, n. 60. The source that outlines the birth of John's daughters also implies that his marriage produced a male heir(s). This heir (or heirs) presumably died young. *Chron. Fordun*, i, 369 n.17.
7. *Chron. Fordun*, i, 369 n.17. The status of John's daughters as potential heiresses may not have been obvious until the premature (?) death of their putative brother(s). John and Johanna were certainly married by August 1362, but it is difficult to calculate with any certainty the dates of birth of their daughters and, therefore, the most likely period for the girls' marriages to the Stewart brothers. *ER*, ii, 106, 114.
8. Sellar, 'MacDougall pedigrees', 7–8.
9. *Lennox Cartularium*, 6–8. A charter issued at Rothesay.
10. *HP*, iv, 17–18. For the dating of this charter to the period May 1385 X August

1388, see A.B.W. McEwan in SWHIHR *Notes and Queries*, xiv, 6–8. The other witnesses were Robert Culquhoun and Walter Buchanan, Duncan Napier and Malcolm MacFarlane.

11. MS. Fairfax 23, f. 116, Bodleian Library, Oxford. The arrest was clearly connected to wider political issues, and it may have been no more than coincidental that David Fleming's father, Malcolm, was married to John Gallda's widow. However, if Malcolm Fleming's wife were alive in 1388, then the issue of the lady of Lorn's terce rights may have been a complicating factor. Malcolm was alive and serving as sheriff of Edinburgh on 1 November 1388. *Mort. Reg.*, ii, 165–6; *ER*, iii, 66.

12. Boardman, *Early Stewart Kings*, 142. Although the interpretation of the Council offered there must be amended in light of the subsequent discovery of the date for Robert II's arrest.

13. *Lennox Cartularium*, 7, 8–9, 9–10.

14. *HP*, iv, 16. Also included were one third of the lands of Gillespic Mac Marten, and a third of the lands of 'Rathnach'.

15. *CPL Clement VII*, 174.

16. Fraser, *Lennox*, ii, 43–5, 49–51.

17. *RMS*, i, no.862.

18. The entail was certainly in favour, first of all, of Duncan's legitimate male heirs, so the subsequent birth of a son and heir would have invalidated the agreement. Duncan was married at this point and his wife was probably well beyond child-bearing age. If, however, he was to be freed by 'aventure' to marry again, the agreement stipulated that he was to marry one of Fife's daughters or one of Fife's kinswomen of sufficient status.

19. See M. Brown, 'Earldom and kindred: the Lennox and its earls, 1200–1458', in S. Boardman and A. Ross (eds.), *The Exercise of Power in Medieval Scotland, c.1200–1500* (Dublin, 2003), 201–224, at 214–8.

20. Boardman, *Early Stewart Kings*, 181–3.

21. *RMS*, i, no. 458. NAS Breadalbane Collection GD112/1/4. Arthur received in February 1376–7 a royal confirmation of a charter by Robert, earl of Fife and Menteith, confirming him in various lands in Glen Dochart.

22. A.B.W.MacEwan, in SWHIHR, *Notes and Queries*, xiv, 6–8. Fife had certainly concluded some sort of deal with Alexander MacDonald of Lochaber before 1394, as Alexander excepted his established obligations to Fife in an agreement of that year with Thomas Dunbar, earl of Moray. Much depends on whether Duncan's negotiations with Alexander MacDonald preceded or post-dated the marriage agreement of February 1392 between Fife and Duncan. If the former, then Fife's intervention in the Lennox succession could be interpreted as a reaction to proposals that threatened to give the formidable Alexander Mac-Donald a potential claim to the earldom. The 1392 agreement between Fife and Duncan could, in that case, be seen as the guardian acting to head off the advance of Clan Donald interests into Lennox.

23. *CPL Benedict XIII*, 75.

24. Duke of Atholl's Muniments, Blair Castle, Blair Atholl, Box 7/ Parcel iv/ Innermeath. Pre-1398 charter by Robert earl of Fife and Menteith to John Stewart of Innermeath. On 20 April 1398 at Perth Robert Stewart, lord of Durisdeer, issued a charter witnessed by Fife, Murdoch, David, lord of

Crawford, John, lord of Lorn, Thomas Kirkpatrick and William Lindsay of Rossie. NAS Buccleuch Muniments, Drawer 3 (lands in the barony of Durisdeer).

25. AT. The document seems to outline established rights in Lorn held by the MacDougalls prior to 1450 since the purpose of the grant was not to give over new privileges, but to protect John Ciar's position as his father's heir against the claims of a younger half-brother.

26. One interesting example of the process can be seen in the Murthly Hours, a devotional manuscript probably held by the Stewart family which had added to it various Gaelic medical charms and rhymes. See John Higgit, *The Murthly Hours Devotion, Literacy and Luxury in Paris, England and the Gaelic West* (British Library, 2000), Appendix 6. (Later Additions in Gaelic), Transcription, Translation and Commentary by Ronald Black, 336–344.

27. Argyll Muniments, Inveraray, Bundle 1107; *RMS*, ii, no. 1431, 24 May 1382. The exact boundaries of the lieutenancy are not given; instead the office was said to cover the area stretching from Carn Drome, near Tyndrum, to Poll Gilb (Lochgilphead?; the north-eastern and south-western limits?) and from Poll Melfurd (Loch Melfort?) to Loch Long (the north-western and south-eastern limits?). Loch Melfort marched with Lorn and Lochgilphead with Knapdale. Whether Cowal was meant to be included in the lieutenancy is wholly unclear, but later Campbell lords seem to have argued that it should be.

28. This was in John's private agreement with John of Islay. *ALI*, 5–8. Documents issued by David II never described John Gallda in this way, noting him simply as Lord of Lorn. *Liber Cartularium Prioratus Sancti Andree* (Bannatyne Club, 1841), p.5. 'Duncano Cambell filio et herede Colini Cambell, domini de Ergadia'. Bannerman suggests that the title 'dominus', when used to describe the overlords of major Gaelic provinces such as Argyll or Galloway, denoted a figure whose title in the east would be Latin *comes* and Scots earl. J.W.M. Bannerman 'The Scots Language and the Kin-based Society', in *Gaelic and Scots in Harmony: Proceedings of the Second International Conference on the Languages of Scotland* (Glasgow, 1988), p.7.

29. In 1423–5 Colin's son and successor, Duncan, appeared as 'Dominus de Argill' and as 'Cambel de Argyle' while in July 1432 Duncan's son and designated heir was styled 'Gillaspy Cambel of Ergile'. *Rot.Scot.*, ii, 242, 244–5, 254; *HP*, ii, p. 174.

30. For discussion, see Sellar, 'Hebridean Sea-Kings', 199, 201, 207, 217 n.155.

31. A. Woolf, 'The Diocese of Sodor', in *A New History of the Isle of Man, volume* 3; the medieval period, ed. Seán Duffy (Liverpool, forthcoming).

32. Sellar, 'Hebridean Sea Kings', 201–2.

33. *Lamont Papers*, no.10, pp.7–8.

34. In one instance it was thought worth recording that a resignation and re-grant of the lands of Benderloch was made in the presence of the 'barons of Argyll'. Was this meant to suggest an extra level of validation? *RRS*, v, no. 366 (p.617), 6 February 1329. Robert I to Sir Duncan Campbell of Benderloch of the lands resigned by his father Sir Donald 'coram nobilibus consilii nostri et baronibus Ergadie'. *HP*, iv, 196–7.

35. *RMS*, i, App.2, no. 692. Appointment between Walter Steward of Scotland and the 'barons of Argyll' on account of the slaying of Ewen Finlayson and other men of said Lord Steward. *The Bruce* (Duncan), 112. 'And he had in his company

the barons of Argyll', *RRS*, v, no.46, pp.333–4. *RMS*, i, App. 1., 106, 'barones nostri in Ergadia'. *RRS*, v, no.46, pp.333–4. (*RMS*, i, App. 1., 106). The recipient of a royal grant to make service for a barony 'just as other of our barons of Argyll make for their baronies'. It is difficult to say with certainty whether royal grants to Argyll landowners that gave lands to be held under the same conditions as 'our other barons of Argyll' provide evidence for the existence of a well-defined set of lordly rights associated with membership of an integrated aristocratic community. They could equally have reflected a charter formula indicating the Crown's willingness to confirm customary privileges in the west in return for political loyalty and military service. Some caution should be exercised in assessing the significance of the term, since it was most often recorded in documents and literature generated by royal administrators and/or by Lowland Scots. In certain cases the characterisation of the inhabitants of Argyll as a separate race was clearly imbued with an element of cultural hostility. An early fourteenth-century verse chronicle description of Robert I's campaigns in the west during 1308 and 1309 incorporated in Walter Bower's *Scotichronicon*, for example, suggested that by his actions Bruce 'had conquered the people of Argyll. This people, reared in arrogant words and deeds, obeyed the king's commands whether willingly or not'. *Chron.Bower* (Watt), vi, 345. See also *The Bruce* (Duncan), 688–9.

36. See K. Simms, *Kings to Warlords*, 16–17, 20, 21–40, 56, 67; E. Fitzpatrick, *Royal Inauguration in Gaelic Ireland,*c. 1100–1600: *A Cultural Landscape Study* (Woodbridge, 2004). I am very grateful to Dr Fitzpatrick for a view of the first chapter of the study ahead of publication.

37. The question will be returned to in discussing the creation of Colin Campbell as the first 'earl' of Argyll in the 1450s, see below pp. 170–171

38. Indeed, the head of the kindred emerged as one of the principal supporters and advisors of Colin's son and successor Duncan. For further details, see Boardman, 'The Campbells and charter lordship', 99–100.

39. *SHS Misc.*, iv, 187; *HP*, iv, 83. It can be argued that the Craignish genealogical tradition reflected a genuine link. Even if this was the case, however, the late adoption of the Campbell surname points to an attempt to suggest that the relationship was far closer than it was.

40. See above, ch. 3, pp, 73–74 *CPL*, iv, 56, 183. In 1372 the pope issued a mandate to the bishop of Argyll to grant a dispensation to Colin and Mary Cambel, who had married despite knowing they were related within the 4th degree of kindred, to re-marry after a suitable period of separation. The offspring of the couple were to be legitimised. An attachment gave the bishop permission to execute the mandate despite the fact that the papal letters did not mention (as Colin and Mary's petition had) that they were related in the 3rd as well as the 4th degree of kindred. When Colin's son and successor, Duncan, granted a charter to the parish kirk of Dunoon in 1440 he asked for masses for the soul of his father Colin and his mother, 'Mariote filie M'Cwill (i.e. MacDougall) Cambel'. NAS RH6/no.304. The seventeenth-century Genealogie of the Campbells is unequivocal in describing Colin's wife as the daughter of John and the granddaughter of Dougall (hence M'Cwill) Campbell.

41. *CPL Benedict XIII*, 243; NLS 'Genealogical material collected by George Crawford', Adv.MSS 35.4.15. Although it is possible that the Duncan Campbell

referred to here was the other Duncan, the eventual heir of Colin Campbell. The Duncan of 1411 was evidently thought also to exercise control over the patronage of the church of St Maelrubha of Melfort, which might favour the latter identification.

42. A 1414 grant by Duncan Campbell of Loch Awe in favour of Ranald Malcolmson of Craignish was witnessed by John Cambell, rector of the church of St Martin, our (Duncan's) brother, Gillespic MacSowarle and Donald his son, Kennito Willalmi Eugenii, lord Celestino Macgillemichal clerico nostro, rector of Melfort, and Martino Malachie capelano nostro. Argyll Muniments, Inveraray, Argyll Charters; NAS RH1/2/87; *AT*, at date; *OPS*, ii, part 1, pp. 97, 125.

43. Chapter 1, pp. 12–13

44. Argyll Muniments, Inveraray, Argyll Charters; *RRS*, vi, 454–5, no.429.

45. It seems probable that the ability to nominate the vicar and rector of the parish kirk of Lochgoilhead was one of the privileges attached to the lordship of Over Cowal. Colin Campbell was certainly attempting to exercise this right before 5 May 1380, but his candidate evidently faced opposition. In May 1380 John de Congallis (Cowal) was said to be rector of the parish church of Kinlochgoil. *CPL Clement VII*, 45. However, on 9 June 1392 Clement VII issued a new mandate to collate John de Congallo to the parish kirk of Kinlochgoil vacant by the transfer of John Malcolm to the parish church of St Peter the Deacon (Kilchrenan). It was narrated that John de Congallo had been 'presented to the living by the true patron, Colin Cambel, and instituted by bishop Martin of Lismore' (i.e. before 1387), 'but his presentation and institution have been contested and he has petitioned the pope for confirmation'. *Ibid.*, 175.

46. *CPL Benedict XIII*, 64; See *Lamont Papers*, nos.19, 20,22, 23, 24 for references to Robert. A tenuous reference suggests that in the same year Colin Óg received a grant of Ardkinglass and other estates from his father.

47. *Lennox Cartularium*, 65–6. The witnesses to the arrangements for the marriage included John Campbell, deacon of Argyll, and Duncan Campbell, lord of Gaunan.

48. *RMS*, i, no.480. At Scone on 7 June 1372 Robert II confirmed a grant by one Malcolm Campbell, son and heir of Dugald Campbell, to his brother 'Dugald' (a scribal slip for Duncan) Campbell of three quarters of Gaunan beside the land of 'Crechan', a quarter of Glen Croe next to Loch Restil, and the land of 'Glenhifren' Mór. The lands were to be held by the said Duncan and his heirs. The beneficiary of this grant was probably the Duncan Campbell of Gaunan who appears as a witness to a number of charters issued by major Argyll/Lennox lords in the closing decades of the fourteenth century. The Campbells of Strachur held the other quarter of Gaunan (Ardgartan) , a quarter of Glencroe, and a pennyland of Kinlochlong. All of these estates were granted by Iver Campbell, lord of Strachur, to his son Arthur Campbell, with the rider that criminals were to be hanged on the gallows of the heir of Malcolm Cambell (presumably the Malcolm son of Dugald mentioned above). So at this stage Malcolm's line were acknowledged as overlords. The arrangements might suggest that there had been a division of a larger lordship between the Strachur and Gaunan Campbells. The landholding of the Campbell families at the northern end of Loch Long was complicated, for there was clearly another Campbell family with lands in the region that failed in the male line in the 1370s.

Certainly Isabel Campbell, described as the daughter and heiress of a Duncan Campbell, was married to William Spens, a burgess of Perth. Duncan's death resulted in Spens' acquiring rights to Glen Douglas, Tarbet, and Tarbet Isles in Arrochar. Isabel also seems to have had a claim to the lands of Drummond in Lennox. In May 1385 Robert Stewart, earl of Fife and Menteith, seems to have exchanged a number of estates in Fife with Isabel and William in return for a grant of the lands of Drummond. Interestingly, Iver Campbell of Strachur had purchased the ward and marriage of the lands of Drummond from Duncan earl of Lennox. Did the MacArthurs arrange the marriage to Spens? It is a possibility that Isabel's father was the brother of Malcolm outlined in the royal grant of 1372. By 1398 it was clear that Colin Campbell had been recognised as the heir to Malcolm as the superior for the lands held by the Strachur Campbells in Over Cowal. *HP*, iv, 18–19.

49. *RMS*, i, no. 866.
50. *HP*, ii, 93–4; *SHS Misc.*, iv, 'The Manuscript History of Craignish', 219–20. Interestingly, the 'Genealogy' seems to have conflated some aspects of the career of Duncan of Ardscotnish, Colin's half-brother, with those of Colin's son Duncan Mór. It is just possible, therefore, that the tale of the attempted assassination of Colin should be placed in the 1390s. It would thus represent an attempt by Duncan Mór, evidently a well-favoured figure within the family, to prevent his father assigning the lordship over to the younger Duncan. Overall, however, the balance of evidence still favours Colin's half-brother as the focus of the assassination plot.
51. Colin Campbell certainly had sons who were far older than Duncan. Most obviously there was the John son of Colin Campbell who had been intended as the marriage partner for Mariota Campbell in 1366. Registrum Aven. vol. 162, f.514. Registrum Vaticanum vol. 255, f.36. It is just conceivable that the John of 1366 was one and the same with John Annan. There was, of course, another (or the same?) brother with the name John who was vicar of Kilmartin in 1414. Argyll Muniments, Inveraray, Argyll Charters; *SHS Misc.*, iv, 292–3.
52. *Liber Cartularium Prioratus Sancti Andree* (Bannatyne Club, 1841), p.5. In addition, papal supplications involving the Campbells seem to have arrived at the papal court at the same time as those dealing with the affairs of Earl Robert. E.g. *CPL Clement VII*, 174–5. A mandate in favour of John of Cowal, presented by Colin Campbell to the parish kirk of Kinlochgoil, was issued on the same day as an order to investigate the marriage of Alexander, earl of Buchan, and Euphemia, countess of Ross, and a mandate to allow the marriage of Earl Robert's son Murdoch to Isabella of Lennox.
53. *CPL Benedict XIII*, p.64 17 June 1396, mandate to confirm, with King Robert's consent, Neil Campbell, deacon of Dunblane diocese, in possession of St Modan in Cowal. Neil doubts the validity of the presentation by Robert king of Scots, patron of the parish, and his institution by John bishop of the Isles.
54. *CPL Benedict XIII*, 79. Robert III supporting the supplication by Robert Duncanson Lamont to marry Anna, daughter of Donald, Lord of the Isles 30 October 1397.
55. *Chron. Wyntoun* (Laing), iii, 69–70; *Chron. Bower* (Watt), viii, 11, 13; *Moray Reg.*, 382.
56. Boardman, *Early Stewart Kings*, 184.

57. At least Alexander's marriage to a daughter of the earl of Lennox and Donald's match with Mary Leslie, the sister of Alexander Leslie, heir to Ross, may both have been made with the consent of Earl Robert. The marriages of Lennox's daughters were expressly to be approved by Fife according to the terms of his deal with Earl Duncan in 1392, while Earl Robert seems to have had custody of Alexander Leslie, the heir to the earldom of Ross, in 1392. Since Leslie's mother Euphemia was also with Fife, it seems most likely her daughter Mary was married to Donald at the Guardian's instigation. Boardman, *Early Stewart Kings*, 184 and notes on pp.192–3.

58. Boardman, *Early Stewart Kings*, 209–214.

59. *Moray Reg.*, 211, 382; R.Nicholson, *Later Middle Ages*, 209–210.

60. *APS*, i, 570.

61. *HP*, iv, 18–19. Robert III had certainly arrived in Dumbarton by 4 August. NLS Fleming of Wigtown Collection, Ch. no. 15730.

62. *APS*, i, 575.

63. *APS*, i, 572–4.

64. Boardman, *Early Stewart Kings*, 235–245.

65. Boardman, *Early Stewart Kings*, 236–237.

66. *ER*, ii, 553. This implies that Duncan was arrested around the time of the seizure of Rothesay and Drummond. It is of course possible that the imprisonment was related to regional disorder around the Firth of Clyde. The sons of Alexander Stewart of Darnley, for example, were also imprisoned in Stirling. Another possibility is that the Duncan Campbell involved was not Colin's heir, but his half-brother Duncan Mór, or even the mysterious Duncan of Gaunan.

67. Boardman, *Early Stewart Kings*, 255–256.

68. Boardman, *Early Stewart Kings*, 278–282.

69. NAS GD 124/1/129.

70. The regality grant presumably indicated that Cowal was not thought to be within the heritable lieutenancy granted to the Campbell lords in 1382.

71. G. Crawford, *The lives and characters, of the officers of the crown and state in Scotland, from the beginning of the reign of King David I to the Union of the two kingdoms: collected from original charters, chartularies, authentick records, and the most approved histories; to which is added, an appendix, containing several original papers relating to the lives, and referring to them* (London, 1736) (hereafter Crawford, *Lives*), p.42. *RMS*, i, App. 2, 1798, 1822, 1857, 1874; *HMC Report*, iv, 478 (20 June 1404); *RMS*, i, Addenda p.651, no.1. John Stewart 'de Achingown filio nostro naturali', witness to Robert III charter issued from Southannan on 28 November 1402. See also *RMS*, ii, no. 3136. Amongst the other witnesses was Alexander, earl of Buchan, the king's brother and Albany's long-time political rival. Within two months of Buchan's appearance at Rothesay his son, also Alexander, would launch a coup against Albany's interests in the inheritance of the earldom of Mar. It is tempting to link this event to the appearance of Buchan at the royal court in June. Boardman, *Early Stewart Kings*, 260–264.

72. *CPL Benedict XIII*, 125–126.

73. Boardman, *Early Stewart Kings*, 290–297. For an argument that suggests that the decision to send the Prince to France came *after* the disaster of Long Hermiston Moor and Fleming's death. Other interpretations are possible,

especially given the contemporary chroniclers' insistence that the *original* aim of the Fleming/Orkney expedition was to convey James to France.

74. *Chron. Bower* (Watt), viii, 63.

75. Karen J. Hunt, 'The Governorship of the First Duke of Albany: 1406–1420' (unpublished Ph.D. Thesis, Edinburgh 1998), esp. Ch. 2.

76. Argyll Muniments, Inveraray, Argyll Charters. Overall, the most significant aspect of this charter may have been the absorption of the lands within Cowal Stewart into the Campbell male descent patrimony. The lands were to descend to Colin and his heirs male, of his body legitimately procreated or to be procreated, whom failing the legitimate and nearest heirs male of said Colin with the surname Campbell and bearing the Campbell arms.

77. *Chron. Bower* (Watt), viii, 75–77

78. *Chron. Bower* (Watt), viii, 77. According to Bower, Albany gathered an army and took Dingwall Castle by the end of the autumn of 1411; *ER*, ii, 213, 239.

79. *Chron. Bower* (Watt), viii, 77. The version of the Scotichronicon known as the Book of Coupar Angus makes Albany's expedition seem rather more aggressive, claiming that the aim was to depopulate all Donald's lands 'citra insulas' Cf. *ER*, ii, 213, 239 which confirms that Albany had been with an army at 'Polgilb contra dominum Insularum' before 27 June 1414.

80. Colin Campbell's charter of 18 June 1412 of the lands of Craignish and others to Ronald Malcolmson of Craignish does not have a place of issue or witnesses. The terms of the charter itself, with specified galley service and the custody of two castles, all to be held under the terms of special retinue service, might reflect the disturbances of that year and/or doubts as to the loyalty of the Craignish kindred.

81. Argyll Muniments, Inveraray, Argyll Charters.

FIVE

The Albany Stewarts

In the years after 1406, held in increasingly dire conditions in the Tower of London, James I may have been tempted, on occasion, to calculate the number and nature of the men he could rely on to work in his interests in his native land. It is unlikely that Duncan Campbell of Loch Awe would have featured prominently in James' thinking. A web of kinship and marital links seemed to make Duncan a natural part of the sprawling Albany Stewart hegemony, presided over by the elderly but formidable Duke Robert, Governor of Scotland. Most importantly, Duncan's son and acknowledged heir, Gillespic, was the product of Duncan's marriage to Duke Robert's daughter (see Table 3).[1] Gillespic, described as the Governor's grandson, was to be found witnessing a charter issued by Duke Robert as early as 1414.[2] In addition, Walter Stewart, the forceful eldest son of Murdoch, 2nd duke of Albany, may have had a liaison with a sister or daughter of Duncan that produced a number of illegitimate children.[3]

Beyond the ties of blood, there were other ways in which Albany lordship came to influence the social and political affairs of Argyll. Of particular import was the advance of one Finlay of Albany to the bishopric of Argyll early in 1420.[4] Finlay had served as chaplain to Duke Robert before leaving Scotland to study in England in or shortly after 1396. Finlay returned to the northern kingdom before 30 August 1409, by which time he had become a Dominican friar, acting as the custodian of the Ayr convent of the Blackfriars and as vicar-general of the order in Scotland. His association with Duke Robert was evidently renewed, as he was styled Albany's confessor in 1416 and 1417. In 1419–20 Finlay was elected as bishop of Argyll and received papal provision to the diocese on 31 January 1420.[5] As a cleric with a long record of service to Duke Robert and his family, Finlay's elevation to the bishopric clearly increased the Albany Stewarts' influence in the diocese. However, the appointment of a Dominican friar also served to resurrect a longer-term link between the Blackfriars and the diocese of Argyll. For most of the century between 1264 and 1362 x 1387 the bishopric of Argyll had been held by three men trained as Dominican friars, two of whom seem to have been drawn from the kindred of the MacDougall lords of Argyll.[6] The origin of the link between the Dominicans and the ecclesiastical and social hierarchy in Argyll may well lie in the career of the charismatic Dominican bishop Clement of Dunblane.[7] Bishop Clement had been given powers to govern the diocese of Argyll during a prolonged vacancy in the 1240s and he seems to have played a major role in encouraging the military expeditions of Alexander II into the province. The thirteenth-century Dominicans were members of a recently founded order still imbued with a steely sense of mission. They regarded themselves as the shock troops of Christian orthodoxy, the 'Hounds of Christ', highly trained and educated preachers capable of combating and extinguishing the growth of heretical thought and practice across Europe. Although primarily seen now as an urban order, the Dominicans possessed an evangelical zeal that also encouraged the Blackfriars to appear in areas where Christian orthodoxy was challenged by heresy, the lack of a regular church structure, and/or the attractions of alternative religious observances. Within two decades of the order's establishment, the 'Hounds of Christ' were prowling along the dangerous marches of Christian Europe.[8] Whether Clement and his Dominican successors regarded or portrayed Argyll as an area that required reform and revitalisation in its spiritual life and observance is impossible to say. The convergence of Alexander II's expeditions into Argyll with the king's support for the foundation of Dominican houses in a number of Scottish burghs may well have knitted together the projects of establishing royal political control in the west and spiritual renewal.[9] It is interesting to note that a collection of *exempla* compiled by an English Dominican c.1263 included an account of two friars sent to preach 'in the Scottish Isles [ad insulas Scocie]' where they taught young women troubled by evil spirits [incubi] how to resist their assaults.[10] The story might have been chosen as an exemplum precisely because, to a Cambridge-based Dominican, the 'Scottish Isles' provided a backdrop of physical remoteness and spiritual and cultural strangeness that highlighted the inspirational endurance and bravery of the preachers. This view in itself might be regarded as significant, and it does not preclude the possibility that underlying the tale was a contemporary (i.e. mid-thirteenth-century) Dominican view that the order's mission *did* embrace the Scottish Isles and west coast. The training of kinsmen of the MacDougall lords of Argyll as friars, presumably in one of the early Scottish foundations such as Stirling, Glasgow, Perth or Ayr, suggests that the aristocratic elite in the province quickly developed, or was forced to develop, an attachment to the order. In the thirteenth century, then, Argyll seems to have become something of a Dominican province, with the region's ruling aristocratic families cultivating links to the order's urban houses, particularly, perhaps, to the foundation in the burgh of Stirling.

The Albany Stewart domination of Stirling and the earldoms of Menteith and Lennox and the multiple marriage links between the Governor's family and the Campbells did not, of course, guarantee an amicable relationship or unquestioning loyalty. Duncan Campbell's paramount concern remained the fortune and security of his own lineage. However, it is difficult to escape the conclusion that, by the time of Duke Robert's death on or around 3 September 1420, the Campbells of Loch Awe were entirely comfortable with Albany governance of the kingdom. After Duke Robert's death his eldest son and heir, Murdoch, took over as Governor of the kingdom in the name of James I.[11] Murdoch, however, was beset by problems within his own kindred. In particular, the new Governor had a strained relationship with his eldest surviving son, Walter Stewart. Murdoch's attempts to secure the earldom of Lennox for a younger son, Alexander, were resisted by Walter, who clearly intended that the three Albany earldoms of Fife, Menteith and Lennox should descend to himself as a unified patrimony. The rivalry between Murdoch and Walter spilled out into other areas, with the Governor's heir also providing the principal opposition to Murdoch's attempts to negotiate the release of James I in the period 1423–4.[12] Murdoch may not have been especially enthusiastic about the prospect of his long-captive cousin returning to assume the crown, but the general political situation within and outwith Scotland after 1420 increasingly encouraged this course of action. The growing support for serious efforts to obtain James' release amongst magnates such as Archibald, 4th earl of Douglas, coincided with the death of Henry V, who had shown no sign of wishing to negotiate over the issue, in 1422. The dominant figures in the administration of the infant English king Henry VI were far more willing to contemplate a settlement with the Scots.[13] Eventually, in a general council of August 1423, Murdoch was forced to commit the Scots to meaningful negotiations over James' deliverance.[14] Opposition to this development appears to have been led by Murdoch's son Walter, who was involved in negotiations with the French crown throughout the winter of 1423–4. Walter's stance seems to have enjoyed the support of his adherents from the earldom of Lennox, including his grandfather, the aged Earl Duncan.[15] Despite Walter's misgivings, arrangements for James I's liberation were successfully concluded after extensive negotiations in York and London. In early April James returned to his long-lost kingdom and received the surrender of Duke Murdoch's seal as governor of the realm at Melrose.[16]

The attitude of Duncan Campbell to the developments of 1423–4 is difficult to discern, for the Campbell lord was not obviously aligned with Duke Murdoch, his son Walter, or those acting in James I's interests during 1423. Moreover, Duncan's social and marital links underwent some possibly significant changes in that year. Duncan's first wife, Duke Murdoch's sister, was still alive in 1420 but seems to have died shortly thereafter. Certainly in 1423 Duncan had obtained a new bride, supplicating the papacy to allow his marriage to Margaret, daughter of John Stewart of Ardgowan.[17] The Stewarts of Auchingowan held land in Cowal and Renfrew and had, some twenty years earlier, sold various estates to Duncan's father. The match may then have been a product of largely local considerations and ambitions, but the fact that John Stewart of Ardgowan was an illegitimate son of Robert III and a half-brother of the about to be released James I may also have been relevant.

Whatever his political affiliation, Duncan was chosen as one of the noble hostages to be sent to England in 1424 to act as a surety for the payment of the king's ransom to the English crown. Duncan probably entered English custody in April 1424 and would be held at various locations in the southern kingdom until at least 16 July 1425.[18] Duncan's enforced absence from his own lordship proved, in the end, to be extremely fortuitous. While the lord of Loch Awe whiled away the dreary hours in a succession of English fortresses, the political landscape of Argyll and Lennox was brutally redrawn by the restored James I.[19] Even before his long-delayed coronation, James took steps to deal with Walter Stewart, the man who had consistently opposed schemes to secure his release. On 13 May Walter was arrested in Edinburgh on the king's orders and consigned to captivity on the Bass Rock.[20] It seems that Walter's father, Duke Murdoch, connived with the king in the arrest of his troublesome son, but the alliance between James and his cousin was a temporary and ill-starred affair. The king's assault on Walter Stewart's Lennox affinity gathered momentum later in 1424 with the arrest (before 7 January 1425) of Walter's grandfather, Duncan, earl of Lennox, and Sir

Robert Graham.[21] By November 1424, James I's agent Sir John Colquhoun of Luss had obtained control of Dumbarton Castle, while Sir John Stewart of Dundonald, James' illegitimate uncle, also seems to have taken on the role of safeguarding royal interests in the Lennox over the winter of 1424–5.[22] While the king busily undercut the established Albany Stewart hegemony in and around the Firth of Clyde, Duke Murdoch's position became increasingly marginal and vulnerable. Eventually, Albany appears to have attempted to organise resistance to the king and his policies in a parliament that opened in Perth on 13 March 1425.[23] Duke Murdoch's defiance provoked James into another tactical pre-emptive strike against the Albany Stewarts. On 21 March, the ninth day of the parliament, Duke Murdoch, his son Alexander, Sir John Montgomery of that Ilk and the duke's secretary Allan of Otterburn were all arrested (although Montgomery and Otterburn were subsequently released). As an almost immediate follow-up to these arrests, the king seized control of the castles of Falkland and Doune, the chief seats of Duke Murdoch's earldoms of Fife and Menteith respectively.[24] In Doune the king's forces apprehended Murdoch's wife Isabella, daughter of the earl of Lennox. Initially imprisoned in St Andrews Castle, the duke and duchess were eventually held in Caerlaverock and Tantallon castles respectively, while the king made arrangements for a trial of the entire Albany Stewart family. The spark that lit the king's anger in March 1424 remains uncertain. The statutes ratified by the parliament on 13 March seem, on the whole, to be rather bland and uncontroversial.[25] Given that the arrests took place over a week after the legislative programme had been drawn up and approved, Brown may well be right to suggest that it was the failure of the assembly to acquiesce in the king's financial demands, or Albany's opposition to the trial of his son Walter, a royal captive since May 1424, in the judicial sessions of the parliament following on from the issuing of legislation, that precipitated the final crisis.[26] At any rate, the confrontation in March apparently sealed the fate of Murdoch and his kinsmen. Around mid-April 1425 James summoned a new parliament, this time to deliver judgement on Duke Murdoch and the other royal captives. This ominous development inspired the few kinsmen of Duke Murdoch left at liberty after the parliament of March 1425 to take direct action in a bid to force the king to compromise. The youngest son of Duke Murdoch, James, who had evaded the royal dragnet in March, raised rebellion in the Lennox aided by Finlay, bishop of Argyll, and on or around 3 May attacked the burgh of Dumbarton. James Stewart's assault resulted in the death of the king's uncle and enforcer in the region, John Stewart of Dundonald, and thirty-two of his men. Crucially, however, Sir John Colquhoun retained control of Dumbarton Castle, and without the protection of the mighty fortress, which proved itself invulnerable to prolonged sieges on a number of occasions in the fourteenth and fifteenth centuries, James' rebellion faltered in the face of determined royal pursuit. Eventually, James and Bishop Finlay were forced to abandon the Lennox and flee to Ireland.[27] The failure of James Stewart's rebellion meant that nothing could now save his imprisoned kinsmen, and the events in and around Dumbarton may have done little more than justify the king's accusations against the Albany Stewarts. On 24 May a parliamentary assise at Stirling condemned to death Walter Stewart, who was immediately beheaded before the royal castle. On the following day Murdoch Stewart, duke of Albany, his son Alexander, and his father-in-law Duncan, earl of Lennox, were similarly condemned and executed.[28] All four men were buried in the Dominican House in Stirling.[29] In the aftermath of the parliament, the king's forces mopped up the last vestiges of open resistance, besieging Inchmurrin Castle on Loch Lomond, still held by men loyal to James Stewart, and forcing its surrender on 8 June.[30]

As reports of the demise of the Albany Stewarts reached Duncan Campbell in England, the reaction of the lord of Loch Awe must have wavered between incredulity and horror. The men executed in 1425 were respectively Duncan's former brother-in-law (Duke Murdoch), his uncle (Duncan, earl of Lennox), and two of his nephews (Walter and Alexander). A third nephew, James, had been forced into exile in Ireland along with the bastard sons of Walter Stewart, who may well have been Duncan Campbell's grandsons. Finlay of Albany, the bishop of Argyll, Duncan's own province, had also become a political refugee.[31] Surveying the wreckage of the political and social elite of Argyll and the Lennox, Duncan Campbell may have been less than overjoyed at the prospect of his imminent return to Scotland as one of a group of hostages scheduled to be released shortly after 16 July 1425. Given Duncan's extensive ties to the Albany Stewarts and the Lennox earls, he could hardly have been sure of the welcome awaiting from a king who had mercilessly annihilated the leading figures in both families and who was still in active pursuit of James Stewart and the disgraced Bishop Finlay. Nevertheless, by 31 March 1427 the lord of Loch Awe had returned to Scotland.[32]

For the half-century from 1371 Campbell lords had enjoyed a generally cordial relationship with the Stewart kings and governors of the realm. After 1426 Duncan faced a rather less appealing political landscape in which he would have to fight to maintain his family's rights and status under the rule of a monarch who seems to have regarded the Campbell hegemony in Argyll with deep suspicion. 'Friendly Duncan' would have to find new strategies and devices to preserve the fortunes of his house.[33]

Given Duncan Campbell's associations with the Albany Stewarts, it was hardly a surprise that James I looked to cultivate new and more trustworthy royal agents to protect his interests in and around the 'rebel' province of Argyll. The return of the exiled James Stewart to avenge his family and, perhaps, assert his own claim to the Scottish crown, remained a very real fear for the king.[34] A parliament of March 1426 passed a number of statutes designed to control and regulate the passage of galleys and other ships between Scotland and Ireland, principally because 'the Kingis notorious rebells are reset [maintained] in the Irischry of Ireland'.[35] However, the final comment on the implementation of the legislation displays an interesting sensitivity to the way in which the action might be perceived by the inhabitants of Gaelic Ireland and the Scottish west. The royal deputies appointed to enforce the regulation of shipping contacts were enjoined to make clear 'that this [action] is not done for hatred nor breaking of the alde frendschip betuix the king of Scotlande and his liegis ande the gude alde frendis of Erschry of Irelande but only to eschew the perils forsaid'.[36] The king's anxiety about the ability of the 'notorious rebels' to re-enter the realm from Ireland presumably reflected a concern that the Albany Stewart cause might yet attract significant support within Scotland. The execution of Duke Murdoch, the former Governor, and his kinsmen had been a traumatic event for many in the kingdom. Although James I had managed to convince the members of the assise of May 1425 to allow the axe to fall, there may well have remained a sense of shock, outrage and sympathy for the Albany Stewarts. Irish chronicles reporting on the events of 1425 saw the death of the Albany Stewarts in terms of the king's 'treachery'.[37] The most curious evidence for the cultivation of a view of 1425 that did not present James I in a favourable light comes from the chronicler Walter Bower's strangely schizophrenic treatment of the events of that year. Bower's major work, the *Scotichronicon*, is wholly supportive of the king and passes over the demise of Duke Murdoch and his family with little comment.[38] However, Bower also produced an abridged version of his chronicle, the so-called Book of Coupar Angus, which incorporated highly positive descriptions of the men executed in 1425. In this version Walter Stewart was noted as 'a man very tall in stature, most loving as a person, very wise in his speech, highly pleasing to everybody and loved by all'. Walter's death 'was lamented not only by those who knew him but also those who had never seen him on account of his admirable reputation'.[39] Similarly, Walter's father and brother were mourned as 'giants among men of noble and refined character'.[40] If the mid-fifteenth-century Book of Coupar Angus reflected in any way the opinions of some sections of the political community around 1425, then James I was right to feel uneasy.

The king's attempt to secure his position in the west inevitably affected the Lord of Loch Awe's dominance of mid-Argyll. There was no dramatic confrontation; instead Duncan steadily found his supremacy in the province undercut in a variety of ways. The first loss may have been the Campbells' hereditary lieutenancy of Argyll. Although there was no explicit recorded annulment of the 1382 grant, events shortly after James I's death in 1437 suggest that the lieutenancy of Argyll may not have been allowed to operate during the king's adult rule.[41] Moreover, it was clear that after 1425 a number of men felt emboldened to challenge the lord of Loch Awe's position in mid-Argyll. One such was Sir John Scrymgeour, lord of Glassary. Before 1424, Neil 'Colini Cambel', the archdeacon of Argyll, had been engaged in a campaign to oust James Scrymgeour, clearly the nominee and a kinsman of Sir John, from the rectorship of the parish church of St Columba in Glassary.[42] The king's return saw the Scrymgeours sweep on to the offensive. By March 1427 Sir John had raised an action before royal courts against Duncan Campbell over possession of a third of Glassary, a case that had apparently lain moribund for some seventy years.[43] James I indicated his willingness and ability to interfere in Campbell's heartland by taking the lands involved into royal possession while the dispute over the estates was decided before the king's council.[44] The quarrel between Scrymgeour and Campbell ground on over the next five years. Duncan's repeated appearances before royal councils and parliaments at Perth (and elsewhere) hammered home the message that the king had both the right and ability to judge the affairs of Argyll. Similarly, the crown's assumption of direct control of the disputed estates provided another indication of the reach and ambition of the new king.[45] By 1428, it was also clear that Sir John Scrymgeour had successfully upheld his right to appoint clerics to the parish kirk of Glassary, apparently with the support of the king.[46]

Campbell reverses in Glassary were indicative of a wider threat to Duncan Campbell's ability to provide men to benefices inside Argyll. As part of his campaign to secure a hold on the province in 1426, James I had initiated proceedings to remove the rebellious and exiled Bishop Finlay from his diocese. By May of the following year George Lauder had been provided to the bishopric.[47] As bishop, Lauder took over the patronage of the parish kirks of Glenorchy and Lochgoilhead, which had previously been in the gift of the lord of Loch Awe. The bishop's appointee in Glenorchy was his own kinsman James Lauder, while Lochgoilhead was assigned over to one Peter of Dalkeith.[48] That Lauder's control of ecclesiastical patronage was a by-product of James I's political agenda in the region and dependent on the king's support is suggested by the Campbell-inspired backlash against the bishop's appointees following James' death in 1437.[49]

On a more general level, James I seems initially to have ignored or bypassed the Clan Campbell in his attempts to govern the west in the years after 1425. The most radical departure from the policies of the Albany Stewarts saw the king develop an understanding with Alexander, Lord of the Isles. The rapprochement between Alexander and the king was fuelled on the one hand by James I's need to find allies prepared to support his actions against the Albany Stewarts and on the other by Alexander's desire to obtain royal recognition for his claims to the earldom of Ross. Differences between the two men over the ultimate destination of the earldom of Ross meant that the alliance was short-lived, and by 1428 the relationship was on the verge of collapse.[50] James I sought to deal with the problem with a typically decisive and duplicitous strike against his opponent and his principal supporters in Ross. Summoning a number of Highland magnates, including the Lord of the Isles, to a meeting at Inverness in August 1428, the king arranged for the wholesale arrest of those who attended.[51] The royal strike against 'nearly all the notable men of the north' was not, however, the only Highland business dealt with by the August 1428 'parliament'. In the aftermath of the mass arrest, a number of magnates were placed in royal custody, while two men, Alexander MacRuairi of Garmoran and a John MacArthur, were singled out for unspecified crimes and beheaded.[52] The identity of MacArthur is uncertain, although it has been suggested that he might have been a member of the Campbell of Strachur family that held a number of estates around the Argyll/Lennox border.[53] More striking is Bower's report of another act of royal justice that he seems to place in the parliament of August 1428. 'Then also James Campbell [Jacobus Cambel] was hanged after being charged and convicted of the killing of John of the Isles [Johannis de Insulis]', now usually taken to be Sir John Mór, lord of Dunivaig and the Glens.[54] The identification of Bower's John of the Isles as John Mór was not made explicitly until the seventeenth-century 'History of the Mac-Donalds' (hereafter the *Sleat History*) provided a great elaboration of the circumstances surrounding John's death, suggesting that it resulted from Campbell's botched attempt to arrest the lord of Dunivaig after the latter's refusal to act against the interests of his captive nephew on the crown's behalf.[55] Even if we accept that the victim of James Campbell was John Mór, the chronology provided by the *Sleat History* remains problematic. Given this unreliable chronology and the fact that the author had several axes to grind in relation to the crown's treatment of the MacDonalds in later ages, the narrative should be treated circumspectly.[56] Most obviously, if Bower was correct in associating the August 1428 'parliament' with the execution of John Mór's killer, then the lord of Dunivaig could hardly have been tempted to act against a nephew who was only made captive by James I at this point. Moreover it seems unlikely that in 1427–8 a Campbell lord would have been entrusted with the sensitive task of either turning the lord of Dunivaig against his nephew or arresting him (indeed the whole scenario of an attempted 'arrest' might only have been suggested because the episode was linked in Bower and later chronicles with James I's operation at Inverness).[57] The king's willingness to execute James Campbell hardly suggests that the culprit was a loyal and valued servant acting in the interests of the crown. Instead, the reported events seem to point straightforwardly towards James I punishing a Campbell lord for his slaughter of a John of the Isles (perhaps, but not certainly, John Mór of Dunivaig) who was under royal protection. Taken as a whole, the events of August 1428 do not suggest that Duncan and his kinsmen were reliable and favoured agents of royal authority in the west.

Alexander of the Isles' imprisonment after August 1428 was short-lived. King James evidently thought that the Lord of the Isles had been thoroughly cowed and allowed his release.[58] By the spring of 1429 it was clear that James had made a major miscalculation. Alexander and his forces launched an assault on Inverness, burning the burgh but failing to take the castle and eventually retreating west. The Clan Donald may originally have intended a far more devastating and ambitious assault on

James I, for very early in 1429 a fleet had appeared in Ireland to convey Murdoch Stewart's son James back to Scotland, presumably to mount a direct dynastic challenge to the king.[59] The looming crisis for James I was averted only by the death of James Mór shortly after the arrival of the fleet intended to return him to Scotland.[60]

The death of Duncan Campbell's kinsman and pretender to the Scottish throne may, in the long term, have been a significant factor in rehabilitating the lord of Loch Awe. Moreover, the king's need for support in his struggle with Clan Donald meant that the crown could hardly afford to ignore the lord of Argyll. As it was, James I's war with Clan Donald in the north raged on for the next two years. The effects of a crushing royal victory on 23 June 1429 in Lochaber or Badenoch were largely negated by an equally spectacular victory by the forces of the lordship over the king's lieutenant Alexander, earl of Mar, at Inverlochy in September 1431.[61]

The attitude of the leader of Clan Campbell to the intrigues involving James Stewart and the great struggle in Ross is unclear. Shocked, perhaps even angered, by the fall of the Albanys and harassed in his own province by the secular and ecclesiastical agents of the crown, Duncan may have felt little affection for the king. The tenor of Campbell/Clan Donald relations in the 1420s is also difficult to gauge. There was, of course, despite the fevered writings of later historians, no natural and entrenched social and political antipathy between the two families. The Campbells and some of their close associates, such as the earls of Lennox and the Lamonts of Cowal, had happily concluded marriage alliances with the ruling dynasties of Clan Donald and other Hebridean kindreds during the fourteenth and early fifteenth centuries. As recently as 1420 papal approval had been sought for a marriage between Duncan's heir Gillespic, and Mariota, daughter of Donald, Lord of the Isles, although the marriage never seems to have been completed.[62] However, two considerations may have encouraged Duncan Campbell to support royal action in and around the Firth of Clyde. One was the realisation that any defiance of royal demands was likely to have disastrous consequences for Campbell interests in mid-Argyll and Cowal. In addition, Duncan had inherited apparently long-moribund claims to a range of estates in 'royal' lordships on the Firth of Clyde, particularly Knapdale and Arran. In these areas it was unclear whether Campbell rights were being disregarded because the crown refused to acknowledge the family's titles, or because parts of both lordships had come under the effective control of Clan Donald. In either case, Campbell involvement in a successful royal campaign in the region held out the possibility of the recovery of these estates. In the spring of 1430 the king may have been making preparations for just such an intensification of his efforts against the lordship in and around the Firth of Clyde. As a result, the parliament of March 1430 in Perth seems to have been something of a watershed in the relationship between Duncan and James. From 1427 onwards Duncan had avoided judgement over the Glassary dispute with Scrymgeour by the simple expedient of not appearing before royal courts when summoned. In March 1430, however, the lord of Loch Awe was clearly confident enough to face the issue head on. The overall political context of the parliament strengthened Duncan's hand. The king was evidently laying plans for summer campaigns against the lordship and required military and political support from Argyll. The legislation of the parliament (which opened on 6 March) included the stipulation that all lands in the west and north, and especially those 'fornent the isles', should provide galleys at the rate of one oar for every four marks of land.[63] The galleys were to be ready by May 1431. Clearly this statute would have had a huge impact on Duncan Campbell, and could only really work across a great stretch of the west coast with the co-operation of the lord of Argyll. Duncan's sojourn at Perth in March/April 1430 also saw the Campbell lord attempt to conclude a number of legal disputes that had dogged him since his return to Scotland in 1426. Most obviously, on 20 March 1430, consideration of the case between Scrymgeour and Campbell was handed over by the parliament to the sheriff of Perth. By 24 April 1431 terms for the settlement had been drawn up that were largely favourable to the lord of Loch Awe. In return for the Campbell lands of Menstrie in Clackmannanshire, Scrymgeour would give Campbell heritable possession of two thirds of Glassary with the patronage of the parish kirk. In addition Duncan was to receive Scrymgeour's right to superiority of a third of Glassary (which seems to have been the initial cause of the dispute).[64] Although the carrying out of the exchange was delayed, it was clear that Scrymgeour was contemplating the abandonment of all his interests inside Argyll if suitable compensation could be arranged. On the same day, 20 March 1430, as the Scrymgeour case was assigned over to the sheriff of Perth, Duncan reached another significant agreement with his kinsman George Campbell of Loudoun, by which Loudoun abandoned any claims that he might have to lands within the parish of Lochgoilhead.[65]

The deliberations of the March parliament bore fruit in the summer of 1430 in the shape of an expedition, perhaps led by the king himself, against his Clan Donald foes in Kintyre and Knapdale.[66] It seems likely that James received the full support of Duncan Campbell and his kinsmen during the summer of 1430, although the lord of Loch Awe may have been less than overwhelmed by the rewards that came his way. In the 1350s Duncan's grandfather, Gillespic, had received charters from Sir John Menteith of extensive estates in Knapdale and Arran, along with the keepership of Castle Sween (Knapdale) and Lochranza (Arran).[67] These Campbell claims were disregarded by the king during 1430. Instead, James turned to men who had proven their personal loyalty to him in the Albany crisis of 1425. At Perth on 10 August 1430, Alexander Montgomery of Ardrossan and Robert Cunningham of Kilmaurs, the men who had captured Inchmurrin in 1425, received a royal charter making them custodians of Kintyre and Knapdale for the next seven years. The islands of Gigha and Danna were included in the grant, along with the keepership of the king's castle of Sween and the fortress at Skipness.[68] The extensive judicial powers given over to Montgomery and Cunningham effectively made them royal lieutenants in Knapdale and Kintyre. Although details of the royal settlement in Bute and Arran have not survived, there was absolutely no indication that Duncan's claims in Arran were allowed. That the lord of Loch Awe still harboured ambitions in Knapdale and Arran is strongly suggested by the fact that he had a notarial copy of Menteith's original charter drawn up at Stirling in May 1433.[69] However, Campbell disappointment with the distribution of royal favour in the Firth of Clyde should not be exaggerated. Duncan's re-engagement with royal government may not have brought a territorial bonanza, but it undoubtedly brought a measure of security to the family's position, particularly perhaps in Cowal. As part of the Stewartry, the lordship of Cowal was held directly by King James. Nevertheless, even if many formal territorial and legal rights lay in the hands of the crown, Duncan Campbell seems to have been the dominant local lord.[70] Royal displeasure could thus have an immediate impact on Duncan's wide-ranging territorial interests in the peninsula.

Part of the change in Duncan's relationship with the crown from around 1430 may be traced to Campbell's deliberate cultivation of links to men close to the king and active in royal government. These links were reflected in, and reinforced by, a profound shift in the marriage strategies pursued by Duncan Campbell. Where Duncan's ancestors over three generations had largely looked for marriage partners in and around the Firth of Clyde, the lord of Loch Awe cast his gaze further east and to the centre of James' court circle and royal administration. Before his death in July x October 1432 Campbell's eldest son and heir, Gillespic, seems to have married Elizabeth Somerville, daughter of Thomas Somerville of Carnwath, a Lanarkshire lord who had risen in royal service and who, in 1430, was the royal justiciar south of the Forth.[71] The Somerville marriage may well have been part of a wider development, namely Duncan's attachment to one of the rising stars in the royal establishment, James Douglas of Balvenie, the future 7th earl of Douglas.[72] From 1430, Balvenie and his associates began to feature as witnesses to Campbell business conducted outwith Argyll.[73]

Friendly Duncan's charm offensive, aimed at men close to the king, was indicative of other subtle changes in the organisation and nature of Campbell lordship during the 1430s. Duncan Campbell's attendance at the March parliament of 1430 and its associated judicial sessions entailed the lord of Loch Awe spending around two months in and around Perth. The commitment perhaps reflected a dawning realisation that in James I's Scotland the successful defence and exercise of aristocratic power required direct representation in and around the royal court. James, an aggressive and interventionist monarch, had brought home to Duncan Campbell the effect which royal indifference or hostility could have on the territorial and political ambitions of Clan Campbell in the west. The interests of Clan Campbell could no longer be defended through a pursuit of regional goals alone; a Campbell presence in the institutions, assemblies and emerging aristocracy centred on the crown was also essential. Although Duncan himself could never be described as a 'court' aristocrat, his exercise of lordship after 1430 clearly set the family on the course that would allow Duncan's grandson Colin, 1st earl of Argyll, to emerge as the most important court politician of the late fifteenth-century kingdom.

On a practical level, Duncan's attendance at meetings of parliaments and general councils in the 1430s raised a number of logistical problems. Where, for example, were the lord of Loch Awe and his retinue to stay when they made their way in from the west? The problem of accommodation may have been partly solved by Duncan's re-invigoration of his family's links to the Carmelite friary of Tullilum near Perth, and the Dominican friaries in Stirling and Glasgow. The Campbell connection with the Carmelites dated back to at least 1387. In that year, Duncan's father Colin and his wife had been admitted to the confraternity of the order, with the provision that on the anniversary of Colin Campbell's death the friars of the order would say masses for the souls of their benefactor, his wife, and children.[74] Thereafter, there was no record of further Campbell generosity to the Carmelites until March 1431, when Dugald Campbell, probably Duncan's brother and foremost counsellor, gave over an annual rent to the Tullilum house. The next year, Duncan himself granted an annual rent to Tullilum from Campbell lands in the earldom of Menteith. Both the grants were made while the Campbell lords were in Perth attending the March parliaments of 1431 and 1432 and may reflect the increasing demands made on the order's hospitality during the early 1430s by Duncan and his kinsmen.[75] A similar association developed between Duncan Campbell and his successors and the Dominican house in Stirling. The loss of the Stirling friars' cartulary means that we have no record of Campbell grants to that particular establishment, but there are certainly indications that Campbell lords were regular visitors to the friary.[76] The development of the Stirling link may have reflected the old bond between the Dominicans and the province of Argyll as well, perhaps, as residual Campbell affection for their kinsmen who had gone under the axe in 1425. The tombs of the Albany Stewarts and the earl of Lennox had been raised beside the high altar of the Stirling house, and the surviving members of the Albany Stewart family seem to have regarded the Dominican house almost as a family mausoleum.[77]

Over the course of 1430–31 Duncan had plotted a course back, if not into the full sun of royal favour, then at least into calmer and less threatening waters. The chief beneficiary of Duncan's careful manoeuvring was clearly his son and acknowledged heir, Gillespic, provided with a bride and an influential father-in-law. However, on a date between 10 July and 28 October 1432 Duncan received a sickening blow, with the premature death of Gillespic, who left behind an infant son, Colin, by his Somerville wife.[78] In the aftermath of Gillespic's death Duncan faced a number of new problems. The succession to Duncan's own lordship was thrown into doubt, with the lord of Loch Awe's remaining adult son a potential danger to the position of his infant grandson. With characteristic care Duncan spent the mournful autumn of 1432 arranging the affairs of the family. In

October 1432 Duncan's eldest surviving son, Colin, received a heritable grant of the Campbell lands in Glenorchy.[79] The grant effectively signalled the emergence of Colin of Glenorchy as the second most powerful figure within the clan, a position he would maintain for most of the next two decades. The gift was also intended to reward, and ensure, Colin's support for the right of his young nephew and namesake to succeed to the wider Campbell lordship. Colin of Glenorchy's long and active role in the governance of the family after his brother's death helped to ensure that by the second half of the fifteenth century the Glenorchy line had emerged as the most powerful and significant cadet branch of the Loch Awe family. At times, indeed, it may have seemed that the personal authority held by Sir Colin and his heirs made them a rival focus for the loyalty and affection of the wider clan. The pre-eminence of the Glenorchy branch in the 1430s and 1440s had another significant long-term effect, in that Sir Colin was able to call on the resources of the kindred to open up a new area of territorial and political expansion in those areas bordering his own personal lordship. Thus began the slow march of Campbell power eastward from Argyll into Breadalbane and Highland Perthshire.

For the remainder of James I's reign, Duncan Campbell's political activity seems to have been rather low-key. But while the relationship between the king and the leading figure in Argyll had been the subject of steady improvement since the opening of the reign, elsewhere problems were multiplying for the monarch. Growing tension produced by the king's aggressive financial policies and interference in the affairs of a number of localities was compounded by the catastrophic failure of an attempted siege of the English-held castle at Roxburgh in August 1436.[80] Duncan Campbell turned out in the royal hosting of 1436 and was belatedly rewarded for his efforts on the king's behalf with a grant of land in 1452.[81] The collapse of the assault on Roxburgh was a blow to the image and authority of a king who was already deeply unpopular with many of his subjects. Over the winter of 1436–7 the king's uncle Walter Stewart, earl of Atholl, was at the centre of a growing conspiracy to take action against his overbearing nephew. On the night of 20–21 February 1437 the earl of Atholl's plans came to fruition when the king was brutally assassinated in his chambers in the Dominican house at Perth by a band largely recruited from former Albany adherents. These men had gnawed on old enmities in the twelve long years since Duke Murdoch and his kin had gone to the gallows, but the guiding hand remained Atholl's.[82] Earl Walter's plan in the wake of James' death may well have been to advance his own right, as the dead king's nearest adult kinsman, to govern the realm in the name of the six-year-old James II. Atholl's schemes were thwarted by his failure to obtain possession of the young king and by the willingness of a number of magnates to support the position of James' widow, Queen Joan, who had fled to Edinburgh shortly after her husband's demise. For a number of weeks there seems to have been a stalemate as Atholl and his supporters dug in in Highland Perthshire and the queen cast around for political and military assistance.

The immediate reaction of Duncan Campbell to the death of James I was likely to have been rather mixed. The lord of Loch Awe may well have sympathised with, if not shared, the vengeful pro-Albany sentiments of the assassins. Yet the simple fact was that, beyond a few irreconcilable individuals, affection for the Albany Stewarts was not the basis on which to rally widespread and effective support in 1437. Nor was Earl Walter, who had happily sat on the assize that condemned Duke Murdoch, the obvious figurehead for those with genuine Albany connections. In February/March 1437 Atholl was not only complicit in an act of regicide, but had failed to attain control of any of the significant levers of power in the realm. Earl Walter's only option would seem to have been to sit tight and build a political and military alliance of sufficient power to convince those in possession of the infant James II that they had to negotiate a settlement with him in order to govern the realm. This was not a position of strength from which to bargain for the support of the Campbell lords of Argyll. Moreover, Duncan Campbell's efforts to develop a working relationship with James I had given the lord of Loch Awe a number of ties to James I loyalists such as Somerville and Balvenie, whose attitude to the murderers of the king was likely to be unequivocal. The Campbells swiftly chose where their loyalties, and advantage, lay. It seems likely that Duncan and his eldest surviving son, Colin of Glenorchy, attended the coronation of the young James II at Holyrood on 26 March 1437 and the parliament, held on either the same or the following day, which tried and sentenced to death the earl of Atholl, who had been apprehended earlier in the month.[83] Colin was certainly in Edinburgh on 27 March, when he received the right to use a portable altar from the papal nuncio Bishop Anthony Altani of Urbino, who seems to have been in constant attendance on the widowed queen after James' death.[84] The papal nuncio clearly regarded the Campbells with some favour in the fraught weeks after 20 February, also supporting the claims of a Campbell cleric to the archdeaconry of Argyll against the wishes of George, bishop of Argyll. Either before or shortly after James II's coronation, the Campbell lords emphasised their loyalty to the new regime by involving themselves in the attempts to capture Earl Walter's fellow conspirators. Colin of Glenorchy was later given a grant of lands in Strathearn for his part in the apprehension of one of the men personally involved in James I's assassination, Thomas Chambers.[85]

Like many others, Duncan Campbell may well have found it easier to express affection and sympathy for James I after the king was dead. The lord of Loch Awe's reaction to the monarch's political legacy was also ambivalent. After 1437, Duncan embarked on a course that involved overt displays of loyalty to those who governed in the name of the young James II on the national stage, and at the same time the destruction of James I's political and administrative settlement in the west. Eleven years spent in search of reconciliation with James I had taught Duncan that the politics of the court could hardly be ignored. Moreover, the connections built up by the lord of Loch Awe with men close to James would serve Duncan well in the hurly-burly of James II's minority. Those who had usurped the authority of the lord of Argyll in his own domain could expect a swift retribution.

Notes

1. Charters issued by Duncan from 1414 onwards were all said to be made with the consent of Gillespic, his son and heir. In addition Duncan, earl of Lennox, the father-in-law of Murdoch Stewart, was married to Helen Campbell, Duncan's aunt
2. NAS RH6/245.
3. *ER*, iv, clxxix; NLS Adv.MSS. 33.2.36.
4. Watt, *Dictionary*, 4–5.
5. *Ibid.*
6. Watt, *Fasti*, 26–7, i.e. Laurence of Argyll (Ergadia) and Martin of Argyll. See also the career of Adam de Lanark, a Dominican friar who became bishop of Galloway and who, in 1357, was associated with his fellow Dominican, Martin of Argyll. Watt, *Dictionary*, 325–6.
7. Janet P. Foggie, *Renaissance Religion in Urban Scotland: The Dominican Order, 1450–1560* (Leiden, 2003), 14–15.
8. C.H. Lawrence, *The Friars: The impact of the early mendicant movement on western society* (London, 1994), Chs. 4, 6, 10, 11; W.A. Hinnebusch, *The History of the Dominican Order*, 2 vols. (New York, 1965–73).

9. Cowan and Easson, *Medieval Religious Houses*, 114–121. See also J.P. Foggie, The Dominicans in Scotland: 1450–1560 (unpublished Ph.D Thesis), Edinburgh 1998, 12–16.

10. Anthony Ross, 'Incubi in the Isles in the Thirteenth Century, *IR*, 13 (1962), 108–9.

11. *Chron. Bower* (Watt), viii, 132–135.

12. Brown, *James I*, 28–9.

13. *Ibid.*, 24–7

14. *Ibid.*, 27–8.

15. *Ibid.*, 28–30.

16. *Foedera*, x, 343.

17. *CPL*, vii, 336 (Duncan Campbell and his first wife supplicating for right to use a portable altar), 259 (dispensation for marriage of Duncan and Margaret Stewart).

18. *CDS*, iv, nos. 941–2, 952–3, 960–1, 964, 973, 981, 983; Brown, *James I*, 40–42.

19. Brown, *James I*, 60–67.

20. *Chron.Bower* (Watt), viii, 241.

21. *Chron. Bower* (Watt), viii, 243; *Glas.Reg.*, ii, no.344; Brown, *James I*, 55.

22. Brown, *James I*, 56–7.

23. *Chron. Bower* (Watt), viii, 243–5.

24. *Chron. Bower* (Watt), viii, 243–5.

25. *APS*, ii, 7–8. The suggestion that an item dealing with the king's granting of remissions to Highlanders was an implicit criticism by Albany and the earl of Mar of James' political rapprochement with Alexander, Lord of the Isles, is not convincing. There is nothing in the statute itself to indicate that it was directed against Alexander in particular. The legislation seems to be a general observation on the difficulty of making the system of remission in return for 'assythment', or compensation of the victim, work in a Highland context. Furthermore the principal victims of the slaughter and theft perpetrated by Highlanders before James I's return were, according to the statute, other Highlanders. Cf. Brown, *James I*, 60–61.

26. Brown, *James I*, 60–61.

27. *Chron.Bower*, viii, 245; *AU*, iii, 99–100.

28. Brown, *James I*, 66; *Chron. Bower* (Watt), viii, 243–5.

29. *Chron. Extracta*, 228; *Chron. Pluscarden*, Bk xi, Ch.3.

30. *Chron. Bower* (Watt), viii, 247.

31. *Rot.Scot*, ii, p.265.

32. *CDS*, iv, no.983; *HP*, ii, 152–7.

33. The byname comes from the early-sixteenth poem addressed to Archibald 2nd earl of Argyll, *Book of the Dean*, xx.

34. Brown, *James I*, 74–5.

35. *APS*, ii, 11.

36. *Ibid.*

37. *AU*, iii, 99–100.

38. For contrasting discussions of Bower's 'political' attitudes as they are represented in his work, see M. Brown, ' "Vile Times": Walter Bower's last Book and the Minority of James I', *SHR*, lxxix (2000), 165–88 and S. Mapstone, 'Bower on kingship' (Chapter 22) in *Chron.Bower* (Watt), ix, 321–338.

39. *Chron. Bower* (Watt), viii, 245. See *Chron. Bower* (Watt), ix, 12–19, 193–96, 322 for notes on the Book of Coupar Angus.
40. *Ibid*. The additional information that Duncan, earl of Lennox was an octogenarian again suggests an account that was sympathetic to the men executed. Amongst the additional details included in the Book of Coupar Angus was the fact that the exiled James Stewart's byname was 'grossus'.
41. Duncan had a notarial copy of the original grant drawn up during the first general council (May 1437) after James I's death in 1437, suggesting that its terms had been ignored prior to the King's demise. Argyll Muniments, Inveraray, Bundle 1107. The lieutenancy could conceivably have come within the terms of a parliamentary statute of March 1426 insisting on the consistent application of the common law of the realm and annulling any 'special privileges' in the judicial sphere. *APS*, ii, 9.
42. *CSSR*, ii, 10–11, 80, 141.
43. *HP*, ii, 152–7. Scrymgeour may well have initiated the action as soon as Duncan Campbell was released from captivity in England. The hostages had probably been guaranteed immunity from legal action in Scottish courts for the period of their captivity.
44. *HP*, ii, 152–174.
45. *Ibid.*, 157–74;
46. *CSSR*, ii, 195–6. A dispensation in favour of a Robert Scrymgeour, described as rector of the kirk of Glassary, and 'kinsman of James King of Scotland'. Scrymgeour's supplication appears to have been part of a bundle of business transmitted to Rome on behalf of clerics close to the King.
47. *Brechin Registrum*, i, 98–104, at 100–102; Watt, *Fasti*, 27; J. Dowden, *The Bishops of Scotland* (Glasgow, 1912), 385–6.
48. *CSSR*, iv, nos. 787 (Lauder), 782, 808, 816, 818, 823, 879 (Peter of Dalkeith).
49. See Ch. 6.
50. See Brown, *James I*, 93–6 for an account of the factors contributing to this worsening relationship.
51. *Chron. Bower* (Watt), viii, 259–61.
52. *Chron. Bower* (Watt), viii, 261.
53. The suggestion is attractive in the sense that a combined execution of a MacArthur Campbell and a MacRuairi of Garmoran might be linked to the competing claims of the ancestors of these families to Garmoran in the fourteenth century. However, it is not entirely clear that the two men executed in 1428 were killed because they were in feud with each other. The chief figures in the Strachur family usually bore the names Arthur or Iver rather than John.
54. *Chron. Bower* (Watt), viii, 261. The name James (Seamus) was an unusual, indeed unprecedented, name within the Campbell kindred and there is no other record of this individual.
55. *HP*, i, 38–9. The lack of any contemporary comment on the violent death of one of the most powerful figures in the Hebrides and the north of Ireland is rather puzzling.
56. The account of John's death, for example, came just after an extended lament on the way in which the arbitrary exercise of royal power could make 'traitors' of the realm's most loyal subjects. Moreover, the *Sleat History* incorporated a number of episodes in which the Crown attempted to undercut powerful Hebridean

lords and lordships by bribing their kinsmen and adherents – the danger of such advances and the virtue of those who rejected them was clearly a major theme within the seventeenth-century work. See *HP*, ii, 9–10 (the assassination of Somerled) and 49. In accepting the gist of the *Sleat History* account, Brown assumes that Bower is simply mistaken in dating Campbell's execution to the Council of 1428 and suggests that John Mór was captured by James alongside his nephew (although Bower does not name him in this group) and then swiftly released. An additional note in Bower's Book of Coupar Angus. (cui paulo ante rex suam dedit remissionem), translated by the *Scotichronicon*'s editors as (who had been released by the king not long before) can be cited in support of this chain of events. The seventeenth-century account of John Mór's death after his refusal of royal offers of his imprisoned nephew's lands and title would thus fit neatly with the idea that these events occurred shortly after August 1428. However, an alternative reading of the additional comment in the Book of Coupar Angus, is that shortly before John's death the king had given him a remission. Thus, Campbell's offence would have been the slaughter of a man who had very recently been taken into royal protection.

57. One of the printed sources known to the producer of the *Sleat History* was George Buchanan's sixteenth-century history, which reproduced Bower's brief account of the execution of James Campbell and specified that his victim was a 'noble islander'. *The history of Scotland/ Rerum Scoticarum historia by George Buchanan*, ed. and trans. J. Aikman, 6 vols. (Edinburgh, 1829–30), ii, 28. It is tempting to suggest that much of the circumstantial detail hung around the episode in the seventeenth-century account was essentially invented.

58. *Chron. Bower* (Watt), viii, 260–63; Brown, *James I*, 101.

59. Brown, *James I*, 101–2.

60. *Annals of the Kingdom of Ireland, by the Four Masters*, vol. iv (2nd edition), ed. John O'Donovan (Dublin, 1856) (hereafter *AFM*), 874–5. Unusually for *AFM* the description of the events of 1429 was not obviously derived from or shared with *AU*. The account in *AFM*, iv, 864–7 of the death of Murdoch and James' exile or banishment to Ireland in 1425 was certainly to be found in *AU*, iii, 99–100. The *AFM* entry for 1429 unhelpfully records that the fleet was sent by unspecified 'men of Scotland'.

61. Brown, *James I*, 102–5, 136–40.

62. *CSSR*, i, 172–3. The initial attempts to arrange a match seem to date from before 17 February 1418. *Ibid.*, n.1. Gillespic eventually married Elizabeth Somerville (see below). This did not result from Mariota's early death as Donald's daughter enjoyed a succession of marriages through the 1420s and 1430s. *CSSR*, iv, no. 154; *ALI*, 301.

63. *APS*, ii, 19 c.17. Duncan evidently attended the parliament from an early stage in proceedings and was also to be found acting as one of the judges for cases brought before the assembly. *APS*, ii, 28.

64. *HP*, ii, 165–172.

65. Argyll Muniments, Inveraray, Argyll Charters. The witnesses were Dugald Campbell (probably Duncan's brother), John Campbell, James Auchinleck of that Ilk, George Campbell of Galstoun, 'Archebald' Campbell and Wat Bet.

66. Brown, *James I*, 135.

67. See above, Ch. 2.

68. RMS, ii, no.163. The grant was to last for seven years from the feast of Pentecost 1430.

69. Argyll Muniments, Inveraray, Bundle 1107. Presumably the notarial copy was drawn up in preparation for some form of legal representation before a royal court.

70. In February 1433, for example, it was Duncan who presided over the arbitration of a dispute within the Lamont kindred at Kyllenan in Cowal. NLS. Lamont Papers, Ch. no. 7364.

71. *HP*, ii, 97; *Records of Argyll*, 10–11.The traditional accounts are backed up by the later claim of Hugh, Lord Somerville, who in March 1549 wrote that the then earl of Argyll 'is cumit of my hous'. *Calendar of the State Papers relating to Scotland and Mary, Queen of Scots, 1547–1603* , vol. I, ed. J. Bain (Edinburgh, 1898), no.344, p.173; *Laing Chrs.*, no.113 (Somerville as justiciar in 1434); *Charters and Writs concerning the Royal Burgh of Haddington, 1318–1543*, 15–16 (Somerville acting as Justiciar south of Forth on 25 September 1430); *Foedera*, x, 487.

72. *RMS*, ii, no.38, 7 March 1425/6, for Somerville as a witness to a Balvenie charter. For Balvenie's rise in James I's service, see Brown, *The Black Douglases* (East Linton, 1998), 233–9. Somerville was a man with extensive Douglas connections.

73. James Auchinleck of that Ilk, one of Balvenie's most trusted associates, witnessed the agreement between Duncan Campbell and George Campbell of Loudoun in March 1430. Argyll Muniments, Inveraray. Auchinleck and Balvenie witnessed the notarial instrument drawn up on Duncan's behalf in Stirling in 1433 while Balvenie was also a witness to another instrument relating to Duncan's lieutenancy of Argyll drawn up in May 1437, again at Stirling. Both in Argyll Muniments, Inveraray, Bundle 1107. In April 1431 Thomas Somerville of Carnwath witnessed a charter issued by Duncan at Perth.

74. AT, at date. See C.H. Lawrence, *The Friars: The impact of the early mendicant movement on western society* (London, 1994), 94–98 for a brief discussion of the early history of the order; Cowan and Easson, *Religious Houses*, 138; J.A. Stone ed., *Three Scottish Carmelite friaries: excavations at Aberdeen, Linlithgow and Perth, 1980–1986* (Edinburgh, 1989), 21–23.

75. NAS Muniments of King James VI Hospital, Perth, GD 79/3/3 and 4.

76. The notarial instrument of 13 May 1433 regarding Campbell claims in Arran was drawn up at the house of the Friars Preachers in Stirling. Argyll Muniments, Inveraray, Bundle 1107.

77. The widowed Isabella, Duchess of Albany certainly maintained a link to the Dominicans, granting the Glasgow house an annual rent to support prayers for her dead husband, sons and father. *Glas. Friars*, 171–2 (no.29). Walter Stewart's son Andrew, who returned to Scotland after the death of James I, became ennobled as Lord Avandale, and enjoyed a spectacular political career culminating in his appointment as James III's chancellor, may have been buried beside his father, uncle and grandfather. Certainly his 'soul mass' was performed in the house of the 'Stirling friars' (probably the Dominican house) in 1488. *TA*, i, 89.

78. Gillespic witnessed a charter of 10 July 1432 (as Gillaspy of Argyll) but thereafter disappeared from record. Grants made by Duncan in favour of his second son Colin in October 1432 were almost certainly made after Gillespic's death. NAS GD 79/3/4.

79. NAS Breadalbane Muniments, GD 112/ 1/5 (sixteenth-century copy), NAS

RH1/2/199 (copy made by Herbert Campbell delivered into the NAS in 1932). Original is now in Guelph University Library. *HP*, iv, 199.

80. Brown, *James I*, 154–166.
81. *RMS*, ii, no.571.
82. Brown, *James I*, 172–88.
83. Brown, *James I*, 197; *APS*, ii, 31.
84. NAS GD 112/3/2.
85. *RMS*, iii, no.316. Thomas was a burgess of Perth and the brother of Christopher Chambers, said to be the first of the conspirators arrested alongside Robert Stewart, Atholl's grandson. Brown, *James I*, 197. It is unclear whether the capture of Thomas preceded the coronation of 25 March or was part of the mopping up of Atholl adherents thereafter. William Douglas, earl of Angus, apprehended Earl Walter himself towards the end of March. For Thomas' involvement in the assassination, see Brown, *James I*, 184, 187–8.

SIX

The Foes of Friendly Duncan

O n 10 May 1437 Duncan Campbell, lord of Loch Awe, was to be found in Stirling attending a meeting of the three estates that made arrangements for the governance of the young King James and his kingdom. The assembly was also notable for the brutal execution of the prominent regicide Sir Robert Graham 'with many other traitours of his couyne".[1] Duncan's presence at this critical meeting seems to confirm the impression that, in the aftermath of James I's death, the Campbells had immediately flung their political and military support behind Queen Joan and her young son. However, Campbell assistance for the minority regime of James II came at a price. During the general council, Duncan had a notarial instrument drawn up recording the royal grant of 1382 that had made Duncan's grandfather hereditary lieutenant of Argyll. Duncan evidently thought that the royal administration should be more than happy to reward men who had helped to root out the earl of Atholl, Sir Robert Graham and the traitorous 'coven' that had undone James I. Duncan's attempt to have the lieutenancy re-established had powerful political backing. The witnesses to the drawing up of the instrument included James Douglas, the newly created earl of Avondale and Lord of Balvenie, Robert Stewart, lord of Lorn, and Alexander Livingstone of Callendar.[2] All of these men were to be significant figures in the intense factional politics of James II's minority. As it was, Duncan Campbell was openly styling himself the king's lieutenant in Argyll by 4 August 1442; whether James II approved of this situation may have mattered little.[3]

The restoration of the lieutenancy paved the way for Duncan to assume control of the crown's extensive interests in the Cowal peninsula. The first addition to the Campbell hegemony in the region may well have been the strategically vital fortress of Dunoon. On 12 March 1440, Duncan Campbell issued a charter from Dunoon Castle, and it seems likely that the castle and its associated estates were in the hands of Duncan and his family between 1437 and 1445.[4] The Campbell lord's interest in Dunoon was more than just short-term predatory opportunism, for the family had owned estates in the neighbouring lordship of Kilmun for more than a century. Yet the years of James II's minority saw a profound deepening of the lord of Loch Awe's links to this part of Cowal. The sense that the Campbell lineage had a long and intimate connection with eastern Cowal was present in Duncan's charter of 12 March 1440 in favour of the parish kirk of Dunoon.[5] In the following year Duncan began a successful campaign to elevate Kilmun kirk on the Holy Loch to the status of a collegiate kirk; from this point on, if not earlier, Kilmun was clearly the principal religious and ecclesiastical focus for Duncan and his family.[6] Quite why Kilmun should emerge as the Campbell mausoleum and family cult centre ahead of kirks in mid-Argyll or Loch Awe is uncertain. It has been speculated that Fionntáin, the saint commemorated at Kilmun, may have been adopted as a patron by the Campbell family at an early stage.[7] However, the first secure link between the family and the cult of St Fionntáin seems to have been the acquisition of the patronage of the kirk of Kilmun on the Holy Loch from the countess of Menteith in the 1350s. Although it is difficult to confirm that they successfully exercised this right, Kilmun kirk certainly featured as a location where, from the mid-fourteenth century onwards, Campbell chiefs issued charters and concluded agreements.[8] A number of personal factors could have influenced Duncan to regard Kilmun with more intense affection. Some traditional tales suggest that the first Campbell to be buried at Kilmun was the son of a lord of Loch Awe who died in the Lowlands and whose body could not be carried beyond the Holy Loch to the traditional Campbell mausoleum at Inishail because of a fierce storm.[9] Duncan's son and heir, Gillespic, as we have seen, died in 1432 and it is certainly tempting to link this event with the embellished narrative of the traditional histories.[10] Regardless of his son's final resting-place, Duncan certainly had a personal link to eastern Cowal through his second wife, Margaret Stewart of Ardgowan. Margaret's family had been patrons of Dunoon as early as 1402, and it seems significant that she was the first named witness of Duncan's 1440 grant in favour of that kirk.[11] On a more general level, Duncan's decision to endow a collegiate kirk at Kilmun reflected wider changes in aristocratic patronage of religious foundations in the fifteenth century. The establishment of kirks served by a small community of priests organised under a provost, providing masses for the souls of the founder and his family, and often acting as a family mausoleum, was increasingly popular in late medieval Scotland.[12] The spread of collegiate kirks testified not only to changing patterns of piety, but also the social pretensions of a 'new' aristocratic elite emerging from the shadows of the great provincial magnates in the fifteenth century.[13] Alexander Grant has drawn attention to the rise of this social elite in the development of a new peerage style and the rank of lord of parliament. The new parliamentary style tended to be based around the family surname rather than a territorial designation. By 1 December 1448, at the latest, Duncan Campbell had begun to use the style 'Lord Campbell' alongside his more familiar designation as lord of Loch Awe.[14] There tended to be a loose correlation between an individual attaining or adopting the status of a lord of parliament and his establishment of a collegiate kirk. In a sense both reflected the nature of the power that underpinned the social pre-eminence of the 'new' elite. The free operation of male entail charters in fourteenth- and fifteenth-century Scotland had produced strong male lineage lordships, in which extensive and inalienable territorial rights, automatic leadership of a wider kin or surname, and perhaps social and political domination of a locality had more or less coalesced. New religious establishments largely dedicated to commemorating the male lineage descended from their founder seem to have been one of the ways in which the social prominence of these lordships was marked, celebrated and confirmed. At any rate, Duncan Campbell could hardly have been unaware of the spiritual and social benefits of the patronage of collegiate kirks. A number of families linked to the Campbells by marriage or political association in the 1430s and 1440s, such as the Douglases of Balvenie and Dalkeith and the Somervilles of Carnwath, had founded or were about to establish collegiate kirks.[15]

The creation of the collegiate kirk at Kilmun also seems to have had an overtly political purpose. Duncan's request in the autumn of 1441 for the elevation of Kilmun to the status of a collegiate kirk proposed the annexation of the revenues of the parish kirks of St. Connan of Dysart (Diseart) (i.e. the parish kirk of Glenorchy at Dalmally) and the 'Three Holy Brethren' of Kinlochgoil to the new institution.[16] Both these kirks were in the hands of men appointed by James I's loyal bishop of Argyll, George Lauder, prior to 1437. With the king dead, Duncan Campbell was clearly determined to reassert his control over these benefices, and annexation to the collegiate kirk at Kilmun was one way to make that control permanent. The Lauder-appointed incumbents of the two kirks intended for appropriation to Kilmun came under attack in papal courts at precisely the same time as Duncan's petition in regard to Kilmun arrived for consideration. The complaints against Lauder's men were interestingly framed around the issue of language rather than any other clerical inadequacy or abuse. As non-Gaelic speakers they could not, it was alleged, adequately minister the sacraments to their parishioners. Duncan Campbell's brother Neil had already deployed this line of argument against the Scrymgeour appointee to the parish kirk of Glassary in the 1420s.[17] The general case against Lowland clerics holding benefices inside Argyll was laid out even more clearly in March 1466 by Duncan's son, Colin Campbell of Glenorchy, who was then in Rome as an ambassador for James III. Colin supplicated the pope to uphold the general principle that no-one should attempt to receive or hold any parish churches in the diocese of Argyll 'unless he understands and speaks intelligibly the language of the greater part of the parishioners'.[18] The consistent use of the language issue by Campbell lords in their litigation over Argyll benefices indicates that Duncan of Loch Awe was undoubtedly the guiding hand behind the attack on the bishop of Argyll's men in 1441. Thus, a 'Morice Patricii Hilarii' supplicated the pope for provision to Dysart, held by James Lauder, 'alleged priest', on the basis that Lauder 'is utterly ignorant of the idiom accustomed to be spoken in that church, whereby he is unable . . . to preach the word of God to the parishioners, hear confessions and administer the sacraments . . .'[19] Similarly, 'Archibald Martini' supplicated for provision to the kirk of Lochgoilhead because 'George bishop of Argyll granted it by his own temerity without the consent of the true patron to one Peter of Dalkeith, alleged priest, . . . who cannot speak intelligibly the idiom of the parishioners, and intruded him by the secular power, . . . by the negligence of the said Peter and his ignorance of the tongue many of the parishioners have died without the sacraments of the church'.[20]

It was clear in fact that George Lauder had fared very badly after James I's death in terms of his ability to appoint to benefices in Argyll. The first trial of strength between the bishop and Duncan Campbell was over the archdeaconry of Argyll after the death of the incumbent, Duncan's kinsman Neil Campbell, c.1436–7. One of Duncan's clerical servants, Dugald of Loch Awe, rector of Loch Awe, was provided to the vacant office by the papal nuncio, Anthony Altani, bishop of Urbino, before the latter left Scotland in 1438.[21] Bishop Lauder had responded by appointing Peter of Dalkeith, the vicar of Lochgoilhead, in opposition to Dugald, but Duncan Campbell's ascendancy inside Argyll ensured that Dalkeith never exercised the office.[22]

A collapse in the influence of men and families who had been very closely associated with James I seems to have been a fairly widespread phenomenon in the lordships around Argyll, particularly the earldom of Lennox. In this area the death of James I brought about a remarkable rehabilitation of the remnants of the Albany Stewart kin. Duchess Isabella, the widow of Duke Murdoch, who may well have spent most of James I's reign in captivity, had returned to the Lennox by May 1437, where she was swiftly joined by her Lennox and Albany Stewart kinsmen.[23] Local opponents of the Lennox/Albany revival were swept aside. The son of Isabella's sister Elizabeth, Allan Stewart of Darnley, returned from France to put forward his own claim to all or part of the earldom. On 20 September 1438 Stewart was killed by Sir Thomas Boyd in a dispute that may, or may not, have been related to the Lennox. An assassination that was perhaps much more directly linked to the Albany revival in Lennox occurred on 24 September 1439 when John Colquhoun of Luss, the man who had acted as James I's local agent, was 'slane in Inchemuryne [Inchmurrin] underneth ane assouerance be Lauchlane McClanis and Murthow Gibson'.[24] Whether Duchess Isabella and her kinsmen were behind Colquhoun's death or not, they were clearly the major beneficiaries, with the duchess swiftly reclaiming Inchmurrin as her own residence. By the time of Colquhoun's demise the Campbells seem already to have aligned themselves with the resurgent Lennox interest. In October 1439 a papal dispensation was issued to allow the marriage of Duncan's eldest surviving son, Sir Colin of Glenorchy, to Isabella's grand-daughter, Marion Stewart, daughter of the Walter Stewart of Albany executed by James I in 1425.[25] By October of 1440 the marriage had been made official.[26] It seems likely that the marriage of Marion Stewart and Colin of Glenorchy reflected Campbell approval, or at least acceptance of the resurrection of Albany/Lennox power that paralleled their own overturning of James I's settlement in Argyll. As it was, the marriage was short-lived since Marion died young and produced no heirs.[27] However, the match may have left a lasting legacy in the good relations established between Marion's brother, Andrew Stewart of Albany, and Duncan's family.

If those around the young James II were worried about the way in which 'royal' strongholds such as Dunoon and Inchmurrin were absorbed into local aristocratic lordships after 1437, the position of the mighty royal fortress at Dumbarton would have been an even more pressing issue. Sir

Robert Erskine had seized the castle because the minority regime refused to acknowledge his claims to the earldom of Mar. In August 1440 Duncan Campbell was one of the men assigned to a royal commission to negotiate Erskine's surrender of Dumbarton. On 6 August Duncan's son (also Duncan) received a precept of sasine of the lands of Achnabrek (Auchenbreck) in the bailiary of Cowal, forfeited by Ferchar Ewenson Lamont, issued by the king at Dumbarton.[28] The timing and location of the issuing of the precept of sasine are significant, for James II and his principal councillors were clearly in Dumbarton to negotiate with Robert Erskine. Within four days the king and his council, accompanied by Duncan Campbell, had returned to Stirling where an agreement was concluded between the king and Erskine.[29] As it turned out, the bargain was never fully carried through and Dumbarton remained in Erskine's hands until c.1444.

The involvement of Duncan Campbell and his son Colin in the negotiations around Dumbarton were typical of the family's dealings in the early minority of James II. The Campbells' field of interest was essentially regional. Between 1437 and 1445 Duncan Campbell effectively restored, indeed enhanced, the Campbell supremacy in Argyll. The lieutenancy of 1382 was re-imposed, the ability of the bishop of Argyll to interfere in Campbell benefices rebuffed, and royal estates in Cowal and the castle of Dunoon effectively annexed. All this was achieved against the background of the highly unstable court politics of James II's minority. It seems likely that for most of the period after 1437 Duncan was not closely involved in the power struggles around the young James II, requiring only tacit acceptance by the royal establishment of his gains in the west. Nevertheless, he and his son Colin were occasional visitors to the royal court, usually when the king and his council were in Stirling and dealing with the affairs of families and regions in which Duncan had an established political or tenurial interest.[30] What evidence there is seems to indicate that in the political sphere Duncan was most often aligned with the powerful and ruthless man of business James Douglas, earl of Avondale and Lord Balvenie.[31] Between 1437 and 1439 Balvenie had been a major influence on the royal administration led by his nephew Archibald, 5th earl of Douglas, who had been appointed lieutenant-general of the kingdom in May 1437.[32] Archibald's death on 26 June 1439 ushered in a period of renewed political discord, from which Balvenie emerged as Earl of Douglas, having engineered the deaths of Earl Archibald's young sons

(James' own grand-nephews), and as the leading figure in the governance of the realm. The chief casualty of Balvenie's rise to power seems to have been Queen Joan Beaufort. The widowed queen had found herself largely frozen out of royal government in the years after 1437 by the influence of the 5th earl of Douglas. Archibald's death thus seemed to present an opportunity for the queen to claim a greater role in the governance of her young son. In July 1439, Queen Joan obtained significant new allies through a marriage to James Stewart, the brother of Robert, lord of Lorn.[33] Lorn was Duncan Campbell's brother-in-law (both men having married daughters of Robert, duke of Albany) and had been one of the men associated with Campbell attempts to resurrect the lieutenancy of Argyll in 1437.[34] There was little to indicate, however, that Campbell supported Queen Joan at this stage. The queen's re-marriage was clearly seen as a threat by other groups that sought to dominate James II's minority government. On 3 August 1439 Sir Alexander Livingstone of Callendar, the constable of Stirling Castle, imprisoned the queen, her new husband and one of his brothers in the royal fortress. The queen and her fellow captives eventually negotiated their release under terms that were ratified by a general council held in the burgh of Stirling on 4 September 1439.[35] The terms of the so-called 'Appointment' of September 1439 saw Livingstone retain custody of the young King James and thus a central role in the political life of the kingdom. Queen Joan's 'men and retenew' were required to swear not to take action against the Livingstones for their seizure of the queen.[36]

If Duncan Campbell seems to have remained aloof from the intrigue around the royal court, his eldest son, Colin of Glenorchy, may have been rather more active. After Mariota Stewart of Albany's early death it swiftly became clear that Glenorchy was not content to restrict his activities to Argyll and Lennox. The execution and forfeiture of Walter, earl of Atholl and Strathearn, in 1437 had allowed Colin's gaze to stray east beyond Drumalban to the fertile lands of the vacated earldom of Strathearn. By c.1442 Colin had some form of bailiary jurisdiction within the earldom, covering estates that were profitable enough to support a £20 pension for Colin's father Duncan.[37] The heart of Colin's jurisdiction may have been Glen Lednock to the north-west of Comrie. Glenorchy's next, and rather mysterious, matrimonial entanglement also pointed to his family's involvement in political struggles in areas far removed from Argyll. On 7 May 1449, at the Dominican house in Stirling, Colin obtained a divorce from Janet Borthwick, Lady Dalkeith, whom he had apparently married sometime after the death of Marion Stewart.[38] Exactly when the match with Borthwick had been contracted and who arranged it is unclear.[39] Janet was the sister of the influential Lothian lord, William Borthwick, and as the widow of James Douglas, lord of Dalkeith (who died between February 1440 and May 1441), she had extensive claims to Dalkeith estates.[40] The Dalkeith inheritance was the subject of an intense dispute in the years after the lord of Dalkeith's death. Douglas's eldest son and heir, also James, appears either to have been mad or slow-witted. Control of the Dalkeith estates was therefore given to James' brother-in-law, James Gifford of Sheriffhall. James Douglas's kinsmen, particularly his younger brother Henry of Borgue, refused to accept this arrangement and by September 1442 the struggle between Gifford and Henry Douglas provoked the intervention of the king's council, which took the Dalkeith estates into royal control.[41] One of the principal backers of Henry Douglas was his father-in-law, James Douglas, earl of Avondale. Given the existing Campbell/Avondale links, it may well have been Earl James who arranged for the match between Janet Borthwick and his 'ally' Colin Campbell. The attractions of the marriage evidently waned swiftly for both parties, and it may well have been little more than a paper arrangement long before the divorce of 1449. Nevertheless, the involvement of the Campbells in the affairs of East Lothian gives an indication of the widening political and social sphere in which the family now operated. However, increased engagement with the political factions around the royal court did not guarantee success, as Duncan Campbell found to his cost during 1445.

Duncan Campbell's problems in 1445 seem to have been linked to the increased influence of the custodian of the king, Alexander Livingstone of Callendar, inside the realm. From August 1443 onwards Livingstone had co-operated with William, 8th earl of Douglas, in the latter's struggle against the chancellor, William Crichton, and his extensive family. In the autumn of 1443 Crichton lost the post of chancellor after violent exchanges in Lothian between members of his kindred and Earl William. In the following year Earl William's hold on the kingdom tightened and others who claimed rights in the governance of the realm found themselves under increasing pressure. Amongst those discomfited by the advance of Livingstone and Earl William was James I's widow, Queen Joan Beaufort.[42] In 1444-5, Queen Joan and her allies found themselves under concerted attack by Livingstone and Douglas, who claimed to be acting in the name of the young king. In November 1444 James II was declared of age, and a general council held in that month approved a revocation of all grants made in the name of the young king since the start of his minority.[43] The revocation allowed the two men to attack their political opponents by selectively cancelling grants of royal land or office given since 1437. The queen mother and her principal ally, James Kennedy, bishop of St Andrews, sought to resist and sent a letter to the burgh of Aberdeen (and no doubt others) demanding that burgh should not answer to 'tha persownis that now has the Kyng in gouernance'.[44] Livingstone and Douglas soon turned to direct action to impose their control on the realm. Early in 1445 the lands of bishop Kennedy in Fife were raided by the earl of Crawford, James Livingstone, 'that tyme kepar to the king and captain of Stirling', and others. Later in the year William Crichton was besieged in Edinburgh Castle while Queen Joan was similarly assailed in Dunbar Castle, eventually dying in the stronghold on 15 July.[45] A parliament that opened in Perth in June 1445 confirmed the ascendancy of the Livingstones and Earl William and prepared the ground for further action against their enemies. On 14 June the assembly decreed that lands held by James I on the day of his death should return to, and remain in, the possession of the young James II 'undemandit and unpleyit of ony man befor ony Juge within the Realme on to the tym of his lauchful age'.[46] The statute may have been a genuine attempt to regularise the administration of royal lands and revenues, but it also allowed the guardians of the young king to move against those of their enemies occupying royal lands since James I's death.

It soon became apparent that the targets for the Livingstone-dominated regime included the leading figures within Clan Campbell. Quite why Earl William was prepared to support moves against Duncan and Colin Campbell is unclear. The Campbells seem to have enjoyed a good relationship with William's father James, earl of Avondale and lord of Balvenie, before James' death in 1443. Moreover, the Campbell marriage links to the families of Somerville and Borthwick would seem to have brought them into the orbit of Douglas influence. The driving force behind the slighting of Campbell interests in 1445 may have been the Livingstone lords of Callendar, whose retainer Robert Callendar had obtained custody of Dumbarton Castle during 1444, perhaps exploiting a dispute between two of Robert Erskine's adherents, Sir Robert Sempill and Patrick Galbraith.[47] Control of Dumbarton renewed the possibility that the Livingstone regime could reassert 'royal' rights in other areas of the Firth of Clyde. At any rate, the new custodian of Dumbarton may swiftly have incurred the displeasure of Duncan Campbell, for on 31 May 1445 Callendar seems to have been involved in the killing of Sir James Stewart of Auchingowan by Robert Lyle of Duchal at Drumglass near Dumbarton.[48] The circumstances behind Stewart's death are unknown, but the slaughter of a close kinsman of Duncan Campbell's wife (probably her brother or nephew) was symptomatic of the challenge to Campbell interests in the region spearheaded by Robert Callendar during 1445. Within two months of the clash at Drumglass, Duncan Campbell lost his hold on the royal castle of Dunoon and the estates of Glendaruel.[49] He was replaced as keeper of Dunoon by Robert of Callendar, who also received the ferms, or rents, of the king's lands of Glendaruel to supplement his fee as custodian of Dumbarton.[50]

Away from the Firth of Clyde, Colin of Glenorchy also ran into trouble in the summer of 1445. In July 1445 the payment of Sir Duncan's Strathearn pension was abruptly stopped while the exchequer audit described Glen Lednock as illegally occupied and laid waste by Colin of Glenorchy.[51] Campbell losses in 1445 were significant, but seem on the whole to have been confined to those areas where the family had blatantly occupied lands and offices after 1437 with little or no legal justification. Duncan was certainly not identified with the irreconcilable political outcasts grouped around Queen Joan and her husband, for he was in Edinburgh as a witness to a royal charter in early July 1445.[52] Later in the year meanwhile, on 2 September, 'Schir Colyn Cambel' of Glenorchy received a discharge from James II of all sums he owed to the crown from 'malis, fermis, eschetis of courtis'. Glenorchy had either stumped up the money he was claimed to owe from Strathearn or the minority regime had decided to abandon its pursuit of the Campbell lord.[53]

The Livingstone regime was to dominate the royal court for a further four years, but the end of James II's minority in 1449 heralded their ruin. On 20 September 1449 James Livingstone, one-time guardian of the king, and a number of his kinsmen and adherents, including Robert Callendar, custodian of Dumbarton and Dunoon, were arrested on the orders of the young monarch.[54] Duncan Campbell received some benefit from the collapse of the Livingstone faction by immediately re-occupying the royal estates of Glendaruel that had been held by Robert Callendar as custodian of Dumbarton. The keepership of Dunoon, however, was assigned to

Walter Graham whose nephew, Patrick, Lord Graham, was made custodian of Dumbarton, the other royal fortress held by Callendar prior to
1449.[55] The Grahams' domination of the Clyde fortresses lasted barely a
year, for in July 1450 Dunoon was handed over to William Turnbull,
bishop of Glasgow, one of James II's key councillors.[56]

The triumph of the young king in 1449 was no guarantee of political
stability, for the monarch increasingly bridled at the power and influence
held by the earl of Douglas and his brothers within the realm. An early
opportunity to take action against Earl William came when the Douglas
earl left Scotland in October 1450 on pilgrimage to Rome to celebrate the
papal jubilee announced by Nicholas V.[57] Amongst the men who accompanied Douglas to Rome over the winter of 1450–1 was Colin Campbell of
Glenorchy.[58] While Earl William was overseas, King James led an
expedition through the Douglas heartlands of the south and south-west,
with the general intention of reinforcing the primacy of royal rights and
interests in the region, and the particular objective of asserting his claim to
the disputed earldom of Wigtown.[59] When Earl William returned to
Scotland in April 1451, an uncomfortable stand-off between the king and
the earl ensued, eventually resolved in the parliament of June 1451. The
king retained his hold on the earldom of Wigtown, but in most other
respects Earl William, who was received back into the king's peace and
had title to his other lands and lordships confirmed, had successfully
defied the royal will.[60]

Although Colin of Glenorchy had accompanied Douglas to Rome, the
political stance of the family during 1451 is not certain. The aged Duncan
of Loch Awe seems to have spent his declining years arranging the affairs
of his lordship in Argyll, in particular strengthening the position of his
grandson as his undisputed heir. Like the rest of the political community,
however, the Campbells were likely to have been perplexed by the next
twist in the simmering dispute between James II and Earl William.
During the course of 1451 James became increasingly irritated by the
refusal of Douglas to assist royal campaigns against John, earl of Ross and
Lord of the Isles. Ross had seized the fortresses of Inverness and
Urquhart, and destroyed Ruthven in Badenoch, in March of 1451. On
22 February 1452, during a fateful meeting between the king and Earl
William in Stirling Castle, James's frustration with Douglas's intransi-
gence overcame his political sense; in a brutal attack initiated by the king
himself, Earl William was set upon and killed by the young monarch and

his courtiers.[61] Earl William may have been eliminated, but the king now faced the prospect of the remaining members of the most powerful magnate family in the realm seeking revenge for the death of their kinsman. The sordid circumstances of Earl William's death, the unarmed earl killed while under a royal assurance explicitly guaranteeing his personal safety, was hardly likely to convince other members of the political community of the justice of the king's cause after February 1452. The immediate aftermath of Earl William's death, then, was a time for shameless royal concessions in order to construct a political and military coalition strong enough for the king to ride out the crisis provoked by his own actions. Earl William's brothers were likewise concerned to find allies to uphold or advance their cause in the months following the fatal events at Stirling. The ripples from the crown/Douglas conflict were soon lapping along the shores of the Firth of Clyde.

In the immediate aftermath of the slaughter of Earl William, the bishop of Glasgow, William Turnbull, diverted 800 merks raised in the diocese for the papal jubilee to support the royal war effort.[62] Turnbull was one of the king's most committed supporters and a fierce opponent of Douglas power. In the mid-fifteenth-century short chronicle of John Law, Turnbull was identified as one of the principal figures who had encouraged James II to attack Douglas lands and interests in 1451.[63] Turnbull's substantial loan required to be repaid, and on 14 April 1452 the king granted the bishop a lease of the royal lands in Bute, Arran and Cowal, along with the great customs of Ayr, Irvine and Dumbarton, until the sum was repaid. In one area Bishop William's chances of making a profit from the royal grant must have seemed remote. The legitimacy of royal rights and agents in Arran had been contested by various figures within Clan Donald long before 1452. From the 1430s onwards nominally 'royal' estates in the north of Arran had been occupied by a Ranald mac Alexander, who clearly did not feel that his title rested on royal assent and who simply refused to render rents to crown officials.[64] For most of the period prior to 1452 the crown seems to have made little or no concerted effort to enforce its supposed 'rights' in the island. Bishop William, however, was made of less forgiving stuff. In May 1452 Turnbull witnessed a royal grant of 'Kinlochransay' (Lochranza) and other lands occupied by Ranald mac Alexander to Alexander, lord Montgomery, and his heirs.[65] Montgomery, who had a proven record as a military campaigner and royal castellan in the Lennox (1425), Kintyre and Knapdale (1430), and who had been constable of Brodick during the 1440s, may well have been brought in at Turnbull's suggestion to break Ranald's hold on the north of Arran.[66] The grants to Turnbull and Montgomery created the conditions for a political and military alliance between the Douglas earls and the Clan Donald in the Firth of Clyde. That there was an engagement between James, earl of Douglas, and the Lord of the Isles in the aftermath of Earl William's death is undoubted; the problem is that the agreement between the two men is very hard to date. The Auchinleck Chronicle records that in May of an unidentified year James Douglas travelled to Knapdale for a meeting with the earl of Ross. Thereafter, in July (presumably of the same year) Donald Balloch, lord of Dunivaig and the Glens, the effective war leader of the Clan Donald, launched a devastating galley raid in the Firth of Clyde 'with the powere of the Isles with him'.[67] The expedition ravaged Inverkip on the Renfrewshire coast, harried the isles of Cumbrae and Arran, and took a tribute or 'crauchment' from the inhabitants of Bute. On Arran, Donald's 'ost of the Isles' also captured and destroyed the royal castle at Brodick.[68] Some doubt lingers as to Earl John's personal enthusiasm for and participation in these events, but the presence of an illegitimate son of Archibald, 4th earl of Douglas, in Donald Balloch's company certainly points to some connection to Ross's conference with Douglas in May. The meeting and Donald Balloch's assault on the islands of the Firth of Clyde have been assigned to every year between 1452 and 1455. The most recent discussion argues strongly for the summer of 1454 on the basis that the chronicle entry between the account of the meeting and the raid concerns a siege of Blackness that demonstrably took place in the summer of 1454. The entry for the siege of Blackness begins with the claim that the incident took place in the same month and year, presumably indicating the preceding entry about Douglas and Ross.[69] However, this is not as conclusive as it appears. The chronology of the various entries in the Auchinleck Chronicle is notoriously jumbled and, very often, 'the same month' or 'the same year' formula is demonstrably wrong.[70] In short, the apparent cross-referencing to surrounding entries does not securely date the meeting and the raid to 1454. Similarly, arguments against the summer of 1452 on the basis that payments were still being made for the upkeep of Brodick Castle in 1453 result from a misreading of the exchequer rolls. It may also be significant that the entry following the account of the July raid is given a precise calendar date in August 1452. Overall, the raid on the Clyde seems to make better sense in the context and chronology of 1452 than the summer of 1454. From April 1452 it was clear that the king's 'principal consolour' against Douglas interests had made a war loan to the king, repayment of which was effectively underwritten by the royal lands in Cowal, Bute and Arran. Turnbull and the king had immediately put pressure on the junior branch of Clan Donald in Arran by encouraging the intervention of the experienced castellan, Alexander Montgomery, in the north of the island. By May 1452, therefore, there were compelling reasons for Douglas and Clan Donald to take joint action in the Firth of Clyde. For Douglas the assault represented a direct strike against the interests of the king and, more particularly, those of the hated bishop of Glasgow. Moreover, James Douglas must have anticipated, and was probably correct in thinking, that the appearance of such a large force in the Firth of Clyde in the summer of 1452 would at the least disrupt and deflect James II's political and military campaign against the Douglas earls. For Donald Balloch the raid fulfilled several objectives. As reported in the Auchinleck Chronicle, the foray appears as little more than an indiscriminate plundering expedition with no long-term strategic aims. The chronicle's horrified and detailed emphasis on the violence employed and the huge losses in terms of livestock from Inverkip and the affected islands may not be unrelated to the fact that the kirk at Inverkip, and that on Great Cumbrae, were appropriated to Paisley Abbey, perhaps the religious house where one of the sources underlying the jumbled Auchinleck Chronicle was compiled. It is certainly not inconceivable that Donald of the Isles and his followers indulged in some profitable harrying of soft targets. The leading figures in Clan Donald were certainly capable of organising massive plunder raids, largely motivated by the prospect of booty. In June 1461, for example, the Orkney isles were subject to a devastating raid by the Lord of the Isles and his 'wild Scots' that may have rivalled or surpassed the assault of 1452 in the scale of forces involved.[71] At any rate the islands and lordships of the Firth of Clyde seem to have been under fairly constant threat of low-key maritime attack.[72] The use of the term 'crauchmet' to describe Donald Balloch's levy from Bute is intriguing in this regard, for the word appears to have been of Gaelic origin, perhaps with the meaning 'raid-measure'.[73] The round figures indicate that it was an organised tribute-taking and not an indiscriminate attack on the island. The fact that the term had crossed over into Scots and was employed with no explanation in the description of the 1452 expedition indicates general familiarity with the concept in and around the Firth of Clyde.

However, the military action of 1452 also seems to have had carefully calculated political and territorial objectives, particularly with regard to the island of Arran. The destruction of Brodick Castle indicates a deliberate assault on the infrastructure that supported royal control of the island.[74] The activities of Donald Balloch in 1452 might then be regarded as an equivalent to the Lordship's assaults on royal fortresses in Badenoch and the Great Glen in March 1451.[75] Both campaigns seem to have been responses to what the Clan Donald regarded as the denial of their legitimate rights in the areas concerned. The family's claims were pursued by the local application of overwhelming military force and the destruction of the strongpoints around which any reassertion of royal influence in the region would be based. That Arran fell into the category of a lordship in which Clan Donald felt they had a legitimate and permanent interest is suggested by the terms of the treaty made a decade later, in 1462, by Earl John and Donald Balloch with the English king Edward IV.[76]

By the end of May 1452 James II must have been aware of the formidable coalition building against him. The parliament held by the king in June 1452 in Edinburgh thus met under the shadow of imminent civil war. The first task of the assembly was to provide retrospective justification for the king's part in the slaughter of Earl William and to mobilise support in the ongoing struggle with the earl's vengeful brothers and their supporters.[77] The Douglas/Clan Donald alliance had effectively opened up a second front in that conflict, and it soon became apparent that the king was willing to dispense significant royal patronage to those in the west prepared to support him in his hour of need. In particular, the king turned to Duncan Campbell of Loch Awe, Colin Campbell of Glenorchy and John Stewart of Lorn. All three lords were the beneficiaries of rather desperate royal largesse during 1452 as the king bought, rather than assumed, their loyalty. The decision of Loch Awe, Glenorchy and Lorn to support James II may well have been prompted as much by distrust of the regional ambitions of Donald Balloch as by any fondness they felt for their sovereign. As we have seen, a Campbell lord may have been responsible for the assassination of Donald's father, John Mór, in 1428. If this old feud was not enough to sour the relationship between Donald and Duncan of Loch Awe in 1452, there were more recent tensions and confrontations to take into consideration. Most notably, John Stewart and his Campbell relatives had recently clashed with Donald Balloch over the succession to the headship of the MacDougall of Dunollie kindred. The dispute seemed to have been resolved in 1451 in favour of the candidate backed by Lorn and the Campbells, but Donald Balloch continued to press the claims of his choice (his own nephew) to the Dunollie inheritance; the dispute was certainly still active in 1460.[78]

At any rate, the Auchinleck chronicler noted that both Duncan and Colin Campbell received grants of dubious legality from the king during the course of the June 1452 parliament.[79] On 19 June the crown lands of one third of Glendaruel were given over as a free barony to Duncan. The flagrant alienation of crown lands evidently offended the sensibilities of many who may not have been convinced by the claim, contained in the preamble to the grant, that the gift represented a much delayed reward for Duncan's service to James I at the siege of Roxburgh Castle in 1436–7. The clause may well reflect an attempt to side-step the criticism noted by the Auchinleck chronicler over the way in which royal lands were alienated in the spring and summer of 1452 in order to secure support in the king's immediate political struggle with the Black Douglases. The suggestion that Duncan had earned the grant by signal service to the crown in 1436–7 was little more than a fig-leaf.[80]

Colin of Glenorchy's rewards for his adherence to the king during 1452 were also substantial, with the Campbell lord obtaining an annuity of forty merks from the crown lands around Loch Tay.[81] Glenorchy's father-in-law, John Stewart, lord of Lorn, was another west-coast lord well favoured by James II during 1452. The Auchinleck chronicler noted that in the parliament of June 1452 'the lord of Lorne John Stewart talzeit all his landis to the male and surname'.[82] In 1452 Stewart had three legitimate daughters (one of whom was already betrothed to Colin Campbell of Glenorchy) but no legitimate male heirs. On 20 June 1452, however, Stewart obtained royal assent for an entailing of his lordship of Lorn and the baronies of Innermeath and Redcastle in favour of his four brothers and their heirs male in succession, whom failing, the male lines descending from John's uncle and cousin.[83] The support of Duncan and Colin Campbell and John Stewart was clearly highly prized by the king. The military resources available to these men from their west-coast lordships must have made them critical allies in the crisis months of 1452, most obviously in countering the threat posed by Clan Donald.

Overall, however, the role of Duncan and his family in the campaigns of 1452 remains obscure. There is no direct evidence that the men rewarded in June 1452 took part in the royal expeditions of the following month. The royal host had been summoned to assemble at Pentlandmuir on 8 July, ready to carry war against the Douglases and their sympathisers in the south of the kingdom. In 1452, in contrast to the account of the 1455 campaign, there was no indication of a hosting at Glasgow (a possible landfall for forces from the Firth of Clyde and Argyll) or the involvement of lords of the 'westland' and 'the ereschery' in attacking Douglas lordships.[84] Indeed, on 6 July 1452, two days before the scheduled hosting at Pentlandmuir, Duncan was at Kilmun in Cowal, on which date he transferred lands within the newly acquired barony of Kinlochruel to one of his grandsons, Colin Neilson Campbell of Ormidale.[85] Revealingly, Duncan's charter laid heavy stress on the importance of Colin Neilson's impending service and loyalty to the king 'that now is'. If Donald Balloch's raid is correctly dated to 10 July 1452, then the grant of Kinlochruel was nothing short of a frontline commission on the fringes of the Kyles of Bute, made only four days before the galleys of Clan Donald swept into the Firth of Clyde. In short, it may be that the Campbells' chief service to the crown in 1452 entailed sitting tight in Cowal to repel the onslaught of Donald Balloch. If this was the case, then it may be significant that Cowal was absent from the Auchinleck chronicler's list of lordships ravaged by the expedition. The presence of a Campbell host in Cowal may also have been sufficient to dissuade Donald Balloch from attempting strikes against targets on the Clyde itself.

Despite the hastily assembled coalition and the campaign by the royal host in July 1452 against Douglas lands and supporters around Peebles, Selkirk and Dumfries, the king was unable to obtain a decisive political/ military victory. In August 1452 the king and Earl James concluded an agreement that brought open hostilities to an end, although the general political situation remained tense and unstable.[86] In the west, the Clan Donald raid in the Clyde also seems to have forced a climbdown by the king's agent, Bishop Turnbull. By the summer of 1453 Turnbull had given up the attempt to extract revenues from Arran and had assigned over his right to all crown rents from the island to Ranald mac Alexander.[87] Yet again, the application of military force had secured Clan Donald sig- nificant concessions from the beleaguered royal government.

The uneasy peace established between James II and the Douglas earls would shatter again in 1455, but by that stage Duncan Campbell was beyond the cares of the world. The man who had dominated Clan Campbell for close on forty years died sometime between February 1453 and 21 May 1454, perhaps quite close to the latter date.[88] Duncan's shrewdness and longevity had paved the way for the smooth succession of his grandson and heir to the collection of territorial rights, jurisdictions and social loyalties that made up Campbell lordship in Argyll. However, Duncan also left a less tangible and perhaps more significant legacy to the young Colin. Over the four decades of his chieftainship, Duncan and his immediate family had engaged more closely with the wider aristocratic society of the realm than his immediate predecessors. Increased interaction with the concerns, habits, institutions and personnel of a noble society beyond the bounds of Argyll and the Hebrides is hinted at in many ways: Duncan's regular personal attendance at parliaments and general councils, his adoption of the title Lord Campbell, the construction of the collegiate kirk at Kilmun and the marriage links to families such as the Stewarts of Ardgowan, the Somervilles, the Cunninghams of Glengarnock and the Borthwicks. However, it would be utterly misleading to portray this process as the result of a series of decisions made with the conscious aim of abandoning a static 'Gaelic identity' and adopting 'Lowland' cultural values and aspirations. As we have seen, many of these developments were in fact intended to shore up and secure the Campbell hegemony inside Argyll against external interference. Nevertheless, by the end of his life the Lord Campbell was clearly accepted as a high-status member of the Scottish political elite in a way that his grandfather had never been. The place of Lord Campbell in the ranking of the Scottish aristocracy was made plain in the mid-fifteenth-century Roll of Arms known as 'The Scots Roll'. Here the arms of the 'Lord Cambell' immediately follow those of the dukes and earls of Scotland, with only the arms of the Lord Keith (hereditary marischal of the realm) allowed precedence.[89] Duncan's status as a natural member of the chivalric aristocracy of the kingdom was also asserted in the construction of his knightly tomb in the collegiate kirk he had founded and endowed at Kilmun.[90] (See plates 1 and 2.) The Kilmun tomb, whether commissioned by Duncan before his death or under the direction of his grandson and heir, was clearly not part of the monumental sculptural tradition supported by other aristocratic families in Argyll and the Hebrides.[91] At one level this might seem to support a view of the earls of Argyll as the vanguard of a process of aristocratic acculturation that threatened the traditional values and culture of the martial elites that dominated Gaelic-speaking areas of the kingdom. However, there is absolutely no indication that the adoption of this type of monumental commemoration was linked to any wider rejection of Gaelic cultural forms or a falling away, for example, of Campbell patronage of the Gaelic learned orders. Moreover, a number of other prominent fifteenth-century Highland lords presented themselves in death (and presumably in life) as knights of the realm, the tomb of Kenneth MacKenzie of Kintail (d.1492) at Beauly priory providing a particularly fine example. The giving and receiving of knighthood also extended into the Hebrides, where it was often associated with particular periods of crisis or dispute, when the crown was anxious to secure the political and social allegiance of leading figures within the Gaelic aristocracy. However, as far as can be told none of these men abandoned the West Highland monumental tradition in order to emphasise their knightly status through their funerary images in the manner of Duncan Campbell's tomb at Kilmun.[92]

At the time of his death, Duncan was lieutenant and sheriff of Argyll and had claimed an uncontested place in the upper echelons of the Scottish aristocracy. The thoughts of those gathered at Inveraray in May 1454 may have been concerned largely with the need to help Duncan's young heir preserve and maintain his grandfather's legacy during difficult and disturbed times. Yet any fears surrounding Colin's capabilities and fortune were soon to be dispelled. As it turned out, Duncan's death was not the point at which the growth of Campbell influence stalled, but rather the juncture at which it went into overdrive. Over the next four decades Colin Campbell would take the family's policies and ambitions into the very heart of royal government. In the west the argent and sable banners of the Campbells came to flap and flutter over new sea- and landscapes. Duncan could sleep easy under the marble at Kilmun.

Notes

1. Argyll Muniments, Inveraray, Bundle 1107. The men executed alongside Graham could have included Thomas Chambers, captured by Colin Campbell of Glenorchy, who was not specified as one of the regicides dealt with in March 1437, M. Connolly 'The Dethe of the Kynge of Scotis': A New Edition, *SHR*, 71 (1992),46–69, at 65.
2. Ibid. The notarial instrument was probably intended to assist Duncan in pleading his case for a restoration of the lieutenancy before the royal council. Others may

not have been as convinced of the validity of Campbell's title, and in May 1439 another notarial instrument recording the 1382 grant had to be drawn up, this time at Otter in Cowal witnessed by Duncan's kinsmen and adherents. However, it is possible that the later instrument was related to opposition within Cowal to Duncan's claim that that lordship fell within the area of the lieutenancy.

3. *RMS*, ii, no.346. Duncan issuing a charter as *locumtenens deputatus domini nostri regis infra partes Ergadie*. There was no suggestion in this title of a jurisdiction limited to the bounds specified in 1382.

4. NAS RH6/304. In July 1445 Duncan Campbell was noted as having received all the rentals from the crown lands of Dunoon and Glendaruel in Cowal for the previous two years, *ER*, v, 202. As this was the first account of the reign for the crown's lands in the Firth of Clyde, the Campbell occupation of Dunoon almost certainly predated 1443.

5. The grant of a half-merk annual rent from the Campbell estate at Ardenslate for the maintenance of candles at the altar of the Virgin Mary in the kirk was intended to benefit the souls of Duncan, his grandfather and grandmother, his father and mother, his deceased spouse, his present spouse (all named) and that of his dead son Gillespic. The witnesses were headed by Duncan's wife Margaret Stewart, and his grandson and heir Colin, the future 1st earl of Argyll.

6. *CSSR*, iv (1433–1447), A.I. Dunlop and D. MacLauchlan eds.(Glasgow, 1983), no.791; *RMS*, ii, no.346.

7. N.D. Campbell, 'The Origin of the Holy Loch', *SHR*, x (1913), 29–34. The 'evidence' cited in support of this argument is the appearance of sites dedicated to Fionntáin near centres of Campbell secular lordship in Argyll. However, the precise chronological relationship between the foundation of the kirks dedicated to Fintan and the appearance of Campbell lords in these localities is very uncertain. *Cf, CPNS*, 307.

8. They also seem to have had a private residence very close to the kirk, 'manerium nostrum de Strathachi' (Strath Eachaig), of which no trace now remains. *Munimenta Fratrum Predicatorum de Glasgu* (Maitland Club, 1846), 163–4, 172–3, 192.

9. N.D. Campbell, 'The Holy Loch', 29–34. In fact, there is no evidence that Inishail was the burial place of Campbell lords prior to the foundation of Kilmun. As we have seen, in the thirteenth century Inishail seems to have been associated with the MacNaughtons. The Lamonts preserve a version of this tale that emphasises the generosity of the Lamont chiefs in allowing the young Campbell lord to be laid to rest in the then Lamont kirk of Kilmun.

10. Prayers for Gillespic's soul were certainly specified as part of the foundation charter for the collegiate kirk at Kilmun. However, the 1440 grant to Dunoon parish kirk was also for the soul of Gillespic Campbell and that charter was witnessed by Gillespic's young son Colin.

11. The lands of Ardenslate assigned over to Dunoon had been a Stewart of Ardgowan estate before being sold to the Campbells in 1402–5. See above, pp. 107–109

12. See D.E. Easson, 'The Collegiate Churches of Scotland', *Scottish Church Hist. Society Recs.*, vi (1938), 193–215; vii (1939), 30–47, at 36–7; D.E.R. Watt, 'Collegiate Churches', in *An Historical Atlas of Scotland, c.400–1600* (St.Andrews, 1975), pp.78–80 and *Atlas of Scottish History to 1707* (Edinburgh, 1996), 346.

13. See A. Grant, 'The development of the Scottish peerage', *SHR* lvii (1978), 1–27.

14. AT, 1/12/1448. Royal sources referred to Duncan as Lord Campbell as early as 1440, but this was the first occasion on which a Campbell-produced document used the style. NAS GD 124/1/147.
15. Easson, 'The Collegiate Churches of Scotland', vi, 193–215; vii (1939), 30–47; Watt, 'Collegiate Churches', in *Historical Atlas* 1, 78–80.
16. *CSSR*, iv, no.791. *CPNS*, 256–7, 282; *OPS*, ii, pt.1, 134.
17. *CSSR*, ii, 10–11.
18. *CSSR*, v, no.1099, p.328.
19. *CSSR*, iv, no.787; I. Fraser, 'The Place-Names of Argyll – An Historical Perspective', *TGSI*, liv , 3–37, at 9.
20. *CSSR*, iv, no.823.
21. The grant of the archdeaconry, combined with the nuncio's grant of a portable altar to Colin Campbell of Glenorchy in March 1437, suggests a real willingness to make concessions to the Campbells. Dugald, as rector of Loch Awe, was one of the witnesses to the notarial instrument drawn up in May 1437. Argyll Muniments, Inveraray, Bundle 1107.
22. *CSSR*, iv, nos. 782, 808, 816, 818.
23. Fraser, *Keir*, 214, no. 18. Isabella issuing a precept of sasine as Duchess of Albany and Countess of Lennox from Inchcailloch on Loch Lomond on 12 May 1437.
24. According to the so-called 'Auchinleck Chronicle', conveniently reprinted in C. McGladdery, *James II* (Edinburgh, 1990), Appendix 2, 160–173, at 160 (hereafter *Chron. Auchinleck* (McGladdery)). By June 1442 Inchmurrin was in use by Duchess Isabella and her large network of male kinsmen. Fraser, *Keir*, 214–6, no. 19.
25. NAS GD 112/25/1 (modern copy).
26. On 4 October 1440 Isabella, Duchess of Albany and Countess of Lennox, gave over to Colin, because of the marriage between Marion and Colin, lands at the head of Gare Loch and others in the earldom of Lennox. On the failure of issue of the marriage the lands were to descend to Marion's brother, Andrew Stewart of Albany. NAS, GD 112/25/2.
27. *Taymouth Bk.*, 10.
28. NAS GD240 Bruce and Kerr W.S. Sasine was to be served by Duncan Gilberti (MacGibbon) of Auchnagarron. For the details of the dispute over Mar, see McGladdery, *James II*, 19–22.
29. NAS GD 124/1/147; *Aberdeen-Banff Illustrations*, iv, 192–3. By the agreement Erskine was to resign Dumbarton in return for possession of Kildrummy, the chief fortress in Mar, for the duration of the king's minority. The witnesses to the 6 August precept were a mixture of royal councillors and local lords. John and Michael, bishops of Glasgow and Dunblane, William, lord Crichton, the Chancellor, William, earl of Orkney, Alexander de Livingstone, lord of Calendare, Sir Colin Campbell, lord of Glenorchy and John Sempill of Eliotston.
30. Aside from the involvement with the Dumbarton dispute Sir Colin Campbell was one of a high-powered council that decided a case between members of the Stirling family in Stirling Castle on 21 January 1443. Fraser, *Keir*, 216–7, no. 20. In the following January Duncan and Colin were both in Stirling and witnessed a royal grant in favour of William Stewart, son of the sheriff of Bute and Arran. *RMS*, ii, no.285.

31. See Ch. 5, notes 72 and 73 for Campbell and Avondale links during the 1430s. *RMS*, ii, no.246. Duncan's only appearance as a witness to a royal charter in the period 1437–1444 occurred on 20 September 1440, the document in question being a confirmation of a charter by William Fraser of Overton in favour of Avondale. Here Duncan appears as 'Dominus Cambell'. The witnesses to the original grant at Lanark on 22 December 1439 included William Somerville, son of Thomas Somerville of Carnwath, and perhaps the uncle of Colin Campbell, Walter Haliburton, lord of Dirleton, George Crichton of Blackness, kts., William de Somerville, son and heir of Thomas Somerville, lord of Carnwath, M. Adam de Achinlek, canon of Glasgow, George Haliburton, and James de Perkle. Lanark, 22 Dec. 1439.

32. McGladdery, *James II*, 12.

33. McGladdery, *James II*, 17; M. Brown, *The Black Douglases* (East Linton, 1998), 257.

34. However, James Douglas, Earl Avondale was also a witness to this instrument and was Queen Joan's principal adversary in 1439.

35. McGladdery, *James II*, 18, 160; *APS*, ii, 54.

36. The reconciliation no doubt explains the presence of Robert, lord of Lorn, and Sir David Murray in Stirling on 5 September. *RMS*, ii, no.205.

37. *ER*, v, 173, 205. There were clearly wide-ranging changes in Strathearn in the wake of Earl Walter's death. David Murray of Tullibardine appears to have replaced Malcolm Drummond of Concraig as Steward of Strathearn in the aftermath of Earl Walter's execution. NAS Drummond Writs, GD 160/1/9 and 10; S. Boardman, 'Politics and the Feud in Late Medieval Scotland' (unpublished Ph.D., St Andrews 1989), 161–2.

38. NAS Breadalbane Collection, GD 112/25/3. The divorce was granted on the basis that Colin had had a relationship with one Alicia Lindsay who was related to Janet within the forbidden degrees of affinity.

39. Most accounts have assumed that Janet Borthwick married George Crichton, Admiral of Scotland and briefly Earl of Caithness, shortly after she was widowed by the death of James Douglas of Dalkeith. That Janet was eventually married to George is undoubted, and the fact that they had a daughter, also Janet, who was mentioned in a charter of 1453 and had borne a child by 1460, would seem to indicate a liaison that must have started soon after James Douglas's death. Crucially, however, the description of the younger Janet as a 'natural' child in the charter of 1453 might indicate that she was born out of wedlock. Moreover, for this Janet to have produced a child old enough to be named in a charter of 1460 might suggest that she was born in the 1430s, prior to her mother's marriage to James Douglas of Dalkeith. George and the elder Janet's formal marriage, then, could indeed date to the period after Janet's divorce from Campbell of Glenorchy in 1449. There is no indication of when George Crichton's first wife died – a feature that may also have prevented a Crichton/Borthwick marriage in the immediate aftermath of the death of James Douglas of Dalkeith.

40. For James Douglas's death before 22 May 1441, see *Mort.Reg.*, ii, 207–209 .

41. Brown, *Black Douglases*, 264–5.

42. *Ibid.*, 272–4.

43. McGladdery, *James II*, 32.

44. *Ibid.*, 34; *Extracts from the Council Register of the Burgh of Aberdeen, 1398–1570* (Spalding Club, 1894), i, 399.
45. *Chron. Auchinleck* (McGladdery), 162.
46. *APS*, ii, 33.
47. *Chron. Auchinleck* (McGladdery), 161.
48. *Chron. Auchinleck* (McGladdery), 161–2. At least, the Auchinleck Chronicle relates how one of the men involved in the slaying had sent Sir Alexander Cunningham, 'chaplane to Robyn kalendare', to persuade Sir James's pregnant widow to come to Dumbarton Castle with the promise of safe-passage home 'in a bait'.
49. *ER*, v, 201–2. On 15 July the exchequer audit noted that the rents of Dunoon and Glendaruel had been uplifted by Duncan Campbell for the previous two years. Cowal had never featured as an area of fiscal account in James I's reign, nor in the years 1437–1443.
50. *ER*, v, 246. For Robert of Callendar's career in the service of the Livingstones, see A.R. Borthwick, The King, Council and Councillors in Scotland, *c.*1430–1460, unpublished Ph.D. (Edinburgh, 1989), vol i, 71–2.
51. *ER*, v, 205, 246–9. Glen Lednock had not appeared on the charge side of the 1444 account for Strathearn, perhaps indicating that it was, at that stage, part of Sir Colin's 'bailiary' within the earldom. *ER*, v, 173.
52. It may be significant that the grant was in favour of the Auchinlecks of that Ilk and was not witnessed by any of the Livingstone lords. Fraser, *Douglas*, iii, no.413.
53. GD 112/3/3.
54. *Chron. Auchinleck* (McGladdery), 172.
55. *ER*, v, 411, 414, 418.
56. *ER*, v, 456; McGladdery, *James II*, 49.
57. Brown, *Black Douglases*, 287.
58. *CDS*, iv, no.1229. A Sir Nicholas Campbell was one of the men named in a group headed by earl William himself allowed to travel through England to Calais in a safe-conduct issued in November 1450; Nicholas was often used in documents of English provenance for the name Colin. Campbell tradition claimed that Colin visited Rome three times, earning his Gaelic byname *Cailean dubh na Roimh* (Black Colin of Rome). At least two expeditions, including the 1450 jubilee trip, can be verified. *Taymouth Bk.*, 13–4.
59. Brown, *Black Douglases*, 288–9.
60. *Ibid.*, 290–1.
61. McGladdery, *James II*, 66–7.
62. *RMS*, ii, no.542.
63. J. Law, 'De Cronicis Scotorum brevia', Edin. Univ. Lib. DC 763, f. 129, alongside William and George Crichton; McGladdery, *James II*, 55, 58, 80, 129.
64. For Ranald mac Alexander's lands, see *ER*, v, 86, 165, 211–2, 251, 289, 333–4, 359, 365, 575–6; vi, 44, 327–8. The identity of Ranald mac Alexander (or MacAlexander?) is uncertain. He may have been a close kinsman of Donald Balloch or a member of the Clan Alexander, a branch of Clan Donald apparently descended from Alexander, son of Angus Mór. *ALI*, Appendix D, 279–81, n.5; K. Nicholls, 'Notes on the Genealogy of Clann Eoin Mhoir', *West Highland Notes and Queries*, Series 2, no.8 (November 1991), 11–24, at 11–12. I should like to thank David Sellar for referring me to this article. See also, N. Murray 'A House

Divided Against Itself: A Brief Synopsis of the History of Clann Alexandair and the early career of 'Good John of Islay' c.1290–1370' in *Rannsachadh na Gàidhlig 2000* eds. C.Ó Baoill and N.R. McGuire (Aberdeen, 2002), 221–230.

65. *RMS*, ii, no.563.

66. The bishop was the first named witness to the royal grant in Montgomery's favour.

67. *Chron. Auchinleck* (McGladdery), 167–8; N.A.T. MacDougall, 'Achilles Heel? The Earldom of Ross, the Lordship of the Isles, and the Stewart Kings, 1449–1507', in E.J. Cowan and R.A. McDonald eds., *Alba: Celtic Scotland in the Middle Ages* (East Linton, 2000), 248–275, at 255.

68. *Chron. Auchinleck* (McGladdery), 167–8.

69. Brown, *Black Douglases*, 303–4. Note, however, that the Knapdale entry does not, in fact, give a year date.

70. Thus the death of William Turnbull (December 1454) is assigned to 'That samyn year', where the preceding entry refers to a duel in 1456. *Chron. Auchinleck* (McGladdery), 164. The death of John Cranach, bishop of Brechin, should, according to the internal logic of the citations in Auchinleck, have occurred in August 1456, yet Cranach's replacement as bishop of Brechin was appointed on 8 March 1454 and was serving as an auditor of exchequer by July 1454; the foundation of Glasgow University, assigned to the 'samyn zere' as the battle of Arbroath (1445), was the achievement of William Turnbull (who only became bishop in 1447). For a discussion of some of the dating problems in the chronicle, see McGladdery, *James II*, 121–4.

71. *Records of the Earldom of Orkney* (SHS 1914), XXII, XXIII; the raid was also commemorated in Clan Donald histories, see below, pp 175–176.

72. See the complaints about '*maledictos invasores*' from Kintyre and Knapdale laying waste estates in Arran. *ER*, v, 167, 213, 253. While this terminology suggests raids, it could refer to the uplifting by Kintyre and Knapdale landowners of the produce of what they regarded as legitimately held estates on the island.

73. *Dictionary of the Older Scottish Tongue*, vol. 1, 818.

74. There is also a faint possibility that the forces of the lordship attempted to take the King's castle of Rothesay on Bute during the campaign that saw Brodick destroyed. In 1475 John, Lord of the Isles, was accused of besieging the King's castle at Rothesay at some point in the past. The dating of this incident is very uncertain and it *might* have occurred in 1452, although the Auchinleck Chronicle makes no mention of John's involvement in its description of the Firth of Clyde raid, assigning leadership to Donald Balloch. Overall it seems more likely that the assault on Rothesay occurred in the 1460s.

75. A.Grant, 'The Revolt of the Lord of the Isles and the Death of the Earl of Douglas, 1451–1452', *SHR*, lx (1981), 169–174.

76. *ALI*, no.75; *Foedera*, xi, 484–7; *Rot.Scot.*, ii, 405–7. By the terms of the treaty Earl John, Donald Balloch and Donald's son, John, were to become liegemen of the English king at Whitsunday 1462. Thereafter, if Edward IV concluded a truce with the government of the young James III then he was to ensure that the three Islesmen and the territories they controlled were included in the peace. The earldom of Ross, the lordship of the Isles and the island of Arran were the areas specified as requiring protection in this eventuality.

77. McGladdery, *James II*, 78–9.

78. S. Boardman, 'Leper John', 233–235.
79. *Chron. Auchinleck* (McGladdery), 166.
80. *RMS*, ii, no.571; *ER*, vi, 48–9, 427–8, 536, 632.
81. *ER*, v, 542, 657; *RMS*, iii, no.316.
82. *Chron. Auchinleck* (McGladdery), 166.
83. *RMS*, ii, nos.573, 574. In addition, Lorn's brother, Robert, was given an annuity from royal lands in the Perthshire Highlands. *ER*, v, 542, 652.
84. *Chron. Auchinleck* (McGladdery), 166–7.
85. *RMS*, iv, no. 791; Colin Neilson Campbell was probably the custodian of the island castle of Eilean Dearg in Loch Ruel, described in the 1440s as an 'impregnable' castle of the lord of Loch Awe.
86. Brown, *Black Douglases*, 299–302.
87. *ER*, vi, 44, 230, 327–9, 419.
88. NAS Society of Antiquaries Charters, GD 103/2/40; *Lamont Papers*, no.35. The charter from May 1454 was witnessed by an impressive array of the leaders of the cadet branches of Clan Campbell assembled at Inveraray and involved Colin's renouncing his family's claims to lands held by a branch of the Lamonts in Cowal. This has the look of a new lord arranging his affairs.
89. C. Campbell, *The Scots Roll: A Study of a Fifteenth Century Roll of Arms* (Heraldry Society of Scotland, 1995), 20–1. For discussion of the date, see pp.6–9.
90. For discussion of the tomb, see RCAHMS *Argyll*, vii (Mid-Argyll and Cowal), no.80 (pp.179–81). For eighteenth-century witnesses to what may have been the original tomb inscription, see *SHS Misc.*, iv, 211; G. Crawford, *Officers of State*, 17. For an analysis that argues for some stylistic connection between the Kilmun effigies and others produced in the mid-fifteenth century for the Houstons of that Ilk (at Houston) and the Stewart Lords of Lorn (at Culross Priory), see M.C. Scott, 'Dress in Scotland, 1406–1460' (unpublished Ph.D. Thesis, University of London, 1987), 132–4, 151, 154–7.
91. See Steer and Bannerman, *Monumental Sculpture*, 28.
92. For MacKenzie's tomb see E. Chisholm-Batten, *The Charters of the Priory of Beauly* (Edinburgh, 1877), 105. The attribution of the tomb may not be entirely reliable.

SEVEN

On the Edge and in the Middle:
The Early Career of Colin, 1st Earl of Argyll

O n 21 May 1454 Colin Campbell, lord of Loch Awe, transacted his first recorded piece of business as the new head of Clan Campbell, a deal over various lands in Cowal, with the representative of a junior branch of the Lamont kindred. Gathered around the young lord was an impressive array of his kinsmen and allies. The first named witness to the document was John Stewart, lord of Lorn, perhaps by this stage Colin's father-in-law.[1] Also present were Colin's uncle, Colin of Glenorchy, and John Campbell of Ardkinglass. The attendance of these experienced kinsmen may have been a comfort to young Colin, but it must also have emphasised the way in which the cadet branches of the family had entrenched their power and authority over the two decades since the untimely death of his father Gillespic Ruadh.

At this point in his career Colin's personal and social circumstances bore many similarities to those of John, earl of Ross and Lord of the Isles. The two men were roughly the same age, Colin perhaps two or three years the senior, and both were surrounded by powerful and charismatic male kinsmen, in Ross's case the fearsome Donald Balloch, lord of Dunivaig and the Glens. In a wider sense the two young men presided over lordships that had developed along similar trajectories over the previous century. The Clan Donald supremacy in the Hebrides and the Clan Campbell lordship in Argyll were both creations of the fourteenth century. The growing domination of one dynastic line, the adoption of charters as a way of expressing the relationship between the head of family and important cadets and dependents, and the development of a definition of lordship in territorial terms were features common to both kindreds.[2] Both families had responded to the pressures of the personal reign of James I by concluding marriage alliances with men favoured by that king. Thus, although John and Colin stood at the pinnacle of a society that was unequivocally Gaelic in language and culture, their mothers, Elizabeth Haliburton and Elizabeth Somerville respectively, were drawn from

Lowland families. In 1449 the Clan Donald's determination to cultivate direct links to individuals of influence at the royal court resulted in John himself being contracted in marriage to Elizabeth Livingstone, daughter of the then royal chamberlain.[3] The regional power of the Campbells and the MacDonalds had also seen the two families acquire and exercise significant royal offices in the previous decade. The Campbells, of course, had acted as sheriffs and as royal lieutenants of Argyll. The earls of Ross were sheriffs of Inverness and Nairn and, in the 1440s, Alexander of the Isles had acted briefly as the royal justiciar North of the Forth.[4] The emphasis placed on Clan Donald's political attitudes as an expression of conscious 'Gaelic separatism' has perhaps tended to obscure the level and nature of MacDonald interaction with other parts of the Scottish kingdom by the middle of the fifteenth century. In particular, the acquisition of the earldom of Ross had given the leader of Clan Donald a natural and incontestable entrée into the highest levels of the Scottish aristocracy. The prominence of Earl John was reflected in the Scots Roll, the armorial dating from the 1450s that displayed the arms of the king of Scots and his major noblemen.[5] Here the arms of the MacDonald, earl of Ross (a galley within a royal tressure for the Isles, quartered with the arms of the earldom of Ross), immediately followed the royal arms and those of the royal dukedoms. The arms of MacLeod of Lewis, a regular witness to Earl John's charters, were also to be found in the Scots Roll.[6] Nor was the profoundly negative imagery surrounding the ambitions and behaviour of the Clan Donald in chronicles such as Bower's *Scotichronicon* the only evidence for the way in which the leaders of the family were regarded. In 1444, while Bower was nearing the end of his work on the *Scotichronicon*, the Provost and council of the burgh of Aberdeen sent a letter in Scots to John's father, Alexander, earl of Ross, requesting that he release English merchants he had taken into custody. The context may have encouraged a certain exaggeration of Alexander's virtues, and the imagery employed may have reflected the concerns of the Aberdonians rather than the leader of Clan Donald. Nevertheless, the missive was clearly framed in an attempt to elicit a positive response from Earl Alexander; its tone hardly suggests that the Aberdonians thought they were addressing a Hebridean isolationist: '. . . for sen, loved be God, heddirtillie [until now] yhe hau al tyme obeit the king alsweil as ony lord of Scotland, and kepit ane hale part til him, for the quhilkis, God will, and yhe sal sone haue grete loving and reward; God forbid that yhe suld, for a litil monee that thir Inglismen has promissit yhou, warpiss your gude name, and the reward and thank yhe have deservide and wonnyn of the king'.[7]

Whatever the similarities between the fledgling Campbell and Clan Donald lords in May 1454, the paths of the two men would soon diverge. Colin Campbell would further develop the mutually reinforcing combination of influence at the royal court and entrenched regional power, enjoying a long career as a court aristocrat and ending his days as chancellor of the kingdom. John, in contrast, would lose the vital ability to defend or enhance his regional interests through the exercise of political influence in the royal administration. Earl John would die a broken man, his vast lordships forfeited to the crown and he and his kinsmen stigmatised in Lowland accounts as little more than the leaders of a barbarian horde. Clan Donald and the Lordship of the Isles came to be presented and regarded in some influential circles as an alien threat on the western and northern fringes of the kingdom, as the representatives of disorder and chaos. Conversely, and at least partly because of the fate of the Lord of the Isles, the leaders of Clan Campbell were increasingly able to claim a special role and status in the kingdom as the defenders of civilisation and order on the dark shores of barbary.

In the years after his elevation to the leadership of his family the general political situation may have presented Colin Campbell with a number of opportunities to demonstrate his loyalty and usefulness to the crown. In 1455 the relationship between the king and the Douglas earls collapsed once more, and war was unleashed again. This time James II had prepared the ground for his assault much more thoroughly; there was to be no second escape for the Douglas earls from the king's animosity. With the neutrality of the earl of Ross and his family bought by careful territorial and political concessions, the way was clear for the military resources of Argyll and Lorn to be utilised against the king's enemies.[8] The Auchinleck Chronicle described how King James organised a hosting at Glasgow in March 1455 that included the 'westland' men and part of the 'ereschery'. This force descended on Lanark and Douglas and burned Douglasdale, Avandale and the lands of Lord Hamilton.[9] It seems more than likely that the Clan Campbell provided a significant proportion of the 'Irishry' that ravaged the lands of the Douglas earl and his allies. Colin was certainly present in the parliament of June 1455 which pronounced the forfeiture of James and his brothers for their various 'crimes' against royal authority.[10] Even before the parliament the Douglas cause was in serious trouble. The royal campaigns of March had intimidated or exiled a number of their followers, and on 1 May 1455 Archibald, earl of Moray, Hugh, earl of Ormond and John, lord Balvenie, had been defeated at the battle of Arkinholm. Moray was killed and Ormond captured and executed, while Balvenie joined his elder brother James in exile in England. Despite a number of attempts to restore their status and authority with the backing of various English regimes, Douglas power had been more or less permanently broken.[11]

James II did not dwell long on his triumph over the Douglases. No doubt partly spurred by the safe haven offered to Douglas in England, the king adopted a thoroughly aggressive diplomatic stance against the English crown. James' diplomacy was backed up by a series of military campaigns aimed at the recovery of three highly symbolic targets, the burgh of Berwick, Roxburgh Castle, and the Isle of Man. The restoration of Scottish rule over the burgh, castle and isle seems to have become something of an obsession for fifteenth-century Scottish rulers as they attempted to return the Scottish realm to what they perceived were its 'natural' (i.e. pre-1286) boundaries. There is nothing to indicate extensive Campbell involvement in these royal campaigns, although Colin may have had some part to play in the assault by a Scottish host on Man sometime before September 1456.[12] The late 1450s also saw royal campaigns in the Firth of Clyde, probably in response to the death of Ranald mac Alexander shortly before July 1457. Ranald's passing re-awakened the king's interest in the settlement of Arran. The year after Ranald's death again saw no fermes rendered from Arran to the crown, but by the time of the exchequer accounts of June 1459 the king's men had managed to establish a foothold on the island. The lands of Blarebeg, Brodick and Dubroch were still classified as 'waste', but Lochead and Catacol were now said to be occupied by Lord Montgomery 'ex dono domini regis', presumably a reference to the charter of 1452.[13] Another crown loyalist, Fergus Foullarton, was excused the grassum and rental of his estate at Clachan beg because of the great quantity of goods he had lost in the service of the king.[14] Montgomery and Foullarton may well have been secured in their Arran lands during an expedition through the Firth of Clyde by the king sometime between 8 July 1457 and 13 June 1458.[15] Here at least, Campbell participation might be expected, and military service to the crown in and around Arran may have contributed to Colin's elevation, before 24 October 1458, to the rank of earl of Argyll.[16]

In some senses Colin's new title can hardly have affected his status *within* Argyll for good or ill. The Campbells had claimed regional overlordship, and the title 'lord of Argyll', for at least sixty years before the creation of the earldom. In 1441 Colin had supplicated the pope for permission to use a portable altar using the style 'master' of Argyll, apparently a reflection of the terminology used to describe the acknowledged heirs to comital and lordly titles elsewhere in Scotland.[17] The extensive practical powers already exercised by Colin as lord of, and royal lieutenant in, Argyll were probably not augmented in the slightest by his creation as earl, but it did represent a significant shift in the way in which Colin's status as a noble was viewed and secured. Since at least the elevation of David Lindsay to the rank of earl of Crawford in April 1398, 'new' comital titles seem to have been made through a belting ceremony conducted in the presence of the king and the assembled peers of the realm in parliament or general council.[18] The will of the crown and the assent of the wider aristocratic community were the mechanisms by which the new status was confirmed and recognised. Colin's standing as 'lord of Argyll' had undoubtedly been secured within Argyll long before 1457–8, yet the achievement of the rank of earl was no empty decoration. Colin had obtained recognition of his place in the aristocratic society of the Scottish realm at the highest level available to men who were not members of the royal dynasty. On the whole, it has been argued, late medieval noble dynasties from within the Gaelic world found it extremely difficult to enter the political and social networks centred on the English and Scottish monarchies with their status and rights intact. Much of the force of this argument is derived from the dealings of the English crown and, more pertinently its local agents, with the native rulers of Ireland and Wales. The barriers preventing the leaders of Gaelic Scotland from obtaining recognition of rights and status from the Scottish crown seem to have been rather more permeable.

Some, of course, might see Colin's acceptance of the comital title as further evidence of the Campbells' abandonment of the 'traditions' of Gaelic lordship. In many – although certainly not all – medieval Irish lordships, inauguration ceremonies and the recognition and acclamation of a wider kin-group, prominent vassals, a recognised overlord, or a provincial community could be critical mechanisms in establishing the legitimacy of claims to wield authority within a given family or area.[19] The Irish evidence, and indications that similar ceremonies were used in the 'creation' of

MacDonald Lords of the Isles, have encouraged the view that inauguration and the rights, rituals and succession practices associated with it were quintessential and defining aspects of 'Gaelic' lordship.[20] The Campbell annexation of the title 'lord of Argyll' in the fourteenth century may also have made some use of the idea of wider communal assent, although here the rights of 'lordship' were, or became, effectively inseparable from the hereditary royal lieutenancy instituted in 1382, the terms of which would therefore determine future succession to the lordship of Argyll.[21] The parliamentary creation of the Campbell 'earldom' of Argyll seems to signal a final, comprehensive rejection of these 'traditional' ways to validate local power. In May 1493, following Earl Colin's death, his son Archibald received possession of the lieutenancy of Argyll through the processing of royal letters of sasine in a low-key conveyancing ceremony at Kilmun.[22] However, we should not overemphasise the coherence of 'traditional' practices or necessarily expect to find them replicated in all areas of the Gaelic-speaking world regardless of local or regional political conditions. The Scottish crown had shown in the case of the Campbells and other west-coast and highland families that it was prepared to support attempts to keep lordships territorially intact by confirming male entail charters.[23] In these circumstances long-lasting and relatively stable aristocratic lineages seem to have developed; the members of these lineages could have seen little real benefit, and a number of potential drawbacks, in the notion of their right to rule being conferred or symbolically confirmed, through ceremonies that involved the implied consent of a wider kin or community.

If the Campbell earldom was a reward for Colin's activities around the Firth of Clyde, then the new earl would soon have further opportunities to display his loyalty, for the gains of the king's servants in Arran fitted into a pattern of restless military and political campaigning typical of James II's regime after 1455. The assertion of royal interests continued apace in all regions of the kingdom, but the campaign had its greatest symbolic weight in the king's promotion of war on the Anglo-Scottish borders and in the Irish Sea. These small-scale but high-profile campaigns may well have had a beneficial effect on the king's standing within his own realm, for they placed James at the centre of what the Scots chronicle tradition regarded as the ongoing and unfinished business of the fourteenth-century Anglo-Scottish wars. The conduct of warfare demanded loyalty and obedience; it also had the useful effect of externalising and vilifying opposition to the crown, regardless of the justice of the complaints about James' dealings with many of his magnate opponents. In the late summer of 1460 James mounted a determined siege of the English-held fortress at Roxburgh (also known as the Marchmont), a stronghold that had resisted his father's ill-fated assault of 1436. On 3 August 1460 the king was struck down and killed when one of the artillery pieces bombarding Roxburgh exploded. The royal forces continued the siege and managed to capture the fortress shortly afterwards, on 8 August. Thereafter, the widowed queen, Mary of Gueldres, arrived in Kelso for the coronation of her infant son, an event that took place on 10 August.[24] The king's untimely death was to have curious repercussions for the new earl of Argyll. In the short term the removal of the king brought war and conflict to Colin's door, but the years after August 1460 also saw the earl of Argyll attain a central role in the beleaguered administration that ran the realm in the name of James II's infant son and heir. For the first time the Campbell lord claimed offices with a wider remit than the exercise of authority within Argyll. Colin Campbell was about to lay hands on the levers of power and he was a man whose grip was not easily dislodged.

The course of events in the six months between James III's coronation in August 1460 and the first meeting of the three estates in February 1461 remains largely uncertain. In the west, the winter of 1460–1 saw Earl Colin immediately embroiled in a renewal of the dynastic struggle in the MacDougall of Dunollie family. Shortly after the king's decease, according to the 'Auchinleck' chronicle, 'John Keir of Lorne . . . was tane be his brother Allane of Lorne of the wod, sister son to downe balloch' and imprisoned on the Isle of Kerrera in Oban Bay. John Ciar had won through to the chieftainship of the MacDougalls of Dunollie in the 1450s as the man favoured by the Stewart lords of Lorn and the earls of Argyll.[25] In 1460–1 that settlement was under direct attack with Allan MacDougall apparently planning to kill his brother and claim 'the heretage'. Earl Colin responded to John Ciar's imprisonment by personally leading a seaborne assault on Allan's forces as they lay at Kerrera. Allan escaped 'richt narowly with his lyf', although most of his retinue and his galleys were destroyed as the Campbell galley-host swept into Oban Bay. Earl Colin's cousin, John Ciar, was freed and restored to his lordship.[26]

Argyll's defeat of the attempted coup against John Ciar in Lorn in the winter of 1460/1 is likely to have increased the tension between Earl Colin and Allan MacDougall's uncle and chief political patron, Donald Balloch.

Argyll and the lord of Dunivaig had conflicting ambitions not just in Lorn, but also around the Firth of Clyde. The contrasting way in which the two men pursued their aims in the latter area is instructive. Both men sought to dominate lordships, Cowal and Arran, that had been inalienably annexed to the royal patrimony since 1404 and in which the crown held or at least claimed extensive rights as a landowner and lord superior. In 1460–1 Earl Colin effectively appropriated the royal castle of Dunoon and the king's estates in Cowal, acquiring the keepership of Dunoon Castle and its associated lands in a move that only received retrospective royal sanction in 1466.[27] At some point in the first year of James III's reign Colin was also made bailie of the king's lordship of Cowal until the monarch reached the age of fifteen.[28] The royal administration may have had little alternative in the face of an effective Campbell takeover of the lordship, as had occurred in the minority of James II, but Earl Colin was evidently concerned to ensure that he had some measure of formal 'royal' assent for his activities in Cowal. The experience of Earl Colin's grandfather Duncan, of course, had been that gains made in Cowal during royal minorities could swiftly evaporate when new factions took control of royal government or when the king came of age. Moreover, the status of Dunoon and the Cowal estates as permanent elements of the royal patrimony that could not be granted away by the crown was re-affirmed by parliamentary statute in 1469.[29] However, Earl Colin's role from 1462 onwards as a more or less permanent 'man of business' around the royal court meant that royal favour was hardly likely to be switched elsewhere with changes of regime or when James III came of age. Indeed, for the remainder of the century the earls of Argyll effectively treated Cowal and Dunoon as part of their private fiefdom. As bailie of Cowal, Earl Colin enforced his 'right' to half of all fines and profits from the office 'ex antiqua infeodacione', presumably a reference to the lieutenancy grant of 1382. James III was more than happy to acquiesce in this arrangement and seems to have regarded the position of Cowal as an inalienable part of his patrimony with some irritation. It was left to the auditors of the royal exchequer and occasionally the three estates in parliament to remind Argyll that his holdings in Cowal were dependent on the will of the crown. The royal financial administrators clearly viewed Earl Colin's position in the lordship as an infringement of royal rights. Argyll's casual approach to answering to the royal exchequer for his activities in Cowal was exemplified by his failure to render any accounts at all between 1468 and 1478.[30]

Earl Colin then gradually absorbed royal rights in Cowal, but Donald Balloch adopted a more fundamental approach to the assertion of his interests in Arran following James II's death. Continuing the policies of the 1450s, Donald engaged in a root and branch denial of royal jurisdiction backed up by military force. Donald's entire career, from his decisive appearance at the battle of Inverlochy in 1431 onwards, had justifiably encouraged him to believe that outright defiance of the Scottish crown could bring real benefits in areas of contention. Where Argyll sought to establish himself as the keeper of Dunoon for the crown, Donald had arranged for the destruction of Brodick Castle on Arran in 1452. Donald's extensive landed interests in the north of Ireland also gave him a political perspective that was not confined to his relations with the Scottish king, and a practical ability to escape the immediate consequences of his actions.[31] Donald's kinsman, John, earl of Ross, sheriff of Inverness and Nairn, was by no means as detached from the affairs of the Scottish realm or invulnerable to direct action by the king or his agents in the north. It is difficult to escape the impression that later in his career Earl John was hopelessly compromised by the behaviour of his kinsmen, for whom he was held responsible without always actually possessing the power to control or discipline them. In the early 1460s, however, Earl John's political and military agenda seems to have coincided roughly with that of Donald Balloch.

It was soon clear that Ross was thoroughly disenchanted with the arrangements made for the governance of the realm after James II's death. By September 1460 a council seems to have emerged for the young king; it included Andrew Stewart, lord Avandale, as chancellor, the bishop of Glasgow, William, earl of Orkney and Caithness, Alexander, Lord Montgomery, and the earl of Erroll.[32] The office of Master of the King's Household had evidently been retained by James Livingstone, who was styled as such in a notarial instrument drawn up in Ayr in December 1460.[33] It seems that the king's council was in Ayr at the same time, for the instrument also noted the presence of Chancellor Avandale, the bishop of Orkney, and William, earl of Orkney.

The composition and behaviour of the king's council established after James II's death seems to have been challenged over the winter of 1460–1. The Auchinleck chronicler noted the appearance of the earl of Ross and 'all the lardis of the Ilis', Lord Darnley, Lord Livingstone and Lord Hamilton, at the first parliament of the reign in February 1461.[34] It is

The tomb of Duncan, 1st Lord Campbell and Lord of Loch Awe (died 1453) at Kilmun. The commemoration of Duncan as a knight in full plate armour marks a departure from the 'West Highland' monumental tradition and hints at the Campbell lord's interaction with the aristocratic society of lowland Scotland. (*RCAHMS*)

The tomb of Duncan's first or second wife at Kilmun. The mason responsible for the Campbell tombs produced very similar effigies for the lord and lady of Houston in Renfrewshire. (*RCAHMS*)

A rough illustration of a clarsach from the manuscript of a fifteenth–century Scottish chronicle, the *Liber Pluscardensis* (Book of Pluscardine). The court of the Campbell earls remained a welcoming venue for Gaelic harpists, poets, bards and tale-tellers throughout the fifteenth century. *Bodleian Library, Fairfax 8, f.190r. reproduced by permission of the Bodleian Library, Oxford*

ABOVE.

Only the arms of the royal dukes of Albany and Rothesay are given precedence
over those of the MacDonald earl of Ross and Lord of the Isles in the mid-fifteenth-
century armorial known as the 'Scots Roll'. The armorial was compiled at the height of
MacDonald power; by 1475 the great earldom of Ross had been lost to the crown.
Add.45133 ff. 47r. reproduced by permission of the British Library

OVERLEAF.

A view of Innis Chonnel Castle, the Campbells' forbidding island-fortress in Loch Awe
and the reputed prison of the infant Donald Dubh in the years after 1490. In the fifteenth
century Innis Chonnel was gradually superseded as a centre for Campbell lordship by the
castles at Inveraray and Dunoon and the collegiate kirk at Kilmun. (*Historic Scotland*)

The social prominence of the Lord Campbell is evident in the appearance of the Campbell arms immediately after those of the earls and the hereditary Marischal in the mid-fifteenth-century 'Scots Roll'. By 1458 Colin Campbell had been elevated to the rank of earl of Argyll. *Add.45133 ff. 47v. reproduced by permission of the British Library*

TOP.

The gatehouse of Dunstaffnage Castle, the principal fortress of Lorn. Possession of Dunstaffnage fell to Colin Campbell, 1st earl of Argyll, when he acquired title to the lordship of Lorn in 1469. The train of events that led to Earl Colin's takeover of Lorn began with the assassination of John Stewart, Lord of Lorn, in Dunstaffnage in the winter of 1463. (*Historic Scotland*)

ABOVE.

The largely rebuilt castle of Menstrie near Stirling. Menstrie was associated with the Campbell family as early as 1263 and remained in the hands of the senior branch of the kindred for most of the middle ages. The origins and significance of early Campbell landholding and social contacts in the area around Stirling and Clackmannan remain obscure. (*Historic Scotland*)

'Black Colin of Rome'. The portrait of Sir Colin Campbell of Glenorchy is one of a series of early-modern depictions of earlier Campbell chiefs to be found in the Black Book of Taymouth. Sir Colin was the uncle of the first earl of Argyll and founder of the Glenorchy (Breadalbane) family.

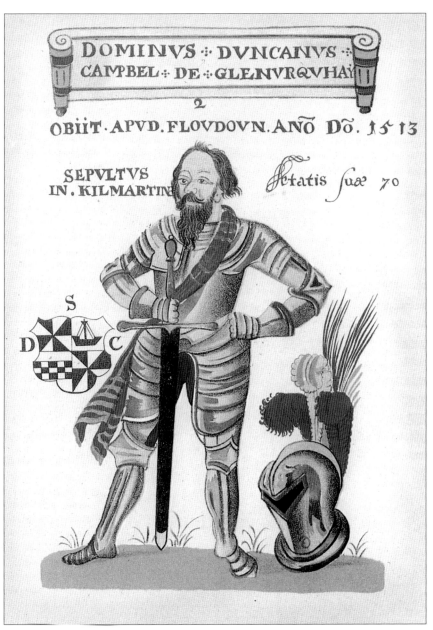

DOMINVS ⁂ DVNCANVS ⁂ CAMPBEL ⁂ DE ⁂ GLENVRQVHAY

2

OBIIT · APVD · FLOVDOVN · ANŌ DŌ · 1513

SEPVLTVS IN · KILMARTIN

Ætatis suæ 70

Duncan Campbell of Glenorchy (d.1513) from the Black Book of Taymouth.
Sir Duncan died fighting alongside the 2nd earl at the battle of Flodden in 1513 and was
buried in the kirk of the earls at Kilmun (despite the claim in the illustration that he was
laid to rest at Kilmartin). Several Gaelic poems composed by Duncan have been
preserved in the sixteenth-century Book of the Dean of Lismore.

'A Campbell trinity'. The relationship of the Campbells of Breadalbane to the
main line of the family is made clear in this illustration from the Black Book of
Taymouth which shows Duncan Campbell of Loch Awe flanked by his son Colin,
first of Glenorchy, and his grandson Archibald (recte Colin), first earl of Argyll.

usually assumed that Ross was named because he had been summoned to answer charges related to his treatment of royal rights, estates and revenues in the north of the kingdom.[35] This could have been the case, as the chronicle certainly went on to detail Earl John's usurpation of royal authority in and around Inverness after James II's death and to link this to a summons to answer charges in a parliament held in the spring of 1462. Moreover, Dunlop's suggestion that the men named were defendants or plaintiffs in the parliament's judicial session receives support from the fact that John Stewart, Lord Darnley, was pursuing claims to the earldom of Lennox around this time, claims which he evidently expected to be dealt with in the parliament.[36] Similarly, Ross might well have been required to attend the judicial sessions to answer charges laid against him by one of the principal members of the new king's council William Sinclair, earl of Orkney and Caithness. Orkney and Ross's half-brother, Hugh of Sleat, were engaged in a ferocious feud that was already in full swing by February 1461. The trouble between the earls seems to have centred on the earldom of Caithness, but the dispute was exacerbated by major maritime raids led by members of Clan Donald on the earldom of Orkney itself.[37] On 29 February 1461 bailies of Kirkwall, writing to the Danish king, informed him that the issues between the earls might soon be resolved; it seems probable that the Orcadians were anticipating the results of the Scottish parliament that had opened in Edinburgh only five days earlier. It thus seems likely that the formal summons delivered to Ross related to his dispute with Orkney. Despite the hopes of the bailies of Kirkwall, the assembly in Edinburgh seems to have inflamed rather than dampened the dispute between the earls. Two Clan Donald histories compiled in the seventeenth century and letters issued by the bishop of Orkney hint at the importance of the Orkney/Ross dispute and attest to the escalating violence in the north in the early 1460s. The *Sleat History* contains a garbled account of a strange competition between Alexander earl of Ross (d.1449) and an unnamed earl of Orkney, while the two men were in Edinburgh, over whose household could provide the earliest and best breakfast. The anecdote is particularly curious when we consider that the Sinclair earls were thought to have held the post of hereditary Pantler (the officer responsible for provisioning the royal household) to the Scottish King.[38] Despite Orkney's underhand dealings the wager was won by MacDonald; the chief result was a complete breakdown in the relationship between the two men. In an angry exchange Alexander challenged Orkney to defend his earldom against an assault that would be led by Earl Alexander's son 'Austin' (i.e. Uisdean or Hugh of the Isles, lord of Sleat). In the ensuing raid Hugh's men were said to have killed the earl of Orkney.[39] William, earl of Orkney, clearly did not die defending his earldom against a Clan Donald raid, but it is interesting to note that William's grandfather Henry, the first Sinclair earl, was said in the fifteenth-century genealogy of the Orkney earls to have 'reterit to the partis of Orchadie, and for the defence of the cuntrie wes sclane thair crowellie be his innimiis", an event that probably took place c.1400.[40] The narrative inventions and confused chronology of the *Sleat History* are obvious, yet there were also clearly elements of the tale that reflected the real rivalry between Hugh of Sleat and Orkney in the 1460s. The Clan Donald raid on Orkney was also briefly commemorated (and fairly accurately dated) in the other seventeenth-century MacDonald history, now known as the 'Book of Clanranald': 'In the same year [as the death of James II] Orkney was plundered by Hugh, grandson of Donald.'[41] The lairds of the Isles who accompanied Ross to Edinburgh in February 1461 probably included Hugh of Sleat, who is likely to have been aggrieved to find his principal local rival secured in a position of authority at the heart of the new regime.

Like Stewart of Darnley, then, Ross and his family had specific disputes with individual members of the royal council and it seems likely that these tensions fed into a wider criticism of royal government in the February 1461 parliament. Indeed, it is possible that the Auchinleck chronicler emphasised the presence of Ross, Darnley, Livingstone and Hamilton in February 1461 because these men were seen as playing a prominent role in the dispute over who should govern the realm in the name of the young king.[42] Over this issue a clear division of opinion had developed during the winter of 1460–1. The men involved in royal government in September included no figures obviously associated with the queen mother, Mary of Guelders. Yet, by the time of the February 1461 parliament many magnates seem to have been prepared to back the claims of Queen Mary to retain (or regain?) possession of the prince and some active role in the governance of the kingdom. However, there was also apparently substantial opposition to any such arrangement. Commenting on the outcome of the parliament, the Auchinleck chronicler suggested that 'thairfor the lordis said that thai war littill gud worth bath spirituale and temporall That gaf the keeping of the kinrik till a woman'. The 'lordis' who dissented from the decision of the parliament were not specified and the alternative to Queen Mary was not identified. However, meaningful opposition to the queen could only have been mobilised by someone claiming to be the young king's nearest adult male relative. The difficulty is identifying exactly who might have deployed such a claim in the immediate aftermath of James II's death. James II had no full brothers but did have a number of sisters. Thus James III was well provided with uncles, but these men were not of royal blood themselves and none featured in the governance of the realm after 1460. Thereafter, the nearest candidates would seem to have been the descendants of the sisters of James I, Margaret and Mary. Margaret had married Archibald, 4th earl of Douglas. Margaret and Archibald's son, also Archibald, 5th earl of Douglas, had briefly acted as lieutenant of the realm during the minority of his cousin James II before Douglas's death in 1439. By 1460 only one representative of the line remained in Scotland, Margaret's daughter Elizabeth, wife of William Sinclair, 3rd earl of Orkney. Orkney could hardly claim authority over the young king on the basis of this marriage, but Earl William himself was of royal descent, being the grandson of Egidia Stewart, Robert III's sister.[43] Orkney's double link to the dynasty and his status as a former chancellor of the kingdom made him a strong candidate for a place in the governance of the realm after August 1460 and, as we have seen, he was a member of the royal council by September. A letter of 28 June 1461 from Thomas Tulloch, bishop of Orkney, to King Christian of Denmark claimed that at that point Earl William was residing with the young king of Scots and had the keeping of the king's person during his 'tender years'. The letter suggested that Orkney's role reflected the desires and wishes of the three estates of the Scottish kingdom.[44] There are no other indications that Orkney was James III's sole tutor or guardian, but Earl William was clearly a member of the king's council that emerged shortly after James II's death. Thereafter, he seems to have been confirmed in the role of counsellor/guardian to the young king by the parliament of February 1461, presumably to assist Queen Mary in the governance of the kingdom. By confirming Orkney's place on the council and, perhaps, giving him a minor role in the prince's care and upbringing, the queen could claim to have acknowledged the rights of a senior male relative of her son, while Earl William secured his position of influence in the minority administration. The entire February 1461 settlement clearly provoked disquiet in some quarters. Amongst the men likely to have been dissatisfied with the outcome of the February 1461 parliament were those who considered that they had a better claim than Queen Mary or Orkney to act as tutor to the young prince. Clan Donald resentment may have been particularly intense if Orkney's position was in any way justified on the basis of Earl William's blood relationship to the young prince, for in that respect Ross seems to have had a better right to a role in government.[45] In addition, the descendants of James I's younger sister, Mary, had effectively been bypassed by the arrangement. Mary had been twice married, first to George Douglas, 1st earl of Angus, and secondly to James Kennedy of Dunure.[46] Both marriages had produced children and in 1460 Mary's line was represented by her grandson George, 4th earl of Angus, and the sons of her second marriage, Gilbert, lord Kennedy, and James Kennedy, bishop of St Andrews. Earl George did emerge as a significant figure in the politics of the minority regime up to his death in 1463, although whether he presented himself or was regarded as a possible alternative regent in February 1461 is uncertain. By far the most active and aggressive of the king's near kinsmen was Bishop Kennedy. However, the bishop was out of the kingdom in February 1461, and did not return until perhaps May 1461 when he immediately emerged as a prominent critic of Queen Mary's government and an alternative leader of the minority administration. Returning to the Auchinleck account of the parliament of February 1461, then, it may be that Ross, Livingstone of Callendar, Hamilton and Lord Darnley were named because they were regarded as the men who objected most strongly to the arrangements put in place by the parliament.[47] The group was certainly more coherent than might appear at first, for James, Lord Livingston, was both Ross's father-in-law and the uncle of James, Lord Hamilton. A regular charter witness for the deceased king, Livingston seems to have been far less influential after August 1460, despite holding on to the offices of royal chamberlain and master of the king's household. Significantly, perhaps, the Auchinleck chronicler noted that shortly after the February 1461 parliament the queen placed her own men in the major royal castles, including one Robert Liddale in Stirling.[48] Control of Stirling had, of course, been the platform on which Livingstone influence in the politics of the kingdom had been based for most of the previous two decades.

Whatever occurred in the February parliament, it soon became evident that the tension between Orkney and Ross had not been resolved. Moreover, Earl John's alienation from, and disregard for, the minority regime seems to have been assured by Orkney's role at the heart of the royal administration. Ross and the Lairds of the Isles retired from Edinburgh to contemplate their next move; the Orcadians would not have to wait long to discover Earl John's intentions. While the threat of further confrontations in the north grew, James Kennedy, bishop of St Andrews, returned from the Continent. Writing later in the 1460s to the French king, Kennedy asserted that he had returned to a realm where he found 'a great division in the said country caused by the queen, whom God pardon, from which there resulted a great dissension between the said queen and me, and great likelihood of slaughter between the kinsmen and friends of either party'.[49] The conflict between Ross and Orkney may not have been uppermost in Kennedy's thoughts here, but it is striking to note that the first task undertaken by the bishop on his return was to head a delegation to meet with Earl John on Bute in June 1461.[50] The aim of the expedition to the Firth of Clyde was probably to resolve the various problems between John, earl of Ross, and the minority government. At any rate it seems that the bishop of Orkney was expecting negotiations of some sort to deal with the dispute between Ross and Earl William in June 1461.[51] The composition of the group, which included James' brother Gilbert, Lord Kennedy, Earl John's father-in-law James Livingstone, and Lord Hamilton, besides men more strongly identified with the queen such as Andrew, bishop of Glasgow, and David, earl of Crawford, suggests a genuine attempt to achieve reconciliation. However, at around the same time as Kennedy met with Ross on the Firth of Clyde, the Orkneys suffered yet another raid from the Hebrides and Ireland. In a letter of 28 June to the king of Norway, the bishop of Orkney asserted that the instigator of the raid was John, earl of Ross, although the evidence from later Clan Donald accounts implies that John's half-brother Hugh was the principal leader.

Earl John and the other leaders of Clan Donald were clearly in no mood to be reconciled to Queen Mary's government in 1461 and the continued disaffection seems to have acquired a more sinister aspect for the regime as the year drew to a close. In April 1461, Mary had offered refuge to the Lancastrian claimants to the English throne, who had been disastrously defeated at the Battle of Towton in March 1461. The presence in Scotland of Henry VI, his wife Margaret of Anjou, and their son Prince Edward was hardly likely to please the new Yorkist king Edward IV. In response, King Edward attempted to pressurise the Scottish government by offering support to the exiled 9th earl of Douglas and entering negotiations with the disaffected earl of Ross and his kinsman Donald Balloch. On 19 October 1461 Earl John appointed commissioners to treat with the English crown.[52] The decision to enter these negotiations may well have been taken by a large meeting of the chief men of the Isles who had been gathered in Ardtornish on 10 October. A charter of lands in Lochaber issued by Earl John on that date in favour of John MacLean of Lochbuie certainly boasted a formidable witness list: Donald Balloch, lord of Dunivaig, Lachlan MacLean of Duart, Celestine of Lochalsh, Hugh of Sleat and Torquil MacLeod of Lewis.[53] Donald Balloch has long been regarded as perhaps the most bellicose member of Clan Donald in the fifteenth century.[54] In 1461 his approach was likely to receive the support of Hugh of Sleat, the leader of the raids on Orkney in 1460–1 and the principal protagonist of Earl William in Caithness; indeed there could have been few voices of restraint around Earl John in the autumn of 1461. Whatever the Kennedy-inspired mission to Bute offered to Earl John in June 1461, it was not sufficient to dissuade Ross from opening negotiations with Edward IV. The talks between the English government and the leading figures in Clan Donald culminated in the famous indenture of 13 February 1462, often called the Treaty of Westminster-Ardtornish.[55] By the terms of the treaty, Ross, Donald Balloch and Donald's son John were to become Edward IV's liegemen by the following Whitsunday (6 June 1462). After Whitsunday the three men would be obliged to serve Edward IV in 'such werres' as the king and his successors 'moved or arreised in Scotlande or ayenste the Scottes in Irlande or ayenste the kynges en-nemyes or rebelles there'. In return for these obligations the three men would receive pensions from the English crown that would be augmented in times of war. It was only after the details of these pensions were laid out that the indenture dealt with the issue that has been fixed on by Scottish historians as the most important aspect of the treaty. If, the document continued, Scotland was conquered by Edward IV with the assistance of Ross, Donald Balloch and James, earl of Douglas, then Earl John and Donald Balloch would thereafter hold all the land north of the Scottish Sea from the English king. In such a scenario Douglas was to receive 'all his owne possessions landes and enheritaunce on this syde the seid Scottyshe see'. This was a more limited but much better defined goal than the vague arrangement for Clan Donald supremacy north of the Forth. Although the arrangements for the post-conquest division of the

Scottish realm have been used to suggest the extent of Clan Donald territorial and political ambitions, there seems little doubt that the agenda of conquest was driven by the exiled James Douglas. Douglas, unlike the earl of Ross, was in no position to bargain with a Scottish regime that was utterly opposed to his restoration. Douglas's goal, the recovery of his wrecked lordship and forfeited estates, could *only* be accomplished by the overthrow of the Scottish kingdom. 'Earl' James was, indeed, already fighting his war against the Scots as the liegeman of Edward IV, and over the autumn and winter of 1462–3 he would lead a series of English-assisted military expeditions across the border, with varying levels of success and support from within the northern kingdom.[56] The earl's most spectacular success involved the defeat of a Scottish force in the western March in the spring of 1463 and the capture of its principal leaders, most notably the earl of Crawford.[57] The fact that the borders of any 'post-conquest' division of Scotland north of the Forth between Ross and Donald Balloch were not given suggests how much detailed thought the leaders of Clan Donald and, indeed, the English king had given to this possibility. The final clause in the indenture returns once again to the specific interests of the Clan Donald and gives a clear indication of some of their activities in 1461–2. It was agreed that if Edward IV concluded a truce with the king of Scots after Whitsunday 1462, then Ross, Donald Balloch and his son and all their men, lands and lordships within Scotland 'and the seid erldom of Isles and also the isle of Arran' would be included, if they wished, in the truce arrangements. The specific reference to Arran in the agreement is highly significant for it implies that the island was, at that stage, under the control of Clan Donald. Royal records confirm that in 1461–2 the island simply dropped off the radar screen in terms of the crown's financial rights. In March 1461 accounts were rendered for Arran at the exchequer audit, while the following year (June) the island was described as 'waste'. In 1475 Earl John would be accused of attacking the king's lieges on Bute and Arran and of besieging Rothesay Castle at some unspecified date. It seems likely that these charges related to the period between March 1461 and February 1462.[58] The driving force behind the annexation of Arran was probably Donald Balloch rather than Earl John. Donald's great raid on the Firth of Clyde in 1452 had demonstrated his long-term interest in the island. The destruction of Brodick in 1452 had obviously been matched in 1461–2 by an attempt to take (and perhaps destroy) the great castle at Rothesay, the chief royal centre on the Firth of Clyde. The assault on the infrastructure of royal lordship was calculated, and Donald's determination to make his hold on Arran permanent was made plain by the island's inclusion in the treaty arrangements with Edward IV.

On the whole the importance of the indenture has been rather exaggerated. There is, for example, absolutely no evidence to suggest that any of the more specific terms were fulfilled. Ross and his kinsmen certainly do not seem to have offered oaths of fealty on 6 June 1462 and it was not until the spring of 1463 that the bishop of Down was despatched by Edward IV to receive the homage of Earl John. Once again, there is no certainty that Ross became the English king's liege at this point and there is no indication that Earl John received any of the annuities specified. Moreover, both Ross and Edward IV were also engaged in independent negotiations with Mary's regime throughout the period and the Westminster-Ardtornish arrangement was simply one of many deals struck by the embattled rivals for the English throne with potential allies that simply withered on the vine as political and diplomatic circumstances changed. In some ways, indeed, the agreement reached in November 1462 between George, earl of Angus, and the exiled Lancastrian King Henry VI was a more remarkable display of ambition and opportunism in a very fluid political environment. Significantly, this deal has not been taken as an indication of the Angus Douglases' long-term policies and ambitions.[59]

Nevertheless Earl John's estrangement from Queen Mary's regime, the Clan Donald assaults on Orkney and the Firth of Clyde, and the earl's negotiations with Edward IV did have some important immediate consequences. The beleaguered minority administration clearly had to respond in some way to the flagrant occupation of Arran. Moreover, although it has been suggested that Ross's dealings with the English king remained unknown to the Scottish government until 1474, this is not certain.[60] Early in 1462 those in control of royal government must have seen a real, immediate and growing threat in the west. It was in these circumstances that, in January 1462, Colin Campbell, earl of Argyll, suddenly appeared as a member of the king's council and as a key figure in the royal administration.[61] By July 1462 Argyll was identified as one of the queen's councillors.[62] Earl Colin may have had many attributes that marked him out as a potential crown administrator, but it seems likely that the queen's council were more attracted by the sheer military power that Argyll had already mobilised to stop the Donald Balloch-inspired coup in Lorn in its tracks. It was certain that Earl Colin very quickly became the spearhead for the reassertion of royal rights in Arran. Moreover, within weeks of his first appearance as a royal councillor, Earl Colin had acquired offices that expanded his influence beyond the confines of Argyll. By 15 February Argyll was in Dumbarton acting as royal justiciar south of Forth in conjunction with Robert, Lord Boyd.[63] Earl Colin's rapid rise in the royal administration was confirmed by his appearance in July 1462 as an exchequer auditor.[64] The review of income from royal lands and estates conducted by the auditors drew attention to a number of areas where royal 'rights' were being challenged or ignored. Of particular interest to Argyll may have been the state of the 'royal' rentals on Arran that he and his colleagues declared to be utterly 'waste'.[65] It was during, or perhaps even before, the exchequer session of July 1462 that the task of uplifting the crown rents from the island was assigned to Earl Colin.[66] Argyll's interest in the commission may not have stemmed solely from a desire to uphold royal rights since Earl Colin's family, as we have seen, had an ancient claim to Lochranza Castle and other estates on the island.[67] On the whole, however, Earl Colin's rapid acquisition of office and responsibilities within the royal lordships of the Firth of Clyde seems to have been justified, implicitly for Cowal and more or less explicitly for Arran, as a way to guarantee the effective exploitation and defence of royal rights in these areas. In taking responsibility for Arran in the summer of 1462, Earl Colin would seem to have been in danger of embroiling himself in a sustained campaign against Clan Donald on the Firth of Clyde, although his first action suggests an attempt to reach an amicable settlement. Sometime in the period July 1462 to August 1463 a delegation headed by Argyll, Lord Montgomery and Lord Kennedy headed north to negotiate with Ross.[68] Given the personnel involved, it was likely that the position of Arran figured prominently in these discussions.[69] The results of Argyll's negotiations are not immediately obvious, but by the close of 1463 it was evident that Earl John was attempting to rein in his brother Hugh. On 8 November 1463 John granted 28 merklands of Sleat to his half-brother Celestine or Gillespic of Lochalsh.[70] Hugh had witnessed a number of Earl John's acts in the 1450s and early 1460s using the territorial designation 'of Sleat', so the arrangements of November 1463 seem to be a direct attack on his lordship. Significantly perhaps, Hugh did not re-appear as a charter witness for Earl John until 1469, when the two men were apparently reconciled. In 1469 the 28 merklands of Sleat that had been assigned over to Celestine were returned to Hugh, but it was stipulated that these had to descend to Hugh's heirs by his marriage to a daughter of MacIan of Ardnamurchan.[71] Further, Hugh was forced to submit himself to the authority of Earl John and named members of his council in arranging any further marriages. The deal had the overall effect of disinheriting Hugh's son Donald Galldach, the product of Hugh's liaison with a woman of the Gunn kindred in Caithness. Earl John, then, had effectively withdrawn support from the branches of Clan Donald involved in the conflict with Orkney in Caithness and Sutherland. John's attempt to undercut Donald Galldach earned him the enduring enmity of Hugh's son, and ensured that Donald would be one of the members of Clan Donald prepared to fight against John in the following decade.

If Earl John's action against Hugh of Sleat resulted from the Argyll-led negotiations of 1462–3, the rapprochement between the two men may have been less successful elsewhere. Colin's influence at the royal court from early 1462 had brought a number of opportunities to expand his interests in the west as men sought his favour and support in their disputes. The most spectacular example of this process occurred within a year of Colin's appearance as a royal councillor. In 1462 a new succession crisis was taking shape in the lordship of Lorn, this time affecting not the MacDougalls of Dunollie but the Stewart overlords of Lorn. On 11 December 1462, at Inistrynich on Loch Awe, Earl Colin came to an agreement with his wife's uncle, Walter Stewart, the brother and 'apperande ayr' of John Stewart, lord of Lorn. John Stewart, as we have seen, had secured Lorn as a male entail in 1452, with his brother Walter as his first named heir. By December 1462 this arrangement was clearly under threat, and the Inistrynich agreement bound Earl Colin to defend Walter and his heirs against any attempt by John to cancel or amend the terms of the 1452 entail.[72] John Stewart had an illegitimate son, Dugald, and the evidence suggests that by 1462 John wished to legitimise Dugald and have him acknowledged as heir to the lordship of Lorn.[73] Any change in the succession arrangements would require royal approval and Walter evidently felt that Argyll was perfectly placed to prevent this occurring. The agreement stipulated that Earl Colin was to allow 'na thing [to] ga throu in preve nor in apertht [openly]'. Argyll exacted a high price for his management of royal patronage on Walter's behalf. In return for Earl Colin's 'supple, mantenans, defens and resisting of al and sundry' Walter agreed that when he inherited Lorn he would give over one hundred merks' worth of land within the lordship to Argyll and his heirs, namely all the lands between Loch Awe and Loch Etive, with the remainder around Ardmaddy and 'Archynaswll' or in Benderloch.[74]

Walter Stewart's desperation to enlist Earl Colin's assistance in December 1462 suggests that the lord of Lorn's attempt to change the succession was imminent. The fact that, as far as can be told, there was no royal recognition for Dugald Stewart as his father's heir indicates that Earl Colin successfully frustrated his father-in-law's plans for the lordship of Lorn. A little over a year later, on 20 December 1463, Dugald Stewart's hopes were dealt a more savage blow when his father was assassinated in Dunstaffnage Castle by Allan MacDougall, probably the man whose claims to the headship of the Dunollie family had been frustrated by John Stewart and Earl Colin.[75] The fact that Earl Colin had such an obvious financial and territorial interest in Walter Stewart's succession to the lordship of Lorn inevitably raises the suspicion that Argyll might have been tempted to hasten the implementation of the December 1462 agreement by arranging for John's forcible removal from the scene. Allan MacDougall, however, was hardly a friend of Earl Colin, and a more obvious backer for his adventures in Lorn in the winter of 1463–4 was his uncle Donald Balloch, lord of Dunivaig and the Glens. Certainly a parliament held early in the following year (perhaps January 1464) pointed the finger of suspicion in the direction of Clan Donald by asking that royal letters should be sent to John, earl of Ross, commanding him not to offer any support to Allan MacDougall, who was continuing to occupy Dunstaffnage. The three estates also made plain their dismay at the death of the king's kinsman and asked that James III should personally lead an expedition to recapture the castle when the weather allowed royal forces to campaign in Lorn.[76]

The parliament of January 1464 had concerns other than the slaughter of the lord of Lorn to address. The assembly had probably been called after the death on 1 December 1463 of Queen Mary to make new arrangements for the governance of the realm. In any case, the queen mother seems to have been gradually excluded from power in the months before her death by the growing influence of Bishop Kennedy. Mary's demise saw a number of men who had prospered because of their association with her vanish from royal government. Earl Colin, however, was not one of those sidelined as the Kennedy family came to dominate the young king's court and administration. Indeed, if anything, Argyll came to play a more prominent role, becoming master of the king's household by 29 March

1464 and increasingly involved in the conduct of Scottish diplomacy.[77]

Earl Colin's burgeoning role at court meant he was well-placed to pursue his ambitions in Lorn. Walter Stewart, John lord Lorn's brother and heir by entail, was given sasine of the lordship and the barony of Innermeath early in 1464.[78] At this point Earl Colin may have expected the terms of his agreement of December 1462 with Walter to be discharged. It quickly became apparent, however, that Walter was not in the least inclined to give over the bulk of his newly acquired lordship to Argyll. The situation in Lorn was made more problematic by the presence of the Clan Donald-backed Allan MacDougall in Dunstaffnage, and the position of John Stewart's son, Dugald. The fact that John Stewart had intended to change the arrangements for the succession to Lorn to benefit Dugald undoubtedly gave the young man a sense of his moral right to all, or at least a part, of his father's inheritance. Moreover, Dugald's claims may well have had extensive support from within the lordship of Lorn and from his mother's kinsmen, the MacLarens of Balquhidder.[79] By the summer of 1464 Dugald was clearly presenting himself as the heir to estates and rights formerly held by his father, and these claims were taken seriously by others. In July 1464, Thomas Rogerson of Drumdrewin paid over a sum of money to Earl Colin, the Campbells of Glenorchy and Marion Stewart as the 'aieris of umquhile John Stewart, Lord of Lorne'.[80] As part of the arrangement Earl Colin and Colin Campbell of Glenorchy granted a bond of maintenance by which they agreed to defend Rogerson against any other men 'that pretendis thaim ayeris to the . . . Lord of Lornis gudis and of all the lave [rest] of the forsaid lordis barnyis', almost certainly a reference to Dugald Stewart.[81]

The struggle over the various elements of the Lorn inheritance was a concern for Earl Colin and Campbell of Glenorchy (married to another of John lord Lorn's daughters) throughout the 1460s. In response to Walter Stewart's failure to implement the terms of the 1462 agreement, Argyll and Campbell of Glenorchy pressed the claims of their wives to various parts of their father-in-law's patrimony, including estates that had been embraced by the entail of 1452. By 15 May 1464 litigation between Lorn and Argyll was underway and the master of the king's household already had the upper hand in the royal courts.[82] Despite Walter's legal objections, Earl Colin's wife and her sisters received sasine in the bulk of their father's unentailed lands during 1464. A more damaging blow came the following year, when countess Isabel, Marion Stewart and Duncan Campbell of

Glenorchy (the son of Janet Stewart, who was probably dead by this point) obtained possession of the entailed lands of Kildinny, Innerdunning and Baldinnies.[83] At around the same time the Stewart heiresses were also given sasine of the lands of Dollar and Gloom in the barony of Dunkeld as heirs to John, lord Lorn.[84] Walter Stewart's frustration spilled over into violence and he and his adherents attacked and burnt the tower of Gloom.[85] The incident served merely to give Earl Colin further ammunition for legal action against the lord of Lorn. These claims were settled on 29 April 1466 in Perth when Lorn granted Argyll various lands in Perthshire in a deal that was probably intended to compensate Earl Colin for Walter's attack on Dollar and the tower of Gloom.[86]

Given Earl Colin's relentless legal assault on Walter Stewart's claims elsewhere in the kingdom, it seems probable that the earl and Glenorchy were also attempting to undermine Walter's hold on Lorn proper. Traditional histories of varying reliability hint at a period of some disorder following Lord John's death. After the parliament of January 1464 no more was heard of John Stewart's assassin, Allan MacDougall. Stewart of Appin histories claimed that Allan died in battle against Dugald Stewart and his MacLaren supporters in Lorn. A less dramatic explanation for Allan's disappearance would be the withdrawal of Clan Donald support as part of a wider settlement concluded in Inverness in August 1464 between James II's administration and John, earl of Ross.[87] Earl Colin was present on the royal expedition as master of the king's household and it seems more than likely that the situation in Lorn was the subject of prolonged discussion. That Earl Colin and Earl John were on reasonable terms by the end of 1464 is suggested by Colin's role, in conjunction with Gilbert, Lord Kennedy, as Ross's procurator at a parliament held in October 1464.[88] The other principal actor in Lorn was Dugald Stewart, although his relationship to the other parties involved in the struggle is unclear. Dugald is reputed to have come to some form of agreement with his half-sisters and their husbands, although this cannot be precisely dated. It is striking to note that Dugald's territorial interests were later concentrated in Appin, north of Loch Creran, i.e. in the area of Lorn that had not been pledged to Colin Campbell in the agreement of December 1462. This might suggest some co-ordination between Dugald and the Campbell lords to cause maximum inconvenience to Walter Stewart.

By the summer of 1466 all of John Stewart's unentailed lands, as well as the estates in Fife, Aberdeenshire, Strathearn and Perthshire that had been annexed to the barony of Innermeath in 1452, had been given over to the Campbells of Argyll and Glenorchy. Walter, lord Lorn, was also heavily in debt to Earl Colin and the guarantee for the payment of this sum was the remaining part of the barony of Innermeath. Only the barony of Redcastle in Angus had passed without dispute to Walter.

In Lorn itself, Walter must have struggled to act as a lord in any meaningful way, given the brooding presence of the Campbell lords in Loch Awe and Glenorchy and the apparently freelance ambitions of his nephew Dugald. Together Argyll and Glenorchy slowly tightened the noose. After the death of Janet Stewart, Colin Campbell of Glenorchy remarried, choosing a daughter of William Stirling of Keir (near Dunblane) as his new partner. Besides his estates at Keir, Stirling also had claims to lands within Lorn from a fourteenth-century marriage between his ancestor John Stirling, and Mary MacDougall, aunt of John Gallda. In 1424 William Stirling's father had initiated legal action to recover possession of these lands from the Stewart lords of Lorn.[89] Given the multiple marriage links already established between the Campbells and the MacDougall of Dunollie kindred, Walter must have been hard pressed to find powerful local allies.[90] The difficulty of his position was exacerbated by the influence of the Campbell lords around the royal court. When Colin Campbell of Glenorchy was employed as a royal ambassador to the papal court over the winter of 1465–6, he clearly used the opportunity to further the Campbell assault on the lord of Lorn. The papal condemnation of Walter Stewart's attack on Castle Gloom obtained in April 1466 presumably reflected Colin of Glenorchy's personal lobbying while he was in Rome.

If Walter hoped that Earl Colin's predominance in royal government might be threatened by the factional politics of the 1460s, then he was to be sorely disappointed. Apparently on good terms with the Kennedy lords during their period of dominance of royal government after the death of Queen Mary, the earl was equally unperturbed by the seizure of the young James III by Robert Lord Boyd after the exchequer session of 1466.[91] The new Boyd regime seems to have had few domestic enemies, with the exception of Gilbert, lord Kennedy, but was notable for three years of reckless and, as it turned out, utterly unsustainable family aggrandisement. In only one area might Boyd ambitions have clashed with those of Earl Colin. Before 22 February 1467, Boyd arranged the transfer of the royal lands in Arran from Argyll to his own son, Thomas, who by 27 April 1467 had been married to James III's sister Mary and created earl of Arran.[92]

From 1462, as we have seen, Earl Colin had been officially charged with the inbringing of the royal rents from Arran. In reality, as the accounting of 1466 revealed, the earl was allowed to keep any revenues raised from the island in return for his 'services'.[93] The arrangement probably reflected the level of military effort required from Earl Colin to maintain the island's nominal status as a royal lordship in the face of the counter-claims of Donald Balloch and his allies in Kintyre and Knapdale. By 1467, however, the threat from Clan Donald may have receded somewhat. Argyll and John, earl of Ross, seem to have reached some form of agreement in 1464, after which Donald Balloch may have been forced to lessen the pressure around the Firth of Clyde. In 1465 Donald experienced a number of setbacks in his Irish lordships, including the death of a son and nephew.[94] These reverses may have curtailed Donald's operations around the Firth of Clyde, although the marriage of Donald's daughter to John Lamont of Cowal in the summer of 1466 pointed towards a continuing involvement in the region.[95]

If Argyll was disturbed by the Boyd annexation of Arran, there was little indication of resentment; Earl Colin remained at court as a witness to all the charters issued by the crown during the period of Boyd ascendancy. The earl retained the office of master of the king's household, and his rights in Cowal were not threatened. In April 1468 Earl Colin was one of the men who bound themselves to support Lord Boyd's governance of the realm, although the fact that the agreement was needed suggests that Lord Robert was already feeling insecure.[96] Boyd's paranoia was not baseless. While he and his son were absent from the realm on two separate diplomatic missions in the early summer of 1469, the network of alliances underpinning Boyd influence unravelled. Despite the bond of April 1468, it is clear that Earl Colin was not an especially enthusiastic supporter of the Boyds, and when their regime collapsed in 1469 Argyll's influence at the royal court seems, if anything, to have been enhanced. Certainly Argyll became custodian of Edinburgh Castle in the summer of 1469, directly replacing Robert, Lord Boyd. Argyll retained the custody of Edinburgh for the following three years.[97] Moreover, the fall of the Boyds in the summer and autumn of 1469 coincided with a number of significant developments for Earl Colin elsewhere in the kingdom. The parliament of November 1469, which confirmed the forfeiture of the Boyds, also saw the final capitulation of Walter Stewart in his long, unequal struggle with the Campbells. Whether Walter's decision to abandon the fight in the west was related to the wider political changes of 1469 is impossible to say; it may simply have been that the long years of litigation and physical confrontation had worn away Walter's will to maintain an increasingly hopeless cause. It is more than likely that further litigation was pending in the judicial sessions of the November parliament. In November 1469, while the parliament met in Edinburgh, the battered lord of Lorn brought to an end his long dispute with Earl Colin. On 30 November Walter agreed to resign Lorn in favour of the earl. In return, Argyll would give over lands that had been held by John Stewart in Fife, Perthshire, Kinross, and Aberdeenshire.[98] In essence, Walter was abandoning the great Highland lordship to obtain possession of his dead brother's Lowland estates. Two additional elements in the agreement confirm the influence that Earl Colin was able to wield in the distribution of royal favour and patronage in 1469. Besides the lands resigned by Earl Colin, Walter was to receive the office of coroner of Perth, and Argyll was to ensure that Walter remained a lord of parliament with the title Lord Innermeath. Walter's new title had evidently been granted by 13 April 1470, and on the following day Walter, Lord Innermeath, resigned Lorn into the hands of James III.[99] On 17 April the king granted the lordship to Earl Colin and his heirs.

One of the immediate effects of Earl Colin's new status as lord of Lorn was probably to increase his interest in the political and social affairs of the Lord of the Isles. In the Hebrides the summer of 1469 had seen further development in Earl John's increasingly troubled relationship with a number of his kinsmen. In June 1469 John was reconciled to his half-brother Hugh of Sleat, but under terms that were to have serious repercussions. On 28 June Earl John issued a charter in Hugh's favour of the lands of Sleat that had been assigned to Celestine of Lochalsh in 1463.[100] Moreover, Hugh was given title to various lands in Benbecula and North Uist that had previously been held by John son of Ranald son of Godfrey of Uist son of John, first Lord of the Isles by Amy MacRuairi. All of the above lands were to be held by Hugh and were to descend to his heirs male by Finvola, daughter of Alexander MacIan of Ardnamurchan. If Hugh and Finvola's heirs failed, then the lands were to descend after Finvola's death to Hugh's male heirs by any other woman who had been approved by John and certain named kinsmen, Donald Balloch, Celestine of Lochalsh, Lachlan MacLean of Duart, and Alexander MacIan of Ardnamurchan. As we have seen, the attempt to ensure the succession of Finvola's heirs to Hugh of Sleat's lordship was aimed against Hugh's sons by previous liaisons, particularly Donald Galldach. However, there were others besides Donald Galldach who would have been upset by the arrangement. Most notably the descendants of Amy MacRuairi's sons undoubtedly regarded themselves as holding claims to the Uist and Benbecula estates superior to there of Hugh of Sleat. In 1469 the senior representatives of this segment of Clan Donald were Ruairi mac Allan, head of Clanranald, and his son Allan. The 1469 settlement thus seems to have sketched the battle lines within Clan Donald that would be drawn up more clearly when external pressures began to take their toll in the next decade. Certainly, when John of the Isles' son Angus Óg rose in rebellion against his father, his principal supporters would include the disinherited Donald Galldach and the leaders of Clanranald.

It was thus just as the internal tensions within Clan Donald were gathering force that Earl Colin's lordship came to the shores of the Firth of Lorn. As in the case of the lordship of Loch Awe in the fourteenth century, we should not exaggerate the instant ability of the new Campbell overlord to control affairs in Lorn by waving parchment. The area seems to have presented special problems to Earl Colin for a considerable period after 1469. In 1467, before Earl Colin had acquired the lordship, it was clearly regarded as the source of damaging raids on surrounding lordships and earldoms such as Menteith. Initially Argyll had no extraordinary judicial powers in Lorn, for the lordship lay outwith the bounds of the hereditary lieutenancy established in 1382. Local conditions soon persuaded Earl Colin (and the king) that he required more extensive rights to control the area, and in May 1471 James III granted Earl Colin the office of justiciar within Lorn, a gift that reflected both the king's favour and the difficulties Argyll was facing.[101] Even with his new powers of justiciary it was evident that Earl Colin faced an uphill task. Not least, the new Campbell overlord would have to deal with the continued social and political coherence and military power of the MacDougalls of Dunollie and the Stewarts of Appin. The MacDougall chiefs certainly retained sufficient status for their affairs to be the subject of occasional comment in the Irish annals. In 1480, for example, one Colla, described as the son of MacDougall of Scotland, was killed in a confrontation between two branches of the de Burgh family in Ireland.[102] For almost two decades the Campbells had backed John Ciar MacDougall against dynastic rivals for the headship of the MacDougall kindred. After 1470 Earl Colin's influence in Lorn probably worked largely through his personal and dynastic links to John Ciar and his family. The situation in the

lordship may, then, have become distinctly less agreeable for both Campbells and MacDougalls following John's death. This may have occurred in
1477, if a terse entry under that year in the *Annals of Connacht* recording that
'Mac Dubgoill mortuus est' refers to John Ciar, rather than the leader of one
of the MacDougall galloglas families established in Ireland.[103] A letter of
protection issued by John, Lord of the Isles, to the prior and monks of
Ardchattan on 22 June 1477 might suggest that there was a major disruption
of secular lordship in Lorn during that year.[104] It was perhaps significant
that the prior of Ardchattan looked, or was forced to look, to John of the
Isles rather than the titular lord of Lorn for protection.[105] Argyll, at least,
could rely on unstinting royal support for his ambitions in the region. Royal
backing for Argyll's acquisition of Lorn had been evident throughout the
period 1469–71. It would seem that Earl Colin was a man whom the king
knew well and trusted, perhaps even liked. The promotion of the local or
regional interests of a court aristocrat was hardly an unusual feature of late
medieval kingship. It may even be that Campbell lordship was by this stage
regarded as playing a wider and essential role in the political structure of the
kingdom. As we shall see, the earl of Argyll seems by the mid-1470s to have
been vigorously promoting an image of his family's power as a bastion
against the dangers that lurked in the west. Given the experiences of his
minority, James III had every reason to take the political and military threat
posed by the great lords of the Hebrides very seriously. Complaints from the
king's lieges on Bute and Arran had no doubt been rehearsed on a number
of occasions before the young monarch in the previous decade. Along the
Firth of Clyde and on the borders of Ross the prince had seen royal
authority openly flouted, his castles attacked and his own estates harried.
The effects of Clan Donald attacks on Orkney, although technically early in
the 1460s a matter for the Danish crown, were almost certainly regularly
lamented at the royal court by Earl William. As an adult ruler James III was
to demonstrate a deep concern with the dignity of the crown and the
fullness of his power as a monarch. The earl of Ross would find that James
also had a long memory. The king's enthusiastic support for Earl Colin's
rapid accumulation of lordships and jurisdictions in and around Argyll may
have been informed by a sense that by building Campbell power he was
addressing a strategic danger or weakness in the Scottish polity.

   Earl Colin would no doubt have been happy to foster that interpretation, but it is also likely that he saw the significance of the acquisition of
Lorn in a rather different way. Lorn was a well-established lordship with a

long and rich history. In the histories of Clan Campbell the rise of the
family to a position of dominance in medieval Argyll and the west was
contrasted with the simultaneous collapse of the great families descended
from Somerled, principally the MacDougalls and the MacDonalds.[106] In a
sense it was inevitable that these processes should eventually be seen as
linked, and Campbell success and expansion be regarded as the cause of
the decline of these 'older' lordships. It seems likely indeed that in the
sixteenth century, for a variety of reasons, the Campbells actively promoted this view of the history of the region to certain audiences, stressing
the way in which their triumph had also established a new and more
amenable type of lordship in the west.

There is a danger in accepting these themes of fifteenth-century
opposition and discontinuity at face value, especially in the case of the
Campbell acquisition of the former MacDougall lordship of Lorn in 1469.
The notion of the Campbell 'conquest' of Lorn seems to have carried with
it the idea of replacement as much as displacement. Campbell accounts,
for example, seem to have treated the period of Stewart lordship as an
almost irrelevant interlude between MacDougall and Campbell domination. The status and memory of the earlier lords of Lorn and Argyll was
co-opted, not undercut, by the Campbell earls. Colin Campbell seems to
have been acutely conscious of the legacy that he inherited with the
acquisition of the lordship of Lorn. Colin certainly accorded Lorn a
special and prominent place within the cluster of lordships that made up
his personal dominion after 1469. The designation 'lord of Lorn' was
employed alongside Colin's established titles of 'earl of Argyll' and 'Lord
Campbell' in the opening clauses of his charters and other documents.[107]
The contrast with the way in which the ancestral title 'lord of Loch Awe'
had gradually slipped out of use as a regular general designation for
Campbell chiefs is striking. Earl Colin's son and heir Archibald, 2nd earl
of Argyll, continued the style 'Earl of Argyll', 'lord Campbell and Lorn',
and employed a seal in which the Campbell gyronny was quartered with
the galley of Lorn.[108] Moreover, the extension of Campbell influence into
Lorn was not simply a question of territorial expansion. Lorn was also a
community with its own traditions, culture and expectations of political
leadership. If the fifteenth century had brought increased involvement in
the business of the Scots-speaking kingdom beyond Argyll, then Earl
Colin's new position as lord of Lorn must have reinvigorated his sense of
himself as a great leader in the affairs of Gaelic Scotland. The Campbells

certainly seem to have enthusiastically adopted and promoted the local historical traditions of the lordship connected to prominent sites such as Dunstaffnage.[109] Aside from the great castle and strategic harbour at Dunstaffnage, however, Colin inherited a wider cultural resource. The Valliscaulian priory at Ardchattan, a religious house founded by the MacDougall lords in the thirteenth century, now fell within the orbit of Campbell lordship.[110] If analogies with the role of religious houses elsewhere are appropriate, we can suspect that Ardchattan was a significant centre of Gaelic learning and culture.[111] Moreover, Lorn had a full range of hereditary learned families, who could now seek the patronage and protection of the new lord. In terms of professional bardic poetry, for example, the acquisition of Lorn may well have signalled the point at which the MacEwens, who seem previously to have acted as poets for the MacDougalls, came into the service of Clan Campbell.[112]

By the end of 1471 the Campbell earl of Argyll and lord of Lorn had only one serious rival for social pre-eminence in the Gaelic world. The next decade would see the last great branch of Clan Sorley, headed by John, earl of Ross and Lord of the Isles, begin its long slide into political disintegration. Although Earl Colin would pick through the wreckage of Clan Donald to his considerable advantage, it is too easy to assume that he was the architect of the great assault that James III was about to unleash. In the struggle between the house of Sorley and the house of Stewart, Earl Colin would play a rather equivocal role. Moreover, Earl Colin, master of the king's household, was also now a court magnate who operated on a wider stage and who had acquired other responsibilities in terms of the governance of the kingdom. A position at court need not imply slavish obedience to the will of the monarch. And James III would find that, in the end, even his most loyal and committed courtiers could be pushed too far.

Notes

1. *Lamont Papers*, no.35, p.17. The exact date of Colin's marriage to John Stewart's daughter Isabella is unknown. They were certainly married by December 1462. NAS RH6/ no.372. The couple's *second* daughter, 'Katrin' (for Catherine or Catriona?), was named in a marriage contract of 6 February 1465. If 'Katrin' was around marriageable age (twelve) when the deal was concluded, this would suggest that Colin and Isabella Stewart may have been married, or at least a couple, prior to May 1454. Argyll Muniments, Inveraray, Argyll Charters.

2. See Grant, 'Scotland's "Celtic Fringe"', 118–141; *ALI*.
3. *Chron. Auchinleck* (McGladdery), 169, 163. This, of course, was a spectacularly mistimed match, made just before the Livingstones lost their hold on power.
4. *ALI*, xliii, no.69; *APS*, ii, 241–2, 249–50.
5. C. Campbell, *The Scots Roll*, 18–19.
6. *Ibid.*, 26–7; *Acts of the Lords of the Isles, 1336–1493*, 41, 53, 71, 108, 119.
7. See *Chron.Bower* (Watt), ix, 207–8 for a chronology of the production of the *Scotichronicon. Abdn. Counc.*, i, 10–11. 14/4/1444. The comparison with 'ony lord of Scotland' could, at a stretch, be interpreted to suggest that the burgh council did not think of Alexander as part of that group, but overall the context suggests otherwise.
8. See *ER*, vi, 124 for the provision of what might have been a silver livery collar to John's half-brother Celestine MacDonald of Lochalsh. Celestine was also given possession of the royal lands and castle of Edderdule at around this time. *Ibid.*, 376, 466, 518, 653.
9. *Chron. Auchinleck* (McGladdery), 166–7. The 'Irishry' were deployed as far south as Ettrick forest, for the exchequer audit of 1456 noted that there had been 'wild Scots' in the King's army in Ettrick forest for whom the warden of Ettrick bought 12 bolls of oatmeal. *ER*, vi, 227.
10. *APS*, ii, 77.
11. See M. Brown, *The Black Douglases*, Ch. 14, for an account of the Douglas earl in exile.
12. *ER*, vi, 204. Kirkcudbright seems to have been the principal centre for the organisation of the expedition, although the death of Patrick Houston of that Ilk on Man indicates that lords from Renfrew and perhaps other Firth of Clyde lordships were also involved. *Ibid.*, 428.
13. *ER*, vi, 533, 534.
14. *Ibid.*
15. R. Tanner, *The Late Medieval Scottish Parliament* (East Linton, 2001), 159.
16. In fact there is an extremely wide window for the creation, running from 23 July 1455 (*ER*, vi, 89) to October 1458 (*RMS*, ii, no.634). In the eighteenth century G. Crawford claimed that the creation took place in 1457 and cited a document held by the earl of Morton. No such document was found in the Morton Papers deposited in the NAS (GD 150). G.Crawford, *The Lives and Characters of the Officers of the Crown and of the State of Scotland* (London, 1736), 43.
17. *CSSR*, iv, no.810, p198. (9 September). The style not only reflected the status of the 'lordship of Argyll', but also emphasised the acknowledged position of Colin as heir to his grandfather.
18. For Crawford's creation as earl during a general council at Scone see *Chron. Wyntoun* (Laing), iii, 69–70; *Chron. Bower* (Watt), viii, 12–13; *Moray Reg.*, 382. The circumstances and ceremonies surrounding the earlier creation of an earldom for William Douglas in the 1350s are unknown, although it seems likely that this would have been the first creation explicitly dependent on an act of royal will in parliament. The *Chron. Auchinleck's* description of the 1452 parliament mentioned the fact that three men were 'beltit erll'. Two of the earldoms involved, Moray and Caithness, were old titles that seem to have long lost their association with active and well-defined regional communities. The third title, Erroll, was a new and avowedly honorific title. *Chron. Auchinleck*

(McGladdery), 166. There is no evidence that the heirs to these titles had to undergo a similar public ceremony when they eventually became earls. Instead the peerage descended automatically according to the rules governing landed inheritances.

19. Simms, *Kings to Warlords*, 16–17, 20, 21–40, 56, 67; E. Fitzpatrick, *Royal Inauguration in Gaelic Ireland, c. 1100–1600: A Cultural Landscape Study* (Wood-bridge, 2004).

20. The notion of a formal well-developed council of the Isles and a solemn inauguration ritual for the Lord of the Isles at Finlaggan finds its clearest expression in accounts dating from the mid-sixteenth and seventeenth century. *Monro's Western Isles of Scotland and Genealogies of the Clans, 1569* ed. R.W. Munro (Edinburgh, 1961), 56–7, 95–110; *HP*, i, 23–4; Bannerman, 'Lordship of the Isles', 224–5.

21. See above.

22. Argyll Muniments, Inveraray, Bundle 1113. Although Archibald was using the title 'earl of Argyll' from the time of his father's death in 1492. It is not impossible that another more locally significant ceremony was conducted elsewhere.

23. See, Boardman, 'The Campbells and charter lordship', 109–110.

24. *Chron. Auchinleck* (McGladdery), 169–170.

25. *Chron. Auchinleck* (McGladdery), 170.

26. *Chron. Auchinleck* (McGladdery), 170; Boardman, 'Leper John', 231, 235.

27. *ER*, vii, 386.

28. *AT*, 1460; *HMC Report*, iv, 480. Since James was born in May 1452, his fifteenth birthday would occur in the summer of 1467.

29. *APS*, ii, 186–7.

30. *ER*, viii, 507–9. The earl's tardiness seems to have encouraged the auditors of exchequer to employ more forthright language in their description of Camp-bell's interests in Cowal.

31. See S. Kingston, 'Delusions of Dál Riada: The Co-ordinates of Mac Domnaill Power, 1461–1550', in *Gaelic Ireland c.1250–c.1650; Land, Lordship and Settlement* eds. P.J. Duffy, D. Edwards and E. FitzPatrick (Dublin, 2001), 98–114, for a review of the family's involvement in Irish affairs.

32. Landesregierungs-Archiv, Innsbruck, Urk.7494. I am grateful to Dr N.A.T. MacDougall for drawing my attention to this document and its likely dating to September 1460.

33. Fraser, *Lennox*, ii, 73–4 (no.51).

34. *Chron. Auchinleck* (McGladdery), 170.

35. Tanner, *Medieval Scottish Parliament*, 170–1; *ER*, vii, 20, xxxix-xl, suggests that Ross was summoned to the parliament in very formal terms, implying that the regime had a number of specific complaints to pursue against him.

36. A.I. Dunlop, *The Life and Times of James Kennedy* (Edinburgh, 1950), 218; Fraser, *Lennox*, ii, 73–4, 49–51.

37. *Diplomatarium Norvegicum*, 5th collection, vol.2, eds. Chr. C.A. Lange and Carl. R. Unger (Christiania, 1861) [hereafter *Diplomatarium Norvegicum*] ii, no.827; *Records of the Earldom of Orkney, 1299–1614* (SHS, 1914), 51–3. The tone of these complaints suggests that Hebridean raids on the Orkneys were a long estab-lished fact of island life.

38. The veracity of the claim that the Sinclairs were hereditary Pantlers is disputed. See *Chron. Bower* (Watt), ix, 41 (and especially discussion on p. 42) where it is argued that a variety of sources misleadingly attributed possession of the office to earlier generations of the Sinclair family. However, the association between the family and the office was obviously entrenched by the time that the various versions of Bower's work were compiled in the 1440s. *Chron. Bower* (Watt), ix, 31. A preface to the Corpus MS of the *Scotichronicon* listed Scottish lords of parliament including 'Synklare panitarius etc.'. *Ibid.*, vii, 413. The Book of Coupar Angus produced by Bower also described William's father, Earl Henry, as 'the king's pantler'. Could the tale in the *Sleat History* have been a coded examination of the struggle between the two families for influence at the royal court?

39. *HP*, i, 35–7. Hugh's involvement in Caithness may have been the starting point for the dispute with Orkney. According to the *Sleat History*, Hugh produced a son by a daughter of the 'Crowner' of Caithness, i.e. of the Gunn family.

40. *Bannatyne Misc.*, iii, 81. See B.E. Crawford, 'The fifteenth-century 'Genealogy of the earls of Orkney' and its reflection of the contemporary political and cultural situation in the earldom', *Mediaeval Scandinavia*, 10 (1977), 156–178 and *Chron. Bower* (Watt), ix, 39–43, for discussion of the genealogy. It seems unlikely that the Clan Donald were responsible for the death of Earl Henry for, as Crawford points out, English chronicles record a great raid on Orkney around 1400 that was probably (although not certainly) the work of an English fleet. B.E. Crawford, 'The Sinclairs in the late Middle Ages', in R. Oram and G. Stell eds. *Lordship and Architecture in Medieval and Renaissance Scotland* (Edinburgh, 2005), 189–203, at 194.

41. 'The Book of Clanranald', in A. Cameron *Reliquiae Celticae*, edd. A. Macbain and J. Kennedy (Inverness, 1892–4), 169 (Hereafter *RC*).

42. Although the selection might simply have reflected the regional bias of the Auchinleck Chronicle which had certainly commented on earlier episodes involving the Darnley Stewarts, the Lord of the Isles, Lord Hamilton and the Livingstones.

43. Earl William's royal descent may have been openly proclaimed in the royal tressure surrounding the Orcadian galley as depicted on his coat of arms in the Scots Roll. *The Scots Roll*, 20–21.

44. *Diplomatarium Norvegicum*, 605–607; *Records of the Earldom of Orkney*, 1299–1614 (SHS, 1914), 53–5 (translation). Since the purpose of the letter was at least partly to explain the earl's tardiness in visiting the court of the Norwegian king, from whom he held Orkney, the bishop may have exaggerated Earl William's prominence at the Scottish royal court.

45. Fraser, *Douglas*, iii, 38–9; NAS Ailsa Muniments GD 25/1/28; *RMS*, ii, no.403.

46. *Vet.Mon.*, 294. Earl John was the great-grandson of Margaret Stewart, the elder sister of Sinclair's grandmother Egidia. Moreover, the MacDonald descent was in a direct male line, whereas Sinclair's relationship depended on a further female link.

47. Unfortunately, the phrasing of the chronicle is very ambiguous and open to a number of interpretations at this point.

48. *Chron. Auchinleck* (McGladdery), 170.

49. Dunlop, *Kennedy*, 211, 219. Whether Kennedy's picture of the situation facing him on his return is in any way accurate is another matter.

50. *ALI*, no.72; *RMS*, ii, no.1196.

51. *Diplomatarium Norvegicum*, ii, no.836; *Records of the Earldom of Orkney*, 1299–1614 (SHS, 1914), 53–5.

52. *ALI*, no.74. As has been pointed out, the driving force behind the negotiations on the Clan Donald side may well have been Donald Balloch rather than Earl John himself.

53. *ALI*, no.73.

54. See Macdougall, 'Achilles' Heel?', 248–275.

55. *Rot. Scot.*, ii, 405–7; *ALI*, no.74.

56. Dunlop, *Bishop Kennedy*, 234–5.

57. *Three Fifteenth-century Chronicles* (Camden Society, 1880), p.159.

58. *APS*, ii, 109–10.

59. Fraser, *Douglas*, iii, 92–3.

60. Nicholson, *Later Middle Ages*, 402, 480. Nicholson argues that Edward IV gave over the details of the agreements he had made with Earl John to James III after the conclusion of an alliance between the two men in 1474. Ross was certainly called to answer charges arising from his treasonable dealings with Edward IV in December 1475. However, the other charges Ross was required to answer were also related to his activities in the 1460s and, by their nature, had been perfectly obvious long before he was prosecuted for them. There is no reason to assume that Earl John's dealings with Edward IV and James Douglas were unknown to the Scottish crown before 1474. *APS*, ii, 109–10.

61. NAS GD 224/890/4/4. The earliest royal charter witnessed by Earl Colin was issued from Linlithgow on 9 January, 1462. After his initial appearance in January, Earl Colin remained around the royal court in the following month and swiftly became a member of the young King's council. On 10 Feb. 1461–2 Earl Colin appeared on the King's council at Linlithgow. NAS GD 12/42. Around this point Argyll was also serving as a Lord of Council, alongside Andrew, bishop of Glasgow, Andrew lord Avandale, the Chancellor, Patrick lord Graham, James, lord Hamilton, Robert, lord Boyd, James Lindsay, Keeper of the Privy Seal and George Ledaile, secretary. NAS, GD 1/1042 (Spens of Lathallan Writs)/5.

62. NAS GD 430/54. 16 July 1462. A grant by Queen Mary to John Napier of Ruskie of lands in Menteith. The witnesses included Andrew, bishop of Glasgow, Andrew, lord Avandale, Chancellor of Scotland, Colin, earl of Argyll and lord Campbell, Robert, lord Boyd, and Mr James Lindsay, provost of Lincluden, keeper of the privy seal, the granter's councillors.

63. NLS Ch. No. 15558.

64. *ER*, vii, 107.

65. *ER*, vii, 109.

66. *ER*, vii, 385–6, 405–6.

67. As recently as 13 May 1433 Colin's grandfather, Duncan, had had a notarial instrument drawn up recording the terms of the original mid-fourteenth century grant. Argyll Muniments, Inveraray, Bundle 1107.

68. *ER*, vii, 204.

69. The Montgomery family had been involved on and off in royal attempts to administer Arran since the 1430s. Like many Ayrshire and Cunningham families the Montgomeries were hardly strangers to Gaelic culture and society. Late in

the fourteenth century John Montgomery of Ardrossan seems to have married a daughter of John of Islay. Fraser, *Eglinton*, ii, no.27, p.21. Confirmation (dated Stirling 9 March, 1413–4) of a charter by John Montgomery of Ardrossan and his deceased spouse Agnes of the Isles. This relationship presumably underlay the strange story reported by Bower of the identification of a man thought to be Richard II working in the kitchen of Donald, Lord of the Isles. Donald sent this man to Robert III in the care of the lord of Montgomery. *Chron. Bower* (Watt), viii, 29. For a slightly different version of this tale see *Chron. Wyntoun* (Laing), iii, 75–6. Interaction between the two families continued in subsequent generations, with Alexander Lord Montgomery being noted as a witness to a charter by the earl of Ross on the isle of Cara in 1456. *ALI*, no.64.

70. *ALI*, no.80.

71. *ALI*, no.96.

72. NAS Register House Charters RH6/ no.372. Argyll was obliged to support Walter against all men except the king and queen and other lords to whom the earl was already bound.

73. See, S. Boardman, 'Leper John' for a detailed examination of the disputes over Lorn. Although the Inistrynich indenture does not specifically name the potential beneficiaries of John Stewart's revision, Earl Colin was charged with preventing the inheritance passing to 'ony man that pertenes to' lord Lorn.

74. NAS Register House Charters RH6/ no.372. Walter also agreed to give Argyll a charter for twenty merks' worth of land in the Perthshire barony of Innermeath. The earl was to receive 'lachfull charter' of the 120 merks' worth of land as soon as Walter received sasine of Lorn, 'be in heyland and lowlande'. Argyll and his wife, Isabel Stewart, also agreed to give up all right and claim they had to the entailed lands associated with the lordship of Lorn. The earl further promised to assist Walter in defending the third of the unentailed lands to which Isabel Stewart had claim as John, lord Lorn's heiress of line.

75. 'Chronicle of Fortingall', in *Taymouth Bk.*, 113; *APS*, xii 31.

76. *APS*, xii, 31. For the dating of the parliament, see R. Tanner, *Scottish Parliament*, 178–9.

77. James Lord Livingston had been Master of the King's Household in December 1460, but whether he held the office up to March 1464 has so far proved impossible to verify. For Argyll's involvement in diplomatic activity, see *CDS*, iv, nos.1337, 1341, 1350, 1362, 1363, 1368; *Foedera*, xi, 517.

78. By 15 May Walter was using the title 'lord of Lorn'. Atholl Muniments, Blair Castle, Blair Atholl, Box 7/Parcel IV/No. 4.

79. See Boardman, 'Leper John'.

80. The payment was a part-payment for the redemption of lands in Strathyre that Rogerson had given in wadset to lord Lorn on 10 January 1463. *Laing Chrs.*, 39. (no.151).

81. Atholl Muniments, Blair Castle, Blair Atholl, Box 2/Parcel xvi/No.3. The lands concerned were in Strathyre and Rogerson was understandably cautious given the proximity of Dugald Stewart's maternal kinsmen in Balquhidder.

82. Atholl Muniments, Blair Castle, Blair Atholl, Box 7/Parcel IV/No. 4.

83. These lands had been annexed to the entailed barony of Innermeath in June 1452. The Lords of Council found in favour of the co-heiresses on 16 August 1465, with Walter, lord Lorn, failing to appear before the lords.

84. *HMC*, iv, Appendix, 483 (nos.187–9).

85. NAS GD112/Box 66/Bundle 1/Item 1.

86. *RMS*, ii, no.876; NAS John MacGregor Collection GD50/1/38. The papal writ obtained by Argyll earlier in April 1466 allowed the bishop of Lismore to threaten Walter and his men with excommunication if they failed to submit themselves to legal judgement.

87. *ER*, vii, 296–7; *RMS*, ii, no.804.

88. *APS*, ii, 84.

89. Fraser, *Keir*, 209–10. Perth 11 Jan 1423–4. A shrieval inquest found that William Stirling, father of Luke Stirling, died in lawful possession of various lands in Lorn. That William Stirling of Keir was part of Campbell of Glenorchy's 'familial' circle by 1466 is suggested by the fact that he was included in a supplication made by Colin Campbell of Glenorchy, while he was in Rome in April 1466, requesting that Colin and his named associates should be allowed the use of portable altars. The other men named were Colin's brothers, Duncan and Gillespic, his kinsmen the Campbells of Ardkinglas and Duntroon and Sir Patrick Graham. *CSSR*, v, no.1116. 10 April 1466.

90. Sir Colin of Glenorchy's daughter was reputedly married to 'McCowle in Lorne'; *Taymouth Bk.*, 11. Duncan Campbell of Auchinbreck, Sir Colin's half-brother, was married in 1456 to Anna, a daughter of John Ciar MacDougall. *HP*, iv, 63–4.

91. N.A.T. Macdougall, *James III*, (Edinburgh 1982), 70–5.

92. *Ibid.*, 75; *CDS*, iv, no.1368; *RMS*, ii, nos. 912–5. Thomas was created Earl of Arran and he and his wife received charters of the island, Meikle Cumbrae, other royal lands on the mainland, as well as estates resigned by Thomas's father.

93. *ER*, vii, 406.

94. It is conceivable that these problems reflected attempts by John, Lord of the Isles to discipline his kinsman as he had with Hugh of Sleat, although they may equally have resulted from internal tensions within the MacDonalds of Dunivaig and the Glens. In the spring of 1465 Donald's son Angus was 'slain . . . by John, son of Alexander. And Domnall, son of the bishop MacDomnaill, it was that mortally struck him with one stroke of a sword'. *AU*, iii, 212–3. K. Nicholls has suggested that the 'bishop MacDomnaill' was Angus, bishop of the Isles, a son of Donald, Lord of the Isles; if this were the case, the assassin would have been a cousin of John, Lord of the Isles. *ALI*, 300–1, but cf. S. Kingston, The Political Development of Ulster and the Lordship of the Isles, 1394–1499 (unpublished D.Phil., Oxford, 1998). Later in the same year the Ulster annalist noted the death of another of Donald Balloch's kinsmen, his nephew 'John, son of Alexander, son of John MacDomnaill Mór', at the hands of the O'Neills of Clandeboye. *AU*, iii, 214–5. S. Kingston, Political Development, 84–5, suggests that the origin of this dispute lay in Donald's negotiations with the English crown in 1462–3, and his subsequent policy of support for the inhabitants of the Anglo-Irish burgh of Carrickfergus, traditional enemies of the O'Neills of Clandeboye. The garrison at Carrickfergus had been under the command of the exiled James, earl of Douglas, since 1463. Douglas had played a leading role in the negotiations that had culminated in the treaty of Ardtornish. M.Brown, *The Black Douglases*, 319.

95. *ALI*, 244.

96. NAS GD8/5. Stirling, 25 April 1468.

97. *ER*, viii, 120, 189, 191.
98. Argyll Muniments, Inveraray, Bundle 1109; *HMC*, iv, Appendix, 474 (no.9). The parliament opened on 20 November. *APS*, ii, 93.
99. Argyll Muniments, Inveraray, Bundle 1109. The exchange of lands and titles proceeded smoothly over the following five months. S.Boardman, Politics and the Feud, 37–8.
100. *ALI*, no.96.
101. Argyll Muniments, Inveraray, Bundle no.110; *HMC*, iv, Appendix, 474 (no.12), 485.
102. 'A spirited encounter took place between the sons of Edmond de Burgh and the sons of Richard de Burgh and rout was put on the sons of Edmond and on the son of Mac Dubgaill of Scotland, namely, Colla, son of Mac Dubgaill, was slain there with one shot of an arrow. And David Mac-in-oirchinnigh and many other good persons were slain there.' *AU*, iii, 271–3; *AFM*, iv, 1114–5. Quite who was being accorded the title MacDougall of Scotland is unclear.
103. *AC*, 578–9.
104. *ALI*, no.112.
105. The identity of the prior in 1477 is uncertain, but in 1489 the prior was Duncan MacDougall and the office seems, at that point, to have been within the patronage of the MacDougall family. Duncan was certainly succeeded as prior by his brother Dugald. Steer and Bannerman, *Sculpture*, 133–4, no.57.
106. e.g. *Records of* Argyll, 9–10.
107. See *RMS*, ii, *passim*.
108. Stevenson and Wood, *Seals*, ii, p.270.
109. See below, 289, notes 94 and 96.
110. Cowan and Easson, *Religious Houses*, 83–4.
111. See M.MacGregor, 'Church and culture in the late medieval Highlands', *The Church in the Highlands*, ed. James Kirk (Edinburgh, 1998), 1–36, at 20, 32, 34; Steer and Bannerman, *Sculpture*, 72–4.
112. *Book of the Dean*, xxi; MacGregor, 'Church and Culture', 16; W. Gillies, 'Gaelic: The Classical Tradition', in *History of Scottish Literature*, vol.1, ed. R.D.S. Jack, (Aberdeen, 1988), 245–62, at 248–9; Angus Matheson, 'Bishop Carsewell', *TGSI*, 42 (1953–59), 182–205, at 200–203. The same text appears as Appendix II, 'The MacEwens', in *Foirm na n-Urrnuidheadh*, ed. R.L. Thomson (Edinburgh, 1970), 183–6.

EIGHT

Courting the Savage?

E arl Colin had arrived as a man of business at the royal court at a time of steady change in the aspirations of government. A greatly expanded royal patrimony, the increasing popularity of the king's own courts, and a new determination to exploit the financial possibilities of royal rights all threatened to modify the relationship between the royal bureaucracy and the kingdom's regional and local communities and lordships.[1] For three decades Colin would successfully navigate through these, sometimes convergent, occasionally conflicting currents of political and administrative development.

The earl seems to have engaged happily with the duties and culture of a royal administrator and the values of an increasingly economically 'progressive' and civilly-minded bureaucracy growing around the crown. At the same time Argyll's position allowed him to peddle influence and royal favour: it was inevitable that Earl Colin should emerge as the focus and representative for factional and regional aristocratic interests. The earl's daughters were much sought after and married into prominent families from across the kingdom. By the 1480s Earl Colin lay at the centre of a network of kinsmen and allies that reached into most areas of the realm. Away from the purely factional aspects of his political power, Argyll also seems to have functioned as the standard bearer for the culture and society of his west-coast lordships. It is usually asserted that late-medieval Scotland saw the growth of a more antagonistic relationship between the principal cultural and linguistic groups within the kingdom. The emergence of a vocabulary that defined and characterised Highland and Lowland societies as quite distinct from each other is seen to date to the fourteenth century. The condemnation of the Scottish Gael in a variety of late-medieval Lowland sources is well known and much highlighted.[2] Less obvious is what seems to have been a consistent counter-argument that found its way into Lowland consciousness at least partly through Campbell lordship. The promotion of the Campbells as crown loyalists may have been self-serving, but it was bound up with wider justifications of the place of Gaelic Scotland in the history, and indeed the future, of the Scottish realm.

In the long run, Argyll's familial and personal reputation for political probity and loyalty proved to be a dangerous combination for James III. In a reign characterised by political strife and a number of direct challenges to the king's authority, James III's most senior councillor would turn his back on the king in 1482 and again in 1488. Argyll's decision to abandon his king undoubtedly included, but probably went beyond, short-term political calculation. For two decades James III's governance of the realm was to be the subject of parliamentary and literary criticism that, in many instances, seemed to commiserate with rather than condemn the King's officers. In the end, Earl Colin's commitment to the good governance of the realm may have been proved not in his twenty-six years of service to James III, but in his appearance at Sauchieburn in the rebel army opposing the king.

The traumatic end of James III's kingship could hardly have been guessed when the young king assumed full control of his government towards the end of 1469.[3] Argyll was by this stage already a permanent fixture in the royal administration. Earl Colin had a near-perfect record of attendance on the monarch, as measured by his appearances as a witness to Great Seal charters, from 1462 until the first great political crisis of the reign in 1482.[4] The earl can reasonably be regarded as a member of the king's 'daily council'. Constant residence near the royal court inevitably restricted Earl Colin's role as an active lord within Argyll itself; and indeed the earl issued only a handful of documents from within the province in the twenty-six years between 1462 and James III's death in 1488.[5] The day-to-day administration of affairs in the west was presumably left in the hands of Argyll's many uncles and cousins, who filled the various hereditary local offices within the lordship.

Earl Colin's prolonged absences from Argyll also created the need for accommodation near the major centres of royal administration. As master of the king's household Argyll may have been allocated his own quarters in the various royal lodgings, although this could hardly have provided for the earl's household and retinue. The Campbells' long-established connections to the Dominican houses at Stirling and Glasgow and the Carmelites at Tullilum may also have been pressed into service, but the earl's needs after 1462 clearly extended beyond occasional hospitality. Of the earl's own residences, Castle Gloom near Dollar (renamed Castle Campbell in 1489), acquired by Earl Colin in the 1460s as part of the Lorn inheritance, was within striking distance of Stirling. The castle was rebuilt during the second half of the fifteenth century and seems to have been used by the earl on a fairly regular basis. However, by the end of his career Earl Colin had adopted the inevitable solution and acquired properties in the burghs of Edinburgh, Stirling and Dumbarton.[6]

Earl Colin's life as a courtier, advisor, diplomat, royal judge and administrator involved more than a change of location. Argyll was now in a social environment where bureaucratic and legalistic visions of the governance of the realm were regularly rehearsed; indeed he was a figure responsible for upholding the functions of royal government (and royal interests) in a wide variety of contexts. Moreover, Earl Colin's network of social contacts and kinsmen by marriage extended far beyond his family's west-coast heartland and it would seem likely that he was increasingly affected by the conventions, attitudes and fashions of this wider group. There are occasional hints that these perspectives affected the way in which Earl Colin dealt with his own regional lordship. On 8 May 1474, for example, James III raised Inveraray to the status of a burgh of barony because of the 'singular favour' that he bore toward Earl Colin.[7] The creation of burghs of barony was a common enough occurrence in fifteenth-century Scotland as a whole, but relatively unusual in the context of Argyll and the Isles. The implication that Earl Colin was interested in the economic exploitation and improvement of certain areas of his lord-ship through commerce seems to fit in well with the aspirations of the royal administration and aristocratic circle of which he was now a part. The newly built residence at Inveraray (probably constructed in the lifetime of Earl Colin's grandfather) dominated a likely harbour site at the point where the Aray flowed into Loch Fyne. The Earl's residence at Inveraray, described by Argyll in 1470 as 'our manor', was demolished in the eighteenth century but the few extant depictions of the building suggest that it was a substantial tower house.[8] The establishment of a burgh of barony in a Highland lordship had a near-contemporary parallel in the Badenoch, where the Gordon earls of Huntly had acquired formal burghal status for Kingussie in 1464.[9]

It would be wrong, however, to suggest that Colin was attempting radical or sustained reform of his Highland lordships. At this point the most important aspect of his position of influence at the centre of royal affairs was that Argyll was able to entrench his position in the west and divert a steady stream of patronage to his own family and allies. Earl Colin was himself the beneficiary of considerable royal largesse during the period after 1469, most notably, of course, in the various negotiations and grants concerning Lorn in 1469–71. There was a further major grant on 18 January 1473 when James III gave over to Earl Colin *and his heirs* the custody of the castle of Dunoon and its associated estates in Cowal.[10] The attempt to give Earl Colin heritable title to Dunoon was bound to provoke opposition, for the grant flew in the face of repeated parliamentary legislation concerned with the preservation of the royal patrimony.[11] The young James III may have been wishing to dispose of what he regarded as his property as he saw fit, but it soon transpired that the auditors of the exchequer were not willing to acquiesce in this endeavour. Despite the grant of 1473 Earl Colin's hold on Dunoon would remain vulnerable to challenge from those intent on the preservation of royal rights.

If Argyll was the object of considerable royal favour, the other great lord of Gaelic Scotland, John, earl of Ross, was less blessed. In 1475 John was accused of a number of offences against the crown, his estates forfeited, and his lordships attacked by magnates to whom the king had devolved extensive military and judicial rights. Despite being widely discussed, the sequence of events leading up to the great royal assault on Earl John in 1475 remains rather mysterious.[12] The charges laid against John in the parliament of November 1475 seem on the whole, and with one significant exception, to refer to events that had occurred at least a decade before. It is difficult to escape the impression that many of these accusations were wheeled out to justify what was, in effect, an aggressive royal campaign to capitalise on Earl John's political difficulties in 1473–5.

As we have seen, there were already deep tensions within Clan Donald by the end of 1469. Donald Galldach and the chief members of Clanranald were thoroughly alienated from Earl John while Donald's father, Hugh of Sleat, was at best a lukewarm supporter dragooned into obedience by the temporary loss of his Skye estates. Around 1473 Earl John's authority suffered a grievous blow with the death of his elder half-brother Celestine (Gillespic) of Lochalsh. Celestine had clearly been one of John's principal allies, a regular witness to John's charters and a member of his council, and had been particularly active in maintaining Earl John's interests in and around Ross and Inverness. Celestine had acted as sheriff depute and as sheriff of Inverness for Earl John in 1450, 1461 and 1467, on two of these occasions also being styled Ross's lieutenant. Celestine had also been the principal agent in John's campaign against Hugh of Sleat and his sons in the 1460s; the lord of Lochalsh's death *c.*1473 suddenly left the earl of Ross vulnerable to his enemies both within and outwith Clan Donald.[13] If, as has been recently suggested, Scottish kings were never wholly reconciled to the triumph of MacDonald claims to Ross, Kintyre and Knapdale, then James III was now presented with an ideal opportunity for action.[14] Earl John's response to his brother's death was to attempt rapidly to build up the power of his own son Angus Óg in Inverness and Nairn as a replacement for the lord of Lochalsh. The only near-contemporary accusation levelled against John in 1475 was that he had (presumably after Celestine's death) promoted his 'bastard son' Angus as his 'lieutenant' and given him jurisdiction over the king's lieges in Inverness and Nairn, with the power to 'justify' (execute) those who defied his authority.[15] The accusation of bastardy levelled at Angus Óg reflected the tangled state of Earl John's personal affairs. In 1449, as we have seen, John had married Elizabeth Livingstone, but the relationship had collapsed by 1464 at the latest. In January of that year Elizabeth lamented to the pope that she had been ejected from her husband's lands and that he was living with an 'adulteress'.[16] Whether the 'adulteress' of 1464 was also Angus Óg's mother is wholly unclear. The only near-contemporary evidence relating to Angus's mother, a Gaelic poem lamenting Angus's death, provides the unhelpfully ubiquitous Christian name Margaret.[17] Curiously, on 6 February 1475 a marriage indenture concluded at Dingwall was finalised in the presence of 'Johne of the Yle erle of Ross and lord of the Ilis, laidy Margret of the Ilis, Huchane of the Ilis of Slet, and utheris gentillis of the saide lordis counsale'.[18] The otherwise unidentified 'laidy Margret' may, of course, have been a kinswoman of John and Hugh. However, it is just possible that she was Angus Óg's mother and effectively Earl John's 'wife', her status recognised in the Isles if not elsewhere. In the seventeenth-century *Sleat History* it was claimed that Angus's mother was the daughter of a Douglas earl of Angus. At first sight this seems rather unlikely and there is certainly no other hint from fifteenth-century sources of such a match.[19] Angus Óg was old enough to act as his father's lieutenant in Inverness and Nairn in the period 1473–November 1475 and it is therefore difficult to envisage that his birth could have occurred after 1460. It seems most probable that Angus was born either in the 1450s (indicating that Earl John had abandoned fidelity in his relationship with Elizabeth Livingstone long before her complaint of 1464) or prior to the Livingstone marriage of 1449. For much of the 1450s, of course, the Scottish crown had been lobbying hard to detach John from the Douglas interest. A liaison at that stage between Earl John and (an illegitimate?) daughter or sister of George, earl of Angus, one of the major figures opposed to James, earl of Douglas, is not inconceivable. An even more intriguing possibility is that the *Sleat History* has confused the earls of Douglas with the Douglas earls of Angus. Was Margaret actually a kinswoman of Earl James Douglas, who was known to have entered a political and military alliance with Earl John in 1452? If this was the case, then the promotion of Earl John's 'Douglas' offspring as his heir in the 1470s might well have alarmed the king. The accusation over Angus Óg would then appear as a natural extension of the charges laid against John in November 1475, the bulk of which related to the period of Ross's co-operation with the Douglases in the early 1460s or 1450s. So much is speculation.

Despite the extensive powers handed over to him, Angus Óg lacked Celestine's established influence and prestige and the Clan Donald supremacy in the region around Inverness was soon under direct threat. The first of Ross's local rivals to take advantage of Celestine's death was George Gordon, earl of Huntly, whose family had contested control of Badenoch and the Great Glen with Clan Donald since the 1450s. By 1474 Huntly and Ross's men were in open conflict.[20] In October 1475 Earl John was summoned to face a variety of charges, including treasonable dealings with Edward IV and the exiled earl of Douglas. However, the charges relating to the position of John's son Angus Óg in Inverness and Nairn probably give a better indication of the battleground between the crown and Earl John in 1475.

In the parliament of November 1475 John, earl of Ross, was found guilty on all charges in his absence and his estates and lordships were forfeited to the crown.[21] In December James III issued a series of grants of lieutenancy instructing a number of his magnates to raise the king's lieges and to execute the sentence of forfeiture. On 4 December Argyll received a letter of lieutenancy that says much about the extent of Campbell political and social influence at this point. Earl Colin's commission covered not only Argyll and Lorn, but also the earldoms of Lennox and Menteith, the lordships of Strathgartney, Balquhidder, Discher and Toyer, Glen Dochart and Glen Falloch, and the leadership of the earl's own tenants in Strathearn. In short, the entire swathe of Highland lordships that had been held by the Albany Stewarts before their forfeiture in 1425 was effectively within the military orbit of Earl Colin. This probably reflected

Argyll's peacetime influence in the same vast area. The grant was not a sole commission, for Laurence Lord Oliphant, John Drummond of Stobhall and William Stirling of Keir were named alongside the earl.[22] However, all three men named were already aligned with the Campbells through marriage and/or service to the earl and they should probably be regarded as the earl's auxiliaries in raising the king's lieges rather than as commanders of equal status. Thereafter, however, the role of Earl Colin in the campaigns that followed over the winter of 1475–6 is thoroughly obscure. The earl was in Inveraray on 24 February 1476 when he created Duncan Campbell of Glenorchy his lieutenant depute in Discher, Toyer, Glen Dochart, Glen Fallach and Glenorchy, presumably in preparation for action in the west.[23] The activities of some of the king's other franchised warlords are better recorded. George, earl of Huntly, for example, is known to have attacked 'the King's rebels' in Lochaber and to have taken Ross's castle of Dingwall by 28 March 1476.[24] It was noted that Huntly had enjoyed the assistance of one Hugh of the Isles, probably, although not certainly, John's own half-brother, freed at last from the oppressive shadow of Celestine of Lochalsh. By the following July the combined pressure of the campaigns launched against his interests in Ross, Lochaber and elsewhere had forced Earl John into an abject surrender of the earldom of Ross and the lordships of Kintyre and Knapdale to the crown.[25] In return John was restored to the Lordship of the Isles (now deemed to be a mere lordship of parliament), which was to descend after his death to his son Angus Óg, whom failing to a second son John. The royal recognition of John's male heirs may have been a minor triumph, but it was reasonably significant in a context where the influence of John's estranged wife Elizabeth Livingstone ensured that John had never been able to secure canonically legitimate heirs.

Earl Colin's part in the traumatic events of 1475–6 is not immediately recoverable. Given the area of his lieutenancy and the sphere of Campbell influence, it seems likely that Clan Donald lordship around the Firth of Clyde, particularly in Kintyre and Knapdale, would have been most vulnerable to Earl Colin and his allies. Unfortunately, the traditional histories of Clan Campbell have next to nothing to say about Argyll's actions in this crucial period. However, Earl Colin looms large in the surviving Clan Donald accounts as a crown agent and as a consistent supporter of the position of John of the Isles against his enemies within Clan Donald. There are, however, intractable problems in squaring the available narrative accounts with the chronology of events suggested by documentary sources. What follows is a necessarily tentative and speculative attempt to reconcile the various pieces of evidence. The two main narrative sources covering the period from the perspective of Clan Donald, the *Sleat History* and the *Clanranald Book*, were both compiled in the seventeenth century but clearly incorporated earlier accounts. From the way in which the *Sleat History* dealt with the Orkney/Clan Donald dispute, we might expect a fairly accurate depiction of discrete events and attitudes within a loose, confused and conflated chronology. The authorship of this history has traditionally been ascribed to a 'Hugh Macdonald, a Skye seannachie', although John Bannerman has suggested that the history as it stands might be the work of a Beaton historian in the service of the MacDonalds of Sleat. More recently Martin MacGregor has advanced the claims of one Captain Hugh MacDonald of Piblesgarry.[26] The *Clanranald Book* is a rather different beast, written in Gaelic and apparently the product of one of the great learned families of the west, the MacMhuirich bards.[27] Where it can be tested against other sources, the Clanranald narrative seems, on the whole, to be much more precise in both the chronology and explanation of events than the *Sleat History*. As we shall see, the fact that both histories were associated with northern branches of Clan Donald may be significant in terms of the interpretation they provide of the problems that beset the fifteenth-century Lordship of the Isles.

In particular, we should be wary of the Clanranald/Sleat perspective underlying both the *Sleat History* and the *Clanranald Book*. The narratives effectively point the finger of blame for the disastrous decline of the lordship after 1460 directly at John of the Isles. Others in Gaelic Scotland were perhaps less inclined to this view, and for the adherents and allies of Lord John it must have seemed that the chiefs of Clanranald and Sleat bore a heavy responsibility for their behaviour. An echo of this viewpoint is perhaps preserved in the scathing satire on Allan mac Ruairi of Clanranald by Finlay the Red Bard.[28]

According to the Sleat and Clanranald histories, the tensions within the lordship initially reflected the partiality in Earl John's distribution of patronage. Earl John showed considerable favour to the MacLeans, granting them the lands of Morvern 'and many of his lands in the north to others'.[29] The *Clanranald Book* remarks succinctly that Angus and his father fell out 'about the division of his territory and land, in consequence of which a war broke out between the chiefs of the Isles and the tribe of MacDonald, the tribe having joined Angus and the chiefs having joined John'. As a result of the conflict John went to the earl of Argyll and gave him all the land 'between the river Add and Altna Sionnach at Braigh Chinntire . . . for going with him before the king to complain of his son'.[30] Certainly, as we have seen, there is some evidence that the northern branches of Clan Donald and some of the offspring of Hugh of Sleat were under direct territorial pressure by the end of the 1460s. The influential position of the MacLeans of Duart in John's council during this period is also undoubted. Lachlan MacLean of Duart was Steward of Earl John's household and a regular witness to his charters.[31] At the time of the promotion of Celestine of Lochalsh at the expense of Hugh of Sleat in 1463 Celestine was married to Finvola, Lachlan MacLean's daughter. The lands given to Celestine in Skye, Sutherland and Inverness-shire in 1463–4 were all to descend in the first instance to the children of this marriage.[32] Angus Óg certainly seems to have come to share the Clanranald antipathy to the influence of the 'upstart' MacLeans within the Lordship of the Isles.[33] A royal grant to the then MacLean of Duart in November 1542 suggested that MacLean's grandfather, Hector, had held a number of estates on Islay at the time of his death. However, the written title for the lands had been burnt and destroyed by Angus, master of the Isles, at the time of the 'mortal enmity' between Angus and Hector.[34]

All the above tends to confirm elements of the 'traditional' accounts. The prominence of the MacLeans in the council of the Lord of the Isles *was* a matter of resentment. The disinherited Donald Galldach and the lords of Clanranald *were* opposed to John's territorial settlement within the lordship and were thus more than likely to support any bid by Angus Óg to displace his father whenever this occurred. However, the sequence of events suggested by these accounts and the motivation ascribed to the principal protagonists may be rather less reliable. The chronology adopted in the Sleat/Clanranald traditions implies that Angus Óg's rebellion against his father preceded the royal assault on the lordship, and that it was John's subsequent petulant resignation of his lands that opened up the lordship to the ambitions of the crown and the earl of Argyll. While a speculative argument can be made for the idea that Earl John was already in serious trouble in the west before the formal royal action against him in 1475–6, the notion of a disastrous split between John and Angus as early as 1475 is difficult to sustain. As they stand, the Clanranald histories manage to suggest that Clanranald support for Angus Óg was designed to reverse the effects of John's malicious and craven surrender to the crown and Argyll. The narrative conveniently absolves the leaders of Clanranald from the charge that it was their opposition to John that fatally undermined the lordship.

Overall it seems most likely that the split between John and Angus Óg occurred some years after July 1476 and that John's attitude to the initial loss of Ross, Kintyre and Knapdale was far from supine.[35] However, the role assigned to Argyll in conveying John to the royal court in order to make his resignation may well be an accurate reflection of Earl Colin's position in the spring/summer of 1476. Colin had a number of social, political and marital links in the Hebrides, had already acted as John's procurator in parliament in the 1460s, and may have been a key intermediary in arranging the deal that saw John lose Ross, Kintyre and Knapdale, while retaining the Lordship itself. After July 1476 Argyll maintained a high degree of involvement in the affairs of the Lordship. The Clanranald histories portrayed the earl as working both in the interests of the crown and in defence of John, Lord of the Isles. The identification with John was important for future Campbell influence in the Isles, for those families who had been part of John's council were increasingly likely to turn to Argyll as the effectiveness of their former patron began to wane. Indeed, by the time of Angus Óg's rebellion, Argyll seems to have been acting alongside John as a political figurehead for the families that had made up the core of the Lord's affinity in the 1460s and 1470s.

Lowland observers seem, on the whole, to have been unaware of, or uninterested in, Argyll's rather equivocal involvement in the politics of the west in the mid-1470s. However, an interesting depiction of the Campbell family and its role in the kingdom from a Lowland perspective emerges from the pages of Blind Harry's verse epic The Wallace. Hary's work was written between 1476 and 1478, at a point where the crown's struggle with the Lordship of the Isles would have been hard to ignore.[36] Given the immediate political context in which it was written, it was perhaps no great surprise that The Wallace tended to portray Gaelic lords as inveterate rebels and troublemakers.[37] However, the work was extremely careful to dissociate the ancestors of Colin Campbell, master of the king's household, from the irresponsible Gaelic lords of Ireland and the Hebrides. In an early episode, a party of Scots treacherously killed by English forces at Ayr included

> . . . kynd Cambellis that nevir had beyne fals
> Thir rabellit nocht contrar thar richtwis croon.[38]

The tale went on to celebrate the virtues of Clan Campbell in a more specifically Highland context by describing Campbell resistance to the depredations of one MacFadzan, an ally of the English crown who descended on Argyll with Irish and Hebridean levies in order to destroy the 'gud Cambell'.[39] The figure of Macfadzan provided a thinly veiled critique of the Hebridean lords of the author's own time. The clash between the Islesmen and Irish in MacFadzan's service, and the 'native true born Scots' who supported Wallace and Campbell was more than a matter of politics, it reflected on the issue of who did, and who did not, belong within the Scottish polity. For the author, men who 'borne war off Argill' were regarded as full members of the Scottish kingdom. Argyll men in MacFadzan's service were still Scots by birth and blood, and therefore accorded rights denied to their Irish and Hebridean allies. The rout that followed MacFadzan's final catastrophic defeat witnessed the pitiless slaughter of the usurper's Irish levies, but

> Born Scottis men baid still in-to the feild
> Keist wappynnys tham fra and on thar kneis kneild.

The words put into Wallace's mouth as a response to the pleas for mercy were, in their own way, a chilling comment in the context of the 1470s:

> Off our awne blud we suld haiff gret pete
> Luk zhe sla nane off Scottis will zoldyn be
> Off outland men lat nane chaip with the liff.[40]

The ethnic distinction made between the 'true born Scots' of Argyll and the 'Outland' men of the Hebrides and Ireland made little real sense in terms of language and culture. It did, however, express in quasi-racial terms what must have seemed an obvious difference between these regions to contemporary Lowland observers in terms of their political relationship with, and loyalty to, the Scottish crown and kingdom in the second half of the fifteenth century.

On another level again, Hary visualised the confrontation between Wallace and Campbell's forces and MacFadzan's men as a straightforward struggle between 'civilisation' and 'savagery'. The Irish and Hebrideans flouted the basic conventions of war through their indiscriminate destruction of non-combatants and property:

> Barnys nor wyff thai peple sparyt nocht
> Wastyt the land als fer as thai mycht ga
> Thai bestly folk couth nocht bot byrn and sla.[41]

Indeed, MacFadzan seems to have been established in Lowland literary circles in the second half of the fifteenth century as an archetype of Highland bestiality and depravity. The poet William Dunbar certainly allowed the Gaelic warlord and his 'Erschemen' an overtly demonic 'guest appearance' in his 'The Dance of the Sevin Deidly Synnis'.[42]

In contrast, the narrative of *The Wallace* presented the Campbells of Loch Awe as full members of civilised society in dress, weaponry and social attitudes. This was plainly expressed in the invented speech attributed to the 'knycht Cambell' shortly before the final confrontation with MacFadzan. Campbell purportedly rallied his troops with the observation that:

> yon bestly folk [the Irish and Islesmen]
> wantis wapynnys [weapons]
> and weid [in this context probably meaning effective armour]
> Swne thai will fle, scharply and we persew.[43]

The portrayal of the Lord of Loch Awe as the determined defender of the Scottish kingdom and civilised society against MacFadzan and his 'beastly' hordes may well have reflected contemporary Campbell depictions of the family's role within the kingdom. Indeed, the provenance of the entire MacFadzan episode in *The Wallace* is intriguing, given the fairly precise geographical knowledge displayed by the author.

The positive picture of Campbell lordship found in *The Wallace* may also have been significant in terms of Earl Colin's position in the wider politics of the Scottish realm. It has long been argued that *The Wallace* was, at least partly, designed as a condemnation of the Anglo-Scottish marriage treaty concluded by James III in 1474 and the king's subsequent development of a pro-English diplomacy.[44] Despite the fact that Argyll had been a member of the royal council throughout the period and one of the king's principal envoys in the negotiation of the treaty, the author of *The Wallace* apparently looked on the earl's family with some favour. That a work apparently so critical of the king could present the master of the king's household's ancestors in such a complimentary way may suggest that the author, or his patrons, did not regard Earl Colin as a man hopelessly in thrall to the policies pursued by the crown.

In truth, however, there was little indication of any significant discord between Argyll and the king prior to the great crisis that engulfed the crown in 1482. Earl Colin maintained his exemplary record of attendance on the king's council and served in a number of other capacities as a royal judge and exchequer auditor. Earl Colin may have been slightly discomfited by the effects of James III's 1478 revocation of grants of royal lands and rights made during his minority. Argyll did not serve as one of the auditors of exchequer in this year, and his absence coincided with a much more critical examination by the royal auditors of the earl's 'rights' in Cowal. For the first time in a decade the earl was actually required to render accounts for Cowal and justify his hold on Dunoon and the lands granted to his grandfather Duncan by James II in 1452. New royal mandates were issued to sanction Argyll's occupation of these 'royal' estates, but for limited terms only. This may have been particularly contentious in the case of Dunoon where, as we have seen, Argyll had effectively been given a hereditary grant of the 'royal' castle. In 1478 it was made clear to Earl Colin that his position in Dunoon, indeed in all the royal estates he held, remained dependent on the king's will. Argyll could hardly object to a principle that had been so openly proclaimed and approved in a series of parliaments from the 1450s onwards.[45]

If Earl Colin himself had no strong reason to feel alienated from the government of which he was an integral part, then the same could not be said of some of the men allied to him by marriage. In the 1470s Earl Colin concluded marriage alliances with John Drummond of Cargill and Hugh Montgomery of Eglinton. Both men were involved in bitter and prolonged disputes over offices that lay in the gift of the crown. The marriages to Earl Colin's daughters may have been partly inspired by the hope that the master of the king's household would be prepared to promote the claims of his sons-in-law at the heart of royal government. The intermittent struggle between the Drummonds and the Murrays of Tullibardine over the Stewartry of Strathearn had been a feature of the politics of the royal earldom from the early 1440s. For most of the period after 1441 the Stewartry had in fact been occupied and exercised by the Murrays of Tullibardine.[46] In 1474, however, the moribund Drummond claim found a new and aggressive champion in the shape of John

Drummond of Cargill. On 19 March 1474 Maurice Drummond of Concraig resigned his rights to the offices of Steward, Coroner and Forester of Strathearn to his kinsman John, a transaction confirmed by the king. On 26 March William Murray of Tullibardine was presented with Privy Seal letters discharging him from the offices. Murray was evidently not inclined to go quietly and at some point over the summer of 1474 all the offices were taken into the king's hands, presumably in order to forestall disputes in the earldom itself. In October 1474 the contesting parties were required to submit the evidence supporting their claims to the king by 8 January 1475.[47] It was clear at this point that Drummond was stressing his hereditary right to the disputed offices while Murray was in fact arguing for the primacy of royal rights and the king's subsequent ability to give the office to whoever he liked. Earl Colin could be expected to display considerable interest in the settlement in Strathearn. Argyll was a substantial landowner inside the royal earldom and his social and political influence was reflected in the commission of lieutenancy of December 1475 that gave Earl Colin military leadership of his servants and tenants inside Strathearn. There is little indication prior to 1475 which of the parties Argyll was inclined to support. However, the seventeenth-century Campbell history presented the Drummonds as an early offshoot of the proto-Campbell O'Duibnes, presumably a reflection of political and social co-operation between the two families at some point prior to the compilation of the genealogy.[48] It remains unclear when the genealogical connection was made and if it could possibly have influenced Argyll's attitude to the unfolding dispute in Strathearn. Of more immediate relevance was the fact that, on 18 January 1475, ten days after Drummond and Murray had been required to deliver their evidence to the royal court, John Drummond sold lands in Lennox and Menteith to Earl Colin. The sale took place at Stirling and was witnessed by Andrew lord Avandale, the Chancellor, as well as lesser men attached to Argyll or Drummond's households.[49] Although the exact import of this transaction is unclear, it would seem that from this point on Earl Colin was generally a supporter of John Drummond's claims in Strathearn, and some time before 5 March 1479 Drummond's son and heir was married to one of the earl's daughters.[50]

The relationship between Earl Colin and another of his sons-in-law, Hugh Montgomery, was even more significant in terms of Argyll's political attitudes during the 1480s. Hugh Montgomery had inherited his family's claim to the bailiary of Cunningham in northern Ayrshire on the death of his great-grandfather Alexander, Lord Montgomery, in 1470. Control of the office had been long contested between the Montgomeries and the Cunninghams of Glencairn, but by 1481 the office was held by John Ross of Montgrenan, James III's lord advocate and favourite.[51] Subsequent events would prove that Hugh Montgomery found the denial of his hereditary rights in Cunningham intolerable. In his long struggle to vindicate his claims Hugh enjoyed the unequivocal backing of Earl Colin, his father-in-law, Hugh having married Helen Campbell at Dollar on 21 April 1478.[52] The Campbell-Montgomery link was perhaps the strongest political association Earl Colin secured through marriage, and Montgomery was frequently to be found as a witness to Argyll's business.

By the end of the 1470s Argyll, loyal royal councillor still, actually sat at the centre of a social and political affinity deeply disenchanted with the distribution of royal patronage. The master of the king's household was no doubt also increasingly aware of the collapsing political position of his king. The breakdown of James III's relationship with his two younger brothers is well attested. In 1479 this resulted in the exiling of Alexander, duke of Albany and earl of March, and the death in mysterious circumstances of John, earl of Mar.[53] At around the same time the king's unpopular policy of co-operation with England failed and the two kingdoms were once again on a war footing in 1480–2.[54] The English crown could attack James III's government on a number of fronts. First, the exiled Albany could be deployed as a direct dynastic threat to James III's hold on the Scottish throne. Second, Edward IV could attempt to use the disaffected elements of Clan Donald to open a second front against the Scottish crown. In 1481 the English king sent Sir Patrick Haliburton to the Western Isles to approach John MacDonald, Lord of the Isles, and his kinsmen John, lord of Dunivaig and the Glens (the son of Donald Balloch), and Donald Gorm (the Blue), the grandson of Donald Balloch's brother Ranald, in an attempt to foment insurrection in the west.[55] There was little in the way of recorded response in the west, but by the summer of 1482 the English crown's plans for action against James III had come to fruition. In May 1482 the king's exiled brother Alexander, duke of Albany, returned to England. On 10 June, styling himself Alexander, king of Scots, he concluded a treaty with Edward IV at Fotheringhay Castle. By the terms of the treaty Alexander was to displace his brother as king of Scots with English military assistance.[56] Once installed as king, he would acknowledge the superiority of the English king, break the Franco-Scottish alliance, resign the burgh and castle of Berwick to the English crown and also surrender Liddesdale, Eskdale, Ewesdale, Annandale and Lochmaben Castle. Shortly thereafter 'King' Alexander headed north alongside a huge English army under the command of Edward IV's brother Richard, duke of Gloucester, to confront James III. The use of Albany as a pretender to the Scottish throne marked a serious escalation in Edward IV's ambitions in the north. As Albany and the English army, commanded by Richard duke of Gloucester, swept into the south-east of Scotland in the third week of July, James III gathered the Scottish host at Lauder. Here the deficiencies of James III's domestic rule caught up with the monarch as a remarkable chain of events unfolded. On 22 July 1482 the king was arrested by a coalition of Scottish nobles who had met in Lauder kirk during the hosting. Subsequently, men associated with the king's own household or with the king's policies in the localities were summarily executed. The most notable casualty of the bloodletting was Thomas Cochrane, who had loyally represented the monarch's interests in the north-east of Scotland and who had thereby earned the fatal enmity of the Gordon earls of Huntly.[57] The fate of Earl Colin, who as master of the king's household and a 'Daily Councillor' of the king was presumably thoroughly identified with the discredited regime, was less dramatic. This may, of course, owe something to the fact that Earl Colin was at the hosting with his intimidating retinue in tow. However, the available evidence suggests that Earl Colin was far from a passive observer of the events of 22 July. What then happened at Lauder? An apparently near-contemporary chronicle suggests that a meeting of the nobility in the parish kirk denounced the devastation and suffering of the 'poor people' of the kingdom as a result of two years of warfare and the king's recent debasement of the Scottish coinage. Thereafter 'thai slew ane part of the kingis housald and other part thai banysyt and thai tuke the king him self and thai put him in the castell of Edynburgh in firm kepyng for he wrocht mair the consaell of his housald at war bot sympill na he did of thame that was lordis'.[58] Earl Colin was neither killed nor banished[59] and it may be that the earl and his kinsmen were in fact willing or at least acquiescent participants in the move against the king and other elements in the royal household. Certainly on 7 January 1483 Argyll and a number of his adherents required a royal remission for their role in seizing the king at Lauder and conveying him against his will to Edinburgh Castle and incarcerating him there.[60] Moreover, the chronicle account can be read to suggest that it was not the aristocracy in general, but the lords in the king's household, who felt that they were being sidelined in favour of those 'at war bot sympill'. If this is the sense of the chronicle, then Argyll's apparent alignment with those prepared to take direct action against the king in July 1482 becomes more understandable. It was clear that while Argyll and the Chancellor Andrew Stewart, lord Avandale, were not in the long run the main beneficiaries of the coup of July 1482, they were still initially regarded post-Lauder as the 'official' representatives of royal government. They were both in Edinburgh in early August and were the principal figures, alongside William Scheves, archbishop of St Andrews, to open negotiations with Gloucester and Albany when the latter reached Edinburgh with the English army. It has been suggested that Argyll, Avandale and Scheves were already sidelined at this point because they had lost possession of James III to a smaller group of conspirators headed by James III's half-uncles. These three men, James Stewart, earl of Buchan, John Stewart, earl of Atholl, and Andrew, bishop of Moray, would certainly emerge as the figures controlling the king by late August, but it is not entirely clear that this was the position in the immediate aftermath of Lauder.[61] Indeed, it seems unlikely that Argyll, Avandale and Scheves had been violently ejected from government at Lauder but had then followed the men who had seized the king and taken him to Edinburgh, to sit and wait outside the castle for the arrival of the English army. More seriously, it is difficult to believe that Albany and Gloucester would have bothered to negotiate a series of specific terms and financial agreements with a displaced faction that did not have access to the king or the apparent ability to deliver on their promises. In short, it would seem that the action against James III at Lauder involved the most senior members of the king's government who were unable to ignore or contain the growing general discontent with his behaviour. In that sense, the coup initiated at Lauder seems to have had a certain political 'legitimacy' and looks, in its early stages at any rate, rather less like an opportunistic strike by a narrow political faction.

What, then, were the hopes of Argyll, Avandale and Scheves for the future governance of the realm as they negotiated with Albany and Gloucester in Edinburgh in early August? On 2 August Argyll, Avandale (styled Chancellor), Scheves and James, bishop of Dunkeld, came to an agreement with Alexander, duke of Albany. By the terms of the deal

Albany agreed to keep 'his trew fath and Allegeance to our Soverane Lord James King of Scotland and his successione' and 'his Fath, Laute, and Band to ws and to the Remanent of the Lordes of the Realme'. In return Albany was to receive a reciprocal obligation allowing him to move around the kingdom free from the threat of 'bodely Harme'. This undertaking (presumably also involving a formal written 'band' or bond) was to be given by the men negotiating with Albany and 'thai', i.e. the 'Remanent of the Lordes of the Realme'. Argyll, Avandale, Scheves and Livingstone thus seem to have been negotiating as representatives of the 'Lordes of the Realme' who had the king in their power in Edinburgh Castle. Their obligation to Albany went on to promise that they would 'cause oure Soverane Lord frely' to restore the duke to the lands, strengths, houses and offices he held on the day of 'his last parting furth of the Realme of Scotland'. In addition they would obtain the king's remission for Albany and 'the Persons being with him, that he will hereafter Neme and desire' provided 'he and thai Remanand and Abidand at the Fath and Obesanse of oure Soverane Lord forsaid as his trew Liege'. All of the above arrangements were to be 'Approvit and Confermmit be oure said Soverane Lord and his hale Thre Estates in the next Parliament but [without] fraud or gyle'.

The political settlement hinted at in the formal language of the agreement was, given the circumstances, astonishingly and perhaps misleadingly conservative. The apparent determination to safeguard the 'authority' of James III in a deal between a man who had openly claimed the throne and noblemen who at that moment held King James against his will in Edinburgh Castle seems rather unconvincing. In reality the arrangements seem to have had the very short-term aim of safe-guarding Albany's position within Scotland once the English army had withdrawn. The longer-term problem of what sort of government could emerge from the shambles was simply not touched on. Albany was to receive pledges guaranteeing his physical safety from the negotiators and the 'Lords of the realm'. Those in charge of the king would also procure the restoration of Albany to the lands and offices he had enjoyed prior to his flight from Scotland in 1479 and a royal remission for the duke's various 'crimes'. These were the minimum guarantees required to allow Albany to re-enter the political life of the Scottish polity and should not be taken as a statement of his ultimate ambitions. Even if the 2 August agreement conceals as much as it reveals about the underlying ambitions and hopes of the signatories, a few general points can be made. Argyll, Avandale, Scheves and Livingstone were linked to, and seemed to speak for, a wider group of noblemen and were in a position, as they thought, to secure royal writs.[62] Far from being amongst the victims of the Lauder coup, Argyll and Avandale appear to have been leading figures in the humbling of the king. Moreover, despite the implication of the August agreement that James III would continue to be king, there was really little to be discerned from the agreement about the underlying political attitudes of the participants. Whether Albany and Argyll and his colleagues discussed future constitutional arrangements at this time is impossible to know.

If the Duke of Gloucester seems to have accepted that the installation of Albany as a puppet Scottish king through military/political conquest as envisaged in the Treaty of Fotheringhay was no longer an immediate possibility, he was clearly determined that other English concerns should be addressed before his departure. On 4 August the provost of Edinburgh, Walter Bartram, and the Edinburgh burgess community agreed to ensure that if Edward IV wished his daughter's marriage to Prince James of Scotland to be concluded, they would work to achieve this. Alternatively – and this surely was the point of agreement with the representatives of the wealthiest burgh in Scotland – if the English king decided that he was no longer interested in the long-delayed marriage, then the burgh was obliged to repay the money already handed over by the English king.[63] The witnesses to this obligation included Gloucester, Albany, the bishop of Dunkeld, the earl of Northumberland, Colin, earl of Argyll, Lord Campbell and Lorn, Thomas lord Stanley and Alexander Inglis, archdeacon of St Andrews. Shortly thereafter, Gloucester's force left Edinburgh to return south, capturing the citadel at Berwick on the way.

The departure of Gloucester allowed internal divisions amongst the magnates who had seized the king at Lauder to surface. Over the course of the next month Argyll, Chancellor Avandale and Archbishop Scheves, the leading figures in the negotiations of early August, found themselves utterly excluded from power. The course of events is very obscure and much hinges on the reliability of sixteenth-century chronicle accounts. By 25 August at the latest a new regime had emerged in which Albany, Argyll, Avandale and Scheves had no place. On that date a Great Seal charter was issued in Edinburgh witnessed by an entirely new set of royal office holders. The earls of Atholl and Buchan and Andrew, bishop elect of

Moray, the king's half-uncles, all appeared as witnesses, Andrew as keeper of the privy seal, and Buchan as chamberlain. The new chancellor was John, bishop of Glasgow, the treasurer the abbot of Holyrood.[64] The authority of this new regime is questionable and its immediate aims unfathomable. As a number of sources indicate that James III was held in ward in Edinburgh Castle until 29 September, Atholl, Buchan and Moray were clearly not men chosen by the king at a point where he had recovered his independence. Atholl was, after Albany, the king's closest adult male relative (although not himself of royal blood) and might have claimed some role in the governance of the king on that basis after Lauder. Overall, however, it is difficult to escape the impression that the sudden emergence of the Stewart half-uncles was the product of a coup within a coup. These men seem to have had possession of the royal seals by 25 August, although whether they also had uncontested possession of Edinburgh Castle and control of the king was less certain.

If the sixteenth-century witness of Bishop John Leslie can be relied on, at some point in this period Albany, Argyll, Avandale and Scheves moved to Stirling, where they negotiated with Queen Margaret and her eldest son, Prince James. It is unclear whether the move west occurred before or after the Atholl/Buchan coup in Edinburgh. Whenever it took place, the assembly at Stirling of James III's brother, queen, heir, former chancellor, former master of household and the archbishop of St Andrews was surely a powerful alternative focus for legitimate government within the realm. Crucially, however, Albany and the queen evidently decided that they could strike a more advantageous, or perhaps more honourable, deal with those who now actually had control of the king, Edinburgh Castle, and the royal seals. According to Bishop Leslie, Albany, with the approval of the queen, 'secretly' left Stirling to 'free' James III from his captivity in Edinburgh. When the king was released (at Michaelmas), Argyll, Avandale and Scheves simply fled to their 'own countries'.[65] Although we cannot press this relatively late source too hard, if the narrative it provides is basically reliable, then a number of intriguing questions arise. Was Albany's 'secret' departure from Stirling an attempt to surprise those holding James III in Edinburgh or needed because he was in effect abandoning his temporary allies Argyll, Avandale and Scheves? The claims of the latter group to a role in government now rested entirely on promoting the rights of Albany, the queen or Prince James, or some combination of the three to exercise royal authority. Leslie and other sources lay great stress on the fact that the queen remained committed to the idea that royal government should be continued in her husband's name. Whether this reflected, as her apologists claimed, the queen's innate goodness and personal loyalty to James III or simply the political choices she made in the autumn of 1482, the result was disastrous for Earl Colin.[66]

As Macdougall argues, the sudden flight of Colin and his associates undoubtedly reflected the nature of the deal struck by Albany in September 1482 in order to obtain the king's release. Albany, who was the man with the best claim to play a role in government if the king was deemed unfit to rule, had no further need to negotiate with Earl Colin. Argyll, Avandale and Scheves simply disappeared from central (and indeed local) record until the following spring. Archbishop Scheves was soon the target of a sustained political campaign to remove him from his arch-episcopacy, with his role to be filled by Andrew Stewart, bishop elect of Moray.[67] Whether the new government also sought to take direct action against Argyll and Avandale over the winter of 1482–3 is difficult to say. That there was some activity in the west is suggested by a charter of 24 October in favour of Malcolm MacCleary to reward him for the 'delivering' of Dumbarton Castle.[68]

By October, then, Albany and the king's half-uncles seem to have been reconciled and a parliament was called for early December. Argyll, Avandale and Scheves were conspicuous by their absence from this assembly. The three estates asked James to 'speke to his bruthir the duke of albany to take apone him to be lieutennant generale of the Realme and to defend the bordouris'. The recommendation hardly amounted to a ringing endorsement of James' abilities as king but neither was it an unequivocal imposition of Albany as lieutenant general.[69] The compromise was hardly likely to last and the tensions between the two royal brothers became manifest early in 1483. It soon became apparent that James III was not inclined to cede any formal powers to his brother. In January 1483 Albany launched a last despairing attempt to seize power. On 2 January the duke and his remaining supporters, including the earls of Buchan and Angus, embarked on a great raid from their base in Dunbar Castle. Their goal was the capture (or the death) of James III, who was resident in Edinburgh. The coup failed and Albany and his band of increasingly isolated supporters retreated to Dunbar Castle and sought assistance from the English crown.[70] It was only in the immediate aftermath of this violent attempt to seize the monarch, as James III cast around for political and military support against his brother, that the king allowed the first steps in the political rehabilitation of Earl Colin. On 7 January Earl Colin and eighteen others, who had presumably been part of Argyll's retinue at Lauder, received a remission for their treasonable actions the previous July.[71] The pressures of the crisis of January 1483 evidently inclined the king to be more forgiving to those who had acted against him in the summer of 1482. By the third week of January James III felt confident enough in the support growing around him to call a parliament to Edinburgh to begin on 1 March and presumably intended to allow action to be taken against Albany and his band of failed conspirators. In the interim, the men who had hijacked the Lauder protest began to disappear from royal government. Late in January Andrew Stewart, bishop of Moray, vanished from the royal council, while Archbishop Scheves returned. Moreover, the king's assembly at Edinburgh in March saw the return of Earl Colin to public life. By 18 March he had reappeared, alongside Avandale, as a witness to the king's Great Seal charters, and on the following day he, Avandale and Scheves were all to be found acting as Lords of Council.[72]

It is, of course, possible to view Earl Colin's return to government simply as a manifestation of James III's recovery of full political freedom in January 1483 and the consequent return of the king's most trusted councillors. Support for this view might be found in the terms of the short-lived agreement reached between the king and Albany on 19 March, the day after Argyll and Avandale reappeared as Great Seal charter witnesses. In return for the king's remission the duke was bound to take the king's (unnamed) councillors in 'hertly favoris frendschip and tendirness'. Moreover, Argyll seems to have enjoyed a frontline role in the gradual assault on the position of Albany as it became apparent that the king's brother was still involved in treasonable negotiations with the English crown throughout March and April 1483. On 29 April Earl Colin received a grant of lands in the barony of Dunbar that had been forfeited by Albany, raised to the status of the barony of Pinkerton.[73] Thereafter, Colin and David, earl of Crawford, acted as the king's justiciars and commissioners 'in that part' in the prosecution of Albany and his adherents in the parliament of June 1483. Finally, when the Chancellor, bishop James Livingstone of Dunkeld, died on 28 August 1483, Earl Colin was appointed as his replacement before 6 September.[74] All this might make it appear that Argyll had simply resumed his 'natural' place as a trusted confidant of the king once the political storms of 1482–3 were spent. However, the role of Argyll and Avandale in July/August 1482 remains deeply ambiguous and the two men had been excluded from government in the winter of 1482 even after the king had recovered some measure of freedom of action. Argyll only received legal indemnity for his actions at a point where James III was once again in fear of his physical safety. It is not inconceivable that the return of Argyll and Avandale to the king's council in March represented a concession by the king in the face of concerns raised by the parliament called earlier in that month. At the least, it is doubtful that Argyll and Avandale were ever again viewed as unquestioning crown loyalists.

What effect Argyll's slide from the king's government in 1482–3 had on the Clan Campbell's interests in the west is difficult to determine. Even before the great crisis following Lauder there were, as we have seen, growing problems in the region. John, Lord of the Isles, was still struggling with the after-effects of the loss of Ross, Kintyre and Knapdale in 1476 and the ambitions of his kinsmen, including apparently his son Angus Óg. The *Sleat History* portrays the young heir to the lordship heading military attempts to reverse the forfeitures of Ross, Kintyre and Knapdale independently of his father, who favoured a less defiant stance towards royal interests. Thus Angus was said to have assembled a host from the Clan Donald chiefs of Lochaber, Glengarry and Knoidart before descending on Ross where he defeated an army led by the earl of Atholl, one of the king's lieutenants.[75] After this, Argyll and Atholl were sent to the islanders, 'desiring them to hold of the king, and abandon Angus Ogg, and that the king would grant them the same rights they had formerly from MacDonald'. Then, 'the Macdonalds, and the heads of their families, saw that their chief and family was to be sunk, they began to look up to Angus Ogg'.[76] Thus the *Sleat History* effectively suggests that Angus Óg was fighting for the preservation of the lordship against the crown quite separately from his father and that this underlay the confrontation between the two men. Curiously, Angus Óg failed to register with either the Scottish or English government as an independent figure in the west in the late 1470s or early 1480s. It was John himself who was accused in April 1478 of holding Castle Sween in Knapdale against the crown and supporting the activities of Donald Gorm and Neil MacNeill who were, it was alleged, attacking the king's lieges on a daily basis.[77] John was apparently reconciled to the king by the time he appeared in

Edinburgh on 22 December 1478. The witnesses to a charter issued by John on that date included Earl Colin and most of the Hebridean leaders loyal to John: Lachlan MacLean of Duart, Hector MacLean of Lochbuie, William MacLeod of Glenelg, Ruairi MacLeod of Lewis, Alexander MacIan of Ardnamurchan and Malcolm MacNeill of Gigha.[78] Nevertheless, when Edward IV attempted to find allies in the Hebrides after the outbreak of Anglo-Scottish hostilities in 1480, he sent envoys in the summer of 1481 to John, Lord of the Isles, John, lord of Dunivaig and the Glens, and Donald Gorm. The last named was a close kinsman of John of Dunivaig, being the grandson of Donald Balloch's brother Ranald Bane. Donald Gorm's lordship seems to have embraced areas of Ulster as well as his interests in Kintyre and Knapdale. He was the 'Domnall the Blue, son of Alexander, *namely* son of Mac Domnaill', whose death was noted by Irish annalists in 1488.[79] Donald had been active in and around Knapdale in 1478 and was clearly regarded by Edward IV as a significant leader in the Isles in 1481–2. 'Donald Gorm mcDonald the principall and bravest gentleman for the tyme of that sirname in the Isles' also appears in the genealogy of Clan Campbell as a reputed marriage partner of a daughter of Earl Colin.[80] The prominence of Donald Gorm in the deliberations of the English and Scottish governments in 1478–81 is in marked contrast to the silence surrounding Angus Óg. If Angus had indeed been brazenly defying Scottish royal interests in Ross and elsewhere since 1476 in opposition to his father, then Edward IV's failure to approach the young lord as a potential ally in 1481 seems bizarre.

The outbreak of open conflict in the Isles between father and son probably, then, dates to the period 1481–2 or later. John's unwillingness to take advantage of Anglo-Scottish hostility and James III's political difficulties during 1481 and 1482 may have been the final straw for the exasperated Angus Óg, but we should not assume that the discord within Clan Donald in the 1480s was based entirely on a split between hawks and doves. The *Sleat History* introduces the war between John and his son with an apparently misplaced and irrelevant obituary. 'About this time Austin [Uisdean], his [Angus's] uncle, died, and was buried in Sand in North Uist'.[81] The death of Hugh or Uisdean of Sleat is usually said to have occurred in 1495–98, on the basis of a royal confirmation of the grant made to him by John, then earl of Ross, in 1469. In fact, however, there is nothing in the 1495 confirmation itself to suggest that Hugh was still alive at the time it was issued.[82] If the death of the lord of Sleat occurred in the early

1480s, then the resentments held in check since John's interference in the Sleat inheritance in the 1460s would have been unleashed, perhaps combining with a wider disapproval of the way John conducted himself during the summer of 1481. It is certainly this period that seems to provide the best 'fit' for many of the undated episodes in the traditional histories. In the *Sleat History* the account of the split between John and Angus opens with an episode in which Angus forced his father from his own house in Islay (a narrative meant as a symbol of the usurpation of lordship?). The humiliated John was compelled to seek assistance from the earl of Argyll at Inveraray. Here John resigned substantial estates in Knapdale in Colin's favour as part of a deal by which Argyll would take John to the king, where he would resign all his lands to the crown in order to punish his son. Intriguingly, Earl Colin did receive a grant of lands in the lordship of Knapdale with the custody of Castle Sween from James III on 26 February 1481.[83] John had, of course, resigned his claims to Ross, Kintyre and Knapdale in 1476. Thereafter, however, in 1478 he had been accused of holding Castle Sween in Knapdale against the crown and allying himself with Neil MacNeill, perhaps the hereditary constable of Castle Sween, and Donald Gorm. Since Knapdale had been officially forfeited to the crown almost five years before the gift to Earl Colin, the charter, as one might expect, gives no indication that the grant was directly dependent on any resignation by John of the Isles.[84] Moreover, Earl Colin's family had longstanding and independent claims to Sween and extensive Knapdale estates dating back to the fourteenth century. The 'traditional' histories thus seem to conflate the resignation of 1476 with events from 1481, perhaps with good cause, since the 1481 grant of Knapdale and Sween did coincide with the emergence of a 'new' relationship between John of the Isles, Argyll and the crown. Certainly by the summer of 1481 there were indications that the crown no longer regarded John of the Isles and *his* adherents as a threat to its interests in the lordships of Kintyre and Knapdale. As we have seen, in June 1481 Edward IV was appointing envoys to try and entice Hebridean lords into political and military action against the Scottish crown. James III's government seems to have responded with a number of concessions to John and his men in the summer of 1481. The man driving this policy of rapprochement was probably Earl Colin, who made a brief visit on 8 June 1481 to Kilmun in Cowal with his son and heir Archibald, his son-in-law Hugh, Lord Montgomery, and various Campbell and Lamont chiefs.[85] On 10 July 1481 one Tearlach MacAlexander was made Steward for his lifetime of the lands of Kintyre within certain given bounds 'pro ejus fideli servitio'.[86] In the following month, on 11 August, John, Lord of the Isles, was given a liferent grant of lands claimed by MacNeill and MacLean in Kintyre and Knapdale again 'pro ejus fideli servitio'.[87] The charter could, of course, have been designed to set John against the MacLean and MacNeill lords but this seems unlikely. At no stage does the charter imply that the MacNeill and MacLean claims were unlawful. If the men referred to were MacLean of Duart and MacNeill of Barra (or the Neil MacNeill whose activities had been the subject of hostile comment in the parliament of 1478), these were individuals reputedly loyal to John of the Isles throughout the 1480s. It may be, indeed, that the charter was intended to allow MacNeill and MacLean possession of these estates while ensuring that they held the lands from John, who thus retained a measure of superiority and remained responsible for their continued 'good behaviour'. If there is any substance to the notion that Donald Gorm was wed to a daughter of Earl Colin, the new custodian of Castle Sween, then the summer of 1481 seems to have witnessed a wide-ranging attempt to settle the disputes that had dominated Kintyre and Knapdale since 1476. It has been reasonably suggested that the king's concessions were prompted by John's rejection of the blandishments of Edward IV's envoys commissioned in June 1481 to enter negotiations with the Lord of the Isles and others.[88] Alternatively, the traditional accounts might suggest that the sequence of grants involving Knapdale and Kintyre represented the point at which Argyll and the crown stepped in to bolster the position of John and his allies in the west in the face of Angus Óg's insurrection. John's abandonment of the struggle to recover Castle Sween and the lordships of Kintyre and Knapdale by force in 1481 may have encouraged the conflation in the *Sleat History* with John's formal resignation to the crown in 1476.

Even if the outbreak of hostilities between John and his son Angus Óg can be credibly placed in the period around 1481–2, it remains difficult to assign even an approximate date to the decisive military encounter of the conflict. The heavy defeat of John's galley fleet at the battle of Bloody Bay off Mull might have occurred at any point in the 1480s, although arguments in favour of the period prior to 14 November 1485 carry some weight.[89] The constituent elements of the opposed fleets as given in the *Sleat History* are entirely convincing. Angus Óg's principal supporters were Donald Galldach of Sleat, defending his claims to part or all of his (perhaps recently deceased) father's lordship, Allan mac Ruairi, lord of

Moidart, head of Clanranald and Allan's son Ranald Bane.[90] Amongst John's supporters it was claimed that MacLeod of Harris and MacLean of Duart were captured and the heir of Torquil MacLeod of Lewis killed.

The great war in the Isles is likely to have affected a number of west-coast lordships in the 1480s. There were certainly indications that Earl Colin was experiencing continuing difficulties in his recently acquired province of Lorn. In 1484 Earl Colin was one of the men sent south to negotiate a three-year truce with Richard III's government. The truce prohibited all manner of military activity by land or sea, but the lordship of Lorn in Scotland and the Isle of Lundy in England were excepted from this arrangement.[91] The stipulation suggests that Earl Colin was antici-pating the need for a military campaign in Lorn that went beyond the conventional form of muscular 'police action' required to exercise lordship in the region. The anxiety may, or may not, reflect the ongoing effects of the war between Angus Óg and his father. If Earl Colin or his agents did undertake action in Lorn over the winter of 1484–5, then one of the results may have been the bond rendered by Dugald Stewart of Appin to Colin, his son Archibald and Duncan Campbell of Glenorchy on 15 October 1485 at Dunoon.[92]

The great breach between Angus Óg and his father seems to have been healed, if not forgotten, by the end of 1485. On 14 November of that year Angus, styled 'Angus of the Isles, master of the same', granted lands in Mull to the abbey of Iona with the consent of his father.[93] Angus' use of the style 'master of the Isles', if not entirely self-bestowed, suggests that he was once more regarded as his father's heir and, conversely, that he recognised John's status as the current Lord. One part of the reconciliation between Angus Óg and those supporting his father may have been a match between Angus and a daughter of Earl Colin. The 'marriage' is mentioned in both Clan Donald accounts, although as they seem to have shared common sources at some points they do not necessarily act as independent witnesses to the suggestion that Angus Óg's partner was the earl's daughter. The woman is unnamed in the Clan Donald histories, but seventeenth-century Campbell genealogies described the earl's 'eldest' daughter as Isabella, 'lady of the Isles', implying a marriage to a figure in the ruling lineage within Clan Donald.[94] That Earl Colin had a daughter bearing his wife's name is not at all unlikely. Martin MacGregor has recently speculated that Colin's daughter may have been the *Iseabal Ní Mhic Cailein* (i.e. daughter of MacCailein Mór – in this context either the first or second earl of Argyll) responsible for two poems preserved in the *Book of the Dean of Lismore* and that one of these works could have referred to her relationship with Angus Óg.[95] If these poems are correctly attributed to Isabella daughter of Earl Colin, then they provide the only contemporary evidence for Angus Óg's partner. If Isabella was indeed Earl Colin's eldest daughter, it seems unlikely that the match with Angus Óg in the 1480s could have been her first marriage, for many of her supposedly younger sisters were married in the 1460s and 1470s.

The Clan Donald histories relate that the relationship between the earl's daughter and Angus Óg produced a son, Donald Dubh, who would emerge as the figurehead for attempts to resurrect the Lordship of the Isles.[96] Since the Scottish government would later insist on Donald Dubh's status as a bastard, it would seem that any liaison between a daughter of Earl Colin and Angus Óg was not a canonically orthodox marriage. There remain difficulties in deciding when the relationship could have been active. The *Clanranald Book* asserts that Donald Dubh was born posthumously after his father's assassination in 1490.[97] If Donald Dubh was the eldest and only child of the union, this might indicate a relatively late date, perhaps *c*.1488, for the conclusion of an alliance between Earl Colin and Angus Óg. The *Clanranald Book* further suggests that Angus's widow was kept a prisoner until she bore her son, who was thereafter confined until he was thirty years of age. The *Sleat History* on the other hand tells of a galley raid on Islay by the earl of Atholl, at Argyll's behest, that captured the then three-year-old Donald while his father was still very much alive, apparently placing Donald's birth much earlier in the 1480s. In the Sleat account Donald was thereafter a prisoner of his grandfather at Innis Chonnell, where he stayed until 'his hair got grey'.[98]

One point that can be made immediately is that the traditional histories clearly conflate two quite separate periods in Donald Dubh's life, his early upbringing prior to the revolt in his name in 1502–1506, and his prolonged spell in royal captivity thereafter. In this, the chronicles may well reflect Donald's own presentation of his life history after his escape from royal custody in the 1540s. Writing to the English king Henry VIII in August 1545 with a certain rhetorical flourish, Donald lamented that 'from our mother's womb we were bound in the yoke and servitude of our enemies: and to this very time overwhelmed with the filth of prison, and with intolerable fetters most cruelly bound'.[99] Despite the apparent continuity suggested here there was, of course, a qualitative difference between

Donald's early 'servitude' and the actual physical imprisonment he endured in the years immediately before his release in 1544. At any rate, in the mid- to late 1480s, Earl Colin and Angus Óg seem to have attempted to patch up their differences through a dynastic union between Angus and one of the earl's daughters.

After March 1483, of course, Earl Colin was once again a lord with concerns far wider than the affairs of Argyll and the Hebrides. After his escape from the nightmare of 1482–3, fortune seemed to smile on the chancellor's royal master as old enemies were steadily removed from the scene by a higher authority than his own. On 9 April 1483 Edward IV died and his young sons were soon eliminated to the benefit of Edward's brother Richard, erstwhile duke of Gloucester, who came to the throne as Richard III. The vulnerability of Richard's regime encouraged the new king to abandon utterly his brother's policy of destabilising the northern kingdom. In September 1484 King Richard's representatives concluded a three-year truce with Scottish envoys and reached an agreement for the marriage of James' son to Anne de la Pole, niece of Richard III and daughter of Anthony, Earl Rivers. In the following year James III's position was strengthened further through the death in a tournament at Paris of his exiled brother and rival Albany.[100] The shadow of an adult male claimant to the throne or the position of lieutenant-general had vanished and James could perhaps face the future with more confidence.

With Argyll now the senior officeholder in James' government, it might be thought that Earl Colin could have little cause for dissatisfaction in the years after 1483. Yet the crisis of 1482–3 seems to have suggested that one of James III's faults was an unwillingness to listen to the advice of senior members of his own government. These tensions and problems may well have resurfaced after 1483; at the least the chancellor must have been acutely aware of the continued widespread dissatisfaction with many aspects of the king's rule.

From 1486 a combination of longstanding grievances about the exercise of royal power and a new set of specific political disputes involving the king began once again to stir thoughts of wider political resistance to James' policies. One flashpoint was the king's attempt to annex the priory of Coldingham in Berwickshire to the chapel royal. The incumbent prior, John Hume, was not in the least inclined to allow this to happen and enjoyed the committed support of his powerful kindred in Berwickshire. In the parliament of October 1487 the king laid down draconian penalties against any men suspected of favouring or supporting the defiance of the Humes. Far from intimidating the opposition, James' heavy-handed crackdown seems to have stiffened the resolve of the Humes and their allies.[101] In January 1488 a large parliamentary committee was asked to proceed with the forfeiture of those who had broken the terms of the royal legislation from October. However, the king's position was made more problematic by the sudden disappearance of his eldest son and heir from Stirling Castle on 2 February 1488.[102] Although it may not have been immediately apparent, the young Duke of Rothesay (and future James IV) had in fact joined with men opposed to the king and was on his way to become a figurehead for the rebellion about to convulse the kingdom.[103] Because we lack any meaningful record of the debates underlying parliamentary statutes it is difficult to discern Earl Colin's attitude towards the king's policies during the 1480s. In February 1488, however, came a clear indication of a political rupture between James and his two senior councillors, Argyll and Avandale. The exact sequence of personnel changes in royal government in that month is not easily reconstructed, but by the end of February William Elphinstone, bishop of Aberdeen, had replaced Argyll as chancellor. Despite the loss of the chancellorship Argyll did not immediately abandon the royal court, with the witness lists for registered Great Seal charters apparently placing both Earl Colin and lord Avandale in Edinburgh on 11 and 20–23 March. However, the witness lists ascribed to these charters by the cross-referencing system used in the Great Seal Register are rather problematic at this point since they have both Argyll and Elphinstone as chancellor on 27 February. Moreover, the appearance of Argyll and Avandale on 11 and 20–23 March would represent a 'return' to court after a period in which they had not witnessed Great Seal charters on 5–7 March.[104]

Were Earl Colin and Andrew, lord Avandale removed from royal office because they were suspected of sympathising with those now gathering around the young heir to the throne? If that was the case, then the king soon had his suspicions confirmed, for by the end of March, if not some time before, Argyll and Avandale, along with Robert Blackadder, bishop of Glasgow, and George Brown, bishop of Dunkeld, vanished from James III's court for the last time. By April Argyll was established as one of the leading figures in the coalition of nobles opposed to the king alongside the bishop of Glasgow, the earl of Angus, and lords Hailes and Lyle.[105] These men were the representatives of Prince James in negotiations that took place in and around Aberdeen seeking to establish some form of settlement between the king and his son. Once again, as in 1482, Argyll found himself as the acceptable and moderate face of rebellion and insurrection. This time, however, there was to be no compromise. Full-blown civil war was gathering and the fate of James III, his son and many of the realm's subjects was to be decided on the battlefield. It would be a long and bloody summer.

Notes

1. Craig Madden, 'Royal Treatment of Feudal Casualties in Late Medieval Scotland', *SHR*, lv (1976), 172–194; Craig Madden, 'The Feuing of Ettrick Forest', *IR*, xxvii (1976), 70–84.
2. Much of the pejorative comment seems to have been generated by the activities of the Clan Donald lords of the Isles, but the depictions of the Gael/Highlander in Lowland sources were also clearly influenced by stereotypes of barbarian society drawn from classical and early medieval writers. See Nicholson, *Later Middle Ages*, 205–8; G.W.S. Barrow, 'The Highlands in the Lifetime of Robert the Bruce', in Barrow, *The Kingdom of the Scots*, 2nd edition (Edinburgh, 2003), 332–349; R.R. Davies, 'The Peoples of Britain and Ireland, 1100–1400', I-IV, *Transactions of the Royal Historical Society* (1994–97); R.R. Davies, 'The English state and the "Celtic" peoples 1100–1400', *Journal of Historical Sociology*, 6 (1993); J. Dawson, 'The Gaidhealtachd and the emergence of the Scottish Highlands', in *British consciousness and identity*, ed.B. Bradshaw (Cambridge, 1998), 259–300; J. Gillingham, 'Foundations of a disunited kingdom', in A. Grant and K. Stringer (eds.), *Uniting the Kingdom?* (London, 1995), 48–64; R. Nicholson, 'Domesticated Scots and Wild Scots', Unpublished article, copies held in Scottish History, University of Edinburgh, and XS1 MS A181, Box 3, file 8, Scottish Collection, University of Guelph; W.R. Jones, 'The Image of the Barbarian in Medieval Europe', *Comparative Studies in Society and History*, 13 (1971), 376–407.
3. Macdougall, *James III*, 88.
4. T. Chalmers, The King's Council, Patronage, and the Governance of Scotland, 1460–1513 (Ph.D., Aberdeen, 1982), 424–28. Chalmers' tables are based on an analysis of witness lists largely of registered Great Seal charters. This analysis often shows Colin as a witness to all registered charters in a given year and with a very high attendance record in other years. In fact, it is clear that Earl Colin was not recorded as a witness to any gifts of which he was himself a beneficiary. These 'artificial' absences actually account for the bulk of the occasions between 1462 and 1482 when the earl was not noted as a witness to registered Great Seal charters.
5. Inistrynich 1(12/1462), Innis Chonnell 1 (7/6/1466), Inveraray 3 (17/12/1470) (20/6/1471) (24/2/1475–6), Kilmun 1 (8/6/1481), Dunoon 1 (15/10/1485). Nearly all of these appearances in the west coincided with substantial gaps in the issuing of Great Seal charters. One exception is the charter issued at Inveraray on 20 June 1471, only two days after the earl had apparently witnessed royal charters in Edinburgh on 18 June. *RMS*, ii, nos. 1030 and 1031.

6. See Chapter 11, below.

7. Argyll Muniments, Inveraray, Argyll Charters; *RMS*, ii, no. 1168. See below, Chapter 11, for a more detailed discussion.

8. *RCAHMS Argyll*, vii, 286–289 (no.132).

9. *RMS*, ii, no.810 (1 September 1464). Before 1501 the Gordon earls also established a Carmelite friary at Kingussie. *RSS*, ii, xxiv; *TA*, ii, 76; Cowan and Easson, *Religious Houses*, 137.

10. Argyll Muniments, Inveraray, Argyll Charters; *RMS*, ii, no.1100. The verb used in the charter 'commissare' is a relatively unusual one, with the sense of committing or entrusting something to the care of another, and was perhaps intended to emphasise the special responsibility given to Argyll and his heirs in relation to the keeping of the 'royal' castle.

11. As recently as 1469, in the wake of the Boyd forfeiture, parliament had confirmed that the castle at Dunoon and the crown's lands in Cowal were permanently annexed to the royal patrimony. *APS*, ii, 186–7.

12. See, e.g., Nicholson, *Later Middle Ages*, 480–2; Donald Gregory, *History of the Western Highlands and Isles of Scotland, from A.D. 1493 to A.D. 1625* (Edinburgh, 1836) (hereafter Gregory, *History*), 50–1; Macdougall, 'Achilles' Heel', 257–62.

13. *ALI*, nos. 55, 71, 76, 80, 82, 89, 91, 96, 98, 128. Celestine was alive as late as 29 November 1472 *ALI*, no.102. His death is recorded under the year 1473 in *AFM*, iv, 1084–5; *ALC*, ii, 174–5; *RC*, ii, 211. If the Clan Donald histories of the seventeenth century are accurate, Celestine was buried in Rosemarkie, a clear indication of his attachment to the eastern lordships of Earl John. See *RC*, ii, 211.

14. Macdougall, 'Achilles' Heel', 249–50.

15. *APS*, ii, 108–9.

16. *CPL*, xi, 671.

17. *Book of the Dean*, no.X, stanza 5.

18. *ALI*, no.104.

19. *HP*, i, 47.

20. TA, i, 48.

21. *APS*, ii, 108–12.

22. Argyll Muniments, Inveraray. Bundle 95; *RMS*, ii, no.1210.

23. NAS GD112/1/14.

24. *Spalding Misc.*, iv, 134.

25. *ALI*, nos.109a, 109b.

26. *HP*, i, 1; J.W.M. Bannerman, *The Beatons: A medical Kindred in the Classical Tradition* (Edinburgh, 1986), 16–20; Martin MacGregor, 'The Genealogical Histories of Gaelic Scotland', in Adam Fox and Daniel Woolf (eds.), *The Spoken Word: Oral Culture in Britain, 1500–1850*, (Manchester, 2002), 196–239, at 212. MacGregor's article provides a fine discussion of the evolution of 'traditional' histories as a genre.

27. For discussion of the text and its sources, see W. Gillies, 'The Clanranald Histories: Authorship and Purpose', in G. Evans, B. Martin and J. Wooding (eds.), *Proceedings of the First Australian Conference of Celtic Studies* (forthcoming); W. Gillies, 'Oral and Written Sources and Effects in the Clanranald Histories', in D.Scheunemann, ed., *Orality, Literacy and Modern Media* (Columbia, 1996), 27–43; W. Gillies, 'Sources of the Books of Clanranald', *Études celtiques*, 29 (1992), part 2, 459–60.

28. *Book of the Dean*, no.XVI. Stanza 10 in particular asserts that 'It was thou that didst stir up evil to the Isles, thou didst impoverish her tribute and her sanctuary'.

29. Macdougall, 'Achilles' Heel', 258, argues for the general validity of the observation.

30. *RC*, ii, 162–3.

31. *ALI*, nos. 19, 21, 29, 34, 42, 51, 54, 64, 73, 76, 78, 80, 87, 89, 91, 96.

32. *ALI*, nos. 80,82.

33. The *Sleat History* has a long and elaborate description of the insult delivered by a member of Clanranald to the MacLeans and MacLeods in assigning seats at a banquet in the Lord of the Isles household. As with the Orkney/MacDonald dispute, genuine political animosities seem to have been represented through a narrative that saw conflict arising from a personal insult and loss of honour. *HP*, i, 45–6.

34. *RMS*, iii, no.2835. Hector seems to have succeeded his father Lachlan as head of the Duart family sometime after 1479. *ALI*, Appendix c, 263–4, 265–6.

35. It is certainly difficult to see an irrevocable breach between John and his son in the period 1475–6, if we accept that Angus's role as his father's lieutenant in Inverness and Nairn was Ross's own policy. Moreover, if John's intention was to disinherit his son, why were Angus and his younger brother John explicitly identified as heirs to the Lordship of the Isles in the settlement of 1476 and (Angus alone) in a confirmation of 1478? *RMS*, ii, nos.1246, 1410.

36. M.P. McDiarmid, 'The Date of the "Wallace"', *SHR*, xxxiv (April 1955), 26–31; Macdougall, *James III*, 54.

37. Nicholson, *Later Middle Ages*, 480–2.

38. *Vita Nobilissimi Defensoris Scotie Wilelmi Wallace Militis*, ed. M.P. McDiarmid (STS, 1968) (hereafter *Hary's Wallace*), i, 144.

39. John of the Isles had of course been charged with treasonable dealings with England and Edward IV in the parliament of November-December 1475 which had seen his forfeiture. Macdougall, *James III*, 121.

40. *Hary's Wallace*, i, 163–4. A. Campbell concern with emphasising the perfidious nature of Islesmen (and by implication the contrasting loyalty and service of the Gaels of mainland Argyll?) was later displayed by Colin, 3rd earl of Argyll, who claimed that in the aftermath of Flodden he had been forced to defend the lands of the young James V against 'the men of the Ylis, quhilkis of ald hes beyn trowbus'. NAS CS5/xxix, f.210.

41. *Hary's Wallace*, i, 157. M. Keen, *Chivalry* (London, 1984), 227–37.

42. *The Poems of William Dunbar*, ed. W.M. Mackenzie (Edinburgh, 1932), 120–23.

43. *Hary's Wallace* i, 162. The distinction implied here was economic as well as moral.

44. McDiarmid, 'The Date of the "Wallace"', 26–31; Macdougall, *James III*, 117–119.

45. *ER*, viii, 507–9, 616; *APS*, ii, 42, 186–7 (1469).

46. Boardman, 'Feud', 160–163.

47. *RMS*, ii, no.1160; NAS Drummond Writs GD 160/1/15 and 16.

48. *HP*, ii, 81.

49. AT, at date. The sale was said to be for money given to John 'in his great necessity' by the earl. This was a standard formula to justify sales that were motivated by many different considerations. The estates were Fynwicke, Casbie in Lennox and Quholloch in Menteith. The witnesses included David Kirpa-

trick of Rokkelhead, William of Drummond, Robert Drummond, Malcolm McCleary (who had interests in Balquhidder), Walter McClere and Sir Patrick Clerkson.

50. Argyll Muniments, Inveraray, Argyll Charters. An acknowledgement of that date by Lord Drummond of a sum of money paid by Argyll for his daughter's marriage. The terms could be read to suggest the original agreement was made either in 1475 or 1477. The document was issued in Edinburgh and was witnessed by Hugh, lord Montgomery, Duncan Campbell of Glenorchy, Duncan Stewart, William of Drummond, Master Walter of Drummond, John of Stirling, Gilbert of Galbraith. It is not certain that the marriage produced any children and John's son and heir may have died young, loosening Argyll's personal ties to the Drummond claim.

51. Boardman, 'Feud', 173–5; NAS Crawford Priory Collection GD 20/1/no.413.

52. Fraser, *Eglinton*, i, 32; ii, 158.

53. Macdougall, *James III*, 128–132.

54. *Ibid.*, 140–145.

55. *CDS*, iv, no.1469; *ALI*, lxxviii.

56. *Foedera*, xii, 156.

57. N.A.T. Macdougall, ' "It is I, the Earle of Mar": In Search of Thomas Cochrane', in *People and Power in Scotland*, eds. R. Mason and N. Macdougall (Edinburgh 1992), 28–49.

58. Macdougall, *James III*, Appendix A. The Short Chronicle of 1482, p.312.

59. Elsewhere the chronicler uses 'banished' in its literal sense of being forced into exile beyond the confines of the realm.

60. NAS GD 112/3/6.

61. Macdougall, *James III*, 165–166.

62. *Foedera*, xii, 160–1; *CDS*, iv, no.1479.

63. *Foedera*, xii, 161; *CDS*, iv, 1480.

64. *RMS*, ii, no.1517. The possibility of these charters being assigned witnesses retrospectively should be borne in mind. Other men who had not featured regularly as charter witnesses before were Lord Erskine, Lord Borthwick, and Patrick Leich, canon of Glasgow as Clerk Register.

65. Lesley, *History*, 49–50. Although the King may have been released on 29 September, the castle was still held by John Stewart, Lord Darnley on 7 October, when the King ordered its surrender to John, earl of Atholl. Darnley seems to have been reluctant to do so without obtaining an indemnity for himself and his men and this was forthcoming on 19 October. If Darnley's role as custodian ended on or around 19 October, then we might assume that the sum paid over to him from an annuity of Queen Margaret's related entirely to the period post-Lauder to early October.

66. Macdougall, *James III*, 170–1.

67. *Ibid.*, 172.

68. *RMS*, ii, no.1521

69. *APS*, ii, 143.

70. Macdougall, *James III*, 178–9.

71. NAS GD112/3/6. The eighteen men who received a remission alongside Earl Colin were an interesting mix of the earl's kinsmen and retainers drawn from Argyll, Stirlingshire and Highland Perthshire. The list included Duncan

Campbell of Glenorchy (and four other Campbells), William Somerville of Plean (Stirlingshire), a kinsman of Earl Colin's mother, Elizabeth Somerville,- who was a not infrequent witness to Earl Colin's charters and acted for the earl in a number of administrative/legal tasks. See GD 112/75/3 (15 August 1481), 112/75/6 (3 September 1491), a Thomas Lumisden of Condelane, Duncan Stewart (of Appin?), and a chaplain Patrick Clerkson, probably the man who by 1486 was Treasurer of the diocese of Argyll. Fraser, *Lennox*, ii, 128.

72. *RMS*, ii, no.1563; *ADC* (1496–1501), cxix.
73. *RMS*, ii, no.1564.
74. *APS*, ii, 147–50; *RMS*, ii, no.1565; Watt, *Fasti*, 98; Myln, *Vitae*, 26.
75. *HP*, i, 48–9. Atholl was indeed one of the men given a commission of lieutenancy in 1475. *RMS*, ii, no.1211.
76. *HP*, i, 49. This tale, involving the rebuff of an underhand royal offer designed to weaken the lordship, has a curious echo of the supposed offer made by James I to Sir John Mór in the 1420s.
77. *APS*, ii, 115.
78. *ALI*, no.113.
79. For Donald's ancestery see *RC*, ii, 303. For Ranald Bane see *ALI*, no 78 and p. 296 and genealogical table on p. 292 (note however, that Donald Gorm is not linked and that the descent of the MacDonalds of Largie from Donald's brother is misreprented); *AU*, iii, 329; *AC*, 590–1; *ALC*, ii, 184–5. Donald *Gorm* was killed in 1488 'in the beginning of Spring by the sons of the abbot, son of Alexander, namely, by the Clann-Domnaill themselves'. For the Irish dimensino of Donald and his family see. S. Kingston *Ulster and the Isles* (Dublin, 2004), 105, 109; *AU*, iii, 395–7; *AFM*, v, 1297.
80. *HP*, ii, 98–99. The earl's daughter is identified in this account as Catharine 'Lady Mull', presumably intended to indicate that her first marriage was to a MacLean of Duart.
81. *HP*, i, 49.
82. *ALI*, 307–8; *RMS*, ii, no.2286.
83. *RMS*, ii, no.1464.
84. This is not to deny the possibility that John had resigned these lands to Earl Colin in 1475–6, that the gift was not allowed by the Crown as an unsuitable piece of private aggrandisement by his royal lieutenant, but that in a time of Anglo-Scottish warfare and intrigue the Crown belatedly allowed the resignation to take effect.
85. *Glas. Friars.* p. 192, no. 45 Brief, at any rate, if his appearance as a witness to royal charters in Edinburgh on 2 and 12 June is reliable. *RMS*, ii, nos. 1478–9.
86. *RMS*, ii, no.1480.
87. *RMS*, ii, no. 1485. The fact that the grant was made for John's lifetime only may indicate that the break with Angus Óg had occurred by this stage.
88. *ALI*, intro., lxxviii.
89. *ALI*, intro., xxii, no.119.
90. *RC*, ii, 166–7. If the *Sleat History* gives the participants at Bloody Bay reasonably accurate titles, then the description of Allan mac Ruairi as lord of Moidart points to a date sometime after the death of Ruairi assigned, in the *Clanranald Book*, to 1481.
91. *Foedera*, xii; Lundy had in the past acted as a base for piratical maritime

lordships. If that was still the case in the 1480s, then the English negotiators may have been aware of an impending military expedition against the island.

92. *AT*, at date. The obligation merely binds Dugald to accept the terms of an arbitration the terms of which are not recorded. Some of the witnesses to the obligation, Robert, bishop of Argyll, John, earl of Lennox and Lord Darnley, John Lamont of Inneryne, John MacLachlan of Strathlachlan and David Rede, notar, may also have been amongst the judge arbiters.

93. *ALI*, no.119.

94. *HP*, ii, 98–9; *Records of Argyll*, 10.

95. M. MacGregor, ' "Surely one of the greatest poems ever made in Britain": The Lament for Griogair Ruadh MacGregor of Glen Strae and its Historical Background', in *The Polar Twins*, eds. E.J. Cowan and D. Gifford (Edinburgh, 1999), 114– 153, at 138. See also p.152, note 122.

96. *HP*, i, 50; *RC*, ii, 163.

97. For Angus's assassination in 1490, see *AU*, iii, 350–1; *AFM*, iv, 1184–5; *ALC*, ii, 186–7; *AC*, 595.

98. *HP*, i, 50; *RC*, ii, 163.

99. *Facsimiles of the National Manuscripts of Scotland* (London, 1867–71), iii, no.29; *Calendar of letters and papers, foreign and domestic, of the reign of Henry VIII* (London, 1862–1932), xx (Part II), no.40. See below Chapter 10, pp. 282–283 for a fuller discussion of Donald Dubh's personal history.

100. *SP*, i, 152.

101. Macdougall, *James IV*, 14–15.

102. *APS*, ii, 223.

103. Macdougall, *James IV*, 2, 24–6 where it is suggested that the young prince had been alienated from the King by James III's preferential treatment of his younger son, also James, in terms of projected marriage alliances and territory and title within the Scottish kingdom. Moreover, Macdougall suggests that the rebel propaganda of early 1488 may have implied that James III intended to forfeit his heir.

104. A registered Great Seal charter of 21 February was witnessed by, amongst others, William Elphinstone, bishop of Aberdeen. *RMS*, ii, no.1707. Argyll and Avandale were not witnesses to this grant. However, of two charters apparently issued under the date 27 February, one (*RMS*, ii, no.1709) included Colin, earl of Argyll, Chancellor and Andrew, Lord Avandale, as witnesses while the other (*RMS*, ii, no. 1711) had Elphinstone as Chancellor but Earl Colin as a witness under his territorial titles (cross-referenced to no. 1719 of 20 March). Argyll and Avandale were not recorded as witnesses to charters issued on 5 (*RMS*, ii, no.1712–3), 6 (*RMS*,ii, 1715–1716) and 7 (*RMS*, ii, no. 1717) March. If this gap represented a genuine withdrawal from the court in early March, then the two men had apparently rejoined the King by 11 March (with Argyll no longer witnessing as Chancellor) (*RMS*, ii, no. 1718, referencing to 1719 of 20 March).

105. *APS*, ii, 210.

NINE

1488–1492: Argyll Ascendant

The death of James III at Sauchieburn ushered in a new king and a new era of Campbell influence in and around the royal court. In the years between Sauchieburn and his death in 1492 Colin Campbell, earl of Argyll, was perhaps the most powerful and influential politician in the minority government of James IV. Swiftly restored to the office of chancellor after James III's demise, Colin's authority at the heart of government brought favour and fortune to the earl's kinsmen and political associates. Colin began gathering the spoils of his victory almost as soon as the dust had cleared from the encounter at Sauchieburn. Supporters of the dead king, on the other hand, could expect little succour from the new regime, and the clear-out of James III loyalists from royal offices and lands began long before the process was officially sanctioned by the first parliament of the new reign in October 1488.

Argyll's prominence in the new regime reflected his contribution to Prince James' war in the summer of 1488. Earl Colin's appearance as one of Prince James' envoys in negotiations with James III in April 1488 was the first unequivocal indication that Argyll had joined the prince's rebel company.[1] Colin's defection may well have been a significant turning point in the struggle between father and son. Earl Colin was, by 1488, a senior statesman with extensive experience of the most important offices in royal government. His position as James III's chancellor was obviously not willingly abandoned, for in applying for an English safe-conduct alongside his fellow rebels in May 1488 Earl Colin was still styled chancellor of the kingdom.[2] If this title were more than just a slip on the part of the English clerk, then it would seem that attempts had been made before the final confrontation with James III to set up an alternative administrative structure based around the person of the young prince at Stirling. The duke of Rothesay's adoption of the national title 'Prince of Scotland' points in the same direction, as does the diplomatic activity of the prince's supporters.[3] The men around the young James were certainly in communication with both the English and Danish monarchs justifying the defiance of their own king in the early summer of 1488.[4] The application for a safe-conduct from Henry VII in May 1488 by Argyll and other rebel lords may suggest an attempt to counter James III's own English diplomacy. The political propaganda produced by those supporting the prince attempted to blacken the king's name by emphasising James III's role in the death of his brother John, earl of Mar, and the (supposed) poisoning of his queen by a royal favourite, John Ramsay, lord Bothwell. The story of Queen Margaret's poisoning was certainly used in rebel approaches and pleas for assistance to her brother King Hans of Denmark.[5] It may have been designed primarily for Danish consumption but it certainly received a wider airing. A garbled version of the tale relayed to King Hans found its way to the compiler of the *Annals of Ulster*, who included an unusually long account of the contest between the king of Scots and his son amidst his description of events in the north of Ireland during 1488. 'The wife of the king of Scotland, . . . daughter of the king of Lochlann [i.e. Denmark/Norway] was put to death this year by poison. The king of Scotland . . . was slain in battle after that, the same year, by his own son . . . because he did not deliver to his son the people on whom it was charged to have given poison to his mother.'[6]

The entire tale of Queen Margaret's assassination strains at the bounds of credibility, yet there may have been some logic behind the rebel association of John Ramsay with the 'crime'. Margaret's death had occurred close to the opening of James III's campaign to conclude an English marriage alliance in 1486; it was a natural step for the rebels of 1488 to link the two events and to implicate the king's most active English envoy, John Ramsay, in the queen's decease. Indeed, the conduct of James III's English negotiations, and particularly the marriages proposed in the period 1486–88, may well have encouraged Prince James to view his mother's death as a major political turning point. The Anglo-Scottish marriage negotiations had begun in July 1486 with the initial proposal that James' younger brother, also James, marquis of Ormonde, should marry Katharine, daughter of Edward IV's widow Elizabeth Woodville.[7] As Macdougall points out, the apparent favouring of Prince James' brother may have been disquieting in itself, but James III's widower status meant that the Scottish king was now also on the marriage market. In November 1487 it was clear that negotiations were underway for James III's marriage to Elizabeth Woodville. Elizabeth's age meant that a match with James III could hardly have produced heirs. However, if both the proposed mar-

riages were successfully concluded, Prince James would be faced with a
new Scottish queen eager to promote the interests of her daughter
Katharine and any children produced in Katharine's marriage to Ormonde. For many it may have seemed that Rothesay's interests in the royal
patrimony and, potentially, his place in the succession, were under threat.
The negotiations of April 1488 certainly raised the issue of the king
guaranteeing the prince's 'honorabill sustentacioun and levin', although
this may be a comment on the enmity caused by the rebellion rather than
an indication of the causes that provoked the struggle.[8]

If Argyll's eminence lent a certain thin dignity to the insurrection, then
the social, political and military resources of Clan Campbell and Earl
Colin's affinity may have been of more immediate relevance in affecting
the outcome of the struggle. The late spring and early summer of 1488 saw
a protracted and messy civil war underpinned by or inflaming local
rivalries and feuds. While some actively sought compromise, and the
majority perhaps sat tight and hoped for some form of political reconciliation, others were desperate and ambitious enough to pursue their
principles or self-interest through violence in their own localities and
in the forces gathering around the king and prince. Local feuds generated
committed partisans for both James III and his son, as victory in the
'national' struggle held out the hope of triumph over local or regional
rivals. Prince James' adherents certainly included any number of men
whose support seems to have been tied to the pursuance of their own local
goals. Two of these men, Hugh, Lord Montgomery, and John, Lord
Drummond, were closely connected to Earl Colin.

Argyll's personal military contribution to Prince James' triumph is
difficult to assess. The earl, of course, might have deployed the considerable military resources of Argyll and the Firth of Clyde in the conflicts of
1488, but there is no evidence to confirm or deny this possibility. Earl
Colin and Campbell of Glenorchy, as the remission for their role at
Lauder Brig in 1482 hinted, also had a wide network of retainers, kinsmen
and supporters in Menteith and Strathearn, and some of these men were
demonstrably involved in the fighting in and around Stirling. One man
with extensive links to Argyll and Glenorchy was Sir William Stirling of
Keir. At some point, perhaps in the immediate run-up to Sauchieburn,
Stirling's residence at Keir was targeted and destroyed by a force under the
command of the loyalist Sir Adam Murray of Drumcrieff.[9] Stirling of Keir
was so closely identified with the rebel cause that he later featured in

sixteenth-century chronicle accounts as one of the suspects thought to have been personally involved in the king's assassination.[10]

However it occurred, James III's death at Sauchieburn transformed the rebels of 1488 into the loyal adherents of the new king. The scale of the victory achieved by Prince James' forces over those of the King on 11 June was evident in the number of James III supporters killed or captured during the battle. According to the Ulster annalist's offhand observation, 'many of the superior lords of Scotland were slain' alongside their king.[11] Alexander Cunningham, newly created earl of Glencairn and Lord Kilmaurs, Thomas, Lord Sempill and William, lord Abernethy were probably all killed in and around Stirling while David Lindsay, duke of Montrose and earl of Crawford, was wounded and captured. The most prominent casualty of course was James III himself, apparently killed in a skirmish with elements of the prince's force around the mill at Bannock-burn. Understandably perhaps, those directly involved in the regicide do not seem to have been eager to advertise the fact. Sixteenth-century chroniclers named a number of individuals who might have played a part. The new regime, however, was eager to bury the uncomfortable implications of James III's death, and the political defiance of royal authority that had preceded it, alongside the slain king in his tomb at Cambuskenneth. The choice of the abbey may have been determined by proximity to the battlefield and by the fact that the abbot, Henry Abercrombie, was a staunch supporter of the new regime.[12] He could be relied on to discourage the growth of any commemoration of James as a 'martyr king' around the royal tomb. Moreover, Cambuskenneth was the resting place of the king's wife Margaret and, despite the rumours encouraged by the rebels of 1488, it might have been thought fitting to reunite the estranged royal couple in death.[13] Once James III had been laid to rest, an official veil of silence fell on the issue of the king's demise, much to the fury of those who had remained loyal to their monarch and now found themselves persecuted by a regime established by an act of regicide.

Argyll himself immediately reclaimed the office of chancellor and possession of the Great Seal.[14] In control of royal resources, the new establishment used the summer and autumn to settle old scores with or make new gains from those who had remained loyal to their king. Earl Colin and his kinsmen and allies certainly rode on this triumphal wave and made many territorial and jurisdictional advances. However, Argyll does not seem to have been associated with the more belligerent, hawkish and self-serving members of the new regime whose activities and vendettas would spark a revolt against the young James IV in the autumn of 1489. In the last four years of his life, between 1488 and 1492, Earl Colin was at the peak of his power and influence, a Chancellor who seems to have enjoyed the backing of a wide cross-section of the political elite, a regional lord whose interests increasingly dominated the affairs of the west.

Earl Colin was clearly at the heart of the post-Sauchieburn regime and was immediately involved in two highly sensitive tasks for the new government. First, Argyll was one of the men charged with overseeing the collection of, and accounting for, the royal hoard. James III had removed much of the hoard from Edinburgh and dispersed it to his supporters in the weeks before Sauchieburn. Some of the royal treasure had been recovered from the field of battle, but significant portions of it remained in the hands of the dead king's supporters or had vanished altogether. Concern over the misuse or misappropriation of the hoard would remain a live political issue in the early years of James IV's reign.[15] Second, on 15 June 1488 and only four days after the victory at Stirling, 'Coline, erle of Ergyle, oure chancellar' was appointed as one of the commissioners for the letting of crown lands. The commissioners were empowered to give tenants of the crown new leases (or 'tacks') for three-or five-year terms and to continue or cancel existing tacks.[16] Unsurprisingly, James III loyalists who held land on fixed-term lease from the crown suffered badly as the commission got to work over the summer of 1488. On 14 July, for example, the letting (or 'assedation') of the royal lands in Strathearn saw a wholesale displacement of Murray tenants and their replacement by John, Lord Drummond (another of the commissioners appointed on 15 June), and his kinsmen.[17] Drummond's pursuit of his long dispute with Murray through the formal mechanisms of royal government was fairly typical of the political atmosphere in the summer of 1488. The general conduct of James IV's government during the months after Sauchieburn was characterised by a mixture of fear, insecurity, vindictiveness and ambition.

The need to reward loyal supporters as well as the drive to remove irreconcilable opponents from positions of influence and authority found its fullest expression in the first parliament of James IV's reign, which opened on 6 October 1488. The meeting of the three estates saw the political ascendancy of the rebels of 1488 translated into an officially sanctioned and systematic displacement of James III loyalists from royal offices. The parliament was thus a busy and profitable occasion for Earl Colin and his kinsmen and associates.

By 17 October the estates had constructed a list of noblemen who were to take responsibility for the searching out and execution of 'trespassers' and other violent offenders within designated areas.[18] The nominated lords gave oaths in the parliament to uphold the terms of their commissions and were given the power to collect similar oaths from lesser lords in the localities and to compel them to assist in the dispensation of justice. At first sight the 1488 legislation looks simply like a repetition of earlier statutes designed to improve the administration of justice. However, the men assigned to take responsibility for large areas of the kingdom, and in effect to wield extensive powers of summary justice, reflected the composition of the triumphant coalition of 1488. In many cases the prosecution of trespassers and the gathering of oaths of good behaviour in the localities must have been a highly contentious affair, for the chief agents in the process were generally partisans of the new regime, whose authority was disputed by local rivals. The legislation, when combined with Item 6 of the October parliament, which insisted that men who had fought against James IV in the summer should be removed from royal offices for the space of three years, threatened a wholesale clear-out of James III loyalists from local office-holding.[19]

The definition of judicial spheres in the October parliament gives a useful indication of the extent of Campbell influence and ambition in the west at the start of James IV's reign. Earl Colin and his son Archibald, 'Master of Argyll', were made responsible for Argyll, half of Lorn, Kintyre and Knapdale. That the Campbell lords offered oaths for only 'half' of Lorn seems rather strange, given that they had held formal title to the entire lordship since 1470 and had been granted regality jurisdiction over the same area in 1471.[20] There is nothing to suggest that Lorn was administratively divided in two; certainly no other magnate was given a role in the other 'half' of Lorn, whatever and wherever that might be. The arrangement may reflect the fact that the Campbells were unprepared to accept responsibility for a large area of the lordship where they had no effective ability to fulfil the terms of the oath. The exemption of Lorn from an Anglo-Scottish truce of 1484 may point in the same direction; Campbell influence in a significant part of Lorn was fairly tenuous and dependent largely on the application of military power through punitive raids and military/judicial expeditions.

The other areas for which Earl Colin and his son gave their oaths in 1488, Kintyre and Knapdale, were likewise regions that required a fairly robust approach to the administration of justice. Further to the north Earl Colin's cousin, Duncan Campbell of Glenorchy, was bound, along with Ewen Campbell and Neil Stewart of Fortingall, for Discher, Toyer (i.e. the north and south shores of Loch Tay), Glenorchy, Rannoch, Appin of Dull, Glenlyon and Glen Falloch. The shared authority exercised by the Campbell lords and Stewart of Fortingall reflected a 'private' deal struck between Duncan Campbell and Neil Stewart only two days before. On 15 October Duncan and Neil Stewart of Fortingall concluded an agreement by which Campbell was bound not to disturb Neil in the lands and offices he held, particularly in the Appin of Dull, Rannoch, Glenlochy, Strathardle and Strathbraan.[21] These were all nominally 'royal' lands that had been set in tack to Neil Stewart and his father John in 1473 for the unusually long period of nineteen years.[22] On 28 June 1488, however, in the immediate aftermath of Sauchieburn, James IV had granted Duncan Campbell 'oure lovit squyare' the bailiary of the Appin of Dull, Glenlyon and Rannoch for his lifetime.[23] In October, in return for Duncan abandoning the pursuit of his claims to the Appin of Dull and Rannoch, Neil agreed not to disturb Duncan in 'Discher, Toyer, Glendochart and Glenlyon', the last of which was to be given over by Neil to Duncan. Glenlyon was another one of the 'royal' lordships assigned to Neil Stewart in 1473. In exchange for Glenlyon, Duncan would give Neil the tacks 'and officis of bailyery and feis of the rannauch, appildull . . .' for which Neil would pay £100. Essentially, Neil Stewart's position as a substantial landholder and chief royal officer across a great swathe of central Highland lordships had been totally undercut by the regime change of 1488. The entire range of rights held by Neil had been transferred to Duncan Campbell. By October the two men were ready to conclude a deal; perhaps Duncan Campbell had been unable or unwilling to enforce his claims against the powerful and well-connected Stewart kindred.[24] As it was, the October agreement still saw Duncan emerge with his influence extended into Strath Tay and Glen Lyon and a sum of £100 from Neil Stewart for the other offices. 'Parchment' gains had been translated into meaningful advances on the ground. Stewart of Fortingall's deal with Glenorchy ensured that two days later Neil Stewart would be included in the parliamentary list of men who should take responsibility for the exercise of justice within their own areas.

Away from the Campbell family itself, the October parliament also saw the advance of a wider circle of men who were part of Earl Colin's political affinity. The most obvious example was Argyll's son-in-law Hugh, lord Montgomery. Montgomery's family had a long-standing claim to the offices of bailie of Cunningham and chamberlain of Irvine. These claims had been contested by the Cunningham lords of Kilmaurs for most of the fifteenth century and, latterly, by James III's lord advocate John Ross of Montgrenan.[25] Hugh, Lord Montgomery's unstinting support for Prince James during 1488 was a remarkable contrast to the behaviour of his principal local rivals Alexander Cunningham, Lord Kilmaurs, and Ross of Montgrenan, both of whom displayed conspicuous loyalty to James III. Cunningham had been particularly prominent in the royal army at Blackness and on 28 May was created earl of Glencairn for his services to the embattled king.[26] Alexander did not enjoy his title long, dying alongside his royal master at Sauchieburn.

Unsurprisingly, Montgomery prospered through the reallocation of judicial responsibilities and offices imposed by the new regime in October 1488. Given sole authority in the long-contested lordship of Cunningham, Hugh was also delegated to exercise justice in Dumbarton, Bute and Arran alongside John Stewart, the earl of Lennox, Lennox's son and heir Matthew, and Robert, Lord Lyle. As Earl Colin's heir Archibald was married to Lennox's daughter the entire settlement placed judicial rights across the Firth of Clyde in the hands of a closely bound aristocratic group. There is no extant grant of the offices of bailie of Cunningham and chamberlain of Irvine in Montgomery's favour, but it seems certain that the offices were assigned to him in the summer of 1488 or after the October parliament.[27]

Despite Montgomery's new authority in Cunningham it was soon clear that the head of the Cunningham kindred was not inclined to let Montgomery exercise his new offices. Montgomery's attempts to hold the bailiary and chamberlain courts provided an obvious flash-point, and in 1489, 1491 and 1492 royal couriers had to be sent to prevent the two lords 'gathering' their men and retainers for confrontations in Irvine. Attempts at royal peace-keeping were not entirely successful as sometime in the late summer or autumn of 1489 Montgomery seems to have killed Robert, Lord Kilmaurs.[28] Just how far Montgomery's ascendancy in Cunningham depended on the influence in government of his Campbell father-in-law would become obvious after Earl Colin's death in 1492.

Another violent feud arising from the change of regime in 1488 and in which Earl Colin and his kinsmen had an interest occurred in Strathearn. Lord Drummond was made judicially responsible for the inhabitants of Strathearn, Balquhidder, and Dunblane in the parliament of October 1488.[29] The new rights allowed Drummond to continue his assault on the interests of the rival Murray family in Strathearn. As we have seen, the assedation of crown lands in Strathearn made in July 1488 resulted in the wholesale removal of Sir William Murray of Tullibardine's kin from their holdings in the earldom. The most devastating blow fell against John Murray of Balloch and Trowan, who lost the lands of Balloch, Cuilt-balloch, Easter and Wester Lochlan, Trowan and the Dry Isle and Loch of Monzievaird despite holding these estates in heritable tenure. All of John Murray's estates were assigned to David Drummond, the second son of John, Lord Drummond. When John Murray tried to obtain redress in the October parliament, his claims were rejected in a series of notably partisan judgements.[30] Tensions between John Murray and David Drummond culminated in a clash at Monzievaird in 1489 that ended with at least nineteen members of the Murray affinity being burned alive in the kirk of Monzievaird. The incident seems to have become something of a *cause célèbre*, perhaps because it was seen as emblematic of the injustice and tyranny underlying the regime established in 1488. The outrage forced the restoration of John Murray to his Strathearn lands and eventually the execution of David Drummond and a number of his accomplices. The judicial dispatch of the son of a prominent lord of parliament was very unusual in fifteenth-century Scotland, where involvement with some form of treason against the crown was normally the only context in which men of David Drummond's status would be sent to meet the executioner.[31] Earl Colin seems to have played no active part in the shocking events in Strathearn, although the seventeenth-century family history of the Drum-monds compiled by William Drummond, Viscount Strathallan, assigned a leading role in the slaughter at Monzievaird to the Drummonds' allies the Campbells of Dunstaffnage.[32] There was some connection between John, Lord Drummond, and Alexander Campbell of Dunstaffnage at around the time of the confrontation in Strathearn. On 12 July 1490 at Perth lord Drummond gave a lifetime grant to Alexander Campbell, captain of Dunstaffnage and baillie of 'Glenyray', of lands in the earldom of Strathearn previously held by Malcolm Drummond.[33] This arrangement seems to have post-dated the slaughter at Monzievaird kirk, so that

Viscount Strathallan's attempt to pin that disaster on the Campbells may not be accurate, although the agreement certainly points toward some measure of Campbell of Dunstaffnage involvement inside Strathearn.[34]

A final confirmation of Earl Colin's widespread influence within the kingdom at the time of the October 1488 parliament came on 18 October when James (Rait), abbot of Culross, made Earl Colin bailie of all the abbey's lands in Scotland for five years.[35] The motivation behind the grant may simply have been the abbot's general concern to have a powerful protector during a period of notable instability, or the monastic community may have made itself particularly vulnerable by offering support to James III during 1488. At any rate the arrangement made Earl Colin responsible for a number of estates scattered through west Fife, Kinross and Stirlingshire.[36] Rait's successor as abbot, John Hog, confirmed Argyll's position as bailie and extended the term of the office to nineteen years. In April 1490 Hog also successfully petitioned for the erection of Culross into a burgh of barony.[37] As bailie of Culross Earl Colin may well have played a leading role in devising and supporting the application. By the end of 1490, then, the Chancellor seems to have been personally involved in the foundation of at least three burghs of barony, Inveraray, Culross and Kilmun. In the post-Sauchieburn period Earl Colin also obtained properties in Edinburgh and Dumbarton. No doubt these purchases were inspired partly by the need to accommodate the household of an earl in almost constant attendance on the king. However, they also suggest a more or less permanent engagement with burghal life, while the earl's foundation of burghs of barony indicates a genuine appreciation of the benefits of commercial organisation and activity.[38]

Overall, the extent of Argyll's authority and influence within the kingdom after Sauchieburn is difficult to overstate. He was undoubtedly the senior figure in James IV's minority government in terms of age, social status and the office he held. Earl Colin's interests and views had directed the distribution of royal patronage and helped to shape the legislation of the October 1488 parliament. All, however, was not well. A minority government founded on an act of regicide could never expect universal acceptance. Moreover, the way in which James III loyalists had been dispossessed of land and office after Sauchieburn had confirmed for many that the new regime was essentially vindictive and unjust. By January 1489 the first murmur of rebellion was heard as Alexander Gordon, Master of Huntly, opened a clandestine correspondence with the English king.[39]

Hostility towards those in charge of James IV's minority government was obviously most intense amongst those who had fought for James III. However, as 1489 wore on it became obvious that a number of men who had been part of Prince James' triumph were also becoming disillusioned with the conduct of royal government. The crisis when it came was in fact sparked by three men who had apparently been major beneficiaries of the events of 1488: John Stewart, earl of Lennox, his son Matthew, and Robert, Lord Lyle.[40] Collectively the three men had come to dominate royal offices in Bute, Arran and Dumbarton during 1488. Most notably, on 20 October Lennox and his son received a life grant of the mighty royal fortress of Dumbarton.[41] However, by 23 April 1489 James IV's government was summoning the royal host to Dumbarton, apparently in an attempt to recover the castle from Lennox's control.[42] The revolt was not so easily suppressed and a parliament was summoned to meet at Edinburgh on 26 June in order to co-ordinate action against the rebel strongholds in the west: Dumbarton, Duchal and Crookston.

Argyll's views on the crisis in an area where he wielded no little influence are difficult to fathom. Earl Colin's son and heir may, by this stage, have been married to Lennox's daughter Elizabeth, but there was little indication that the chancellor was swithering in his commitment to James IV's government.[43] Argyll seems to have offered no dissent to the first act of the June parliament, the forfeiture of Lennox, Matthew Stewart and Lord Lyle.[44] Indeed, on 3 July the earl's son Archibald received a number of estates around the Clyde forfeited by Lyle.[45] Moreover, the chancellor was assigned to play a leading role in the prosecution of the war that James IV's regime intended to unleash against the rebels in the west. The operation was to begin on 19 July with the king laying siege to Crookston and Duchal while Earl Colin was to begin the unenviable task of investing Dumbarton. Argyll was to impose the siege with the men of his earldom of Argyll, and levies from Lennox, Menteith and Strathearn. After twenty days Earl Colin's men were to be relieved by a force from Fife, Atholl, Angus and Perth east of the Tay. Finally, after a further twenty days a third force gathered in the north-east by the earls of Huntly, Marischal, Errol, and lord Forbes with all the men from north of the Mounth would relieve the second.[46] The system of staggered arrivals was clearly meant to allow the government to sustain a long siege of Dumbarton, but in the event it also allowed those opposed to James IV's regime to plan open resistance. In particular the hosting of the north-eastern lords became a rallying point for rebellion and the force that eventually arrived at Dumbarton in early September came to reinforce the rebels in the fortress rather than support the crumbling siege.[47] The arrival of the northern rebels, led by the Earl Marischal, Lord Forbes and the Master of Huntly, allowed Lennox, Matthew Stewart and Lord Lyle to break the siege of Dumbarton. On 11–12 October the combined rebel force was defeated, or at least halted, at Gartloaning near Aberfoyle by James IV's army.[48] The rebels fell back to Dumbarton Castle from where they sent a detailed 'apologia' to the king, detailing the faults of the regime established after Sauchieburn and suggesting how these might be remedied. In many areas the document sent to the king after Gartloaning mirrored the terms of a declaration made by the Earl Marischal, Lord Forbes and the Master of Huntly shortly before they committed themselves to rebellion in September. In summary the complaints were that no action had been taken against the killers of James III; that the royal treasure, castles and artillery had been misused and were in unsafe hands; that the regime had extorted unjustified ransoms from its opponents; and that royal justice should be administered in a less partisan way.[49] Both documents insist that the problems of the kingdom had to be addressed through a full meeting of the three estates in parliament. The 'apologia' issued after the battle of Gartloaning had the additional feature of naming a number of 'parciall personis' who were said to be chiefly responsible for the mis-government of the kingdom.[50] Unsurprisingly, the list of 'guilty' men included all the major office holders in James IV's government with the glaring exceptions of Earl Colin and Alexander Hume, the chamberlain. The apparent unwillingness to blame Argyll for the iniquities of the post-Sauchieburn regime may reflect the earl's familial ties to Lennox and his family, or a perception that he was a mere figurehead for an administration actually dominated by Patrick Hepburn, earl of Bothwell, and his sup-porters. However, in the context of a letter sent to James IV in the wake of Gartloaning, it seems more likely that the rebels were looking to Argyll as a powerful and possibly sympathetic figure at the heart of royal govern-ment who shared many of their concerns. The pressure for a compromise solution was certainly growing in the autumn of 1489 as James IV's government struggled to re-impose the siege of Dumbarton. In Decem-ber, financially and politically crippled by the ongoing insurrection, James IV's government saw sense and concluded a settlement with the besieged lords that involved the calling of a new parliament to begin on 3 February

1490.[51] Between the end of the siege of Dumbarton and the opening of the parliament Argyll received a reward for his loyalty to the king during 1489. On 9 January Earl Colin was granted the lands of Rosneath on the northern shores of the Clyde. The terms of the charter were exceptionally fulsome, narrating that the lands were given because of Argyll's labours in defence of the king and crown and the common weal and tranquillity of the kingdom.[52]

The parliament that opened in February 1490 began with the cancellation of the forfeitures of Lennox, Matthew Stewart and Lord Lyle. Thereafter the assembly seems to have been concerned with addressing many of the rebel complaints of 1489 and establishing something approaching equitable government.[53] One aspect of this was an attempt to regulate the distribution of royal patronage by the nomination of a panel of men from which the king was to draw his privy councillors until the meeting of the next parliament. This group included many of the men condemned as 'parcial persounis' in the rebel apologia of 1489, but also a number of prominent James III adherents. Royal grants would only be accepted as valid if they had the express approval of at least six of this group, 'the chancellor being one'. This stipulation may simply reflect the general expectation that the Chancellor should be at the heart of the government by virtue of his office. However, the arrangement might also imply that Argyll was regarded as the key figure in ensuring the probity and even-handedness of royal patronage. That Argyll was viewed in this light might help to explain his otherwise puzzling absence from the rebel 'hit-list' of the previous year.[54]

The failure to crush swiftly the rebellion of 1489 had thus forced political reconciliation on many of James IV's administration. Moreover, by this stage a weariness with and distaste for civil discord may have settled on a kingdom wracked by war and rebellion for most of the previous two years. The faults in government that had led to the downfall of James III combined with the traumas of the period 1488–1490 seem to have produced a regime unusually determined to address what were perceived as long-term failings in the administration of justice. In the early 1490s the young James IV emerged as a vigorous suppresser of the baronial feuds that had arisen from, and contributed to, the political discord of the previous decade.[55]

One area where the ideals of 'luf, amity and frendship' may have seemed especially remote was the Hebrides. The attitude of the dominant figures within Clan Donald to the civil war that had gripped the Scottish kingdom in 1488 was, if the experience of previous fifteenth-century minorities is any guide, likely to have been unrestrainedly opportunistic. Argyll's influence may have maintained some level of contact between the new regime and John, Lord of the Isles, but John was essentially a broken man, his authority eroded through external pressures and the long internal war within Clan Donald.[56] John's fortunes may not have been helped by the assassination in the spring of 1488 of the influential ulster-based Donald Gorm. Donald, who had been associated with John in 1478 and 1481 and may have been married to Argyll's daughter Catherine, was despatched by other members of Clan Donald.[57] Thereafter, the most active lord in the Hebrides between 1488 and 1490 was John's son, Angus Óg. The fact that no magnate was named in the parliament of October 1488 as giving oaths for the suppression of 'trespassers' in the Isles was probably a comment both on John's powerlessness and the estrangement between James IV's regime and Angus Óg. Indeed, Angus seems to have made a determined bid to restore the fortunes of Clan Donald in the earldom of Ross in the troubled years of 1488 and 1489.[58] Angus was certainly resident in Inverness during 1490, for it was there that he was assassinated by his Irish harpist Diarmaid Ua Cairbre. The event inspired at least two Gaelic poems, one a lament for Angus, the other a vicious condemnation addressed to the severed head of the executed Diarmaid.[59]

Angus Óg's death threw the governance of the Isles back into a state of confusion. While this undoubtedly would have disturbed Earl Colin, the chancellor might have had more personal and immediate concerns in the wake of Angus' unhappy demise. In particular, the fate of his daughter, Angus Óg's partner, may well have loomed large in Argyll's thoughts. Unfortunately, the two Clan Donald accounts upon which most narratives of the period are based not only seem to offer a highly coloured interpretation of Argyll's behaviour, but as we have seen differ crucially from each other in terms of the chronology they offer. The *Sleat History* implied that Angus Óg's partner and his three-year-old son Donald Dubh had been seized by Argyll in the immediate aftermath of the Battle of Bloody Bay and while Angus was still alive. The Clanranald version of the tale narrated that Argyll's daughter was pregnant with Donald Dubh at the time of Angus' death and that thereafter she was captured by Earl Colin's agents and taken into the 'care' of the chancellor.[60] The inference in both accounts is that Argyll was seeking to secure Angus Óg's son in an attempt to control the destiny of the Lordship of the Isles, latterly by preventing the release of the young man regarded as the legitimate heir to the headship of Clan Donald. The chronicle accounts seem to reflect Donald Dubh's own interpretation of his childhood when, in the 1540s, he was in negotiations with the English crown for military and financial support. In this context Donald was keen to stress both his unquestioned but long-denied right to the Lordship and his hostility to the chief representative of the Scottish government in the west, the then earl of Argyll. In order to portray himself as a reliable potential ally to Henry VIII Donald may have been tempted to embroider the narrative of his early life in order to assure the English of his implacable hostility towards Argyll and the Scottish crown. Donald's communications with the English crown and its agents during 1545 also tend to support the 'Clanranald' account in that Donald consistently suggested that he had been under the control of his enemies from before his birth.[61] Returning to 1490, then, it seems more than probable that after Angus Óg's death Argyll's pregnant daughter simply returned to her father's care. Whether this actually required a forcible military intervention and effective kidnap as suggested in the Clan Donald histories must be debatable.[62] Moreover, if Earl Colin's actions were designed to capture and frustrate the obvious heir to the lordship, then the chancellor certainly possessed Campbell perspicacity in abundance. Over-all, it seems unlikely that Colin successfully predicted the safe arrival of a male child, his survival to adulthood, the forfeiture of the Lordship of the Isles to the crown in 1493 (after Colin's own death), and the elimination of all the alternative leaders of Clan Donald active in 1490.

Curiously, and perhaps coincidentally, in the very year that Angus Óg died the earl of Argyll *was* implicated in a seaborne operation that resulted in the forcible kidnap of a major Gaelic lord. An entry in the *Annals of Ulster* recorded that in June 1490 Sean Ua Catháin 'was taken by a ship that came from Scotland' or, more precisely, *hinber-air* (Inveraray?).[63] An Ua Catháin lord was certainly in Scotland by 22 October 1490 when Duncan Campbell of Glenorchy was required by royal judges to stand surety for the appearance of the Irish lord 'Okane' to answer charges brought by a Peter Colquhoun.[64] It must be doubtful that Ua Catháin was ever called to account in Scotland, for the Irish annals record that in 1491 Sean was 'let out from his captivity' and returned to Ireland. In the following year Sean's sons were killed in a dispute with members of his own family, a neighbouring lord and John Cathanach, son of the Lord of

Dunivaig and the Glens.[65] What the precise strategic objective of the Campbell abduction and release of Sean Ua Catháin in 1490–91 might have been is impossible to say; indeed the Irish annals seem to imply that the seizure of Ua Catháin was opportunistic rather than planned. Nevertheless, the incident points toward direct Campbell involvement in the politics of Ulster early in the 1490s. It was part of a pattern that suggested a growing Campbell interest in the affairs of the north of Ireland, an entanglement that presumably grew naturally from Argyll's attempts to control and protect his interests in Kintyre and Knapdale. As we shall see, in the years after 1491–2 the Campbells seem increasingly to have regarded Ua Domhnaill of Tír Conaill (O'Donnell of Tirconnell) as a potential ally in the region.

The arrival of Donald Dubh and his mother in the care of Earl Colin after Angus Óg's death, whether as a result of abduction or, as seems more likely, a widowed daughter's homecoming, had important long-term consequences. In 1490, however, Earl Colin and his tiny charge were more or less bystanders as the various powerful figures within Clan Donald fought to control, disregard or usurp the vestigial authority still exercised by John, Lord of the Isles. The apparent 'disorder' in the Isles featured in the legislation of a parliament held in April/May 1491. Amongst the tasks delegated to a large committee assigned to deal with government business after the close of the parliament was 'the mater of the Ilis and uther pertis brokin within his realme'. The committee was 'to provide sua that the kingis lyegis may lif in quiete and peax According to Justice and the lawis of his Realme'.[66] Parliamentary injunctions such as this have normally been viewed as essentially cynical, representing the covert bureaucratic voice of the Stewart monarchy or the interests of those, such as Argyll or the earl of Huntly, wishing to justify their own expansion in the Isles as a search for 'law and order'. Behind the professions of crisis and concern for the 'king's lieges' or 'poor folk' lay a determination to extend royal authority into the furthest reaches of the realm and to suppress social and legal structures at variance with those favoured by the royal administration. However, Roland Tanner's recent study of the late medieval Scottish parliament has suggested that we should not automatically assume high levels of royal control over representative assemblies in terms of the issues raised in debate or passing through to the statute stage.[67] There is no reason to suggest that the plea to the king to deal with the 'broken parts' of the realm did not reflect the genuine

concerns of many attending the parliament. The relentless expansion of
the royal patrimony during the late medieval period increasingly laid a very
direct obligation on the crown to provide defence and protection for a
larger number of communities within 'royal' lordships, such as Ross,
Kintyre and Knapdale, directly affected by disorder. In short, there is little
reason to doubt that in the immediate aftermath of Angus Óg's death
there was considerable anxiety in many quarters about the situation in the
Isles.

In the Isles itself Angus Og's death saw the emergence of Alexander of
Lochalsh, John of the Isles' nephew, as John's effective co-lord and,
perhaps, most likely heir. In August 1492 Alexander issued a joint charter
with his uncle and the consent of 'their' council.[68] Alexander of Lochalsh
was thus the dominant player inside the Lordship at the time of Earl
Colin's death sometime between 24 October and 10 November 1492,
although the curious misdating of a number of documents has rather
obscured the sequence of events in the autumn/winter of 1492.[69]

Argyll's demise proved to be a huge blow not only to his network of
kinsmen and allies, but also the interests of Clan Donald. While Earl
Colin was alive and at the centre of royal government the possibility of the
forfeiture of the Lordship of the Isles must have been remote, not least
because Argyll may already have been thinking about the potential future
claims of his infant grandson. However, the regime which came to
dominate James IV's minority government in 1492/3 was not simply less
well disposed towards Campbell interests but actively hostile towards the
new earl, Archibald, and his associates. As the position that Earl Colin
had built up after 1488 crumbled, one of the first casualties may have been
the Clan Donald lordship; in May 1493 the Lordship was forfeited to the
crown.[70] It is ironic, given the partly self-proclaimed reputation of the
Campbells as the family that brought down the Clan Donald, that the
final forfeiture of May 1493 was pushed through by a regime in which they
had little or no influence. Earl Archibald would in fact maintain a rather
ambiguous attitude towards royal policy in the Isles long after 1493. The
Campbell unease may have extended beyond a simple calculation of
familial interest. In the west Argyll's kinsmen and dependants inhabited
the same cultural and social world as the Clan Donald; they were aware of
the latter's persuasive claims to be the natural heirs to great historical and
mythological figures in the narratives maintained by Gaelic scholarship.
The Campbell earls sought to wield influence over men who looked on the

political and judicial structures associated with the lordship as part of the natural order of things. In the years after 1493 Earl Archibald would attempt both to appropriate and contest the symbols and narratives that had underpinned or grew from Clan Donald power. It was not always a comfortable situation. The viability of the earl's combined role as a representative of the interests of the west at the royal court and the representative of royal policies in the locality was severely tested on a number of occasions. The second earl, perhaps more than any Campbell lord before him, would experience conflicting calls on his sense of duty and responsibility. Dealing with the immediate aftermath of his father's death was simply the first of the trials of Earl Archibald.

Notes

1. *APS*, ii, 210.
2. *CDS*, iv, no.1539.
3. Macdougall, *James IV*, 41.
4. *Ibid.*, 39–40.
5. *Ibid*, 39.
6. *AU*, iii, 334–5. This version of events obviously mirrored the claims made in the letter to Hans. It may have been transmitted to the compiler of the Ulster annals direct from Scotland or from a Danish or English source. The narrative digression may indicate a written source.
7. Macdougall, *James IV, 13*.
8. *APS*, ii, 210.
9. *RMS*, ii, no.1811; *TA*, i, 96; *ADA*, 130.
10. For an evaluation of the conflicting accounts of the king's death, see Macdougall, *James IV*, 43–4. In the 1540s the English privy council thought that the chief culprits in James III's death were the Humes, Hepburns and the Carrys (the Kerrs?). *Letters of Henry VIII*, xx, Part 1, from 13 February 1545. In 1487 it was noted that Stirling of Keir was bound in manrent to Argyll's associate Andrew, Lord Avandale. NAS GD 124/7/8.
11. *AU*, iii, 334–5.
12. D.E.R. Watt and N. Shead, eds., *The Heads of Religious Houses in Scotland from Twelfth to Sixteenth Centuries*, (SRS, 2001), 26. Abbot Henry was noted as having given Prince James financial support prior to Sauchieburn. *TA*, i, 93, 134. His abbey had been subject to a physical assault by James III loyalists in the same period. He had also witnessed a bond of manrent given by William Stirling of Keir to Lord Erskine on 22 August 1487. NAS GD 124/7/8.
13. *Cambuskenneth Registrum*, no.129; *The Letters of James the Fourth*, 1505–1513, ed.R.L. Mackie (SHS, 1953) (Hereafter *James IV Letters*), no.542.
14. An entry for 11 August 1488 in the Treasurer's Accounts makes it clear that the earl had physical possession of the seal. *TA*, i, 93. 'to Mussche to pass in Argyle to the Chanslare to get a commission seylit to the Bordouris'.

15. *TA*, i, 80; Macdougall, *James IV*, 50–1.
16. *ER*, x, 629–30.
17. *ER*, x, 639. Argyll was not actually named as one of the men making the assedation in July.
18. *APS*, ii, 208.
19. *Ibid.*, 207.
20. Argyll Muniments, Inveraray, Bundle 1110; *HMC*, iv, Appendix, 474 (no.12), 485. (although the grant of regality may not have survived James III's revocations).
21. NAS GD112/Section 1/24: C.P. Stewart, *Historic Memorials of the Stewarts of Forthergill, Perthshire* (Edinburgh, 1879), Appendix 77–8; *Taymouth Bk*, 177–8.
22. *RMS*, ii, no.866.
23. NAS GD112/56/1/1.
24. The guarantors for the October agreement were Earl Colin (for Duncan) and George, earl of Huntly (for Neil).
25. For the background to the dispute, see Boardman, 'Feud', 171–78.
26. NAS Cunninghame-Graham Muniments GD22/2/2.
27. *APS*, ii, 208.
28. Boardman, 'Feud', 177. Robert Cunningham's death at the hands of Hugh, Lord Montgomery, is referred to obliquely in a court case of 1508 in which the then Lord Kilmaurs, Cuthbert Cunningham, referred to the death of his father. It is just possible that Cuthbert was Robert's brother rather than his son, and that the reference is therefore to Alexander Cunningham's death at Sauchieburn.
29. *APS*, ii, 208.
30. Boardman, 'Feud', 289–291.
31. *Ibid*, 292–299. The exact date of the clash at Monzievaird and of David Drummond's execution remain unclear.
32. *Ibid.*, 292–3; William Drummond, Viscount Strathallan, *The genealogy of the most noble and ancient House of Drummond* (Edinburgh, 1831), 157–160.
33. AT, at date. The grant was made during an exchequer audit at Perth that saw many of the Murray kindred restored to their rentals in the earldom of Strathearn.
34. The Campbells of Dunstaffnage are said (*SP*, i, 329) to be descended from Dugald, brother of Sir Duncan Campbell of Loch Awe (d.1452–3). Earl Colin also seems to have concluded a series of deals with William Murray of Tullibardine relating to lands in the barony of Tullibardine in the years 1490–91.
35. AT, at date. The gift of the bailieship was made at the monastery and was attested by all the monks. For Rait as abbot, see Watt and Shead, *Heads of Religious Houses*, 51.
36. See W. Douglas, 'Culross Abbey and its Charters', *PSAS* (1925–6), 67–104 for a discussion of the abbey's landholdings.
37. *RMS*, ii, no.1944.
38. See Chapter 11, below.
39. Macdougall, *James IV*, 61–62.
40. *Ibid.*, 63–65, for a summary of the activities of Lennox and Lyle in 1488–9 and a discussion of their possible motives in rebelling.
41. *RMS*, ii, no.1794.
42. *TA*, i, 109.
43. In the run-up to the parliament Earl Colin returned briefly to Argyll, issuing a

charter on 9 June from Inishail kirk in Loch Awe. NAS GD 116/1/256. The witnesses to Earl Colin's charter included his son and heir Archibald, Duncan Campbell of Glenorchy, Duncan (MacDougall), prior of Ardchattan, John Stewart, John Dewar, provost of Kilmun, and Andrew Cunningham. The charter was issued on the feast day of St Columba.

44. *APS*, ii, 215.
45. Argyll Muniments, Inveraray, Argyll Charters; *RMS*, ii, nos. 1868, 1869.
46. *APS*, ii, 214–5.
47. Macdougall, *James IV*, 69–70.
48. For a detailed account of the campaigns of the year, see Macdougall, *James IV*, 72–6.
49. *Abdn. Counc.*, 45–6; Fraser, *Lennox*, ii, 128–131; Macdougall, *James IV*, 70–71; Boardman, 'Feud', 234–239.
50. Fraser, *Lennox*, ii, 128–131.
51. Macdougall, *James IV*, 75–76; *APS*, ii, 216.
52. Argyll Muniments, Inveraray, Bundle 1092; *RMS*, ii, no.1918. The grant also gave Earl Colin a significant foothold on the north of the Clyde near Dumbarton. It could, of course, have been designed to compensate Argyll for the imminent loss of the estates about to be handed back to Robert, lord Lyle.
53. *APS*, ii, 217–8; Boardman, 'Feud', 239–251.
54. *APS*, ii, 220–21. The insistence on the Chancellor's presence might also imply that in previous years Argyll had been bypassed by those with a more direct hold on the young King.
55. Macdougall, *James IV*, 83–86.
56. In August 1488 James IV's regime was in communication with John of the Isles. *TA., i*, 92.
57. *AU*, iii, 329; *AC*, 590–1; *ALC*, ii, 184–5.
58. Macdougall, 'Achilles' Heel', 264.
59. For the rough dating of the assassination, see *AU*, iii, 350–1; *AC*, 593–5; *ALC*, ii, 186–7. For the poems, see *Book of the Dean of Lismore*, X, XII. Intriguingly the lament for Angus was linked by the poet to a well-known tale concerning the death of Conlaoch at the hands of his father Cú Chulainn. The tale of Conlaoch may have been considered suitable in the general sense that it dealt with the tragic death of a young lord. However, was the element of paternal involvement in the death seen as especially appropriate by the poet given the estrangement between Angus Óg and his own father?
60. *HP*, i, 50; *RC*, ii, 163.
61. *Calendar of letters and papers, foreign and domestic, of the reign of Henry VIII* (London, 1862–1932), vol xx, part 2, no.294. (4/9/1545).
62. See Bannerman, 'Lordship', 211 for an intelligent discussion of these issues. The idea of a galley raid and kidnap might have been added by later commentators to square with the notion of Donald's pre-natal imprisonment?
63. *AU*, iii, 348–9; *AFM*, iv, 1176–7; *ALC*, ii, 188–9; *AC*, 594–5. LC and *AC* suggest only that the ship involved came from Scotland. *AU* and (following *AU*) *AFM* add the detail that the ship came from *hinber-air*. The editors of *AU* suggested that *hinber-air* represented Inveraray (rather than Ayr); the fact that Earl Colin's cousin, Duncan Campbell of Glenorchy, was held responsible for the behaviour

of Ua Cathain in Scotland might support this notion. The correlation between *AU* and *AFM* is obvious in the shared identification of Sean as the 'son of Aibne son of Dermot', whereas *ALC* and *AC* describe Sean as son of Dermot son of Aibne.

64. *ADC*, i, 153–4.

65. *AU*, iii, 352–3, 364–5; the role of John Cathanach is recorded only in *AFM*, iv, 1192–3. The involvement of a member of the Dunivaig and Glens' family in the deaths of the sons of a man who had recently been in the custody of the Campbells is suggestive. There is, however, nothing else that might suggest this was a deliberate Campbell attempt to interfere with the Lord of Dunivaig's interests in the north of Ireland.

66. *APS*, ii, 228.

67. Tanner, *Late Medieval Scottish Parliament* 264–78

68. *ALI*, no.123. The witnesses to the grant included the abbot of Iona, John MacIan of Ardnamurchan, Ruairi MacLeod of Lewis and Colin MacNeill of Gigha.

69. Earl Colin was alive on the first date, when he issued a precept of sasine directed to his son Archibald, master of Lorn and Argyll. *SHS Misc.*, iv, 258, no.4. He had evidently died by 10 November when, at Glendaruel, Archibald, earl of Argyll, made Duncan Campbell of Glenorchy his bailie for all his lands in the Lowlands of Scotland. NAS GD112/1/26. The dating of Colin's death is made problematic by the appearance of Earl Colin as one of the commissioners named to set tacks of royal lands, a document apparently drawn up on 12 December 1492. *ER*, x, 710–11. It seems likely, however, that this date is a mistake for 12 September, because the named commissioners, minus Argyll and the bishop of Aberdeen, were actually in Perth on 14 September and beginning to set lands according to the terms of the commission. *ER*, x, 711. Oddly, an entry in the printed Aberdeen Council Records seems to err in the opposite direction. The Aberdeen register has Archibald, earl of Angus, Lord of Douglas appearing as Chancellor on 11 September 1492 at a point when Earl Colin was still very much alive. *Abdn. Counc.*, i, 421. On the same page, under the date 6 August 1492, it was noted that a William Gibson, bellman, had passed through the town enjoining the inhabitants to come to the tolbooth to pay their tax contribution to 'furnyss the personis furtht to the meting of my lord Huntlie, locumtenant, to pas with him to the asseging of the of the strinthis of the Ilis'. Again this seems to refer to the summer of 1493, when there was a royal campaign in the Isles, rather than the given year date of 1492 from which we have no evidence of royal action in the Hebrides.

70. Macdougall, 'Achilles' Heel', 265–66.

TEN

The Fall of the House of Sorley

I n the weeks after Earl Colin's death his son and heir faced a number of immediate problems. The sudden loss of influence at the heart of the minority administration was made far worse by the fact that the man who eventually replaced Earl Colin as chancellor, Archibald Douglas, earl of Angus, seems to have been determined to undermine Campbell interests at every opportunity. The Angus/Argyll animosity might seem strange given that the two families were not obvious regional rivals, but the marital and kinship links of the two earl Archibalds did clash in one crucial region. The Campbell lords, as we have seen, were staunch supporters of Lord Montgomery's ambitions in Cunningham and northern Ayrshire. Angus, on the other hand, was tied by marriage to two of Lord Montgomery's rivals in the region. Archibald himself had married Elizabeth Boyd, sister of Thomas Boyd, earl of Arran, shortly before 19 May 1468, at the height of Boyd influence over royal government in the minority of James III.[1] The Boyds' forfeiture and fall from power in November 1469 clearly lessened the political advantages of the match, but the Angus connection to the Boyd family remained close. Thomas, earl of Arran, is thought to have died sometime before 1474 but his marriage to James III's sister, Princess Mary, produced at least two children, James (a name reflecting his royal bloodline) and Margaret. The fortunes of James Boyd, nephew by marriage to the earl of Angus and James III's nephew by blood, looked to have been revived in the wake of the Lauder crisis of 1482. In October 1482 James was restored to many of the Boyd estates forfeited by his father and grandfather, including the barony of Kilmarnock.[2] The Boyd revival was short-lived for it depended on the temporary ascendancy of the duke of Albany and the earl of Angus in royal government in 1482–3. After Albany was forced from the realm in February 1483 the Boyd estates were reclaimed by Queen Margaret on behalf of her son Prince James. James Boyd was not apparently forced to follow his uncle Albany into exile although, as it turned out, this was hardly an advantage.[3] At some point, perhaps c.1487, James was killed by Hugh, Lord Montgomery.[4] If James

III did not mourn for his nephew the earl of Angus may have been less willing to forget the incident.

Aside from any lingering animosity deriving from the death of James Boyd, Angus was drawn into the politics of the region in the 1490s by his initially reluctant acquisition of the former Boyd lordship of Kilmarnock in 1491.[5] By June 1492 Angus was openly identified with Montgomery's enemies through the marriage of his daughter Marion to Cuthbert Cunningham, Lord Kilmaurs.[6] In the following month Angus also acquired the Ayrshire lands and castle of Bothwell. By August 1492 Lord Montgomery was faced in Ayrshire by a powerful and politically active earl closely identified with Boyd and Cunningham interests. The involvement of Angus may well have encouraged the lord of Kilmaurs to resume his open defiance of Montgomery's claim to be bailie of Cunningham. On 10 August royal messengers were dispatched to prevent Montgomery and Cunningham 'gathering' their men for a further confrontation in Irvine. Angus could hardly have been unaware of the plans of his new son-in-law, for on 7 August Cunningham had acknowledged receipt of a dowry payment from Angus at the earl's own castle of Kilmarnock. The agreement at Kilmarnock was witnessed not only by a large group of Ayrshire lairds but also by a number of royal courtiers.[7] The potential clash in Irvine was clearly more than just a local problem. After the difficulties of James III's reign and the experience of 1489 James IV's minority regime was acutely aware of the dangers of leaving local or regional feuds to fester. By 12 August the king himself was present at Angus's castle at Kilmarnock.[8] However, James' appearance in Ayrshire was more than a simple royal show of force to keep the peace for it soon became clear that the king was increasingly sympathetic to the position of Montgomery's local enemies. The men with Angus in Kilmarnock on 7 August had included a number of royal officers and courtiers, and during the autumn of 1492 Angus and his supporters claimed an even more prominent place in royal government. Argyll remained as chancellor and as a witness to royal charters, but during September and October he was joined on the royal council by a number of men attached to the earl of Angus.[9] Moreover, the Boyd/Angus/Cunningham faction had another card to play in terms of securing royal favour for at some point in 1492 Angus's niece, Marion Boyd, became the young king's mistress.

Thus even before Earl Colin's death Hugh Montgomery's brutal ascendancy in northern Ayrshire was starting to be questioned at the

heart of royal government; the disappearance of Montgomery's chief
patron hastened and confirmed the reversal of fortune. As we have seen,
Earl Colin died between 24 October and 10 November, perhaps as early as
28 October.[10] Angus seems to have become chancellor immediately on
Argyll's death. Thereafter Angus's kinsmen were the beneficiaries of
considerable royal largesse.[11] At first the ambitions of Chancellor Angus
and his Douglas, Boyd and Cunningham allies were curtailed by the terms
of the various royal grants made in favour of Montgomery and others in
the period after 1488. The restrictions placed on the new regime in terms of
their ability to control the disposition of royal lands and office could be
removed, however, by a formal royal 'revocation'. Accordingly in May 1493
the young king issued a sweeping annulment of all grants made to the
crown's prejudice in his own minority and the reign of his father.[12] Lord
Montgomery's office-holding in Cunningham, Bute and Arran was swept
away in the wake of the revocation. By 8 June 1493 the earl of Angus
himself had replaced Montgomery as bailie of Cunningham while Lord
Hugh also demitted his claims to liferents and offices in Arran and Bute at
around the same time.[13]

The collapse of Montgomery's position was clearly a blow to the
regional interests of the earl of Argyll, and brought a new political force
to the fore in the Firth of Clyde. Earl Archibald would soon have more
pressing concerns, for it is clear that the assembly of May 1493 also laid the
foundations for a major military and political campaign by the Angus
regime in the Hebrides. The attitude of Argyll to the 'royal' campaigns of
1493 is hard to fathom. It would be wrong to suggest that the Campbells
had been utterly excluded from royal service after Earl Colin's death. Over
the winter of 1492–3 Earl Archibald and Duncan Campbell of Glenorchy
had both served as royal judges and Argyll was one of the Lords of the
Articles in the May 1493 assembly and must, therefore, have had some part
to play in initiating or reviewing the legislative programme.[14] Earl
Archibald could, conceivably, have been eager for the intervention of a
royal host if the Campbells' adversaries had been particularly active after
the death of Earl Colin. Moreover, the political problems in the Isles and
their impact on surrounding regions had already been raised in a parliament of 1491, long before the Angus regime came to power. Yet the
political context of the May 1493 assembly, with the deliberate undercutting of the power of Argyll's brother-in-law on the Firth of Clyde,
hardly suggests a government intent on bolstering Earl Archibald's

position, or following his preferred policies, in the west.[15] Like a loyal subject Argyll may well have given his support to royal forces active in the Hebrides during the summer of 1493, but his enthusiasm for the project may be doubted.

The campaign of 1493 is usually seen as marking a distinctive new phase in governmental policy towards the management of the affairs of the Isles. Attempts to influence the behaviour of the great men of the region through the intermediary of a figure enjoying the prestige and authority of the Lord of the Isles seem to have been abandoned. Instead the Hebrides were to be governed directly by the crown, with the title and lands of the Lordship annexed to the royal patrimony. It is assumed that the May 1493 parliament saw a final forfeiture of John, Lord of the Isles, the terms of which have been subsequently erased from the record.[16] In order to enforce the new dispensation and to bring the Hebridean chiefs to obedience a major military campaign was planned for the summer of 1493 in which the government expected to besiege 'the strinthis [castles] of the Ilis'.[17] Details of the conduct of the campaign are almost entirely lacking, although the Earl of Huntly at least may have been given a commission of lieutenancy similar to those issued by James III in 1475-6.[18] The young king himself was taken briefly on campaign, issuing one charter on 18 August from the Campbell fortress of Dunstaffnage.[19]

In the wake of the appearance of royal armies in the west many of the leading figures in Clan Donald sought to establish new arrangements with James IV's government. Amongst the first to submit may have been the Lord of the Isles himself, for later entries in the Exchequer Rolls imply that he became a royal pensioner, and resident at the royal court, early in 1494 or 1495.[20] John's new status as a 'guest' (or hostage) of the Scottish court was part of a wider settlement. Alexander of Lochalsh, the man who had been exercising authority in the Isles in partnership with John in 1492, appears to have negotiated a submission which guaranteed that the leading men within the Isles would maintain possession of estates previously held from the Lord of the Isles.[21] The young king's dubbing of Alexander as a knight may have reinforced Lochalsh's submission to James IV. By the summer of 1494 Lochalsh and his kinsman John of Dunivaig and the Glens had both become knights.[22] The symbolism of leading figures within Clan Donald becoming royal knights and accepting the personal bonds and abstract values associated with that status is striking. Lochalsh's immediate good behaviour may have been further assured by the handing over of his young son and heir, Donald, to be brought up outwith the Isles. Donald's byname Gallda (foreign) reflected a childhood and adolescence spent in the Lowlands, perhaps at the royal court or in the household of a Scots magnate.[23] In the long term, the education of Lochalsh's heir in the Lowlands held out the hope of a dominant lineage in the Isles sympathetic to the political aims and cultural life of the Scottish crown. At any rate, the royal perception of a new order in the west was confirmed by the appearance around this time of new heraldic officers, Islay Herald and Kintyre Pursuivant, taking their titles from the lordship territories now directly 'subject' to the king.[24]

The regime's aims in the west were not swiftly achieved, and in the following summer the military pressure was reapplied. In May 1494 James IV made a swift visit to the Isles, but a much more prolonged and serious campaign was launched in July-August 1494. The expedition concentrated on the lordships in and around the Firth of Clyde and saw the reconstruction of the strategically vital royal castle of Tarbert which dominated the narrow isthmus between Kintyre and Knapdale. Royal forces were also sent to the castle of Dunaverty further down the Kintyre peninsula.[25] Earl Archibald could hardly fail to be interested in the conduct of this particular campaign for it affected areas and lordships in which he had extensive claims. Argyll was in Edinburgh in the month before the expedition was launched and was clearly involved in the preparations if still not part of the inner circle of government. In early June 1494 Argyll was to be found pursuing a legal case against the MacNeills of Gigha that may well have related to Castle Sween and estates in Knapdale. Earl Archibald was still in Edinburgh on 28 June when Elizabeth Menteith, Lady of Ruskie, resigned various estates in Cowal in the earl's favour. The witnesses to the transaction included Ninian Stewart, the sheriff of Bute (and Arran), and more notably Ruairi MacLeod of Lewis, presumably in Edinburgh and attending the earl in anticipation of the campaign about to conducted in the Firth of Clyde.[26]

MacLeod was not the only Hebridean aristocrat limbering up for the royal expedition to the Firth of Clyde. On 14 June John MacIan of Ardnamurchan, the leader of an ancient and powerful cadet branch of the Clan Donald, received a grant of lands in Islay with the office of bailie of the island as he had held them from John, one-time Lord of the Isles.[27] The confirmation was presumably intended to encourage MacIan's co-operation with royal forces in the summer of 1494. However, MacIan was

not the most significant member of Clan Donald to whom the crown
looked for assistance. All the available evidence suggests that throughout
the summer and autumn of 1494 Sir Alexander of Lochalsh remained the
pivotal figure around whom the crown settlement in the Isles was to be
constructed. 'Sir' Alexander's willingness to adhere to the terms of his
submission to the crown may well be indicated by the fact that he was
prepared to acknowledge and respond to legal processes raised in royal
courts. In June he submitted a deposition relating to a case between the
earl of Argyll and Gillecallum MacNeill of Gigha to the Lords of Council.
On 5 July Hugh Rose of Kilravock was noted as standing surety for Sir
Alexander of Lochalsh in a claim for damages probably arising from one of
Alexander's earlier raids in and around Ross.[28] Overall, there seems no
reason for James IV's government to have regarded Lochalsh with a
particularly unfriendly eye in the summer of 1494.[29] Despite this, Lochalsh's brutal assassination, probably on a date between 5 July and 8
November 1494, at the hands of a member of the Dunivaig and the
Glens family and John MacIan of Ardnamurchan is sometimes attributed
to the machinations of the crown.[30] In fact, the evidence relating to
Alexander's death suggests quite otherwise. The charter issued in favour of
John MacIan of Ardnamurchan of lands in Islay on 14 June 1494 can hardly
have been, as is sometimes claimed, a royal reward for MacIan's elimination of Lochalsh given that Sir Alexander was still alive as late as 5 July.
Indeed, it is tempting to link Lochalsh's death with an incident recorded
under the date 14 October 1494 in the *Annals of Ulster*. There, the annalist
noted the assassination of an Alexander son of Gillespic MacDonald,
described as a 'representative' or 'deputy' (*Fer inaid*) of MacDonald, by
John Cathanach of Dunivaig and the Glens. A recent study has argued
that the man killed on 14 October was not, as is usually thought, Alexander
of Lochalsh, but a member of a MacDonald galloglass family based in
Ulster. The suggestion is plausible, but requires the coincidence of John
Cathanach and his son independently killing prominent MacDonald
kinsmen bearing the same patronymic in July–November 1494.[31] At
the least, we can be reasonably certain that Alexander of Lochalsh's
killers included a leading member of the Clann Eóin Mhóir. None of
the men responsible for Lochalsh's death appear likely to have been
operating under royal instruction. John of Dunivaig and the Glens, the
senior figure in Clann Eóin Mhóir had in fact been summoned by James
IV's government sometime before 8 September 1494 to answer for his

alleged treason 'in Kintyre'.[32] John MacIan of Ardnamurchan would certainly go on to earn a reputation as a violent 'hatchet man' in the west for the Scottish crown, but his stance in 1494 is far less clear. A note in the treasurer's accounts for 8 November 1494, within a month of the likely date of Lochalsh's death, records a payment made to masons who went 'to cast down M'Kanys house with the Lord Gordon'. If, as seems probable, this refers to MacIan of Ardnamurchan, then the reaction of the royal administration to Lochalsh's death was one of shock and outrage.[33] There is little to indicate that MacIan enjoyed significant royal favour until March 1499, when he captured John of Dunivaig and the Glens and his family and handed them over to the tender mercies of the king's executioner.[34] As to the motivation for the assassination, the earliest direct comment is provided by the seventeenth-century *Sleat History*, which sketches a very hostile picture of Alexander of Lochalsh as a man of dubious descent with pretensions to lord it over the other branches of Clan Donald. The remarkably partisan account attributes the actions of the MacDonalds of Dunivaig and the Glens and MacIan of Ardnamurchan to fear of Lochalsh's territorial ambitions and resentment at his usurpation of the rights properly vested in Donald Dubh.[35] Much of this is clearly a retrospective gloss attributing noble principles and aims (in terms of the preservation of the lordship and its 'legitimate' ruling dynasty) to those branches of the kin most favoured by the seventeenth-century compiler of the narrative. In terms of the immediate context of 1494 it is evident that the MacDonalds of Dunivaig and the Glens had been thoroughly alienated by, and offered resistance to, the royal campaigns in the Firth of Clyde during July and August. If, as seems probable, Lochalsh had maintained his policy of co-operation with the crown during this period then the animosity of John of Dunivaig and his family would be understandable. However, the wider issue of succession to the Lordship of the Isles raised by the seventeenth-century accounts may still have been relevant. To many Hebridean kindreds neither the finality nor the relevance of the royal forfeiture of the Lordship in 1493 could have been obvious. Despite the supposed transformation of the Lordship into a parliamentary title in 1475-6, for many the process of creating or removing a 'Lord of the Isles' was one that depended on the assent and recognition of the chief men of the Hebrides, however obtained. Until 1493-4 Alexander's authority within the Isles and his exercise of the wider rights of lordship apparently rested on his association with the moribund John,

Lord of the Isles.[36] The royal intervention of 1493–4 must have strained the convenient fiction that underpinned this arrangement by placing John, Lord of the Isles, in royal custody. The final humiliation and removal of John may well have stimulated discord over who had the right to govern in his absence, with Lochalsh presumably claiming, fatally as it turned out, that he was still entitled to exercise leadership in the Isles. John of Dunivaig and the Glens had pretensions of his own in that regard if the Irish chronicle that decribed him on his death in 1499 as 'king of the Hebrides' (ri Innsi Gall) was not engaging in poetic hyperbole.[37] In that sense the vicious rubbishing of the legitimacy and conduct of the entire Lochalsh line in much later accounts seemed to reflect genuine tensions within the Clan Donald late in the fifteenth century.

The attitude of Argyll to the unfolding drama in the Isles during 1494 is simply unknown. The earl was not at the centre of royal government yet the available sources give no hint that he actively or passively opposed the strategies adopted in 1493–4. Argyll, as the uncle and 'guardian' of Donald Dubh, could be expected to maintain more than a passing interest in any dispute relating to the leadership of Clan Donald but it is difficult to see his hand behind the assassination of Lochalsh. MacIan of Ardnamurchan was married at some point to the earl's sister, but the MacDonalds of Dunivaig were hardly likely to follow any agenda but their own. Nevertheless, Lochalsh's murder seems to have had some unforeseen and inadvertent benefits for Earl Archibald. It was clear by the end of 1494 that the Angus regime's intervention in the west had ended in a more or less complete failure. The ineffectiveness of the crown's Hebridean intervention may have helped to persuade many that the new Earl of Argyll should claim a role in government. In any case wider circumstances were beginning to loosen Chancellor Angus's grip on power. James IV was displaying more and more signs of independence from the councillors who had guided him since 1488 and it was also clear that the young king's infatuation with Chancellor Angus's niece Marion Boyd, who had borne James two children, was beginning to wane. A suitable marriage to John Muir of Rowallan was arranged for James' discarded mistress over the winter of 1494–5, after which the young king's eye eventually wandered to the daughter of John, Lord Drummond.[38] In March 1495 Argyll followed his father into the heart of the royal establishment by claiming the office of master of the king's household, a post that earl Colin himself had held before becoming chancellor.[39]

Argyll joined a royal administration already gearing up to renew its military endeavours in the west. Over the winter of 1494–5 James IV maintained a modest ship construction and refitting programme at Dumbarton, presumably in preparation for the naval expedition into the Isles that was in its planning stage as early as January 1495.[40] In early May 1495 the royal fleet, complete with artillery pieces and gunners for siege work, set sail from Dumbarton. What were the likely targets for this demonstration of royal power and displeasure? If James's expedition was intended to discomfit the assassins of Alexander of Lochalsh, then the lord of Dunivaig and the Glens and MacIan of Ardnamurchan could both expect less than friendly visitations during 1495. In that light James IV's appearance at MacIan's stronghold of Mingary Castle on 18 May might have been less agreeable to the lord of Ardnamurchan than is usually assumed.[41] The display of royal military might in the heart of his own lordship persuaded MacIan to offer his submission to James IV. Certainly by October of 1496 MacIan was included amongst a group of Hebridean lords bringing their disputes before the royal courts.[42] The lord of Dunivaig and the Glens might also have felt increased pressure from the Scottish crown in the summer of 1495, but there is little indication that it brought Sir John to bay. The progress of the royal fleet through the Firth of Clyde would have allowed campaigning against Sir John's interests in Knapdale, Kintyre and Islay, and James IV may even have contemplated a strike against the family's lordships in the north of Ireland. When the king returned to Dumbarton and then Glasgow in June 1495, one of his first duties was to greet the great Ulster lord Aedh Ua Domhnaill of Tír Connail.[43] As Macdougall has pointed out, the main purpose of the Uí Dhomhnaill embassy may have been to interest the Scottish king in the political and military cause of Perkin Warbeck, the Yorkist pretender to the English throne who was about to launch an ill-fated assault on Henry VII's kingdom.[44] However, both Ua Domhnaill and the Scottish king may have had more limited and specific aims that they hoped could be furthered by co-operation across the Irish Sea. For King James, Ua Domhnaill was an ally who could potentially inconvenience the MacDonalds of Dunivaig and the Glens in their Antrim fastness and/or the bastion of English power in the north of Ireland, the burgh of Carrickfergus and its castle.[45] For the Uí Dhomhnaill, the Scottish king represented a powerful military confederate. The lords of Tír Connail may have envisaged Scottish support as critical in one key area, namely the family's determined and prolonged campaign to wrest control of the town of Sligo from the Ui Conchobhair (O'Connors).[46] In 1494 Ua Domhnaill had mounted a siege of Sligo Castle with the assistance, amongst others, of one Donald of Arran, 'a Scottish captain', who was killed during the operation. While Aedh was in Scotland during 1495 his son made a renewed, and similarly unsuccessful, attempt to take Sligo.[47] For Aedh the favour of James IV may have held out the prospect of a more regular supply of Scottish manpower to assist Ui Dhomhnaill campaigns. However, the most intriguing possibility from the viewpoint of the lord of Tír Connail may have been the Scottish king's capacity, demonstrated in both 1493 and 1494, to attack and take Hebridean castles through the use of ship-borne artillery. Much later in his reign James IV would prove willing to lend artillery pieces to the Uí Dhomhnaill and such logisitical support may have been in Aedh Ua Domhnaill's mind in 1495.

Whatever the precise aim of Ua Domhnaill's mission, it seems indicative of James IV's determination to control or disrupt access between the north of Ireland and Kintyre and Knapdale. As Macdougall has noted, James IV and his agents embarked on an extensive building programme on the Firth of Clyde during the 1490s. A new royal fortress appeared at Kilkerran (modern Campbeltown) at the southern tip of Kintyre which, combined with the rebuilt royal castle at Tarbert, would have presented new challenges to John of Dunivaig and others as they sought to operate in and around Kintyre and Knapdale.[48] Other strategic fortresses in the area, such as Skipness, were placed in the hands of trusted royal familiars. On 3 July 1495, shortly after his return to Glasgow from Mingary, James IV created a free barony of Skipness (including possession of the castle) for his comptroller (the financial officer responsible for the accounts of the royal household), Duncan Forrester. Forrester was essentially a minor laird, a former provost and custumar of Stirling, whose principal estates lay at Torwood near the burgh.[49] Besides placing the fortress in the care of a trusted royal servant, the grant may have had a symbolic aspect to it, a demonstration of the king's ability to dispense with his lordships and lands in the west as he saw fit. Forrester had few, if any, previous ties to Knapdale, but in the wake of James IV's recently demonstrated military and political supremacy in the region the gift was surely meant to suggest that the king's patronage was as effective there as it was anywhere else in the realm. Moreover, Forrester with his extensive links to the burgh of Stirling and financial experience as comptroller may have seemed like a man likely to subject his new Knapdale estates to planned economic development. Certainly later in the 1490s James IV seems to have used his financial officers to spearhead attempts to introduce new and more onerous feu-ferm tenure to 'royal' lands. In 1499, for example, Forrester's successor as comptroller, Sir Patrick Hume of Polwarth, and the Treasurer, Robert Lundy of Balgony, received Strathbraan and other Perthshire estates formerly occupied by Neil Stewart of Fortingall in feu-ferm for doubled rents.[50] In the end, the ability of the royal administration to deal with the crown's landed resources unrestricted by the demands, ambitions and entrenched interests of local lords and power structures was overestimated. Forrester for one soon found it necessary to bolster his position by enlisting local support through the marriage of his daughter Margaret to James Campbell of Lawers. Eventually, indeed, Forrester would abandon his barony in the west to the Campbells, granting Skipness to Earl Archibald in September 1502.[51] Similarly Hume of Polwarth and Lundy of Balgony were forced to give over their grants of Strathbraan to more powerful local lords in the face of the opposition of the previous occupant, Neil Stewart of Fortingall, to the change in tenurial arrangements.

All the royal activity in Knapdale and Kintyre during 1495 seems to have had little effect on the lord of Dunivaig's ability to raise substantial forces and to operate freely in the Irish sea. In October 1496 a letter from an Anglo-Irish knight claimed that 'Jhon of the oute Iles' had descended on the country around Carrickfergus Castle in Ulster with a thousand men and 'keterykes' in order to free one of his sons who had been taken prisoner by a local Irish lord. As Conway observes, John of the Outer Isles was almost certainly John of Dunivaig (or perhaps his son John Cathanach).[52]

Although not a direct beneficiary of the 1495 campaign, there seems little doubt that Argyll was involved in the expedition and that his participation confirmed the revival of Campbell influence at the centre of royal government. The earl may have acted as an intermediary for some of the Hebridean lords who, during the summer of 1495, sought royal confirmation of the lands and offices previously held from the Lords of the Isles.[53] The submission of these kindreds evidently encouraged James IV to regard the situation in the Isles as a problem solved. Increasingly, the king turned his attention to European diplomacy, the steadily worsening relationship with England, the search for a suitable marriage partner, and the quest to increase royal revenues.[54] Argyll, as a royal councillor, was no doubt fully involved in all these areas of activity, but his interests as a regional lord obviously remained bound up with the situation in the west. Archibald's more or less constant attendance on the king from 1495 onwards meant that, as in the case of his father, the earl was something of an absentee lord. This did not, however, imply that Argyll was out of touch with the affairs of his province. Earl Archibald's 'Edinburgh' household was dominated by clerical administrators holding benefices in Argyll and servants and familiars drawn from Campbell lordships in the west. In the early stages of his career as master of the king's household Earl Archibald's most important household men (as measured by their witnessing the earl's charters and other legal business) were John Dewar, provost of the collegiate kirk at Kilmun, Andrew Cunningham, parson of Loch Awe, Charles MacArthur and Archibald Uchtre (a name anglicised as Ochiltree). Uchtre/Ochiltree was the earl's ubiquitous and hyperactive 'man of business' who, amongst many other tasks, appeared regularly in Argyll and elsewhere dealing with the earl's conveyancing or carrying letters on behalf of his lord or the king.[55] The bulk of Argyll's household in 1495–7, with the exception of Andrew Cunningham, parson of Loch Awe, were drawn from Argyll and were regular returnees to the province.[56] John Dewar, provost of Kilmun, as his name suggests, may well have been a member of the family of hereditary relic keepers associated with the cult of St Fiontáin in and around Kilmun. John's ecclesiastical career seems to have been spent entirely in Campbell-controlled benefices; before attaining the provostry of Kilmun he had been rector of Loch Awe.[57] Archibald Uchtre and his family were also connected to Cowal and the kirk of Kilmun. A probable kinsman, David Uchtre (Ochiltree), had served as provost in the 1460s and 1470s, while in 1481 a notarial instrument drawn up at Kilmun was witnessed by, amongst others, Alan 'Oghtre', vicar of Glenorchy and a William 'Oghtre'.[58] Moreover, it is evident that Earl Archibald, despite his familiarity with the many able administrators floating around the royal court, continued to recruit into his household direct from Argyll. By the time of his death in 1513 the core of Earl Archibald's curia was still made up of clerics holding major benefices inside the diocese of Argyll.[59]

Surrounded by Argyll men and provided with a constant flow of information from the west, Earl Archibald was hardly detached from the affairs of his province. Moreover, the earl was occasionally able to journey into Argyll and consult with his kinsmen and adherents in person, although in normal circumstances these visits seem to have been confined to the Campbell centres in eastern Cowal, Kilmun and Dunoon. For a while after the royal expedition of 1495 Argyll's informants seem to have had little of an alarming nature to report. Both John of Dunivaig and MacIan of Ardnamurchan seem to have gone to ground. Other potential claimants to the leadership of Clan Donald were in no position to act. John, the broken Lord of the Isles, was in royal custody. John's grandson Donald Dubh was in the care of Argyll, and Donald Gallda the son of Alexander of Lochalsh was either at the royal court or in the household of a Lowland magnate. Royal legislation addressing the Isles was no longer concerned with crisis management, but with attempting to make the leading figures in the region more responsive to the crown's financial, judicial and administrative machinery.[60] That there was no perception of imminent danger from the Hebrides may be reflected in the commitment of Earl Archibald's military resources to James IV's campaigns in northern England during 1496 and 1497. Under the pretext of supporting the claims of the pretender Perkin Warbeck to the English throne King James had unleashed a war of swift raids and sieges against Henry VII's realm. Macdougall argues that King James was not deeply committed to, or even convinced by, Perkin's claims, but that the pursuit of war served his own diplomatic, military and political purposes and ambitions.[61] From the very start of the royal campaign the king made it plain that he expected his Hebridean subjects to participate. Early in 1496 'servants of my Lord of Ergilis' took letters demanding attendance at the king's planned hosting at Lauder to the 'heidis of the Ilis'.[62] James eventually launched a short-lived campaign in September 1496 and it would seem that the Scottish host included an impressive turn-out of leading figures from the west. Shortly after the conclusion of the campaign MacLean of Duart, MacIan of Ardnamurchan (apparently restored to royal favour), Alan mac Ruairi of Moidart, Ewen mac Allan of Clan Cameron and Donald mac Angus (MacDonald of Lochaber) were all personally present in Edinburgh, where they delivered oaths of good behaviour to Argyll as the king's representative.[63] In the following summer the king was in the field again, and on this occasion Earl Archibald can be shown to have brought an intimidating retinue of Argyll lords to serve in James' border wars. On 17 June 1497 Argyll was at Melrose where he concluded a series of transactions with Gilchrist Lamont concerning lands and offices in Cowal.[64] Two days later, in the presence of Earl Archibald, in St Mary's kirk in the

Cistercian monastery at Melrose, one Malcolm Salmond resigned any right he might have to the deanery of Lismore.[65] The conclusion of this piece of ecclesiastical business was witnessed by Duncan Campbell of Glenorchy, John MacDougall of Rarey (Lorn), and Alexander Campbell 'Keir' (i.e. Alexander Ciar Campbell, Captain of Dunstaffnage). The appearance of these men in the royal host at Melrose alongside what appears to have been another large Hebridean contingent suggests that there was little apprehension about potential disorder in the west in the summer of 1497.[66] The Spanish ambassador to Scotland, Don Pedro de Ayala, accompanied James IV on his 1497 military adventure and was deeply fascinated by the large number of 'savage' troops that accompanied the king into England.[67] De Ayala's lavish praise of the king's ability to control and harness the Islesmen as no other king before him should not, perhaps, be dismissed out of hand. The evidence seems to suggest that the sustained efforts of 1495–6 had persuaded many in the west that the Scottish king's claims on their miltary service at least could not be lightly ignored. Meanwhile, the oath-giving of October 1496 also revealed the influential position claimed by Argyll as an intermediary between the king and his subjects in the west. Indeed, in many cases James IV's communications with individual Hebridean chiefs or the aristocrats of the Isles as a collective were directed through Argyll's household.[68]

In the spring and summer of 1498 James IV appeared in the west once again, although this time confining his activities largely to the Firth of Clyde. The king's chief interest seems to have been in the construction of his new royal fortress at Loch Kilkerran in the south of Kintyre.[69] James made at least four separate visits to Kilkerran during the year in March (including stops in Bute and Arran), May, June-July and July-August.[70] Kintyre was the area where the resistance of the MacDonalds of Dunivaig and the Glens had been most effective; the completion of Kilkerran gave the crown a significant new weapon in its struggle with Clan Donald south. Royal policy happily dovetailed with the interests and ambitions of Earl Archibald and his kinsmen on the Firth of Clyde. That the king was sympathetic and responsive to the plans of Earl Archibald in the west is made plain in a privy seal letter of 1 April 1498. The letter, said to have been requested by earl Archibald, was directed to the pope and asked that the abbey of Iona should become the seat of the bishopric of the Isles until the head church of the diocese (in the Isle of Man) was recovered from English control.[71] The arrangement could have reflected Argyll's genuine concern for the state of the diocese of the Isles, but the fact that the Bishop of the Isles in 1498 was John Campbell, the brother of Duncan Campbell of Glenorchy, may also have been relevant.[72] The plea to make Iona the cathedral chapter for the Isles was not allowed, but in June 1499 the abbey was granted in commend to Bishop John. Campbell attempts to gain control of the key ecclesiastical centre of the former Clan Donald lordship were clearly supported by the king in 1498–99 as part of his general promotion of proven royal allies in the west.[73] In other areas too, 1498 saw Earl Archibald's star in the ascendant. Over the winter of 1497–8 the earl received a number of resignations of lands and offices in Cowal from Gilchrist Lamont of Inverneilbeg, John Colquhoun of Luss and Robert Fleming, all of which the king was happy to confirm.[74] More striking were the various transactions concluded while the royal fleet sailed down the Firth of Clyde to Kilkerran in June 1498. On 24 June Argyll was at Inveraray accepting the resignation of various lands in Lorn from one Ranald son of John son of Allan Dubh MacDougall.[75] Four days later Argyll was with the king at the 'new castle' of Kilkerran witnessing a royal grant in favour of Torquil MacLeod of Lewis.[76] The grant was of the office of bailie of Trotternish in Skye with the lands attached to that office said to be in the king's hands by reason of the forfeiture of John, Lord of the Isles. The office and lands were to be held by Torquil and any heirs produced between himself and Catriona Campbell, Earl Archibald's sister. If there were no heirs produced in this marriage, then the office and lands were to revert to the crown. Clearly the royal gift was dependent on Torquil's Campbell connection and provided an incentive for Torquil to privilege the heirs of Catriona Campbell in the succession to his wider lordship. The flow of patronage to Campbell and his kinsmen and allies continued through the summer of 1498, at least partly reflecting the service rendered by the family to the king during his stay in Kintyre. On 4 July at Kilkerran Duncan Campbell of Glenorchy received a feuferm grant of lands in the royal lordship of Discher and Toyer, while on 3 August Colin Campbell 'Knychtsone' was given lands in Gareloch and Rosneath specifically for his service to the king 'in the Isles'.[77] By 27 August James IV had left the Firth of Clyde and was in Stirling, but the master of the king's household continued to receive significant royal favour. On 27 August Argyll received the marriage and ward of the heir of the recently deceased John Caldor, son and heir of William, Thane of Cawdor.[78] The grant provoked a fierce feud between Argyll and John Caldor's father and brothers who refused to recognise the claims of John's infant daughter to the family's estates.[79]

James IV may well have sailed from Kilkerran in August 1498 confident that the successive military expeditions of the 1490s and the construction of the great royal fortresses at Tarbert and Kilkerran had reduced the political challenge to royal rights in the Firth of Clyde and elsewhere. Hebridean chiefs had bent their knee to the king at Mingary, Dunstaffnage, Tarbert and Kilkerran and had brought their men to fight and die in royal hosts in northern England. Pedro de Ayala's 1498 report may well have reflected the genuine self-assurance of the king's advisers when it suggested that he exercised greater authority over the Isles than any previous Scottish monarch. The optimism of James' government could only have been increased by the news that came from the west as the winter of 1498–99 ebbed away. At some point before 29 March 1499 the crown's most implacable opponent in the Hebrides, John of the Isles, Lord of Dunivaig and the Glens, was 'arrested' at Finlaggan on Islay by John MacIan of Ardnamurchan. Captured alongside the lord of Dunivaig were his son John Cathanach and a number of other kinsmen.[80] In March 1499 James IV sailed from Ayr to Tarbert Castle where he may have taken personal custody of MacIan's prisoners.[81] The Lord of Ardnamurchan was handsomely rewarded for the prize he brought the king. In a charter of 29 March at Tarbert MacIan received 'for his good and faithful service' in capturing John of the Isles and the Glens and his son and accomplices the lands of Sunart, lands in Jura, and extensive lands in Islay.[82] Argyll accompanied the King on his triumphant visit to Tarbert and took the opportunity to conclude some business of his own at Kilmun on 25 March.[83] Earl Archibald was likely to have little sympathy for the leaders of Clann Eóin Mhóir, a family that had presented a challenge to the Campbells' ambitions in the Firth of Clyde throughout the fifteenth century. Nor could Sir John anticipate mercy from James IV, for the lord of Dunivaig had been the one figure openly and consistently to deny the authority of the Scottish king in the lordship territories after 1493. Sir John's proud stance reflected not only his ability to escape the wrath of the Scottish monarch by retreating to Ireland, but the inherited outlook of the Clann Eóin Mhóir. The family had long regarded itself as second only to the Lords of the Isles themselves in terms of status and prestige within the Hebrides.[84] The five years of defiance of the Scottish king's right to govern in the west ensured that Sir John and his family were doomed from the moment that they were handed over to James IV. A point was to be made about the passing of the old order: there was to be no prolonged imprisonment or the taking of hostages or the acceptance of a no doubt temporary submission. In July 1499 Sir John, his son John Cathanach and other members of the family were hanged like common thieves, probably at Stirling. If the Lord of Dunivaig was unlamented in the royal burgh, the Irish annals at least roused themselves to mourn the passing of the 'king of the Hebrides' and his kin.[85]

At first sight the shabby death of Sir John seemed to signal the final triumph of King James in the west. Who now would or could stand against the will of the crown? James himself seems to have regarded Dunivaig's death as the final act of his war in the west. Indeed, the king was never to reappear in Tarbert or Kilkerran let alone the Hebrides after July 1499. The war won, the king looked to his loyal vassals to maintain his interests in the region without the need for direct royal involvement. James' disengagement from the affairs of the west was almost symbolised in the handing over of the reconstructed royal fortress at Tarbert to the custody of Earl Archibald in the month after Sir John's execution.[86] James' self-confidence was misplaced, for the defiance of royal policies in the west was far from over; and dangers lurked in the most unlikely places. Within three years of the leading members of Clann Eoin Mhóir going to the gibbet the crown would face a great rebellion nominally led by Donald Dubh, son of Angus Og, that attracted wide support within the Hebrides. The leading figures in the rebellion, Donald Dubh and Torquil MacLeod of Lewis, were men initmately connected to the earl of Argyll, the Master of the King's Household and the king's most powerful and trusted lieutenant in the Firth of Clyde and southern Hebrides. How did the political situation in the west deteriorate so rapidly after the King's apparently succesful campaigns in the 1490s? In the end, two quite divergent aspects of royal policy seem to have ensured the alienation of men who had looked as if they might be wooed or coerced into accepting the disappearance of the MacDonald Lordship of the Isles.

One problem was the king's personal lack of interest in the Isles after 1499. From 1493 the monarch claimed to be directly responsible for the territories and lordships forfeited by the Lord of the Isles. Lordship carried with it responsibilities and obligations as well as rights and the men who had provided military service to the crown in 1496–7 could reasonably expect their 'lord' to act as lawgiver, secure their rights, and arbitrate their disputes. Pedro de Ayala certainly suggested that James IV's visits to the

Isles prior to 1498 had been concerned with dispensing justice as well as advancing the king's political agenda.[87] Whether the inhabitants of the region necessarily regarded the appearance of the king and his intimidating retinue as a type of novel, oppressive and 'alien' tyranny may be open to doubt. Lordship in the west prior to 1493 had always involved a fair degree of coercion. Across much of the region Clan Donald power had rested on punitive expeditions, tributary raids and meddling with uncertain successions. Now the king himself employed those techniques in order to make good his claims in the west. However, after 1499 it became clear that James IV was unwilling or unable to sustain the investment of his time and the crown's financial resources in these annual expeditions to the Isles. For a monarch increasingly concerned with cutting a dash on the European diplomatic stage personal campaigning in the Isles may have held few appeals. William Dunbar's sardonic description of Sir William Norny's military adventures in the Highlands gives little sense that this was an area where chivalric renown could be won.[88] The rapid withdrawal of the king as an active overlord hardly served to consolidate the advances made by the crown in the 1490s and did little to inculcate a sense of loyalty. However, a much more significant factor in stoking resentment in the Isles was the financial strategies being adopted by the crown late in the 1490s. These policies were designed to maximise the financial return to the king from his rights as a feudal overlord and to exploit 'royal' land in a more aggressive and systematic way.[89] The recently forfeited territories of the Lordship of the Isles thus came into crown control at precisely the same time as a new and more stringent fiscal regime came into operation. The leading aristocrats in the Lordship were by no means unique in their resentment at the practical application of these policies. The 'market' in casualties and feu-farm leases of 'royal' lordships developing around the crown favoured those with connections to the royal court and the ability to raise disposable capital. In places the implementation of the new fiscal policy actually resulted in the wholesale displacement of established aristocratic interests. A spectacular manifestation of the enmity that could be built up against the local agents of the administration was the assault on Sir Robert Menzies of Weem by Neil Stewart of Fortingall in October 1502.[90] Stewart's family had held estates and judicial offices in the nominally royal lordships of Rannoch and Appin of Dull for most of the second half of the fifteenth century. In reality neither lordship had actually rendered any significant rents to the crown, with the fee allowed to the Stewarts of Fortingall for their office-holding more or less equivalent to sums supposed to be given in to the king. In the 1490s this type of arrangement, justified at some level by the effort required to establish and maintain local order in these Highland lordships, was no longer acceptable to the crown. As the royal administration sought to increase revenues from these non-productive lordships, Neil Stewart found himself steadily out-manoeuvred by his neighbour Sir Robert Menzies of Weem. Menzies proved willing to offer greater rental returns to the crown on various parcels of land granted out in feu-farm during the 1490s. Moreover, Menzies had a wider range of economic and territorial interests than Stewart of Fortingall which meant, for example, that he was able to use his Dumfriesshire barony of Enoch as security when concluding deals with the king's agents. Matters came to a head in September 1502 when Rannoch and the Appin of Dull were assigned to Menzies as feu-farm baronies.[91] From the crown's viewpoint this was a good piece of business, transforming two lordships that had effectively produced no income for the monarch over the previous fifty years into real financial assets. At the local level, however, the results were disastrous, for the move threatened to displace not just the Stewarts of Fortingall but the network of kinsmen and dependent tenants and farmers long established under them. The reaction of this threatened community was not long delayed; in October 1502 Stewart and his men ravaged the crown lands recently granted to Menzies, attacked and destroyed Sir Robert's castle of Weem and took the no doubt shocked Menzies into captivity on 10 October.[92]

The Donald Dubh rebellion should thus be viewed against this wider background of sustained and intensive crown interference in the rights of local landowners and gathering discontent and resentment at the insensitive implementation of royal financial policy. The scope for the arbitrary displacement of Highland lords and their dependents was particularly wide because few areas of the recently annexed lordship had previously been granted out under chartered tenure. Even where the crown's commissioners were prepared to offer leases to major lords there may have been little inclination to accept what must have been regarded as unprecedented and unjustified financial demands and conditions of tenure. Earl Archibald's enthusiasm for the crown's increasingly aggressive financial and political policies in the former lordship territories is uncertain. Argyll, of course, was a trusted member of the royal government who could be expected to have made a direct contribution to the formulation of royal policy. There were indications that Argyll and his kinsman the lord of Glenorchy made a limited attempt to introduce commercially and fiscally 'progressive' tenurial arrangements promoted by the crown, such as feu-farm grants, within their own lordships. Moreover, some aspects of early sixteenth-century histories of the kingdom might suggest that the Campbells sympathised with a 'crown' view that regarded the Highlands and the Hebrides as an area where economic potential was vast but underdeveloped because of the prevailing social structures and attitudes.[93] The chronicle of Hector Boece and the vernacular translation and 'adaptation' of Boece's work produced by John Bellenden openly acknowledged their dependence on Campbell sources for their account of early Scottish history.[94] It may be no surprise then that the Boece/Bellenden tradition reflected a remarkably upbeat history of Gaelic Scotland in general, and Argyll in particular. In these narratives Argyll became a region noted from earliest times for its adherence to the king and its role as a bulwark against the rebels and thieves of the Isles.[95] One of the great conventions of medieval and indeed classical historical writing was that disorder was linked to and largely explained economic underdevelopment. The sixteenth-century chroniclers emphasised their point by suggesting that some areas of the Highlands, such as Inverlochy, had once been great economic and commercial centres before falling into decay.[96] Inverness, on the other hand, had survived 'howbeit it sustenis importabill damage be perpetualle weeris of undantit pepill lyand aboute the samyn'. The depiction of Inverlochy as a ruined trading town was not a historical lament, but a forward-looking statement of intent and aspiration of the recoverable potential of the Highlands, a potential held back implicitly and explicitly by the 'undaunted' inhabitants of the region.

Against these hints that the Campbell lords were 'on message' in terms of the crown's commercial, financial and judicial policies in the Isles might be set suggestions that Earl Archibald was in fact less than comfortable with spearheading these initiatives. In April 1500 Earl Archibald, Hugh, Lord Montgomery, John, Lord Drummond, Duncan Campbell of Glenorchy, John Stirling of Craigbernard and Henry Allan archdean of Dunblane were given a commission to lease out all the lands belonging to the forfeited John, Lord of the Isles, in the Isles and the 'fermland'.[97] On the same day Argyll was made lieutenant general within the bounds of the Isles and terra firma of the same formerly belonging to John, Lord of the Isles for the term of three years.[98] From the crown's viewpoint neither

Argyll's lieutenancy nor the leasing of royal lands seems to have been entirely satisfactory. The only known results of the leasing commission are described as the lands 'set in Lochaber' by the earl of Argyll.[99] Argyll's commission had been highly conservative and seems, largely, to have left established local aristocrats undisturbed in the lands they had held in the lordship. A vast area of land was simply described as unset, including Glengarry, Invergarry, and tracts of Knoidart occupied by Allan mac Ranald Bane. Earl Archibald's laid-back approach to the inbringing of the revenues owed to the crown from these areas was evidently not acceptable. The crown in fact had an alternative to the Campbells in its attempts to exploit its claims in the former lordship, particularly in the central Highland lordship of Lochaber. In 1501 Alexander Gordon had succeeded his father as earl of Huntly. Alexander was a notably bellicose individual who had already displayed a vigorous approach to the advance and protection of his family's political and territorial interests. The Huntly earls were also lords of Badenoch on the north-eastern marches of Lochaber. The most powerful kindreds in Badenoch were part of a great rambling confederacy known as the Clan Chattan that also harboured ancient claims and ambitions to territory and office inside Lochaber. On 11 August 1501 the king, perhaps disappointed with the earl of Argyll's approach to the prosecution of royal rights in the region, granted Huntly the right to pass to the king's lordship of Lochaber to collect the royal rents and to raise the king's lieges against any who resisted.[100] On the same day, Huntly obtained a royal letter allowing him to receive, in the King's name, the 'bands and oblissingis of erlis, lordis, baronis and hed kinnysmen . . . on the North parts of the Month'.[101] These bonds and obligations were presumably similar to the bonds which the king had already extracted from the magnates and local lords across much of the rest of Scotland in May/June 1501, collective undertakings to support the work of royal officials and to act against those defying or evading royal justice. The bonds were an attempt to curtail the widespread evasion of the King's laws by men maintained and protected by local magnates, but they also seem to have been concentrated in areas where the crown was simultaneously unleashing campaigns to increase the economic exploitation of royal lands and rights. A bond of May 1501, by which the earl of Atholl and a host of other Perthshire lords were bound to the king for their own behaviour and that of the inhabitants of their lands gives some indication of the tenor of these contracts.[102]

In August 1501, then, Earl Alexander had been given what amounted to carte blanche to inbring the king's rents from Lochaber, to wage war on anyone who resisted and, more generally, to extract bonds for their good behaviour from clan chiefs in the area 'north of the Mounth'. The combination of powers swept Gordon's authority into areas which, the year before, had clearly been regarded as lying within Argyll's sphere of influence. Local families had every reason to be apprehensive, particularly those, such as the Camerons and Macleans, whose rights to land in Lochaber had been long disputed by the Clan Chattan allies of the Gordon earl. Tenurial insecurity may well have been heightened by a fear of the consequences of admitting the crown's claims in the region. Would the king's agents seek to recover all rents that they judged had been withheld from the crown since the 'official' forfeiture of the lordship of the Isles in 1493? Given the aggressive attitudes being followed by crown agents elsewhere, this must have been seen as a distinct possibility.

The acid test of Huntly's ability to implement his new commission would arrive with the attempt to collect the Martinmas rents from Lochaber in November 1501. With a potentially violent confrontation brewing, the crown made moves to neutralise resistance. The king himself appeared in Inverness in the early weeks of November, granting at least three charters in favour of Huntly's kinsmen and allies.[103] By this stage James IV and his advisers were aware of a new danger, namely that the lords of Lochaber and the Hebrides might react to royal pressure by throwing their political and military support behind an attempt to create a new 'Lord of the Isles'. The fact that the king demanded that Donald Dubh should be delivered into royal custody during the November visit to Inverness suggests that rumours of possible rebellion in the west had already reached the royal court.[104] Despite James IV's personal intervention, it soon became clear that the aristocracy of the central Highlands and Hebrides were not inclined to submit to the king's demands. On 10 December 1501 a host of Hebridean lords were found guilty in their absence of wrongfully occupying royal lands in Morvern, Moidart, Morar, Knoldart, Glenelg, Lochaber, Glengarry, and Glenconnich which they were instructed to abandon and pay the byrun (uncollected) rents.[105] More tellingly, Donald Dubh was not surrendered to royal safe-keeping by Torquil MacLeod of Lewis who was said to have Donald at his 'rewle and governance' over the winter of 1501–2. On 15 March 1502 MacLeod was outlawed because of his refusal to hand over Donald.[106] The crown's determination to obtain possession of the man described in March 1502 as merely Angus of the Isles' bastard son surely reflected the fear that Donald remained a potent rallying point for those eager to reject James' demands on inhabitants of former lordship lands. Although Argyll was with the royal court in Inverness in November and was one of the men who approved the outlawing of MacLeod in March 1502, he could hardly have enjoyed the prospect of Huntly's ascendancy in Lochaber and elsewhere. Moreover, many of the men affected by the royal campaign of 1501 were closely tied to Argyll's lordship and may have appealed directly to Earl Archibald for his assistance; Argyll was, after all, Torquil's brother-in-law and the uncle of Donald Dubh. Given this general context, there may be merit in a recent argument by Máirtín Ó Briain that the so-called 'Flodden' poem directed to Earl Archibald dates from this period rather than 1513.[107] The interpretation of the poem, which urges Earl Archibald to provide leadership for the Gael and strike down the Gall (foreigners) who threaten their land, depends crucially on the way in which 'Gall' is translated. The idea that the term was being used to denote the Saxons (i.e. English) and that the poem reflected preparations for James IV's military campaign of 1513 was established by one of the earliest editors of the poem, Thomas McLauchlan, in 1862.[108] There is nothing in the poem itself to support this dating and context. If, however, we accept Ó Briain's suggestion that the term 'Gall' might refer to non-Gaelic-speaking Lowland Scots, then the tone and tenor of the poem would fit very well with the period around 1501–2. The plea that Argyll should help to ward off a direct threat to the landholding of the Scottish Gael makes little sense in the context of Anglo-Scottish conflict, but would have been deeply resonant given royal fiscal policies in 1501–2. The dark nemesis bearing down on the homeland of the Gael as envisaged by the poet was surely more likely to be the earl of Huntly than Northumbrian levies. Moreover the poem also seems to hint that for various reasons Earl Archibald might be reluctant to respond to the poet's supplication. 'The race of the Gael from the land of Greece have no spot in their keeping, should it come to pass that thou shouldst deem it no reproach to disregard the race of the Gael.' Similarly the recitation of Archibald's genealogy reads almost like a challenge to the earl's sense of duty and honour. After the listing of his ancestors the earl is asked to remember 'that those men made no submission for dread to Foreigners [Ghallaibh]; why shouldst thou, more than they, make submission now?'

If the re-dating and recontextualisation of the poem stands, it becomes very difficult to characterise Argyll simply as an agent imposing royal policies in the west. There must also be some doubt as to whether the relationship between Earl Archibald and Donald Dubh prior to 1502 was as hostile as the traditional Clan Donald narratives suggest. A particular point to ponder is exactly how Donald came to be in the care of Torquil MacLeod of Lewis prior to November 1501. The usual answer, derived from a particular (mis)reading of the traditional histories, is that Donald was freed from Innis Chonnell Castle by the men of Glencoe through a 'Fenian exploit'.[109] It seems more likely that the description of Donald's jailbreak referred to his much later escape from royal custody after a prolonged imprisonment, c.1544. However, that Donald Dubh presented (and perhaps thought of) his childhood in Campbell care in terms of oppression and misuse is readily confirmed by correspondance from and relating to Donald from 1545. In May 1545 the Council of Ireland wrote to Henry VIII informing him that Donald Dubh wished to enter the king's service. In a rather garbled explanation of Donald's personal history the Council claimed that he was 'mortal enemy to the earl of Argyle and all that were friends to the Scottish king that dead is [James V?] who put to death his father and many of his friends and kept him in prison for 30 years'.[110] Some of these claims were reiterated in a letter to Henry VIII on 5 August 1545 where Donald asserted that 'from our mother's womb we were bound in the yoke and servitude of our enemies, and to this very time overwhelmed with the filth of the prison, and with intolerable fetters most cruelly bound'.[111] This storyline was repeated in yet another letter from Donald's representatives to the English Privy Council in which the iniquities inflicted on the inhabitants of the Hebrides by the Scottish crown were listed. The atrocities included the charge that Donald Dubh lay in prison before he was born 'and nocht releiffet wyth thair will, but now laitlie by the grace of God'.[112] Here certainly were all the elements to be found in the seventeenth-century MacDonald histories, the capture before birth, the long imprisonment at the hands of the crown and the escape 'laitlie by the grace of God'. However, some caution should be exercised in evaluating these claims since they were made in a very specific context. Early in 1545 the English crown was uncertain of Donald's loyalty and had heard rumours that he was about to conclude an agreement with the then earls of Argyll and Huntly. In March 1545 the English king had a 'golden handshake' of 1,000 ducats awaiting Donald Dubh if the Earl of

Lennox, the English crown's principal Scottish supporter, returned a favourable report on Donald's commitment to Henry's cause.[113] While Donald's lamentable tale may have been true in parts, it may also have been embellished in order to emphasise that Donald would never be reconciled to the then earl of Argyll and the Scottish government. In particular, it seems more than likely that prior to 1501 Donald Dubh had been set at liberty, or at least sent to Torquil MacLeod's household as part of a fosterage arrangement, by Earl Archibald. Torquil's marriage to Archibald's sister (and Donald's aunt) Catriona, before August 1498 may well have encouraged such a development.[114] In any case the statement that Donald was in Torquil's 'rule and governance' in 1501 does not seem to imply any illegality in the arrangement as would have been the case had the youth been broken out of Innis Chonnell for the sole purpose of raising rebellion.

By the end of 1501 Earl Archibald faced an awkward and embarrassing dilemma. Master of the King's Household, hereditary lieutenant of Argyll, keeper of Dunoon and Tarbert, Argyll was unambiguously a lord whose interests lay with serving the crown and implementing its policies in the Hebrides. As we shall see in the following chapter, Argyll's own economic advantage and attitudes would also seem to have made him a natural supporter of James IV's ambitions in the west. Yet the earl's effectiveness in his own heartland in part rested on his reputation and status as a great lord of the Gael. The gathering crisis asked new questions of the ability of the Campbell lordship to reconcile the expectations of the various social and political arenas in which the earl moved. When the simmering resentments broke into full-scale rebellion in the winter of 1503–4, would Earl Archibald be able to supply answers?

Notes

1. Fraser, *Douglas*, iii, 96.
2. NAS GD8 nos. 14 (Original document missing), 15, 16.
3. Boardman, 'Feud', 261–2; *RMS*, ii, no.1573.
4. NAS CS5/xix/f132r; GD 8/74; Boardman, 'Feud', 262–3.
5. Boardman, 'Feud', 264–5; Macdougall, *James IV*, 90–91. The earl was essentially forced to exchange his strategic border lordship of Liddesdale for Kilmarnock because of treasonable dealings with the English crown earlier the same year.
6. Fraser, *Douglas*, iii, 131.
7. Fraser, *Douglas*, iii, 135–6. Angus himself, despite his political problems in 1491, was described as one of the king's 'councillors' in a charter of July 1492.

8. *RMS*, ii, no.2111.
9. *RMS*, ii, nos.2112, 2113. Boardman, 'Feud', 268–70.
10. *RMS*, ii, no.2115. A royal charter of that date was assigned a witness list by cross-referencing with a charter issued in January 1493. This witness list had Archibald, earl of Angus, as Chancellor. If the cross-referencing is secure, Argyll was probably dead by 28 October.
11. Again, if the witness list assigned to the 28 October charter (*RMS*, ii, no.2115) is correct; Boardman, 'Feud', 270.
12. *APS*, ii, 235–7.
13. NAS Crawford Priory Collection GD20/7/190; *ER*, x, 710–11.
14. *ADC*, i, 260–3, 265, 267, 269–71, 274–81, 283, 285–6, 288; *APS*, ii, 231.
15. Aside from the new regime's hostility to Hugh, Lord Montgomery, other Campbell adherents in Ayrshire lost out in 1492–3, most notably one William Campbell, whose lands in the lordship of Kilmarnock were reclaimed by Angus' Boyd kinsmen as a result of the young king's personal intervention in the dispute. See Boardman, 'Politics and the Feud', 273–4 for details. The new earl of Argyll also lost his father's hold on the bailiary of Culross abbey to Patrick Blackadder of Tulliallan, the brother of the bishop of Glasgow, who was politically aligned with the earl of Angus in the 1490s. The dispute between Argyll and Blackadder was resolved by arbitration in August 1495. NAS Cadross Writs, GD 15/153.
16. *ALI*, lxxii, 311; *RMS*, ii, nos. 2172, 2200, 2201, 2202, 2216. It is possible that the 'forfeiture' did not require a specific new indictment of John, but depended instead on a stringent application of the terms of James IV's revocation in the May parliament. James III's 'restoration' of John to the lordship of the Isles in 1475 was technically an alienation of lands and rights held by the crown at the time and was therefore within the terms of the 1493 revocation. *APS*, ii, 231–4.
17. *Abdn. Counc.*, i, 421. An entry of 6 August 1493 apparently misdated to 1492.
18. *Ibid.* The Aberdeen Council entry describes attempts to raise a tax in the burgh to 'furnyss the personis furtht to the meting of my lord Huntlie, locumtenant, to pas with him to . . . the strinthis of the Ilis'.
19. *RMS*, ii, no.2171.
20. *TA*, i, 233–35; *ER*, x, 534. Technically this accounting by the custumars of Edinburgh was for the period from 17 December 1494 to 27 August 1496. However, the custumars were allowed the sum of £133 6s 8d, i.e. 200m, for the expenses of John, lately Lord of the Isles, for the sustenance of himself and his servants 'for one year before the feast of the Purification of the Blessed Mary [2 February] in this account'. John seems to have been joined as a crown dependent by a number of his illegtimate sons or grandsons and other kinsmen, including a Ranald Ruadh and a Donald Odhar (Sallow). The latter seems to have served with royal forces in 1494 but was also the subject of a stinging satirical poem by William Dunbar, 'Epetaphe for Donald Owre', that implied he had died as a traitor. *The Poems of William Dunbar*, ed.W.Mackay MacKenzie (Edinburgh, 1932), no.36. It is tempting to speculate that there may have been some conflation in later accounts of the careers of Donald Odhar (who could have been another son of Angus Og) and that of Donald Dubh. However, the fact that the Donald at the centre of the 1502 rebellion seems to have been a minor probably precludes the idea that the events of 1502–6 were inspired by Donald Odhar.

21. *RMS*, ii, no.2438.
22. Alexander was a knight by 5 July 1494. *ADC*, i, 327, 359. Kingston argues that there is no evidence to support the idea that John of Dunivaig and Glens was ever knighted. See Kingston, *Ulster and the Isles*, 110. However, a royal charter of 1499 rewarding MacIan of Ardnamurchan for the capture of John and his son specifically refers to the elder John as 'militis'. G.G. Smith, *The Book of Islay* (Edinburgh, 1895), 28–30.
23. Although Donald's time in the Lowlands may have post-dated rather than preceded his father's death. The name is found in the *Clanranald Book*, (*RC*, ii, 165), which also implied that Donald had spent his minority years in the Lowlands. See also *ALI*, p. 306. Here, however, all references to a Donald 'of the Isles' in and around the royal court are assumed to relate to Donald of Lochalsh. This is by no means certain.
24. *ER*, x, 449 (Islay Herald – created by 18/6/1494); *TA*, i, 237 (Kintyre Pursuivant), *TA*, i, ccxciii–ccxcv.
25. Macdougall, *James IV*, 104–5.
26. *ADC*, i, 327; Argyll Muniments, Inveraray, Bundle 1114.
27. *RMS*, ii, no.2216.
28. *ADC*, i, 327, 359.
29. The fact that Lochalsh received a gift of royal marts from Bute in the accounting year 1494–5 may indicate personal involvement in the Firth of Clyde campaign. *ER*, x, 550.
30. Gregory, *History*, 92–3. The killers are identified in both the seventeenth-century MacDonald accounts, the *Sleat History* and the *Clanranald Book*, as MacIan of Ardnamurchan and Alexander, son of John Cathanach, son of John of Dunivaig and the Glens, *RC*, ii, 164–5; *HP*, i, 56. However, it is clear that the compiler of the *Sleat History*, at least, was horribly confused in regard to the various generations of the Dunivaig family at this point, most notably conflating the careers of Alexander and his grandfather John. *HP*, i, 58–9, 60–1. The Clanranald account may be more trustworhty but, like the *Sleat History*, seems to have treated the rivalry between the Dunivaig, Lochalsh and Ardnamurchan families as an ongoing feud that reached a resolution early in the sixteenth century when Alexander was indeed the leading member of Dunivaig kindred. Alexander's personal role in earlier clashes may have been exaggerated as a result of this narrative perspective. In short, the seventeenth-century sources should probably not be regarded as entirely reliable in terms of identifying those personally involved in Lochalsh's death.
31. *AU*, iii, 382–3; *AFM*, iv, 1212–3; Kingston, *Ulster and the Isles*, 117, 120–1. Kingston points out that in 1494 the MacDonald constable of the UíNeill galloglass had a brother named Gillespic who *may* have had a son Alexander. According to Kingston the putative Alexander 'might reasonably be described as '*Fer inaid*', in that he was in some way regarded as the representative of his uncle the MacDonald constable. The existence of this Alexander mac Gillespic and any role he might have played as a 'deputy' to his supposed uncle are not otherwise attested. The argument also depends on the accuracy of the seventeenth-century Scottish sources in differentiating between John Cathanach and his son Alexander as the killer, a precision which is not guaranteed (see note 30). The strongest point in favour of Kingston's identification of the Alexander

killed in 1494 as an Ulster-based MacDonald is the fact that the Irish annalist does not specify that he (or his uncle) was a MacDonald of Scotland, a description usually applied to leading members of the Clan Donald in the *Annals of Ulster*. The last observation is interesting, but hardly conclusive.

32. *TA*, i, 238.
33. *Ibid.*, 239. MacIan's name was variously rendered in royal accounts, e.g. *RMS*, ii, p.961. Makane, Mackane, Makcane, Makcayne, Makcayn.
34. See below, pp 00–00.
35. *HP*, i, 53–59. The Sleat account makes a consistent effort to undercut and disparage the status and claims to authority within the Isles of Alexander, his father and his son Donald Gallda.
36. *ALI*, 123.
37. *AU*, iii, 442–3; *ALC*, ii, 198–201; *AC*, 604–5. See Kingston, *Ulster and the Isles*, 119–21 for a discussion of the Dunivaig family's ambitions in this regard.
38. Macdougall, *James IV*, 107.
39. *RMS*, ii, no.2240. It is not certain who had exercised the office immediately prior to Argyll's promotion. Patrick Hepburn, earl of Bothwell, had been Master of the Household after 1488 but whether he retained the office until 1495 is unclear.
40. *TA*, i, 240–1, 245–54; Macdougall, *James IV*, 115.
41. *RMS*, ii, no.2253. Although, curiously, two charters are also listed on the same date with Glasgow as the place of issue. *Ibid.*, nos.2254, 2255. The witness list assigned to the Glasgow charters does not have Argyll as a witness.
42. *ADC*, ii, 41.
43. If the chronology of the Ulster annalist is correct Ua Domhnaill left Ireland a month before Lammas (1st August) and returned a few days after Lammas. *AU*, iii, 388–91; *ALC*, ii, 192–3; *AC*, 598–599; *TA*, i, 227, 242.
44. Macdougall, *James IV*, 116–123.
45. Carrickfergus had been the most significant northern base for English naval forces throughout the fourteenth and fifteenth centuries. The Ui Dhomhnaill of Tír Connail could occasionally threaten the castle and burgh with assault from the west. In 1428, for example, the then Ua Domhnaill lord was said to have sent to Scotland (the Hebrides?) for forces to attack Carrickfergus. A. Cosgrove (ed.), *Medieval Ireland, 1169–1534* (*A New History of Ireland*, vol. II; Oxford, 1987) (hereafter Cosgrove, *Medieval Ireland*), 535. In 1481 the mayor of Carrickfergus played a critical role in negotiations between the English crown and MacDonald lords.
46. Cosgrove, *Medieval Ireland*, ii, 626.
47. *AU*, iii, 382–3, 388–93.
48. Macdougall, *James IV*, 116.
49. Argyll Muniments, Inveraray, Bundle 1114; *RMS*, ii, no.2261; *ER*, x, 62, 72, 132, 149, 303, 361.
50. Boardman, 'Feud', 388–90.
51. *Book of the Dean*, XIV stanzas 30 and 31; *RMS*, ii, nos.2669, 2670.
52. A. Conway, *Henry VII's relations with Scotland and Ireland, 1485–1498* (Cambridge, 1932), 96 and Appendix xliii.
53. *RMS*, ii, nos. 2264 (MacLean of Duart), 2281 (Alan, captain of Clan Cameron), 2287 (MacNeill of Barra).

54. Macdougall, *James IV*, chs. 5, 6.

55. *TA*, i, 288. e.g. Argyll Muniments, Inveraray, Bundle 1101 and *passim*.

56. In 1497 Cunningham was described as a priest of Glasgow diocese. Argyll Muniments, Inveraray, Bundle 1115. He may possibly have been a kinsman of Earl Archibald, for earlier in the century Margaret Campbell, one of Archibald's great-aunts, had married an Andrew Cunningham, son of the laird of Glengarnock. *Chron.Auchinleck* (McGladdery), 163.

57. NLS Lamont Papers, Ch. no. 7364; *Lamont Papers*, no.63 (25 May 1481); GD 112/75/5. December 18 1485.

58. *CSSR*, v, nos.1067, 1105; GD 112/75/2 (1470). David was evidently in Campbell service as early as 1455 when he rendered the shrieval accounts of Earl Colin to the exchequer. *ER*, vi, 89. He may have been one and the same as the David 'Ouchtour', priest of Dunblane diocese, who drew up an instrument relating to the transfer of lands by John Stewart, lord of Lorn, to Sir Colin Campbell of Glenorchy in December 1456. NAS GD 112/2/37/1; NLS Lamont Papers, Ch. no. 7364; *Lamont Papers*, no.63.

59. Patrick Clerkson, treasurer of Argyll by 1486, was probably the man included in the remission granted in 1483 to Earl Colin and his adherents for their role in the seizure of James III at Lauder in 1482. GD 112/3/6; Fraser, *Lennox*, ii, 128. Malcolm MacGilleker, Dean of Lismore in 1494, was to be found in association with Earl Archibald on a number of occasions in the 1490s and the first decade of the sixteenth century. See *RMS*, ii, no.2221; Argyll Muniments, Inveraray, Bundles 26 (1498), 1091 (1502), 1092.(1504–5); Duncan MacFadzean, precentor of Lismore, and Archibald Leech, chancellor of Lismore were also occasional witnesses to Earl Archibald's charters. See e.g. AT, 24/6/1498; *RMS*, ii, no.3622. For the cultural impact of these Campbell-maintained clerics, see MacGregor, 'Church and Culture', 27–29; J.W.M. Bannerman, 'The MacLachlans of Kilbride and their Manuscripts', *SS*, 21 (1977), 1–34.

60. See *ADC*, ii, 41, 101–2.

61. Macdougall, *James IV*, 123–141.

62. *TA*, i, 269.

63. *ADC*, ii, 41. On the same day the king issued letters of legitimation for Hector MacLean's son Lachlan. *RSS*, i, no.68.

64. *RMS*, ii, nos.2363, 2264; Argyll Muniments, Inveraray, Bundle 1115. A summons also seems to have been sent to the Isles on 16 May. *TA*, i, 335.

65. Argyll Muniments, Inveraray, Bundle 1115. The notary was Andrew Cunningham, probably the parson of Loch Awe, here described as a priest of Glasgow diocese. Salmond had obviously been contesting possession of the benefice with Argyll's preferred candidate, Malcolm MacGilleker, who had appeared in Earl Archibald's company as Dean of Lismore in 1494. *RMS*, ii, no.2221.

66. Although entries in the Treasurer's Accounts for 1496 and 1497 make reference to a tax levied elsewhere in the kingdom for the 'Isles', presumably indicating some form of prolonged military action in the region. *TA*, i, 312, 315.

67. *Calendar of Letters, Despatches and State Papers relating to the negotiations between England and Spain*, vol. i (1485–1509), ed. G.A. Bergenroth (London, 1862) (hereafter *State Papers (Spanish)*), no.210. De Ayala, for all his tendency to exaggeration, was an eye-witness to James IV's campaign of 1497. Indeed the

ambassador may have been one of the Spaniards with whom the king played cards at Norham on 7 August 1498. *TA*, i, 350.

68. *TA*, i, 374 (30 December 1497) 9s to the master of the Household to give to a man to pass to 'McLoyd in the Ilis'.

69. Macdougall, *James IV*, 176–77.

70. *TA*, i, 382; *RMS*, ii, nos. 2406, 2424, 2425, 2428, 2429, 2435, 2436, 2437, 2439, 2440.

71. *RSS*, i, no.184.

72. Watt, *Fasti*, 204.

73. *HP*, iv, 185–7. John Campbell eventually died on Iona in June 1510 and was buried in the abbey. *Taymouth Bk.*, 115.

74. Argyll Muniments, Inveraray, Bundle 1115; *RMS*, ii, nos.2402, 2403.

75. Argyll Muniments, Inveraray, Bundle 26. Ranald's brothers Dugald and John confirmed the resignation. It is difficult to place these men in the established MacDougall geneaologies. The notary for the resignation was Malcolm McGilleker, the Dean of Lismore. The witnesses included John Dewar, Provost of Kilmun, Alexander MacNachtan of Lettir, Alexander son of John Campbel of Inverliever, Alexander McIver of Pennymore and his son Ivor, Duncan McLucas and Patrick Faber.

76. *RMS*, ii, no.2424.

77. AT, at date; *RMS*, ii, no.2428; *RSS*, i, no. 242.

78. *Cawdor Bk.*, 94–5.

79. *Cawdor Bk.*, 103–4.

80. *ALI*, 230–1; *AU*, iii, 442–3; *ALC*, ii, 198–201; *AC*, 604–5; *HP*, i, 59; *RC*, ii, 163.

81. The king was at Ayr on 17 March and at Tarbert by 29 March. By 1 April James had sailed on to the castle of Rothesay on Bute. *RMS*, ii, nos.2484, 2485; *RSS*, i, no. 368.

82. Argyll Muniments, Inveraray, Bundle 1115; *ALI*, 230–31. In addition, and on the same date, MacIan was confirmed in his lands of Ardnamurchan and his castle of Mingary. The grant of Sunart, Jura and Islay was justified by MacIan's resignation of claims to land in Mid-Kintyre and the Stewartry of the same region as well as his capture of John of Dunivaig. Three days later, on 1 April, the King confirmed Colin McEachern in lands in South Kintyre and the office of mair or baillie, of the region. *RSS*, i, no.368. MacEachern may also have been involved in Sir John's capture.

83. AT, at date.

84. See Kingston *Ulster & the Isles*.

85. *AU*, iii, 442–3; *ALC*, ii, 198–201; *AC*, 604–5. Sir John was almost certainly dead by 27 August. *RMS*, ii, no.2500. In *AU* it was claimed that the executed men included one Ranald Ruadh. A 'Ranald Roy de Insulis' had been at James IV's court (as a prisoner?) in 1496 (*ER*, x, 567, 589), although this man has also been claimed as a son of John, last Lord of the Isles. *ALI*, 315.

86. *RSS*, i, no.413. The grant also gave Argyll the bailiary of the king's lands in Knapdale 'for the [duration of] the King's will'.

87. *State Papers (Spanish)*, no.210.

88. Dunbar, *Poems* (MacKenzie), no.35.

89. Macdougall, *James IV*, Ch. 6; Craig Madden, 'Royal Treatment of Feudal Casualties in Late Medieval Scotland', *SHR*, lv (1976), 172–194; Craig Madden, 'The Feuing of Ettrick Forest', *Innes Review*, xxvii (1976), 70–84.

90. Boardman, 'Feud', 377–415.

91. NAS GD 247/27/4/1; Boardman, 'Feud', 386–88.

92. Boardman, 'Feud', 391; *Taymouth Bk.*, 114; NLS Charter no.10634. Robert Menzies' account of the events of the previous three months recorded on 17 January 1503.

93. See below, Ch. 11, 'The Economy of Campbell Lordship'.

94. R.A.Mason, 'Civil Society and the Celts: Hector Boece, George Buchanan and the Ancient Scottish Past', in E.J. Cowan and R.J. Finlay, eds., *Scottish History, The Power of the Past* (Edinburgh, 2002), 95–119, at 100–101 and note 14; Bellenden, *Chronicles*, i, 67, 99. A fair bit of the 'inventive' early history of the Scottish realm was localised in Campbell fortresses such as those at Innis Chonnell and Dunstaffnage. Bellenden, *Chronicles*, 57. Council and election of a king at Innis Chonnell, 80–1, 100, Dunstaffnage as burial place of the great King Ewen.

95. Bellenden, *Chronicles*, i, 30, 65, 76–7.

96. Bellenden, *Chronicles*, i, 88–9. Here Inverlochy was claimed as a foundation of 'King Ewen' who built a town, 'ane commoun port till all merchandis of France or Spanze, for the incredible fertilitie of fische swommand in thai seyis'. All was now ruined 'bot the brokin wallis, brocht to rewyn be the weirs of Danys'.

97. *RSS*, i, no.513. It was specified that any three commissioners could set the lands but that Argyll had to be one of the three.

98. Argyll Muniments, Inveraray, Bundle 95; *RSS*, i, no.520.

99. *ER*, xi, 460.

100. *RSS*, i, no.723.

101. *RSS*, i, no.722.

102. Fraser, *Menteith*, ii, 303. For other examples, see NAS CS5/xviii/f302,v (Annandale); *APS*, ii, 247 (Teviotdale and Dumfries). Argyll and Glenorchy were bound for the behaviour of the inhabitants of their own areas of influence at around this time. See 1 June 1501 A general remission to the inhabitants in the bounds of Argyll, Cowal, Lorn and the half of Knapdale at the request of Earl Archibald who is 'bound for the good rule of them in time to come'*RSS*, i, no.697. On the same day Duncan Campbell of Glenorchy obtained a similar remission for the inhabitants of Discher, Toyer, Glen Lyon, Glen Dochart, Glen Lochay and Glen Coich. *RSS*, i, no.698.

103. *RMS*, ii, nos.2612–4.

104. *ADC*, iii, 141–2.

105. *ADC*, iii, 87–88.

106. *ADC*, iii, 141–2. On the same day Torquil was ordered to pay the king 80 merks of the byrun mailes (uncollected or unpaid rents) of Trotternish for the three years from 3 July 1498.

107. Máirtín Ó Briain, 'Snaithín san uige: "Loisc agus léig a luaith le struth"', in *Téada Dúchais: Aistí in ómós don Ollamh Breandán Ó Madagáin* (Inverin: Cló Iar-Chonnachta, 2002), 245–72. I am grateful to Dr Wilson MacLeod for bringing this article to my attention and for providing a translation.

108. Reverend Thomas McLauchlan, *The Dean of Lismore's Book* (Edinburgh, 1862), 134, note 4. McLauchlan's note shows that he did consider the possibility that the Galls referred to in the poem were Lowlanders before he eventually concluded that the term indicated Saxons or Englishmen. W.J. Watson, editing

the poem in the 1930s, accepted McLauchlan's hypothesis. *Book of the Dean*, xx (pp.158–165), notes pp.290–1.

109. E.g. Gregory, *History*, 95–6. This narrative derives from the conflation of the Sleat and Clanranald accounts. The *Sleat History* asserts that after his capture by Colin, earl of Argyll, Donald was confined at Innis Chonnel until his hair went grey, a chronology that obviously makes little sense in terms of the young Donald's involvement in the rebellion of 1502–6. Sleat has no account of Donald's release. *HP*, i, 50, 55. The Clanranald account mentions Donald's release by the men of Glencoe (but does not suggest he was liberated from Innis Chonnel) and then moves immediately into a discussion of the events of 1545. *RC*, ii, 163, 167.

110. *Letters and Papers, Foreign and Domestic, of the Reign of Henry VIII*, xx (Part I), nos. 665, 865.

111. *Nat. MSS. Scot.*, iii, no.29; *Letters and Papers Foreign and Domestic, Henry VIII*, xx (Part II), no.40.

112. *Letters and Papers, Foreign and Domestic, Henry VIII*, xx (Part I), no. 294.

113. *Letters and Papers, Foreign and Domestic, Henry VIII*, xx (Part I), no. 436

114. *RMS*, ii, no.2424. The charter of the bailiary of Trotternish in Skye emphasised the importance of Torquil's Campbell match by insisting that the office should descend to any heirs produced between Torquil and Catriona (who was referred to in the charter as the sister of Earl Archibald). If the marriage failed to produce heirs, the office was to return to royal control. Catriona is also mentioned in a Gaelic praise poem composed for Torquil. *Book of the Dean*, XIII, Stanzas 16, 17. Catriona does not appear as a daughter of the first earl in any of the seventeenth-century Campbell genealogies, unless she was the 'Catherine' who was claimed to have been the partner of a MacLean of Mull and then Donald Gorm MacDonald (k.1488). *HP*, ii, 98–99; *Records of Argyll*, 10. Earl Colin did have a daughter 'Katrin' who was contracted in marriage to the Haldanes of Gleneagles as early as 1465. Argyll Muniments, Inveraray, Bundle 26.

ELEVEN

Loch, Stock and Barrel:
The Economy of Campbell Lordship

I n March 1424 at Durham a number of Scottish noblemen were handed over to English custody as hostages and financial sureties for the payment of James I's ransom.[1] Amongst the no doubt disconsolate group was Duncan Campbell 'lord of Argile'. Each nobleman was assigned a financial value, presumably indicating the sum for which the individual was liable in the event of the non-payment of the ransom.[2] Strikingly, the value attached to Duncan, 1,500 marks, was greater than that assigned to any of his fellow hostages, with the exception of William Douglas, son and heir of the Lord of Dalkeith. Duncan's redemption value thus outstripped that of all of the men of comital rank listed before him in the agreement: David Stewart, son and heir of the earl of Atholl (1,200 marks), Thomas Dunbar, earl of Moray (1,000 marks) and Alexander Lindsay, earl of Crawford (1,000 marks). That the Campbell lords of Argyll and the Douglas lords of Dalkeith had, in the judgement of their peers, the wealth to support a lifestyle appropriate for the highest levels of the Scottish aristocracy was confirmed in the 1450s when the heads of the two families were elevated to the rank of earl (the Douglases of Dalkeith as earls of Morton).[3] The contemporary impression of Campbell wealth was re-inforced through the lord of Loch Awe's financial and social interaction with noble society outwith Argyll. Throughout the fifteenth century Campbell lords displayed the ability to provide substantial cash dowries for their numerous daughters. The 'Auchinleck' chronicler, reporting on the death in the 1450s of Andrew Cunningham, son and heir to William Cunningham of Glengarnock, found that the most noteworthy fact relating to Andrew's life was that he had 'spousit Margaret Campbell, Sir Duncan lord Campbell's dochter and tuke viiic [800] merkis of touchers'.[4] Similar periodic outlays of large sums of hard cash to persuade prospective grooms of the virtues of Argyll's daughters were a feature of Campbell dealings for the remainder of the century. In 1467 Colin, earl of Argyll, gave over 1,000 marks to secure a marriage to the son and heir of

Lawrence, Lord Oliphant, while only two years later he offered another 1,000-mark tocher as part of a marriage contract with George, Lord Seton. In 1479 John, Lord Drummond, gratefully acknowledged receipt of 400 marks of 'new coined silver' from Earl Colin as part-payment of the dowry owed for the marriage of Drummond's son and heir and the earl's daughter.[5] Fifteenth-century Campbell lords were also active in the purchase of land and offices and the burgeoning and highly competitive market in feudal rights and casualties that grew up around the royal court in the second half of the century.[6] There was expenditure in other areas, with Duncan Campbell and his successors able to fund extensive building programmes that saw the construction or reconstruction of castles, kirks, and townhouses from Argyll to Lothian. In the fifteenth century major work was completed or initiated at Kilmun, Inveraray, Innis Chonnell, Inishail, Eilean Dearg, Castle Campbell and Dunstaffnage.[7] The Campbell earls were also able to meet the running costs of a large and presumably expensive household that, after 1460, spent the bulk of the year in the major centres of royal government, far distant from the agricultural resources of their lordships in the west.[8]

Did the post-1460 status of the Campbell earls as almost absentee lords of Argyll engaged in commercial and social transactions that depended on the ability to generate relatively large amounts of ready cash have implications for the organisation and exploitation of their lordships in Cowal, mid-Argyll, Lorn and Loch Awe? In the absence of detailed financial or estate records it is impossible to detect or trace changes in the level of income the earl derived from his western lordships, although there are occasional isolated indications of the revenues generated in these areas. After the death of Earl Colin in 1492, for example, his son and heir did not recover full legal title to his estates until late the following spring. In the interim the lands had, in theory, passed to the control of the crown. When, on 25 April 1493, Earl Archibald received a royal precept of sasine allowing him to be served as his father's heir, it was noted that the king's officials were to take financial sureties from Archibald that he would pay the half-year rents owed to the crown as well as the normal entry fee (a sum equivalent to a year's income from the named estates).[9] How far the sums detailed for the individual lordships were an accurate reflection of the earl's income is difficult to know, but the royal demands estimated the combined ferm of the baronies of Loch Awe, Glenorchy and Over Cowal at 690 marks per annum and that of Lorn at 549 marks. The annual ferms of smaller properties were also detailed; Kilmun (24 and a half marks); 'Orchart' (20 marks); Strath Eachaig and Lochstrivenhead (48 marks); Glassary (50 marks); Otter (30 marks); Melfort (40 marks); Craignish (65 marks), giving a total of just over 1,500 marks. To this total we can add the revenues from the earl's lands in Kintyre, Knapdale, Highland Perthshire and elsewhere that were not detailed in the same way in 1493. In most of these areas the unrecorded profits of 'justice' and the exercise of other lordly rights may have been as lucrative to the earl as rental income. Certainly when Duncan Campbell of Glenorchy raised an action against Earl Colin for one third of the profits from the lord's courts in Lorn he claimed that the sum involved was £100 Scots per annum. Glenorchy may well have been exaggerating for the sake of the legal process, but if we provisionally accept the figure as a basis of calculation, then enforcing 'justice' in Lorn would have raised around 450 marks per annum, almost matching the value of the lordship's rents as given in 1493. On the whole, these rough figures give no more than a vague sense of the revenues available to Campbell earls and tell us nothing about the way in which the family managed and exploited their estates.

Analysis of the much fuller evidence for the economy of Highland lordships in the early modern period makes it seem unlikely that the earl's western heartlands could have made a significant contribution to increased levels of expenditure during the fifteenth century, for the very limited resources of Highland lordships tended to be tied up in supporting the distinctive social structures of the area. Current models of the economy of Highland society in the medieval and early modern period emphasise the way in which, through networks of kinship and clientage, clan chiefs exerted social and political control over the collection, redistribution and consumption of the scarce resources that sustained life.[10] Agricultural surpluses might be traded directly for luxury goods; used to sustain a large and intimidating military retinue; to reward and retain professionals from the Gaelic learned orders; to maintain a lord's kin and adherents and dependents through times of dearth; to entertain and woo new and established followers through lavish feasting. There has been a tendency to see this type of social behaviour and the structures associated with it as being quintessentially Gaelic, representing a form of society physically distant from and culturally, almost spiritually, opposed to the world of the burgh and the merchant. Recent work has perhaps laid more stress on the way in which chieftainship and the practices through which it was expressed and maintained, such as guesting, feasting, raiding, tribute-taking, feuding and clanship, can be explained as a 'logical', indeed unavoidable, response to regional economic conditions, opportunities and costs.[11] The ability to obtain supplies of wine and other luxury imports need not, of course, imply that there were any fundamental changes in the social and political structures underpinning Campbell lordship. The surpluses traded could be generated through established structures and methods of lordship rather than any wider spread of commercial opportunities or market-orientated attitudes through society. Moreover, this type of aristocrat-led trade could strengthen rather than undermine the power of Gaelic lords. Robert Dodgshon has certainly suggested that one of the ways in which relationships of lordship and dependence could be established, consolidated and extended in the western Highlands and Islands was through the ability to obtain a monopoly over the redistribution of prestige items. In that sense commercial activity and trade leading to the procurement of luxury goods could have sustained and enhanced the status and influence of the Campbell lords within Argyll in entirely traditional ways.[12]

Campbell earls in the second half of the fifteenth century were obviously both part of this clan-based 'chiefly' economy of largely localised consumption and redistribution and, in their guise as royal courtiers resident in Edinburgh and elsewhere for long periods, partly divorced from it. Clearly, the needs and ambitions of one noble house could not transform the economic and social realities of areas such as Lorn and Loch Awe. Here, opportunities for commercial development were severely limited and resources tended to be absorbed in maintaining the 'clan' structures through which the earl exercised control. However, Campbell lordship also embraced areas with a rather different social, cultural and commercial history and organisation. Most obviously the Firth of Clyde was a region where Gaelic lords and communities potentially enjoyed easy access to a number of major burghs involved in international or local trade. By the end of the fifteenth century Campbell earls were operating within a maritime world particularly well served by convenient marketing outlets for the surplus production of their lordships. Within a day's sail of the Campbells' own recently established burghs of barony at Inveraray (1474) and Kilmun (1491) there was an impressive array of larger royal burghs, such as Glasgow, Dumbarton, Irvine and Ayr, as well as lesser centres such as Rothesay, Renfrew and Rutherglen. Dumbarton had, since its thirteenth-century foundation, enjoyed extensive trading privileges covering an area that extended to the head of Loch Long. The Dumbarton burgesses faced a number of challenges for control of this wide hinterland, particularly from the burgh of Glasgow.[13] The Clyde burghs (and non-burghal ports) had trading links to Ireland, the west of England, Brittany, Spain and France that could also be traced back into the thirteenth century. In October 1274, for example, a Bristol merchant, William de Canville, landed merchandise at the unidentified 'port of Loch Fyne' (*portu de Loghfyn in Scocia*) where a Scottish merchant 'Bryan de Dunbrecan' (for Dunbretan, i.e. Dumbarton?) arrested Canville's ship and goods.[14] That Canville pursued his case against Bryan when he next came across the Scottish trader in Dublin tells us something of the sphere of operations of these west-coast merchants. That Dublin was a regular port of call for Scottish merchants in the thirteenth century is suggested by the appearance of a number of Scots in the Dublin Guild Merchant Roll.[15] The vitality of this west-coast trade would clearly have been affected by the general downturn in the European economy in the fourteenth century and, more particularly, by the outbreak of Anglo-Scottish warfare that made access to Bristol and Irish ports under the control of the English crown problematic. If these conditions restricted the development of the Clyde burghs during the fourteenth century, then the fifteenth century potentially offered a more favourable environment. Anglo-Scottish warfare was intermittent and there were long periods of truce during which Scots merchants could legitimately trade direct with Bristol, Chester and Dublin. Yet Scottish trading contacts with these ports never seem to have been very significant in the late medieval period.[16] Despite the restrictions on trade with English-controlled centres the growth in the Irish Sea and Atlantic herring fisheries during the second half of the fifteenth century attracted Breton, French and Spanish merchants to the ports of Ireland and the Scottish Isles and west coast in increasing numbers, and it may not be coincidental that, as the economic liveliness of the Firth of Clyde became more obvious, Campbell lordship came to be centred on castles and settlements in this region.[17]

The Herring Fisheries[18]

On 8 May 1474 the settlement associated with the earl of Argyll's castle at Inveraray was granted the status of a burgh of barony with the right to hold a weekly market and to have two annual fairs on the feasts of St Michael the Archangel (29 September) and St Brendan (16 May).[19] It seems possible that the weekly markets and the fairs were an established feature of the life of the community at Inveraray long before the royal grant of 1474.[20] The range of dates within which fairs were held were inevitably dictated by the rhythms of an agricultural society with surpluses to dispose of or essential goods to be obtained at certain times of the year. Yet the particular saint's feast chosen could often reflect real local devotion. It is interesting, therefore, to note that the summer fair at Inveraray was associated with the feast of St Brendan. Brendan's cult had long been popular in the Firth of Clyde and in the thirteenth and fourteenth centuries the saint had been particularly favoured by the Campbells' political patrons, the Stewart lords of Bute.[21]

Earl Colin's wish to attain burghal status for the port at Inveraray may well have been inspired by an awareness of increased opportunities for properly constituted trading communities around Loch Fyne and the Firth of Clyde as Breton, French and Spanish merchants became more regular visitors to the area. Certainly within a few years of Inveraray's 'foundation', royal customs revenue from the export of salted herrings through the Firth of Clyde began to increase dramatically. The fifteenth-century growth in the Atlantic herring trade seems partly to have been attributable to a corresponding decline in the productivity of the herring fisheries of the Baltic, perhaps triggered by climatic change or the migration of herring shoals to new areas.[22] Herring fishing had been part of the economic life of the Clyde burghs for a considerable time prior to the fifteenth century, but the trade certainly quickened in the period after 1450 as merchants sought new sources to supply salted fish to the great Lent markets of mainland Europe.[23] It is also possible that the Atlantic coasts benefited from a natural increase in easily accessible herring stocks in the second half of the fifteenth century which made exploitation on a larger scale economically attractive.

One of the features of the growth of the herring fisheries in the west of Ireland was that the English crown and its agents found it very difficult to regulate and control the way in which trade was conducted. Local Irish lords and communities tended to be the direct beneficiaries of contact with foreign merchants, a situation seen as an infringement of the English crown's economic rights and a potential threat to its wider political interests.[24] Indeed it has been suggested that the wealth generated by the trade underpinned the building or rebuilding of new and established monasteries and castles across 'Gaelic and Gaelicised areas of the western seaboard [of Ireland]'.[25]

If similar conditions prevailed in the Gaelic lordships around the Firth of Clyde, it may be that the apparent surge in herring exports from the region in the 1480s reflected only the increased ability of the Scottish crown to extract customs revenue from a long-established and expanding industry which had previously lain outwith the reach of the king's tax-collectors. The grant of burghal status to Inverary in 1474 may have been a crucial step in the crown's attempt to achieve some level of control over the herring trade, for it gave Earl Colin an obvious incentive to police and protect the rights of officially sanctioned burghs in the region against infringement. The increasing value of the herring trade for royal finances and the emergence of Loch Fyne as a centre for that trade were obvious in the run of customs accounts from 1480 onwards. In 1480 the custumar of Irvine, David Blair, began, for the first time, to account for customs revenue levied on the export of salted herring custumed at Loch Fyne.[26] In 1481 Blair was described as custumar of Irvine and Loch Fyne, and the value and volume of the custumed herring exports had doubled.[27] In the same year the Dumbarton accounts also registered a dramatic leap in customs revenue from Loch Fyne herring.[28] The escalating value of the herring customs prompted a redistribution and reorganisation of responsibility for the levying and collection of the sums due to the crown. In 1483 the custumar of Dumbarton was renamed the custumar of Dumbarton and the 'Lowis'. Later entries make clear that the new area of fiscal assessment embraced Loch Fyne and the other sea lochs of the Firth of Clyde.[29] In the 1480s the value of the herring customs from the region steadily rose. By 1487 the custumar of Dumbarton accounted for the duty on 397 lasts of herring from which the crown was owed £286 4s.[30] The royal customs revenue represented only a small fraction of the total value of the herring traded, so that the profits of the men who dominated the trade in the Firth of Clyde were likely to be substantial. In 1492 salted herring sold in Scotland at the rate of 240s per last.[31] Using this as a very rough guide, the retail value in Scotland of the herring custumed at Loch Fyne and Dumbarton during 1487, admittedly an exceptionally productive year, would have been just under £4,800.[32] It is perhaps no surprise that the protection against infringement of the lucrative rights and monopolies of the burghs and lords involved in the trade became a regular feature of parliamentary legislation in the closing decades of the fifteenth century. Besides defending burghal and aristocratic interests, the parliamentary legislation also sought to promote investment in more advanced fishing vessels after the Dutch model in an attempt to improve the efficiency and extend the scope of the fisheries.[33] In 1491, the estates even passed legislation that envisaged a forced conscription of 'idlemen' to work in the fishing fleets of their nearest burghs.[34] While there is little indication that west-coast lords and burghs did invest in new vessels and fishing methods, they probably took the parliamentary protection of their privileges very seriously. Indeed, James III's rather cavalier treatment of these rights may have provoked some of this legislation and contributed to the growing hostility to the king in the final years of his reign. The parliament of January 1488 seemed to criticise the king's preparedness to grant concessions to foreign merchants and others which allowed them to bypass established burghs.[35] The king was enjoined not to 'graunt letters in tyme tocum' that might allow foreign merchants to circumvent the free burghs. The first parliament held after the death of James III at Sauchieburn returned to this issue and produced legislation that took a very robust line against those evading royal customs.[36] The parliament insisted that all foreign merchants should trade only at royal burghs such as Dumbarton, Ayr, Irvine, Wigtown, Kirkcudbright and Renfrew or other 'free' burghs. These merchants were forbidden to buy unsalted and unbarrelled fish and were not to trade at any location 'at the Lowis nor uthir Mane land' other than free burghs where the appropriate duties and customs could be levied. The 'free burghs' through which the herring trade was to be channelled no doubt included Earl Colin's burgh of barony at Inveraray, which was confirmed as one of the few locations within the 'Lowis' where salted and barrelled herring could legitimately be sold to the Breton and French merchants who were the main carriers involved in the trade. Campbell interest in, and domination of, the western fisheries had been confirmed as early as the month after James III's death when the new king's councillors (headed by Earl Colin) gave a three-year lease of the assise of the 'herrings of the western sea' to the earl's kinsman Colin Campbell 'Knightson'.[37] In 1490 Earl Colin established yet another commercial outlet in the Firth of Clyde when he successfully petitioned James IV for Kilmun to be given the status of a burgh of barony with a fair on 21 October, the feast day of St. Fionntáin.[38]

A further development saw the acquisition of a substantial interest in

Dumbarton burgh. On 9 May 1491, Colin, earl of Argyll, purchased a tenement on the south side of the High Street in the burgh from the burgess John Smolat.[39] The purchase may have been part of a wider move by Earl Colin to obtain appropriate accommodation in centres of royal governance to support his role as a full-time councillor. Certainly, within a few months, on 18 November 1491, Earl Colin had obtained possession of another urban property, this time in Edinburgh. The 'great mansion and backland' bought by Argyll in Edinburgh lay on the north side of the High Street. The use of this property as a residential townhouse was made explicit on 6 November 1495 when Colin's son Earl Archibald sold the mansion and backland to a kinsman, Donald Campbell, an Edinburgh burgess, with the proviso that the earl and his heirs were to be 'received into the said tenement as oft as they happen to be in said burgh'.[40] Other urban properties inherited by Earl Archibald from his father included two tenements in the burgh of Stirling, originally obtained by Earl Colin in 1481.[41] Unlike Edinburgh and Stirling, however, Dumbarton was not a major centre for the conduct of royal business in the reign of James IV, and Earl Colin's chief aim in establishing a presence in the burgh may have been to protect his interests in the herring trade which was monitored, assessed and taxed by royal officials based in the town.[42]

An agreement of 2 November 1482 involving John Dalrymple of 'Laight' and two Breton merchants, John 'Bulwart' and Nicholas David, provides a particularly interesting insight into aspects of the burgeoning west-coast herring trade.[43] From September 1481 to June 1483 Dalrymple acted as the deputy of George Maxwell, the custumar of Dumbarton and the 'Lochs'. The terms of the 1482 agreement recorded that Dalrymple, in order to settle a debt of £581 he owed to the Bretons, promised to deliver to them eighty lasts of fresh herrings to be barrelled 'as in Flanders'. If the Bretons did not come 'to the lochis at the west sey' to receive payment, the obligation would be annulled. In the following year Bulwart and Nicholas David returned to Scotland where, on 1 October 1483, they acknowledged that they had received twenty lasts of herring from Dalrymple.[44] The timing and terms of the initial agreement and discharge suggest that the Breton merchants were, or were expected to be, annual visitors to the 'lochis at the west sey' in late autumn. The fairs of St Michael the Archangel (29 September) at Inverary and St Fionntáin (21 October) at Kilmun may thus have coincided with the period in which Spanish, French and Breton merchants were most likely to be in the Firth of Clyde.

Both Bulwart and Nicholas David were described as merchants of Le Croisic, a port at the mouth of the River Loire in Brittany. From the fourteenth century onwards the area surrounding Le Croisic, the Bay of Bourgneuf, was noted for salt production, and it may be that these men were well placed to become involved in the export of herring because they were shipping in the sea-salt used in the processing and preservation of the fish.[45] However, the most important and popular commodity brought in from Spain, France and Brittany to the burghs of the west in exchange for herring was undoubtedly wine. Prior to the second half of the fifteenth century there was little indication that the west-coast burghs were significant players in the import of wine into Scotland. The increasing evidence for the arrival of wine through Firth of Clyde and Galwegian ports from *c.*1450 onwards may well be directly related to the expansion of the herring trade.[46]

That the western fisheries were seen by the opening decades of the sixteenth century as a resource that attracted foreign merchants to Scotland and brought prosperity to the region is suggested in a roundabout way in Bellenden's vernacular translation (1532) of Hector Boece's *History of Scotland.* According to Bellenden, the town of Inverlochy had been founded by the mythical 'King Ewen' whose protection ensured that it became 'ane commoun port till all merchandis of France or Spanze, for the incredibill fertilitie of fische swommand in thai seyis'.[47] This sixteenth-century view of Scotland's ancient past was clearly informed by a contemporary understanding of the importance of the fishing trade in the region.

Herring may have been the main draw for the continental merchants who were regular visitors to the Clyde at the close of the fifteenth century, but the trade in fish was complemented by markets in other commodities. The most important of these was probably that in cow-hides.[48] Throughout the medieval period observers commented on the fact that the west was a pastoral country rich in cattle. John Barbour's description of Robert I's harrying of the lordship of Lorn, for example, emphasised the huge number of beasts captured by the king and his followers during the expedition.[49] In 1367 David II's government, attempting to rectify what they saw as the unfairly light contribution made by Highland Scotland to the payment of the king's ransom and the other expenses of monarchy suggested levying new export taxes on the typical produce of the region. The items picked out were cattle, fish, oats and barley.[50] Over a century later the account of the 'savage' parts of Scotland provided by the Spanish ambassador, Don Pedro de Ayala, also commented on the great herds of the region.[51]

There is little doubt that Campbell lords played an active role in the commercial export market in hides that built up around burghs such as Dumbarton. In February 1507, for example, Earl Archibald received a royal grant that allowed him to export (custom-free) herring, cod and hides through the burghs of Dumbarton, Irvine and Ayr.[52] However, the importance of the rearing of cattle to the economy and society of medieval Argyll extended beyond the opportunity to trade surpluses for imported luxuries. In these pastoral areas the number of cows owned by an individual often acted as a basic measure of wealth and social status while the beasts themselves functioned as a type of currency underpinning a variety of social transactions and exchanges. In that sense, the export of hides through burghs such as Dumbarton, Stirling and Perth was a thin veneer covering the much more fundamental way in which Highland lordship functioned through the ability to control the redistribution of livestock. The bulk of these exchanges and the relationships they established or entrenched went unrecorded except where specific property rights were involved. Thus a couple of transactions involving fourteenth- and fifteenth-century Campbell lords display the use of cattle alongside cash as a medium of exchange to buy out tenurial rights. One of the resignations made by Christina of Craignish in favour of Colin Campbell in 1361, for example, seems to have involved the handing over of livestock as well as coinage.[53] In 1432 Gillespic Campbell, Duncan Lord Campbell's son, entered into a complicated transaction involving the lands of the MacEwen lord of Otter in Cowal in which the latter seems to have received sixty marks in cash and twenty-five cows in exchange for effectively signing over the inheritance of Otter to Gillespic.[54] The gifting of cattle herds in exchange for claims to land was also found in the earldom of Carrick, another upland zone dominated by pastoral farming.[55]

A complicating factor in the treatment of the agricultural and mineral resources of Firth of Clyde lordships was the expansion of direct royal 'ownership' of land in the region in the second half of the fifteenth century. The spread of the crown's territorial interests into former lordship territories such as Kintyre during the fifteenth century may have provided an early stimulus to the practice of driving live cattle from the west to centres of consumption further to the east. The king was entitled to a ferm or rent of cattle and other agricultural produce from both long-held lordships, such as Bute, and more recently acquired lands. In the fifteenth century the monarch was not a regular visitor to these lordships so the produce rents were never likely to be consumed directly by the royal household. The solution adopted for the Bute ferms saw the marts (cattle to be slaughtered in the autumn for winter consumption) owed to the king crossing to the mainland at Largs (by swimming) before being driven to royal centres in Edinburgh, Stirling or Linlithgow.[56] The intention seems to have been to extend this practice into the new crown lands taken from the Lord of the Isles. The earl of Argyll as the king's chamberlain in Kintyre from 1505 became the effective local enforcer of these policies. Certainly Earl Archibald's accounts as chamberlain of Kintyre recorded the driving of marts from Kintyre to Edinburgh, Stirling and Dumbarton.[57] More ambitiously in 1506 it was suggested that the marts due for the royal fermes of Islay and Colonsay should be delivered to the 'Ross' in Knapdale on 8 August of that year.[58] Since it was specified that the king and his comptroller (the financial officer in charge of household income) were prepared to risk the sea-crossing, it seems that the cattle were to swim across to Knapdale. The flow of livestock from the west was miniscule and was generated by the demands of lordship rather than the market. However, the type of organisation and co-ordination required and the connections established may well have made the development of a commercial cattle trade in response to the population growth in sixteenth-century Scottish burghs much more likely. The attitude toward the transportation of marts reflected the general determination of James IV's administration to exploit the king's new lands in a vigorous and imaginative way. One telling indication of the new outlook came in 1498, when the king sent colliers to survey Kintyre to see 'gif colis may be wonnye thare'.[59]

Although the economy of Campbell lordships was dominated by cattle and fish, there were occasional glimpses of other products. An isolated reference from the first decade of the sixteenth century records Sir Duncan Campbell of Glenorchy preparing to send salted and barrelled venison to Spain, but there is nothing to indicate this was a regular or significant export from Highland areas.[60] There was, however, a market for Highland mantles, large and vibrantly coloured woven cloaks. The use of mantles as an item of exchange was obvious in the Auchinleck chronicler's account of the meeting between John, earl of Ross and Lord of the Isles, and James 9th earl of Douglas in 1452.[61] The trade of gifts accompanying the meeting saw Douglas give over 'wyne, clathis, silver, silk and English cloth' to which Ross responded by presenting Douglas with 'mantillis'. The apparent disparity in the value and variety of the goods exchanged has sometimes been used to confirm the economic backwardness of Hebridean magnates (and Hebridean society in general) in comparison to their wealthier and better connected Lowland counterparts. Clearly relative levels of wealth and access to luxury goods were greater in the more fertile and populous regions of the kingdom, well-served by prosperous trading communities. However, the 'inequality' in the exchange of 1452 surely also reflected the relative political strength of the parties involved. Douglas's brother had just been killed by James II, and the earl's lordships scattered through southern Scotland remained vulnerable to royal action. In blunt terms Douglas needed a political and military alliance more than Ross did. Moreover, Earl John was hardly incapable of accessing these types of goods on his own account. As earls of Ross, John and his father actually seem to have spent a great deal of their time in and around the burghs of Inverness and Dingwall. The numerous branches of Clan Donald also seem to have maintained links to merchants in a variety of Irish and English ports while Scottish central records occasionally hint at the presence of Spanish and French traders active in 'the Isles' in the fifteenth century.[62] Finally, we should note that mantles were, like the goods offered by Douglas, potentially expensive and prestigious items.[63] An interesting indication of the social and financial value attached to high-quality mantles is the appearance of a red cloak or mantle as the blench-ferm render owed to the crown from the Campbell lordship of Lorn.[64] In 1470–1 the earl of Argyll sold the red mantle owed to the king for 13 shillings and 4 pence and accounted for the sum to the exchequer, while in the 1490s the Lorn mantle was considered to be an appropriate gift for the king to bestow on William Elphinstone, bishop of Aberdeen.[65]

Without full estate management and/or household account books for any one late medieval Scottish magnate it is very difficult to assess in any convincing way the economic life and ambitions of the aristocratic class or to trace and explain fluctuations in their relative levels of wealth and prosperity. The discussion above does little more than suggest that the Campbell earls displayed a real interest in the economic exploitation of their lordships and attempted to respond to new opportunities and pressures. The Campbells, of course, were not unique in this and the policies they pursued have to be seen against the background of increased royal interest in maximising revenues and expanding and encouraging economic activity throughout the realm. Even in the regional context of the Firth of Clyde the Campbells do not appear particularly unusual in becoming involved in mercantile activity and/or maintaining burghal properties. On 1 August 1474, for example, Duncan Lamont was one of the merchants given a three-year English safe conduct to allow their ship *the Trinity*, to trade in English ports. Lamont may well have been the brother of John Lamont, lord of Inveryne in Cowal.[66] In July 1489, 'Archebald Makelar of Argile Scottyshman' received a similar safe-conduct to allow him to trade in England, France, Flanders and Burgundy with 'almaner goodis and merchaundises'.[67] Little else is known of MacKellar, but in 1502 a man of the same name appeared as a witness to a charter issued by Earl Archibald at Inveraray.[68] If this figure was one and the same with the Archibald MacKellar of 1489 it is tempting to suggest that his trading base might have been the earl's own burgh of Inveraray. Perhaps the most significant aspect of the 1489, safe-conduct was that it was granted at the request of Thomas Grafton, a prominent London trader and sometime merchant and lieutenant of the English king's staple at Calais.[69] Quite how MacKellar knew Grafton is unclear, but the Argyll merchant clearly had some impressive commercial connections.

The emergence of a small Gaelic mercantile elite fostered through the long interaction between the burgh of Dumbarton and the principal landowners within the burgh's hinterland in Argyll and the Firth of Clyde seems a natural development. It remains mildly surprising only because studies of medieval Scotland have tended to emphasise lack of engagement or outright hostility towards commercial development and trade through urban settlements as one of the defining and enduring features of Gaelic social organisation. The impression has been reinforced by the pejorative descriptions of the Gael scattered through a number of late medieval Scottish and English sources that portrayed a people unable or unwilling to engage in the forms of economic activity that underpinned 'civilised' society.[70] The stereotypes seem to bear little relation to the situation in the Firth of Clyde by the end of the fifteenth century. Here, a number of local landowners, regardless of cultural or linguistic affiliation, were active in promoting and exploiting trade. The most obvious participants and beneficiaries were the earls of Argyll with their urban townhouses, their burghs at Inveraray and Kilmun, and their interests in Dumbarton, Stirling, Irvine and Ayr. However, the Campbells' good fortune reflected wider regional developments and opportunities in which others shared. The government of James IV, about to unleash its programme of political, judicial and economic reform in its newly acquired Highland and Hebridean lordships, may well have viewed the modest prosperity of Campbell regional lordship in the sea lochs of the Firth of Clyde as further proof of the misuse of resources by Gaelic magnates in other areas. In the end the rhetoric of economic improvement and social justice that accompanied the wide-ranging assault by crown agents on established aristocratic interests and social structures across the territories forfeited by the Lordship of the Isles was horribly misplaced. The economic advances made in the Firth of Clyde were the product of a quite distinct mix of historical and geographical conditions that could not be transferred to other regions on the point of a sword.

Notes

1. *CDS*, iv, 952; *Foedera*, x, 327.
2. The basis of the evaluation is unknown, the currency (English or Scots) unspecified, and the accuracy of the estimation uncertain, but at some level it must have reflected perceptions of the relative wealth of the individuals concerned. For discussion see A.Grant, *Independence and Nationhood: Scotland, 1306–1469* (London, 1984), 132–3.
3. The creation of the title earl of Morton occurred in a parliament of March 1458. *APS*, ii, 78. It is not inconceivable that the Campbell earldom was also instituted in this assembly.
4. *Chron. Auchinleck* (McGladdery), 163.
5. Argyll Muniments, Inverary, Bundle 1109 (Oliphant); British Library, HL 4693 f.9. 14 September 1469 (Seton); AT, at date (Drummond); Ibid., 2/11/1509. An acknowledgement by Lord Erskine that he had received 600 marks in part payment of a larger sum for 'tochir gude' for the bond of marriage between Erskine's son and heir and Margaret Campbell, daughter of Archibald, 2nd earl of Argyll.
6. E.g. *TA*, i, 197, 205. Purchase of the ward of the heir of Andrew, Lord Avandale cost a sum well in excess of £454.
7. RCAHMS *Argyll*, ii, no.247 (Inishail), no.287 (Dunstaffnage), no.292 (Innis Chonnell), *Ibid.*, vii, no.80 (Kilmun), no.129 (Eilean Dearg), no.132 (Inveraray).
8. See Chalmers, 'The King's Council', 424–8 for tables indicating the attendance of Earl Colin and Earl Archibald as witnesses to royal great seal charters.
9. Argyll Muniments, Inveraray, Bundle 1113.
10. See in particular R.A. Dodghson's detailed analysis of the changing economic and social structures underlying Hebridean and Highland lordship and society

in this period. R.A. Dodghson, *From Chiefs to Landlords: social and economic change in the Western Highlands and Islands*, c.1493–1820 (Edinburgh, 1998); R. Dodgshon, ' "Pretence of blude" and "place of thair duelling": the nature of Scottish clans, 1500–1745', in R.A. Houston and I.D. Whyte, eds., *Scottish Society, 1500–1800* (Cambridge, 1989).

11. Dodghson, *Chiefs to Landlords*, Chs. 1–3. For an insightful discussion of guesting and feasting in the context of medieval Ireland, see K. Simms, 'Guesting and feasting in Gaelic Ireland', *Journal of the Royal Society of Antiquaries of Ireland*, 108 (1978), 67–100.

12. R.A. Dodgshon, 'West Highland chiefdoms, 1500–1745' in R. Mitchison and P. Roebuck, eds., *Economy and Society in Scotland and Ireland, 1500–1919* (Edinburgh, 1988).

13. *RMS*, vii, no.190 (1); ix, no.601; *Glas. Reg.*, no.183. For some reason, perhaps connected to the nature of aristocratic colonisation of the area in the twelfth and thirteenth centuries, the Lordship of Kilmun and other lands in eastern Cowal and mid-Argyll seem to have developed links to Glasgow rather than Dumbarton. The blench-ferm renders of Kilmun, for example, were to be offered to the superior at the fair of Glasgow, held around 6 July, if required. AT 25/3/1499. The Campbells also maintained a link to the Dominican house in Glasgow that revolved around lands held by the family in Cowal. In 1429 and 1451, for example, Duncan Campbell granted the Glasgow house rents from lands in Cowal. *Glas. Friars*, pp.163–4, 172–3 (nos.21,30) while Earl Colin gave them a further gift in the form of an annual rent from the escheats of the bailiary of Cowal that was also to be paid over at the fair of Glasgow. *Ibid.*, p.192, no.40. The MacLachlans of Strathlachan also gave the Glasgow Dominicans rents from their Argyll lands to be rendered at Glasgow fair. *Ibid*, pp 152–3, 178–9 (nos 9, 33)

14. *Select cases concerning the law merchant: A.D. 1270–1638*, 3 vols. (Selden Society, 1908–1932), ii (Selden Society, 46) ed.H.Hull, 18–19; *CDS*, v, no.62.

15. 'The Dublin Guild Merchant Roll, c.1190–1265', ed. P. Connolly and G. Martin (Dublin, 1992), 13 (Robertus de Salan (Salen, Argyll?) – undated); 55 (Baudric de Dunbretan) (in 1226–7); 74, Gilbertus de Sadewelle (Saddel?); 85, Thomas de Argeythel (in 1246–7).

16. See D.Ditchburn, *Scotland and Europe: The Medieval Kingdom and its Contacts with Christendom, c.1215–1545*, i (East Linton, 2000), 147.

17. For a discussion of the impact of the fisheries on Ua Domhnaill lordship in Tír Connail, see Darren Mac Eiteagáin, 'The Renaissance and the late Medieval lordship of Tír Chonaill 1461–1555', in *Donegal: History and Society*, ed. W. Nolan, L. Ronayne and M. Dunlevy (Dublin, 1995), 203–228, at 206–9. Also in the same collection, Katherine Simms, 'Late Medieval Donegal', 183–201, at 195–7; Timothy O'Neill, *Merchants and Mariners in Medieval Ireland* (Dublin, 1987), 30–36.

18. Much of the following discussion has already appeared in print in S. Boardman, 'Pillars of the Community': Campbell lordship and architectural patronage in the fifteenth century', in *Lordship and Architecture*, ed. R. Oram and G. Stell (Edinburgh, 2005).

19. Argyll Muniments, Inveraray, Argyll Charters; *RMS*, ii, no. 1168.

20. See G.W.S. Barrow, 'The sources for the history of the Highlands in the Middle Ages', in *The Middle Ages in the Highlands* (Inverness, 1981), 11–12, for the

observation that, despite the absence of burghs in the Highlands, economic activity may have been sustained at some level through fairs and weekly markets.

21. See S. Boardman, 'The Early Stewart court and the Gaelic world', in *Miorun Mór nan Gall: The great ill-will of the Lowlander*, ed. D. Broun and M. MacGregor (forthcoming). The kirk at Inveraray was the parish kirk of Kilmalieu, named for a St. Liubha or Liba and with no obvious connection to Brendan. *CPNS*, 304–5.

22. J.R. Coull, *The Sea Fisheries of Scotland: A Historical Geography* (Edinburgh, 1996), 54–78; O'Neill, *Merchants and Mariners*, 30; D. Ditchburn, *Scotland and Europe*, 144–5.

23. In 1306, for example, Scottish fishing boats from Rutherglen were trading herrings in Dublin and Drogheda. O'Neill, *Merchants and Mariners*, 31.

24. O'Neill, *Merchants and Mariners*, 33, where it is argued that the Atlantic herring trade was regarded by the authorities as a development that strengthened the king's Irish enemies 'in victuals and harness and diverse gear'.

25. O'Neill, *Merchants and Mariners*, 36. Although the point is asserted rather than proved.

26. *ER*, ix, 65. 56 lasts (1 last=12 barrels) generating £16 16s of customs revenue for the Crown.

27. *Ibid.*, 144–5. 115 lasts with a customs value of £34 10s.

28. *Ibid.*, 146. 76 lasts 2 barrels, customs value of £22 17s.

29. *Ibid.*, e.g. 210, 292, 339, 438, 542, xi, 371, xii, 371, 462, 592, xiii, 226. The custumar of the 'Lowis' received an unusually high fee for the 'great labours and expenses' involved in collecting the customs of the area, indicating that his duties involved visiting multiple sites around the 'Lochs' where herring was being processed and traded. *Ibid.*, 543.

30. *Ibid.*, 542–3. This sum represented the fifteenth-century peak of royal revenues from the western fisheries. In James IV's reign the annual sum collected only rarely exceeded £100.

31. E. Gemmill and N. Mayhew, *Changing values in medieval Scotland : a study of prices, money, and weights and measures* (Cambridge, 1995), 322.

32. The extent and value of the Scottish domestic market for west-coast herring cannot be calculated. There is, of course, no guarantee that the price per last in 1487 would have been at the rather high 1492 level.

33. *APS*, ii, 179, 183, 209, 235, 237, 242.

34. *APS*, ii, 235, 237.

35. *Ibid.*, ii, 183. The terms of the statute (Item 15) should probably be read in conjunction with the act passed in the parliament of October 1488 after James III's death.

36. *Ibid.*, ii, 209.

37. *ER*, x, 374, 499, 570, 638.

38. *RMS*, ii, no.1993. The October fair would have allowed for the purchase of grain and perhaps also salt in preparation for the processing of a winter herring catch for sale in the Lent markets. I am grateful to Dr Martin Rourke for this suggestion. The Campbell habit of consuming as well as overseeing the trading of fish, a form of food traditionally considered rather 'ignoble' in Gaelic society, drew pejorative comments from the seventeenth-century Gaelic poet Iain Lom MacDonald of Keppoch. *Orain Iain Luim: Songs of John MacDonald, Bard of*

Keppoch, ed. A.M. Mackenzie (SGTS, 1964), pp.42–3. In his 'Oar-Song to MacLean of Duart', MacDonald describes the Campbells (*sliochd Dhiarmaid*) as the 'dirty rabble of the fishing' (*prasgan salach an iasgaich*). I am grateful to Dr Wilson McLeod, Department of Celtic, University of Edinburgh, for bringing this reference to my attention.

39. Argyll Muniments, Inveraray, Bundle 1112. The burgage plot was defined as lying between the lands of James Law on the east, Thomas Ranald's on the west, the King's way on the north, and the Water of Leven on the south. Sasine was not delivered until the following March. For Smolat, see *ER*, x, 242, 368.

40. Argyll Muniments, Inveraray, Bundle 1112; AT, 6/11/1495.

41. Argyll Muniments, Inveraray, Bundle 1111; sasine delivered to Earl Archibald in 1494, Ibid., Bundle 1114.

42. It may not be coincidental that Earl Colin was also heavily involved, through his support of Hugh, Lord Montgomery, in the political struggle to control the burgh of Irvine. See above, p. 245.

43. NAS Napier Charters GD 430/185. See also GD 430/43 and the *Protocol Book of John Foular, 1501–1503* (SRS, 1930), no.201.

44. The discharge was witnessed by burgesses from Ayr (Thomas Tait) and Irvine (John and Walter Scott).

45. P. Galliou and M. Jones, *The Bretons* (Oxford, 1991), 209. The connection to Le Croisic was evidently still in place in 1486–7 when Master 'Eugenius la Pyne' exported forty-six lasts of herring in his ship the *Maria-de Crosik*. *ER*, ix, 542. The same exchequer account (for Dumbarton and the 'Lowis') mentioned other Breton merchants from La Rochelle and St. Malo. Some of these men had evidently evaded paying royal customs on their cargoes. *Ibid.*, 542, 544. See H. Touchard, *Le Commerce Maritime Breton à la fin du moyen age*, (Paris, 1967) for a general discussion of Breton trading links. Ditchburn, *Scotland and Europe*, 185 makes the point that French salt was better than Scottish-produced salt for preserving fish.

46. See example *TA*, iii, 279. A payment to Andrew Barton to 'mak hering to send in France for wyne, and to furnis the schip biggit in Dunbertane to Burdeous' (ie. Bordeaux). The heavy involvement of the burghs of south-western Scotland in the importation of wine is obvious in the central judicial and fiscal records of the Scottish crown from the second half of the fifteenth century onwards. For example see *ADA*, 9, a legal dispute between the Bishop of Glasgow and the burgh of Dumbarton caused by the refusal of the Dumbarton burgesses to allow Glasgow men to purchase wine from the ship of the Frenchman 'Peris Cokate' in the water of Clyde as they claimed they were entitled to do; *ADA*, 122*-123*. A Spanish merchant pursuing his trading partners for payment in relation to wine shipped into the port of Wigtown; see *ER*, viii, 343, 345, 373 for Galloway as a region in which the Scottish royal house regularly bought wine; Ditchburn, *Scotland and Europe*, 154–6.

47. Bellenden, *Chronicles*, i, 88.

48. Hides were, behind wool, the most important and valuable Scottish export in the Middle Ages. See Ditchburn, *Scotland and Europe*, 162–3, for a brief survey of the trade.

49. *The Bruce* (Duncan), 366. (Book 10, ll. 108–111)

50. *APS*, i, 508.

51. *CSP (Spain)*, i, no.210.
52. E.g. *ER*, xii, 156, 371, 598; xiii, 87, 226; *RSS*, i, no.1436. See O'Neill, *Merchants and Mariners*, 77–83 for the trade in hides in medieval Ireland. Like herring, Irish hides were traded in exchange for Gascon wine but also found their way to the leather-processing centres in the Low Countries and Italy. See Ditchburn, *Scotland and Europe*, 162–3 for a discussion of the apparently less extensive European markets for Scottish hides.
53. NAS RH1/2/87; *SHS Misc.*, iv, 292.
54. Argyll Muniments, Inveraray, Bundle 1107. In March 1432 Suibne MacEwen of Otter resigned his lands to the Crown and received a new charter in favour of himself and any lawfully procreated male heirs. By the terms of the charter, if the lord of Otter's male line failed the lands were to go to Gillespic Campbell, Duncan's son and heir. The resignation and insertion of a new Campbell heir seems to have been secured through the handing over of the cash and cows detailed in the text, for a separate agreement of June 1432 (also Bundle 1107) specified that these payments were to be given to Gillespic should the MacEwen lord actually produce a lawful heir. Why the lord of Otter was prepared to hand over his inheritance to the Campbells is unclear.
55. *Laing Charters*, nos.64 (1370–1380) and 69 (c.1385).
56. E.g., *ER*, x, 123, xii, 66, 246, 319, 512, xiii, 80, 138, 313.
57. *ER*, 352, 363, 365.
58. *ER*, xii, 709. Presumably the cattle were to be driven across Jura. The 'Ross' of Knapdale is not easily identified but may have been one of the promontories on the west of the Loch Sween peninsula. Once in Knapdale the cattle were probably to be driven, like those from Kintyre further to the south, to major burghs or royal centres.
59. *TA*, i, 388. 27 April 1498. To ane cole man, to pas in Kyntyr to vesy; *Ibid.*, 389. 4 May 1498 to Davidson, colyar, to mak werklumys and to pas in Kintyr.
60. *TA*, iii, 209.
61. *Chron. Auchinleck* (McGladdery), 167.
62. For a review of the place-dates associated with the issuing of charters by John and his father see *ALI*, xlix; *CDS*, iii, no.1244 (1337). A galley of John of Islay mistakenly arrested at 'Coupeland' (Cumbria or Belfast Lough?); *Rot. Scot.*, i, 534, 535; *CDS*, iii, 1606; *Foedera*, vi, 59; *Cal. Pat. Rolls* 1354–7, 589. 1357 safe-conducts obtained by John of the Isles from Edward III for six 'merchants of the Isles'. All those named appear to be based in the north of Ireland; O'Neill, *Merchants and Mariners*, 121. A merchant of Drogheda negotiating a safe-conduct in 1443 with Donald Balloch; *TA*, i, 377. Alms given to five 'Spanyartis' taken in the Isles; *ER*, viii, 540 John 'Begarson', Frenchman, his ship arrested on the way to the Isles.
63. H.F. McClintock, *Old Irish and Highland dress* (Dundalk, 1950); O'Neill, *Merchants and Mariners*, 68–70.
64. *RMS*, ii, no.989. The 1470 grant specifies only a cloak (clamedem), but later references make clear that a red cloak was expected. *ER*, viii, 20, 35.
65. *ER*, viii, 20, ix, 311*. In addition, it might be noted that in 1361 the financial penalty to be paid by Christina of Craignish if she retracted her resignation of Craignish in favour of Colin Campbell was to be rendered 'on a red cloak' at the altar of Kilmartin kirk.

66. *Rot.Scot.*, ii, 443; *Lamont Papers*, nos.57, 58.
67. *CDS*, iv, no.1550. In 1498, meanwhile, Earl Archibald's brother-in-law, Matthew Stewart, earl of Lennox, obtained safe passage for his own vessel, the *Mary of Dumbarton*, to the English west-coast ports of Bristol and Chester. *CDS*, iv, no.1647.
68. Argyll Muniments, Inveraray, Bundle 1091; *AT* 16/9/1502. He was listed after a series of local landowners, Colin Campbell of Barbreck, Alexander Campbell of Inverlevir, Alexander MacIvor of Pennymoir and a priest, Malcolm MacGilliker, and alongside a John 'Herd'.
69. For Grafton, see *Petty Customs Account*, 1480–1, ed. H.S.Cobb (London, 1990), no.599, 602; A.Hanham, *The Celys and their World* (Cambridge, 1985), 241. The link is not easily explained through the type of commodities in which Grafton dealt, for he was principally connected with the grain and wool trade rather than hides or fish.
70. See Boardman, 'Pillars of the Community', for an extended discussion of these representations.

TWELVE

The Red Road

Trouble was coming. Across the kingdom a range of men who felt themselves dispossessed or harried by those who had snapped up feudal rights or feu-farm grants through the power of the purse fought their corner at the local level in a series of bruising petty feuds. These confrontations were certainly violent, but were usually localised and unco-ordinated with no wider political agenda or support.[1] In some areas, however, where the impact of change was especially widespread or disruptive, resistance could assume a more extensive, almost communal, aspect as Sir Robert Menzies of Weem could unhappily attest. Of all the various flashpoints, the central Highland lordship of Lochaber was potentially the most serious. Here, as in the Appin of Dull, the implementation of the crown's policies threatened the widespread displacement of established landowners and their dependents. Over the course of 1500–2 the crown had effectively sanctioned the earl of Huntly's personal war in Lochaber after the earl's commission of August 1501 to set leases of the lands in the lordship had run into fierce opposition. The roll-call of lords charged with 'illegally' occupying royal lands in Lochaber and elsewhere in December 1501 reflected the resistance Huntly had encountered. There was to be no compromise. On 21 March 1502 Huntly, Thomas, Lord Fraser of the Lovat and William Munro of Foulis were re-appointed to set the king's lands of Lochaber and Mamore in five-year leases. At the same time Huntly received permission to set Torquil MacLeod's lands of Assynt and Cogeach forfeited to the crown because of Torquil's 'rebellion'.[2]

The language of the letters appointing the Lochaber commission indicated the way in which the determination to maximise royal revenue, attested in the crown's dealings with all areas of the kingdom, was thought to face particular obstacles in the social, economic and political structures of Highland lordships. The lands were to be set to 'gud trew and sufficient men for the plenysing thairof'. It was essential that 'trespassouris and brokin men' were expelled and the lands set 'to as gret avale as thai can for our soveran lordis proffitt'. The commission, in linking successful economic exploitation and development of royal lands with the removal of a disruptive element (trespassers and broken men) in local society reflected a characteristic concern of royal legislation from the period.[3] We should not exaggerate the impact of these pious policy aspirations on the actual conduct or effect of the royal-backed campaigns in the Highlands after 1500. Huntly and his allies were hardly likely to bring about the root and branch social, judicial and economic re-organisation anticipated by royal legislators through simple force of arms. Yet at the least the government could hope for a local lordship that was more responsive to royal demands in judicial and economic terms and perhaps enjoyed the modest attempts at development seen in Huntly's own lordship of Badenoch, with its burgh of barony and Carmelite friary at Kingussie. The seriousness with which Earl Alexander approached the task of realising the economic potential of Badenoch is indicated by an agreement of 17 March 1501 between Huntly, the earl of Atholl and Robert Ayson of Tullimet.[4] The agreement stipulated that Atholl and Ayson (whose estates at Tullimet lay on the main route between Badenoch and Atholl) should not obstruct or levy tolls from the men of Badenoch or other lands belonging to Huntly north of the Mounth when they took their goods and carriages through Atholl. Three categories of produce, cattle, timber and iron (presumably bog iron), were specified. The likely destinations for these goods were the burghs of Dunkeld and Perth. Earl Alexander was apparently paying more than lip service to the notion that Highland Scotland was a land ripe for development if the resources of the region could be freed from the wasteful domination of established lords.

Huntly's advance would have repercussions well beyond the marches of Lochaber. The establishment of Clan Donald control of the region in the fourteenth century had left a number of Hebridean families with extensive, and often conflicting, territorial claims inside the lordship. In the 1490s, for example, the MacLeans of Duart and the MacLeans of Lochbuie fought each other and occasionally combined to harry the Captains of Clan Cameron.[5] It was a measure of the threat posed by Huntly after 1501 that, for a while at least, these local rivals made common cause against Earl Alexander and his allies.[6] The king had other willing agents whose activities aroused resentment, such as Duncan Stewart of Appin, who seems to have become something of a favourite of James IV in the period after 1500. In a little over two years Stewart received royal grants of Duror, Glencoe and the adjoining lands of Mamore, pushing along the southern shore of Loch Linnhe into Lochaber to complement Huntly's drive from the north and east.[7] As James IV's administration identified itself completely with the interests of Huntly and Stewart in the region, Earl Alexander's enemies in Lochaber would eventually be forced to embrace a cause that struck at the very validity of royal rights. It is no surprise that the thoughts of the beleaguered Lachlan MacLean and Ewen mac Allan, Captain of Clan Cameron, turned to Lewis, where the grandson of the last Lord of the Isles resided in the care of Torquil MacLeod, another man under pressure from the rampant Earl of Huntly.

Argyll's attitude towards the development of royal policy in the areas north of the Firth of Lorn is difficult to fathom. In a strictly territorial sense this was not Argyll's war. Campbell's gaze remained firmly fixed on the Firth of Clyde and the southern Hebrides. Here, Earl Archibald continued to enjoy royal favour. On 13 September 1502, for example, the king confirmed to Earl Archibald the lands and castle of Skipness resigned by Duncan Forester of Skipness.[8] Duncan Forester's resignation may be indicative of a wider process, the steady withdrawal of the crown servants who had been given extensive but perhaps rather speculative grants of territory and office in lordships acquired by the king in the 1490s. The Firth of Clyde remained an arena where vigorous local lordship was required. Skipness Castle looked out on the north of Arran, and pillaging attacks on the island were a persistent feature in the period 1500–1503.[9] When Earl Archibald granted Skipness to his younger son Archibald in 1511, the terms of the grant suggest that the stronghold was very much viewed as an active military centre.[10]

As a member of the royal government influential in the drawing up of crown policy and as a protector of the crown's interests in the Firth of Clyde Earl Archibald might have been expected to show commitment to, and support for, the king's methods and allies elsewhere in the Highlands. One tenurial innovation vigorously promoted by the crown as a means of encouraging commercial, financial and economic development within the kingdom was the granting out of land under feu-farm tenure.[11] It was no surprise that the master of the king's household sought to introduce feu-farm tenure to some of his highland properties after 1500. However, the great conversions of large areas of crown or kirk land to feu-farm tenure depended on an active and competitive land market, in which lesser men were willing and able to offer capital sums and increased rentals in the expectation that they would still be able to market the produce of the land at a profit. This type of tenurial, financial and commercial context simply did not exist in most of Argyll. Moreover, local conditions meant that the earl himself would have been extremely cautious about alienating ownership of land to men outwith his own direct political and social control. The Campbell use of feu-farm tenure, then, tended to be highly conservative. On the whole the beneficiaries of Campbell feu-farm charters were the earl's kinsmen or long-established landowners. The terms of the grants, moreover, make it clear that the process did not entail any fundamental change in the economic relationship between granter and grantee or any direct commercialistion of the estates granted out. In some cases feu-farm grants were made in which the economic rights of lordship (in the shape of renders of foodstuff to be given over to the earl) were highlighted at the expense of other forms of personal service, such as galley service.[12] However, it seems likely that the increased renders were absorbed and used in the traditional way, i.e. the produce was consumed by the earl and his household or redistributed to dependents, although theoretically a greater surplus may have allowed the earl more scope for commecial marketing. A striking example of the terms of one of these feu-farm grants was Earl Archibald's charter of 24 June 1502 in favour of Alexander Ciar Campbell, the Captain of Dunstaffnage. The grant gave over lands surrounding Dunstaffnage and custody of the fortress to Alexander and his heirs male, with the usual reversion in favour of the Earl's line should Alexander's heirs male fail. The charter did display a fine awareness of the economic rights attached to the lands granted away and asked for a substantial annual render of 32 bolls of oatmeal and 2 bolls of barley. In addition Alexander was given one third of the fishings of 'KenLochfechyne' (i.e. the head of Loch Feochan) with the stipulation that he and his heirs should provide a third of the nets and a third of a fishing boat ('le cobill'). The rest of the charter, however, dealt with the duties of Alexander and his heirs as custodians of Earl Archibald's mighty castle of Dunstaffnage. Here the difficulties of treating estates in Lorn as simple units of economic resource were made more apparent. Alexander was always to have in that place six good men with bows and weapons for war and the keeping of the castle as well as a door ward and watchman, in total eight people in times of peace. If it happened that war existed in those parts through which the country was wasted, then Earl Archibald and his heirs would meet half the expenses required to maintain the defence of the castle. In addition Alexander and his heirs would find annually for the earl and his heirs fuel for the chamber, kitchen, bakehouse and 'le brouhous' and the first night for the 'court' whenever the Earl or his heirs visited Dunstaffnage.[13] On the whole, the terms of the Dunstaffnage grant and others seem to show both the willingness of Earl Archibald to embrace the tenurial forms associated with the commercial development of royal and monastic estates elsewhere in the kingdom, and the difficulties of adapting 'feu-farm' tenure in any meaningful way to the social and economic conditions in his Highland lordships.

If Earl Archibald was happy with the ideology and rhetoric surrounding royal policies in the west, in political terms Argyll had little reason to welcome the developments in and around Lochaber and little inclination to interfere in an area at the edge of Campbell interests. In many ways the promotion of Huntly and Stewart of Appin adversely affected the interests of Earl Archibald. The Stewarts of Appin nominally held their estates in Appin from Argyll and Duncan Campbell of Glenorchy. Duncan Stewart's father Dugald, and indeed Duncan himself, had occasionally witnessed Campbell charters, but the relationship between the two families was by no means straightforward. For the most part Campbell lordship seems to have lain lightly on Appin, indeed on much of Lorn, and the period after 1470 was punctuated by formal agreements in which Argyll and Glenorchy confirmed the Stewarts in their Appin lands in return for guarantees as to their behaviour.

From 1500, however, tensions between Stewart and Earl Archibald over the exact nature of the duties owed to Argyll as Lord of Lorn were exacerbated by a separate dispute over Duror and Glencoe. In January 1500 James IV gifted the lands of Duror and Glencoe to Duncan for the service of a galley of 24 oars. The grant was not heritable but for the duration of the King's will.[14] However, Duror and Glencoe had already been assigned prior to 1498 to John MacDougall of Rarey. MacDougall had been one of the men with Earl Archibald on the Anglo-Scottish border in 1497 and it was clear that Argyll was not in the least inclined to see his adherent dispossessed. On 26 November 1500 MacDougall and Earl Archibald, described as John's tenant in Duror and Glencoe, brought an action against Stewart and John of the Isles 'alias Abrochson' (i.e. MacIan of Glencoe) for troubling them in possession of Duror and Glencoe. The Lords of Council found in favour of Argyll and MacDougall and asked them to produce details of their losses at the hands of Duncan Stewart on 16 January 1501.[15] However, on 14 January 1501, two days before Argyll and MacDougall were due to appear before the Lords of Council to establish the damages owed to them, James

IV made a direct intervention in the dispute. The king issued a great seal charter confirming that the lands were to remain with Duncan for his lifetime because the assignation made to MacDougall was invalidated by the terms of the revocation of 1498.[16] The king's overturning of a decision of his own judges was one indication of his obvious partiality for Stewart of Appin, who seems to have become the crown's preferred 'man of business' in the west.[17] Earl Archibald may have been none too amused with the independent line adopted by his tenant in Appin, and in the autumn of 1501 Argyll attempted to re-impose his authority on Duncan Stewart. In August Earl Archibald issued a charter confirming Duncan Stewart in the lands of Appin with an entail in favour of his brothers Robert and Allan.[18] In the following month at Stirling, Argyll and Glenorchy concluded a wide-ranging agreement with Stewart that dealt with a number of issues. It was made plain that the dispute over Duror and Glencoe was still not closed, with the two parties agreeing to pursue their claims by law and binding themselves to accept the situation if the decision went against them.[19] Despite the agreement and Stewart's position as Argyll's tenant it is difficult to agree with Gregory that the lord of Appin was a mere pawn of Argyll's ambitions in Lochaber. Indeed, Stewart seems to have taken a thoroughly independent line in the years after 1500, bolstered by his obvious personal closeness to James IV. As a family the Stewarts of Appin were more than capable of holding their own ground in the rough and tumble of local feud and raid. Duncan's father seems to have been responsible for the death of Donald Angusson, the leader of the Lochaber MacDonalds, c.1498. That Duncan himself was a significant and aggressive military figure in the maritime warfare of the west is suggested by the sequence of royal gifts giving Duncan land in return for galley service. We can at least be certain that Duncan maintained a large 32–oared galley at Appin.[20]

Throughout 1503 Earl Archibald must have been aware of the growing likelihood of a co-ordinated response to the activities of Huntly, Clan Chattan and Stewart of Appin. Late in the year the men gathered around Donald Dubh made their move. At Christmas 1503 Huntly's lordship of Badenoch was subject to a great hership (a deliberately destructive raid) by forces led by Lachlan MacLean of Duart, Donald his son, Ewen mac Allan of Clan Cameron and Ewen's brother John.[21] Earl Alexander and his Clan Chattan adherents did not suffer alone, for at some point Duncan Stewart's lands in Appin and Duror were ravaged by the MacLeans of Duart, Coll and MacQuarrie of Ulva.[22]

The devastation of Badenoch, Appin and Duror, like the assault on Sir Robert Menzies at Weem in September/October 1502, represented a direct challenge to the crown's financial and judicial programmes. That James IV regarded the situation as approaching a crisis was shown by his decision to call a parliament in March 1504 after an eight-year period in which the government of the kingdom had been conducted with no recourse to large formal assemblies of the king's subjects.[23] The immediate business of the parliament was to condemn those guilty of the attacks on Badenoch and Appin and to organise a military response for the summer of 1504.[24] However, the parliamentary legislation also revealed wider and longer-term plans to revamp the judicial/military structures through which the crown sought to govern in the Isles. It was clear that Earl Archibald was expected to play a prominent part both in the immediate suppression of the rebellion and the long-term 'pacification' of the Isles. However, the surviving records of the parliament also seem to include a copy of the draft legislation presented by the preparatory committee (the Lords of the Articles) to the full assembly.[25] The differences between the early draft and the final statutes reveal some level of disquiet over the role of Earl Archibald as the chief agent of royal justice in Lorn and Argyll. It is certain that Argyll's heritable jursidictions in Lorn and Argyll were the subject of heated debate.

The draft legislation began with a clarification of judicial responsibilties in the areas most affected by the Donald Dubh rebellion. The lands of Duror and Glencoe were to answer at the justice ayre of Perth, Mamore and Lochaber at Inverness. Thereafter it was decreed that the justice ayre of Argyll should be held in Perth 'when the king's grace please' where both 'heland' men and 'lawland' men might come and ask for justice. The implication here, of course, was that an ayre held in Argyll itself made it very difficult for Lowland men to attend and obtain redress. There then followed a long explanation of the arrangements surrounding the Argyll justiciary that has subsequently been scored through. The deleted section makes it clear that the Earl of Argyll had countered the proposed shift of the Argyll justiciary to Perth by asserting that he held the offices of justiciar and sheriff in Lorn and Argyll in heritage and that his justice ayre should be held within Argyll. Moreover, it was noted that Argyll was already bound for the inhabitants of Argyll and Lorn and, as far as the lords of the Articles could ascertain, he had, since then, competently 'reulit' the region. The Lords of the Articles therefore thought it 'expedient' that as long as Argyll 'keeps good rule and does justice' he should be allowed to hold his ayres within the bounds of Argyll and Lorn. However, should the king be securely informed that Argyll and Lorn 'brekis be vak and falt of justice through him [Argyll], it shall be lefull to his hienes to command and charge said Earl to cry his said justice ayres be holden in Perth so that the King and the Lords of Council may consider and see that justice be ministered'. The arrangement was to last only for the king's lifetime.[26] In the end the long elaboration of possible circumstances in which Argyll's justice ayre might be held under royal supervision at Perth was deleted. What remained in the final legislation was the bald statement that the justice ayre of Argyll should sit at Perth whenever the king required so that both Highlanders and Lowland men might receive justice.

There are some problems in interpreting the significance of the long discussion of the Argyll justice ayre and its subsequent deletion. The terms of the discussion seem to indicate that one body of opinion wanted direct royal supervision of Argyll's judicial activities. The concern clearly went beyond the feeling that a justice ayre held in Argyll itself was inconvenient for 'Lowland' men, for the deleted statute eventually linked any transfer to Perth to the proven failure of the Earl's 'rule' in Argyll and Lorn. The widespread unrest in the Highlands over the winter of 1503–4 partly explains the disquiet over the fate of 'Lowland men' with cases to bring against the inhabitants of Argyll and Lorn. That the activities of men based in Lorn could affect landowners far to the east was obvious in a letter written by James IV to Argyll, Campbell of Glenorchy and Stewart of Fortingall in response to a complaint brought before the king by Sir Robert Menzies in February 1495. The letter narrated that while Robert Menzies 'our lovit servitor' had been in Glen Lyon on his lawful business the previous May, a man named Alexander Menzies came to Robert's estates at Weem, slew 30 cattle and wounded some of Robert's servants. Alexander Menzies and his accomplices were described as the king's rebels and at his horn for other slaughters, and as residing in Lorne for the previous two to three years, where they were supported by 'diverse hieland men'.[27] At any rate Argyll had responded to the challenge to his judicial privileges in 1503 by playing a powerful card; the move to Perth would represent an intolerable and illegal infringement of the established rights of a hereditary office-holder. The argument against arbitrary interference in aristocratic rights presumably won the concession that if the king did require the justice-ayre to move to Perth, the arrangement should last only for James' lifetime. Overall it is difficult to escape the impression that Earl Archibald's judicial rights were under pressure for precisely the same reason as that which caused James IV to suspend the Earl of Atholl's justiciar court after the attack on Robert Menzies in 1502.[28] Argyll, like Atholl, may have been suspected of sympathising, if not actually colluding, with men who had launched full-scale assaults on the crown's agents, and without direct supervision Earl Archibald could not be relied on to pursue or punish the perpetrators with the necessary vigour. The striking out of the various safeguards for Argyll's position might reflect the amendment of the solution proposed by the Lords of the Articles in the face of wider parliamentary criticism of the exemptions proposed for Earl Archibald. There were other hints of a strained relationship between the crown and senior figures within Clan Campbell in 1504 with the issuing of a summons of treason against Duncan Campbell of Glenorchy on 8 June.[29] The exact nature of Glenorchy's 'treason' is unclear; it may have been related in some way to the problems experienced by the crown in implementing its financial and judicial programme in Highland Perthshire.[30] Alternatively the challenge to Argyll's hereditary jurisdictions may have been inspired by the general concern for the primacy and effective implementation of the King's Law throughout the realm evidenced in the rest of the parliamentary legislation, rather than a particular distrust of Earl Archibald.[31]

It is clear that despite the dispute over Argyll's exercise of justice in Lorn and Argyll, Earl Archibald remained an essential part of the king's plans for the military subjugation of the Hebridean rebels in the summer of 1504. At the conclusion of the parliament on 19 March 1504 it was specifically noted that James was to consult with Argyll over the strengthening and garrisoning of the castles of Dunaverty and Loch Kilkerran in Kintyre. On the same day it was suggested that royal letters should be sent to MacIan of Ardnamurchan, MacLean of Lochbuie, MacLeod of Dunvegan, Ranald mac Allan (of Clanranald), MacNeill of Barra, MacKinnon, MacQuarrie and Torquil MacLeod informing these men of the forfeiture of MacLean of Duart and Ewen mac Allan. These Hebridean chiefs, who were presumably regarded at this stage as potential allies of the crown, were encouraged to attack Duart and the Clan Cameron with the promise that if they captured one of the chief 'rebels' they would receive half their lands. If, however, they failed to take action against MacLean and Ewen mac Allan, then they would be treated as rebels and punished accordingly 'be oure soverane lord at his cuming'.[32] Argyll was to be responsible for delivering this ultimatum to MacIan and MacLean of Lochbuie. The recipients of the king's letters could hardly be in doubt about the seriousness of the situation they faced, for by mid-April 1504 a great royal war fleet well supplied with artillery had gathered at Dumbarton.[33] Around 20 April the fleet sailed, rounding the Mull of Kintyre and labouring north to strike MacLean of Duart's remote fortress of Cairn-na-Burgh on the Treshnish Isles. The castle seems to have been taken by the time the royal fleet returned to Dumbarton in June, and Macdougall may well be right in suggesting that the fall of the fortress encouraged the submission of Lachlan MacLean of Duart.[34] However, few of MacLean's Hebridean neighbours seem to have aided the royal assault, for by 4 June MacLean of Lochbuie, MacQuarrie of Ulva and MacNeill of Barra (all encouraged to attack Duart by the terms of the royal letters of April) had also been summoned for treason.[35] The King's agents did not have it all their own way in the summer and autumn of 1504. In August or September of that year William Munro of Foulis, one of the men assigned by the crown to help Huntly set the lands of Lochaber and the estates of Torquil MacLeod in 1501, was killed in an encounter with the Camerons of Lochiel at a place called 'Achonasellache'. The name seems to indicate 'the field or settlement of the willows' and there are a number of sites bearing the name in and around modern Wester Ross and Glenelg.[36] Whether any of these was the location of Munro's death is now impossible to say.

Despite the tensions evident in the March 1504 parliament Argyll played a leading military and political role for the crown throughout the summer of 1504. By 1505 Earl Archibald was holding Cairn-na-Burgh for the king, a post he had probably assumed as soon as the castle had been captured.[37] Royal reliance on Campbell power in the region was made plain on 8 August 1504 when Earl Archibald was confirmed as royal lieutenant within the lands of Argyll, Lorn, Knapdale, Kintyre, Discher, Toyer, Glen Lyon and Balquhidder. In particular Argyll was to take action against rebels within the bounds of his lieutenancy and also 'within our Isles and utheris the north parts of our realm, commiters of herships, slaughters, depredations and burnings on our true lieges'.[38] In addition, in February 1505 James IV made Earl Archibald Justiciar, sheriff, coroner and chamberlain of Knapdale and Kintyre and captain of Tarbert Castle. With these wide-ranging jurisdictions went the lands of south half of Knapdale and the patronage of the kirk of Kilberrie all united into a free barony. All the offices and lands were to be held heritably by the earl and his successors under the Campbells' usual franchise arrangement with the crown, i.e., the earl would deliver half the profits of justice and half of the fees and casualties of the office of coroner to the king.[39]

The fate of Donald Dubh in the wake of the 1504 campaign remains elusive. It is usually assumed, perhaps correctly, that Donald was not captured during 1504 but instead escaped to the relative sanctuary of Lewis and the care of Torquil MacLeod. From then until the summer of 1506, it is argued, he was supported by a dwindling band of diehards who were protected from the full wrath of the crown and the earl of Huntly by sheer distance and inaccessibility. MacLeod was certainly forfeited in February 1506 for, amongst other things, his treasonable assistance to 'Donald yla bastard sone of. . . Angus of the Ilis . . . bastard sone of. . . Johne lord of the Ilis' and for failing to deliver Donald into royal custody despite the king's demands to that effect.[40] It is strange, however, that there is no indication of Torquil being pursued for the withholding of Donald Dubh until late in 1505, over a year after the assault on Lachlan MacLean's fortresses. Moreover, the charges relating to defiance of royal demands for Donald's surrender could easily have referred to the period prior to MacLeod's earlier forfeiture in 1501–2 when Torquil was demonstrably guilty of this offence. It must be a possibility, then, that the prosecution of February 1506 represented the revival of old charges and that Torquil might not actually have had possession of Donald Dubh at that point. MacLeod may have been targeted in 1506 simply because he was still offering fierce resistance to the Earl of Huntly's claims in areas such as Assynt and Cogeach[41]

By the close of 1505 James IV had evidently decided on a further great campaign to break MacLeod's defiance of the royal lieutenant. A parliament was summoned to meet in February 1506. One of the first pieces of parliamentary business, on 3 February, was the forfeiture of the lord of Lewis.[42] The sentence of forfeiture was followed by yet another summer expedition in the Hebrides spearheaded by Huntly but mobilising the king's own naval and artillery resources. In late June the king's guns were freighted out from Dumbarton to support Huntly's forces.[43] In July and August Earl Alexander carried the war to Torquil's own heartland. By late August the Gordon earl seems to have been campaigning on Lewis itself and by mid-September MacLeod had fled.[44] If MacLeod did indeed have custody of Donald of the Isles, then it would have been at this point that the 'heir' to the Lordship of the Isles began his long and apparently bitter captivity as a guest of the Scottish king.[45]

Shortly before the opening of Huntly's campaign Earl Archibald and other royal commissioners were in the west on an intriguing judicial/ political tour of Knapdale, Kintyre and Argyll that involved mass gatherings of Hebridean lords at Lochgilphead, Dunadd and Dunstaffnage. At each of these locations Argyll and his fellow commissioners assigned 'crown' estates and offices to loyal lords and attempted to settle feuds by forcing the protagonists to pursue their claims before royal courts.[46] The royal commission, however, had a more ambitious agenda than discharging by proxy the king's duties as overlord of the former Clan Donald lordships. The commission demanded not just political obedience, but judicial and social reform aimed at refiguring and 'taming' the fractious and rebellious society of the west. The three locations used by Argyll may hint at the appropriation of older practice, for Dunadd, Lochgilphead and Dunstaffnage were all ancient sites well placed to act as meeting points for men sailing in from the Hebrides. There is no evidence for large late medieval building complexes at either Lochgilphead or Dunadd, but both places seem to have been used for open-air public ceremonial in this period. In 1412, for example, the Lord of the Isles and the Duke of Albany concluded an agreement at Lochgilphead (Polgilb) designed to settle the animosity between the two men over the earldom of Ross.[47] Lochgilphead may have had an established role as a meeting place where political/ judicial business could be concluded as it lay on the boundary between Argyll and Knapdale. Argyll's appearance at Dunadd in 1506 is the only documentary reference to the use of the early medieval fort/inauguration site as an assembly place at a later period.[48] Dunstaffnage was thus the only location used by the commission for the proclamation of the terms of the king's imposed settlement on the west that was actually a Campbell stronghold. Even here the excellent natural harbour and Dunstaffnage's association with older Kings of Argyll and the Isles was probably a more important consideration in choice of venue.

The terms under which Earl Archibald and the rest of the commissioners granted out land and office in the west to MacIan of Ardnamurchan at Dunadd on 10 June reveal the royal government's concerns and strategy.[49] The document seems to have been drawn up in Argyll's name as the royal lieutenant in Argyll, Lorn, Kintyre, Knapdale, Morvern and Ardnamurchan 'and all pairtis of the Ilis for gude reule and governance of his [the king's] liegis'. The letter demanded that MacIan ensure that all kirk lands within the bounds of his office should be free from unjust secular exactions, and also that MacIan should hold regular bailie courts at four fixed terms in the year. At these courts inquests of the 'best and worthiest persons of the cuntre' were to give up to MacIan 'the names of all thevis, pikaris, and sornaris that oppress the cuntre and the pure commonys or that takis mete, drink or ony uthir thing without payment'. MacIan was also to hold further courts on fifteen days' notice for the 'stanching of slauchtir, sornyng, and oppression' whenever he received a particular complaint. The lord of Ardnamurchan and his bailies were to 'caus all sornaris and oppressouris of the kingis liegis within your boundis and all uthiris idill persons that wirkis nocht nor has to leve apon of thair awin to be expellit and put furth . . . of your boundis or ellis caus thame to wirk and labour for thair leving'. If such persons were found on the lands in the future, the king would 'reput and hald you and your deputis manteinaris, assistaris, and defendaris of thame and mak you be punyst thairfor'. The composition of the court was specified (judge, clerk, sergeant, suitor, dempstar and a lawful assise) and it was stipulated that all procedures should follow 'the ordour of oure soverane lordis lawis'. Finally 'na convocation [gathering] of the kingis liegis be maid bot for resisting his rebellis defence of the cuntre or to the kingis special service and nocht uthirwayis'.

It seems likely that the commission to MacIan replicated the terms under which all Hebridean lords were confirmed in the lands they held of the king as Lord of the Isles during the summer of 1506. The attempt to provide a judicial structure modelled on that of Lowland Scotland was clearly part of a sustained programme in which learned men from the Hebrides were earmarked for training in the Scots common law. On 11 April 1508 one 'Kanoch Williamson' was assigned a rental from the 'royal' lands of Terunga of Kilmartin and Terunga of 'Baronsmor' in Trotternish. The money was to support his studies 'at the schools to lere [learn]' the king's laws of Scotland and 'eftirwart to exers and use the sammyn within the bondis of the Ilis'.[50] At a wider social level the attempt to make Highland lords responsible not just for their own behaviour but also for the judicial reform of their lordships and the expulsion of a 'disruptive' element within the local population was ambitious but unrealistic. The 'problem' population was variously described as trespassers, broken men, idle men, masterful beggars or 'sorners'. The difficulty was that these pejorative terms potentially embraced a number of social groups including outright bandits, the itinerant poor, the dependent soldiery and adherents of local lords, and the minor kinsmen of chiefs who supplied the military, political and social backbone of their respective clans.[51] In short, many of the people identified as obstructing the proper exploitation of royal lordships had an accepted place, status and function within local society. The origin of the pejorative Scots term 'sorner' as a description of a class of 'idle men' who 'illegally' oppressed tenants with demands for meat and drink hints at the fundamental dilemma. Gaelic *sorthan* seems initially to have been used to denote the perfectly legal obligation of a free tenant to provide hospitality for a superior lord and/or his officers and men. There was certainly a cluster of fourteenth-century charters dealing with lands in Galloway and Carrick in which estates were to be held free of 'sorryn/ sorren' in a context that makes clear the link to hospitality and guesting.[52] By the sixteenth century in Ireland the same Gaelic noun had spawned the Anglo-Irish term 'sorren'. Shortly after the death in 1597 of MacCarthaigh Mór, 1st earl of Clancare, a description of the rights exercised by the earl outlined 'sorren' as 'a nightes meat upon any such landes as the earle of Clancarty passeth through with his force and companies'.[53] Thus, despite the condemnation of 'sorning' in the 1506 agreement with MacIan at Dunadd, the name itself suggests a practice that grew from and may still have played a role in sustaining local political and social lordship and hierarchies. A number of the poems preserved in the *Book of the Dean of Lismore* suggest that there was a large group with direct or indirect claims on the largesse of an individual lord. The position was, if not exactly a cause for concern and/or reform, at least a suitable subject for satire.[54] Nevertheless, the most obvious and direct criticism seems to have been generated by individuals or institutions with interests and ambitions beyond Argyll and the Isles. Royal bureaucrats homed in on the groups of 'idle men' sustained by sorning as a source of manpower that allowed rebellion and feud to prosper and as a parasitic presence that prevented the proper economic exploitation of the king's lands. Bishops and clergymen holding benefices in Argyll and the Isles could also complain bitterly of the unjust exactions made on their church's lands by sorners.[55] The remark-ably detailed petition of James Scrymgeour and John Scrymgeour, re-spectively the rector and lay patron of the parish kirk of Kilneuair, sent to the pope in 1501 made clear that 'sorning' was a phenomenon entrenched even in the very heart of Earl Archibald's lordship in mid-Argyll.[56] Kilneuair parish corresponded to the secular lordship of Glassary at the southern end of Loch Awe. The Scrymgeours complained that their kirk was afflicted because 'even within the limits of its parish live wild men who cannot be coerced or punished by secular judge or power'. The offenders were based at a variety of named sites that included the castle of Fincharn, 'Lochquho' (Loch Awe), and Ford. Aside from homicides, thefts, robberies and burnings the offenders were responsible for 'oppressions, vulgarly called [i.e. known in the vernacular as] *lesornyng*'. In response to the Scrymgeours' petition, the pope gave permission for the excommunication of those responsible for any similar activity after the papal command had been advertised in the parish.

The agreements imposed on west-coast and Hebridean lords by the crown commission in June 1506 and the assault on Lewis later in that summer were not the only means by which the king sought to influence the affairs of the west. A less coercive approach to the management of the aristocracy of Highland Perthshire and the Hebrides was evident in late August and early September, even as Huntly's gunners battered Torquil MacLeod's last fastness in Lewis. During these months James IV embarked on a hunting tour that took him through Lennox, Menteith, Atholl and Badenoch on his way to Inverness. James IV was no stranger to these areas, for he had covered the same ground in a number of autumn hunting tours in previous years.[57] The role of royal hunting expeditions in allowing Scottish kings to fraternise with and cultivate the loyalty of their Gaelic-speaking subjects should perhaps receive greater emphasis.[58] The men who attended the king's hunts in September 1506 included the usual suspects such as Argyll and Campbell of Glenorchy, but also a more varied cast drawn both from the local aristocracy and the Hebrides. In some cases the men socialising with the king had played prominent roles in the defiance of royal policies over the previous four years. Neil Stewart of Fortingall, ravager of the Appin of Dull and burner of Weem, provided two hunting dogs for James' entourage while on 3 September 'Maklanis clarscha' (probably the harpist or clàrsair of MacLean of Duart rather than MacLean of Lochbuie) received a payment from the king.[59] Indeed, the royal entourage seems to have been bombarded with artistic offerings from the servants of local lords. Besides MacLean's harper the first week of September saw payments to the Earl of Argyll's clàrsair, Campbell of Glenorchy's 'bard' and 'ane tale teller'.[60] The king's familiarity with the culture and language of Gaelic Scotland is evident in the fact that he himself maintained a branch of the McBhreatnaich family of hereditary harpists as entertainers around the royal court and as envoys to conduct royal business in Highland Scotland.[61] King James who, according to de Ayala, happily spoke the 'language of the savages who live in some parts of Scotland and the islands', was thus not estranged from the aristocratic elite of Gaelic society because of an unbridgeable linguistic and cultural antagonism.

From 1506 to the end of King James' reign in 1513 the situation in the west seems to have been relatively calm, with little indication of major figures continuing to offer outright and co-ordinated defiance of the king or his lieutenants. A number of Hebridean lords exhibited a new responsiveness to or awareness of royal views and policies. In 1507, for example, MacIan of Ardnamurchan referred a request from Aedh Ua Domhnaill of Tír Connail for MacIan to provide 4,000 men for Ua Domhnaill use in the north of Ireland to James IV.[62] It seems more than likely that in previous years the traffic in Hebridean manpower for summer campaigns in Ireland would not have come under the scrutiny of the Scottish king. MacIan was, in fact, adhering to the terms of the settlement he had made the previous June with Argyll and the rest of the crown's commissioners at Dunadd which had stipulated that he should make no convocation (gathering) of the king's lieges without the express consent of the monarch. Ua Domhnaill seems to have been intent on using the Scottish king's new authority in the west not only to sanction MacIan's intervention in the north of Ireland but also to deny other Irish lords similar support. Ua Domhnaill certainly asked that the Scottish king should prevent other 'Clandonnell' lords from assisting his enemies.

There were other indications of the willingness of Hebridean lords to respond to royal demands after 1506. The men most badly affected by the great raids of 1503 raised legal actions before the king's courts in Edinburgh, and men such as MacLean of Duart and Ewen mac Allan, Captain of Clan Cameron, unwilling to risk provoking further royal expeditions to the west, submitted themselves to judgement. It soon became obvious in the judicial process that Earl Archibald was to some extent representing the interests of Lachlan MacLean of Duart.[63] The royal courts may have delivered sentence but the reality of regional power in the Highlands was acknowledged in the way in which the rights established by these judgements were traded between the great regional lords with the power and influence to enforce the penalties. Thus, Huntly received an assurance from Argyll that Lachlan MacLean would assign over lands as compensation for the raid of 1503 (which he did). Earl Alexander 'bought' Argyll's co-operation by assigning over to Earl Archibald the right to pursue Huntly's claims, established before the Lords of Council, against Ewen mac Allan of Clan Cameron.[64]

Aside from championing Lachlan MacLean before the Lords of Council, Earl Archibald acted on behalf of a number of Hebridean lords as an intercessor for royal favour or forgiveness in the period after 1506.[65] For many in the west, however, the submission to 'royal' authority must have been indistinguishable from a submission to the personal lordship of Earl Archibald. Indeed, an ability to influence the king and to represent followers and adherents in the legal and social world of the royal administration may have been viewed increasingly as an essential aspect of effective lordship in the west.[66] There was thus no particular incongruity in Campbell bards proclaiming Argyll's leadership of the Scottish Gael and the earl acting as Master of the King's Household and royal lieutenant in the west. In a sense the royal offices allowed the idea of leadership and protection to be both practical and demonstrable rather than a vague rhetorical aspiration to military and social dominance.

The Campbells were also at the forefront of another process that brought important religious, social and cultural centres associated with Clan Donald lordship, such as the monastic communities at Saddell and Iona, into a closer relationship with royal authority.[67] In 1507–8 the property of the Cistercian abbey at Saddell was annexed to the bishopric of Argyll with the subsequent (unfulfilled) proposal that the abbey should replace the church on Lismore as the cathedral of the diocese.[68] The then bishop of Argyll, David Hamilton, was a prominent figure in the implementation of royal policies in the west. Similarly, the abbey of Iona was granted in commend to John Campbell, bishop of the Isles, a half-brother of Duncan Campbell of Glenorchy, on 15 June 1499.[69] The handing over of effective control of monastic houses (and their lands and revenues) to bishops was not a development confined to the Hebrides, although the process may have had a particularly severe impact on cultural activity in the west by removing resources from local control and direction.[70] By the seventeenth century Clan Donald histories linked Campbell control of Iona with the deliberate stripping away of physical icons that represented the ancient spiritual and cultural legacy of the house. In a sense this was part of a propaganda effort that sought to portray the medieval Clan Donald as guardians of the culture of the Gael, the end of the lordship allowing a wider assault on institutions dependent on Clan Donald patronage, such as Iona, that supported Gaelic scholarship and learning. Thus, in describing (and probably partly inventing) the functions of the council of the Lord of the Isles, the *Sleat History* claimed that the 'table of stone where the council sat in the Isles of

Finlaggan . . . with the stone on which Macdonald sat, were carried away by Argyle with the bells that were at Icolumkill [Iona]'.[71] The notion that the Campbells were at the forefront of a drive to suppress not just the political structures of the lordship but also the culture and scholarship previously maintained by Clan Donald patrons in great ecclesiastical centres is very deceptive. The late fifteenth century and early sixteenth century saw a general shift of control of monastic houses and their resources to bishops and/or secular figures. In that sense the suppression of Saddell and the new status of Iona as a commend were not really connected to the political collapse of the Lordship, nor were the changes specifically intended as an assault on the cultural activities pursued there. Like other commendators, Campbell and Hamilton were keen to maximise the revenues from the annexed abbeys. That there was resistance to the process is suggested by the fact that royal letters had to be issued commanding the inhabitants of the region to support the two bishops in the exploitation of their rights.[72] This was not necessarily opposition to what the bishops represented in political or cultural terms. It was, rather, the determination of the clerics and their officials to challenge the hold of local families on 'clerical' rights and property that seems to have aroused resentment. Similarly, both bishops were likely to be enthusiastic supporters of the wider crown campaign to curb 'unjust' secular exactions on church property.

Far from neglecting the centres at Iona and Saddell, both bishops harboured hopes that their new acquisitions might also become cathedral churches for their respective dioceses. John Campbell, at least, seems to have regarded his commendatorship as initiating a real relationship with Iona, for he died and was buried on the island in 1510.[73] Nor was the new bishop-abbot likely to be hostile to the great traditions of learning built up around the monastic house, for John was part of a highly literate family. By the second half of the fifteenth century Campbell lords and ladies were not simply the patrons of bardic poets trained in the classical manner, but were also capable of producing vernacular poems on their own account. The most notable practitioner was in fact Bishop John's elder half-brother, Duncan Campbell of Glenorchy, whose output included at least six poems, most with a thoroughly satirical edge.[74] If the demise of monastic centres in James IV's reign did threaten the vitality of a number of Gaelic literary genres, then the slack seems to have been taken up by Campbell lords and the clerics reliant on their patronage. By the 1520s the chronicler Hector Boece would claim that Campbell lords were supplying him with

ancient histories from Iona. Although the statement is usually regarded
with deep suspicion, a Campbell role in preserving and reworking
historical accounts derived from Iona and elsewhere would chime well
with the sixteenth-century gathering of contemporary and earlier Gaelic
poetry by James MacGregor, Dean of Lismore. As has been pointed out,
MacGregor's collection seems to reflect a geographical and social perspective rooted in areas of Campbell lordship at the time of compilation,
while the Deanery of Lismore had long been a benefice dominated by
Campbell appointees.[75] An interest in economic development and commerce, social planning and improvement, in history and vernacular
literatures, and engagement with a range of cultural and social activities
formerly dominated by a clerical or scholastic elite would, in other
contexts, have the earls of Argyll described as 'renaissance' lords. Modern
scholarship is far less inclined to see the 'renaissance' as a single coherent
movement or as representing a decisive break from the 'medieval' past.
Nevertheless, we can suggest that Campbell lordship in the opening
decade of the sixteenth century exhibited, in a Gaelic cultural context, at
least some of the features to which the term 'renaissance' has been applied
elsewhere in Scotland.

For the remainder of James IV's reign Earl Archibald maintained his
relentless attendance at the royal court and discharged a variety of judicial
and bureaucratic tasks for the king.[76] In a development typical of the
Campbells' careful preparation for the succession of lordship, Archibald's
eldest son and heir emerged as an active leader in his own right, associated
with his father in the discharging of royal business both at court and in the
west. 'Colyn maister of Ergile' was cited alongside his father for supporting the outlawed John, Master of Montgomery, in January 1506.[77] A more
typical example of Colin's relationship to the crown came in the summer
of 1512 as James IV conducted a judicial/social tour along the Ayrshire
coast. The royal expedition seems to have involved a sea trip to Ailsa Craig
(Ilsay?) and perhaps other locations in the Firth of Clyde. Some level of
military activity seems to have been anticipated, for cross bows, gunpow-
der, artillery and armour were brought to the King at Ayr for use on 'Ilsay',
the last two items in particular suggesting something rather more than a
hunting party. Moreover on 6 May messengers were sent to summon the
Master of Argyll to come with his 'army' to join his father in Ayr.[78] In the
same month the king, a noted naval enthusiast, began the construction of a
great galley at Ayr.[79] On 1 May an 'Ersche rynnar' was dispatched to the

Isle of Arran to summon a shipwright to Ayr to 'mak ane galay', and work on the vessel continued through the summer of 1512.[80] The galley was presumably primarily intended to aid the type of small-scale military activity that the king had undertaken in the Firth of Clyde during the summer of 1512. By the end of the year, however, it must have seemed increasingly likely to all James' subjects in the west that the Ayr galley would find its first serious use in a far wider conflict, for war with England now loomed.

The evolution of James' foreign policy has been covered in detail in a recent biography of the king.[81] Although the evidence is slight, it would appear that Earl Archibald was one of the 'hawks' in James' government. The English ambassador dispatched to Scotland in April 1513, Nicholas West, dean of Windsor, informed Henry VIII of numerous conversations he had had with the Scottish king over the possible effects of an outbreak of Anglo-Scottish warfare on the plans of the English monarch to invade France. West also told Henry that he had clashed with the earl of Argyll when he had rehearsed the same arguments in the King's Council.[82] At the least, then, Argyll seems to have been speaking with the same voice as the king prior to the outbreak of war. Moreover, Earl Archibald appears to have been the driving force behind plans to include an assault on English interests in the north of Ireland in the military planning for 1513. It was certainly Argyll who played host to Aedh Ua Domhnaill of Tír Connail when the Ulster lord travelled to Scotland in the early summer of 1513 to renew his family's alliance with James IV.[83] The Ua Domhnaill had been in communication with the Scottish crown for at least two decades and James IV, at least, seems to have viewed the relationship as one in which the lords of Tír Connail were effectively his liegemen.[84] A formal agreement between Ua Domhnaill and James was drawn up on 25 June by which James promised to support Aedh with ships and men when they were required.[85] At the least the agreement cleared the way for Va Domhnaill to recruit Hebridean and west-coast forces for his wars in Ireland, as he had already requested in 1507. There may, however, have been a more specific strategic objective underlying the co-operation between Ua Domhnaill and his Scottish allies. It seems evident that the Scots expected Ua Domhnaill to be involved in a major military operation during the summer of 1513, for James IV provided the lord of Tír Connail with the artillery and workmen required to mount a sustained assault on a major stronghold.[86] One possibility is that the intended target was Carrickfergus Castle, a fortress critical for English naval operations in the Irish Sea. As part of their military alliance with Louis XII the Scots were to send a naval force to join with a French fleet in attacking the English ships supporting and supplying Henry VIII's army in France. The Scots ships sailed on 25 July and rounded the Pentland Firth before coming down the west coast in search of an uncontested passage to the rendezvous with the French fleet in Normandy.[87] A well-informed and near-contemporary Italian poem on the Flodden campaign included the observation that the Scottish fleet 'plundered the shores of Ireland'.[88] The sixteenth-century Scottish chronicler Robert Lindsay of Pitscottie asserted that on its way south the Scottish fleet under the command of James Hamilton, earl of Arran, a figure with more than a passing personal interest in the security of the North Channel, swept into Belfast Lough and burnt Carrickfergus.[89] The assault on the Ulster burgh was also the subject of a long digression in Sir David Lindsay of the Mount's 'Squyer Meldrum'. The hero of the poem reputedly displayed his chivalric qualities by defending the life and honour of a young woman of the burgh from fellow Scots during the attack.[90] The fact that Ua Domhnaill was supplied with Scottish artillery and quarriers to undermine walls early in July may have been an indication that a co-ordinated land and sea assault on the Ulster castle and burgh was being prepared. However, an equally plausible target for Ua Domhnaill was Sligo on the west coast of Ireland. Ua Domhnaill had, in fact, spent the early months of 1513 imposing an unsuccessful siege on Sligo and travelled to Scotland almost as soon as he had admitted defeat in his attempts to take the castle and town.[91] When Ua Domhnaill requested Scottish guns and quarriers in the summer of 1513, the defences that had defied him in the preceeding months may have been uppermost in his thoughts. It is interesting to note that three years later, in 1516, Ua Domhnaill *did* capture the burgh and castle of Sligo with the aid of artillery pieces supplied by the then Scottish regent.[92]

There are no indications that the ordnance supplied by James IV was successfully deployed by Ua Domhnaill either at Carrickfergus or Sligo in July/August 1513, but it seems likely, contrary to the assertion of the editor of the Treasurer's Accounts, that the guns did leave Scotland.[93] Circumstances may have prevented Ua Domhnaill making use of the gift, but James IV and his principal advisors were unlikely to make a mess of the timetabling of the transport of men and artillery given their extensive experience of mounting very similar amphibious operations in the Hebrides. There is also little doubt that the great Scottish fleet moving down through the Hebrides had been instructed to strike at targets in Ireland. Pitscottie's account of Arran's assault on Carrickfergus managed to imply that the earl's actions countermanded James IV's orders, but this seems unlikely. Indeed, it may be that the Scottish king was originally contemplating a far more ambitious Irish campaign. Certainly the Irish annalists claimed that during his visit to Scotland in 1513 Ua Domhnaill had 'changed the king of Scotland's intent as to going to Ireland'.[94] The meaning of this statement is not immediately obvious, but it is just possible that the ever-ambitious James had originally intended to take a personal role in a more extensive and sustained Scottish campaign in Ulster and the north of Ireland. As it was, the assault on Carrickfergus (and Sligo?) and the plundering of the 'shores of Ireland' seem to have left no impression on Irish annalists.

Aside from any role in promoting James IV's interest in the fortunes of Ua Domhnaill, the Campbell earl was obviously the major figure in the general mobilisation of the military resources of Argyll and the west in the service of James IV. On 24 July 1513 royal messengers were sent to Bute and Argyll summoning the inhabitants to the hosting of the royal army at Ellem in Berwickshire.[95] There is no record of a formal summons to the inhabitants of the Isles but there can be little doubt that there was a significant contingent from the Hebrides in the king's final muster. The royal expectation of military service from the region was made plain in the summer of 1512 when letters of 'wappingshawings' were sent to the Isles.[96] There is perhaps a general tendency to downplay or ignore the contribution of Gaelic-speaking areas of the kingdom to royal armies in the medieval period. It has been assumed that Highland and Hebridean magnates, even if loyal to the crown, faced more severe logisitical problems in reaching muster points on the Anglo-Scottish border than their Lowland counterparts. Geographical remoteness, let alone political and cultural estrangement, would seem to have placed limits on the participation of lords from the west in Scottish hosts. However, for the men of Argyll, Cowal, Kintyre, Knapdale and the islands of the Firth of Clyde, the Clyde itself could function as a great maritime routeway into the south of Scotland. When James II made use of a force drawn from the 'Irishry' to attack Douglasdale and Douglas interests in the south of the kingdom in 1455, he met his Highland allies at Glasgow. The 'Irishry' had presumably arrived at the burgh aboard galleys, and within days the Highland forces

were encamped in the Forest of Ettrick.[97] A similar mobilisation of
Campbell forces through the Clyde was organised by a later earl of Argyll
in 1547, when it was noted that some 4,000 men under the command of the
earl and a Hebridean lord had successfully landed 'a little fra' Glasgow and
were 'campand' while waiting for the arrival of 2,000 more troops.[98]

The manpower of the lordships around the Firth of Clyde might thus
have been more easily mobilised for service on the Anglo-Scottish border
than, say, contingents from Aberdeenshire and Banffshire, and it is more
than likely that when James IV rode to war in August 1513 the Master of
his Household brought to the field a sizeable array from Argyll. Along
with Earl Archibald came the head of the second most powerful Campbell
family, Duncan Campbell of Glenorchy, leading the levies of broad
Breadalbane. Amongst the west-coast lords who took part in James' final
military adventure were John MacIan of Ardnamurchan, the king's red-
handed enforcer in the Hebrides, and Lachlan MacLean of Duart, who
had carried steel and fire into the lordship of Badenoch in 1503.[99]

The chief target of James' host and large artillery train was the great castle
of Norham on the Tweed. In a blitzkrieg campaign the Scots stormed
Norham on 28 or 29 August and captured the smaller fortresses of Etal and
Ford shortly thereafter. The English king's northern lieutenant, Thomas
Howard, earl of Surrey, hurried north from his base at Pontefract to confront
James' force. The Scottish king was in no mood to slink north and abandon
the gains he had made. Over the course of his reign James had displayed a real
appetite for the organisation and culture of war and conflict; the army he
commanded was large and well-equipped; if Surrey's approaching host could
be shattered, Henry VIII would have no alternative but to abandon his
French adventures. Victory on the barren hills of Northumberland would
confirm James' status as a figure of consequence and esteem in the diplomacy
of western European rulers; to await Surrey's arrival was a risk, but a
calculated risk, and the potential rewards were great.[100]

By the afternoon of Friday 9 September James IV looked down from the
heights of Branxton Hill on Surrey's army. A number of contemporary or
near-contemporary accounts of the ensuing battle survive, although several
episodes and the disposition of various elements in the two forces remain
uncertain. Most modern interpretations of the conflicting evidence suggest
that Earl Archibald and Argyll's brother-in-law Matthew, earl of Lennox,
commanded a battalion on the far right of the Scottish battlefront.[101] It
seems likely that Argyll's force included men from his own earldom and

perhaps the contingents led by MacIan and MacLean. If King James glanced across to the right flank before starting down Branxton Hill, the sight of the Campbell banners may have offered some reassurance. The master of the king's household, the royal lieutenant of Argyll and the Isles, would not lightly abandon his sovereign. However, the lairds of Clan Campbell and the men of the west ranged behind Earl Archibald may have seen a rather different figure at their head. MacCailein Mór, chief of Clan Campbell, the Head of the Gael, had called his men and friends to war and they had answered; from rocky Ardnamurchan and Cowal, the gentle glens of mid-Argyll, from the long shores of Loch Awe and the tumbled hills of Lorn. That so many took the red road to spill their blood on a bleak Northumbrian hillside stands as a sombre testament to the role and effectiveness of Campbell lordship in tying large sections of Gaelic society to the fortunes of Scottish kingship. As the Scots advanced down Branxton Hill it soon became clear that there would be little for the Campbell bards to celebrate and plenty to lament. The King's own battle was fought to a standstill and then brought to ruin by Surrey's men; fighting desperately, the Scottish king went down under the English halberds. On the left of the Scottish host Alexander, earl of Huntly, surrounded by the veterans of his long campaigns in Lochaber and Lewis, smashed through the Cheshire division commanded by Surrey's brother Edward Howard. Surveying the wreck of the rest of James IV's army, Huntly and his co-commander Alexander, Lord Hume, turned their faces to the border and began the long run for home. There was to be no such escape for Argyll and Lennox, who seem to have been outflanked by Sir Edward Stanley and his Lancashire levies and driven across the hill through the shambles of James IV's already defeated battle; somewhere in the grim and bloody mess Earl Archibald and his poet-cousin Duncan of Glenorchy fell.[102] If MacIan and MacLean were in Argyll's command, then the defeat was obviously not total, for the two west-coast lords somehow managed to carve their way off the field despite their appearance in the lists of Scottish dead included in the exultant English reports on the battle. An evocative and no doubt embellished account of MacLean's heroic and unlikely escape found its way to Robert Lindsay of Pitscottie, who gleefully seized on the incident to relieve the overall gloom of his description of Flodden.[103]

Earl Archibald and Duncan of Glenorchy took a different road home to the west. At some point the bodies of the two great men of Clan Campbell were also returned to the Scots and taken to lie at rest in the family mausoleum on the shores of the Holy Loch.[104] For all the emphasis on the life of Highland lords as a weary round of strife and war, few of Earl Archibald's ancestors had lost their lives in battle. Indeed, in the direct line of Campbell chiefs the only man to share Archibald's dubious distinction was Colin Mór, who had died at the Red Ford on the boundary between Loch Awe and Lorn over two centuries before Flodden. There was, in truth, little else to link the two men, for the circumstances of their deaths were very different and serve to illustrate the great transformation of Campbell lordship in the intervening period. Colin was the leader of a locally powerful kindred, eliminated when he had the temerity to mount a challenge to the regional supremacy of the MacDougall lords of Argyll. In the years after Colin's death it was not entirely obvious that the family's influence and coherence would survive the stress of dynastic infighting and the civil wars of the early fourteenth century. Earl Archibald, in contrast, died as one of the most prominent lords in the Gaelic world and as a figure of national importance within the Scottish realm. The great regional lordship that he bequeathed to his son played too important a role in the political structure of the kingdom, carried too great a weight of jurisidictional, economic and social power, represented too many entrenched interests, to be destroyed by the passing of one man. The final comment on the status of Earl Archibald and the family he headed might be left to the annalists of Gaelic Ireland as they reported on news of the Scottish disaster at Flodden. The deaths of only three men were thought worthy of note: James IV, for the demise of a king was of import to all; the archbishop of St Andrews, for the slaying of a primate in battle was a shock and a sensation; and MacCailein Mór, for the Campbell earl was a great lord of the Gael.[105]

Notes

1. For an example, see the death of John Dunbar of Mochrum at the hands of the Gordons of Lochinver after he obtained (in September 1502) the custody of Threave Castle and the Stewardship of Kirkcudbright previously held by the Gordons. *RSS*, i, no.873. Dunbar was dead by 15 May 1503. *ER*, xii, 656. For further details of the feud, see *RSS*, i, nos.1321, 1723, 2626.
2. *RSS*, i, no.792. Torquil was summoned to show his rights to the holdings of Lewis, Vaternish in Skye, Assynt and Coigach and the title by which he claimed to hold them of the king. In August 1502 the Lords of Council decided possession of these lands should stay with the King until Torquil produced title to recover them. NAS CS5/xi/f.143/4.
3. See below, pp. 323–325 for an extended discussion.

4. *ADC*, ii, 488–9.
5. In February 1500 the MacLeans of Lochbuie, Duart and Coll received remissions for their 'hership' of Ewan mac Allan. *RSS*, i, nos.486–7.
6. The Camerons had a long-running dispute with the Clan Chattan over the lands of Glenloy and Loch Arkaig and the office of Steward of Badenoch. CS5/xvii, f.76r.
7. *RSS*, i, no.448 20 January 1500. James IV grant to Duncan Stewart of lands of Duror and Glencoe Duncan doing service owed and wont and to have a galley with 24 oars to do the king's service in peace and war; *Ibid.*, no.844; *RMS*, ii, no.2565.
8. *RMS*, ii, no.2669. This appears to have been arranged in exchange for lands held by Earl Archibald in Menteith. *RMS*, ii, no.2670.
9. *ER*, xii, 247–8.
10. *RMS*, ii, no.3622.
11. R.G. Nicholson, 'Feudal Developments in Late Medieval Scotland', *Juridical Review* (1973), 1–21, at 3–8; *APS*, ii, 244.
12. GD 112/ 2/8/106. A feu-farm grant of Balygrundle in Lismore by Duncan Campbell of Glenorchy which concentrated on the rendering of cereal crops (May 1507); GD 112/ 18/8/1502 (Glenorchy) Earl Archibald feu charter to Duncan Campbell of Glenorchy of the 4merkland of Inverneill in Knapdale. AT, 9/9/1501 (Strathfillan) charter of confirmation Earl Archibald to Gillemory McFederane of land of Sonachan in feu-farm with the office of 'Ferrier' and Portarship as predecessors had held them, in the lordship of Loch Awe.
13. AT, at date. Substantial foodstuff renders were also a feature of the (non feu-farm) grant made by Earl Archibald of Skipness Castle in favour of his younger son in 1511. *RMS*, ii, no.3622.
14. *RSS*, i, no.448.
15. *ADC*, ii, 447.
16. *RMS*, ii, no.2565.
17. *TA*, ii, 138, 371, 390, 417, 149, 348, 461, 474, 306, 353, 355, 377, 364.
18. AT 4/8/1501. The charter was issued at Edinburgh.
19. AT 24/9/1501.
20. For the death of Donald Angusson, see Gregory, *History*, 108; for the 32-oared galley CS5/xx/f. 189r. Later in the reign James IV would confirm Duncan Stewart of Appin in liferent in the lands of Inverlochy, Terelondy, Drummiffoure and Auchintoir in the Lordship of Lochaber, for good service and the service of a galley of 36 oars. *RMS*, ii, no.3753.
21. *APS*, ii, 263 for date. The direct involvement of Torquil MacLeod of Lewis is asserted in charges laid against MacLeod in 1505, although interestingly this charge was not noted as an explanation of his formal forfeiture. CS5/ xvii, f.77/8. Action pursued by MacIntosh of Dunachton against Ewen mac Allan for spoliation from William from his lands in the Lordship of Badenoch of 600 ky (cattle), 600 sheep, 60 horses, 400 bolls of oats and 200 bolls bere. 16/2/1507–8 CS5/xix/f.174r/v. Ewen mac Allan and John mac Allan his brother and 92 others were decerned to pay Archibald, earl of Argyll, as assignee to Alexander, Earl of Huntly, and Gillespy MacWiliam goods spoiled from them by John and Ewen from the Brae of Badenoch, at the 'time of the hership of the same'. 14/2/1507–8 CS5/xix/f166r/v. Archibald earl of Argyll granted to William Scot of Balwearie as procurator to Alexander, earl of Huntly, that William had presented a letter

of assignation of said Earl of Huntly and his tenants of Badenoch for the goods spoiled and destroyed by Lachlan Maclean of Duart and his accomplices by the which there is a decreet given for Argyll against Ewen and John mac Allan and ohers at the spoliation and hership.

22. CS5/xx/f.189r-v. 9 May 1509. Summons by Duncan Stewart of Appin and his tenants of Duror and Appin against Lachlan MacLean of Duart, MacLean of Coll and MacQuarrie of Ulva for damages for cows, horses and the taking from Appin of a galley of 32 oars.

23. Macdougall, *James IV*, Ch. 7.

24. On 13 March it was ordained that the earl of Huntly should besiege the castles of Strome and Eilean Donan with the King providing a ship and artillery for the siege. On the following day it was confirmed that John MacLean of Lochbuie, Lachlan MacLean of Duart, and Ewen mac Allan had been summoned for treason. *APS*, ii, 240–1.

25. For a discussion of the significance of these variant versions, see R. Tanner, 'The Lords of the Articles before 1540: A Reassessment', *SHR*, 79 (2000), 189–212, at 206–8.

26. NAS PA2/7 f 4r-v.

27. NAS John MacGregor Collection GD 50/186/1/14. It was presumably this type of activity, which involved the perpetrators travelling through several jurisdictions (with or without the connivance of the local office-holders) that encouraged the development of the system of regional bonds through which lords were made liable for the behaviour of the men inhabiting their own lordship.

28. Boardman, 'Feud', 392.

29. *APS*, ii, 255.

30. Glenorchy may have been liable for prosecution for his failure to implement the terms of the general bond he had made to the Crown for the behaviour of his tenants. Certainly in 1503 he had tried to evade the implications of the bond on the eve of a royal justice ayre in Perth. Alternatively, Glenorchy could have been summoned because of his failure to pay the increased sums due for the feu-farm barony of Glen Lyon. *ER*, xii, 299–300. Cf. *RMS*, ii, no.2664.

31. *APS*, ii, 249–254.

32. *APS*, ii, 248.

33. Macdougall, *James IV*, 185. *APS*, ii, 248 for the gathering of ships and artillery pieces.

34. Although it was not until 31 May 1505 that James IV issued a formal respite to Lachlan MacLean of Duart 'suisque parentoribus, for art and part . . . bastardo filio Angusii Ylis, in convocatione ligeorum'. The respite was to last for 19 years provided Lachlan discharged the obligations he had made to the king. *RSS*, i, no.1083.

35. *APS*, ii, 255.

36. My thanks to Dr Simon Taylor for the identification of the placename elements and information on the distribution of the name in the present day. R.W. Munro, *The Munro Tree (1734)* (Edinburgh, 1978), 13–4. The traditional Munro genealogy gives the year of William's death as 1505 at 'Achnaselach' and identifies his killer as 'Locheal'. However, the sixteenth-century Calendar of Fearn describes the death of one Hugh Ross 'qui occisus fuit apud Achonasellache 1504'. The editor of the Calendar points out that a Hugh Ross is to be

found acting as a procurator for William Munro in November 1503 and it seems probable that this was the man killed alongside William. The Calendar seems to record Hugh's death under two different dates in 1504, one in August and the other on 19 September. Since William Munro was alive on 26 July 1504 and dead by 16 July 1505, if the dating to August/September is secure, then William and Hugh must have been killed in the autumn of 1504. *The Calendar of Fearn : text and additions, 1471–1667* (SHS, 1992), 108; *Calendar of writs of Munro of Foulis, 1299–1823* (SRS, 1940), no.34; *ER*, xii, 246, 308.

37. *ER*, xiii, 224.
38. GD 112/1/32.
39. AT, at date. For the accounts rendered by Argyll as royal chamberlain for Kintyre, see *ER*, xii, 352, 576, xiii, 221, 319.
40. *APS*, ii, 263–4.
41. In September 1507 James IV issued a letter to the Earl of Huntly assigning to him lands that had been given to Margaret, sister of Alexander of the Isles of Lochalsh. Margaret had lost the King's favour because she had since subjected herself, lands and goods to 'Donald Makcarle Maklauchlane Doue' who had assisted Torquil MacLeod of Lewis, passing with him on raids and spoliations of the King's true lieges. *RSS*, i, no.1532.
42. *APS*, ii, 263–4. Macleod had been summoned for a variety of offences including the hership of Badenoch. Intriguingly, however, he was convicted only on the basis of his support for Donald Dubh and for handing him over to Lachlan MacLean of Duart. As we have seen above, the government appealed to MacLeod in March 1504 to help enforce the forfeitures imposed on MacLean of Duart and Ewnen mac Allan. It would seem at that stage that the Lord of Lewis was not thought to have been directly involved in the hership of Badenoch. A clause in the judgement of 1506 convicting Torquil of appearing in manner of war in action against the King's lieges was, in fact, subsequently struck through. It thus appears that Torquil was not a leading light in the violence of 1503.
43. *TA*, iii, 200.
44. MacLeod's fate remains mysterious. If a letter transcribed in the Argyll Transcripts is dated accurately, then as late as 27 July 1508 Catriona Campbell, lady of Lewis, was using the seal of her husband, 'ane goud and honourable man torquell mc cloyd of lous', to attest an agreement with her brother Earl Archibald. AT, at date.
45. Macdougall, *James IV*, 189. Donald's career is particularly difficult to trace because there seem to have been a number of men around the royal court bearing the name 'Donald of the Isles'. In March 1508, for example, a payment was made to a 'Donald of the Ilis', about to pass in the Isles. *TA*, iv, 105. It was unlikely, but not impossible, that this was Donald Dubh, who had so recently been a figurehead for revolt in the Isles. The individual concerned may have been Donald Gallda of Lochalsh. If the 1508 reference was to Donald Dubh, or indeed if he was the Donald of the Isles' 'hench boy' who appeared in the records of James IV's household in 1511–13, then the great lament of 1544 about the conditions in which he was kept by Scottish kings would seem to be thoroughly overdrawn. Other Clan Donald pensioners at the royal court in 1511 included Margaret of the Isles (*TA*, iv, 229–230), and the King's henchmen Ranald of the

Isles, and Donald of the Isles (*ibid.*, 238–9). In, April 1513 a payment was made to Donald of the Isles the 'Kingis hensboy'(*TA*, iv, 443).

46. *ER*, xii, 709–710. At Dunadd on 10 June and in the presence of the king's commissioners, (David, bishop of Argyll, John, Bishop of the Isles, Earl Archibald, Henry Abbot of Jedworth, James Redheuch, Duncan Campbell of Glenorchy, John Stirling and Duncan Forester) MacIan assured Lachlan MacLean of Duart that he would take no action against him before 1 May following. The same promise was extended to John MacLean of Lochbuie, his kin and friends. The penalty for any infraction of the promise involved the payment of 3,000 merks to the King, 1,000 merks to the kirk of the Isles, and 1,000 merks to party sustaining damage. MacIan and John MacLean promised to appear before the King and his Council on 15 October next, as they were lawfully summoned, to pursue claims actions and injuries in form of law and underly sentence and decreet of law and justice. In particular they were to bring all charters they intended to use to pursue claims against Lachlan MacLean in relation to the occupation of 'royal' lands within the bounds of the Isles. Lachlan MacLean was likewise bound to keep others harmless and to appear on 15 October. The drive to bring these disputes before the King's courts met with some success, for the MacLeans of Duart and Lochbuie brought their dispute over the lands and bailiary of Morvern to the Lords of Council in Edinburgh. CS5/xix/f.221v.

47. *Chron.Bower* (Watt), viii, 76–7.

48. A. Lane, *Dunadd : an early Dalriadic capital* (Oxford, 2000).

49. *ER*, xii, 703–4.

50. *RSS*, i, no.1654.

51. See *An lasair: anthology of* 18th century Scottish Gaelic verse, ed. R. Black, (Edinburgh, 2001), Introduction, xxix-xxxv, for a fascinating discussion of the 'benign' social role of 'sorning' and 'thigging' in a later period.

52. See *RMS*, i, no 192, preface xiii-xiv (barony of Terregles); *RSS*, vi, no.235 (lands of Sweetheart Abbey); Skene, *Celtic Scotland*, iii, 234. For a discussion of the significance of guesting in the context of medieval Irish lordships, see K. Simms, 'Guesting and feasting in Gaelic Ireland', *Journal of the Royal Society of Antiquaries of Ireland*, 108 (1978), 67–100.

53. W.F.T. Butler, *Gleanings from Irish History* (London, 1925), 20. I should like to thank Dr Katharine Simms, Department of Medieval History, Trinity College, Dublin, for this reference. Aside from the provision of foodstuffs for the lord and his men the same text describes another exaction 'sorrenmore . . . a certayne charge of meat which if the earls would not come in place to spende yt, yet there was a certayne knowne quantitie . . . paid yearelie therefore' (*Ibid.*)

54. *Book of the Dean*, I (stanzas 2–5), III, and especially IX.

55. *RSS*, i, no.1797 In January 1509 Agnes MacLean, Prioress of the Nunnery of the Virgin Mary on Iona, received a letter of protection from James IV. The King's command to protect the prioress and the nunnery and its estates from a variety of impositions and dangers, including 'le sornyng', was relayed to all King's subjects in the Isles, and especially Lachlan MacLean of Duart, Ranald son of Alan MacRuairi and John MacLean of Lochbuie.

56. *CPL*, xvii, Part 1 1495–1503, ed. Anne P. Fuller (Dublin, 1994), no.493.

57. *TA*, ii, 119–121 (1501), 388 (1503).

58. For a detailed study of the royal hunting reserves, see J.M. Gilbert, *Hunting and hunting reserves in medieval Scotland* (Edinburgh, 1979).

59. *TA*, iii, 339.

60. *TA*, iii, 339. Earlier royal visits to the hunting grounds had seen a similar mix of entertainment. In 1503 the King had also seen a performance by Argyll's Clàrsair (*TA*, ii, 388) and in 1501 a presentation by 'tua Heland bardis' (*TA*, ii, 119).

61. J.W.M. Bannerman, 'The Clàrsach and the Clàrsair', *SS*, 30 (1991), 1–17, at 6–7. *RSS*, i, no.1195.

62. *James IV Letters*, nos. 89, 104, 106. Ua Domhnaill probably wrote to James after an initial contact with MacIan himself.

63. In particular during the hearing of a dispute between the MacLeans of Duart and Lochbuie before the Lords of Council in February 1508. CS5/xix/f.214, f.221v.

64. CS5/ xvii, f.76r. Action pursued by Ferchar MacIntosh v. Ewen mac Allan for the wrongful occupation of lands of Glenloy and Loch Arkaig for space of eight years bygone (to 1497/8); CS5/ xvii, f.77/8. CS5/xix/f.174r/v. Ewen mac Allan and John mac Allan his brother were decerned to Archibald earl of Argyll as assignee to Alexander Earl of Huntly, and Gillespy MacWiliam goods spoiled from them by John and Ewen from the Brae of Badenoch during the hership of the same. 14/2/ 1507–8 CS5/xix/f166r/v. Archibald earl of Argyll granted to William Scot of Balwearie as procurator to Alexander earl of Huntly, that William had presented a letter of assignation of said Earl of Huntly and his tenants of Badenoch for the goods spoiled and destroyed by Lachlan Maclean of Duart and his accomplices by the which there is a decreet given for Argyll against Ewen and John macAllan and others at the spoliation and hership. Therefore Argyll will cause Lachlan MacLean to infeft Huntly in 25 merks of land in Lochaber according to the indenture made between the two earls, before 8 May. If this was not carried through, then Argyll would remit the privileges of the decreet given for him against Ewen and John and would allow Huntly to follow the claims against Lachlan MacLean himself. *RSS*, i, no.1790. Licence to Lachlan MacLean to sell to Alexander, earl Huntly, lands lying in Badenoch. *RSS*, i, no.1792 letters of regress.

65. January 1506. *RSS*, i, no.1208 Remission to Donald makranald vane and his tenants and household men. 'Gratis comiti de Ergile'. Argyll seems to have been particularly active on behalf of female members of Clan Donald. January 1507 *RSS*, i, no.1420. Letter to Elizabeth of the Isles, 'dochter to umquhil Johne lord Ilis' of lands in Islay for a year. 'Gratis comiti de Ergile'. In April 1508 Argyll clearly acted as a negotiator for Archibald 'Huchonson' (i.e.son of Hugh) of Sleat, outlawed for the murder of his brother. *RSS*, i, no.1649. A respite to Archibald of the Isles and 28 others because they had captured 'Auchane Duncan Dowsone, Sorle his son, and Donald Mule Makalester', his rebels and for delivering of them to his grace or his assignee. Archibald was to receive a remission for the death of his brother Donald 'Galdlauch', providing the rebels were delivered to royal custody. Again this was said to be 'Gratis comiti de Ergile'.

66. See *Book of the Dean*, xxxiii, stanza 2, where the poet asserted that 'Not good is an earl without English'. The rest of the poem offers an extended list of similar, and in most cases self-evident, observations: 'not good a harp without strings: not good is war without courage'.

67. See MacGregor, 'Church and Culture', where the role of these institutions as centres of 'cultural production' in sculpture and manuscript is discussed.

68. *James IV Letters*, no.446; Watt, *Fasti*, 38–9; Macdougall, *James IV, 216*; A.L. Brown, 'The Cistercian Abbey of Saddell, Kintyre', *Innes Review* xx, 1969, 130–7.
69. *HP*, iv, 185–7; Watt, *Fasti*, 264–5.
70. Macdougall, *James IV,* 215–7.
71. *HP*, i, 24–5.
72. In January 1506 James IV issued letters to Lachlan MacLean of Duart and a number of other island lords instructing them not to interfere with the rentals owed to John, as Bishop of the Isles and commendator of Iona. *RSS*, i, nos.1203, 2069.
73. *Taymouth Bk.*, 115.
74. John was the son of Colin of Glenorchy and a woman from the Atholl-based Clann Donnchaidh, probably the Elizabeth Robertson, wife of Colin of Glenorchy, who died on 12 August 1470. *Taymouth Bk.*, 11, 113. For discussion of Campbell of Glenorchy's output, see W.Gillies, 'Courtly and Satiric Poems in the Book of the Dean of Lismore', *SS*, 21 (1977); W.Gillies, 'The Gaelic Poems of Sir Duncan Campbell of Glenorchy (III)', *SGS*, xiv, part I (1983), 71–6.
75. MacGregor, 'Church and culture', 27–8.
76. Chalmers, 'King's Council'; *RSS*, i, nos. 1228, 1263. A particularly notable example was the earl's 46 days of continuous service on the 'westland' justice ayres between 19 October and 4 December 1512. *TA*, iv, 319.
77. *RSS*, i, no.1194. See also *RSS*, i, no.1192.
78. *TA*, iv, 345. Two days later on 8 May the royal expenses included 'In Aire, to ane schip boit to have the king to Ilsay and to convoy his folks home again'. *Ibid.*, 343 for the provision of harness, cross bows, gun powder to Aire and Ilsay. It may be entirely unconnected to the military activity of the Campbell chiefs in the Firth of Clyde, but in May 1512 a Duncan MacDougall (probably of Dunollie) was killed by 'Collinun M'Enos [Campbell] de Barbrek'. *Taymouth Bk.*, 116.
79. See Macdougall, *James IV*, Ch. 9, for an examination of James's obsession with the development of the kingdom's naval forces.
80. *TA*, iv, 344, *TA*, iv, 345. On 5 May the treasurer paid 'for a tree in Aire to the new galay'. *TA*, iv, 292 payments in July 1512 to David Lindsay for the building of a galley and £66 13s 4d to John Brown of Ayr in part-payment of the building of a new galley and to Henry Cornetoun builder of the galley for his expenses during June and July.
81. Macdougall, *James IV*, 247–276.
82. *James IV Letters*, Appendix II, 320–324, at 324.
83. *TA*, iv, 415–6, 12 July 1513 to a servant of the Earl of Argyll's for the expenses of Ua Domhnaill made the time he was in Scotland £50, 6s, 8d. *AU*, iii, 506–7. *AFM* agreed that Ua Domhnaill was in Scotland for three months, but also noted that he had been besieging Sligo until Pentecost (16 May in 1513). *AFM*, v, 1320–23. *ALC*, ii, 215; *AC*, 623 briefly note Ua Domhnaill's visit to Scotland.
84. *TA*, i, 339; *TA*, iv, 135, hawks sent by Ua Domhnaill to James IV in July 1508.
85. *RMS*, ii, no.3586.
86. *TA*, iv, 527.
87. Macdougall, *James IV*, 268.
88. *La Rotta de Scocesi* translated in W. Mackay Mackenzie, *The Secret of Flodden with 'The Rout of the Scots'* (Edinburgh, 1931), 97.
89. Robert Lindsay of Pitscottie, *The Historie and Cronicles of Scotland*, vol.1 (Edinburgh, 1899), 256.

90. *Sir David Lyndsay: Selected Poems*, ed. Janet Hadley Williams (Glasgow, 2000), 130–34.

91. *AFM*, v, 1320–23; see D.B.Quinn, '"Irish" Ireland and "English" Ireland', in *Medieval Ireland, 1169–1534*, ed. A.Cosgrove (Oxford 1987), 619–636 at 625–627, for Ua Domhnaill ambitions in and around Sligo in the fifteenth and sixteenth centuries.

92. At the request, it is said, of a French knight who befriended Ua Domhnaill while on pilgrimage to St Patrick's Purgatory. *AU*, iii, 520–23; *AFM*, v, 1334–5, *ALC*, ii, 224–5; *AC*, 631. The Scottish connection is mentioned only in *AU*.

93. *TA*, iv, lxxx,-lxxxi, 527. Ua Domhnaill seems to have left Scotland around 15 July with gunners and artillerymen prepaid for a month's work. The artillery pieces themselves had to be carted to Glasgow where they were presumably transferred to waiting ships. The empty carts used to transport the guns were then employed to bring back wine from the burgh. The next reference to the guns in Scotland is almost exactly a month later (as envisaged in the prepayment to the gunners and quarriers). On 14 August arrangements had to be made to send further carts to Glasgow to pick up the artillery. These were obviously not the carts originally used on the westward journey. Overall it seems likely that the guns arrived back in Glasgow by boat according to the intended schedule.

94. *AU*, iii, 506–7.

95. *TA*, iv, 417.

96. *TA*, iv, 350.

97. *Chron. Auchinleck* (McGladdery), 166–7; *ER*, vi, 227.

98. *Calendar of the State Papers relating to Scotland and Mary, Queen of Scots, 1547–1603*, vol. i, ed. J. Bain (Edinburgh, 1898), 9.

99. Curiously, English accounts of the battle list amongst the prominent Scottish dead 'MacKeyn' and 'MacCleen'. 'A Contemporary Account of the Battle of Flodden, 9th September 1513. From a Manuscript in the possession of David Laing, Esq., LL.D., V.P.AS.A.Scot' , *PSAS*, vii, 1867–1868, 141–152, at 149. MacIan, however, certainly survived the battle and, if Pitscottie is to be believed, MacLean also made a near-miraculous escape from the carnage. See John Finlay, *Men of Law in Pre-Reformation Scotland* (East Linton, 2000), 22 for MacIan pursuing claims relating to the loss of a box of money and jewels from the field of Northumberland in March 1514. Quite why MacIan brought the hoard to the field is unclear.

100. Macdougall, *James IV*, 272–3.

101. *La Rotta de Scocesi* for example places Argyll and Lennox together and has Argyll killed before earl Matthew. Argyll, however, then reappears to mount a last-ditch defence of the royal banners.

102. *Letters and Papers, Foreign and Domestic, of the Reign of Henry VIII*, vol. i, Part ii, no.2246 (1) 'At the same time, Lennox and Argyle joined battle with Sir Edward Stanley and were put to flight'; *Taymouth Bk.*,16, iii. Glenorchy's brother John Campbell of Lawers was also killed.

103. Pitscottie, *Historie*, i, 274–76. Pitscottie seems to have had a high estimation of the martial qualities of the Highlanders in general, attributing the Earl of Huntly's limited success to the contribution of his 'hieland men witht thair bowis and tua handit svordis'. *Ibid.*, 270–1.

104. *Taymouth Bk.*,16, iii.

105. *AU*, iii, 508–9.

Bibliography

PRIMARY SOURCES
Private Collections

Duke of Atholl's Muniments, Blair Castle, Blair Atholl
Argyll Muniments, Inveraray Castle

Bodleian Library, Oxford
MS. Fairfax 23

British Library
Harleian MSS. 4693

Edinburgh University Library
DC 763. John Law, 'De Cronicis Scotorum brevia'

Innsbruck
Landesregierungs-Archiv, Urk.7494

National Archives of Scotland
CS5 Court of Session Records

E34 Exchequer Rolls

GD 1 Spens of Lathallan Writs
GD8 Boyd Papers
GD 12 Swinton Charters
GD 20 Crawford Priory Collection
GD22 Cunninghame-Graham Muniments
GD 25 Ailsa Muniments
GD50 John MacGregor Collection
GD 79 Muniments of King James VI Hospital, Perth
GD 103 Society of Antiquaries Charters
GD112 Breadalbane Muniments
GD 116 Campbell of Duntroon
GD 124 Mar and Kellie Collection
GD 160 Drummond Writs

GD 224, Buccleuch Papers.
GD 240, Bruce and Kerr W.S
GD 247, Records of Brodies, W.S.
GD 430, Napier Charters.

PA 1 and 2 Parliamentary Acts

RH1 Register House Transcripts
RH6 Register House Charters

National Library of Scotland
Adv.MSS. 33.2.36.
Adv.Ms.35.3.7
Adv.MSS 35.4.15
Fleming of Wigtown Collection
Lamont Papers

PRINTED PRIMARY SOURCES

Accounts of the Lord High Treasurer of Scotland, edd. T. Dickson and Sir J. Balfour
    Paul (Edinburgh, 1877–1916).
The Acts of the Lords Auditors of Causes and Complaints, ed.T. Thomson (Edin-
    burgh, 1839).
The Acts of the Lords of Council in Civil Causes, edd. T. Thomson and others
    (Edinburgh, 1839 and 1918–).
The Acts of the Lords of the Isles, 1336–1493, ed. J. and R. W. Munro (SHS, 1986).
The history of Scotland/ Rerum Scoticarum historia by George Buchanan, ed. and
    trans. J. Aikman, 6 vols. (Edinburgh, 1829–30).
The Acts of the Parliaments of Scotland, edd. T. Thomson and C. Innes (Edin-
    burgh, 1814–75).
Analecta Scotica (ed.J.Maidment) (Edinburgh, 1834–7).
An lasair: anthology of 18th century Scottish Gaelic verse, ed. R. Black, (Edinburgh,
    2001).
Annála Connacht: the Annals of Connacht, AD 1224–1544, ed. A.M. Freeman
    (Dublin, 1944).
The Annals of Loch Cé, ed.W.M. Hennessy (Rolls Series, 1871).
Annals of the Kingdom of Ireland, by the Four Masters (2nd edition), ed. John
    O'Donovan, 5 vols. (Dublin, 1856).
Annals of Ulster, ed. W.M. Hennessy and B. McCarthy (Dublin, 1887–1901).
The Bannatyne Miscellany (Bannatyne Club, 1827–55).
John Barbour: The Bruce, ed. A.A.M. Duncan (Edinburgh, 1997).
The Book of Bon-Accord (Aberdeen, 1839).
'The Book of Clanranald', in A. Cameron *Reliquiae Celticae*, edd. A. Macbain and
    J. Kennedy (Inverness, 1892–4).
The Book of the Thanes of Cawdor (Spalding Club, 1859).

Walter Bower, *Scotichronicon*, ed. D.E.R. Watt, 9 vols. (1987–1998).

Calendar of Chancery warrants preserved in the Public Record Office (London, 1927–).

Calendar of Documents Relating to Scotland, ed. J. Bain (Edinburgh, 1881–8).

Calendar of Entries in the Papal Registers relating to Great Britain and Ireland: Papal Letters, edd. W.H. Bliss and others (London, 1893–).

Calendar of Entries in the Papal Registers relating to Great Britain and Ireland: Petitions to the Pope, ed. W.H. Bliss (London, 1896).

The Calendar of Fearn: text and additions, 1471–1667 (SHS, 1992).

Calendar of the Laing Charters, 854–1837, ed. J. Anderson (Edinburgh, 1899).

Calendar of Letters, Despatches and State Papers relating to the negotiations between England and Spain, vol. i (1485–1509), ed. G.A. Bergenroth (London, 1862).

Calendar of letters and papers, foreign and domestic, of the reign of Henry VIII (London, 1862–1932).

Calendar of Scottish Supplications to Rome, 5 vols. (SHS and others, 1934–).

Calendar of the State Papers relating to Scotland and Mary, Queen of Scots 1547–1603, edd. J.Bain and others (Edinburgh, 1898–).

Calendar of writs of Munro of Foulis, 1299–1823 (SRS, 1940).

Cartularium Comitatus de Levenax (Maitland Club, 1833).

The Cartulary of Holy Trinity Aldgate, ed. G.A.J. Hodgett (London, 1971).

Charters, Bulls and other Documents relating to the Abbey of Inchaffray (SHS, 1908).

Chartularies of St Mary's Abbey, Dublin, ed. J.J. Gilbert (London, 1884).

The Chronicle of Walter of Guisborough (Camden Society, 1957).

The Chronicles of Scotland compiled by Hector Boece, translated into Scots by John Bellenden 1531 (STS, 1938–41).

'A Contemporary Account of the Battle of Flodden, 9th September 1513. From a Manuscript in the possession of David Laing, Esq., LL.D., V.P.AS.A. Scot', *PSAS*, vii, 1867–1868, 141–152.

G.Crawford, *The Lives and Characters of the Officers of the Crown and of the State in Scotland* (London, 1736).

Dictionary of the Older Scottish Tongue.

Diplomatarium Norvegicum, 5th collection, vol. 2, edd. Chr. C.A. Lange and Carl. R.Unger (Christiania 1861).

Documents and Records illustrating the History of Scotland, ed. F. Palgrave (London, 1837).

Documents Illustrative of the History of Scotland 1286–1306, ed. J. Stevenson (Edinburgh, 1870).

The Dublin Guild Merchant Roll, c.1190–1265, edd. P. Connolly and G. Martin (Dublin, 1992).

The Exchequer Rolls of Scotland, edd. J. Stuart and others (Edinburgh, 1878–1908).

Extracts from the Council Register of the Burgh of Aberdeen (Spalding Club, 1844–48).

Extracta e Variis Cronicis Scocie (Abbotsford Club, 1842).

Facsimiles of the National Manuscripts of Scotland (London, 1867–71).

Foedera, Conventiones, Litterae et Cuiuscumque Generis Acta Publica, ed. T. Rymer, Record Commission edition (London, 1816–69).

W. Fraser, *The Douglas Book* (Edinburgh, 1885).

W. Fraser, *The Lennox* (Edinburgh, 1874).

W. Fraser, *Memorials of the Montgomeries Earls of Eglinton* (Edinburgh, 1859).

W. Fraser, *The Stirlings of Keir* (Edinburgh, 1858).

The Frasers of Philorth, ed. A. Fraser, Lord Saltoun (Edinburgh, 1888).

George MacKenzie, *The lives and characters of the most eminent writers of the Scots nation; with an abstract and a catalogue of their works; their various editions; and the judgment of the learn'd concerning them*, 3 vols. (Edinburgh, 1708–22).

Highland Papers, ed. J.R.N. Macphail (SHS, 1914–34), 4 vols.

Illustrations of the Topography and Antiquities of the Shires of Aberdeen and Banff, 4 vols. (Spalding Club, 1847–69).

An Inventory of Lamont Papers (SRS, 1914).

G.H. Martin ed. and trans., *Knighton's Chronicle, 1337–1396* (Oxford, 1995).

La Rotta de Scocesi, translated in W. Mackay Mackenzie, *The Secret of Flodden with 'The Rout of the Scots'* (Edinburgh, 1931).

J. Lesley, *The History of Scotland from the Death of King James I in the Year 1436 to the Year 1561* (Bannatyne Club, 1830).

The Letters of James the Fourth, 1505–1513, ed. R.L. Mackie (SHS, 1953).

Liber Cartarum Sancte Crucis (Bannatyne Club, 1840).

Liber Cartularium Prioratus Sancti Andree (Bannatyne Club, 1841).

Liber Pluscardensis, ed. F.J.H. Skene (Edinburgh, 1867).

Liber Sancte Marie de Lundoris (Abbotsford Club, 1841).

Sir David Lyndsay: Selected Poems, ed. Janet Hadley Williams (Glasgow, 2000).

The Works of Sir David Lindsay of the Mount, 1490–1555, ed. Douglas Hamer (STS, 1931).

Robert Lindsay of Pitscottie, *The Historie and Cronicles of Scotland*, vol.1 (Edinburgh, 1899).

Memoranda de Parliamento, 1305 (Rolls Series, 1893).

Miscellany of the Maitland Club (Maitland Club, 1833–47).

The Miscellany of the Scottish History Society (SHS, 1893–).

Miscellany of the Spalding Club (Spalding Club, 1841–52).

Munimenta Fratrum Predicatorum de Glasgu (Maitland Club, 1846).

A. Myln, *Vitae Dunkeldensis Ecclesiae Episcoporum* (Bannatyne Club, 1831).

Oeuvre de Ghillebert de Lannoy, voyageur, diplomate et moraliste (Louvain 1878).

Oeuvres de Froissart publiées avec les variants des divers manuscrits, ed. Baron H. Kervyn de Lettenhove, 25 vols. (Brussels, 1867–77).

Orain Iain Luim: Songs of John MacDonald, Bard of Keppoch, ed. A.M. Mackenzie (SGTS, 1964).

Origines Parochiales Scotiae (Bannatyne Club, 1851–5).

Petty Customs Account, 1480–1, ed. H.S. Cobb (London, 1990).

The Poems of William Dunbar, ed. W.M. Mackenzie (Edinburgh, 1932).

Records of the Earldom of Orkney (SHS 1914).

Regesta Regum Scotorum, edd. G.W.S. Barrow and others (Edinburgh, 1960–).

Registrum Episcopatus Brechinensis (Bannatyne Club, 1856).

Registrum Episcopatus Glasguensis (Bannatyne and Maitland Clubs, 1843).

Registrum Episcopatus Moraviensis (Bannatyne Club, 1837).

Registrum Honoris de Morton (Bannatyne Club, 1853).

Registrum Magni Sigilii Regum Scotorum, edd. J.M. Thomson and others (Edinburgh, 1882–1914).

Registrum Monasterii de Passelet (Maitland Club, 1832).

Registrum Monasterii S. Marie de Cambuskenneth (Grampian Club, 1872).

Registrum S. Marie de Neubotle (Bannatyne Club, 1849).

Registrum Secreti Sigilii Regum Scottorum, edd. M. Livingstone and others (Edinburgh, 1908–).

Reports of the Royal Commission on Historical Manuscripts (London 1870–).

Rotuli Scotiae in Turri Londinensi et in Domo Capitulari Westmonasteriensi Asservati, edd. D. Macpherson and others (1814–19).

Scalacronica, by Sir Thomas Gray of Heton Knight (Maitland Club, 1836).

Scottish Verse from The Book of the Dean of Lismore, ed.W.J. Watson (SGTS, 1937).

Select cases concerning the law merchant: A.D. 1270–1638, 3 vols. (Selden Society, 1908–1932)

J.H. Stevenson and M. Wood (eds.), *Scottish Heraldic Seals* (Glasgow, 1940).

Three Fifteenth-century Chronicles (Camden Society, 1880).

K.A. Steer and J.W.M. Bannerman, *Late Medieval Moumental Sculpture in the West Highlands* (RCAHMS, Edinburgh, 1977).

N. Trivet, *Annales*, ed.T. Hog.

Vetera Monumenta Hibernorum et Scotorum Historiam Illustrantia, ed. A. Theiner (Rome, 1864).

Vita Nobilissimi Defensoris Scotie Wilelmi Wallace Militis, ed. M.P. McDiarmid (STS, 1968).

William Worcestre, *Itineraries,* ed. John. H. Harvey (Oxford, 1969).

Androw of Wyntoun, *The Orygynale Cronykil of Scotland*, ed. D. Laing (Edinburgh, 1872–79).

SECONDARY SOURCES

Bannerman, J.W.M., *The Beatons: A medical Kindred in the Classical Tradition* (Edinburgh, 1986).

Bannerman, J.W.M., 'The Clàrsach and the Clàrsair', *SS*, 30 (1991), 1–17.

Bannerman, J.W.M., 'The Lordship of the Isles', in J. Brown (ed.), *Scottish Society in the Fifteenth Century* (London, 1977), 209–240.

Bannerman, J.W.M., 'The Lordship of the Isles: Historical Background', Appendix II, in K.A. Steer and J.W.M. Bannerman, *Late Medieval Moumental Sculpture in the West Highlands* (Edinburgh, 1977), 201–213.

Bannerman, J.W.M., 'The MacLachlans of Kilbride and their Manuscripts', *SS*, 21 (1977), 1–34.

Bannerman, J.W.M., 'The Scots Language and the Kin-based Society', in *Gaelic and Scots in Harmony: Proceedings of the Second International Conference on the Languages of Scotland* (Glasgow, 1988).

Barron, E.V., *The Scottish War of Independence*, 2nd edition (Inverness, 1934).

Barrow, G.W.S., *The Anglo-Norman Era in Scottish History* (Oxford, 1980).

Barrow, G.W.S., 'The Highlands in the Lifetime of Robert the Bruce', in *The Kingdom of the Scots*, 2nd edition (Edinburgh, 2003), 332–349.

Barrow, G.W.S., *The Kingdom of the Scots: Government, Church and Society from the eleventh to the fourteenth century* (London, 1973).

Barrow, G.W.S., *Kingship and Unity: Scotland, 1000–1306* (London, 1981).

Barrow, G.W.S., *Robert Bruce and the Community of the Realm of Scotland*, 3rd edition (Edinburgh, 1988).

Barrow, G.W.S., 'The sources for the history of the Highlands in the Middle Ages', in *The Middle Ages in the Highlands* (Inverness, 1981).

Barrow, G.W.S. and A. Royan, 'James Fifth Stewart of Scotland, 1260(?)- 1309', in K. Stringer (ed.), *Essays on the Nobility of Medieval Scotland* (Edinburgh, 1985), 166–194.

Boardman, S., 'The Campbells and charter lordship in medieval Argyll', in S. Boardman and A. Ross (eds.), *The Exercise of Power in Medieval Scotland, c.1200–1500* (Dublin, 2003), 95–117.

Boardman, S.,'Chronicle Propaganda in Fourteenth-Century Scotland: Robert the Steward, John of Fordun and the 'Anonymous Chronicle'', *SHR*, lxxvi (1997), 23–43.

Boardman, S., 'Late Medieval Scotland and the Matter of Britain', in E.J. Cowan and R.J. Finlay, eds., *Scottish History: The Power of the Past* (Edinburgh, 2002), 47–72.

Boardman, S., *Robert II and Robert III: The Early Stewart Kings* (East Linton, 1996).

Boardman, S., 'The Tale of Leper John and the Campbell Acquisition of Lorn', in E.J. Cowan and R.A. McDonald (eds.), *Alba, Celtic Scotland in the Middle Ages* (East Linton, 2000), 219–247.

Broun, D., 'A New Look at *Gesta Annalia* attributed to John of Fordun', in *Church, Chronicle and Learning*, ed. Barbara E. Crawford (Edinburgh 1999), 9–30.

Brown, A.L., 'The Cistercian Abbey of Saddell, Kintyre', *IR*, xx (1969), 130–7.

Brown, M., *The Black Douglases* (East Linton, 1998).

Brown, M.,'Earldom and kindred: the Lennox and its earls, 1200–1458', in S. Boardman and A. Ross (eds.), *The Exercise of Power in Medieval Scotland, c.1200–1500* (Dublin, 2003), 201–224.

Brown, M., ''Vile Times': Walter Bower's last Book and the Minority of James I', *SHR*, lxxix (2000), 165–88.

Butler, W.F.T., *Gleanings from Irish History* (London, 1925).

Campbell, Lord Archibald, *Records of Argyll* (Edinburgh, 1885).

Campbell, C., *The Scots Roll; A Study of a Fifteenth Century Roll of Arms* (Heraldry Society of Scotland, 1995).

Campbell, N.D., 'The Origin of the Holy Loch', *SHR*, x (1913), 29–34.

M. Connolly, '*The Dethe of the Kynge of Scotis*: A New Edition', *SHR*, 71 (1992), 46–69, at 65.

Contamine, P., 'Froissart and Scotland', in G.G. Simpson (ed.), *Scotland and the Low Countries, 1124–1994* (East Linton, 1996), 43–58.

Conway, A., *Henry VII's relations with Scotland and Ireland, 1485–1498* (Cambridge 1932).

Cosgrove, A, (ed.), *Medieval Ireland, 1169–1534 (A New History of Ireland,* vol. II; Oxford, 1987).

Coull, J.R., *The Sea Fisheries of Scotland: A Historical Geography* (Edinburgh, 1996).

Cowan, E.J., 'Norwegian sunset-Scottish dawn: Hakon IV and Alexander III', in N. Reid, ed., *Scotland in the Reign of Alexander III* (Edinburgh, 1990).

Cowan, I.B., and D.E. Easson, *Medieval Religious Houses Scotland* (London, 1976).

Crawford, B.E., 'The fifteenth-century 'Genealogy of the earls of Orkney' and its reflection of the contemporary political and cultural situation in the earldom', *Mediaeval Scandinavia,* 10 (1977), 156–178.

Cregeen, E.R., 'The Changing Role of the House of Argyll in the Scottish Highlands', in *History and Social Anthropology,* ed. I.M. Lewis (London, 1968), 153–192.

Crick, J.C., *The Historia Regum Brittannie of Geoffrey of Monmouth,* vol. iv: *Dissemination and Reception in the Later Middle Ages* (Cambridge, 1991).

Davies, R.R., 'The English state and the "Celtic" peoples 1100–1400', *Journal of Historical Sociology,* 6 (1993).

Davies, R.R., 'The Peoples of Britain and Ireland, 1100–1400', I-IV, *Transactions of the Royal Historical Society* (1994–97).

Dawson, J., 'The Gaidhealtachd and the emergence of the Scottish Highlands', in *British consciousness and identity,* ed. B. Bradshaw (Cambridge, 1998), 259–300.

Ditchburn, D., *Scotland and Europe: The Medieval Kingdom and its Contacts with Christendom, c.1215–1545,* i (East Linton, 2000).

Diverres, A.H., 'The Geography of Britain in Froissart's *Meliador*', in *Medieval Miscellany Presented to Eugene Vinaver* (New York, 1965), 97–112.

Diverres, A.H., 'Froissart's *Méliador* and Edward III's Policy towards Scotland', *Mélanges offerts à Rita Lejeune* (Gembloux, 1969), 1399–1409.

Dodghson, R.A., *From Chiefs to Landlords: social and economic change in the Western Highlands and Islands, c.1493–1820* (Edinburgh, 1998).

Dodgshon, R.A., ' "Pretence of blude" and "place of thair duelling": the nature of Scottish clans, 1500–1745', in R.A. Houston and I.D. Whyte, (eds)., *Scottish Society, 1500–1800* (Cambridge, 1989).

Dodgshon, R.A., 'West Highland chiefdoms, 1500–1745', in R. Mitchison and P. Roebuck, (eds)., *Economy and Society in Scotland and Ireland, 1500–1919* (Edinburgh, 1988).

Douglas, W., 'Culross Abbey and its Charters', *PSAS* (1925–6), 67–104.

Dowden, J., *The Bishops of Scotland* (Glasgow, 1912).

Drummond, William, Viscount Strathallan, *The genealogy of the most noble and ancient House of Drummond* (Edinburgh, 1831).

Duffy, S., 'The Bruce Brothers and the Irish Sea World', *Cambrian Medieval Celtic Studies*, 21 (Summer 1991), 55–86.

Duffy, S., 'The "Continuation" of Nicholas Trevet: a new source for the Bruce invasion', *Proceedings of the Royal Irish Academy*, xci (1991).

Duffy, S., *Ireland in the Middle Ages* (London, 1997).

Dunbar, J.G., and AA.M. Duncan, 'Tarbert Castle; a contribution to the history of Argyll', *SHR*, l (1971), 1–17.

Duncan, A.A.M., 'The "Laws of Malcolm MacKenneth"', in A. Grant and K. Stringer (eds)., *Medieval Scotland: Crown, Lordship and Community* (Edinburgh, 1993), 264–5.

Duncan, A.A.M., *The Nation of the Scots and the Declaration of Arbroath* (Historical Association, 1970).

Duncan, A.A.M., *Scotland: The Making of the Kingdom* (Edinburgh, 1975).

Duncan, A.A.M., Review of Barrow's *Robert Bruce*, *SHR*, xlv (1965), 184–201.

Dunlop, A.I., *The Life and Times of James Kennedy* (Edinburgh 1950).

Easson, D.E., 'The Collegiate Churches of Scotland', *Scottish Church Hist. Society Recs.*, vi (1938), 193–215.

Easson, D.E., 'The Collegiate Churches of Scotland', *Scottish Church Hist. Society Recs.*, vii (1939), 30–47.

Finlay, J., *Men of Law in Pre-Reformation Scotland* (East Linton, 2000).

Fitzpatrick, E., *Royal Inauguration in Gaelic Ireland, c.* 1100–1600: A Cultural Landscape Study (Woodbridge, 2004).

Foggie, J.P., *Renaissance Religion in Urban Scotland: The Dominican Order, 1450–1560* (Leiden, 2003).

Fraser, I., 'The Place-Names of Argyll – An Historical Perspective', *TGSI*, 54 (19), 3–37.

Galliou, P. and M. Jones, *The Bretons* (Oxford, 1991).

Gemmill, E., and N. Mayhew, *Changing values in medieval Scotland: a study of prices, money, and weights and measures* (Cambridge, 1995).

Gilbert, J.M., *Hunting and hunting reserves in medieval Scotland* (Edinburgh, 1979).

Gillies, W., 'Some aspects of Campbell History', *TGSI*, 50 (1978), 265–295.

Gillies, W., 'The Clanranald Histories: Authorship and Purpose', in G. Evans, B. Martin and J. Wooding (eds)., *Proceedings of the First Australian Conference of Celtic Studies* (forthcoming).

Gillies, W., 'Courtly and Satiric Poems in the Book of the Dean of Lismore', *SS*, 21 (1977),

Gillies, W., 'The Gaelic Poems of Sir Duncan Campbell of Glenorchy (III)', *SGS*, xiv, part I (1983), 71–6.

Gillies, W., 'Gaelic: The Classical Tradition', in *History of Scottish Literature*, vol.I ed. R.D.S. Jack (Aberdeen, 1988), 245–62.

Gillies, W., 'Oral and Written Sources and Effects in the Clanranald Histories', in D.Scheunemann (ed.), *Orality, Literacy and Modern Media* (Columbia, 1996), 27–43.

Gillies, W., 'Sources of the Books of Clanranald', *Études celtiques*, 29 (1992), part 2, 459–60.

Gillingham, J., 'Foundations of a disunited kingdom', in A. Grant and K. Stringer (eds.), *Uniting the Kingdom?* (London, 1995), 48–64.

Grant, A., 'The development of the Scottish peerage', *SHR*, lvii (1978), 1–27.

Grant, A., *Independence and Nationhood: Scotland, 1306–1469* (London, 1984).

Grant, A., 'The Revolt of the Lord of the Isles and the Death of the Earl of Douglas, 1451–1452', *SHR*, lx (1981), 169–174.

Grant, A., 'Scotland's "Celtic Fringe" in the late middle ages: the MacDonald Lords of the Isles and the kingdom of Scotland', in R.R. Davies (ed.), *The British Isles, 1100–1500* (Edinburgh, 1988).

Grant, A., 'Thanes and Thanages, from the Eleventh to the Fourteenth Centuries', in A. Grant and K.J. Stringer, (eds)., *Medieval Scotland: Crown, Lordship and Community* (Edinburgh, 1993), 39–79.

Gregory, D., *History of the Western Highlands and Isles of Scotland, from A.D. 1493 to A.D. 1625* (Edinburgh, 1836).

Handbook of British Chronology, 3rd edition (1986).

Hanham, A., *The Celys and their World* (Cambridge, 1985).

Hayes-McCoy, G.A., *Scots mercenary forces in Ireland (1565–1603)* (Dublin, 1937).

Higgit, J., *The Murthly Hours; Devotion, Literacy and Luxury in Paris, England and the Gaelic West* (British Library, 2000).

Hinnebusch, W.A., *The History of the Dominican Order*, 2 vols. (New York, 1965–73).

Jones, W.R., 'The Image of the Barbarian in Medieval Europe', *Comparative Studies in Society and History*, 13 (1971), 376–407.

Keen, M., *Chivalry* (London, 1984).

Kingston, S., *Ulster and the Isles in the Fifteenth Century* (Dublin, 2004).

Kingston, S., 'Delusions of Dál Riada: The Co-ordinates of Mac Domnaill Power, 1461–1550', in *Gaelic Ireland c.1250–c.1650: Land, Lordship and Settlement* (eds). P.J. Duffy, D. Edwards and E. FitzPatrick (Dublin, 2001), 98–114.

Lane, A., *Dunadd : an early Dalriadic capital* (Oxford, 2000).

Lawrence, C.H., *The Friars: The impact of the early mendicant movement on western society* (London, 1994).

Lydon, J.F., 'Edward I, Ireland and Scotland, 1303–4', in *England and Ireland in the later Middle Ages*, ed. J.F. Lydon (Dublin, 1981), 43–61.

Lynch, M., *Scotland: A New History* (Edinburgh, 1990).

McClintock, H.F., *Old Irish and Highland Dress* (Dundalk, 1950).

McDiarmid, M.P., 'The Date of the "Wallace"', *SHR*, xxxiv (April 1955), 26–31.

McDonald, R.A., *The Kingdom of the Isles, Scotland's Western Seaboard, c.1100–c.1336* (East Linton, 1997).

Macdougall, N.A.T., 'Achilles Heel? The Earldom of Ross, the Lordship of the Isles, and the Stewart Kings, 1449–1507', in E.J. Cowan and R.A. McDonald (eds)., *Alba: Celtic Scotland in the Middle Ages* (East Linton, 2000), 248–275.

Macdougall, N.A.T., *James III* (Edinburgh 1982).

Macdougall, N.A.T., *James IV* (Edinburgh, 1989).

Macdougall, N.A.T., ' "It is I, the Earle of Mar": In Search of Thomas Cochrane', in *People and Power in Scotland*, edd. R.A. Mason and N. Macdougall (Edinburgh 1992), 28–49.

Mac Eiteagáin, D., 'The Renaissance and the late Medieval lordship of Tír Chonaill 1461–1555', in *Donegal: History and Society*, edd. W. Nolan, L. Ronayne and M. Dunlevy (Dublin, 1995), 203–228.

MacKechnie, H., *The Lamont Clan, 1235–1935* (Edinburgh, 1938).

MacLean-Bristol, N., *Warriors and Priests: The History of the Clan Maclean, 1300–1570* (East Linton, 1995).

Mapstone, S., 'Bower on kingship', in *Chron. Bower* (Watt), ix, 321–338.

McGladdery, C., *James II* (Edinburgh, 1990).

MacGregor, M., 'Church and culture in the late medieval Highlands', in *The Church in the Highlands*, ed. James Kirk (Edinburgh 1998), 1–36.

MacGregor, M., 'The Genealogical Histories of Gaelic Scotland', in Adam Fox and Daniel Woolf (eds)., *The Spoken Word: Oral Culture in Britain, 1500–1850* (Manchester, 2002), 196–239.

MacGregor, M., 'Surely one of the greatest poems ever made in Britain': The Lament for Griogair Ruadh MacGregor of Glen Strae and its Historical Background', in *The Polar Twins*, edd. E.J. Cowan and D. Gifford (Edinburgh, 1999), 114– 153.

McLauchlan, Reverend T., *The Dean of Lismore's Book* (Edinburgh, 1862).

MacInnes, J., 'Gaelic poetry and historical tradition', in *The Middle Ages in the Highlands* (Inverness, 1981), 142–163.

McNamee, C., *The Wars of the Bruces* (East Linton, 1997).

Madden, C., 'The Feuing of Ettrick Forest', *IR*, xxvii (1976), 70–84.

Madden, C., 'Royal Treatment of Feudal Casualties in Late Medieval Scotland', *SHR*, lv (1976), 172–194.

Mason, R.A., 'Civil Society and the Celts: Hector Boece, George Buchanan and the Ancient Scottish Past', in E.J. Cowan and R.J. Finlay (eds)., *Scottish History, The Power of the Past* (Edinburgh, 2002), 95–119.

Matheson, A., 'Bishop Carsewell', *TGSI*, 42 (1953–59), 182–205.

Matheson, A., Appendix II 'The MacEwens', in *Foirm na n-Urrnuidheadh*, ed. R.L. Thomson (Edinburgh, 1970), 183–6.

Munro, R.W., *The Munro Tree (1734)* (Edinburgh, 1978).

N. Murray 'A House Divided Against Itself: A Brief Synopsis of the History of Clann Alexandair and the early career of 'Good John of Islay' c. 1290–1370', in *Rannsachadh na Gàidhlig 2000*, edd. C. ÓBaoill and N. R. McGuire (Aberdeen, 2002), 221–230.

Nicholls, K., 'Notes on the Genealogy of Clann Eoin Mhoir', *West Highland Notes and Queries*, Series 2, no.8 (November 1991).

Nicholson, R., 'Domesticated Scots and Wild Scots', unpublished article, copies held in Scottish History, University of Edinburgh, and XSi MS A181, Box 3, file 8, Scottish Collection, University of Guelph.

Nicholson, R., *Edward III and the Scots; the formative years of a military career, 1327–1335* (London, 1965).

Nicholson, R., 'Feudal Developments in Late Medieval Scotland', *Juridical Review* (1973), 1–21.

Nicholson, R., *Scotland: The Later Middle Ages* (Edinburgh, 1974).

Ó Briain, M., 'Snaithín san uige: "Loisc agus léig a luaith le struth"', in *Téada Dúchais: Aistí in ómós don Ollamh Breandán Ó Madagáin* (Inverin: Cló Iar-Chonnachta, 2002), 245–72.

O'Neill, T., *Merchants and Mariners in Medieval Ireland* (Dublin, 1987).

Oxford Dictionary of Saints, ed. D.H. Farmer (Oxford, 1992).

Penman, M.A., *David II, 1329–71* (East Linton, 2004).

Penman, M.A., 'A fell conuiracioun agayn Robert ye douchty king: the Soules conspiracy of 1318–20', *IR*, 50 (1999), 25–57.

Penman, M.A., 'The Scots at the Battle of Neville's Cross, 17 October 1346', *SHR*, lxxx (2001), 157–80.

Prestwich, M., *Edward I* (London, 1988).

Quinn, D.B., '"Irish" Ireland and "English" Ireland', in *Medieval Ireland, 1169–1534*, ed. A. Cosgrove (Oxford 1987),

Royal Commission on the Ancient and Historical Monuments and Constructions of Scotland, *Inventory of the Ancient Monuments of Argyll*, 7 vols., (Edinburgh, 1971–92).

Ross, A., 'Incubi in the Isles in the Thirteenth Century, *IR*, 13 (1962), 108–9.

Sellar, W.D.H., 'The Earliest Campbells – Norman, Briton or Gael?', *SS*, 17 (1973), 109–126.

Sellar, W.D.H., 'Family origins in Cowal and Knapdale', *SS*, xv (1971), 21–37.

Sellar, W.D.H., 'Hebridean Sea Kings: The Successors of Somerled, 1164–1316', in *Alba: Celtic Scotland in the Middle Ages* (East Linton, 2000), edd. E.J. Cowan and R.A. McDonald, 187–218.

Sellar, W.D.H., 'MacDougall pedigrees in MS 1467', *SWHIHR*, 1st series, xxix (1986), 3–16.

Simms, K., *From Kings to Warlords* (Woodbridge, 1987).

Simms, K., 'Guesting and feasting in Gaelic Ireland', *Journal of the Royal Society of Antiquaries of Ireland*, 108 (1978), 67–100.

Simms, K., 'Late Medieval Donegal', in *Donegal: History and Society*, edd. W. Nolan, L. Ronayne and M. Dunlevy (Dublin, 1995), 183–201.

Sims-Williams, P., 'The visionary Celt: the construction of an ethnic preconception', *Cambridge Medieval Celtic Studies*, 11 (1986).

Skene, W.F., *The Highlanders of Scotland* (Stirling 1902).

Smith, B., 'Lionel of Clarence and the English of Meath', *Peritia* 10 (1996), 297–302.

Stewart, C.P., *Historic Memorials of the Stewarts of Forthergill, Perthshire* (Edinburgh, 1879).

Stewart, M., 'A Recently-Discovered Manuscript: "ane taill of Sir colling ye knyt"', *SS*, 16 (1972), 23–39.

Stone, J.A., ed., *Three Scottish Carmelite friaries: excavations at Aberdeen, Linlithgow and Perth, 1980–1986* (Edinburgh, 1989).

Stones, E.L.G., *Anglo-Scottish Relations, 1174–1328, Some Selected Documents* (London, 1965).

Stones, E.L.G., 'The Submission of Robert Bruce to Edward I, c.1301–2', *SHR*, xxxiv (1955), 122–34.

Tanner, R., *The Late Medieval Scottish Parliament* (East Linton 2001), 159.

Tanner, R., 'The Lords of the Articles before 1540: A Reassessment', *SHR*, 79 (2000), 189–212.

Thomson, O., *The Great Feud: The Campbells and the MacDonalds* (Stroud, 2000).

Touchard, H., *Le Commerce Maritime Breton à la fin du moyen age* (Paris, 1967).

Watson, W.J., *The History of the Celtic place-names of Scotland* (Edinburgh, 1926).

Watt, D.E.R., *A Biographical Dictionary of Scottish Graduates to A.D. 1410* (Oxford, 1977).

Watt, D.E.R., 'Collegiate Churches', in *An Historical Atlas of Scotland, c.400–1600* (St.Andrews, 1975), 78–80.

Watt, D.E.R., 'Collegiate Churches', in *Atlas of Scottish History to 1707* (Edinburgh, 1996), 346.

Watt, D.E.R., *Fasti ecclesiae Scoticanae medii aevi ad annum 1638, 2nd draft (SRS, 1969).*

Watt, D.E.R., and N. Shead (eds.), *The Heads of Religious Houses in Scotland from Twelfth to Sixteenth Centuries* (SRS, 2001).

Woolf, A., 'The Diocese of Sodor', in *A New History of the Isle of Man, volume 3: the medieval period*, ed. Seán Duffy (forthcoming).

Young, A., *Robert the Bruce's Rivals: The Comyns, 1212–1314* (East Linton, 1997).

THESES

Boardman, S., Politics and the Feud in Late Medieval Scotland unpublished Ph.D. Thesis (St Andrews 1989).

Borthwick, A.R., The King, Council and Councillors in Scotland, c.1430–1460, unpublished Ph.D. Thesis (Edinburgh, 1989).

Chalmers, T., The King's Council, Patronage, and the Governance of Scotland, 1460–1513', unpublished Ph.D. Thesis (Aberdeen, 1982).

Foggie, J.P., The Dominicans in Scotland: 1450–1560, unpublished Ph.D Thesis (Edinburgh 1998).

Hunt, K.J., The Governorship of the First Duke of Albany: 1406–1420, unpublished Ph.D. Thesis (Edinburgh 1998).

Scott, M.C., Dress in Scotland, 1406–1460, unpublished Ph.D. Thesis (University of London, 1987).

Index

Abercrombie, Henry, abbot of
    Cambuskenneth, 241
Aberdeen, 109, 149, 167, 232; shire 333
Abernethy, William, Lord Abernethy, 241
'Achonasellache', 320
Ailsa Craig, 47, 329
Albany, dukes of, see Stewart, Alexander;
    Stewart, Murdoch; Stewart, Robert
Albany, Finlay of, Dominican bishop of
    Argyll, 118
  rebels against James I and flees into
    exile, 122–123
  removed from his diocese, 126
Albany Stewarts,
  links to Argyll, 118–120
  destroyed by James I, 120–123
  sympathy for, 124–125, 133–134
Alexander II (1214–1249), 17, 20, 19
Alexander III (1249–1286), 13, 17, 20
Alexander, earl of Menteith, 20–21, 37
Alan, Henry, archdean of Dunblane, 278
Allan, earl of Menteith, 38
Allan mac Ranald Bane, 279
Allan mac Ruairi (I), 46
Allan mac Ruairi (II), 209, lord of
    Moidart, 227–228, 271
Altani, Anthony, bishop of Urbino, papal
    nuncio, 134–135, 144
Ane Taill of Sir Colling ye Knyt, 42
Angus, 79
Angus, earl of, see Douglas, Archibald;
    Douglas, George; Stewart, Thomas
Anjou, Margaret of, wife of Henry VI,
    179
Annandale, 217
Appin, 45, 48, 95, 96, 187, 315–317
Appin of Dull, 244, 276–277, 311, 325
Aray, 204
Arbroath, 41
Ardchattan, priory of, 192, 194
Ardenslate, 108
Ardmaddy, 185
Ardnamurchan, 322, 334

Ardscotnish, 12, 67, 74, 75, 80, 82, 102,
    103, 104
  status of as a royal bailiary, 20–21, 40–
    41
  annexed by Dugald Campbell and his
    heirs, 43–44
Ardstaffnage, 45
Ardtornish, 180
Argyll, 17, 37, 39, 43, 48, 56, 57, 59, 60, 65,
    66, 74, 75, 77, 80, 82, 94, 99, 100, 101,
    110, 118–120, 121, 124, 133, 145, 157, 158,
    166, 168, 204, 211–213, 243, 248, 320–
    322, 332
Argyll, barons of, 20, 40, 68, 101
Argyll, bishops of, 118–120
Argyll, earldom of, 169–171
Argyll, earls of, see Campbell, Archibald;
    Campbell, Colin
Argyll, justice ayre of, 317–319
Argyll, lord of, use of title, 66, 67–68, 94,
    99–102, 109
Argyll, mid, 14, 47, 68, 74, 75, 82, 99, 102,
    109, 125, 142, 292
  as a centre for royal lordship in Argyll,
    62, 82–83
Argyll, sheriffship of, 4, 44, 45;
  lieutenancy of, 82–83, 99, 109, 125,
    141, 146, 147
Arisaig, 46
Arkinholm, battle of (1455), 169
Arran, 15, 39, 61, 63, 64, 81, 84, 105, 107,
    128, 130, 152–154, 155, 157, 169, 171, 173,
    181–183, 188, 189, 192, 245, 248, 261,
    313, 330
Arran, Donald of, 268
Arthur, legendary king, Campbell claim
    of descent from, 11, 13–14,
Assynt, 311, 321
Atholl, earl of, see Campbell, John;
    Stewart, John; Strathbogie, David
    (I) of; Strathbogie, David (II), of
Atholl, earldom of, 44, 48, 57, 63, 77, 79,
    325

Atlantic, the, 99

Auchinleck chronicle, 153, 154, 156, 157, 168, 172, 174, 176, 178, 291

Avandale, 168

de Ayala, Don Pedro, Spanish ambassador, 272, 274–275, 301, 325

Ayr, 20, 41, 62, 152, 174, 211, 274, 294, 298, 301, 305, 329–330; sheriffdom of, 25; Dominican friary of, 118

Ayson, Robert, of Tullimet, 312

Badenoch, 20, 77, 128, 155, 204, 207, 279, 312, 316–317, 325, 333

Baldinnies, 187

Balliol, Edward, 76
  his attempts to reclaim the Scottish throne, 56–60

Balloch, 246

Balquhidder, 207, 246, 320

Banffshire, 333

Bannerman, John, 4

Bannockburn, battle of (1314), 40

Bannockburn, mill of, 241

Barbour, John, author of *The Bruce*, 9, 36, 39, 42, 45, 95, 300

Barrow, Geoffrey, 26

Bartram, Walter, provost of Edinburgh, 220

Bass Rock, 108, 121

Beaufort, Queen Joan, widow of James I, her involvement in the politics of the minority of James II, 134–135, 141, 147, 148–149, 150

Beauly, priory of, 159

Belfast Lough, 331

Bellenden, John, 278, 300

Benbecula, 190–191

Benderloch, 45, 47, 48, 95, 96, 97, 185

Bergen, 18

Berwick, 18, 19, 57, 169, 217, 220; Treaty of, 75

Blackadder, Robert, bishop of Glasgow, 231

Blackfriars, see Dominicans

Blackness, 153; skirmish at (1488), 245

Blair, David, 297

Blarebeg, 169

Blind Harry, author of *The Wallace*, 211–213

Bloody Bay, battle (date unknown), 227–228, 251

Boece, Hector, 278, 300, 328–329

Book of Coupar Angus, the, 125

Book of the Dean of Lismore, 229

Borthwick, Janet, Lady Dalkeith, 148

Borthwick, William, 148

Botetourte, Sir John, justiciar of Galloway, 22

Bothwell, castle of, 260

Bourgneuf, Bay of, 300

Bower, Walter, 76, 79, 124–125, 126–127, 167

Boyd, Elizabeth, 259

Boyd, James, son of the earl of Arran, 259–260

Boyd, Margaret, daughter of the earl of Arran, 259

Boyd, Marion, James IV's mistress, 260, 266

Boyd, Robert, Lord Boyd, 183, 188–189

Boyd, Sir Thomas, 145

Boyd, Thomas, earl of Arran, 188–189, 259

Branxton Hill, 6, 333–334

Breadalbane, 133, 333

Bristol, 295

Brittany, 295

Brittany, John of, 25

Brodick, lands of, 169; castle of, 47, 153, 155, 174, 181

Brown, George, bishop of Dunkeld, 231

Bruce, Edward, 40, 42, 46

Bruce, Isabella, queen of Norway, 18

Bruce, Mary, 40, 42

Bruce, Robert, father of Robert I, 18

Buchan, earl of, see Comyn, John; Stewart, James

Buchanan, John, 109

Buchanan, Walter, 109

'Bulwart', John, Breton merchant, 299–300

Burgh, Egidia de, 17

Burgh, Isabella de, wife of Robert I, 23

Burgh, Richard de, earl of Ulster, 17, 23

Bute, 13, 14, 20, 59, 104, 105, 107, 108, 130, 152, 153, 154, 179–181, 192, 245, 248, 261, 302, 332; Kyles of, 157

Caerlaverock, castle of, 122

Cairn na Burgh Beg, castle of, 48, 66, 320

Cairn na Burgh Mór, castle of, 48, 66, 320

Caithness, earldom of, 175, 180, 184

Caldor, John, son of William, thane of Cawdor, 273–274

Callendar, Robert, 149–150

Cambuskenneth, abbey of, 13, 22, 40, 241

Campbell, Alexander Ciar, of
  Dunstaffnage, 246, 272, 314–315

Campbell, Sir Andrew, 83

Campbell, Archibald, 2nd earl of Argyll, 6,
  42, 171, 193, 226, 228, 245, 248, 301, 304
  his ambivalent attitude toward the
    Lordship of the Isles, 254–255
  Campbell interests threatened by
    Archibald, earl of Angus, 259–262
  involvement in royal campaigns in the
    west, 263–270
  returns to government, 266
  his links with the Ui Dhomhnaill, 267–
    268, 332–334
  his Edinburgh household, 270–271
  involved in Anglo-Scottish warfare,
    271–272
  his plans for Iona, 272–273
  acts as a link between the king and
    Hebridean lords, 272
  his ambivalent attitude to royal policy
    prior to the Donald Dubh rebellion,
    275, 277–283, 313
  the 'Flodden' poem an appeal for his
    assistance?, 281–282
  attempts at economic reform?, 313–315
  at odds with Duncan Stewart of
    Appin, 315–316
  the three estates suspicious of his role
    in 1503–4?, 317–319
  his leading role in royal campaigns of
    1504–1505, 320–321
  his expedition of 1506 and attempted
    reform of Hebridean lordship, 321–
    325
  his clàrsair entertains the king, 325
  representing Hebridean lords at court,
    326–327
  the Campbell earls as patrons of
    Gaelic culture, 328–329
  Anglo-Scottish diplomacy, warfare and
    the earl's death at Flodden, 330–335
  plans for an attack on Ireland, 332–334

Campbell, Archibald, son of the 2nd earl,
  313

Campbell, Sir Arthur (I),
  his ambitions in Lorn and Garmoran,
    45–47, 48, 96

Campbell, Sir Arthur (II),
  his claims to Garmoran, 45–47, 48, 59,
    62

Campbell, Arthur (III), 97

Campbell, Catherine, 251

Campbell, Catriona, 273, 283

Campbell, Christian, 103

Campbell, Colin Mór (d.c.1296?), 335
  the individual from whom the style
    MacCailein Mór derived, 10, 12, 42
  relationship to the Stewart and Bruce
    families, 17–18
  his death at the hands of the
    MacDougalls of Argyll, 21, 37

Campbell, Sir Colin (d. by 1323), 39, 58,
  67, 80, 83
  receives grant of Loch Awe and
    Ardscotnish, 40–41, 44, 69
  his brief career and early death, 42, 43,
    48

Campbell, Colin, putative heir of Colin
  Mór? (d.c.1305), 24–25

Campbell, Colin 'Iongantach' (d.c.1412/
  13), 11, 82, 94, 99, 105, 106, 107, 108,
  109, 301
  territorial gains of in Glassary, 68–70
  in Craignish, 70–71
  position in Cowal threatened, 72–73
  his reclamation of Ardscotnish through
    marriage, 73–74
  attempted assassination of, 74–75, 102
  consolidation of his family's lordship in
    Argyll, 94, 102–104
  his use of the title Lord of Argyll, 99–
    102
  his links to the Albany Stewarts, 109
  his death and legacy, 109–110
  patronage of the Carmelites, 132

Campbell, Colin Óg, founder of
  Campbells of Ardkinglas, 103–104

Campbell, Colin, 1st earl of Argyll, 131,
  158, 159, 166, 189, 291–293, 297
  his father's early death and
    arrangements to assure his
    succession, 132–133
  his success as a court aristocrat, 168,
    172, 185–186, 202–203
  supports James II's assault on Douglas
    power, 168–169
  his creation as earl of Argyll, 169–171
  conflict with Donald Balloch over
    MacDougall succession and Arran,
    172–173
  his position in Cowal, 173–174, 214
  brought in to government because of
    regional power, 182–183

his defence of Arran, 183, 189

his acquisition of the lordship of Lorn, 184–190

importance of Lorn, 191–194

record of, as royal administrator, 203–204, 214

new views on estate management?, 204

action against John, earl of Ross, 207–208

role of, in politics of Clan Donald, 209–211, 224–230

portrayal of his lordship in the lowlands, 211–213

his relationship with James III, 213–216, 222–223, 230–232

his role in Lauder crisis and aftermath, 217–223

his rehabilitation and promotion to the Chancellorship, 223–224

his relationship with Donald Dubh, 228–230, 251–253

involved in rebellion of 1488, 231–232, 238

favour shown to his affinity by the post-Sauchieburn regime, 238, 241–247

his founding of burghs of barony and purchases of urban properties, 247, 299

the rebellion of 1489, 247–250

his death in 1492 and its effect on the Lordship of the Isles, 254–255, 261–262

Campbell, Colin, 1st of Glenorchy, 146, 147, 150, 166

increased influence because of his brother's early death, 133

captures one of the assassins of James I, 134–135

royal ambassador, 144, 188

his matrimonial adventures, 145, 147–148, 156, 188

visits Rome with William, earl of Douglas, 151

supports James II during 1452, 155–156

involved in dispute over Lorn, 186

Campbell, Colin Neilson, of Ormidale, 157

Campbell, Colin 'Knightson', 273, 298

Campbell, Colin, master of Argyll, later 3rd Earl, 329

Campbell, Donald, son of Colin Mór, 21–22, 38, 40, 45, 47

his service to the future Robert I, 21–27

Campbell, Donald, burgess of Edinburgh, 299

Campbell, Dugald, the man to whom the byname Caimbeul was first applied, 10, 16

Campbell, Dugald, elder brother of Gillespic of Arran, 42–43

control of Ardscotnish lost to his uncle? Dugald, 43–44

supporter of Robert the Steward, 58

leaves Bruce allegiance and suffers forfeiture, 60–61, 67

Campbell, Dugald, uncle? of Gillespic of Arran, 69

his emergence as the leading figure in Clan Campbell, 43–44, 48

founder of the Ardscotnish Campbells, 44, 73

Campbell, Dugald, brother of Duncan, 1st Lord Campbell, 132

Campbell, Duncan, son of Thomas, 47

Campbell, Duncan, ('of Scotnish'), 74–75, 102

Campbell, Duncan Mór, founder of Campbells of Duntroon, 102–103

Campbell, Duncan, 1st Lord Campbell, 104, 107, 147, 173, 214, 291–292

son-in-law of Robert, duke of Albany, 104, 106, 109–110, 118

relationship with the Albany Stewarts, 109–110, 118, 120–121, 123–124

James I suspicious of, 118, 123–124, 127

2nd marriage of, to Margaret Stewart, 121

a hostage for James I's ransom, 121

returns to Scotland, 123

authority in Argyll undercut by the king, 124–126

lieutenancy revoked?, 125

dispute with the Scrymgeours of Glassary, 125–126, 129

dispute with George Lauder, bishop of Argyll, 126, 143–144

reconciled with James I, 128–130, 132–133, 135

cultivation of links with the royal court, 130–132, 135

interest in the Carmelite and Dominican orders, 132

death of his son and heir Gillespic, 132–133

support for Queen Joan after James I's assassination, 134–135, 141 lieutenancy restored, 141, 146

his interests in Dunoon and Cowal, 141–142

his foundation of a collegiate kirk at Kilmun, 142–144, 158

adoption of the style 'Lord Campbell', 143, 158

links to Douglas earl of Avondale and Lord Balvenie, 146–147

his position in Cowal undermined by the Livingstones, 148–150

is rewarded for his support of James II during 1452, 155–157

his death and summary of career, 158–159

Campbell, Duncan, of Auchenbreck, son of the 1st Lord Campbell, 146

Campbell, Duncan, 2nd of Glenorchy, 186–187, 208, 228, 244, 252, 261, 272–273, 278, 293, 302, 315, 319, 328, 333–334

Campbell, Ewen, 244

Campbell, George, of Loudoun, 130

Campbell, Gillespic, on record in the 1260s, 10, 13, 15, 16, 17

Campbell, Gillespic (of Arran), 36, 42–43, 61, 62, 66, 69, 73, 76, 103

his good relationship with Robert the Steward, 48–49, 61, 64–65, 82, 95

his critical role in the expansion of Campbell lordship, 56, 83–85

territorial gains in Arran, Knapdale, Cowal and mid-Argyll, 64–65, 68, 70–73, 130

his lordship in Loch Awe, 67, 80–81

his status as a leading lord in Gaelic Scotland recognised, 75, 79, 82, 83–84

stands as surety for the men of his lordships, 79–81

attempts to increase burden of royal taxation on, 81

significance of contact with new royal dynasty after 1371, 82–83, 85, 94

created royal lieutenant in Argyll, 82–83, 99, 101–102

the nature of his lordship, 83–84

becomes provincial lord of Argyll, 94, 99–102

involved in struggle for control of Lorn, 96–97

his death, 97

Campbell, Gillespic (d.1432), son and heir of Duncan, Lord Campbell, 128, 301

his relationship with his Albany Stewart kinsmen, 118

his marriage to Elizabeth Somerville, 131

his early death, 132, 142, 166

Campbell, Helen, 216

Campbell, Isabella, partner of Donald Dubh?, poetess?, 228–229

Campbell, Iver (I), 59

Campbell, Iver (II), of Strachur, 96, 97

Campbell, James, 127

Campbell, James, of Lawers, 269

Campbell, John, earl of Atholl, 40, 41–42, 44, 48

his death at Halidon Hill, 57

Campbell, John, of Ardscotnish (and Menstrie?), 75

dispute with Gilbert of Glassary, 68–69, 73

his death, and transfer of Ardscotnish and Glenorchy to the Loch Awe Campbells, 73–74

Campbell, John, son of Colin 'Iongantach', 74, vicar of Kilmartin?, 103, the same as John 'Annan'?, 104

Campbell, John, of Ardkinglas, 104, 166

Campbell, John, bishop of the Isles, 273, 327–328

Campbell, Margaret, 291

Campbell, Mariota, heiress of Ardscotnish and Glenorchy, 73–74, 102, 104

Campbell, Sir Neil (d.c.1316), 9, 10, 12, 13, 38, 42, 83

possibly the same man as Master Neil, 21–22

his service to Robert Bruce, earl of Carrick, 21–27

dispute with Sir Robert Keith and fall from favour of Edward I, 24–27

his close relationship with Robert I during and after 1306, 36–37, 39–40

marriage to the king's sister, 40

his death c.1316, 41–42, 43

Campbell, Master Neil, 18, 22

Campbell, Neil (son of Colin), archdeacon of Argyll, 107, 125, 144

Campbell, Thomas, 12, 38, 45, 47

Campbells, of Gaunan, 103–104

Campbells, Loch Awe, 69, 70–71, 74, 75, 82, 100, 102, 103

Campbells, Loudoun, 67, 68

Campbells, MacArthur (Strachur), 47, 62, 67, 68, 98, 103, 106, 126

ambitions in Lorn, 95–97
Campbells, MacDougall, of Ardscotnish, 44, 48, 61, 67, 69, 102
Canville, William de, 295
Carlingford Lough, 59
Carlisle, 57
Carmelites, Campbell connections to, 132
Carrick, earl of, see Neil; Robert I; Robert III
Carrick, earls of, 47
Carrick, earldom of, 37, 107, 301, 324
Carrick, Effrica of, 18
Carrick, Marjorie of, 18
Carrickfergus, castle and burgh of, 267, 269, 330–332
Castle Campbell, 292 (see Gloom)
Castle Sween, 15, 47, 64, 130, 224, 226–227, 263
Catacol, 169
Cattle trade, 300–302
Chambers, Thomas, 135
Chester, 295
Christian, king of Denmark, 177
Clachan Beg, 169
Clackmannan, 13, 129
Clan Campbell, the, 39, 48, 57, 68
    historical reputation of, 1–7, 82–84, 211–213
    early history of , 10–12
    claims to Arthurian descent, 13–14
    military strength of, 84–85
    relationship with Clan Donald, 128–129
'Clanchallum', the, 74–75
Clan Chattan, 279–280, 316
Clan Donald, the, 39, 45
    historical reputation of, 1–7, 82, 168
    conflict with Stewart monarchy, 104–106, 127–128, 130, 151, 153–157
Clan MacDougall of Craignish, 102
Clanranald, 190–191, 208–211
    see Ruairi mac Allan, Allan mac Ruairi
Clanranald, Book of, 208–211, 224–231, 251–152
Clan Sorley, 44, 45, 194
Clement, bishop of Dublane, 20–21, 119
Clyde, 13, 58, 59, 157, 332; Firth of, 13, 14, 17, 38, 44, 47, 48, 49, 58, 59, 63, 68, 83, 84, 94, 104, 105, 106, 108, 122, 128, 129, 130, 150, 154, 157, 169, 173, 182, 189, 193, 272, 313; the economy of the Firth of Clyde, 294–305
Cochrane, Thomas, 217
Cogeach, 311, 321

Coldingham, priory of, 230
Colin 'Doncandouesone', 25
Coll, 66
Colonsay, 302
Colquhoun, Humphrey, 109
Colquhoun, Sir John, of Luss, supporter of James I in Lennox, 122–123
    assassinated in 1439, 145
Colquhoun, John, of Luss, 273
Colquhoun, Peter, 252
Comrie, 147
Comyn, John, earl of Buchan, 26
Comyn, John, lord of Badenoch and Lochaber (k.1306), 18, 20, 23, 38
    killed by Robert Bruce in 1306, 25–26, 36–37
Comyn, Walter, earl of Menteith, 15–16
Comyns, the, 45
Connacht, lordship of, 76
Cornwall, duke of (literary figure), 76
Cowal, 12, 14, 15, 16, 17, 20, 48, 58, 61, 63, 64, 68, 71, 72, 73, 84, 100, 102, 103, 104, 105, 107, 121, 128, 130, 141–142, 146, 152, 154, 157, 166, 173–174, 183, 205, 214, 270, 292, 332, 334; Over, 80, 102, 103, 108; Stewart, 109
Craignish, Christina of, 70–71, 301
Craignish, Dugald of (I), 12,
Craignish, Dugald of (II), 62, 70
Craignish, Malcolm of, 70–71
Craignish, 12, 70, 74, 80, 102, 293
Crawford, Alice, co-heiress of Loudoun, 24
Crawford, Andrew of, 22
Crawford, earl of, see Lindsay, Alexander; Lindsay, David (3rd earl); Lindsay, David (5th earl)
Crichton, Sir William, 148–149
Crookston, 248
Cuiltballoch, 246
Culloden, 2
Culross, 247
Cumbraes, the, 107, 153, 154
Cunningham, 59, 107, 216, 259, 261; bailie of, 245, 260–261
Cunningham, Alexander, earl of Glencairn, 241, 245
Cunningham, Andrew, son of laird of Glengarnock, 291
Cunningham, Andrew, parson of Loch Awe, 270
Cunningham, Cuthbert, Lord Kilmaurs, 260

Cunningham, Robert, of Kilmaurs, 130
Cunningham, Robert, Lord Kilmaurs, 245
Cunninghams of Glencairn, 216, 245

Dail Righ, battle of (1306), 9, 36
Dalilongart, 108
Dalkeith, Peter of, 126, 144
Dalmally, 143
Dalrymple, John, 'of Laight', 299
Danna, 130
Darcy, John, justiciar of Ireland, 59
David I (1124–1153), 1
David II (1329–1371), 11, 13, 56, 58, 62, 64,
    69, 74, 75, 81, 99, 103, 300
  in exile, 58, 60
  his return to Scotland, 60–61
  his hostility towards Robert the
    Steward, 60, 72, 78
  his capture and imprisonment in
    England, 62–63, 66
  his release and support for
    MacDougall lordship, 65–67, 94–95
  negotiations with Edward III over the
    Scottish succession, 72, 75–76
  his marriage, 73
  his difficulties with Highland Scotland,
    77–82
  his death, 82, 94
David, Nicholas, Breton merchant, 299–
    300
Denmark, Margaret of, queen of James
    III, 221–222, 239, 241, 259
Desmond, earl of, 59
Dewar, John, provost of Kilmun, 270
Dingwall, 206, 208, 303
Discher and Toyer (Loch Tay), 207, 208,
    244, 273, 320
Diverres, A.H., 76
Dodgshon, Robert, 294
Dollar, 187, 203, 216
Dominicans,
  the order's connection to Argyll, 118–
    120, 132
  their houses at Stirling, Glasgow,
    Perth and Ayr, 120, 203
Donald (I), earl of Mar, 46
Donald (II), earl of Mar, 57
Donald mac Angus, 271, (Angusson), 316
Douglas, 168
Douglas, Archibald (d.1333), guardian of
    the realm, 57
Douglas, Archibald, 4th earl of Douglas,
    120, 153, 177

Douglas, Archibald, 5th earl of Douglas,
    146–147, 177
Douglas, Archibald, earl of Moray
    (k.1455), 169
Douglas, Archibald, earl of Angus, 222,
    231
  his action against the Campbells, 259–
    262
Douglas, Elizabeth, wife of the 3rd
    Sinclair earl of Orkney, 177
Douglas, George, 1st earl of Angus, 178
Douglas, George, 4th earl of Angus, 178,
    182, 207
Douglas, Henry, of Borgue, 148
Douglas, Hugh, earl of Ormond, 169
Douglas, James, 2nd earl of Douglas, 96,
    97
Douglas, James, of Balvenie, earl of
    Avondale, later 7th earl of Douglas,
    107, 141
  attachment of Duncan Campbell to,
    131, 134, 143, 146–149
Douglas, James, 9th earl of Douglas, 153–
    154, 157, 207, 303
  forced into exile, 168–169
  attempt to recover lordships, 180–181
Douglas, James (I), lord of Dalkeith, 148
Douglas, James (II), 148
Douglas, John, lord Balvenie, 169
Douglas, Marion, 260
Douglas, William (d.1384), 1st earl of
    Douglas, 72
Douglas, William, 8th earl of Douglas,
    148–149
  killed by James II, 151–153, 155
Douglas, William, son and heir of lord of
    Dalkeith, 291
Douglasdale, 168, 332
Douglases of Dalkeith, 143, 148
Doune, castle of, 122
Dovedale, Sir John, 24–25
Down, bishop of, 182
Draffan, 22
Drumalban, 147
Drumglass, 150
Drummond, David, 246
Drummond, John, of Concraig, 71–72
Drummond, John, of Cargill/Stobhall,
    later Lord Drummond, 208, 214–215,
    240, 242, 245, 266, 278, 292
Drummond, Malcolm, lord of Mar, 106
Drummond, Malcolm, 246
Drummond, Margaret, 72–73

Drummond, Maurice, of Concraig, 215
Drummond, William, Viscount
    Strathallan, 246
Dublin, 59, 77, 295
Dubroch, 169
Duchal, 248
Dugald, son of Somerled, 100
Duibne, putative founder of the proto-
    Campbell MacDuibne kindred, 11
Dumbarton, 20, 38, 106, 123, 183, 245, 247–
    248, 267, 294–295, 297–299, 301–302,
    304–305, 320–321; castle of, 58, 59,
    122, 123, 145–146, 149–151, 152, 204,
    222, 248–250
Dumbarton?, Bryan of, 295
Dumfries, 157
Dunadd, 322, 324, 326
Dunaverty castle of, 47, 263, 319
Dunbar, 223; battle of (1296), 19, 37; castle
    of, 149, 222
Dunbar, Patrick, earl of March, 72
Dunbar, Thomas, earl of Moray, 291
Dunbar, William, poet, 213, 276
Dunblane, 188, 246
Duncan, Archie, 16
Duncan Dubh, putative ancestor of the
    MacArthurs of Strachur, 12
Duncan, earl of Lennox, 96, 109
    alliance with Robert, earl of Fife and
        Menteith, 97–98
    supports claims of his grandson Walter
        to Lennox, 121
    arrested and executed by James I, 121–
        123
Duncan, son of the earl of Mar, 46
Dun Chonnuil, 66
'Dungall the parson', 62
Dunkeld, 187, 312
Dunollie, castle of, 45
Dunoon, castle of, 13, 44, 47, 58, 59, 61,
    141–142, 145–146, 150–151, 173–174, 205,
    214, 228, 271, 283; kirk of, 142
Dunstaffnage, castle of, 39, 44, 45, 185–
    186, 194, 262, 274, 292, 314–315, 322
Dupplin Moor, battle of (1332), 57
Durham, 62, 291
Duror, 312, 315–317
Dysart, parish kirk of, St Connan, see
    Glenorchy

Earl Rivers, Anthony, 230
Ederline, 70
Edinburgh, 60, 81, 82, 96, 121, 134, 150,

155, 175–176, 179, 190, 204, 218, 220,
    222–223, 225, 242, 247–248, 263, 294,
    299, 302, 326; castle of, 149, 189, 217–
    221
Edward I, 22
    his campaigns in Scotland, 19–21, 23, 41
    his growing antipathy to Robert Bruce,
        24–27, 36
    his support of Sir John Menteith, 37–
        38
Edward II, 65
Edward III,
    his support for Edward Balliol and the
        'Disinherited', 56–60
    his negotiations with David II over the
        Scottish succession, 71, 75–76
Edward IV, 217, 220, 230, 239
    negotiations with Clan Donald, 155,
        179–182, 207, 216, 225–227
Edward, prince, son of Henry VI, 179
Eigg, isle of, 46
Eilean Dearg, 292
Eilean Tioram, 46
Elgin, 20
Ellem, hosting at, 332
Elphinstone, William, bishop of
    Aberdeen, 231, 303
Enoch, 277
Erroll, earl of, 174, 248
Erskine, Sir Robert (I), 63–64, 73
Erskine, Sir Robert (II), 146, 149
Eskdale, 217
Etal, castle of, 333
Ettrick, Forest of, 333
Ewen mac Allan (of Clan Cameron), 271,
    313, 316, 319, 326
Ewesdale, 217

Falkirk, battle of (1298), 22
Falkland, castle of, 106, 122
Fanad (Ireland), 15
Faslane, Walter of, lord of Lennox, 96, 98
Fife, 72, 104, 120, 122
Fife, earl of, see Stewart, Robert
Fincharn, castle of, 325
Finlaggan (Islay), 274
Finlay, rector of Loch Awe, 107
Finlay, the Red Bard, 209
Flamborough Head, 108
Fleming, Sir David, of Biggar, 96, 107–
    108
Fleming, Sir Malcolm, 58
Fleming, Robert, 273

Flodden, battle of (1513), 6, 334–335
Fochart, battle of (1318), 42, 43, 44, 45, 46
Forbes, Alexander, Lord Forbes, 248–249
Ford, 325
Ford, castle of, 333
Forrester, Duncan, 268–269, 313
Forrester, Margaret, 269
Fotheringhay, castle of, 216; treaty of, 220
Foullarton, Fergus, 169
France, 295
Fraser, Thomas, Lord Fraser of the
    Lovat, 311
Froissart, Jean, 13, 76

Galbraith, Patrick, 149
Galloway, 76, 324
Gareloch, 273
Garmoran, 46, 48, 68
Gartloaning, battle of (1489), 249
Gartney, earl of Mar, 46
Geoffrey of Monmouth, author of
    Historia Regnum Britanniae, 14
Gibson, Murdoch, 145
Gifford, James, of Sheriffhall, 148
Gigha, 130
Gillies, Willie, 6
Glasclune, 79
Glasgow, 20, 59, 157, 168, 267–268, 294–
    295, 332–333
Glassary, 12, 69, 70, 74, 129, 293, 324
Glassary, parish kirk of, St Columba, 125,
    129, 144
Glassary, Gilbert of, 62, 68–70, 73
Glassary, John of, 44, 69
Glassary, Margaret of, 44, 69
Glen Add, 69
Glen Breackerie, 47
Glencoe, 312, 315–317
Glenconnich, 280
Glendaruel, 150, 156
Glen Dochart, 36, 98, 207–208
Glenelg, 280, 320
Glen Falloch, 207–208, 244
Glengarry, 224, 279–280
Glen Kin, 109
Glen Lean, 109
Glen Lednock, 147, 150
Glenlochy, 244
Glenlyon, 244, 318, 320
Glenorchy, 12, 74, 102, 104, 108, 208, 244,
    292; parish kirk of, 126, 143–144
Glenorchy, John of (I), 12
Glenorchy, John of (II), 74

Glenorchy, Mariota of, 74
Gloom, castle of (renamed Castle
    Campbell), 187, 188, 203
Godfrey mac Aulay, 100
Gordon, Alexander, as master of Huntly,
    247–249
    as earl of Huntly, 321, 325–326, 334
    provokes Donald Dubh rebellion?, 279–
        281, 311–313, 316
    his lordship of Badenoch attacked,
        316–317
Gordon, George, earl of Huntly, 207–
    208, 248, 262
Gordon, earls of Huntly, 204, 217
Grafton, Thomas, 304
Graham, John, earl of Menteith, 64
Graham, Margaret, heiress of Menteith,
    64–65, 71–72
Graham, Patrick Lord, 151
Graham, Sir Robert, 122, 141
Graham, Walter, 151
Grant, Alexander, 6, 143
Gray, Sir Patrick, 79
Great Glen, 105, 155, 207
Greyfriars kirk (Dumfries), 26
Gueldres, Mary of, widow of James II,
    172, 176–179, 182, 185, 188
Gunn family, 184

Haakon IV, 15
Haliburton, Elizabeth, 166
Haliburton, Sir Patrick, 216
Halidon Hill, battle of (1333), 57, 58
Hamilton, David, bishop of Argyll, 327–
    328
Hamilton, James, Lord Hamilton, 168,
    174, 176, 178–179
Hamilton, James, earl of Arran, 331–332
Hans, king of Denmark, 239
Harlaw, battle of (1411), 2, 109
Hastings, Sir John, 38
Hebrides, the, 56, 59, 66, 75, 77, 83, 84,
    158, 166, 179, 192, 211–213, 250–251, 261
Henry III, 16
Henry IV, 108
Henry V, 120
Henry VI, 120, 179, 182
Henry VII, 239, 267, 271
Henry VIII, 229, 252, 282, 330, 333
Hepburn, Patrick, earl of Bothwell, 249
Hereford, earl of, 40
Hermond (literary figure), 76
Hermondine (literary figure), 76

Herring fisheries, Irish Sea and Atlantic, 295–300
  Breton, French and Spanish merchants attracted to, 295–296
Highland Scotland, royal 'governance' of, 77–82
Highlanders, 78
Hog, John, abbot of Culross, 247
Holy Island, 64
Holy Loch, 58, 142, 335
Holyrood, 134; abbot of, 221
Howard, Edward, 334
Howard, Thomas, earl of Surrey, 333–334
Hume, Alexander, 249
Hume, Alexander, Lord Hume, 334
Hume, John, prior of Coldingham, 230
Hume, Patrick, of Polwarth, 269
Hunting, 325–326
Huntly, earl of, see Gordon, Alexander; Gordon, George

Iain Lom (poet), 3
Inchaffray, abbey of, 20
Inchmurdo, 73
Inchmurrin, castle of, 123, 130, 145
Inge, Sir William, 25
Inglis, Alexander, archdeacon of St Andrews, 220
Inishail, parish and church of, 12, 20, 70, 142, 292
Inistrynich, 184
Innerdunning, 187
Innermeath, 156, 186, 188
Innes, Cosmo, 1–2
Innis Chonnell, 229, 282–283, 292
Inveraray, 159, 204, 208, 226, 247, 252?, 273, 292, 294–298, 304–305
Inverawe, 45
Invergarry, 279
Inverkip, 153, 154
Inverleckan, 69
Inverlochy 278, 300; battle of (1431), 128, 174
Inverness, 105, 126, 127, 167, 175, 187, 205–207, 251, 280–281, 303, 325; castle of, 151; justice ayre of, 317
Iona, abbey of, 228; annexed to the bishopric of the Isles, 272, 327–329
Ireland, 39, 42, 46, 75, 76, 77, 84, 101, 123, 124, 174, 179, 211–213, 252–253, 267–268, 326, 330–332; trading links, 295
Irvine, 152, 245, 260, 294, 297–298, 301, 305; chamberlain of, 245

Isaac, Janet, niece of David II and wife of John Gallda, 66
Islay, 12, 60, 210, 226, 229, 263–264, 267, 274, 302
Islay Herald, 263
Islay, John of, see MacDonald, John
Isles, the, 17, 100, 253–254 (see also the Hebrides)
Isles, the, lords of, 83; see MacDonald, Alexander; MacDonald, Donald; MacDonald, John (see also Clan Donald)
Isles, lordship of the, 84
Isles, Donald of the, see MacDonald, Donald
Isles, John of the, see MacDonald, John
Islesmen, 78

Janet, niece of David II, see Isaac, Janet
James I (1406–1437), 141, 144, 145, 156, 166, 177–178, 291
  forced to flee the kingdom, 107–108
  his imprisonment in England, 108, 110, 118
  his hostility towards the Albany Stewarts, 110, 121
  his return to Scotland, 110, 121
  negotiations for his release, 120–121
  arrests and executes the Albany Stewart family, 121–123
  anxious about rebellion in the west, 124–125
  his clashes with Alexander, lord of the Isles, over Ross, 126–128, 130
  political opposition to and eventual assassination, 125, 133–134
James II (1437–1460), 214, 332
  his father's death and his own coronation, 134
  factional politics of his minority, 141, 145–147, 148–150
  end of his minority, 150–151
  collapse of the Livingstone regime, 150–151
  his confrontation with the Douglas earls, 151–153, 157, 168–169
  faced by a Douglas/Clan Donald coalition, 153–155
  campaigns to recover Berwick, Roxburgh and Man, 169, 171–172
  killed at siege of Roxburgh, 172, 174, 177
James III (1460–1488), 144, 172, 173, 190, 194, 203, 259–260, 298

conflict over his minority council, 172–178

seized by Lord Boyd, 188

supports Colin Campbell in the west, 192, 205, 214

his antipathy to John, earl of Ross, 205–206

criticism of, 213–214, 216

conflict with his brothers, 216–217, 222–223

his arrest at Lauder and imprisonment, 217–222

English marriage negotiations, 230, 239–240

final crisis of his reign and death at Sauchieburn, 230–232, 238–241

James IV (1488–1513) (1488–1513), 79, 220–221

figurehead of rebellion against James III, 231–232, 238–241

acts of his minority regime create opposition, 242–247

rebellion of 1489 forces compromise, 247–250

attached to Angus faction, 260–262

forfeiture of the Lordship and royal campaigns in the west, 261–275

assassination of Alexander of Lochalsh not planned by, 264–265

his links with the Uí Dhomhnaill, 267–268, 326

the crown's attempts to increase revenue, 268–269, 271, 275–283, 311–312

his apparent triumph in the Hebrides, 274–275

his culpability for the rebellion of 1502–1506?, 275–283

his support for Stewart of Appin, 312–313, 315–316

his military response to the Donald Dubh rebellion, 319–321

royal attempts to remodel Hebridean lordship and society, 321–325

royal hunting tours as a means of governance, 325–326

his preparation for war and the Flodden campaign, 330–335

James VI, (1567–1625) 79

John, archdeacon of Argyll, 70

John (Balliol), king of Scots, 12, 18, 19, 22, 24, 47, 56, 68

John son of Ranald son of Godfrey of Uist, 190

John of Gaunt, son of Edward III, 76

John mac Allan (of Clan Cameron), 316

Jura, 66, 274

Keir, 188, 240

Keith, Edward, 63

Keith, Janet, 63

Keith, Sir Robert,
in dispute with Neil Campbell, 24–25

Kelso, 172

'Keneltone', 15

Kennedy, Gilbert, lord Kennedy, 178–179, 183, 187, 188

Kennedy, James, of Dunure, 178

Kennedy, James, bishop of St Andrews, 149, 178–179, 185

Kerrera, 172

Kilberrie, kirk of, 320

Kilchrenan, 12, 80

Kildinny, 187

Kilkerran, 268, 272–275, 319

Kilmarnock, 259–260

Kilmartin, parish and church of, 12, 44, 75, 103

Kilmorich, parish and church of, 12, 20, 103

Kilmun, 65, 74, 142–143, 157, 158–159, 171, 226, 270–271, 274, 292–294; burgh of barony, 247, 298, 305

Kilneuair, parish of, 324

Kinghorn, 57

Kingston, John de, 25

Kingussie, burgh of barony, 204, 312; Carmelite friary at, 312

Kinlochgoil, see Lochgoilhead

Kinlochruel, 157

Kinlochstriven, 61, 109, 293

Kintyre, 15, 38, 44, 45, 47, 60, 62, 63, 81, 105, 130, 152, 189, 206–208, 211, 224–227, 243, 253–254, 263, 267–269, 272, 293, 301–302, 320, 322, 332; sheriffdom of, 12, 19, 47

Kintyre Pursuivant, 63

Kirkcudbright, 297

Kirkwall, 175

Knapdale, 12, 14, 15, 19, 39, 60, 61, 63, 64, 68, 81, 84, 99, 107, 128, 130, 152, 153, 189, 206–208, 211, 224–227, 243, 253–254, 263, 267–269, 293, 320, 322, 332

Knighton, Henry, English chronicler, 76

Knoidart, 224, 279–280

'Kyldachanane', see Kilchrenan

Kyle, 17, 59; Kyle-Stewart, 107

Laing, John, bishop of Glasgow, 221
Lamlash Bay, 64
Lamont, Christian, 103
Lamont, Duncan son of John, 69
Lamont, Duncan, 304
Lamont, Fercher Ewenson, 146
Lamont, Gilchrist, 271, 273
Lamont, Isabella, 61, 68
Lamont, John (I), 17
Lamont, John (II), 189
Lamont, Robert, of Inveryne, 103
Lamonts, the, 14, 128, 166
Lanark, 168; sheriffdom of, 25
Largs, 302
Lauder, hosting at, 271; hosting and
    James III's arrest at, 217–221, 223–224,
    240, 259
Lauder, George, bishop of Argyll,
    James I loyalist, 126
  contests right to appoint to benefices
    with Duncan Campbell, 126, 135,
    143–144
Lauder, James, 126, 144
Law, John, chronicler, 152
Leckie, Murdoch of, 109
Le Croisic, Breton port, at mouth of the
    Loire, 300
Lennox, earldom of, 9, 11, 38, 98, 110, 122,
    145, 152, 207, 215, 248, 325
  disputes over 95–97, 120–121, 175
  rebellion in, 122–123
Lennox, earls of, see Duncan; Faslane,
    Walter of; Malcolm; Stewart, John;
    Stewart, Matthew
Lennox, Elizabeth of, 98, 145
Lennox, Isabella of, Duchess of Albany,
    97–98, 122, 145
Lennox, Margaret of, wife of Walter,
    lord of Lennox, 96
Lennox, Margaret of, 98
Leslie, John, Bishop, chronicler, 221–222
Lewis, 313, 321, 325, 334
Liddale, Robert, 178
Liddesdale, 217
Lindores, abbey of, 13
Lindsay, Alexander, earl of Crawford,
    291
Lindsay, Sir David, lord of Glen Esk, 1st
    earl of Crawford, 79, 170
Lindsay, David, 3rd earl of Crawford, 149
Lindsay, David, 5th earl of Crawford,
    179, 223; as duke of Montrose, 241
Lindsay, David, of the Mount, 331

Lindsay, Robert, of Pitscottie, chronicler,
    331–332, 334
Linlithgow, 302
Lionel, duke of Clarence, 75–76
Lismore, 65, 96, 100, 327
Livingstone, Alexander, of Callendar,
    constable of Stirling castle, 141, 147,
    his influence during the minority of
    James II 148–150
Livingstone, Elizabeth, 167, 206, 208
Livingstone, James, 149–150, 174, 176, 178–
    179
Livingstone, James, bishop of Dunkeld,
    218–220, 223
Lochaber, 20, 77, 128, 180, 208, 224, 278,
    334
  epicentre of the Donald Dubh
    rebellion, 279–280, 311–312, 315, 317
Loch Awe, 11, 12, 47, 58, 67, 68, 69, 70,
    74, 80, 81, 84, 99, 108, 142, 184–185,
    292, 294, 324–325, 334–335
  status of as royal bailiary, 20–21, 40–41
Loch Awe, Dugald of, rector of Loch
    Awe, 144
'Lochbren', 39
Loch Creran, 187
Loch Etive, 185
Loch Feochan, 314
Loch Fyne, 13, 69, 103, 204, 296–297; port
    of, 295
Lochgilphead, 109, 322
Lochgoilhead, 103, 130; parish kirk of,
    126, 143–144
Lochlan, Easter and Wester, 246
Loch Linnhe, 47, 313
Loch Lomond, 123
Loch Long, 9, 13, 58, 99, 103, 294
Lochmaben, castle of, 217
Lochmartnaham, 22
Loch Melfort, 43
Lochranza, castle of, 47, 64, 130, 183
Loch Tay, 36, 156
Logie, Sir John, 72
London, 75, 121; Tower of, 118
Long Hermiston Moor, 108
Lords of the Isles, the, 4–6
Lorn, 45, 48, 65, 67, 68, 69, 78, 95, 99,
    100, 156, 168, 173, 182, 191–194, 205,
    228, 243, 292–294, 300, 303, 314–315,
    317–320, 322, 334–335; Firth of, 47,
    191; sheriffdom of, 12, 19, 68; struggle
    over lordship of, 95–98, 184–190
Lorn, John of, see MacDougall, John

Lothian, 81, 107, 148
Loudoun, 22
Louis XII, 331
Lundy, Isle of, 228
Lundy, Robert, of Balgony, 269
Luss, Sir John of, 17
Lyle, Sir Robert, of Duchal, 150
Lyle, Robert, Lord Lyle, 245, 248–250

MacAlexander, Tearlach, 226–227
MacArthur Campbells of Strachur, 12
MacArthur, Charles, 270
MacArthur, John, 126
MacCarthaigh Mor, earl of Clancare, 324
MacCleary, Malcolm, 222
MacDonald, Alexander (k.1299), 21, 37
MacDonald, Alexander, son of Angus
     Óg, 45
MacDonald, Alexander, lord of
     Lochaber, 97–98, 105–106
MacDonald, Alexander, earl of Ross, lord
     of the Isles, 167, 175
   dispute with James I over Ross, 126–127
MacDonald, Alexander, of Lochalsh, son
     of Celestine, 254, 262–263, 265–266
   his assassination in 1494, 264–265, 267
MacDonald, Angus Mór, 12
MacDonald, Angus Óg, 45
MacDonald, Angus Óg, son of John, earl
     of Ross, 206, 208
   rebellion against his father, 191, 209–
     211, 224–228
   identity of his mother uncertain, 206–
     207
   reconciled with father and Argyll, 228–
     230
   assassinated in 1490, 251–253
MacDonald, Celestine (Gillespic), of
     Lochalsh, 180, 183–184, 190, 210
   impact of his death, 205–208
MacDonald, Donald, lord of the Isles,
     105–106, 128, 322
   struggle with Albany Stewarts for
     control of Ross, 109, 322
MacDonald, Donald Balloch, lord of
     Dunivaig and the Glens, 166, 190,
     216, 225
   raids Firth of Clyde, 153–154, 157
   his interest in Arran, 155, 174, 181–182,
     189
   dispute with Campbells over Dunollie
     inheritance and Arran, 156, 172–173,
     185

negotiations with Edward IV, 180–182
MacDonald, Donald Dubh, son of
     Angus Óg, 265, 271, 316
   problems with traditional accounts of,
     229–230
   his relationship with the 1st and 2nd
     earls of Argyll, 251–253, 282–283
   1502 rebellion in his name, 275, 277–278,
     280–283, 316–317
   his capture and imprisonment, 321
MacDonald, Donald Gallda, son of
     Alexander of Lochalsh, 263, 271
MacDonald, Donald Galldach, son of
     Hugh of Sleat, 184, 191, 205, 210,
     227–228
MacDonald, Donald Gorm, 216, 224–227
   assassinated in 1488, 251
MacDonald, Hugh, of Sleat, 180, 183–184,
     190–191, 205, 208, 210, 225–226
   his feud with the earl of Orkney, 175–
     176, 179
MacDonald, Hugh, author of the Sleat
     History?, 209
MacDonald, Captain Hugh, of
     Piblesgarry, 209
MacDonald, John (d.c.1387), 56, 75, 79, 81,
     82, 84, 190
   agreement with Edward III and
     Edward Balliol, 60
   reconciled with David II, 62
   marriage alliance with Robert the
     Steward, 63, 95
   agreement with MacDougalls of Lorn,
     65–67
MacDonald, John, earl of Ross and last
     Lord of the Isles, 166–168, 174, 185,
     187, 192, 194, 206–207, 251, 271, 303
   action against royal castles of Inverness
     and Urquhart, 151
   coalition with the Douglas earls, 153–155
   unhappy with composition of James
     III's minority council, 174–179
   feud with earl of Orkney, 175–176, 178–
     179
   negotiations with Edward IV, 180–182,
     216
   attempts to control Hugh of Sleat,
     183–184
   agreement with James III's minority
     regime, 189
   his problems with Sleat and
     Clanranald, 190–191, 209, 225–226
   his clashes with James III, 205–207

loss of Ross, Kintyre and Knapdale, 207–208
unjustly blamed for collapse of the Lordship?, 209
rebellion of his son Angus Óg, 209–211, 224–228
reconciliation with Angus Óg, 228–229
Lordship forfeited, John taken into royal custody, 261–262, 265–266
MacDonald, John Mór, lord of Dunivaig and the Glens, 105
his assassination in 1428?, 127, 155
MacDonald, John Mór, lord of Dunivaig and the Glens, son of Donald Balloch, 180, 216, 225, 262, 267–269, 271–272
his capture and execution, 265, 274–275
his ambitions in the lordship, 266, 274–275
MacDonald, John Cathanach, son of John, lord of Dunivaig and the Glens, 252–253, 269
involved in death of Alexander of Lochalsh?, 264
captured and executed in 1499, 274
MacDonald, John, son of John, last Lord of the Isles, 208
MacDonald, Mariota, 128
MacDonald, Ranald, brother of Donald Balloch, 216, 225
MacDougalls, the, 3, 38, 41, 44, 45, 47, 60, 65, 68, 70, 84, 95, 99, 100, 119, 193–194
continued influence of the Dunollie family in Lorn, 191–192
MacDougall, Allan (I), 65
MacDougall, Allan (II), 95, 98
MacDougall, Allan (III), 'of the Wood', 172, 185–187
MacDougall, Alexander, Lord of Argyll, 18, 19–20, 41, 67
conflict with the Campbells and MacDonalds, 20–21, 37
his struggle against Robert I, 36–37
MacDougall, Colla, 191
MacDougall, Ewen, 65
MacDougall, John, 20–21
an implacable opponent of Robert I, 36–37, 39, 65, 95
MacDougall, John Gallda, 69, 75, 76, 79, 80, 81, 82, 99
his good relations with David II, 66–67, 94

his part in the restoration of MacDougall lordship, 65–68
the collapse of MacDougall lordship after his death, 94–96, 99–100
MacDougall, John Ciar, 98, 191–192
rescued by Earl Colin, 172
MacDougall, John, of Rarey, 272, 315–316
MacDougall, Mary, 65, 188
MacDougall, Ranald son of John son of Allan Dubh, 273
MacDuibne (or mac Duibne), Duncan, putative ancestor of Clan Campbell, 10–11
his role in justifying later claims to Loch Awe, 20, 80–81
MacDuibne kindred, the, 16–17
MacEwens, bardic family, 194
MacFadzan (literary figure), 211–213
MacFarlane, Duncan, 103
MacFarlane, Malcolm, lord of Arrochar, 103
MacFirbis, Duald, 10, 16
MacGilchrist, John, 12
MacGilchrist, John son of Ewen, 62
MacGilchrists, 14, 41, 70
MacGillemichael, Celestine, rector of St Maelrubha of Melfort, 107
MacGregor, James, Dean of Lismore, 329
MacGregor, Martin, 6, 228
MacIan, Alexander, of Ardnamurchan, 184, 190, 225
MacIan, Finvola, 190
MacIan, John, of Ardnamurchan, 270–271, 319, 322–323, 326, 333–334
assassinates Alexander of Lochalsh, 263–265, 267
captures the MacDonalds of Dunivaig, 274
MacIan, John, of Glencoe, 315
MacIver, Ewen, 47
MacIver, Malcolm, 12
MacIvers, the, 41, 67
MacKellar, Archibald, 304
MacKenzie, Kenneth, of Kintail, 159
MacKenzie's 'shirt of mail', 49
MacLachlan, Gillespic, 12
MacLachlans, 14
MacLarens, of Balquhidder, 186–187
MacLean, Donald (I), 47
MacLean, Donald (II), 316
MacLean, Finvola, 210
MacLean, Hector, 210

MacLean, Hector, of Lochbuie, 225, 319?
MacLean, John, 47
MacLean, John, of Lochbuie, 180
MacLean, Lachlan (I), of Duart, 145?, 180, 190, 210
MacLean, Lachlan (II)?, of Duart, 225, 227
MacLean, Lachlan (III), of Duart, 228?, 313, 316, 319-321, 325-327, 333-334
MacLean, Neil, 47, 48
MacLeans, the, 39, 209-210
  relationship to Robert I, 47-48
MacLeod, of Harris, 228
MacLeod, of Lewis, 167
MacLeod, Ruairi, of Lewis, 225, 263
MacLeod, Torquil (I), of Lewis, 180, 228
MacLeod, Torquil (II), of Lewis, 273, 275, 319-320, 325
  his role in the Donald Dubh rebellion, 280-283, 311-313, 320
MacLeod, William, of Glenelg, 225
MacMhuirich, bardic family, 209
MacNaughton, Alexander, 47, 62, 70
MacNaughton, Gilbert, 12
MacNaughtons, the, 20, 41, 62, 67, 70
MacNeill, Gillecallum, of Gigha, 263-264
MacNeill, Malcolm, of Gigha, 225
MacNeill, Neil, 224, 226, 227?
MacQuarrie of Ulva, 316
MacRaes of Kintail and Wester Ross, 49
MacRuairi, Alexander, 126
MacRuairi, Amy, 190-191
MacRuairi, Christina, 46, 47
MacRuairi, Lachlan, 46
MacRuairi, Ranald, 46, 62
MacRuari, Ruari, 45, 46; see also Allan mac Ruairi
MacRuairies, the, of Garmoran, 19, 45
MacSweens, 14, 15
Malcolm, earl of Lennox, 17, 38, 39
Malise, earl of Strathearn (I), 20
Malise, earl of Strathearn (II), 26
Mamore, 311-312, 317
Man, isle of, 76, 169
Mantles, 302-303
Mar, earldom of,
  dispute over, 146
Mar, earls of, see Donald (I); Donald (II); Gartney; Thomas; Stewart, Alexander; Stewart, John
Mar, Isabella of, first wife of Robert I, 46
Mar, Ruairi of, 46

March, earls of, see Dunbar, Patrick
Margaret, widow of Hubert de Multon, 22
Marischal, earl, 248-249
Maryenknecht, 108
Maxwell, George, 299
McBhreatnaich, family of harpists, 325
McKechnie, Hector, 1, 3
McLauchlan, Thomas, 281
Melfort, 61, 62, 80, 293
Meliador, 76
Meliador (literary figure), 76
Melrose, 121, 271-272
Menstrie, 13, 15, 16, 43, 44, 73, 74, 129
Menteith, Christian, 63, 64
Menteith, Elizabeth, Lady of Ruskie, 263
Menteith, Isabella, countess of, 16
Menteith, John (I), 61
  his links to Edward I and eventual reconciliation with Robert I, 37-38
  his service to Robert I, 38-39
  his ambitions in the west and links to Clan Campbell, 39, 45, 47?
Menteith, John (II), 45, 47?
Menteith, John (III), 63, 64, 130
Menteith, Mary of, 15-16
Menteith, Mary, countess of, 64-65, 71, 73
Menteith, Maurice of, elder, 15-16
Menteith, Maurice of, younger, 15
Menteith, earldom of, 15-16, 38, 39, 71, 79, 120, 122, 132, 191, 207, 215, 240, 248, 325
Menteith, earls of, see Alexander; Allan; Comyn, Walter; Graham, John; Maurice; Murdoch; Stewart, Robert; Stewart, Walter
Menteiths of Knapale and Arran, 47
Menteiths of Rusky, 71
Menzies, Alexander, 318
Menzies, Sir Robert, of Weem, 276-277, 311, 317-319
Methven, battle of (1306), 9, 36, 38
Mingary, castle of, 267-268, 274
Mo Laise, island of, see Holy Island
Moidart, 46, 280
Montgomery, Alexander, of Ardrossan, 130
Montgomery, Alexander, lord Montgomery, 152-154, 169, 174, 183, 216
Montgomery, Hugh, of Eglinton, later Lord Montgomery, 214-216, 226, 240, 245, 259-262, 278

Montgomery, Sir John, 122
Montgomery, John, master of
    Montgomery, 329
Monzievaird, 246; slaughter at kirk of,
    246
Morar, 46, 280
Moray, 105
Moray, earl of, see Dunbar, Thomas;
    Randolph, John; Randolph, Thomas
Morvern, 280, 322
Mowbray, Sir John, 23
Muir, John, of Rowallan, 266
Muirhead, Andrew, bishop of Glasgow,
    174, 179
Mull, 48, 66, 228; Sound of, 47
Multon, Hubert de, 22
Munro, Billie, 6
Munro, Jean, 6
Munro, William, of Foulis, 311, 320
Murdoch, earl of Menteith, 39
Murray, Adam, of Drumcrieff, 240
Murray, Andrew, guardian of the realm,
    60
Murray, John, 64
Murray, John, of Balloch and Trowan, 246
Murray, William, of Tullibardine, 215, 246
Murrays of Tullibardine, 214–215, 246

Nairn, 167, 206–207
Neil, earl of Carrick, 18
Neville's Cross, battle of (1346), 62, 64,
    66
Nicholas V, pope, 151
Norham, castle of, 333
Norny, Sir William, 276
North Channel, 58
North Uist, 190–191, 225
Northumberland, earl of, 220

Oban Bay, 172
Ó Briain, Maírtín, 281
Ogilvy, Sir Walter, sheriff of Angus, 79
Oliphant, Laurence, Lord Oliphant, 208,
    292
Orkney, 154, 175, 179–180, 182, 192
Orkney, earl of, see Sinclair, Henry (I);
    Sinclair, Henry (II); Sinclair,
    William
Ormond (Ireland), earl of, 59
Ormonde, marquis of, see Stewart, James
Otter, 293, 301
Otterburn, battle of (1388), 97
Otterburn, Allan of, 122

Paisley, abbey of, 14, 16, 17, 154
Paisley, Blackhall of, 17
Paris, 230
Peebles, 157
Pentland Firth, 331
Pentlandmuir, 157
Perth, treaty of (1266), 19
Perth, 36, 59, 60, 65, 77, 81, 107, 122, 125,
    129, 130, 131, 132, 149, 246, 301, 312;
    shire, 83, 95, 133, 187; Dominican
    house at, scene of James I's
    assassination, 133; justice ayre of, 317
Pinkerton, barony of, 223
Pole, de la, Anne, niece of Richard III,
    230
Pontefract, 333

Rait, James, abbot of Culross, 247
Ralph of Dundee, Master, 12
Ramsay, John, lord Bothwell, 239
Ranald Bane, son of Allan mac Ruairi, 228
Ranald mac Alexander,
    occupies Arran, 152–153, 157
    death of, 169
Ranald mac Allan (of Clanranald), 319
Randolph, John, earl of Moray, 60
Randolph, Thomas, earl of Moray, 56, 57
Rannoch, 244, 276–277
Redcastle, 156, 188
Red Ford, 335
Renfrew, 14, 20, 107, 121, 294, 297; shire,
    64
Richard III, 228, 230; as Richard, duke of
    Gloucester, 217–220, 230
Rí Innse Gall, 46
Robert I (1306–1329), 9, 13, 18, 36, 66, 67,
    68, 80, 300
    patron of the Campbells as earl of
        Carrick, 21–22, 82
    breakdown of his relationship with
        Edward I, 23–27
    involved in death of John Comyn, 25–
        26
    his resurrection of Scottish kingship
        and initial setbacks, 36–37
    his campaigns against the MacDougall
        lords of Argyll, 36–37, 39, 95–96, 101
    marriage of his sister to Neil
        Campbell, 40
    his campaign in Ireland, 42
    his settlement of Argyll and the Isles,
        42–48
    effect of his death, 56

Robert II (1371–1390), 36, 97, 99
  career as Robert the Steward, 13, 69
  patron of Dugald and Gillespic
    Campbell, 48–49, 58–59, 61, 63–65,
    71, 82, 94
  expansion of lordship and influence
    within Gaelic Scotland, 56, 63, 75,
    78–79, 94
  resistance to, and accommodation with,
    Edward III in 1333–4, 58–60
  guardian of the realm, 60, 63, 65
  poor relationship with David II, 60,
    62, 66–67, 72, 78
  his rebellion against David II, 72–73
  threatened by proposals to alter the
    succession, 75–76
  forced to render sureties for the
    inhabitants of his highland
    lordships, 79–80
  becomes king, 82, 94
  'arrested' in 1388, 96
Robert III (1390–1406), 97, 104, 106, 121
  as John, lord of Kyle, in rebellion
    against David II in 1363, 72–73
  as John, earl of Carrick, organises 1388
    coup against his father, 96
  his loss and recovery of political
    influence, 106–107
  his death, 108
Rogerson, Thomas, of Drumdewin, 186
Rome, 151, 188
Rose, Hugh, of Kilravock, 264
Rosneath, 250, 273; castle of, 59
Ross, earldom of, 6, 49, 57, 77, 105, 109,
    126, 167, 192, 205–208, 211, 224–226,
    251, 254; sheriffship of 12
'Ross', the, in Knapdale, 302
Ross, earls of, see MacDonald,
    Alexander; MacDonald, John;
    William
Ross, John, of Montgrenan, 216, 245
Rothesay, 20, 294; castle of, 47, 58, 59,
    107, 181
Roxburgh, castle of, 133, 156, 169, 172
Ruairi mac Allan, 191
Rum, isle of, 46
Russell, Isabella, heiress? of Menteith, 16
Russell, John, 16
Rutherglen, 294
Ruthven, castle of, 151

Saddell, abbey of, 327–328
St Andrews, parliament at, 38, 40

St Andrews, bishop of, 25
St Andrews, castle of, 122
St Brendan, fair of, 296
St Fionntáin, 142, 270, 298–299
St Michael, the Archangel, fair of, 296,
    299
Saline, 15
Salmond, Malcolm, 272
Sand, 225
Sandale, John de, 25
Sauchie, 13
Sauchieburn, battle of (1488), 203, 238,
    240–242, 245, 249
Scheves, William, archbishop of St
    Andrews, 218–223
Scone, abbey of, 26, 43, 57
Scotichronicon, 124, 167
Scots Roll, the, 158, 167
'Scraburgh', castle of (see Cairn na Burgh
    Mór/Beg), 48
Scrymgeour, James (I), rector of parish
    kirk of Glassary, 125
Scrymgeour, James (II), rector of parish
    kirk of Kilneuair (Glassary), 324
Scrymgeour, Sir John, lord of Glassary,
    125, 129
Scrymgeour, John, patron of parish kirk
    of Kilneuair (Glassary), 324
Selkirk, 157
Sellar, David, 10, 11, 18
Sempill, Sir Robert, 149
Sempill, Thomas, Lord Sempill, 241
Seton, George, Lord Seton, 292
Sinclair, Henry (I), 176
Sinclair, Henry (II), earl of Orkney, 107–
    108
Sinclair, William, earl of Orkney and
    Caithness, 174–179, 180, 184, 192
Skene, W.F., 1–3
Skipness, castle of, 15, 47, 130, 268–269,
    313
Skye, 205, 210; sheriffdom of, 19
Sleat, 183, 190
Sleat History, 208–211, 224–231, 251–252
Sligo, 268, 331–332
Smolat, John, 299
Snowdon, 13
Solway, the, 59
Somerled, 100, 193
Somerville, Elizabeth, 131, 132, 166
Somerville, Thomas, of Carnwath, 131,
    134, 143
Sorning, action against custom of, 323–325

Spain, 295
Steward, Alexander the, 15, 17
Steward, James the, 12, 17, 19, 20
Steward, Walter the, 47, 58
Steward, Robert the (see Robert II)
Stewart, Alexander, earl of Buchan and
  lord of Badenoch, 105
Stewart, Alexander, son of Murdoch,
  duke of Albany, 120
arrested and executed, 122–123
Stewart, Alexander, earl of Mar, 128
Stewart, Alexander, duke of Albany,
  brother of James III, 216–223, 230,
  259
Stewart, Allan, of Darnley, 145
Stewart, Andrew, lord Avandale, 145, 217–
  224, 231; chancellor, 174, 215
Stewart, Andrew, bishop of Moray, 218–
  223
Stewart, David, duke of Rothesay, 104,
  105, 107
rivalry with the duke of Albany, 106
Stewart, David, son of the earl of Atholl,
  291
Stewart, Dugald, 1st of Appin, 184–188,
  228
Stewart, Duncan, 2nd of Appin,
  a favourite of James IV and an agent
    of royal policy, 312–313, 315–316
his lands attacked, 316–317
Stewart, Egidia, sister of Robert III, 177
Stewart, Elizabeth, 248
Stewart, Isabel (of Lorn), countess of
  Argyll, 186–187
Stewart, James, of Durisdeer, 58
Stewart, James, son of Murdoch, duke of
  Albany
raises rebellion against James I, 122–123
flees to Ireland, 123
potential dynastic threat to James I,
  124, 128
Stewart, James, brother of Lord of Lorn
  and 2nd husband of Joan Beaufort,
  147
Stewart, James, of Auchingowan, 150
Stewart, James, earl of Buchan, 218–223
Stewart, James, marquis of Ormonde,
  239–240
Stewart, Janet (of Lorn), 187–188
Stewart, John, brother of James the
  Steward, 17
Stewart, John, lord of Kyle, earl of
  Atholl, see Robert III

Stewart, John (I), lord of Lorn, 96
his struggle to establish himself in
  Lorn, 98–99
settlement with the duke of Albany,
  98–99
Stewart, John (II), lord of Lorn, 166, 186,
  190
rewarded for support of James II
  during 1452, 155–156
at odds with Donald Balloch, 156
his succession problems, 184
assassinated, 185, 187
Stewart, John, of Ardgowan/
  Auchingowan, 107, 109 121?
Stewart, John (I), of Darnley, 109
Stewart, John (II), of Darnley, 174–176,
  178; later earl of Lennox, 245, 248–
  250
Stewart, John, of Dundonald, 122–123
Stewart, John, earl of Atholl, 218–221,
  224, 229?, 279, 312, 319
Stewart, John, earl of Mar, 216, 239
Stewart, John, of Fortingall, 244
Stewart, Johanna, 98
Stewart, Margaret, of Ardgowan, 2nd
  wife of Duncan Campbell, 121, 142
Stewart, Margaret, sister of James I, 177
Stewart, Marion (of Albany), 145, 148
Stewart, Marion (of Lorn), 186
Stewart, Marjory, 104, 107
Stewart, Mary, sister of James I, 177
Stewart, Mary, sister of James III, 188
Stewart, Matthew, son of John, earl of
  Lennox, 245, 248–250; later earl of
  Lennox, 333–334
Stewart, Murdoch, duke of Albany, 97,
  120, 128, 134, 145
marriage to Isabella, heiress of Lennox,
  97–98
secures the release of James I, 120–121
problems with his son Walter, 120–121
his arrest and excution, 122–124
Stewart, Neil, of Fortingall, 244, 269,
  276–277, 325
Stewart, Ninian, 263
Stewart, Robert, son of Robert II, earl of
  Fife and Menteith, duke of Albany,
  71, 147, 322
rebels against David II, 72–73
growing influence in south-western
  Highlands, 97–99
marriage and political links to Clan
  Campbell, 104, 118

campaigning against Clan Donald, 105–106
rivalry with David, duke of Rothesay, 106
becomes governor of the realm, 108
dispute with Donald of the Isles over Ross, 109
his influence in Argyll, 118–120
his death, 120
Stewart, Robert, of Innermeath, 96
Stewart, Robert, lord of Lorn, 98, 141, 147
son-in-law of the duke of Albany, 98
Stewart, Thomas, earl of Angus, 72
Stewart, Walter, earl of Menteith, 15–16, 17, 37
Stewart, Walter, son of Murdoch, duke of Albany, 118
disputes with his father over Lennox, 120
resists return of James I, 120–121
his arrest and execution, 121–123, 145
posthumous sympathy for, 125
Stewart, Walter, earl of Atholl,
conspires in assassination of James I, 133–134
captured, tried and executed, 134–135, 147
Stewart, Walter, lord of Lorn, 184–190
becomes Lord Innermeath, 190
Stewartry, the, 58; as royal patrimony, 107–108
Stewarts, the, 17, 58
ancestry and early history of, 14–15
growing influence of, in fourteenth-century kingdom, 48–49
Stewarts, of Innermeath, 95–96
Stirling, 13, 96, 108, 123, 130, 141, 146, 147, 152, 215, 221, 238, 240, 242, 268, 273, 275, 299, 301–302, 305, 316; castle of, 23, 106, 147, 151, 178, 204, 231
Stirling, Dominican friary of, 120, 123, 132, 147
Stirling, John, 65, 188
Stirling, John, of Craigbernard, 278
Stirling, William, of Keir, 188, 208, 240–241
Strachur, 80, 102
'Stradlochlin', 15
Strathardle, 244
Strathbogie, David (I) of, earl of Atholl, 40
Strathbogie, David (II) of, earl of Atholl, 58

Strathbraan, 244, 269
Strathclyde, British kingdom of, 11
Strath Eachaig, 293
Strathearn, earls of, see Malise
Strathearn, earldom of, 63, 135, 147, 150, 207, 215, 240, 242, 246, 248; stewartry of, 214–215
Strathgartney, 61, 63, 207
Strathlachlan, 12
Sunart, 274
Sutherland, 184, 210

Tanner, Roland, 253
Tantallon, castle of, 122
Tarbert, 44, 45, 48; castle of, 263, 268, 274–275, 283, 320
Terunga of 'Baronsmor' (Trotternish), 323
Terunga of Kilmartin (Trotternish), 323
Thomas, earl of Mar, 64, 71, 72, 78
Thomas, lord Stanley, 220
Tiree, 66
Torsay, island of, 43, 44
Torwood, 268
Towton, battle of (1461), 179
Treshnish Isles, 48, 320
Trinity, The, merchant vessel, 304
Trotternish (Skye), 273
Trowan, 246
Tullilum, Carmelite friary of, 132, 203
Tulloch, Thomas, bishop of Orkney, 174, 177, 179
Turnbull, William, bishop of Glasgow, his anti-Douglas activity, 151–154, 157
Tyndrum, 36

Ua Cairbre, Diarmaid, harpist, 251
Ua Catháin, Sean, 252–253
Ua Domhnaill of Tír Conaill, 253
Ua Domhnaill, Aedh (I), of Tír Connail, 267–268
Ua Domhnaill, Aedh (II), of Tír Connail, 326, 330–332
Uchtre, Alan, vicar of Glenorchy, 270
Uchtre, Archibald, 270
Uchtre, David, 270
Uchtre, William, 270
Ui Conchobhair, the, 268
Ui Dhomhnaill, the, 330–332
their campaign against Sligo, 267–268
Ulster, 225, 253; earldom of, 76
Umfraville, Ingram de, 25
Urquhart, castle of, 151

Uther Pendragon, 11

Valence, Aymer de, 36–37
Venison, 302

Wales, 76
Wallace, William, 22, 38, 211–213
Warbeck, Perkin, 267, 271
Weem, 318, 325
West, Nicholas, dean of Windsor, 330
Wester Ross, 320
Westminster, parliaments at, 23, 24
Westminster-Ardtornish, treaty of, 180–182

Wigtown, burgh of, 297; sheriffdom of, 25
Wigtown, earldom of,
    disputed by James II and the earl of Douglas, 151
William, earl of Ross, 19
Williamson, 'Kanoch' (Kenneth?), 323
Wine trade, 300
Wishart, Robert, bishop of Glasgow, 23
Woodville, Elizabeth, 239–240
Woodville, Katharine, 239–240

York, 121